LANGUAGE, LITERATURE, AND LIFE

A FOREIGN-LANGUAGE PROGRAM

LATIN BOOK TWO

BY

HARRY FLETCHER SCOTT
OHIO UNIVERSITY, ATHENS, OHIO

FREDERICK WARREN SANFORD
LATE OF THE UNIVERSITY OF NEBRASKA

JOHN FLAGG GUMMERE
WILLIAM PENN CHARTER SCHOOL, PHILADELPHIA

SCOTT, FORESMAN AND COMPANY
CHICAGO   ATLANTA   DALLAS   NEW YORK

ACKNOWLEDGMENTS

For permission to reproduce pictures, grateful acknowledgment is made to: A. & C. Black, Ltd., London, England, for those on pages 194 and 211; the sculptor Gutzon Borglum and The Metropolitan Museum of Art for that on page 77; Museum of Fine Arts, Boston, for the picture by John Singer Sargent which is reproduced on page 72; The Colonial Art Company, Oklahoma City, Oklahoma, for those on pages 117 and 229; Czechoslovak State Railways, New York, for that on page 278; ENIT, Italian Tourist Information Office, Chicago, for those on pages 11, 21, 60, 228, 261, 309, 330; Miss Georgia T. First, Rock Island, Illinois, for those on pages 142 and 147; Fratelli Alinari, Florence, Italy, for that on page 317; Philip D. Gendreau, New York, for that on page 188; German Railroads Information Office for those on pages 134, 168, 169, 170, and 275; Longmans, Green & Co. for that on page 249; Metro-Goldwyn-Mayer for that on page 153; The Metropolitan Museum of Art for those on pages 71, 74 86, 90, 92, 93, 95, 102, 107, 198, 313, and 315; Paramount Pictures for those on pages 13, 26, 210, and 226; The Pennsylvania Railroad for that on page 14; Railways of France, New York, for that on page 219; Sovfoto, New York, for that on page 262; Swiss Federal Railroads for those on pages 83, 138, and 212; University of Cincinnati for that on page 47. The pictures on pages 29 and 30 are reproduced by courtesy of the U. S. Bureau of Public Roads, and the maps on pages 32 and 264 are after maps issued by the Bureau. The picture on page 253 is taken from the series of Latin Picture Cards by Grainger, by permission of G. Bell and Sons, London, England, and that on page 38 is reproduced by permission of the Columbia University Press.

Many of the illustrations, both in black and white and in color, were made especially for this book by Herbert Rudeen, who also designed the end sheets. The cover is by Ernest E. King.

PREFACE

Latin Book Two is a companion volume to *Latin Book One*, which has been widely welcomed as bringing a new spirit and purpose into first-year Latin.

The enthusiastic reception of *Book One* indicates that emphasis on the social values of Latin is an important need of today. To meet this need, the second book recognizes, as does the first, that pupils should gain from the study of Latin not only an acquaintance with a great language and literature, but also an understanding of a civilization to which we owe important elements in our culture.

Not only does the Latin reading material of *Book Two* contribute to the social values of the course, but thirteen cultural essays in English help to bring out the social values of the classical studies. These deal with such topics as Roman engineering accomplishments, the civilization of the Gauls, the influence of Rome on present-day thought. An aspect of the cultural inheritance which is often neglected in the Latin course—our inheritance from the Greeks through the Romans—is adequately treated by means of discussion and pictures.

All the illustrations in the book —about one hundred seventy-five in number—have been selected to bring Roman life closer to the student. They are made meaningful by descriptive titles that show vividly likenesses and differences between the ancient world and our

world today. Not only are these illustrations of generous size, but twenty-eight of them are in full color.

The Latin reading is presented in such a way that the pupil is enabled to profit by the social values. It is of graded difficulty, beginning with an interesting, functional review of first-year work, in the form of ten easy stories, with correlated grammar review. This review is flexible, so that a class can devote to forgotten constructions whatever time is necessary and pass rapidly over other points.

After the review material, comes the story "Ulysses." Because of the rapid action of the narrative and the many dramatic illustrations, this story is well adapted to arouse the student's interest. The vocabulary and constructions in this tale are mainly those of the first year, but easy second-year forms are introduced.

In connection with the reading, new grammatical material is taught, not as lessons, but as a functional part of the study, each construction being taken up and developed where it is met. *Book Two* continues the plan of *Book One* by furnishing for every new grammatical principle full explanations built on the pupil's knowledge. Each new point is made clear by examples in both English and Latin.

"Hercules" and "The Argonauts" follow, with progressively more difficult constructions and additional correlated grammar. Thus, by the time the pupil comes to the reading of Caesar, he has learned the necessary constructions and—more important—he has met these often in connected reading.

The seven books of Caesar's *Gallic War* are presented in nine thought units, with lively chapter heads. Where portions of the Latin are omitted, English summaries carry the thread of the narrative. Thus the pupil is enabled to follow Caesar's account in complete form, without being asked to read an amount of Latin which he cannot cover in a reasonable length of time. In Book I of Caesar and a few especially difficult passages in Book II the text has been somewhat simplified.

Though more than enough of the *Gallic War* is provided for the requirements of the College Entrance Examination Board and of various states, the pupil is not required to memorize indiscriminately a large mass of vocabulary. Words which occur only once or twice are defined in parentheses or in footnotes on the pages where they occur. This "visible vocabulary" will save the time of looking up these words in the Vocabulary at the back of the book, as well as making the Vocabulary smaller, and so, easier to use. Thus the pupil is enabled to read without keeping a finger constantly in the vocabulary pages and is free to devote his learning time to acquiring the important basic words which recur again and again in Latin reading.

On the other hand, the words of the second-year list prescribed by the College Entrance Examination Board (with sufficient additions to meet the requirements of various states) are adequately repeated to insure mastery. Special provision is made for review and drill on these words. Attention has also been given to vocabulary correlation between *Book One* and *Book Two*.

"Stories from Roman History" have been placed last, in the belief that they furnish the most satisfactory reading for the closing weeks of the course. However, if the teacher wishes to devote the entire second semester to Caesar, these stories may be read at the close of the first semester. In addition, a play is provided, which may be read or given at any time.

At the end of each reading unit of the book, derivative work is provided.

Lessons in Latin composition are furnished for those who prefer to have such material available in the textbook.

It has been the authors' aim to supply the needs of the teacher who wants a direct, easily-followed method of achieving results of permanent value in the Latin class.

The authors wish to express their appreciation for valuable suggestions to Professor Arthur Tappan Walker, of the University of Kansas, who read the review stories, and to Miss Annabel Horn, of the Girls' High School, Atlanta, Georgia, who read the proofs of the entire book.

CLASSIFIED TABLE OF CONTENTS

Review of First-Year Work

PAGE

ANCIENT AND MODERN TOURISTS IN ITALY 16

ANCIENT AND MODERN TOURISTS IN ITALY (*continued*) 34

CONSPECTUS OF FIRST-YEAR FORMS. 42

Latin Reading

ULYSSES 47

HERCULES. 66

THE ARGONAUTS. 101

CAESAR'S GALLIC WAR

    CAESAR AND THE HELVETIANS 136

    THE WAR WITH ARIOVISTUS 165

    THE CRUSHING OF THE BELGIAN LEAGUE 189

    A SHORT CAMPAIGN IN THE ALPS 212

    UPRISINGS IN THE WEST AND SOUTH 220

    CAESAR IN BRITAIN 230

    A ROMAN CAMP BESIEGED 251

    THE CUSTOMS OF THE GAULS 265

    A GREAT GALLIC LEADER ARISES 281

STORIES FROM ROMAN HISTORY 296

TRŌJA CAPTA (A Play) 333

English Essays

ANCIENT ROME LIVES TODAY. 12

THE ROADS OF ROME 29

OUR INHERITANCE FROM THE GREEKS 61

LIFE IN ANCIENT GAUL. 132

JULIUS CAESAR—THE RISE OF A POLITICAL LEADER 162

CAESAR'S ARMY IN ACTION 185

CAESAR'S ARMY ENCAMPED. 208

CAESAR, THE DICTATOR 225

THE ROMANS IN BRITAIN 247

English Essays—Continued

PAGE

THE ROMAN EMPIRE AND ITS TRADE 262
ROME AND ITS PROVINCES 277
ROMAN BRIDGES AND AQUEDUCTS 293
THE REPUBLIC AND THE EMPIRE 329

Word Study

I — SOME IMPORTANT PREFIXES 59
II — ENGLISH WORDS FROM LATIN 99
III — WORDS DERIVED FROM LATIN 126
IV — WORDS FROM LATIN THROUGH OTHER LANGUAGES 159
V — PERSONAL NAMES OF LATIN ORIGIN 183
VI — PLACE NAMES OF LATIN ORIGIN 207
VII — SIX IMPORTANT PREFIXES 218
VIII — WORDS OF INTERESTING DERIVATION 223
IX — SUFFIXES IN LATIN AND IN ENGLISH 245
X — LATIN WORDS WITH NUMEROUS DERIVATIVES 260
XI — MORE LATIN WORDS WITH NUMEROUS DERIVATIVES 276
XII — ENGLISH WORDS OF INTERESTING DERIVATION 287
XIII — ABBREVIATIONS OF LATIN WORDS AND PHRASES 325

Exercise and Reference Material

CLASSIFIED LIST OF ILLUSTRATIONS   7
CONSPECTUS OF FIRST-YEAR FORMS 42
CONSPECTUS OF SECOND-YEAR FORMS 128
THE CONQUEST OF GAUL — THE STORY IN BRIEF 289
ROMAN HISTORY IN BRIEF 327
EXERCISES — LATIN-ENGLISH AND ENGLISH-LATIN 339
GRAMMATICAL SUMMARY 359
THE ROMAN CALENDAR 408
LATIN-ENGLISH VOCABULARY 411
ENGLISH-LATIN VOCABULARY 467
INDEX OF GRAMMAR 475

CLASSIFIED LIST OF ILLUSTRATIONS

The illustrations of this book are here classified in groups which show how each picture contributes to a knowledge of ancient life.

INFLUENCE OF THE CLASSICS ON MODERN TIMES

	PAGE		PAGE
Roman Shop in Moving Pictures	13	Modern Pontoon Bridge	147
Pennsylvania Railroad Station	14	Roman Cavalryman in Moving Pictures	153
Baths of Caracalla	15		
Death of Caesar as Shown in Moving Pictures	26	Centurion in Moving Pictures	210
Greek Temple in Ohio — Old Court House at Dayton	64	Roman Triumph in Moving Pictures	226
		Gardens of the Villa d'Este	330

FAMOUS LANDMARKS AND SCENES

	PAGE		PAGE
Roman Forum	11	Site of Ancient Bibracte	152
Baths of Caracalla	15	Scene on the Rhine	169
Bay of Naples	21	Besançon, Ancient Vesontio	171
Circus Maximus (color)	28	Soissons, Ancient Noviodunum	199
Ancient Buildings along the Via dell' Impero	38	Martigny, Ancient Octodurus	212
		Forum of Caesar	228
Site of Ancient Troy	47	Roman Fortress in Czechoslovakia	278
Temple of Concord at Segesta, Sicily	60	Mulvian Bridge	293
Restoration of the Acropolis	63	Arches of an Aqueduct	294
Ancient Corinth	124	Arches of the Claudian Aqueduct	295
Lake Geneva	138	Palatine Hill	309
The Pass	142	Cloaca Maxima	312

IN THE ROMAN HOME

Scene in the Atrium of a Roman House	19	Dinner in a Roman Villa	34
		Courtyard of a House in Pompeii	261

TRAVEL AND TRADE IN ANCIENT DAYS

Merchant Ship Entering a Harbor	17	Laying Out the Appian Way	30
Gentleman in a Litter	18	Roman Carriage	31
Street Scene in Pompeii	23	Early Greek Galley	101
On the Appian Way (color)	25	Roman Seaport in Russia	262
Construction of the Appian Way	29	Roman Storage Houses in Africa	280

RELIGION IN ANCIENT TIMES

Head of Mercury	56	Sacred Inclosure at Delphi	102
Temple of Concord at Segesta, Sicily	60	Head of Jupiter	108
Head of Athena	62	Gallic Goddess	134
Head of Juno	66	Druids of Ancient Gaul	268
Head of Apollo	70	Statue of Janus	302
Statue of Vulcan	75	Vestal Virgin	302

Roman History and Legend

	PAGE		PAGE
Roman Senators (*color*)	160	The Tarquins before the Oracle at	
Sulla	162	Delphi	314
Pompey	164	Cincinnatus (*color*)	317
A Roman of Caesar's Time	198	Manlius Saves Rome (*color*)	320
Flight from Troy (*color*)	297	Tarquin Consulting the Oracle at	
Battle with the Sabines (*color*)	300	Cumae	329
Oath of the Horatii	304	The Emperor Augustus	331
Members of the Roman Senate	308	Marcus Aurelius as a Young Man	332

In the Roman Provinces

Roman Arena in Paris	135	Roman Brooches Found in Britain	248
Ruins of Roman Baths in Trier	170	On the Roman Wall	249
Roman Arch in Rheims, France	190	Roman Baths in the City of Bath	250
Roman Amphitheater in Arles,		Roman Seaport in Russia	262
France	219	Roman Amphitheater in Trier	275
Libation Pan Used in Roman Brit-		Roman Fortress in Czechoslovakia	278
ain	248	Roman Storage Houses in Africa	280

Ancient Warfare

Greek Spear-Heads	95	Plea for Mercy (*color*)	200
Greek Dagger	107	Constructing a Roman Camp	208
Gallic Helmet	132	Plan of a Camp	209
Roman Cavalryman Shown in Mov-		Roman Centurion as Shown in	
ing Pictures	153	Hollywood	210
Plan of the Battle with the Helvetians	154	Foot-Soldier	211
Caesar and His Soldiers (*color*)	157	Roman War-Ships	216
Roman Soldiers Crossing a Bridge		Roman Cavalryman	222
of Boats	159	Roman Triumph in Moving Pictures	226
German Swords	167	Transport Ships	233
Reconstruction of a Roman Camp	168	Landing in Britain	236
Roman Soldier	174	Attacking a Town (*color*)	253
Roman Javelins	176	Large Stone-Thrower	254
Caesar and Ariovistus (*color*)	177	Vorenus and Pullo (*color*)	256
Roman Eagle	185	Gallic Standard	267
Dressing Station	186	Caesar's Fortifications before Alesia	287
Catapulta	187	Caesar's Siege Works before Avari-	
Ballista	187	cum	292
Besieging a Town	188	Oath of the Horatii	304
Archer and Slinger	194	Etruscan War Chariot	313
Cavalryman (*color*)	197	Attack on an Ancient Town	318

Julius Caesar, Soldier and Statesman

Death of Caesar	26	Crossing the Rubicon (*color*)	225
Caesar and His Soldiers (*color*)	157	Bust of Caesar	227
Statue of Caesar	163	Forum of Caesar	228
Caesar and Ariovistus (*color*)	177	Death of Caesar (*color*)	229

LIFE IN ANCIENT GAUL

PAGE

Gallic Helmet 132
Gallic Chief 133
Gallic Goddess 134
Roman Arena in Paris 135
Helvetians Planning Their Migra-
tion (*color*) 140
The Pass 142
Young Gaul 143
Site of Bibracte 152

PAGE

Besançon, Ancient Vesontio 171
Roman Arch in Rheims, France . . 190
Soissons, Ancient Noviodunum . . 199
Martigny, Ancient Octodurus . . 212
Amphitheater in Arles, France . . 219
Gallic Standard 267
Druids of Ancient Gaul 268
Statue of Vercingetorix. 281
Modern Painting of Vercingetorix . 286

LIFE IN ANCIENT BRITAIN

Life in Ancient Britain (*color*) . . . 232
Bridle Bits 239
British Dagger and Sheath 240
British Chariots in Action 241
British Helmet 247

British Shield 247
Libation Pan 248
Roman Brooches Found in Britain 248
On the Roman Wall (*color*) 249
Roman Baths in the City of Bath 250

LIFE IN ANCIENT GERMANY

German Swords 167
Ruins of Roman Baths in Trier . . 170

Scene in Ancient Germany (*color*) . 180
Roman Amphitheater in Trier . . 275

LEGENDS OF ULYSSES

The Sailors of Ulysses Free the
Winds 46
In the Land of the Lotus 48

In the Cave of Polyphemus . . . 50
Statue of Ulysses 52
Blinding the Giant, Polyphemus . . 53

LEGENDS OF HERCULES

Battling the Amazons (*color*) 65
The Infant Hercules 67
Map of Adventures of Hercules . . 68
The Hero Frees Himself from His
Bonds (*color*) 69
Hercules Wearing the Lion Skin . 71
Fighting with the Hydra (*color*) . . . 72
Hercules with the Boar. 74
Horses of Diomedes 77
Statue of an Amazon 78

Battle of the Amazons 81
Pass in the Alps 83
Hercules with Atlas 86
Atlas Holding Up the Sky 88
Comic Statuette of Hercules . . . 90
Hercules Seizing Cerberus 91
Statue of Hercules 92
Statuette of a Centaur 93
Building the Funeral Pyre (*color*) . 97
Temple of Hercules at Cori, Italy . . 98

LEGENDS OF THE ARGONAUTS

Battling the Harpies (*color*) 100
Jason before Pelias 103
Jason Yoking the Bulls 112
Warriors from the Dragon's Teeth . 115

Map of the Voyage of the *Argo* . . . 116
Flight of Medea (*color*) 117
Jason Returns with the Golden
Fleece (*color*) 120

MAPS

Region around the Bay of Naples . 20
Roads of the Roman Empire (*color*) 32
City of Rome 39
Languages That Come from Latin 40
Colonies of the Ancient Greeks . . 61
Adventures of Hercules 68

Voyage of Jason 116
Gaul (*color*) 137
Britain 237
Roads Leading to Rome 264
Roman Empire 277
Central Italy 305

WHY READ LATIN?

During the first year you learned many Latin words and forms and read a good deal of easy Latin. Now you are about to read some interesting stories in Latin, and then a great classic—Caesar's story of his conquest of Gaul. This story has been read for centuries, not only because it is a masterly account, but also because it contains so much information about the people of Gaul, Britain, and Germany. Its author was a keen observer, and he was interested in all that he saw.

While you are reading, you will see more and more how closely Latin and English are connected. Your knowledge of Latin grammar and vocabulary will help you to understand and use your own language better.

Nor is this all. Your increasing knowledge of Roman times will enable you to see how our civilization has borrowed from the past. In that light you will understand present conditions better, and perhaps you will think of ways in which you can help to improve future ways of living.

THE FORUM—THE HEART
OF ANCIENT ROME

ANCIENT ROME LIVES TODAY

HAVE the language and the life of the Romans any significance for us today beyond the mere matter of interest in a people of long ago? Is their language a dead language, and are their customs nothing but an object of curiosity? Or on the other hand, is the influence of Rome on modern life so vital that we cannot understand clearly the world of today without knowing something of the city that "sat on her seven hills and from her throne of beauty ruled the world"?

These are questions of importance in connection with our education. We can scarcely be satisfied to study the life of the world about us without wishing to know something of the source from which many of its features have come.

Each day every one of us comes in contact, directly and indirectly, with the culture of the ancient Romans.

In virtually every sentence of our daily speech we borrow from their language, for modern English is more than half Latin in its origin. For instance, the sentence you are now reading contains seven examples of words that have come down to us in modified form from the Latin. These words are underlined.

The printed letters in our books and periodicals and on our type-writer keys have been developed from those used by the Romans. And when we write in longhand, we are using characters derived from these ancient letters.

The Latin book before you is concrete evidence of the influence that Rome wields today, for throughout the world, and especially in America and Europe, millions of students are studying the life, language, and writings of the Romans.

Not only through the study of Latin, but also through that of such modern languages as French, Spanish, and Italian, we become acquainted with a speech and a culture that are Roman in origin. As you know, these important languages are merely modern Latin. Though the languages of Egypt and Babylon and many other ancient countries became in a true sense dead languages, the language of the Romans lives on in the speech of Italy, France, Spain, Portugal, and Rumania.

In the days of the Roman Empire Latin was spoken in the lands that are now France, Belgium, Spain, Rumania, and Italy; and Roman civilization was dominant there. After the fall of Rome the languages spoken in these regions changed somewhat, but these Romance (or Romanic) languages are still a form of Latin.

In the study of English gram-

ROME LIVES TODAY IN MOVING PICTURES

Notice the loaves of bread in this shop of ancient Rome. The scene is taken from the film "The Sign of the Cross."

mar, language, and literature, we constantly encounter reminders of our heritage from the Romans. Our grammatical terms are taken from those used by the ancients, and our study of words and their use and meanings constantly carries us back to ancient Rome. In our literature English writers of every period make numerous references to classical mythology. Famous poets of modern times have written whole works that are based on Roman legends, such as Macaulay's *Lays of Ancient Rome.*

There is no escaping frequent associations with the life of the ancient Romans. In our study of history and the social sciences, we learn that modern society has borrowed largely from the Romans in laws, government, and politics. In fact, one of the greatest achievements of the Romans was the development of a code of laws on which have been based the legal systems of most European countries. Though the common law, founded on custom and precedent, is the basis of the legal code in the United States and in other English-speaking countries, our lawmakers have often borrowed from other modern systems of law that follow the Roman code. In Louisiana, which was occupied by both the Spanish and the French, the state law is based on the Roman code.

In the study of geometry, we meet many terms that come from

IN A REPLICA OF THE BATHS OF CARACALLA COMMUTERS CATCH THE 5:15
The design of the busy Pennsylvania station in New York City was inspired by that of the Baths of Caracalla in ancient Rome. The call of the train announcer echoes in vast halls like those where Romans exercised and played games after bathing.

the Latin, such as "rectangle," "triangle," "circle." Our knowledge of the subject itself is based on principles formulated by the ancient Greeks and handed down through the Romans.

The Roman school-boy of ancient Rome, if he were alive today, would see many familiar words in our science books.

The word "science" comes from the Latin *sciō*, "to know," and the language of science is full of Latin terms; in biology, chemistry, and physics we meet such words as "flora," "fauna," "sodium," "calcium," "momentum," "inertia."

Not only are reminders of the Romans met in the classroom today, but outside of school we encounter them everywhere. On the way to a moving picture, the setting of which may be ancient Rome, we may drive over highways planned by engineers who have studied Roman methods of road-building. Among the roadside signs we pass may be advertisements of products named for Atlas, a strong man of ancient mythology; Mercury, the swift-footed messenger of the gods; Venus, the goddess of beauty; or Vulcan, the blacksmith of the gods.

If, instead of driving, we go on a bus (short for Latin *omnibus*, "for all") or a street-car, we may hand the conductor a dime, a coin which is adorned with the *fascēs*, a bundle of rods inclosing an ax, which was carried before Roman magistrates as a symbol of power.

If we spend an evening reading the latest novel, we may find that the scene of the story is ancient Rome, and that some of the characters actually lived; or the novel may be a tale of modern life in which references are made now and then to ancient Roman times.

When we look at a calendar to

PUERĪ NĀVEM PATRIS VĪDĒRUNT

suās habēbant, in quibus prope ōram maritimam saepe nāvigābant. Natāre (*how to swim*) bene sciēbant.

Ubi puerī ad portum pervēnē- 5 runt, nāvis patris eōrum nōn erat in cōnspectū, quod ventō ā lītore dētinēbātur (*it was held back*). Itaque puerī duās hōrās eam expectāvērunt. Tandem nāvem longē ā 10 portū vīdērunt. Ubi nāvis ad lītus appropinquāvit, puerī clāmāvērunt: "Salvē, pater! Gaudēmus quod tūtus redīs."

"Heu (*alas*)!" inquit pater, "numquam anteā tanta perīcula in 15 marī vīdī. Ubi ad vīllam redierimus, omnia vōbīs nārrābō. Nunc dēfessus sum. Statim in vīllam properābimus, et posteā multās rēs dē itinere meō et dē praedōnibus audiētis." 20

REVIEW

1. What is the genitive singular ending of nouns of the first declension? 2. Of what gender are most first-declension nouns? 3. Give the declension of **īnsula** and **via**. (For model see Gr. S., 1.) 4. Give the present, imperfect, and future of the verb **sum**. (Gr. S., 39.) 5. Give the verb forms meaning *we are, we were, we shall be*. 6. What is the genitive singular ending of nouns of the second declension?

7. Write the declension of **perīculum**. (For model see Gr. S., 2.) 8. What is the gender of all nouns ending in **-um** in the nominative singular? 9. Give the Latin phrases for *a large island, a large temple*, in the nominative form. (Gr. S., 9, 47.) 10. On page 16 in the first line of the story find the words **Sicilia** and **prōvincia**. What is the case of each, and why is it in that case? (Gr. S., 51.)

QUĪNTUS IN LECTĪCĀ VECTUS EST

Pursued by Pirates

TUM pater et fīliī ad vīllam properāvērunt. Quod vīlla longē ā portū aberat, Quīntus mercātor in lectīcā[1] vectus est. Uxor Quīntī cum servīs reditum ejus domī expectābat. Omnēs servī, ubi lectīcam vīdērunt, clāmāre coepērunt: "Salvē, domine." In trīclīniō (*dining-room*) mēnsa ā servīs parāta erat, atque in ātriō erant flōrēs. Servī et servae (*women slaves*) gaudēbant quod dominus salvus redierat.

Post cēnam omnēs in ātrium convēnērunt, atque cēterī circum patrem sēdērunt; nam ejus cōnsuētūdō erat multa dē itineribus suīs nārrāre. Quārē omnēs silēbant (*were silent*) quod verba patris audīre studēbant. Inter aliās rēs pater hās nārrāvit:

"Audīverāmus praedōnēs hāc aestāte in marī esse, sed nihil timēbāmus, quod ōlim Pompeius Magnus[2] praedōnēs multīs proeliīs vīcit. Ita mare tūtum reddidit atque praedōnēs ē marī expulit. Sed ubi ad mare Aegaeum[3] vēnimus, magnam nāvem lītorī propinquam vīdimus. In eā nāve erant multī virī quī barbarī esse vidēbantur. Hastīs gladiīsque armātī erant et magna scūta portābant.

"Gubernātor (*pilot*) magnā vōce, 'Praedōnēs sunt!' inquit. 'Perīculum maximum est. Paucī sumus neque arma bona in nāve habēmus. Impetum facient et nōs capient. Nāvem nostram frangent et mergent. Nōs erimus servī. Statim fugere dēbēmus.'

[1] In cities and on short journeys the Romans usually rode in litters, which were carried by slaves.

[2] *Pompey the Great*, a Roman general of the first century B.C.

[3] *the Aegean Sea*. See map, page 61.

PATER MULTA DĒ ITINERIBUS SUĪS NĀRRĀVIT

"Ubi praedōnēs nāvem nostram vīdērunt, statim ad nōs cursum dīrēxērunt. Nostrī nautae rēmīs contendere jussī sunt, et vēla quam 5 prīmum ventō dedimus.

"Sed ventus levis erat neque nōs juvābat. Quod numerus praedōnum magnus erat, nāvem suam celeriter ēgērunt. Mox nōn longē 10 ā nōbīs aberant. Eōrum clāmōrēs horribilēs audīre et vultūs crūdēlēs vidēre poterāmus. Paene omnem spem āmīserāmus. Ventus autem validior flāre (*to blow*) coepit et vēla nostra implēre. Jam nostra 15 nāvis celerius per undās (*waves*) cucurrit. Praedōnum nāvis, quae vēla nōn habēbat, nostrum cursum aequāre nōn poterat. Mox magnum intervāllum inter duās nāvēs 20 erat. Dēnique illī cōnātū suō dēstitērunt et ad lītus rediērunt.

"Grātiās dīs omnibus ēgimus, quī nōs servāvērunt. Posteā sine timōre nāvigāvimus. Post duōs 25 diēs in cōnspectum Siciliae vēnimus. Nunc gaudeō quod salvus vōs in patriā nostrā iterum videō."

REVIEW

1. Write the declension of **servus** and **puer**. (Gr. S., 2.) 2. What is the gender of these two nouns? 3. Decline the adjective **magnus**. (Gr. S., 9.) 4. What are the nominative and genitive forms of the phrase meaning *a good sailor?* 5. Decline the possessive adjective **noster**. (Gr. S., 25.) 6. Give the present, imperfect, and future active of **juvō, properō,** and **videō**. (Gr. S., 33, 35.) 7. What case is used as object of each of the following prepositions: **ē (ex), cum, in, sine?** (Gr. S., 152-153.) 8. What is the case of **lectīcam**, page 18, line 7? Why is this case used? (Gr. S., 67.) 9. Decline **vir**. (Gr. S., 2.) 10. Give the accusative plural of **nauta, vēlum,** and **ventus.**

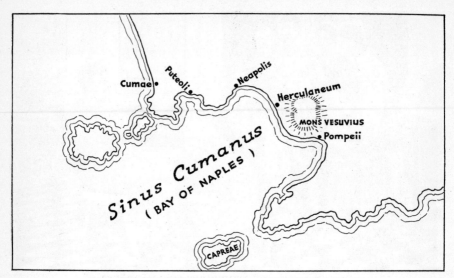

MARCUS AND SEXTUS VISITED THIS PART OF ITALY

Sailing for Italy

POSTERŌ diē pater ad sē puerōs vocāvit. "Vōs, meī fīliī," inquit, "mox adulēscentēs eritis. Certē sciō vōs itinera facere cupere. Itaque mēcum ībitis cum iterum ad Ītaliam ībō. In eā parte maris nunc sunt nūllī praedōnēs, atque sine perīculō nāvigābimus."

Ubi puerī haec verba audīvērunt, magnō gaudiō quaesīvērunt: "Quandō (when) discēdēmus?"

Pater respondit, "Proximō mēnse ad Ītaliam ībimus."

"Omnēs viātōrēs," inquit Mārcus, "dē eīs terrīs quās vidēre cupiunt multa scīre dēbent. Ego multās rēs dē historiā (history) et dē geōgraphiā (geography) Ītaliae jam cognōvī. Quārē spērō mē posse intellegere multa quae aliīs ignōta sunt.

"Librōs Horātiī,[1] poētae clārī, quī multa dē Ītaliā et dē Rōmā scrīpsit, iterum legam."

Longī vidēbantur diēs illīus mēnsis, quod Mārcus et Sextus alacrēs ad profectiōnem erant.

Kalendīs Septembribus[2] trēs comitēs, Quīntus pater et fīliī duo, ad portum Syrācūsārum vēnērunt, ubi nāvis jam parāta erat. Nāvem cōnscendērunt atque ē portū discessērunt. Per mare nāvis celerrimē cucurrit.

Nautae autem vigilāvērunt (kept watch), quod angustum fretum inter Scyllam[3] et Charybdim[4]

---

[1] of Horace, a famous Roman poet.
[2] September first. The first day of the month was called **Kalendae**, *Kalends.* See page 408.

[3] *Scylla* (sil'ä), a dangerous rock on one side of the Strait of Messina.
[4] *Charybdis* (ka̤-rib'dis), a whirlpool on the other side of the Strait.

ONE OF THE WORLD'S MOST BEAUTIFUL HARBORS

When modern travelers sail into the famous Bay of Naples, they often exclaim, as did the Roman boys, "Never have I seen a more beautiful sight!"

perīculōsum erat. In eō locō lītora ā dextrā et ā sinistrā nōn longē absunt. Sed Scylla et Charybdis brevī tempore relictae sunt, et nāvis in mare apertum sine injūriā pervēnit.

Tandem ad īnsulam Capreās[1] appropinquāvērunt, ubi puerī sinum Cūmānum (*the Bay of Cumae*)[2] prīmum vīdērunt.

"Mihi[3] in mentem," inquit Mārcus, "veniunt verba ā Vergiliō (*Vergil*), poētā clārissimō, scrīpta. Ubi Aenēās, dux Trōjānus, et comitēs ejus ad Ītaliam appropinquāvērunt:

'Ītaliam!' prīmus clāmāvit Achātēs.[4]
Ītaliam laetō sociī clāmōre salūtant.[5]"

Ventus erat levis; itaque nautae jussī sunt nāvem rēmīs agere. Quod lentē (*slowly*) prōcēdēbant, puerī poterant diū spectāre oppida, vīllās, tēcta, agrōs in lītore. Montem Vesuvium (*Vesuvius*), quī nōn longē ā lītore stat, vīdērunt.

"Tandem ad Ītaliam vēnimus," inquit Sextus. "Terram pulchriōrem umquam vīdistī?"

"Minimē," respondit Mārcus. "Quamquam in īnsulā nostrā multa loca pulchra vīdī, tamen hic sinus (*bay*) multō pulchrior est."

[1] *Capri* (kä′prē—see pronunciation key, p. 410).
[2] Now called the Bay of Naples.
[3] With **mentem**—*my*.
[4] *Achates* (a̯-kā′tēz).
[5] *greet*.

REVIEW

1. Give the present, imperfect, and future passive of **vocō** and **videō**. (Gr. S., 34, 36.) 2. What are the person endings of verbs in the passive voice? 3. Decline the demonstrative pronoun **hic**. (Gr. S., 26.) 4. Give the accusative singular of the phrases meaning *this book, this land, this danger*. 5. Give the declension of the relative pronoun **quī**. (Gr. S., 29.) 6. Write two English sentences containing relative pronouns and tell what their case would be in Latin. 7. What case is used in Latin to denote the time in which or at which an act takes place? (Gr. S., 79.)

In the Shadow of Vesuvius

Postquam nāvis ad portum Puteolōrum[1] appulsa est, Quīntus et fīliī vīllam Cornēliī petīvērunt. Cornēlius, quī erat amīcus Quīntī, eōrum adventum expectābat. Quīntus ad eum epistulam mīserat, in quā scrīpserat: "Mēcum erunt meī fīliī duo, quī prīmum iter ad Ītaliam facient."

Viātōrēs dēfessī ūnum diem in vīllā Cornēliī mānsērunt. Haec vīlla proxima oppidō Herculāneō stābat. Prope Herculāneum multī hominēs magnae dignitātis et potestātis vīllās pulchrās in lītore aedificāverant.

"Vidētis," inquit Cornēlius, "hoc oppidum in ipsō lītore stāre. Nōs omnēs quī hīc habitāmus ōram maritimam amāmus. Ē fenestrīs (*windows*) vīllārum nostrārum undās (*waves*) spectāre potestis.

"Multī incolae hujus regiōnis parvās nāvēs habent, ex quibus piscēs (*fish*) capiunt. Herī ego cum duōbus amīcīs tōtum diem in marī fuī, et multōs piscēs (*fish*) cēpimus."

Proximō diē Quīntus et fīliī itinera ad loca propinqua facere parāvērunt.

"Prīmum iter nostrum," inquit Quīntus, "erit ad oppidum Cūmās.[2] In librō Vergiliī (*of Vergil*) lēgistis dē Sibyllā[3] quae prope Cūmās[2] magnum antrum incolere dīcitur."

"Fortasse," inquit Mārcus, "Sibylla nōbīs futūra (*the future*) aperiet. Ōlim illa Aenēae, clārissimō ducī Trōjānō, fāta aperuit."

Itaque puerī cum patre antrum Sibyllae petīvērunt. Eō sextā hōrā pervēnērunt. Quamquam undique quaesīvērunt, Sibyllam nūllam invenīre potuērunt.

Posterō diē ad oppidum Pompeiōs iter fēcērunt. Hoc oppidum nōn longē ā vīllā Cornēliī aberat. Quamquam Pompeiī[4] multa templa et alia magna aedificia habēbant, tamen pauciōrēs cīvēs dīvitēs habēbant quam Herculāneum. Ibi autem multī mercātōrēs habitābant.

---

[1] *Puteoli* (pu-tē'ọ-lī), modern Pozzuoli (pọt-sö-ō'lē—see pronunciation key, p. 410). This noun, like **Syrācūsae**, takes a plural verb, since it is plural in form.

[2] *Cumae* (kū'mē). See map, page 20.

[3] *the Sibyl*, a priestess of Apollo.

[4] Another example of a city name which takes a plural verb.

AD OPPIDUM POMPEIŌS ITER FĒCĒRUNT

Tertiō diē ad īnsulam Capreās[1] nāvigāvērunt. Īnsula erat pulcherrima, sed Quīntus et fīliī nāvem ad eam appellere nōn potuērunt, 5 quod ibi imperātor Tiberius habitābat.

Is duodecim vīllās in īnsulā habēbat. Ibi eō tempore ultimōs annōs vītae agēbat. Īnsula 10 ā mīlitibus custōdiēbātur. Itaque Quīntus et fīliī circum īnsulam nāvigāvērunt et ad vīllam Cornēliī rediērunt.

"Quid dē Tiberiō putās?" ā 15 Cornēliō quaesīvit Quīntus.

Cornēlius respondit: "Multī putant eum esse crūdēlem et atrōcem (*savage*). Ego autem exīstimō eum esse ēgregium imperātōrem. Ante mortem Augustī ipse fortiter bella 20 cum barbarīs gentibus gessit. Pāx Augusta[2] Rōmānīs multa beneficia dedit, atque crēdō Tiberium ea beneficia intellegere. Semper fīnēs imperiī Rōmānī custōdīvit." 25

"Dē hīs rēbus," inquit Quīntus, "rūmōrēs in Siciliam pervēnērunt. Aliī Tiberium culpant (*blame*), aliī laudant. Quid dē eō posterī jūdicābunt? Dī sōlī id intellegunt." 30

Posterō diē grātiās maximās Cornēliō ēgērunt pater et fīliī quod tam bene acceptī erant, et dīxērunt, "Valē."

---

[1] *Capri* (kä′prē — see pronunciation key, p. 410), an island in the Bay of Naples. See map, page 20.

[2] *of Augustus.* This refers to the long period of peace in the reign of Augustus.

REVIEW

1. In what do the present infinitives of the first and second conjugations end in the active? In the passive? 2. Give the present active and passive infinitives of **expectō** and **timeō**. (Gr. S., 33, 35.) 3. Decline the demonstrative pronoun **ille**. (Gr. S., 26.) 4. Give the accusative of the Latin phrases meaning *that letter*, *that town*, *that year*. 5. Give the nominative of the Latin phrases meaning *these islands*, *these wars*, *those temples*. 6. What case is used in Latin to denote duration of time? (Gr. S., 68.) 7. Write an English sentence containing a direct object and an indirect object, and give the name of the case in which the indirect object would stand in Latin. 8. Find an example of the ablative of time in the story "In the Shadow of Vesuvius," which begins on page 22.

Avē Rōma Immortālis! (*Hail, Immortal Rome!*)

Nunc, puerī," inquit pater, "iter nostrum ad urbem Rōmam erit. Scītis nūllam aliam urbem in omnī orbe terrārum tam
5 clāram esse. Brevī tempore oculīs vestrīs illud clārum 'caput mundī' (*of the world*) vidēbitis.

"Multa ex hīs aedificiīs quibus Rōma nunc ōrnāta est ab Augustō,
10 illō imperātōre potentissimō, aedificāta sunt. Is multa et magna opera in urbe cōnfēcit. Inter haec est novum forum, quod Forum Augustī[1] appellātur. In hōc forō
15 Augustus templum Mārtis, deī bellī, aedificāvit, postquam magnō proeliō eōs virōs vīcit ā quibus Jūlius Caesar interfectus est."

"Dē Forō Augustī atque dē Forō
20 Rōmānō quoque multa lēgī," inquit Mārcus. "Sed nārrā aliquid nōbīs dē templō Jovis (*of Jupiter*) Capitōlīnī.[2]"

"Melius erit haec omnia vidēre," respondit pater. "Paucīs diēbus 25 urbem ipsam vidēbitis."

Hōrā decimā ejus diēī ad urbem Capuam pervēnērunt. Ex hāc urbe Via Appia ad urbem Rōmam dūcit, atque Quīntus hāc viā iter facere 30 in animō habēbat. Capua magnum amphitheātrum habēbat, in quō saepe gladiātōrēs pugnābant.

Illō ipsō diē quō Quīntus cum fīliīs in urbem pervēnit, fuerat 35 spectāculum in hōc amphitheātrō. Pater et fīliī vīdērunt multōs hominēs ex agrīs et ex vīcīs. Hī in urbem convēnerant quod spectāculum vidēre studēbant. 40

Domum cīvis ejus urbis petīvērunt, quī erat amīcus Cornēliī, atque ibi eam noctem mānsērunt.

Proximō diē iter prīmā lūce facere coepērunt. Via Appia erat 45 clārissima omnium viārum Rōmānārum. In eā Quīntus fīliīque multōs viātōrēs vīdērunt, quī aut

---

[1] Augustus provided another forum in addition to the Roman Forum, which was in his time too small to accommodate the increased business of the city.

[2] The temple of Jupiter Capitolinus, on the Capitoline Hill, was one of the most famous in the city. A museum now occupies part of the site.

IN VIĀ APPIĀ MULTŌS VIĀTŌRĒS VĪDĒRUNT

ex urbe aut ad urbem properābant.

Eā nocte in tabernā (*inn*) mānsērunt, ubi male dormīvērunt.
5 Viātōrēs antīquī nōn saepe taber-
nās (*inns*) bonās invēnērunt.

Post duōs diēs ad oppidum Arī-
ciam[1] pervēnērunt. Nōn longē ab
hōc oppidō templum antīquissi-
10 mum Diānae in lītore lacūs Ne-
morēnsis[2] stābat.

Dēnique pater et fīliī Rōmam
cōnspexērunt.

"Quam pulchra est illa urbs!"
15 clāmāvit Sextus. "Ecce mōns Pa-

lātīnus,[3] in quō Rōma ā Rōmulō
prīmum condita est."

Et Mārcus, "Ecce flūmen Tiberis, ā sinistrā."

Mox Circum Maximum cōn- 20
spexērunt. "Crās (*tomorrow*)," inquit Quīntus, "mīrābile spectāculum in Circō vidēbitis."

Mox per Sacram Viam (*Sacred
Way*) ad Forum iter vertērunt, 25
quod quam prīmum Forum Rōmānum vidēre cupiēbant.

"Nōmina omnium templōrum et
basilicārum[4] in memoriā teneō,"
inquit Sextus, "sed maximē volō 30

---

[1] *Aricia*, a city of Italy. See map,
page 305.

[2] *of Lake Nemi* (nā′mē—see pronunciation key, p. 410). See map, page 305.

[3] For the location of the various places

in Rome mentioned in this story, see
map, page 39.

[4] *of basilicas.* These were used like
modern court-houses, in that legal business was transacted in them.

CAESAR DIES AGAIN IN HOLLYWOOD
The Sicilian boys Marcus and Sextus would have been interested in this moving-picture version of the assassination of Julius Caesar.

vidēre templum Jūliī Caesaris. Dē ejus morte multa lēgī. Mārcus Antōnius,[1] amīcus Caesaris, clārissimam ōrātiōnem prō amīcō suō in Forō habuit."

5 "Estne illud aedificium ōrnātissimum, quod in monte Palātīnō vidēmus, templum Apollinis?" quaesīvit Mārcus.

Pater respondit: "Ita est. Au- 10 gustus templum Apollinis in eō monte aedificāvit. Multōs diēs in urbe manēbimus, et alia nōta aedificia vidēbimus."

[1] *Mark Antony*, a supporter of Caesar in the war between Pompey and Caesar, and later, one of the leaders in the civil war that followed Caesar's death.

REVIEW

1. Conjugate **intrō, habeō,** and **vincō** in the perfect indicative active. (Gr. S., 33, 35.) 2. What is the tense sign of the past perfect indicative active? 3. Conjugate **spectō, maneō,** and **videō** in the past perfect indicative active. (Gr. S., 33, 35.) 4. What is the tense sign of the future perfect indicative active? 5. Give the third person singular and the third person plural of **nārrō** and **teneō** in the perfect, past perfect, and future perfect indicative active. 6. Decline the demonstrative **is.** (Gr. S., 26.) 7. Decline the nouns **pater, viātor,** and **nōmen.** (Gr. S., 3, 4.) 8. What is the case of **cīvis** in line 41 on page 24? (Gr. S., 52.)

Cheers for the Winner

POSTERŌ diē Quīntus et fīliī ad Circum Maximum iērunt. Ibi Rōmānī cursūs equōrum et alia certāmina spectāre solēbant. 5 Magna multitūdō jam convēnerat, et hominēs dē celeritāte equōrum et dē arte aurīgārum multa dīcēbant. Puerī Syrācūsānī audīverant hominem Syrācūsānum esse inter 10 aurīgās.

Subitō Sextus exclāmāvit: "Ecce Līber![1] Vidēsne virum quī illōs equōs nigrōs (*black*) agit? Sine dubiō ille est Līber, quī ōlim in 15 urbe nostrā habitāvit. Saepe eum in Siciliā vīdī."

Spectātor vīcīnus haec verba Sextī audīverat. "Ille homō," inquit, "hīc paene ignōtus est. Num-20 quam fuit victor, neque erit inter prīmōs hodiē. Nē ipse quidem in hōc certāmine victōriam spērat."

"Fortasse errās," inquit Mārcus. "Līber est Syrācūsānus; nōs quoque 25 Syrācūsānī sumus. Sciō eum aurīgam perītissimum esse, et putō eum hodiē facile vincere posse."

Jam equī et aurīgae in carceribus signum expectābant. Tandem tuba 30 signum dedit. Equī carcerēs relīquerunt, et certāmen inceptum est. Magnus erat fremitus[2] spectātōrum, quī nōmina aurīgārum clāmābant. Vōcēs puerōrum Syrācūsānōrum 35 vix audīrī poterant. Mox prīmum locum habēbat Crēscēns,[1] aurīga Rōmānus, quī plūrimōs fautōrēs

(*backers*) habēre vidēbātur; secundum locum Hispānus (*a Spaniard*); tertium locum Gallus; quārtum lo-40 cum Līber, ille Syrācūsānus.

In Circō erat mūrus, quī spīna appellābātur. Circum hanc spīnam aurīgae cursum dīrigēbant.

Necesse erat septem spatia 45 (*laps*) circum spīnam cōnficere. In utrōque fīne spīnae erant mētae. Semper is currus quī proximus mētīs erat brevissimum spatium habēbat. Quārē aurīgae in om-50 nibus spatiīs locum interiōrem petēbant. Saepe in certāminibus currūs mētīs frangēbantur atque aurīgae et equī vulnerābantur.

Post prīmum spatium equī Līberī 55 longē post cēterōs currēbant. Spectātōrēs vīcīnī puerōs irrīsērunt (*laughed at*): "Ecce vester aurīga Syrācūsānus! Etiam nunc Līberum aurīgam perītissimum esse crēditis? 60 Omnēs eum antecēdunt."

Līber autem spem nōn āmīserat. Equōs magnā cum arte agēbat. Mox, ubi facultās data est, Gallum praeterit.[3] Deinde Hispānum 65 (*the Spaniard*) petit et eum quoque post tergum relinquit. Nunc sōlus Crēscēns eum antecēdit, et intervāllum inter duōs currūs est nōn magnum. Nunc certāmen est inter 70 eōs duōs hominēs, quōs omnēs intentī spectant. Fautōrēs (*the backers*) Crēscentis nōmen ejus saepe clāmant.

---

[1] There actually were famous drivers named **Līber** and **Crēscēns**. Their names appear in Latin inscriptions.

[2] *uproar.*

[3] *he passes.* The present tense is used to make the action more vivid.

"NUNC, LĪBER, MĒTĀS PETE!"

Dēnique currūs in ultimō spatiō ad mētās appropinquābant.

"Nunc contende! Nunc, Līber, mētās pete!" clāmāvit Mārcus, 5 quī spērābat Līberum audīre posse.

Crēscēns nimis (*too*) longē mētās vītāvit. Līber occāsiōnem vīdit et equōs inter Crēscentem et mētās 10 ēgit. Līberī currus paene frāctus est, sed mētās vītāvit.

Nunc Līber prīmum locum cēperat. Crēscēns equōs flagellō (*with a whip*) cecīdit (*lashed*), sed Līberum praeterīre (*pass*) nōn po- 15 tuit. Līber prīmus calcem (*chalk line*) trānsiit, quae fīnem certāminis indicābat (*marked*). Ita ignōtus Syrācūsānus vīcit.

Puerī et pater clāmāvērunt: 20 "Euge (*Bravo*)! Bene fēcistī. Nōs Syrācūsānī tē maximē laudāmus."

REVIEW

1. Decline the nouns **urbs, fīnis, ars, animal.** (Gr. S., 3, 5.) 2. Compare the adjectives **perītus** and **brevis.** (Gr. S., 16.) 3. Compare the irregular adjectives **bonus, magnus, parvus.** (Gr. S., 17.) 4. How is the superlative formed for adjectives ending in **-er?** 5. Compare the adverbs **lātē, fortiter, ācriter.** (Gr. S., 19.) 6. Decline the reflexive pronoun of the third person. (Gr. S., 24.) 7. Explain the case of **hominem,** page 27, line 9. (Gr. S., 72.) 8. Give the genitive plural of the following nouns: **collis, cīvis, homō, victor, certāmen.** (Gr. S., 3, 5.)

A ROAD CREW BUILDING THE APPIAN WAY

The ancient Roman highways were so excellent that even today the U. S. Bureau of Public Roads studies the methods of the builders. This model and the one on page 30 were constructed by the Bureau. Notice the different stages of construction shown in this picture.

THE ROADS OF ROME

"ALL roads lead to Rome!" This statement was no exaggeration, for in the time of the Roman Empire, all through Italy and the provinces—north, south, east, and west—there was a network of highways, all leading toward Rome.

Just as the federal highways unite the various parts of our country, so these ancient roads united Rome and the different provinces. They were an important means of spreading Roman civilization throughout the Empire.

No sooner did the Romans conquer a region than they began to build roads there. These roads made possible the quick movement of troops and supplies from one point to another as well as the rapid sending of communications.

They encouraged travel and the development of commerce.

One of the oldest and most famous Roman roads was the *Via Appia*, which ran south from Rome to Capua, a distance of one hundred thirty-two miles. This "queen of roads" was built in 312 B.C. under the direction of Appius Claudius, in whose honor it was named. Later the *Via Appia* was extended to the city of Brundisium —modern Brindisi—a busy seaport in the heel of the Italian "boot."

The great road known as the *Via Flaminia* ran in a northeasterly direction to the Adriatic Sea, continuing under another name to the city that is now Milan. The *Via Aurelia* followed the west coast of Italy into Gaul. In time this highway was extended through

A ROMAN SURVEYOR AT WORK

The toy figure in this model is shown with a level such as was used in laying out a Roman road.

southern Gaul into Spain. There it followed the eastern coast and eventually was carried to Gades —modern Cadiz—on the coast beyond the Strait of Gibraltar. From this road, many branches led to towns in the interior of Spain.

The Roman roads were especially notable for their excellent construction. Certain definite and high standards were followed, and to this day no roads have ever been more solidly built. The methods of construction, however, naturally varied somewhat with the nature of the regions through which the roads ran.

The most common method was to dig a shallow trench from ten to fifteen feet wide for the road-bed. In this trench was placed a layer of small stones. Over them was spread coarse concrete, about nine inches thick, made of broken stones mixed with lime. Next came a six-inch layer of cement, in which large paving stones were set.

The paving stones which formed the actual surface of the road were blocks of volcanic rock or other hard stone. Usually they were cut to an edge or point on the under side, instead of being flat, so that they would be held firmly in the cement. The upper parts of the blocks were joined tightly together, to make as smooth a surface as possible. The middle of the road was made higher than the sides, so that rain and melting snow would run down to the curbstones which lined both sides and finally be drained off through the nearest culvert.

Slaves—and frequently natives drafted from the province through which the road was to run—labored through wind, sun, and rain. Often soldiers stationed in the locality also worked on the roads.

Roman roads were remarkable for running as nearly straight as possible over hills and valleys. Roman engineers did not, as a rule, try to avoid obstacles by making curves, as our highway engineers do. They cut through hills instead of going around them, and kept grades easy by carrying the roads across valleys and marshes on great viaducts.

It has been estimated that the Romans constructed nearly fifty thousand miles of highways. In Gaul alone there were almost fourteen thousand miles of roads. Though the Roman roads did not, of course, equal our modern ones, they were far better than those in Europe and America thirty years ago, and the rate of travel was fully as high. When speed was necessary, the Romans could make as much as fifty or sixty miles a day, provided they changed horses often enough.

A great historian has said that during the Empire the Roman world was in motion. Over the highways streamed a constant procession of travelers. Merchants hurrying to close a business deal, a legion of Roman soldiers on the march, provincial officials going to and from their duties, couriers dashing along on horseback, students on their way to finish their education, people journeying to shrines, watering-places, and festivals, farmers hauling their produce to market—all of these and many others continually passed up and down the great roads of the Empire.

The vehicles in which people traveled varied according to their station in life. Rich people often traveled with as great a display as they could manage. The emperor rode in a richly carved and decorated cloth-covered carriage, drawn by six or eight horses. Outriders and soldiers guarded him, and baggage wagons came lumbering along behind. The grandeur of the imperial traveler was far greater than his comfort, for his elegant carriage had no springs.

There were many different kinds of two- and four-wheeled vehicles, ranging from light carriages and carts to heavy transport wagons.

WEALTHY ROMANS TRAVELED IN CARRIAGES LIKE THIS
This picture represents a Roman relief of a luxurious carriage. The stone-cutter carefully showed the elaborate decorations of the carriage, but omitted the wheels on the farther side.

HIGHWAYS
OF THE
ROMAN EMPIRE

These were drawn by horses, donkeys, mules, or slow-plodding oxen. A traveler might even journey in a litter, carried by slaves, such as that shown on page 18. For a long trip a litter was sometimes fitted in front and back with shafts, so that horses or mules could be used to carry it.

As a rule, the Romans made only short trips on horseback. This was not a very comfortable way to travel, for the saddles had no stirrups. Folded blankets were often used instead of saddles. The road-builder, however, did not forget the horseman, for at intervals along the road there were stone blocks where he could mount and dismount.

When traveling, a public official or a wealthy Roman usually lodged for the night at the home of a friend or some local official to whom he had a letter of introduction. If such a haven could not be reached, he slept either on a bed in his carriage or in a tent.

Travelers without money, influence, or friends slept at inns or on the ground, with only the sky for a roof. Since the inns were often crowded and usually filthy, those who slept under the stars must have rested more comfortably than those inside. An ancient inscription recommending an inn at Lugdunum — modern Lyons, in France — ends with the wise caution, "Traveler, take heed where you stay!"

On all important roads the Emperor Augustus installed a courier service, to carry not only official communications, but also private letters. This service was much like that once afforded by the pony express in the western part of our own country, for the "mail" was relayed from one station to the next by young men on horseback. Many people, however, sent their dispatches by slaves, freedmen, or privately hired couriers. There were also places along the roads where travelers could obtain supplies and fresh horses as well as the services of a blacksmith or wheelwright.

In outlying desolate parts of the Empire travel was often very dangerous, for people ran great risk from bandits, who might rob them and then either kill them or sell them into slavery. In such regions travelers usually proceeded in groups, often accompanied by armed guards. How eagerly they must have counted the milestones along the way, in their anxiety to reach the end of their journey!

Remains of Roman roads are still to be found today throughout the regions which once formed the Empire. Often a modern highway follows the line of one of these ancient roads. The traveler of the present day, passing over these thoroughfares, still benefits from the work done by the Roman engineers centuries ago.

AULUS ET HOSPITĒS CĒNĀVĒRUNT

Roman Hospitality

Tum Quīntus et fīliī montem Ēsquilīnum (*Esquiline*) petīvērunt. Amīcus Quīntī, quī in eā regiōne habitābat, eōs in domum 5 suam invītāverat. Ubi pater et fīliī in tēctum pervēnērunt, is amīcus, quī Aulus appellābātur, eōs cum magnō gaudiō accēpit. Servī balneum (*bath*) parāre jussī 10 erant. Quod hospitēs dēfessī erant, balneum (*bath*) eīs erat grātissimum.

Deinde Aulus et hospitēs cēnāvērunt. Post cēnam colloquium fuit 15 breve, quod dormīre cupiēbant.

Aulus, quī vīllam rūsticam (*country*) prope Tusculum[1] habēbat,

hospitēs eō dūcere cōnstituerat. Quod iter erat quīndecim mīlium passuum,[2] carpentum parārī jussit. 20

Sed quod viae Rōmae angustae erant, per eās vehicula (*vehicles*) equīs ducta īre prohibēbantur ā prīmā lūce usque ad decimam hōram.[3] Itaque Aulus et amīcī 25 lectīcīs ad portam urbis vectī sunt, ubi servī cum carpentō adventum eōrum expectābant.

In eā regiōne per quam via ā tēctō Aulī ad portam urbis dūcēbat, 30 erant multa aedificia altissima. Ea aedificia "īnsulae" ā Rōmānīs appellābantur, quod viīs undique ab aliīs aedificiīs dīvīsa erant. In

[1] *Tusculum* (tus′kū-lum—see pronunciation key, p. 410). See map, page 305.

[2] *miles;* literally, *thousands of paces.*

[3] The tenth hour after sunrise.

eīs īnsulīs multī cīvēs pauperēs (*poor*) habitābant. Numquam Syrācūsānī in suā urbe tam alta aedificia vīderant.

5 Ubi ad portam urbis pervēnērunt, in carpentum ascendērunt et ad vīllam īre coepērunt. Servī tēla portābant; nam interdum latrōnēs in viātōrēs impetūs faciē-
10 bant, et sine comitibus armātīs itinera facere nōn erat satis tūtum.

Per Viam Latīnam[1] celeriter vectī sunt. Ab utrōque latere viae erant sepulcra (*tombs*) nōbilium Rōmā-
15 nōrum, quod cōnsuētūdō Rōmānōrum erat mortuōs extrā urbem prope viās sepelīre (*to bury*). Aulus sepulcra (*tombs*) virōrum clārōrum comitibus mōnstrāvit.

20 Aulus fundum centum jūgerum[2] habēbat, in quō erat vīlla magna et pulcherrima. Circum eàm vīllam erant fontēs, flōrēs, hortī, arborēs. Vīgintī servī agrum
25 colēbant et animālia cūrābant. Fundus multās rēs ferēbat, sed maximē vīnum. Hoc vīnum Aulus

in urbe vēndēbat. Vīlicus Aulī Syrācūsānīs multa dē fundō nārrāvit. Inter aliās rēs magna dolia 30 (*jars*) mōnstrāvit, in quibus vīnum conditum erat.

Rōmānī dīvitēs exīstimābant agricultūram esse optimum (*most honorable*) ūsum pecūniae. Saepe 35 complūrēs fundōs habēbant. Vīlicī fundōs cūrābant. Dominī in urbe habitābant sed in fundīs multōs diēs agēbant.

Aulus hospitēs ad eam vīllam 40 dūxit quam Cicerō ōlim habuerat et maximē amāverat. In eā vīllā, quam Tusculānum[3] appellābat, Cicerō multum tempus ēgerat.

Post trīduum Syrācūsānī amīcō 45 suō "Valē" dīxērunt. Per Viam Latīnam[1] ad urbem Capuam rediērunt. Inde Via Campāna[4] ad portum Puteolōrum[5] eōs dūxit, ubi nāvem suam iterum cōnscendē- 50 runt. Ventīs secundīs ad Siciliam nāvigāvērunt. Posteā puerī omnibus amīcīs multa dē itinere nārrāvērunt.

[1] *the Latin Way*, a road which ran southeast from Rome.
[2] Since a **jūgerum** was about two-thirds of a modern acre, the farm had about sixty-seven acres. The form here is genitive plural of **jūgerum, -ī**, with the genitive ending **-um** instead of **-ōrum**.

[3] *Tusculanum* (tus-kū-lā′num — see pronunciation key, p. 410).
[4] *the Campanian Way*. It ran from Capua to Cumae, with a branch to Puteoli.
[5] Genitive plural of **Puteolī**. See page 22, note 1.

REVIEW

1. Conjugate **amō, videō,** and **dīvidō** in the perfect indicative passive. 2. Give the third person singular and the third person plural of **parō** and of **dūcō** in the past perfect and the future perfect passive. 3. Decline the adjectives **omnis** and **fēlīx**. (Gr. S., 11, 12.) 4. Conjugate **eō** in the present, imperfect, and future indicative. (Gr. S., 43.) 5. Give the third person singular and plural of **trānseō** in the present, imperfect, and future indicative. 6. Explain the case of **eīs**, page 34, line 11. (Gr. S., 60.)

Nineteen Hundred Years Later

Mārcus et Mārcella, frāter et soror, in urbe Americānā[1] hodiē habitant. Haec inter sē dīxērunt.

5 "Multās rēs," inquit Mārcus, "dē Italiā in librīs meīs lēgī. Maximē illam terram vidēre cupiō. Nōnne tū, Mārcella, eō iter facere cupis?"

10 "Id iter," inquit Mārcella, "facere cupiō, sed sine parentibus nostrīs in Eurōpam īre nōn possumus."

"Ita est," inquit Mārcus, "sed 15 ad patrem ībimus et dē hāc rē eum interrogābimus. Fortasse nōs audiet."

Deinde puer et puella ad patrem accēdunt, atque Mārcella ita dīcit: 20 "Sentiō, pater, tē dēfessum esse. Per tōtum annum labōrāre nōn dēbēs. Certē ōtium meruistī.

"Ego et Mārcus Italiam vidēre magnopere cupimus, quod multās 25 rēs dē eā terrā et urbibus ejus audīvimus et lēgimus. Nōnne tū hāc aestāte nōs eō dūcēs?"

Ubi haec audīvit, pater rīsit (*laughed*) et hoc respōnsum dedit: 30 "Putō vōs dē vestrā voluntāte plūs cōgitāre quam dē meō ōtiō. Sed nihilō minus id quod rogātis nōn sine ratiōne est. Prīmum autem dē impēnsā (*expense*) tālis 35 itineris quaeram."

Post paucōs diēs pater ad sē Mārcum et Mārcellam vocāvit. "Cum mātre vestrā," inquit, "om-nia dē impēnsā (*expense*) itineris ēgī (*I have discussed*). Hāc aestāte 40 in Italiam īre poterimus."

Mox omnia parāta sunt, atque dē portū Novī Eborācī (*of New York*) Kalendīs Jūliīs (*July first*) omnēs discessērunt. 45

Post quīnque diēs viātōrēs in cōnspectum Hispāniae vēnērunt. Nāvis cursum inter duōs montēs tenuit, quōs Rōmānī columnās Herculis appellāvērunt. 50

Hodiē oppidum *Gibraltar* in lītore est, atque fretum dē hōc oppidō nōmen habet. Ferē omnēs nāvēs quae per fretum eunt hunc portum intrant, ubi complūrēs hōrās ma- 55 nent. Post longum cursum in marī, viātōrēs in "terrā firmā" libenter ambulāvērunt.

Contrā hoc oppidum frāter et soror lītus Āfricae vīdērunt. Eam 60 regiōnem Rōmānī Maurētāniam[2] appellāvērunt. Quārē hodiē incolae *Moors* appellantur.

Inde nāvis ad oppidum *Algiers*, quod est in *Algeria*, prōcessit. 65

Ab *Algeria* viātōrēs ad orientem sōlem[3] nāvigāvērunt. Cursus nāvis nōn longē aberat ab illā parte lītoris ubi urbs Carthāgō antīquitus stābat. Ea urbs potentissima vix 70 ā Rōmānīs superāta est. Postquam Carthāgō dēlēta est, Rōmānī in Āfricam colōnōs (*colonists*) mīsē-runt, quī ibi magnās urbēs aedificā-vērunt. 75

Dēnique nāvis ad Siciliam per-

---

[1] *American.* While **Americānus** was not a word known to the Romans, it is Latin in form.

[2] *Mauretania* (mâ-rē-tạ′ni-ạ̈). See map, page 277.

[3] *the east;* literally, *the rising sun.*

vēnit. Haec īnsula multa oppida habet, quōrum Panormus[1] et Tauromenium[2] viātōribus bene nōta erant. Quod nāvis in portū Tauromeniī[2] complūrēs hōrās mānsit, omnēs viātōrēs in summum (*top of*) collem ascendērunt, unde montem Aetnam[3] vidēre potuērunt. In hōc locō est clārum theātrum (*theater*) antīquum.

REVIEW

1. Conjugate the verbs **dīcō** and **cupiō** in the present and future tenses of the indicative, active and passive. (Gr. S., 35, 36.) 2. Conjugate **faciō** in the imperfect indicative active, and **capiō** in the imperfect indicative passive. 3. Decline **currus** and **cornū** in the plural. (Gr. S., 6.) 4. Decline **cursus** and **cōnspectus** in the singular. 5. Decline the personal pronouns **ego** and **tū** in the singular and plural. (Gr. S., 23.) 6. Explain the case of the word **Rōmānīs**, page 36, line 71. (Gr. S., 76.)

Yesterday and Today

VIĀTŌRĒS Siciliam relīquērunt, et gubernātor (*pilot*) ad portum Neāpolis cursum dīrēxit. Prīmā lūce viātōrēs Neāpolim cōnspexērunt.

Inter Neāpolim et Rōmam est iter multōrum mīlium passuum. Hoc iter autem viātōrēs hodiē paucīs hōrīs cōnficiunt.

"Omnēs," inquit pater, "quī historiam (*history*) Ītaliae bene intellegunt Rōmam amant. Multī ad eam urbem iterum iterumque redīre cupiunt. In memoriā teneō verba Rutiliī Namātiānī,[4] quī haec scrīpsit ubi ab urbe in Galliam, patriam suam, redīre coāctus est: 'Hospes, nēmō potest immemor (*forgetful*) esse tuī.' Et vērē (*truly*) dīxit."

"Maximē gaudeō," inquit Mārcella, "quod Rōmam vidēbimus."

"Ubi prīmum adveniēmus," inquit pater, "eam regiōnem urbis vidēbitis in quā thermae (*the baths*) Dioclētiānī (*of Diocletian*), imperātōris clārī, stetērunt. Magnam ecclēsiam (*church*) et mūsēum (*museum*) nōtissimum et alia aedificia vidēbimus in eō spatiō quod ōlim intrā mūrōs thermārum (*of the baths*) continēbātur."

Postquam viātōrēs urbem intrāvērunt, in mediam urbem iter vertērunt. Ibi vīdērunt montem Capitōlīnum, quem statim ascendērunt. Hīc antīquitus stābat templum Jovis (*of Jupiter*) Capitōlīnī. Montem trānsiērunt atque per clīvum (*sloping street*) Capitōlīnum ad Forum Rōmānum dēscendērunt.

In Forō aedificia jam eīs nōmine

---

[1] *Palermo* (pạ-lèr'mō—see pronunciation key, p. 410). See map, page 61.

[2] *Taormina* (tä-ọr-mē'nạ). See map, page 61.

[3] *Mount Aetna* (et'nạ), a volcano on the island of Sicily. See map, page 61.

[4] *of Rutilius Namatianus* (rö-til'i-us nạ-mä-shi-ā'nus). He was a Gallic poet who lived in Rome in the fifth century A.D.

A FINE MODERN BOULEVARD LEADS TO THE COLOSSEUM

The old and the new rub elbows in Rome today. The broad street leading to the Colosseum is the *Via dell' Impero*, down which our American travelers went. Some of the landmarks they saw are Trajan's Column and the Forum of Trajan. At the right of the picture, behind the Victor Emmanuel Monument, is the Roman Forum.

(*by name*) nōta vīdērunt. Tum montem Palātīnum ascendērunt. In hōc monte vīdērunt multa loca eīs ex librīs nōta. Hīc imperātor Caligula[1] ā mīlitibus interfectus est.

Illīc (*there*) Augustus domum suam habuit; illīc Tiberius et aliī imperātōrēs habitāvērunt. Quod hic collis altior est, ex eō tōta urbs spectārī potest.

"Flūmen Tiberim[2] videō," inquit Mārcus, "et ultrā flūmen in monte altō multa et magna aedi- ficia videō. Estne Jāniculum?" Et digitō magnum montem ā sinistrā mōnstrāvit.

Pater respondit: "Sine dubiō est Jāniculum."

Tum pater mūrum Aurēliānum[3] mōnstrāvit, quī multīs in locīs cōnspicī poterat. Hodiē ultrā hunc mūrum urbs longē patet.

Viātōrēs per Forum Rōmānum ad novam viam lātam vēnērunt, quae *Via dell' Impero*[4] appellātur. Ab utrōque latere hujus viae ruīnās aedificiōrum vīdērunt quae ā clārīs

[1] *Caligula* (kạ-lig′ū-lạ̈—see pronuncia-tion key, p. 410), the third Roman emperor, successor of Tiberius (see p. 23).
[2] This is one of a few third-declension nouns with the accusative singular in **-im**, instead of **-em**.
[3] *Aurelian's Wall*. It was built around the city about A.D. 275.
[4] *"Empire Street."*

imperātōribus Rōmānīs extrūcta sunt.

Inter haec sunt ruīnae templī Veneris (*of Venus*), quae in Forō 5 Jūliī Caesaris nūper inventae sunt.

Nōn longē abest columna Trajānī (*of Trajan*), quae omnibus viātōribus nōta est. Ea in Forō Trajānī (*of Trajan*) stat. In aliā 10 parte hujus forī, mercātōrēs multās rēs vēndidērunt.

Ad Colossēum (*the Colosseum*) iērunt, quod omnēs intrāre vehementer cupiēbant; nam clārissimum aedificium est in tōtā urbe. In 15 hoc ingēns amphitheātrum circiter XLV mīlia hominum convenīre potuērunt.

"Hīc," inquit Mārcus, "ōlim gladiātōrēs cum bēstiīs (*beasts*) et 20 interdum cum aliīs gladiātōribus pugnāvērunt. Hīc Chrīstiānī (*Christians*) sub crūdēlibus oculīs multitūdinis ad mortem missī sunt. Putō etiam nunc mē posse clāmōrēs 25 spectātōrum audīre."

REVIEW

1. Conjugate **veniō** in the present, imperfect, and future active indicative. (Gr. S., 35.) 2. Give the third person singular of **audiō** in the passive in all six tenses of the indicative. (Gr. S., 36.) 3. Conjugate **possum** in the present, imperfect, and future indicative. (Gr. S., 40.) 4. Give the third person plural of **possum** in all six tenses of the indicative. 5. Decline **diēs** and **rēs**. (Gr. S., 7.) 6. Explain the case of **digitō**, page 38, line 16. (Gr. S., 82.)

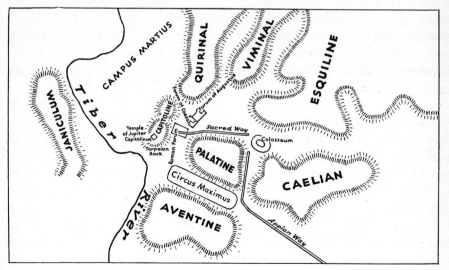

ROME IN ANCIENT TIMES

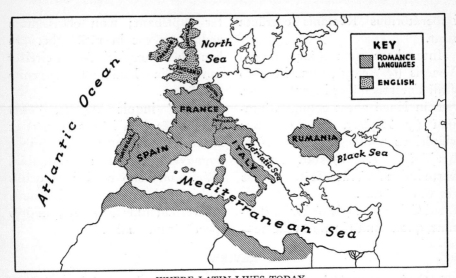

WHERE LATIN LIVES TODAY

In much of the territory once occupied by the Roman Empire, Latin still lives. Countries where Romance languages are now spoken are shown by shaded lines, while the English-speaking countries—the language of which has been greatly influenced by Latin—are indicated by dots.

The Language That Has Never Died

IN EŌ locō ubi Mārcus et Mārcella cum patre urbem intrāvērunt erat magnum aedificium novum. Id nōndum cōnfectum
5 erat atque multī hominēs ibi labōrābant. Suprā jānuam ejus aedificiī haec verba in signō scrīpta erant: *Pericolo di morte.*

"Nōnne, pater," inquit puer,
10 "errāvit scrīptor (*writer*) eōrum verbōrum? Ego linguam Latīnam in scholā (*school*) didicī. Mihi haec verba dēbēre esse videntur: Perīculum mortis."

15 Pater respondit: "Gaudeō quod hoc rogāvistī. In hōc signō verba vidētis ejus linguae quam *Italian* appellāmus, quae autem 'nova Latīna' est."

20 "Fortasse igitur," inquit Mār-
[1] -ve added to a word means *or.*

cella, "nōs hanc novam linguam facile intellegere possumus. Plūs dē eā scīre cupiō."

Et pater "Antīquitus," inquit, "lingua Latīna apud eās gentēs 25 audiēbātur quās Rōmānī vīcerant. In magnā parte Eurōpae atque etiam in Āfricā incolae linguam Latīnam sciēbant.

"Post ruīnam imperiī Rōmānī 30 lingua apud eās gentēs paulātim mūtāta est. Itaque eadem lingua, plūs minusve[1] mūtāta, in multīs locīs nunc audītur.

"Sed in Ītaliā nova lingua est 35 simillima antīquae. Multa verba eandem fōrmam habent in linguā antīquā atque in eā linguā quae hodiē in Ītaliā audītur; exemplī grātiā: *porto, portare, dico, Roma,* 40 *patria, fortuna, bene.*"

"Quid dīcunt Italī (*Italians*) hodiē prō 'vīlla' aut 'via,' pater?" inquit Mārcus.

Pater respondit: "Haec verba
5 eīsdem litterīs hodiē scrībuntur. Sed littera 'v' nōn habet eundem sonum quī apud antīquōs Rōmānōs audiēbātur. Haec littera habet eum sonum quem in nostrīs
10 verbīs *voice* et *very* habet.

"Alia verba parvās mūtātiōnēs (*changes*) exhibent (*show*). Nōmina (*nouns*) autem semper dē cāsū accūsātīvō[1] dērīvārī (*be derived*)
15 possunt. Ea verba Latīna quae in -*m*, -*n*, -*t* fīniuntur, in linguā Ītaliae sunt sine hāc litterā; e.g.,[2] 'montem' nunc est *monte;* 'pontem,' *ponte;* 'nōmen,' *nome;* 'erat,' *era.*"

20 "Itaque, pater," inquit Mārcus, "sine dubiō incolae Ītaliae hodiē dīcunt *simile,* nōn 'similem.' "

"Ita est, Mārce," inquit pater. "Ea verba autem quae litteram
25 -*u*- ante ultimam litteram in linguā Latīnā habuērunt nunc in -*o* fīniuntur; e.g., 'numerum,' *numero;* 'librum,' *libro;* 'possum,' *posso.*

"Jam intellegere potestis hanc
30 linguam esse facillimam. Quī linguam Latīnam cognōvit, linguam

Ītaliae facile intellegere poterit. Multa verba aliās parvās mūtātiōnēs (*changes*) exhibent (*show*), sed facillimē cognōscentur; e.g., 35 'īnsulam,' *isola;* 'longum,' *lungo;* 'patrem,' *padre;* 'aestātem,' *estate;* 'scrīptum,' *scritto;* 'dīxī,' *dissi.*"

"Quid igitur prō 'aurum' hodiē habēmus?" inquit Mārcus. 40

"Prō 'au' nunc *o* habēmus. Itaque 'aurum' nunc *oro* est."

"Nōnne poterimus," inquit Mārcella, "hanc linguam legere?"

Et pater "Ita" inquit. "Spec- 45 tāte id quod scrīpsī."

In estate la[3] vita in Italia è (est) buona (bona).
Il[3] re (regem) d' (*of*) Italia è Vittorio Emmanuele III. 50
In questo (*this*) libro è la storia (historia) d'Italia.
Una nuova (nova) via importante in Roma è la Via dell' (*of the*) Impero.
Il nome di (*of*) mio (*my*) padre è Carlo. 55
Il secondo mese (mēnsis) dell' anno è febbraio.
Il libro fu (fuit) scritto nel (*in*) 1715.
"Madre!" disse Carlo, "non posso aprire (aperīre) la porta!" 60

Nunc viātōrēs in urbe relinquēmus. Ad multās urbēs Ītaliae adībunt. Tum in Americam[4] redībunt.

---

[1] Roman grammarians used the phrase **cāsus accūsātīvus** for *accusative case.*
[2] Abbreviation for **exemplī grātiā.**
[3] *the.* A form of the Italian definite article, which is derived from **ille, illa, illud.**
[4] *America.* **America,** like **Americānus** (p. 36, note 1), is Latin in form.

REVIEW

1. Decline the interrogative pronoun. (Gr. S., 30.) 2. Explain the case of **quid,** line 1 of this page. 3. Decline **īdem.** (Gr. S., 27.) 4. Give the accusative of the phrases meaning *the same boy, the same language, the same word.* 5. Name the case used after each of the following prepositions: **apud, ex, sine, ad, inter, cum, ab, trāns.** (Gr. S., 152, 154.)

CONSPECTUS OF FIRST-YEAR FORMS

DECLENSION OF NOUNS

I		II			
SINGULAR			SINGULAR		
ros-a	amīc-us	puer	ager	vir	templ-um
ros-ae	amīc-ī	puer-ī	agr-ī	vir-ī	templ-ī
ros-ae	amīc-ō	puer-ō	agr-ō	vir-ō	templ-ō
ros-am	amīc-um	puer-um	agr-um	vir-um	templ-um
ros-ā	amīc-ō	puer-ō	agr-ō	vir-ō	templ-ō
PLURAL			PLURAL		
ros-ae	amīc-ī	puer-ī	agr-ī	vir-ī	templ-a
ros-ārum	amīc-ōrum	puer-ōrum	agr-ōrum	vir-ōrum	templ-ōrum
ros-īs	amīc-īs	puer-īs	agr-īs	vir-īs	templ-īs
ros-ās	amīc-ōs	puer-ōs	agr-ōs	vir-ōs	templ-a
ros-īs	amīc-īs	puer-īs	agr-īs	vir-īs	templ-īs

III					
			SINGULAR		
lēx	mīles	flūmen	host-is	gēns	īnsign-e
lēg-is	mīlit-is	flūmin-is	host-is	gent-is	īnsign-is
lēg-ī	mīlit-ī	flūmin-ī	host-ī	gent-ī	īnsign-ī
lēg-em	mīlit-em	flūmen	host-em	gent-em	īnsign-e
lēg-e	mīlit-e	flūmin-e	host-e	gent-e	īnsign-ī
			PLURAL		
lēg-ēs	mīlit-ēs	flūmin-a	host-ēs	gent-ēs	īnsign-ia
lēg-um	mīlit-um	flūmin-um	host-ium	gent-ium	īnsign-ium
lēg-ibus	mīlit-ibus	flūmin-ibus	host-ibus	gent-ibus	īnsign-ibus
lēg-ēs	mīlit-ēs	flūmin-a	host-ēs, -īs	gent-ēs, -īs	īnsign-ia
lēg-ibus	mīlit-ibus	flūmin-ibus	host-ibus	gent-ibus	īnsign-ibus

IV		V	
SINGULAR		SINGULAR	
exercit-us	corn-ū	di-ēs	r-ēs
exercit-ūs	corn-ūs	di-ēī	r-eī
exercit-uī	corn-ū	di-ēī	r-eī
exercit-um	corn-ū	di-em	r-em
exercit-ū	corn-ū	di-ē	r-ē
PLURAL		PLURAL	
exercit-ūs	corn-ua	di-ēs	r-ēs
exercit-uum	corn-uum	di-ērum	r-ērum
exercit-ibus	corn-ibus	di-ēbus	r-ēbus
exercit-ūs	corn-ua	di-ēs	r-ēs
exercit-ibus	corn-ibus	di-ēbus	r-ēbus

DECLENSION OF ADJECTIVES

I *and* II (*-us*)   I *and* II (*-er*)

MASC.	FEM.	NEUT.	MASC.	FEM.	NEUT.
	SINGULAR			SINGULAR	
bonus	bona	bonum	pulcher	pulchra	pulchrum
bonī	bonae	bonī	pulchrī	pulchrae	pulchrī
bonō	bonae	bonō	pulchrō	pulchrae	pulchrō
bonum	bonam	bonum	pulchrum	pulchram	pulchrum
bonō	bonā	bonō	pulchrō	pulchrā	pulchrō
	PLURAL			PLURAL	
bonī	bonae	bona	pulchrī	pulchrae	pulchra
bonōrum	bonārum	bonōrum	pulchrōrum	pulchrārum	pulchrōrum
boʟīs	bonīs	bonīs	pulchrīs	pulchrīs	pulchrīs
bonōs	bonās	bona	pulchrōs	pulchrās	pulchra
bonīs	bonīs	bonīs	pulchrīs	pulchrīs	pulchrīs

I *and* II (*-er*)

MASC.	FEM.	NEUT.
	SINGULAR	
miser	misera	miserum
miserī	miserae	miserī
miserō	miserae	miserō
miserum	miseram	miserum
miserō	miserā	miserō
	PLURAL	
miserī	miserae	misera
miserōrum	miserārum	miserōrum
miserīs	miserīs	miserīs
miserōs	miserās	misera
miserīs	miserīs	miserīs

III

Three Terminations   Two Terminations   One Termination

MASC.	FEM.	NEUT.	M. AND F.	NEUT.	M. AND F.	NEUT.
	SINGULAR			SINGULAR		SINGULAR
ācer	ācris	ācre	omnis	omne	fēlīx	fēlīx
ācris	ācris	ācris	omnis	omnis	fēlīcis	fēlīcis
ācrī	ācrī	ācrī	omnī	omnī	fēlīcī	fēlīcī
ācrem	ācrem	ācre	omnem	omne	fēlīcem	fēlīx
ācrī	ācrī	ācrī	omnī	omnī	fēlīcī	fēlīcī
	PLURAL			PLURAL		PLURAL
ācrēs	ācrēs	ācria	omnēs	omnia	fēlīcēs	fēlīcia
ācrium	ācrium	ācrium	omnium	omnium	fēlīcium	fēlīcium
ācribus	ācribus	ācribus	omnibus	omnibus	fēlīcibus	fēlīcibus
ācrēs, -īs	ācrēs, -īs	ācria	omnēs, -īs	omnia	fēlīcēs, -īs	fēlīcia
ācribus	ācribus	ācribus	omnibus	omnibus	fēlīcibus	fēlīcibus

CONJUGATION OF VERBS, ACTIVE VOICE

PRESENT SYSTEM

PRESENT

I	II	III *(-ō-verbs)*	III *(-iō-verbs)*	IV
port-ō	mone-ō	dūc-ō	capi-ō	audi-ō
portā-s	monē-s	dūci-s	capi-s	audī-s
porta-t	mone-t	dūci-t	capi-t	audi-t
portā-mus	monē-mus	dūci-mus	capi-mus	audī-mus
portā-tis	monē-tis	dūci-tis	capi-tis	audī-tis
porta-nt	mone-nt	dūcu-nt	capiu-nt	audiu-nt

IMPERFECT

I	II	III *(-ō-verbs)*	III *(-iō-verbs)*	IV
portā-ba-m	monē-ba-m	dūcē-ba-m	capiē-ba-m	audiē-ba-m
portā-bā-s	monē-bā-s	dūcē-bā-s	capiē-bā-s	audiē-bā-s
portā-ba-t	monē-ba-t	dūcē-ba-t	capiē-ba-t	audiē-ba-t
portā-bā-mus	monē-bā-mus	dūcē-bā-mus	capiē-bā-mus	audiē-bā-mus
portā-bā-tis	monē-bā-tis	dūcē-bā-tis	capiē-bā-tis	audiē-bā-tis
portā-ba-nt	monē-ba-nt	dūcē-ba-nt	capiē-ba-nt	audiē-ba-nt

FUTURE

I	II	III *(-ō-verbs)*	III *(-iō-verbs)*	IV
portā-b-ō	monē-b-ō	dūc-a-m	capi-a-m	audi-a-m
portā-bi-s	monē-bi-s	dūc-ē-s	capi-ē-s	audi-ē-s
portā-bi-t	monē-bi-t	dūc-e-t	capi-e-t	audi-e-t
portā-bi-mus	monē-bi-mus	dūc-ē-mus	capi-ē-mus	audi-ē-mus
portā-bi-tis	monē-bi-tis	dūc-ē-tis	capi-ē-tis	audi-ē-tis
portā-bu-nt	monē-bu-nt	dūc-e-nt	capi-e-nt	audi-e-nt

PERFECT SYSTEM

PERFECT		PAST PERFECT		FUTURE PERFECT	
portāv-ī	*(so,* monuī	portāv-era-m	*(so,* monueram	portāv-er-ō	*(so,* monuerō
portāv-istī	mānsī	portāv-erā-s	mānseram	portāv-eri-s	mānserō
portāv-it	dedī	portāv-era-t	dederam	portāv-eri-t	dederō
	dūxī		dūxeram		dūxerō
portāv-imus	cēpī,	portāv-erā-mus	cēperam,	portāv-eri-mus	cēperō,
portāv-istis	*etc.)*	portāv-erā-tis	*etc.)*	portāv-eri-tis	*etc.)*
portāv-ērunt		portāv-era-nt		portāv-eri-nt	

CONJUGATION OF VERBS, PASSIVE VOICE

PRESENT SYSTEM

PRESENT

I	II	III (*-ō-verbs*)	III (*-iō-verbs*)	IV
port-or	mone-or	dūc-or	capi-or	audi-or
portā-ris	monē-ris	dūce-ris	cape-ris	audī-ris
portā-tur	monē-tur	dūci-tur	capi-tur	audī-tur
portā-mur	monē-mur	dūci-mur	capi-mur	audī-mur
portā-minī	monē-minī	dūci-minī	capi-minī	audī-minī
porta-ntur	mone-ntur	dūcu-ntur	capiu-ntur	audiu-ntur

IMPERFECT

I	II	III (*-ō-verbs*)	III (*-iō-verbs*)	IV
portā-ba-r	monē-ba-r	dūcē-ba-r	capiē-ba-r	audiē-ba-r
portā-bā-ris	monē-bā-ris	dūcē-bā-ris	capiē-bā-ris	audiē-bā-ris
portā-bā-tur	monē-bā-tur	dūcē-bā-tur	capiē-bā-tur	audiē-bā-tur
portā-bā-mur	monē-bā-mur	dūcē-bā-mur	capiē-bā-mur	audiē-bā-mur
portā-bā-minī	monē-bā-minī	dūcē-bā-minī	capiē-bā-minī	audiē-bā-minī
portā-ba-ntur	monē-ba-ntur	dūcē-ba-ntur	capiē-ba-ntur	audiē-ba-ntur

FUTURE

I	II	III (*-ō-verbs*)	III (*-iō-verbs*)	IV
portā-b-or	monē-b-or	dūc-a-r	capi-a-r	audi-a-r
portā-be-ris	monē-be-ris	dūc-ē-ris	capi-ē-ris	audi-ē-ris
portā-bi-tur	monē-bi-tur	dūc-ē-tur	capi-ē-tur	audi-ē-tur
portā-bi-mur	monē-bi-mur	dūc-ē-mur	capi-ē-mur	audi-ē-mur
portā-bi-minī	monē-bi-minī	dūc-ē-minī	capi-ē-minī	audi-ē-minī
portā-bu-ntur	monē-bu-ntur	dūc-e-ntur	capi-e-ntur	audi-e-ntur

PERFECT SYSTEM

PERFECT	PAST PERFECT	FUTURE PERFECT
portātus (monitus, *etc.*) sum	portātus (monitus, *etc.*) eram	portātus (monitus, *etc.*) erō
portātus (monitus, *etc.*) es	portātus (monitus, *etc.*) erās	portātus (monitus, *etc.*) eris
portātus (monitus, *etc.*) est	portātus (monitus, *etc.*) erat	portātus (monitus, *etc.*) erit
portātī (monitī, *etc.*) sumus	portātī (monitī, *etc.*) erāmus	portātī (monitī, *etc.*) erimus
portātī (monitī, *etc.*) estis	portātī (monitī, *etc.*) erātis	portātī (monitī, *etc.*) eritis
portātī (monitī, *etc.*) sunt	portātī (monitī, *etc.*) erant	portātī (monitī, *etc.*) erunt

THE SAILORS OF ULYSSES RELEASE
THE UNFAVORABLE WINDS

ULYSSES

Ulysses, much-experienced man,
Whose eyes have known this globe of ours,
Her tribes of men, and trees, and flowers.

TENNYSON: TO ULYSSES

Starting Home

Urbs Trōja ā Graecīs decem annōs obsessa est. Dē hōc bellō Homērus (*Homer*), quī maximus poētārum Graecōrum erat, Iliadem (*the Iliad*), opus nōtissimum, scrīpsit.

Trōja tandem per īnsidiās capta est, et Graecī, longō bellō[1] dēfessī, in patriam suam redīre mātūrāvērunt. Postquam omnia ad profectiōnem parāvērunt, nāvēs dēdūxērunt. Ventus erat secundus,[2] et magnō cum[3] gaudiō solvērunt.[4]

Erat inter prīmōs Graecōrum quīdam vir summae virtūtis et prūdentiae, Ulīxēs nōmine, quī ex īnsulā Ithacā ad bellum Trōjānum vēnerat.

Rēgnum Ithacae obtinuerat, et ante bellum Trōjānum puellam pul-

A STORIED HILL

In days so long ago that we know about them not from history, but from legend and poetry, the Greeks captured the citadel of Troy. In recent years scientists have excavated the site and learned at first hand about the people of ancient Troy.

cherrimam, Penelopēn (*Penelope*) nōmine, in mātrimōnium dūxerat. Quod decem annōs quasi in exiliō cōnsūmpserat, magnopere patriam et uxōrem vidēre cupiēbat.

The Land of the Lotus-Eaters

Postquam nāvēs pauca mīlia passuum ā lītore Trōjae prōcessērunt, magna tempestās furere (*to rage*) coepit. Nūlla nāvium cursum tenēre poterat.

Nāvis quae Ulīxem vehēbat, vī[5]

---

[1] *by the long war.*

[2] *favorable.*

[3] A monosyllabic preposition may stand between a noun and its modifier.

[4] Translate, *they set sail;* literally, *they loosed* (the ship).

[5] Ablative singular of the noun **vīs.** (See Gr. S., 8.)

EŌS QUĪ LŌTUM ĒDERANT AD NĀVEM REPORTĀVIT

tempestātis ad merīdiem dēlāta,[1] ad lītus Libyae appulsa est. Ancora jacta est, et Ulīxēs nōnnūllōs ē sociīs in terram expōnere cōnstituit. Eōs aquam referre et nātūram regiōnis cognōscere jussit.

Dum hī fontem quaerunt,[2] ā quibusdam[3] incolīs vīsī sunt, quī eōs hospitiō[4] accēpērunt. Cibus eōrum hominum paene omnīnō ē quōdam mīrō frūctū cōnstābat, quem lōtum appellābant.

Nautae, simul atque hunc cibum gustāvērunt (*tasted*), memoriam patriae et sociōrum statim dēposuērunt. In eā terrā jūcundā (*pleasant*) semper manēre et illum cibum dulcem (*sweet*) edere cupiēbant.

Homeland and Friends Forgotten

Ulīxēs ab hōrā septimā[5] ad vesperum expectāvit, sed sociī ejus nōn rediērunt. Id mīrum esse vidēbātur, et aliī complūrēs nautae in eandem regiōnem dēnique missī sunt.

Hī ad vīcum, quī nōn longē aberat, iērunt, ubi comitēs suōs mox invēnērunt. Sed eī redīre ad nāvēs nōlēbant.[6] Neque patriam neque domōs neque amīcōs in memoriā jam habēbant. Nihil praeter lōtum et illam terram jūcundam (*pleasant*) dēsīderābant.

Tum nūntiī haec[7] ad Ulīxem rettulērunt, quī statim ad eum locum sē contulit.[8] Manūs eōrum vīnxit quī lōtum ēderant et in eā terrā manēre volēbant, et eōs ad nāvem invītōs reportāvit. Deinde ancoram sustulit[9] et portum relīquit.

FERŌ AND ITS COMPOUNDS*

The verb **ferō**, *I bear, I carry*, is irregular. Its principal parts are: **ferō, ferre, tulī, lātum.** In the present indicative it is conjugated as follows:

ACTIVE		PASSIVE	
SINGULAR	PLURAL	SINGULAR	PLURAL
ferō, I bear	ferimus, we bear	feror, I am borne	ferimur, we are borne
fers, you bear	fertis, you bear	ferris, you are borne	feriminī, you are borne
fert, he, she, it bears	ferunt, they bear	fertur, he, she, it is borne	feruntur, they are borne

In the imperfect and future indicative **ferō** is conjugated as a regular -ō-verb of the third conjugation: **ferēbam, ferēbas,** etc.; **feram, ferēs,** etc.

The perfect system is formed like that of regular verbs.

There are many compounds of **ferō**. Forms of two of these, **dēferō** and **referō**, appear in the first chapter on page 48. Other compounds are **auferō, cōnferō, differō, efferō,** and **īnferō.** Observe carefully the spelling of the principal parts of these compounds as they occur.

THE VERBS *VOLŌ* AND *NŌLŌ*

The principal parts of the irregular verb **volō**, *I wish*, and its compound **nōlō**, *I am unwilling*, are as follows: **volō, velle, voluī; nōlō, nōlle, nōluī.**

The stem vowel -o- in **volō** appears as -e- in the infinitive **velle**, but the -ō- of **nōlō** is unchanged in the infinitive **nōlle.**

Volō and **nōlō** are conjugated as follows in the present indicative:

SINGULAR	PLURAL	SINGULAR	PLURAL
volō, I wish	volumus, we wish	nōlō, I am unwilling	nōlumus, we are unwilling
vīs, you wish	vultis, you wish	nōn vīs, you are unwilling	nōn vultis, you are unwilling
vult, he, she, it wishes	volunt, they wish	nōn vult, he, she, it is unwilling	nōlunt, they are unwilling

In the imperfect and future indicative, **volō** and **nōlō** are conjugated as regular -ō-verbs of the third conjugation: **volēbam, volēbās,** etc., **volam, volēs,** etc.; **nōlēbam, nōlēbās,** etc., **nōlam, nōlēs,** etc.

The perfect system of these verbs is formed like that of regular verbs.

NOTES ON THE TEXT

[1] From **dēferō**. See the conjugation of **ferō** and its compounds above.

[2] *were seeking*. As was explained in note 2, page 16, the present tense is always used with **dum** meaning *while*, even though the main verb denotes past tense.

[3] **quīdam**, *a certain, some*. For the declension of **quīdam**, see Gr. S., 32.

[4] *with hospitality*.

[5] See page 409.

[6] The conjugation of **nōlō** and **volō** is given above.

[7] With **rettulērunt**—*reported this fact*. The neuter plural of **hic** may often be translated *this* or *this fact*.

[8] *made his way*; literally, *betook himself*.

[9] From **tollō**.

*NOTE TO THE TEACHER. Additional drill on this and subsequent grammar topics is given on page 339.

DUŌS Ē NUMERŌ GRAECŌRUM CORRIPUIT

An Inhospitable Reception

Posteā ad terram vēnit ubi gigās habitābat, quī tantum[1] ūnum oculum habēbat. Is crūdēlissimus erat et saepe hominēs dēvorābat. Nōmen ejus erat Polyphēmus.

Ulixēs et comitēs ejus ingēns antrum invēnērunt in quō Polyphēmus noctū dormiēbat, sed is tum ab antrō aberat. Graecī multās rēs quās ibi vīdērunt mīrābantur.[2]

Mox Polyphēmus rediit et Graecōs vīdit, quamquam hī sē cēlāre cōnābantur.[3] Sine morā duōs ē numerō eōrum corripuit et interfēcit. Tum carnem eōrum avidē (*ravenously*) dēvorāvit. Omnēs Graecī magnopere territī sunt, sed Polyphēmus validissimus erat neque quemquam verēbātur.

Posterō diē duōs aliōs interfectōs dēvorāvit. Deinde ex antrō excessit et ovēs caprōsque (*sheep and goats*) ad montēs ēgit[4] ubi eōs pāscēbat (*he pastured*).

[1] *only;* an adverb.
[2] A deponent verb. See page 51.
[3] Another deponent verb.
[4] *drove,* from **agō.**

DEPONENT VERBS

There is an important class of Latin verbs which are passive in form but active in meaning. Examples are **cōnor**, *I try;* **polliceor**, *I promise.* These are called *deponent verbs.* They have only three principal parts:

PRESENT INDICATIVE	PRESENT INFINITIVE	PERFECT INDICATIVE
cōnor	cōnārī	cōnātus sum
polliceor	pollicērī	pollicitus sum

Deponents have only two stems, the present and the participial.

The present infinitives of deponent verbs of the four conjugations have the same endings as the present passive infinitives of the four conjugations.

I	II	III	IV
-ārī	-ērī	-ī	-īrī

The present indicative of deponents of the first and second conjugations is formed exactly like the present passive of **portō** and **moneō**.

I	II

SINGULAR

cōnor, I try	polliceor, I promise
cōnāris, you try	pollicēris, you promise
cōnātur, he, she, it tries	pollicētur, he, she, it promises

PLURAL

cōnāmur, we try	pollicēmur, we promise
cōnāminī, you try	pollicēminī, you promise
cōnantur, they try	pollicentur, they promise

In the imperfect and future, the use of tense signs and person endings is the same as in the passive of the corresponding tenses of **portō** and **moneō**: **cōnābar, cōnābāris**, etc., **cōnābor, cōnāberis**, etc.; **pollicēbar, pollicēbāris**, etc , **pollicēbor, pollicēberis**, etc.

The perfect tense of deponent verbs of the first and second conjugations is formed like the perfect passive of **portō** and **moneō**.

I	II

SINGULAR

cōnātus sum, I tried, I have tried	pollicitus sum, I promised, I have promised
cōnātus es, you tried, you have tried	pollicitus es, you promised, *etc.*
cōnātus est, he, she, it tried; he, she, it has tried	pollicitus est, he, she, it promised, *etc.*

PLURAL

cōnātī sumus, we tried, we have tried	pollicitī sumus, we promised, *etc.*
cōnātī estis, you tried, you have tried	pollicitī estis, you promised, *etc.*
cōnātī sunt, they tried, they have tried	pollicitī sunt, they promised, *etc.*

The past perfect and future perfect are formed like the corresponding tenses of the passive of **portō** and **moneō**: **cōnātus eram**, etc., **cōnātus erō**, etc.; **pollicitus eram**, etc., **pollicitus erō**, etc.

The Escape

ULĪXĒS VĪNUM IN MAGNŌ
PŌCULŌ POLYPHĒMŌ DEDIT

Deinde Polyphēmō, quī cum 5
ovibus (*sheep*) et caprīs (*goats*) sub[1]
vesperum in antrum redierat, vī-
num in magnō pōculō dedit. Polyphēmus libenter id pōculum accēpit et Ulīxī grātiās ēgit. Multum 10
vīnum bibit et mox somnō oppressus est.

Tum Ulīxēs et comitēs ejus
Polyphēmum circumvēnērunt et
oculum ejus pālō acūtō trānsfōdē- 15
runt (*gouged out*). Gigās magnōs
clāmōrēs sustulit[2] et in antrō vagā-
tus est, sed quod jam caecus
erat, Graecōs capere nōn poterat.

Porta antrī autem magnō saxō 20
obstrūcta est (*was stopped up*),
neque Graecī hoc saxum āmovēre
poterant. Sed posterō diē māne[3]
Polyphēmus saxum āmōvit et pecudēs ex antrō mīsit. Tum Graecī 25
effūgērunt et tūtī ad nāvēs contendērunt.

Sᴇᴅ Ulīxēs dolum callidum ex-
cōgitāvit (*devised*). Magnum
pālum, quem praeacūtum effēce-
rat, in igne posuit.

The Home of the Winds

Sᴛᴀᴛɪᴍ profectī sunt[4] et ad
aliam īnsulam pervēnērunt, in
30 quā rēx ventōrum habitābat. Is
rēx Aeolus appellātus est, et īnsula
ejus erat patria ventōrum.

Hīc Graecī benignē ab Aeolō
acceptī sunt, et paucōs diēs ibi
35 mānsērunt. Septimō diē, quod
omnēs ē labōribus sē recēperant,[5]
iterum proficīscī volēbant.

Tum rēx Ulīxī saccum ē coriō
(*of leather*) cōnfectum dedit, in
quō omnēs ventī praeter ūnum 40
inclūsī erant.

Hoc dōnum Ulīxēs libenter accēpit. Ille ūnus quem rēx nōn in-
clūserat erat Zephyrus (*the gentle
west wind*). Merīdiānō tempore 45
(*at midday*) Graecī discessērunt, et
Zephyrus eōs per flūctūs ferēbat.

[1] *toward.*
[2] From **tollō.**
[3] *the next morning;* literally, *on the
next day in the morning.*

[4] For this form of **proficīscor** see the
conjugation given in the last paragraph
on page 53.
[5] With **sē**—*had recovered.*

OCULUM POLYPHĒMĪ PĀLŌ ACŪTŌ TRĀNSFŌDĒRUNT

DEPONENTS OF THE THIRD AND FOURTH CONJUGATIONS

The present tense of deponents of the third and fourth conjugations is formed like the present passive of **dūcō** and **audiō**.

III	IV
SINGULAR	
sequor, I follow	**partior,** I share
sequeris, you follow	**partīris,** you share
sequitur, he, she, it follows	**partītur,** he, she, it shares
PLURAL	
sequimur, we follow	**partīmur,** we share
sequiminī, you follow	**partīminī,** you share
sequuntur, they follow	**partiuntur,** they share

In the imperfect and future indicative the use of tense signs and person endings is the same as in the passive of the corresponding tenses of **dūcō** and **audiō : sequēbar, sequēbāris,** etc., **sequar, sequēris,** etc.; **partiēbar, partiēbāris,** etc., **partiar, partiēris,** etc.

There are also deponent verbs corresponding to the **-iō**-verbs of the third conjugation. An example is **prōgredior, prōgredī, prōgressus sum.** It is conjugated like the passive of **capiō : prōgredior, prōgrederis,** etc.

The perfect system of all deponent verbs is like that of the regular passive system of other verbs: **secūtus sum, secūtus eram, secūtus erō,** etc.; **partītus sum, partītus eram, partītus erō,** etc.

Too Much Curiosity

Novem diēs cursum tenuērunt atque jam in cōnspectum Ithacae vēnerant. Sed comitēs Ulīxis putābant aurum et argen-
5 tum (*silver*) in eō saccō cēlārī.[1] Hās rēs inter sē partīrī volēbant.

Itaque dum dux eōrum dormit,[2] saccum solvērunt. Extemplō (*im-*
10 *mediately*) ē saccō ventī ērūpērunt (*burst forth*), et magna tempestās coorta est. Ulīxēs, ē somnō excitātus, vīdit nāvem in perīculō esse, et īrātissimus erat.

Sed nūllum auxilium invēnit, et 15 tempestās Graecōs ad īnsulam Aeolī rettulit.[3] Aeolus dīxit omnēs deōs Ulīxī et comitibus ejus inimīcōs[4] esse, atque Graecōs iterum juvāre nōlēbat. 20

A Famous Sorceress

Ulīxēs cāsum suum dolēns[5] ā rēgnō Aeolī cum comitibus discessit et ad aliam īnsulam pervēnit, quam Circē, fīlia Sōlis, in-
25 colēbat.

Graecī ibi frūmentum petere cōnstituērunt, quod cōpia frūmentī in nāve dēficiēbat. Nōnnūllī nautae igitur frūmentum petentēs[6] in
30 partem interiōrem īnsulae profectī sunt.

Mox ad vīllam pulcherrimam vēnērunt. Ibi vōcem fēminae canentis (*singing*) audīvērunt. Jā-
35 nuam pulsāvērunt, et ipsa Circē eōs salūtāvit (*greeted*) et benignē accēpit.

Sed ūnus ex eīs,[7] Eurylochus[8] nōmine, dolum timēns, nōn cum reliquīs intrāvit, sed ad ōstium 40 sedēbat.

Eī quī intrāverant convīvium (*feast*) magnificum parātum invēnērunt.

Sed Circē, quae magicae artis 45 summam perītiam (*knowledge*) habēbat, vīnum eīs dedit in quō medicāmentum (*drug*) quoddam posuerat.

Tum postquam Graecī vīnum 50 bibērunt, Circē capita eōrum virgā (*with a wand*) aureā tetigit. Statim omnēs in porcōs conversī sunt.

Ulysses to the Rescue

Eurylochus,[8] quī extrā ātrium sedēbat neque vīnum biberat, sine morā ad Ulīxem contendit atque haec omnia nūntiāvit. Ulīxēs, ubi haec audīvit, gladium cēpit et in īnsulam prōgressus 60

[1] *was concealed.*

[2] This use of the present tense is explained in note 2, page 49.

[3] From **referō.**

[4] *unfriendly.*

[5] *grieving* (*over*). The present active participle is explained on page 55.

[6] Nominative plural of the present participle, agreeing with the noun **mīlitēs.**

[7] *one of these.* With **ūnus** and some other numerals (and also with **quīdam**) the ablative with **ex** or **dē** is regularly used instead of the genitive.

[8] *Eurylochus* (ū-ril'ọ̄-kus—see pronunciation key, p. 410).

PRESENT ACTIVE PARTICIPLE

In addition to the perfect passive participle (**portātus,** *having been carried*), there are also participles in the active voice. The present active participles of regular verbs in the four conjugations are as follows:

I	II	III		IV
(portō)	(moneō)	(dūcō)	(capiō)	(audiō)
portāns	**monēns**	**dūcēns**	**capiēns**	**audiēns**
carrying	*warning*	*leading*	*taking*	*hearing*

The present active participle of a Latin verb is formed on the present stem and has the ending **-ns** in the nominative singular. Observe that the present participle of **-ō**-verbs of the third conjugation is exactly like that of the second conjugation. In the fourth conjugation and in **-iō**-verbs of the third conjugation the stem ending appears as **-iē-.**

A deponent verb has the present active participle: **cōnāns,** *trying.*

The English present participle must not be confused with the progressive form of the verb.

> *Progressive:* The man *is standing* in the street.
> *Participle:* The man *standing* in the street is my brother.

In the first sentence the expression *is standing* is the progressive form of the verb, and is translated by one Latin word, **stat.** In the second sentence the word *standing* is a participle modifying *man,* and is expressed by the Latin present participle, **stāns.**

While the English verb has a present passive participle (*being carried, being warned*) as well as a present active, there is no present passive participle in Latin.

DECLENSION OF PRESENT PARTICIPLE

Like other participles, the present participle agrees in gender, number, and case with the noun or pronoun it modifies. It is declined as an adjective of the third declension.

SINGULAR

	MASC. AND FEM.	NEUT.	MASC. AND FEM.	NEUT.
Nominative:	portāns	portāns	monēns	monēns
Genitive:	portantis	portantis	monentis	monentis
Dative:	portantī	portantī	monentī	monentī
Accusative:	portantem	portāns	monentem	monēns
Ablative:	portante, -ī	portante, -ī	monente, -ī	monente, -ī

PLURAL

	MASC. AND FEM.	NEUT.	MASC. AND FEM.	NEUT.
Nominative:	portantēs	portantia	monentēs	monentia
Genitive:	portantium	portantium	monentium	monentium
Dative:	portantibus	portantibus	monentibus	monentibus
Accusative:	portantēs	portantia	monentēs	monentia
Ablative:	portantibus	portantibus	monentibus	monentibus

est. Ad vīllam Circēs statim ac-
cessūrus[1] erat.

Sed deus Mercurius eum convēnit et dē arte magicā Circēs omnia

DEUS MERCURIUS

docuit. Herbam quandam quoque 5
eī dedit. Haec herba contrā artem
magicam maximē valēbat.[2]

Post breve tempus Ulīxēs in cōnspectum vīllae vēnit. Ibi Circēn
vīdit et eam dē comitibus suīs in- 10
terrogāvit. Circē eum quoque per
magicam artem suam in porcum
vertere cōnāta est, sed propter
herbam illam[3] nihil efficere potuit.
Deinde Ulīxēs gladium dēstrīnxit 15
(*drew*) et eam interfectūrus erat.
Circē, magnopere territa, veniam
(*pardon*) petīvit, et eōs porcōs quī
hominēs fuerant in propriam fōrmam hūmānam convertit.　　　　20

Sine morā omnēs Graecī magnō
cum[4] gaudiō ad lītus rediērunt et
statim ex īnsulā discessūrī[5] erant.
Sed Circē, quae nunc benigna
facta erat, magna beneficia Ulīxī 25
et comitibus ejus dabat; et per
ūnum annum ibi mānsērunt.

Setting Out Once More

Propter dēsīderium (*longing*)
patriae et amīcōrum quī in
30 Ithacā eum expectābant Ulīxēs ex
īnsulā discēdendī[6] cupidus erat.
Nāvem refēcit, quae tempestāte
afflīcta erat (*had been damaged*), et
omnia ad proficīscendum[7] parāvit.
35　Tum nautae vēla ad ventōs pan-
dērunt et rēmōs manibus rapuērunt. Ventī secundī vēla implē-

bant, et nāvis per flūctūs celeriter
cucurrit.

Sed mox in nāvigandō in alia 40
perīcula incidērunt, et omnēs praeter Ulīxem vītam āmīsērunt.

Is multa incommoda accēpit,
quae in hōc locō longum est perscrībere. Ad postrēmum (*at last*) 45
in Ithacam pervēnit, ubi magnō
cum gaudiō acceptus est.

---

[1] Future participle of **accēdō**. Its
use with **sum** is explained on page 57.

[2] With **maximē**—*was very powerful.*

[3] For special emphasis a form of **ille**
may follow the word it modifies.

[4] See page 47, note 3.

[5] Nominative plural, agreeing with
Graecī.

[6] *of departing.* The gerund is explained
on page 57.

[7] A deponent verb may have all the
forms of the gerund.

FUTURE ACTIVE PARTICIPLE

In addition to the perfect passive participle (**portātus**) and the present active participle (**portāns**), Latin verbs have a future active participle, which is formed on the participial stem. It is declined like the perfect passive participle, from which it is to be distinguished by **-ūr-**, preceding the case ending.

> **portātūrus, -a, -um,** *about to carry,* or *going to carry*
> **monitūrus, -a, -um,** *about to warn,* or *going to warn*

Like other participles the future active participle agrees in gender, number, and case with the noun or pronoun it modifies.

Some verbs which have no perfect passive participle have a future active participle. The future active participle of such verbs is given as the fourth principal part. The future participle of **sum** is **futūrus,** and the principal parts are **sum, esse, fuī, futūrus.** The fourth principal part of **stō** is **statūrus.**

The future participle is often combined with the forms of **sum** to refer to something which someone intends to do or is about to do.

> **Laudātūrus est,** *He is about to praise,* or *He intends to praise.*
> **Ad vīllam accessūrus erat,** *He was about to come to the villa.*

Deponent verbs have future active participles.

> **cōnātūrus,** *about to try*   **pollicitūrus,** *about to promise*

THE GERUND

The English present participle ends in *-ing*, as we have already seen.

> *The boy standing in the street is my brother.*

In the preceding sentence, *standing* tells something about the *boy* and is therefore a participle.

There is, however, another verb form in English which also ends in *-ing*.

> *I am fond of fishing.*

In the sentence above, *fishing* is the object of the preposition *of* and is therefore used as a noun. Such a verb form used as a noun is called a *gerund.*

The Latin gerund is declined as a neuter noun of the second declension. It is formed on the present stem as it appears in the present participle (see p. 55). It has no nominative and is used only in the singular.

	I	II	III	IV
Genitive:	portandī	monendī	dūcendī	audiendī
Dative:	portandō	monendō	dūcendō	audiendō
Accusative:	portandum	monendum	dūcendum	audiendum
Ablative:	portandō	monendō	dūcendō	audiendō

The gerund of **capiō** is declined like that of **audiō: capiendī,** etc.

The genitive of a gerund is used with adjectives or nouns and is translated *of carrying, of warning,* etc.

> **cupidus discēdendī,** *desirous of departing*

The genitive of the gerund is also frequently employed with the ablative **causā,** *for the sake of, for the purpose of.*

<u>effugiendī **causā,** *for the purpose of escaping*</u>

The ablative without a preposition is translated *by carrying* or *with carrying,* etc. The ablative is also used with prepositions. The accusative is used only with prepositions. The dative does not often occur.

COMPREHENSION QUESTIONS

The incidents told in the story of Ulysses are frequently referred to in English literature. The following questions deal with some of the more important of these incidents.

1. How long did the siege of Troy last?
2. What was the name of Ulysses' wife?
3. What did the sailors who had eaten the lotus wish to do?
4. Who was Polyphemus?   Describe his appearance.
5. Why did Ulysses not wish to kill Polyphemus in the cave?
6. Who was the king of the winds?   Where did he live?
7. Which of the winds was left free?   What did it do?
8. Why did the sailors open the bag in which the winds had been inclosed?
9. Who was Circe?   How did Ulysses meet her?
10. What magic power did she have?
11. How did Ulysses escape the power of Circe?
12. On what island was the home of Ulysses?
13. What finally happened to the companions of Ulysses?

QUESTIONS ON GRAMMAR

1. Conjugate **ferō** in the present indicative, active and passive. (Gr. S., 42.) 2. Translate: *I was bearing, he will bear, they bore.* 3. Write a synopsis of **dēferō** in the third person singular, active voice, and give the meaning of each form. 4. Conjugate **volō** and **nōlō** in the present indicative. (Gr. S., 45.) 5. Give the principal parts of **volō** and write a synopsis of it in the third person singular. 6. What is a deponent verb? (See p. 51.) 7. Give a synopsis of **cōnor** in the third person plural. (Gr. S., 38.) 8. Conjugate **sequor** in the present and the future indicative. (Gr. S., 38.) 9. Conjugate **partior** in the future indicative. (Gr. S., 38.) 10. Give the Latin for *carrying, saying, coming.* What is this form of the verb called? (See p. 55.) 11. Decline the present active participle of **videō.** (Gr. S., 14.) 12. Give the Latin for the following: *about to plan, about to see, about to touch,* and *about to come.* What is this form of the verb called? (See p. 57.) 13. Give the gerund of **expectō** and of **sentiō.** (See p. 57.)

WORD STUDY I
Some Important Prefixes

In Latin, as in English, a new word is often formed by adding a prefix to a simple word. Four important prefixes used in forming Latin compounds are: **in-**[1] (**il-, im-, ir-**), meaning *not;* **inter,** *among, between;* **prae,** *before, in front;* **prō,** *before, forward, for.* Examples of these appear in "Ancient and Modern Tourists in Italy" and "Ulysses," e.g., **inimīcō,** page 54, line 18; **praeacūtum,** page 52, line 3; **prōcēdēbant,** page 21, line 21.

Some other Latin words of frequent occurrence which are formed with these prefixes are the following:

indignus, *not worthy*
īnfēlīx, *not fortunate*
īnfīnītus, *not limited*
injūstus, *not just*

immortālis, *not mortal,*
  not subject to death
imprūdēns, *not foreseeing*

interjaceō, *lie between*
interpōnō, *place between*
interrēgnum, *(interval) between reigns*
interserō, *plant among*
interveniō, *come between*

praecurrō, *run before*
praedīcō, *tell beforehand*
praeferō, *carry before one*
praeficiō, *put before, put in charge of*
praemittō, *send before (one)*
praestō, *stand before, excel*
praesum, *be before, be in charge of*

prōcēdō, *go forward*
prōdūcō, *lead forward, bring forward*
prōfluō, *flow forth*
prōjiciō, *throw forward*
prōmoveō, *move forward*
prōpellō, *drive forward*

These same prefixes also appear in many English words.

inconvenient	intercede	predict	promote
indivisible	interval	prejudice	provoke
illegal	interrupt	premature	provide
impure	interfere	prepare	propose
irregular	intermittent	preview	prospect

EXERCISES

1. Give some additional English words in which the following prefixes appear: **in-** (**il-, im-, ir-**), **prō.**

Idioms and Phrases

Latin has a number of phrases which cannot be satisfactorily translated into English, word by word, but which must each be taken as a whole. Some of these are of frequent occurrence. A few such phrases are given below. These should be carefully learned, so that their meanings will be easily recognized when they appear in later reading.

grātiās agere, *to thank*
in memoriā habēre, *to remember*
mīlia passuum, *miles*

sē cōnferre, *to make one's way, to go*
simul atque (or **ac**), *as soon as*
sī quid, *if anything*

[1] This must not be confused with the adverbial prefix **in**, meaning *in* or *into*. The hyphen shows that the prefix is inseparable; i.e., it is not found as a separate word.

Vocabulary Review

The following words, which appear frequently in this book, are important in second-year work. Their meanings should be thoroughly learned.

adulēscēns	cōnferō	fīniō	obsideō	rapiō
aequō	cōnspiciō	ignōtus	oculus	redeō
alacer	cōnstō	interior	passus	rūmor
angustus	cōnsuētūdō	levis	pateō	secundus
antecēdō	cupidus	lūdō	perītus	spērō
aperiō	cūrō	memoria	portus	tam
ascendō	differō	mēnsis	postquam,	tangō
aut . . . aut	digitus	mercātor	posteāquam	tuba
caedō	dīligēns	mūtō	potestās	vertō
cēterī	dīrigō	nē	praeter	vīcīnus
circum	dominus	nēmō	profectiō	vītō
cōgitō	efferō	numquam	prōvincia	voluntās

A GREEK TEMPLE IN SICILY

In the long-ago days when Rome was a small settlement and Greek colonies were numerous in Sicily and southern Italy, worshipers passed in and out of this impressive Temple of Concord at Segesta.

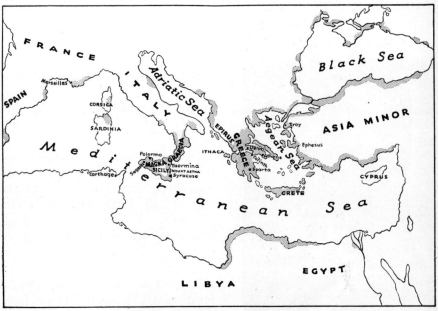

GREEK CIVILIZATION SPREAD FAR

The Greeks were a seafaring and trading people, whose colonies—shown here by the dotted areas—fringed the Mediterranean Sea and the Black Sea. Notice the large Greek domain in Sicily and Italy.

OUR INHERITANCE FROM THE GREEKS

Two thousand years ago Roman boys were studying the *Odyssey*, the Greek poem that tells of the wanderings of Ulysses, and reading the *Iliad*, which gives an account of the ten-year siege of Troy by the Greeks. These poems were already hundreds of years old and belonged to a civilization much more ancient than that of the Romans.

The Greeks, or Hellenes, were a daring and enterprising people, who in very early days ventured out on the Mediterranean and into the Black Sea. They planted colonies from Asia Minor to Spain. There were so many Greek cities on the coasts of southern Italy and Sicily that these colonies came to be known as *Magna Graecia*. The ruins of splendid Greek buildings still to be seen in *Magna Graecia* show us how remarkable was the civilization which flourished there.

This highly developed Greek culture so near to Rome could not fail to leave its mark on the young town. Greek ships were sailing along the coast of Italy, and Hellenic merchants were trading with the Italian tribes there while Rome was still a village. From these very early times, all through the many centuries of Roman history, contacts with the Greek culture of southern Italy were an important factor in Roman life.

In both *Magna Graecia* and Greece itself, many beautiful things

MODELED ON A GREEK ORIGINAL

From a statue made by the famous Greek sculptor Phidias, a Roman copied this Athena, which represents the Greek goddess of wisdom.

a Greek was to seek to know." The ancient Greek was eager to observe the world of nature and of men, to organize his knowledge, and to find explanations for what he saw. He made investigations in the fields of zoölogy, botany, history, geography, and mathematics.

In mathematics the Greeks discovered and stated principles which have been important in the thinking of all later peoples. The geometry studied in our high schools is based on the work of a famous Greek mathematician, Euclid. Many of our mathematical terms come from the Greek; for instance, "isosceles" comes from two Greek words meaning "equal" and "legs." Thus an isosceles triangle is one with two equal legs, or sides.

Greek astronomers were so skilled that one of them was able to predict accurately the time of an eclipse of the sun, and another reached the conclusion that the earth is a sphere.

A Greek scholar found and stated some of the laws of language, and wrote a grammar that formed the basis for all later works. The grammatical relations which he pointed out underlie our study of grammar today—his principles apply to languages, such as our own, which did not even exist in his time.

Greek writers produced not only the *Iliad* and the *Odyssey*, but histories, lyric poems, comedies, and tragedies which rank among the greatest literature of the world.

have been found that testify to "the glory that was Greece." Some of the greatest art treasures of the world are a heritage from the Greeks. The Parthenon, the most marvelous of all Greek temples, still looks down on modern Athens from the Acropolis, the high rock on which it was built. Famous Greek statues, or reproductions of them, are to be found in art museums all over the world, for the wonders in marble which the Greek sculptors produced have never been surpassed.

The Greeks were interested in knowledge and ideas, as well as in art. It has been said that "to be

THE ANCIENT GREEKS LIVED AMID BEAUTY

This restoration shows the Acropolis, the hilltop where the Athenians walked, talked, and worshiped. From its fortified height they defended their city when necessary.

The stories of Hercules and of the Argonauts given in this book were originally Greek tales.

Greek philosophers wrote much about the manner in which one should live, and the modern world still finds these writings worthy of study. Of course, not all these philosophers agreed, but certain ideas were generally accepted by the Greeks, such as that one should serve the state; be fair to other citizens; cultivate the mind by education in science and the arts, and the body by athletic sports; not be a slave to a desire for wealth and material possessions, but seek to know the truth and do one's duty.

Great as is our debt to the Greeks for the statues and buildings they left us, still greater is our indebtedness for the foundation of our knowledge in science and for many of the ideals on which modern society is based.

In the middle of the second century B.C., Greece fell before the relentless progress of the Roman armies. But though the legions of Rome had conquered the people, they could not destroy Greek civilization. On the contrary, the culture of the Greeks so influenced the Romans that the poet Horace wrote, "Greece, taken captive, captivated her savage conqueror."

For centuries after the conquest of Greece many an educated Roman spoke Greek almost as well and as frequently as he spoke his native Latin. The beautiful objects in his house—the wall-paintings, mosaics, statues, vases, silver dishes, graceful pieces of furniture, and rich draperies—either were of Greek origin or showed the influence of Greek artists and craftsmen. His children attended a school in which Greek was taught, or they had Greek tutors. A Roman's education was not complete until he had visited Greece. The most valued of his slaves were Greeks, often more highly educated than their master.

Learned Romans studied the scientific and historical works of Greece, and on this foundation built their own contributions to science and history.

Thus the Romans absorbed a part of the Greek culture. In fact, the civilization of the Mediterranean from the time of the conquest of Greece is usually referred to as Graeco-Roman.

If the Romans had not made the Greek culture part of their own civilization and thus preserved for the western world much that is beautiful and great, life in Europe and in our own country today would be quite different. Perhaps our knowledge of the natural sciences would be less, our ways of organizing knowledge different, our standards of beauty of another sort. In your own school, geometry might be an entirely different kind of course; in your study of grammar you might not meet the same ideas and terms; probably you would never have heard of Ulysses or of Troy.

The English poet Shelley wrote: "We are all Greeks. Our laws, our literature, our religion, our arts have their roots in Greece. But for Greece, Rome—the instructor, the conqueror, or the metropolis of our ancestors—would have spread no illumination with her arms."

A GREEK TEMPLE IN OHIO

If there were no peanut stand, memorial cannon, street lamps, or modern figures, this might be taken for a temple in ancient Greece, instead of the Old Court House in Dayton.

HERCULES AND HIS MEN
BATTLE THE AMAZONS

HERCULES

But Hercules with faith sublime
Pursued his many labors.

GUITERMAN: HERCULES AND COMPANY

An Infant Prodigy

A FOE OF HERCULES
An ancient sculptor carved this head of Juno,
queen of the gods.

Hercules, Alcmēnae fīlius, ōlim in Graeciā habitābat. Hic dīcitur omnium hominum validissimus fuisse.[1]

At Jūnō, rēgīna deōrum, Alcmēnam ōderat,[2] et Herculem adhūc īnfantem (*infant*) necāre voluit. Mīsit igitur duās serpentēs saevissimās.

Hae mediā nocte[3] in cubiculum (*bedroom*) Alcmēnae vēnērunt, ubi Herculēs cum frātre suō dormiēbat. Nec tamen in cūnīs (*cradle*) sed in scūtō magnō cubābant (*they were lying*).

Serpentēs jam appropinquāverant et scūtum movēbant; itaque puerī ē somnō excitātī sunt.

Hercules and the Serpents

Frāter Herculis magnā[4] vōce exclāmāvit; at Herculēs ipse, puer fortissimus, haudquāquam (*not at all*) territus est. Parvīs manibus serpentēs statim prehendit et colla eārum magnā vī com-

---

[1] With **Hic dīcitur**—*he is said to have been.*
[2] *hated.* The verb **ōdī** has only the tenses formed on the perfect stem. The perfect form, however, is translated as a present, the past perfect is translated as imperfect, and the future perfect is translated as future.
[3] *in the middle of the night.*
[4] Do not translate here by "great." What is the best equivalent you can find?

THE FIRST TRIAL OF HERCULES' STRENGTH

pressit. Tālī modō serpentēs ā puerō interfectae sunt.

Alcmēna autem, māter puerōrum, clāmōrem audīverat et ma-
5 rītum suum ē somnō statim excitāverat.

Ille lūmen accendit et gladium suum rapuit; tum ad puerōs properābat. Sed ubi ad locum vēnit, rem mīram vīdit; Herculēs enim 10 rīdēbat (*was laughing*) et serpentēs mortuās mōnstrābat.

The Music Lesson

Herculēs ā puerō[1] corpus suum dīligenter exercēbat.[2] Mag-
15 nam partem diēī in palaestrā (*exercise-ground*) cōnsūmēbat; didicit[3] etiam arcum intendere et tēla con-

jicere. Hīs exercitātiōnibus vīrēs[4] ejus cōnfirmātae sunt.

In mūsicā (*music*) etiam ā Linō 20 Centaurō[5] ērudiēbātur. (Centaurī autem equī erant, sed caput ho-

[1] *from boyhood;* literally, *from a boy.*
[2] The imperfect is often used to express repeated or habitual action; another example is **cōnsūmēbat** in line 16.
[3] From **discō.** What are its principal parts?
[4] For the declension of **vīs**, see Gr. S., 8.
[5] In apposition with **Linō.**

minis habēbant.) Huic tamen artī minus dīligenter studēbat.[1] Hic Linus Herculem ōlim culpābat (*reproached*) quod parum studiōsus 5 (*studious*) erat. Tum puer īrātus citharam[2] subitō rapuit et sum-mīs vīribus caput magistrī īnfēlīcis percussit.

Ille[3] ictū prōstrātus est, et pau-lō[4] post ē vītā excessit, neque 10 quisquam posteā id officium susci-pere voluit.

A Narrow Escape

DĒ HERCULE haec etiam inter alia[5] nārrantur. Ōlim, dum 15 iter facit,[6] in fīnēs Aegyptiōrum (*of the Egyptians*) vēnit. Ibi rēx quīdam, nōmine Būsīris,[7] illō tem-pore rēgnābat; hic autem, vir[8] crū-dēlissimus, hominēs immolāre cōn-20 suēverat.[9] Herculem igitur cor-ripuit et in vincula conjēcit. Tum nūntiōs dīmīsit et diem sacrificiō[10] ēdīxit.

Mox ea diēs appetīvit, et omnia 25 rīte (*properly*) parāta sunt. Manūs Herculis catēnīs ferreīs (*of iron*) vīnctae sunt, et mola salsa (*salted meal*) in caput ejus īnspersa est (*was sprinkled*). Mōs enim erat apud antīquōs salem et fār (*ground* 30 *meal*) capitibus[11] victimārum im-pōnere.

Jam victima ad āram stābat; jam sacerdōs cultrum (*knife*) sūmp-serat. Subitō tamen Herculēs 35 magnō cōnātū vincula rūpit. Tum ictū sacerdōtem prōstrāvit; alterō[12] rēgem ipsum occīdit.

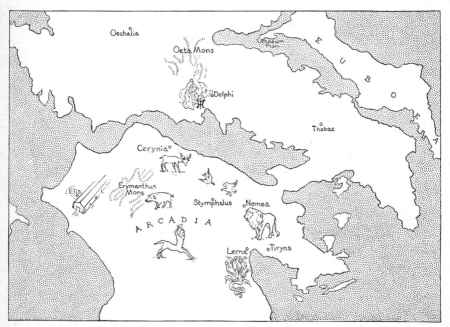

GREECE — SCENE OF MANY OF HERCULES' ADVENTURES

SUBITŌ HERCULĒS MAGNŌ CŌNĀTŪ VINCULA RŪPIT

DATIVE WITH SPECIAL VERBS

Most verbs meaning *to please, displease, trust, distrust, believe, persuade, serve, obey, favor, resist, envy, threaten, pardon,* and *spare* govern the dative.

> **Liber tibi placet,** *The book pleases you.*
> **Huic artī studuit,** *He devoted himself to this art.*

The verbs **imperō,** *command,* **noceō,** *injure,* and a few others also govern the dative.

The English equivalents of these verbs take direct objects, but the Latin words did not suggest to the Romans a direct object. Thus **placēre** meant *be pleasing to,* and **persuādēre** meant *make attractive to.*

NOTES ON THE TEXT

[1] With **Huic artī**—*he devoted himself to this art.* This use of the dative **artī** is explained above.

[2] *a cithara,* a kind of stringed instrument.

[3] *he,* meaning **Linus.**

[4] With **post**—*a little later;* literally, *later by a little.*

[5] With **haec**—*these things among others.*

[6] Translate as an imperfect.

[7] *Busiris* (bū-sī′ris—see pronunciation key, p. 410).

[8] In apposition with **hic.**

[9] *was accustomed.*

[10] *for the sacrifice;* dative.

[11] *on the heads;* dative.

[12] Supply **ictū.**

Hercules in Thebes

FOR a time Hercules made his home in the Greek city of Thebes. The Thebans had at one time been defeated in war by the Minyae, and as a result they were compelled to pay tribute to their conquerors. Hercules determined to put an end to this situation, and on one occasion when the representatives of the Minyae came to demand the annual payment, he seized them and cut off their ears.

In the war that followed, the Theban king, Creon, left the leadership to Hercules, who gathered an army and routed the Minyae, thus freeing the Thebans from the payment of tribute. Hercules then married the daughter of the king, but after a few years of peaceful life he was stricken with temporary insanity.

While in this condition he killed his children. He soon regained his reason, but since the Thebans shunned all association with him as a result of his terrible deed, he was compelled to leave the city.

Atoning for a Deed of Madness

HE SPOKE TO HERCULES
Through the famous oracle Pythia, Apollo gave advice to Hercules—advice which led him into a life of dangerous adventures.

HERCULĒS magnopere cupiēbat scelus expiāre. Cōnstituit igitur Delphōs[1] īre, in quā urbe erat ōrāculum celeberrimum (*very famous*). Ibi templum erat Apollinis, plūrimīs dōnīs ōrnātum. Hōc

5

in[2] templō sedēbat fēmina quaedam, nōmine Pȳthia, et cōnsilium dabat eīs quī ad ōrāculum veniēbant. Haec autem fēmina ab ipsō Apolline docēbātur, et voluntātem deī hominibus ēnūntiābat. 10

Herculēs igitur, quī Apollinem praecipuē (*especially*) colēbat, hūc vēnit. Tum rem tōtam exposuit, neque scelus cēlāvit. 15

Ubi Herculēs fīnem fēcit, Pȳthia diū tacēbat. Tandem tamen jussit eum Tīryntha[3] īre, et Eurystheī rēgis omnia imperāta facere. 20

Herculēs, ubi haec audīvit, ad urbem illam contendit et Eurystheō rēgī sē in servitūtem[4] trādidit.

Duodecim annōs in servitūte Eurystheī tenēbātur, et duodecim 25 labōrēs, quōs ille imperāverat, cōnfēcit; hōc enim ūnō modō tantum scelus expiārī potuit. Dē hīs labōribus plūrima[5] ā poētīs scrīpta sunt. Multa tamen quae poētae nārrant 30 vix crēdibilia (*credible*) sunt.

The First Labor—Killing the Nemean Lion

PRĪMUM ab Eurystheō jussus est Herculēs leōnem occīdere, quī illō tempore vallem Nemaeam[6] reddēbat īnfestam (*dangerous*).

5 In silvās igitur quās leō incolēbat statim sē contulit. Mox feram (*wild beast*) vīdit, et arcum quem sēcum[7] attulerat intendit; ejus tamen pellem, quae dēnsissima erat, 10 trājicere nōn potuit.

Tum clāvā (*with a club*) magnā, quam semper gerēbat, leōnem percussit. Frūstrā tamen, neque enim hōc modō eum occīdere po- 15 tuit.

Tum dēmum collum mōnstrī manibus suīs comprehendit,[8] et faucēs (*throat*) ejus summīs vīribus compressit. Hōc modō leō brevī 20 tempore exanimātus est.

THE VICTOR WEARING THE LION SKIN

Tum Herculēs cadāver (*body*) ad oppidum in umerīs rettulit et pellem quam dētrāxerat posteā prō veste[9] gerēbat. Omnēs autem quī eam regiōnem incolēbant, ubi fā- 25 mam dē morte leōnis accēpērunt, vehementer gaudēbant, et Herculem magnō in honōre habēbant.

PLACE TO WHICH

With names of cities and towns, and also with **domus**, when meaning *home*, place to which is denoted by the accusative without a preposition.

    Cōnstituit Delphōs īre, *He decided to go to Delphi.*

    Consul domum rediit, *The consul returned home.*

With other words **ad** or **in** is used with the accusative to denote place to which.

NOTES ON THE TEXT

[1] *to Delphi.* The use of the accusative is explained above.

[2] A monosyllabic preposition may stand between a noun and its modifier.

[3] A Greek accusative form. The word is of Greek origin; hence the Greek case-ending is kept. The nominative is **Tīryns**, *Tiryns* (tī′rinz—see pronunciation key, p. 410).

[4] *into slavery.*

[5] *a great many things.*

[6] *of Nemea* (nē-mē′a). Nemea was a city in Greece. See map, page 68.

[7] The preposition **cum** regularly follows, and is attached to, a personal, a reflexive, or a relative pronoun.

[8] What tense?

[9] *as a garment.*

HERCULES FIGHTING WITH THE HYDRA

The Second Labor—Slaying the Hydra

Post haec jussus est ab Eurystheō Hydram necāre. Hoc[1] autem mōnstrum erat quod novem capita habēbat.

5 Herculēs igitur cum amīcō ad palūdem Lernaeam[2] contendit, quam Hydra incolēbat. Mox mōnstrum invēnit et, quamquam rēs erat magnī perīculī, collum ejus laevā (*with his left hand*) prehen- 10 dit. Tum dextrā capita novem abscīdere coepit. Quotiēns tamen hoc fēcerat, nova capita prōveniēbant (*came forth*). Diū frūstrā labōrāvit; tandem hōc cōnātū[3] dē- 15 stitit. Cōnstituit deinde arborēs succīdere (*to cut down*) et ignem accendere.

Hoc celeriter fēcit, et postquam ligna ignem comprehendērunt,[4] face (*with a torch*) ārdente colla adussit (*seared*), unde[5] capita prōveniēbant (*came forth*). Nec tamen sine magnō labōre haec fēcit. Auxilium enim Hydrae tulit can-cer (*crab*) ingēns, quī, dum Herculēs capita abscīdit, crūra (*legs*) ejus mordēbat (*was biting*). 10

Postquam mōnstrum tālī modō[6] interfēcit, sagittās suās sanguine ejus imbuit (*soaked*), itaque mortiferās (*deadly*) reddidit.

The Third Labor—Capture of the Cerynian Stag

Postquam Eurystheō caedēs Hydrae nūntiāta est, magnus timor animum ejus occupāvit. Jussit igitur Herculem cervum quendam ad sē referre; nōluit enim virum tantae audāciae in urbe retinēre. Hic autem cervus, cujus cornua aurea erant, omnia animālia celeritāte[7] praecessit. Herculēs igitur prīmum vēstīgia ejus in silvīs animadvertit. Deinde, 25 ubi cervum ipsum vīdit, summīs vīribus (*with all his might*) currere coepit. Usque ad vesperum cucurrit, neque nocturnum tempus sibi[8] ad[9] quiētem relīquit. Tandem, 30 postquam tōtum annum cucurrerat (ita trāditur[10]), cervum cursū exanimātum cēpit et vīvum ad Eurystheum rettulit.

ABLATIVE OF MANNER

The ablative is used to show in what way or manner something is done. The preposition **cum** is commonly used with a noun in the ablative when the noun has no modifier, but need not be used if the noun is modified by an adjective or a genitive.

Mōnstrum tālī modō interfēcit, *He killed the monster in this way.*

ABLATIVE OF RESPECT

The ablative without a preposition is used to show in what respect a statement is true.

Hae gentēs inter sē linguā differunt, *These nations differ from one another* (literally, *among themselves*) *in language.*

NOTES ON THE TEXT

[1] The reference is to **Hydram,** a feminine noun, but the demonstrative, as usual in Latin, takes its gender from the predicate noun, **mōnstrum.**

[2] *Lernaean* (lèr-nē′an—see pronunciation key, p. 410). For Lerna, see map, page 68.

[3] Ablative of separation. See Gr. S., 74.

[4] *caught.*

[5] *from which;* equivalent to **ex quibus.**

[6] Ablative of manner. This use is explained above.

[7] Ablative of respect. This use is explained above.

[8] Dative with **relīquit.** It may be omitted in translation.

[9] *for.*

[10] *so the story goes.*

The Fourth Labor—Capturing the Erymanthian Boar

HUNTER AND HUNTED

The story of Hercules was handed down to the Romans by the Greeks. The adventures of Hercules inspired many Greek painters and sculptors.

THE fourth labor which Hercules was ordered to perform was the capture of a famous wild boar that was terrifying the inhabitants of the region near the Erymanthus[1] Mountains.

On the approach of Hercules the boar took to flight, but the hero succeeded in throwing a noose over the animal and pulling him out of a ditch into which he had jumped in his panic. Hercules then carried it back alive to the king.

While on his way to the haunt of the Erymanthian boar, Hercules came into the land where the centaurs[2] lived. Here he was courteously received by Pholus, one of the centaurs, who dwelt in a cave. In this cave was kept a cask of wine under the care of Pholus. Although Pholus objected, Hercules drew a cup of wine from this cask. The odor of the wine attracted the other centaurs, who came to the cave and attacked Pholus, trying to kill him.

Hercules beat off the attackers, using in defense of his host some of the arrows which he had poisoned with the blood of the Hydra. He pursued the centaurs until he had driven them to a safe distance.

Meanwhile, Pholus picked up one of the poisoned arrows Hercules had shot. While handling the weapon, he accidentally dropped it on his foot, and the poison on the point of the arrow caused his death in a short time. Hercules returned to find Pholus dead. The hero gave his friend's body fitting burial and then rested awhile after the vigorous exertions of the battle.

The Fifth Labor—Cleansing the Augean Stables

DEINDE Eurystheus Herculī[3] hunc labōrem graviōrem imposuit.

Augēās[4] quīdam, quī illō tempore rēgnum in Ēlide[5] obtinēbat, tria mīlia boum[6] habēbat. Hī

[1] Pronounced er-i-man′thus—see pronunciation key, p. 410. See map, page 68.

[2] A centaur was a mythical creature with a horse's body and a man's head. See picture, page 93.

[3] *upon Hercules.*

[4] *Augeas* (â-jē′as).

[5] *Elis* (ē′lis), a city in Greece. See map, page 68.

[6] *three thousand cattle.* The singular **mīlle** is regularly an adjective; the plural **mīlia** is always a noun, used with a genitive of the whole. The form **boum** is the genitive plural of **bōs**. See Gr. S., 8.

in stabulō ingentis magnitūdinis inclūdēbantur. Stabulum autem illuviē (*with dirt*) ac squālōre (*filth*) obsitum erat (*was filled*); neque 5 enim ad hoc tempus umquam[1] pūrgātum erat. Hoc jussus est Herculēs intrā spatium ūnīus diēī pūrgāre.

Ille, etsī rēs erat multae ope- rae,[2] negōtium suscēpit. Prīmum, 10 magnō labōre fossam duodēvīgintī pedum[3] fēcit, per quam flūminis aquam dē montibus ad mūrum stabulī perdūxit. Tum, postquam mūrum perrūpit (*he broke through*), 15 aquam in stabulum immīsit (*he let*), et tālī modō, contrā opīniōnem omnium, opus cōnfēcit.

The Sixth Labor—The Birds of Stymphalus

Post paucōs diēs Herculēs ad oppidum Stymphālum iter fē- cit; jusserat enim eum Eurystheus avēs Stymphālidēs[4] necāre. Hae avēs rōstra aēnea habēbant et carnem[5] hominum edēbant.

25 Ille, postquam ad locum per- vēnit, lacum vīdit. In hōc lacū, quī nōn procul erat ab oppidō, avēs habitābant.

Nūllō tamen modō ad eās ap- 30 propinquāre poterat; lacus enim nōn ex aquā sed ē līmō (*mud*) cōnstitit.[6] Herculēs igitur neque pedibus[7] neque lintre prōcēdere potuit. Tandem postquam mag- 35 nam partem diēī frūstrā cōnsūmp- sit, hōc cōnātū dēstitit et ad Vul- cānum[8] sē contulit auxiliumque ab eō petīvit.

Vulcānus, quī ā fabrīs maximē 40 colēbātur, crepundia,[9] quae ipse ex aere fēcerat, Herculī dedit. Hīs

Herculēs dīrum crepitum (*noise*) fēcit, et avēs perterritae āvolāvē- runt. Ille autem, dum āvolant, magnum numerum eōrum sagittīs 45 trānsfīxit.

VULCAN, THE BLACKSMITH GOD

---

[1] With **neque**—*never*.

[2] *was (one) of great labor.*

[3] *eighteen feet (wide).*

[4] *of Stymphalus* (stim-fā'lus—see pro- nunciation key, p. 410). See map, page 68.

[5] From **carō, carnis**, *flesh.*

[6] From **cōnstō.**

[7] *on foot*; ablative of means, but sug- gesting, in addition, the idea of manner.

[8] *Vulcan*, the god of fire and metal work.

[9] *a rattle.* The form is plural; the meaning, singular.

The Seventh Labor—The Cretan Bull

Postquam Herculēs Stymphālō[1] rediit, Eurystheus eum jussit taurum quendam ferōcissimum[2]
ex īnsulā Crētā[3] vīvum referre.

5 Ille igitur nāvem cōnscendit, et
cum prīmum[4] ventus idōneus fuit,
solvit. Ubi tamen īnsulae[5] jam
appropinquābat, ventus subitō vehementer flāre (*to blow*) coepit, nā-
10 visque cursum tenēre nōn poterat.

Nautae paene omnem spem salūtis dēposuērunt; tantus timor
animōs eōrum occupāverat. Herculēs tamen haudquāquam (*by no*
15 *means*) territus est.

Sed post breve tempus mare
tranquillum (*calm*) factum est, et
nautae, quī sē ex timōre jam recēperant,[6] nāvem incolumem ad
terram perdūxērunt. Herculēs 20
statim ad rēgem Crētae[3] sē contulit et causam itineris docuit.

Deinde, postquam omnia parāta
sunt, ad eam regiōnem contendit
quam taurus vāstābat. Mox tau- 25
rum vīdit, et quamquam rēs erat
magnī perīculī, cornua ejus prehendit. Tum ingentī labōre mōnstrum ad nāvem trāxit et cum
praedā in Graeciam rediit. 30

The Eighth Labor—The Horses of Diomedes

The eighth labor of Hercules was to bring from Thrace the horses of Diomedes. These horses were fed on human flesh. Their victims were strangers who had been found in the region ruled by Diomedes. Hercules demanded that the horses be given to him, and when his demand was refused, he killed the owner and threw his body to the horses to be eaten. As a result of this exploit he was offered the kingship in place of Diomedes, but he refused and returned to Greece, taking the horses with him.

The Ninth Labor—The Girdle of Hippolyte

Gēns Amāzonum dīcitur om-
nīnō ex mulieribus cōnsti-
tisse.[7] Hae summam scientiam reī
mīlitāris[8] habēbant et maximam
35 virtūtem praebēbant; nam etiam
cum virīs proelium committere[9]
audēbant.

Hippolytē,[10] Amāzonum rēgīna,
balteum habuit celeberrimum (*very
famous*), quem Mārs eī dederat. 40
Admēta[11] autem, Eurystheī fīlia,
fāmam dē hōc balteō accēperat,
et eum possidēre vehementer cupiēbat. Eurystheus igitur Hercu-

[1] This ablative expresses place from which and is explained on page 77.
[2] *very savage.*
[3] *Crete* (krēt—see pronunciation key, p. 410), an island in the Mediterranean Sea. See map, page 61.
[4] *as soon as.*
[5] Dative with **appropinquābat.**
[6] With **sē**—*had recovered.*

[7] *to have consisted,* perfect infinitive of **cōnstō.** The form is explained on page 77.
[8] *of military science,* or *of the art of war.*
[9] *to engage in battle.*
[10] A Greek form in the nominative singular.
[11] *Admeta* (ad-mē′ta).

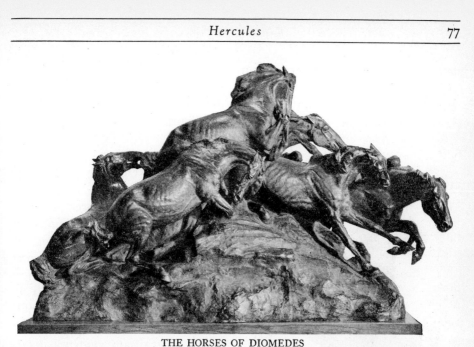

THE HORSES OF DIOMEDES

This is the work of the American artist Gutzon Borglum, whose gigantic head of Washington is carved in the living rock of Mount Rushmore in South Dakota. The spirited group is in the entrance of the Metropolitan Museum in New York City.

PLACE FROM WHICH

With names of cities and towns, and also with **domus** (when meaning *home*), place from which is denoted by the ablative without a preposition.

Mīlitēs Rōmā profectī sunt, *The soldiers set out from Rome.*
Herculēs Stymphālō rediit, *Hercules returned from Stymphalus.*

With other words, **ab, dē,** or **ex** is used with the ablative to denote place from which.

PERFECT AND FUTURE ACTIVE INFINITIVES

The Latin infinitive has three tenses, the present, perfect, and future. The present active infinitive has already been given.

Present Active Infinitive: **portāre,** *to carry*

The perfect and the future active infinitives of **portō** are as follows: perfect, **portāvisse,** *to have carried;* future, **portātūrus esse,** *to be going to carry,* or *to be about to carry.*

The perfect active infinitive is formed by adding **-isse** to the perfect stem. The future active infinitive consists of the future active participle with **esse.** The active infinitives of the model verbs of the four conjugations are as follows:

	I	II	III	IV
Present:	portāre	monēre	dūcere	audīre
Perfect:	portāvisse	monuisse	dūxisse	audīvisse
Future:	portātūrus esse	monitūrus esse	ductūrus esse	audītūrus esse

lem jussit cōpiās cōgere et bellum Amāzonibus īnferre.[1] Putābat Herculem balteum relātūrum esse.

Ille nūntiōs in omnēs partēs dīmīsit et, postquam magna multitūdō convēnit, eōs dēlēgit quī maximum ūsum in rē mīlitārī habēbant.

The Girdle Refused

A DANGEROUS WOMAN

This ancient statue shows one of the famous women warriors against whom Hercules battled. Stories of the Amazons were favorite subjects for Greek and Roman artists.

Hīs virīs[2] Herculēs causam itineris exposuit. Illī auctōritāte[3] ejus adductī iter cum eō facere cōnstituērunt. Tum, cum eīs quibus[4] persuāserat, nāvem cōnscendit, et ventum idōneum nactus, post paucōs diēs ad ōstium flūminis Thermōdontis[5] appulit.

Postquam in fīnēs Amāzonum vēnit, nūntium ad Hippolytam mīsit, quī causam veniendī docuit et balteum poposcit. Ipsa Hippolytē balteum trādere volēbat,[6] quod dē Herculis virtūte fāmam accēperat. Quod tamen reliquae Amāzonēs[7] nōlēbant,[8] negāvit. At Herculēs, ubi haec[9] nūntiāta sunt, bellī fortūnam temptāre cōnstituit.

A Battle with Women Warriors

Proximō igitur diē cōpiās ēdūxit. Tum locum idōneum dēlēgit et hostēs ad pugnam ēvocāvit (*challenged*). Amāzonēs quoque cōpiās suās ex castrīs ēdūxērunt et nōn magnō intervāllō aciem īnstrūxērunt. Palūs erat nōn magna[10] inter duōs exercitūs. Neutrī[11] tamen initium trānseundī facere volēbant. Tandem Herculēs signum dedit, et ubi palūdem trānsiit, proelium commīsit.

Amāzonēs impetum virōrum fortissimē sustinuērunt et, contrā opīniōnem omnium, magnam virtūtem praestitērunt.[12] Multōs quidem eōrum occīdērunt; multōs etiam in fugam conjēcērunt.

Virī enim novō genere pugnae perturbābantur, nec[13] solitam virtūtem praestābant. Herculēs autem, ubi haec vīdit, dē suīs fortūnīs dēspērāre coepit. Mīlitēs igitur vehementer cohortātus ad prīstinam virtūtem, tantum dēdecus dēprecātus est;[14] quibus[15] verbīs animī omnium ērēctī sunt; nam multī, etiam quī[16] vulneribus cōnfectī erant, proelium sine morā redintegrāvērunt (*renewed*).

PERFECT AND FUTURE PASSIVE INFINITIVES

The present passive infinitive has already been given in this book.

Present Passive Infinitive: **portārī,** *to be carried*

The perfect passive and the future passive infinitives of **portō** are as follows: perfect, **portātus esse,** *to have been carried;* future, **portātum īrī,** *to be going to be carried,* or *to be about to be carried.*

Observe that the perfect passive infinitive consists of two words, the perfect participle and **esse.** The participle agrees with the subject of the infinitive in gender, number, and case.

Dīcit urbem captam esse, *He says (that) the city was captured.*

In this example **captam** is feminine accusative singular to agree with **urbem,** the subject of the infinitive.

The future passive infinitive, which is seldom used, consists of a form called the *supine* (usually the same as the neuter of the perfect participle) followed by **īrī.**

The passive infinitives of the model verbs of the four conjugations are as follows:

	I	II	III	IV
Present:	portārī	monērī	dūcī	audīrī
Perfect:	portātus esse	monitus esse	ductus esse	audītus esse
Future:	portātum īrī	monitum īrī	ductum īrī	audītum īrī

INFINITIVES OF DEPONENT VERBS

The present and perfect infinitives of deponent verbs are passive in form. Their future infinitives are active in form as well as in meaning.

	I	II
Present:	cōnārī, *to try*	verērī, *to fear*
Perfect:	cōnātus esse, *to have tried*	veritus esse, *to have feared*
Future:	cōnātūrus esse, *to be about to try*	veritūrus esse, *to be about to fear*

NOTES ON THE TEXT

[1] *to make war on the Amazons.*
[2] Dative of indirect object.
[3] Ablative of cause. See Gr. S., 88.
[4] Dative with **persuāserat.**
[5] *Thermodon* (thér-mō'don—see pronunciation key, p. 410). A river in Pontus, a country on the southern coast of the Black Sea.
[6] *was willing.*
[7] This word has the nominative plural ending **-es** with **e** short because it is a Greek form.
[8] Supply **balteum trādere.**
[9] Neuter plural—*these things.*
[10] *of no great extent.*
[11] The plural of **neuter** is employed with reference to two groups. The masculine is here used, though one of the groups was feminine.
[12] The verb **praestō** may be transitive, as here, in the sense of "exhibit, display."
[13] Translate *and . . . not.*
[14] The meaning of **tantum . . . est** is *he prayed (the gods) to avert such a great disgrace.* The word **dēdecus,** *disgrace,* is accusative singular.
[15] Translate by a demonstrative, *these.*
[16] *even those who.*

Defeat of the Amazons

Dīū et ācriter pugnātum est.[1] Tandem tamen ad sōlis occāsum[2] magna commūtātiō rērum facta est, et mulierēs terga vertērunt atque fugā salūtem petīvērunt. Multae autem vulneribus dēfessae, dum fugiunt, captae sunt. In quō numerō ipsa erat Hippolytē. Herculēs summam clēmentiam praestitit, et postquam balteum accēpit, lībertātem omnibus captīvīs (*the captives*) dedit. Post haec sociōs ad mare redūxit et, quod nōn multum aestātis[3] supererat, in Graeciam proficīscī mātūrāvit. Nāvem igitur cōnscendit et, tempestātem idōneam nactus, statim solvit. Antequam tamen in Graeciam pervēnit, ad urbem Trōjam nāvem appellere cōnstituit; frūmentum enim quod sēcum habēbat jam dēficere coeperat.

The Story of a Sea Serpent

Lāomedōn quīdam illō tempore Trōjae[4] rēgnābat. Ad hunc Neptūnus[5] et Apollō annō superiōre vēnerant et, quod Trōja nōndum moenia habēbat, ad hoc opus auxilium obtulerant. Postquam tamen hōrum auxiliō moenia cōnfecta sunt, nōlēbat Lāomedōn praemium quod prōposuerat persolvere (*to pay*).

Neptūnus igitur et Apollō, ob hanc causam īrātī, mōnstrum quoddam mīsērunt speciē horribilī, quod cotīdiē ē marī veniēbat et hominēs pecudēsque vorābat (*devoured*). Trōjānī igitur, timōre perterritī, in urbe continēbantur,[6] et pecora omnia ex agrīs intrā mūrōs compulerant.

Lāomedōn, hīs rēbus commōtus, ōrāculum cōnsuluit. Ā deō autem jussus est fīliam Hēsionem[7] mōnstrō objicere.

The Rescue of a Princess

Lāomedōn, ubi hoc respōnsum renūntiātum est, magnum dolōrem percēpit. Sed tamen, quod cīvēs suōs tantō perīculō līberāre volēbat, ōrāculō[8] pārēre cōnstituit et diem sacrificiō[9] dīxit.

Sed, sīve cāsū sīve cōnsiliō deōrum, Herculēs tempore opportūnissimō Trōjam attigit; ipsō enim temporis pūnctō quō[10] puella catēnīs vīncta ad lītus dēdūcēbātur ille nāvem appulit.

Herculēs, ē nāve ēgressus, dē rēbus quae gerēbantur certior factus est.[11] Tum, īrā commōtus, ad rēgem sē contulit et auxilium suum obtulit.

Rēx libenter ejus auxilium accēpit. Deinde Herculēs mōnstrum interfēcit et puellam, quae jam omnem spem salūtis dēposuerat, incolumem ad patrem redūxit. Lāomedōn magnō cum gaudiō fīliam suam accēpit, et Herculī prō tantō beneficiō meritam grātiam rettulit.

AMAZONS IN BATTLE

LOCATIVE CASE

In addition to the five cases already given, a few nouns have another case, called the *locative*. This case denotes place where. Names of cities and towns and **domus** are the most important words which have a locative case.

The locative singular of the first and second declensions has the same form as the genitive singular.

Nominative: **Trōja,** *Troy*   *Locative:* **Trōjae,** *at Troy,* or *in Troy*

In the plural of these two declensions and in the singular and plural of other declensions, the locative regularly has the same form as the ablative.

Nominative: **Athēnae,** *Athens*   *Locative:* **Athēnīs,** *at Athens,* or *in Athens*

NOTES ON THE TEXT

[1] *the battle was long and fierce;* literally, *it was fought long and fiercely.*

[2] *about sunset.*

[3] *not much of the summer.*

[4] The case of this word is explained above.

[5] *Neptune,* god of the sea.

[6] *were confining themselves.* The passive voice is sometimes used in a reflexive sense, i.e., it denotes an act done by the actor to or for himself. Instead of the passive, **sē continēbant** might have been used in this sentence.

[7] *Hesione* (hē-sī'ọ-nē—see pronunciation key, p. 410).

[8] Dative with **pārēre.**

[9] *for the sacrifice;* dative.

[10] The phrase **ipsō temporis pūnctō quō** may be translated *at the very moment when.*

[11] *was informed;* literally, *was made more certain.*

The Tenth Labor—The Oxen of Geryon

Post haec jussus est Herculēs ad īnsulam Erythīam[1] īre bovēsque Gēryonis arcessere. Rēs erat summae difficultātis, quod bovēs ā gigante Eurytiōne[2] et ā cane bicipite (*two-headed*) custōdiēbantur. Ipse autem Gēryōn speciem horribilem praebēbat; habēbat enim tria corpora inter sē[3] conjūncta. Herculēs tamen, etsī intellegēbat perīculum magnum esse,[4] negōtium suscēpit et, postquam per multās terrās iter fēcit, ad eam partem Libyae pervēnit quae Eurōpae proxima est. Ibi, in utrāque parte[5] fretī quod Eurōpam ā Libyā dīvidit, columnās cōnstituit, quae posteā Herculis columnae[6] appellātae sunt.

Post breve tempus ad īnsulam Erythīam[1] pervēnit atque ā rēge Gēryone bovēs postulāvit. Quod tamen ille hōs trādere nōlēbat, Herculēs et rēgem ipsum et gigantem Eurytiōnem[2] statim interfēcit. Tum per Hispāniam et Liguriam[7] bovēs compellere cōnstituit.

Across the Alps

Celerrimē prōgressus est, et post paucōs diēs ad Alpēs pervēnit. Necesse erat hās trānsīre, quod in Ītaliam bovēs dūcere volēbat. Rēs tamen summae erat difficultātis; hī enim montēs, quī Galliam ulteriōrem[8] ab Ītaliā dīvidunt, nive perennī (*by perpetual snow*) teguntur. Quam ob causam[9] neque frūmentum neque pābulum in hīs regiōnibus invenīrī potest. Herculēs igitur, antequam ascendere coepit, magnam cōpiam frūmentī et pābulī comparāvit, et bovēs onerāvit (*loaded*).

Postquam in hīs rēbus trēs diēs cōnsūmpserat, quārtō diē profectus est et, contrā omnium opīniōnem, bovēs incolumēs in Ītaliam trādūxit.

A Cattle Thief

Post breve tempus ad flūmen Tiberim vēnit. Illō tamen tempore nūlla erat urbs in eō locō; Rōma enim nōndum condita erat. Herculēs, itinere fessus (*tired*), cōnstituit ibi paucōs diēs morārī atque

---

[1] *Erythia* (er-i-thī'ặ—see pronunciation key, p. 410), an island in the Mediterranean, off the coast of Spain.

[2] *Eurytion* (ū-rish'i-ọn).

[3] *together, to one another*. What does **inter sē** mean literally?

[4] *was.* The translation of the tenses of the infinitive in indirect discourse is explained on page 83.

[5] *on both sides.*

[6] The Rock of Gibraltar and a hill on the opposite side of the strait doubtless gave rise to this legend.

[7] *Liguria* (li-gū'ri-ặ), a district in northern Italy and southern France. See map, page 137.

[8] Gaul north and west of the Alps. The valley of the Po in Italy was also inhabited at one time by a Gallic population and was known to the Romans as **Gallia Citerior**, *Nearer Gaul.*

[9] *for this reason.*

LEADING A HERD OF OXEN ACROSS ALPINE PEAKS SUCH AS THESE WAS
A TASK FIT FOR A HERCULES

TENSE OF INFINITIVES IN INDIRECT DISCOURSE

In indirect discourse the present infinitive expresses an act occurring at the time shown by the tense of the main verb.

> **Dīcit sē perīculum timēre,** *He says that he fears danger.*
>
> **Dīxit sē perīculum timēre,** *He said that he feared danger.*

The act expressed by the perfect infinitive in indirect discourse is represented as already past at the time shown by the tense of the main verb.

> **Hostēs fūgisse videō,** *I see that the enemy have fled.*
>
> **Hostēs fūgisse vīdī,** *I saw that the enemy had fled.*

The act expressed by the future infinitive in indirect discourse is represented as future in relation to the time denoted by the main verb.

> **Puer dīcit frātrem ventūrum esse,** *The boy says that his brother will come,* or
>
> *is going to come.*
>
> **Puer dīxit frātrem ventūrum esse,** *The boy said that his brother would come,* or
>
> *was going to come.*

The future infinitive is regularly translated with *shall* or *will* after a main verb in the present tense and with *should* or *would* after a main verb in any past tense.

> **Putāvit Herculem bovēs nōn inventūrum esse,** *He thought that Hercules would*
>
> *not find the cattle.*

sē ex labōribus recreāre.[1] Haud procul ā valle ubi bovēs pāscēbantur (*were feeding*) antrum erat, in quō gigās quīdam, nōmine Cā-
5 cus, tum habitābat. Hic speciem terribilem praebēbat, nōn modo quod ingēns corpus habēbat, sed quod ignem ex ōre expīrābat (*he breathed out*).

Cācus autem dē adventū Her- 10 culis fāmam accēperat; noctū igitur vēnit, et dum Herculēs dormit, quattuor pulcherrimōrum boum abripuit (*he carried off*). Hōs caudīs (*by their tails*) in antrum trāxit; 15 hōc enim modō putāvit Herculem vēstīgiīs dēceptum bovēs nōn inventūrum esse.[2]

A Giant at Bay

Posterō diē, simul atque ē somnō excitātus est, Herculēs fūrtum (*theft*) animadvertit. Cum bovēs āmissōs undique quaereret,[3] eōs tamen nusquam reperīre poterat, nōn modo quod locī nātūram
25 ignōrābat, sed quod vēstīgiīs falsīs dēceptus est.

Tandem, ubi magnam partem diēī frūstrā cōnsūmpsit, cum reliquīs bōbus prōgredī cōnstituit. At
30 dum proficīscī parat, ūnus ē bōbus[4] quōs sēcum habuit mūgīre (*to bellow*) coepit.

Extemplō (*immediately*) eī quī in antrō inclūsī erant mūgītum
35 reddidērunt.[5] Hōc modō Herculēs locum invēnit. Tum vehementer īrātus, ad spēluncam quam celerrimē sē contulit.

At Cācus saxum ingēns dējēce-
40 rat et aditum spēluncae omnīnō obstrūxerat (*had closed*). Herculēs, quoniam nūllum alium introitum

(*entrance*) reperīre poterat, hoc saxum āmovēre cōnātus est; sed propter ejus magnitūdinem rēs 45 erat difficillima. Diū labōrābat, neque[6] quicquam efficere poterat. Tandem tamen magnō cōnātū saxum āmōvit et spēluncam patefēcit.   50

Cum āmissōs bovēs statim cōnspiceret,[3] Cācum ipsum vix cernere potuit, quod spēlunca replēta erat (*was filled*) fūmō quem ille mōre suō[7] ēvomēbat (*was breathing out*). 55 Herculēs, inūsitātā speciē turbātus, breve tempus[8] haesitābat (*hesitated*). Mox tamen in spēluncam irrūpit et collum mōnstrī bracchiīs complexus est (*clasped*).   60

Ille multum relūctātus est (*struggled*), sed nūllō modō sē līberāre potuit; et quod nūlla facultās respirandī (*of breathing*) dabātur, mox, quod[9] necesse fuit, exanimā- 65 tus est.

The Eleventh Labor—The Golden Apples

Eurystheus, postquam bovēs Gēryonis accēpit, labōrem ūndecimum Herculī imposuit, graviō-

rem quam[10] quōs suprā nārrāvimus. 70 Jussit enim eum aurea pōma ex hortō Hesperidum auferre.

THE SUBJUNCTIVE MOOD

The indicative mood of the verb, as has already been explained, is used to state a fact or to ask a question which implies as answer a statement of fact. The Latin verb has also a mood called the *subjunctive*. This mood is most frequently used in subordinate clauses. No general statement can be given as to how the Latin subjunctive is translated. Its translation in different kinds of clauses will be explained as these are introduced.

The Latin subjunctive has only four tenses, the present, imperfect, perfect, and past perfect. The forms of the imperfect are given first.

ACTIVE OF THE IMPERFECT SUBJUNCTIVE

The imperfect subjunctive of all Latin verbs can be formed by adding the regular person endings to the present active infinitive.

I	II	III		IV
		SINGULAR		
portārem	monērem	dūcerem	caperem	audīrem
portārēs	monērēs	dūcerēs	caperēs	audīrēs
portāret	monēret	dūceret	caperet	audīret
		PLURAL		
portārēmus	monērēmus	dūcerēmus	caperēmus	audīrēmus
portārētis	monērētis	dūcerētis	caperētis	audīrētis
portārent	monērent	dūcerent	caperent	audīrent

THE SUBJUNCTIVE IN *CUM* CONCESSIVE CLAUSES

A subordinate clause introduced by **cum** meaning *although* has its verb in the subjunctive. The subjunctive in clauses of this kind is translated in the same manner as the indicative.

Cum bovēs āmissōs undique quaereret, eōs tamen nusquam reperīre poterat,
Although he hunted for the lost cattle everywhere, nevertheless he could find them nowhere.

Frequently **tamen** is found in the main clause to which a concessive clause is attached.

NOTES ON THE TEXT

[1] With **sē**—*to recover.*

[2] Another example of the future infinitive in indirect discourse.

[3] This form and its use here are explained above.

[4] With cardinal numbers and with **quīdam** the ablative with **ex** or **dē** is regularly used instead of the genitive of the whole, as explained on page 54, note 7. The latter, however, sometimes occurs, as on page 84, line 13.

[5] *bellowed in answer;* literally, *gave back the bellowing.*

[6] *but . . . not.* Occasionally **neque** is used as the equivalent of **sed nōn.**

[7] *according to his custom.*

[8] Accusative of duration of time. See Gr. S., 68.

[9] (*a thing*) *which.* The pronoun is neuter, because it refers to the thought of **exanimātus est.**

[10] Supply **eī erant.**

DON'T LET THE SKIES FALL!
This decoration from an ancient mirror shows Hercules taking over
from Atlas the crushing burden of the sky.

Hesperides autem quaedam nymphae erant fōrmā[1] praestantissimā, quae in terrā longinquā (*distant*) habitābant, et quibus 5 aurea quaedam pōma ā Jūnōne commissa erant. Multī hominēs, aurī cupiditāte inductī, haec pōma auferre jam anteā cōnātī erant. Rēs tamen difficillima erat; nam 10 hortus in quō pōma erant mūrō ingentī undique circumdatus est. Praetereā dracō quīdam, quī centum capita habēbat, portam hortī dīligenter custōdiēbat.

Opus igitur quod Eurystheus 15 Herculī[2] imperāverat erat summae difficultātis, nōn modo ob eās causās quās memorāvimus (*we have stated*), sed quod Herculēs situm hortī omnīnō ignōrābat.   20

Upholding the Sky

Hercules, cum quiētem vehementer cuperet, cōnstituit tamen Eurystheō[3] pārēre; et simul ac jussa (*commands*) ejus accēpit, 25 proficīscī mātūrāvit. Multōs mercātōrēs interrogāverat dē sēde Hesperidum; nihil tamen certum reperīre potuerat.

Frūstrā per multās terrās iter fēcit, et multa perīcula subiit.[4] 30 Tandem, postquam in hīs itineribus tōtum annum cōnsūmpsit, ad extrēmam partem orbis,[5] quae proxima erat Ōceanō, pervēnit.

Hīc stābat vir quīdam, nōmine 35 Atlās, ingentī magnitūdine[6] corporis, quī caelum (ita trādunt[7]) umerīs[8] suīs sustinēbat et in terram

PASSIVE OF THE IMPERFECT SUBJUNCTIVE

I	II	III		IV
		SINGULAR		
portārer	monērer	dūcerer	caperer	audīrer
portārēris	monērēris	dūcerēris	caperēris	audīrēris
portārētur	monērētur	dūcerētur	caperētur	audīrētur
		PLURAL		
portārēmur	monērēmur	dūcerēmur	caperēmur	audīrēmur
portārēminī	monērēminī	dūcerēminī	caperēminī	audīrēminī
portārentur	monērentur	dūcerentur	caperentur	audīrentur

Observe that -e- is long before the endings of the second person singular and the first and second person plural in both active and passive and in the third person singular of the passive.

IMPERFECT SUBJUNCTIVE OF *SUM* AND *POSSUM*

SINGULAR	PLURAL	SINGULAR	PLURAL
essem	essēmus	possem	possēmus
essēs	essētis	possēs	possētis
esset	essent	posset	possent

ABLATIVE AND GENITIVE OF DESCRIPTION

The ablative modified by an adjective may be used to describe a person or thing.

homō **magnā virtūte,** *a man of great courage*

Hesperides quaedam nymphae erant **fōrmā praestantissimā,** *The Hesperides were certain nymphs of very attractive appearance.*

The genitive modified by an adjective may also be used to describe a person or thing.

homō **magnae virtūtis,** *a man of great courage*

The genitive is employed in this construction to express measure.

mūrus trium pedum, *a three-foot wall (a wall of three feet)*

In many phrases, such as *a man of great courage*, either the genitive or the ablative may be used. But physical characteristics are usually expressed by the ablative, and measure always by the genitive.

In lines 16-17 on page 86 **summae difficultātis** is an example of the genitive of description.

NOTES ON THE TEXT

[1] This use of the ablative is explained above.

[2] Dative with **imperāverat**—*had imposed upon Hercules.*

[3] Dative with **pārēre.**

[4] A compound of **eō.** What are its principal parts?

[5] Supply **terrārum.** The two words together mean *the world.*

[6] Another ablative of description.

[7] *so legend has it,* or *as the legend goes;* literally, *so they hand down.*

[8] Ablative of means, but to be translated *on his shoulders.*

dēcidere[1] prohibēbat. Herculēs, tantum labōrem magnopere mīrātus,[2] post paulō in colloquium cum Atlante vēnit, et postquam causam 5 itineris exposuit, auxilium ejus petīvit.

Atlās autem potuit Herculī[3] maximē prōdesse; ille enim, quoniam ipse erat pater Hesperidum, 10 situm hortī bene scīvit.

Postquam igitur audīvit causam itineris Herculis, "Ipse," inquit, "ad hortum ībō. Ego sī hortābor, fīliae certē pōma suā sponte[4] trādent." 15

Herculēs, ubi haec audīvit, magnopere gāvīsus est; cupiēbat enim rem sine vī fierī.[5] Cōnstituit igitur oblātum auxilium accipere.

Sed quod Atlās abitūrus erat, ne- 20 cesse erat aliquem[6] caelum umerīs sustinēre. Hoc igitur negōtium Herculēs libenter suscēpit, et quamquam rēs erat summī labōris, tōtum pondus caelī continuōs com- 25 plūrēs diēs sōlus sustinuit.

A Persuasive Father

ATLĀS intereā abierat et ad hortum Hesperidum, quī pauca mīlia passuum[7] aberat, sē quam 30 celerrimē contulerat. Eō ubi vēnit, causam veniendī exposuit, et ā fīliābus[8] suīs pōma vehementer petīvit.

Illae diū haerēbant (*hesitated*); 35 nōlēbant enim hoc facere, quod ab ipsā Jūnōne, dē quā ante dictum est, hoc mūnus jam prīdem accēperant.

Atlās tamen post multa verba 40 eīs persuāsit, et pōma ad Herculem rettulit.

Herculēs intereā, quī plūrēs diēs expectāverat, neque ūllam fāmam dē reditū Atlantis accēperat, hāc 45 morā graviter commōtus est. Tandem quīntō diē Atlantem vīdit redeuntem, et mox magnō cum gaudiō pōma accēpit. Tum, postquam grātiās prō tantō beneficiō 50 ēgit, ad Graeciam proficīscī mātūrāvit.

A WEIGHTY RESPONSIBILITY

Upon his straining shoulders Atlas bears the sky, which the ancient sculptor portrayed as a globe. The goat, the fish, and other figures on the globe are symbols of constellations we know. According to legend, Atlas was transformed into a mountain. A range of mountains in Africa bears his name.

The Twelfth Labor—The Three-Headed Dog

Postquam aurea pōma ad Eurystheum relāta sunt, ūnus modo relinquēbātur ē duodecim labōribus quōs Pȳthia Herculī prae-
5 cēperat.[9]

Eurystheus autem, cum Herculem magnopere timēret,[10] sē ab eō in perpetuum[11] līberāre volēbat. Jussit igitur eum canem
10 Cerberum ex Orcō in lūcem trahere.

Hoc opus omnium difficillimum erat; nēmō enim umquam ex Orcō redierat.

Praetereā Cerberus iste erat 15 mōnstrum horribilī speciē, quī tria capita serpentibus saevīs cīncta habēbat. Is canis portam Orcī custōdiēbat, et omnēs terrēbat quī eō advēnērunt. Herculēs autem, 20 quī nihil umquam timēbat, nōn hoc negōtium recūsāvit.

ACCUSATIVE OF EXTENT OF SPACE

The accusative is used to denote extent of space.

Hic locus ab hoste passūs DC aberat, *This place was six hundred paces from the enemy.*

Ad hortum Hesperidum, quī pauca mīlia passuum aberat, sē contulerat, *He had gone to the garden of the Hesperides, which was a few miles away.*

THE SUBJUNCTIVE IN *CUM* CAUSAL CLAUSES

A subordinate clause introduced by **cum,** meaning *since*, has its verb in the subjunctive. The subjunctive in clauses of this kind is translated in the same manner as the indicative.

Cum Herculem magnopere timēret, eum dīmīsit, *Since he feared Hercules greatly, he sent him away.*

NOTES ON THE TEXT

[1] *from falling.* Supply **caelum** as the subject of **dēcidere** and take **caelum dēcidere** as object of **prohibēbat.**

[2] A perfect participle, to be translated as a present.

[3] Dative with **prōdesse** (from **prōsum**).

[4] *of their own accord,* or *without compulsion.*

[5] *to be done.* The forms of **fīō** will be explained later.

[6] For declension of **aliquis** see Gr. S., 32.

[7] *a few miles.* The use of the accusative **mīlia** is explained above.

[8] If the dative and ablative plural of **fīlia** were written **fīliīs,** with what other word might it be confused in those cases?

[9] *which Pythia had prescribed for Hercules.*

[10] This use of the subjunctive is explained above.

[11] *forever.* The neuter adjective is used as a noun.

The Kingdom of the Dead

A COMIC STATUETTE OF HERCULES

An ancient Greek sculptor with a sense of humor made this caricature of Hercules.

ORCUS, or Hades, the realm of the dead, from which the dog Cerberus was to be brought, lay beneath the earth. On their way to Hades the spirits of the dead were guided by the god Mercury.

First they came to the River Styx, over which they were carried by Charon[1] in a boat. The ancients sometimes placed a coin in the mouth of the dead to pay the fare across the Styx.

Those who had not been properly buried had to wait for a hundred years on the bank of the river before they were allowed to enter Charon's boat and cross.

After crossing the Styx the spirits came to the River Lethe.[2] They drank from this river and at once forgot all their past lives.

Next they came to the palace of Pluto, which was guarded by Cerberus. Pluto was the king of Hades, and his wife was Proserpina, daughter of Jupiter and Ceres.[3]

Near the throne of Pluto and Proserpina were seated three judges of the dead, Minos,[4] Rhadamanthus,[5] and Aeacus,[6] who assigned rewards or punishment to the spirits. The good were given a home in the Elysian Fields, the land of happiness, while the wicked were sent down to Tartarus to suffer punishment.

Charon's Ferry

HERCULĒS postquam imperia Eurystheī accēpit, in Lacōniam[7] ad Taenarum[8] statim sē contulit; ibi enim spēlunca erat ingentī magnitūdine, per quam (ut trādēbātur[9]) hominēs ad Orcum dēscendēbant. Eō[10] ubi vēnit et ex incolīs situm spēluncae cognōvit, sine morā dēscendere cōnstituit. Nec tamen sōlus hoc iter faciēbat; Mercurius enim et Minerva sē sociōs[11] eī adjūnxerant.

5

10

[1] Pronounced kā′rǫn (see pronunciation key, p. 410).

[2] Pronounced lē′thē.

[3] Pronounced sē′rēz. Ceres was the goddess of agriculture.

[4] Pronounced mī′nos.

[5] Pronounced rad-ạ-man′thus.

[6] Pronounced ē′ạ-kus.

[7] *Laconia* (lạ-kō′ni-ạ), a region of ancient Greece.

[8] *Taenarum* (ten′ạ-rum), a promontory of Laconia.

[9] The clause has the same sense as **ita trādunt**, page 86, line 37.

[10] *to that place.*

[11] *as companions.*

THE LAST OF THE LABORS

This carving in rock crystal shows Hercules in the very act of subduing the three-headed dog, Cerberus.
As often, Hercules wields a club—fitting weapon for a strong man.

Ubi ad rīpam Stygis[1] vēnit, Herculēs scapham Charontis cōnscendit. Cum tamen Herculēs vir esset ingentī magnitūdine corporis, Charōn solvere nōlēbat; arbitrābātur enim tantum pondus scapham suam in mediō flūmine mersūrum esse.[2]

Tandem tamen, minīs (*by the threats*) Herculis territus, Charōn scapham solvit et eum incolumem ad ulteriōrem rīpam perdūxit.

The Twelve Labors Accomplished

Postquam flūmen Stygem[3] tālī modō trānsiit, Herculēs in sēdem ipsīus Plūtōnis[4] vēnit, et postquam causam veniendī docuit, ab eō facultātem Cerberum auferendī[5] petīvit.

Plūtō, quī dē Hercule fāmam accēperat, eum benignē excēpit, et facultātem quam ille petēbat libenter dedit. Jussit tamen Herculem imperāta Eurystheī facere et posteā Cerberum in Orcum rūrsus redūcere.

Herculēs haec pollicitus est, et

---

[1] *of the Styx.*
[2] *would sink;* future active infinitive.
[3] *the Styx;* accusative.

[4] *of Pluto.*
[5] A gerund with a direct object, **Cerberum.**

Cerberum, quem nōn sine magnō perīculō manibus prehenderat, summō cum labōre ex Orcō in lūcem et ad urbem Eurystheī 5 trāxit.

Eō ubi vēnit, tantus pavor animum Eurystheī occupāvit ut ex ātriō statim refugeret.[1] Postquam autem paulum sē ex timōre recē- 10 pit,[2] multīs cum lacrimīs clāmitāvit (*he cried out*) sē velle mōnstrum sine morā in Orcum redūcī.

Sīc, contrā omnium opīniōnem, duodecim illī labōrēs quōs Pȳthia praecēperat cōnfectī sunt. Her- 15 culēs enim tam validus erat ut nūlla perīcula vītāret, nūlla mōnstra timēret. Itaque Herculēs, servitūte[3] tandem līberātus, magnō cum gaudiō Thēbās rediit. 20

A Dangerous Journey

Post haec Herculēs multa alia praeclāra (*very famous*) perfēcit, quae[4] nunc perscrībere longum est.[5]

HERCULES IN BRONZE
The ancient sculptor thought of our hero as a youth, though he already wears the famous lion skin.

Tandem, jam aetāte prōvectus 25 (*advanced in age*), Dēianīram, Oeneī[6] fīliam, in mātrimōnium dūxit.

Post tamen trēs annōs puerum quendam cāsū occīdit. Mōre an- 30 tīquō[7] necesse erat Herculem ob eam rem in exilium īre; itaque cum uxōre suā ē fīnibus ejus cīvitātis exīre mātūrāvit.

Dum tamen iter faciunt, ad 35 flūmen quoddam pervēnērunt in quō nūllus pōns erat, et dum quaerunt modum trānseundī, accurrit Centaurus quīdam, nōmine Nessus, quī auxilium viātōribus obtulit. 40 Herculēs igitur uxōrem suam in tergum Nessī imposuit; tum ipse flūmen nandō[8] trānsiit.

At Nessus, paulum in aquam prōgressus, ad rīpam subitō re- 45 vertit et Dēianīram auferre cōnābātur.

Quod ubi animadvertit Herculēs,[9] ita īrātus erat ut arcum intenderet et pectus Nessī sagittā 50 trānsfīgeret.

A STATUETTE IN MODERNISTIC STYLE

One might easily see a book-end or decorative figure similar to this on some department-store counter. It is a statue of a centaur made thousands of years ago by a Greek sculptor.

THE SUBJUNCTIVE IN CLAUSES OF RESULT

A subordinate clause expressing result is regularly introduced by **ut**, *that*, and has its verb in the subjunctive. The subjunctive in clauses of this kind is translated in the same manner as the indicative.

Tantus pavor animum Eurystheī occupāvit ut ex ātriō statim refugeret, *Such great fear seized Eurystheus* (literally, *the mind of Eurystheus*) *that he fled from the atrium immediately.*

NOTES ON THE TEXT

[1] This use of the subjunctive is explained above.

[2] With **sē**—*recovered.*

[3] Ablative of separation. See Gr. S., 74.

[4] Object of **perscrībere.**

[5] *it would take too long.*

[6] *Oeneus* (ē'nūs — see pronunciation key, p. 410).

[7] *according to ancient custom.* Ablative expressing accordance.

[8] *by swimming;* ablative of the gerund expressing means and manner.

[9] *when Hercules had observed this.*

The Poisoned Robe

Nessus igitur, sagittā Herculis trānsfīxus, moriēns humī (*on the ground*) jacēbat; at nōlēns occāsiōnem Herculem ulcīscendī[1] dīmittere, ita locūtus est.

"Tū, Dēianīra, verba morientis[2] audī: sī vīs amōrem (*love*) marītī tuī cōnservāre, aliquid sanguinis hujus[3] quī ē pectore meō effunditur (*is flowing*) sūme ac repōne (*keep*); tum, sī umquam suspīciō in mentem tuam vēnerit, vestem marītī hōc sanguine īnficiēs.[4]"

Haec locūtus, Nessus animam efflāvit.[5] Dēianīra, cum haec audīvisset, nihil malī[6] suspicāta est, et statim imperāta fēcit.

Post breve tempus Herculēs bellum contrā Eurytum,[7] rēgem Oechaliae,[8] suscēpit, et cum rēgem ipsum fīliōsque interfēcisset,[9] Iolēn,[10] fīliam Eurytī, captīvam (*as a captive*) redūxit.

Antequam tamen domum[11] vēnit, nāvem ad Cēnaeum prōmunturium[12] appulit. Ibi in terram ēgressus quod Jovī sacrificāre (*to sacrifice*) volēbat, āram in eō locō cōnstituit.

Dum tamen sacrificium parat, Licham, comitem suum, domum īre et vestem albam referre jussit; mōs enim erat apud antīquōs in sacrificandō (*sacrificing*) vestem albam gerere.

At Dēianīra, arbitrāta[13] Herculem amōrem (*love*) ergā[14] Iolēn[10] habēre, vestem, priusquam Lichae dedit, sanguine Nessī īnfēcit.

Received among the Immortals

Herculēs, nihil malī suspicātus, vestem quam Lichās attulit[15] statim induit. Post tamen breve tempus dolōrem acūtum per omnia membra sēnsit, sed quod causam ejus reī ignōrābat, magnopere mīrābātur. Dolōre paene exanimātus, vestem dētrahere cōnātus est. Illa tamen in corpore haesit (*stuck fast*), neque ūllō modō dīvellī (*be torn away*) potuit.

Tum dēmum Herculēs, quasi

---

[1] The genitive of the gerund with a direct object, as on page 91, line 17.

[2] *of one who is dying;* a present participle (from **morior**) used as a noun.

[3] *some of this blood.*

[4] *dye;* literally, *you will dye.* The future indicative is sometimes employed both in Latin and in English as a substitute for the imperative.

[5] The words **animam efflāvit** are equivalent to **mortuus est**—*died.*

[6] *no harm;* literally, *nothing of evil.*

[7] *Eurytus* (ū´ri-tus—see pronunciation key, p. 410).

[8] *Oechalia* (ē-kā´li-ạ), an ancient Greek city. See map, page 68.

[9] This use of the subjunctive is explained on page 95.

[10] *Iole* (ī´ọ-lẹ).

[11] *home.* The accusative of this noun is used without a preposition to express place to which, as explained on page 71.

[12] *the Promontory of Cenaeum* (sē-nē´um), a cape on the island of Euboea. See map, page 68.

[13] *thinking.*

[14] *for.*

[15] *brought.*

THE PAST PERFECT SUBJUNCTIVE

The past perfect subjunctive active of all verbs, regular and irregular, is formed on the perfect stem with the tense sign -issē.

I	II	III	IV
		SINGULAR	
portāvissem	monuissem	dūxissem	audīvissem
portāvissēs	monuissēs	dūxissēs	audīvissēs
portāvisset	monuisset	dūxisset	audīvisset
		PLURAL	
portāvissēmus	monuissēmus	dūxissēmus	audīvissēmus
portāvissētis	monuissētis	dūxissētis	audīvissētis
portāvissent	monuissent	dūxissent	audīvissent

The past perfect subjunctive passive is made up of the perfect participle and the imperfect subjunctive of **sum.**

I	II	III	IV
		SINGULAR	
portātus essem	monitus essem	ductus essem	audītus essem
portātus essēs	monitus essēs	ductus essēs	audītus essēs
portātus esset	monitus esset	ductus esset	audītus esset
		PLURAL	
portātī essēmus	monitī essēmus	ductī essēmus	audītī essēmus
portātī essētis	monitī essētis	ductī essētis	audītī essētis
portātī essent	monitī essent	ductī essent	audītī essent

DESCRIPTIVE CLAUSES OF SITUATION

The imperfect or the past perfect subjunctive is often used in a clause introduced by **cum** meaning *when.* Such a clause describes the situation in which the act of the main clause takes place.

The subjunctive in clauses of this kind is translated in the same manner as the indicative.

Cum pōns factus esset, exercitus trāductus est, *When the bridge had been made, the army was led across.*

Cum haec audīvisset, nihil malī suspicāta est, *When she had heard this, she suspected no evil* (literally, *nothing of evil*).

GREEK SPEAR-HEADS

furōre impulsus, in montem Oetam[1] sē contulit et in rogum, quem summā celeritāte extrūxit, sē imposuit. Cum hoc fēcisset, voluit eōs quī 5 circumstābant (*were standing about*) rogum quam celerrimē accendere. Nam morī mālēbat[2] quam dolōrem diūtius perferre. Omnēs diū re-cūsābant; tandem tamen pāstor quīdam, ad misericordiam (*pity*) 10 inductus, ignem subdidit (*applied*). Tum, dum omnia fūmō obscūrantur (*were obscured*), Herculēs, dēnsā nūbe vēlātus (*veiled*), ā Jove in Olympum[3] abreptus est.[4] Itaque 15 inter deōs relātus est.

[1] *Oeta* (ē'tä—see pronunciation key, p. 410), a mountain in Greece. See map, page 68.

[2] From **mālō**. See Gr. S., 45.

[3] *Olympus*, a mountain north of Greece.

[4] *was taken.* Since Hercules was the son of Jupiter, it was not unnatural, in view of his marvelous exploits, for legend to represent him as deified and free from the death usual to mortals.

COMPREHENSION QUESTIONS

The story of Hercules, like that of Ulysses, has often been drawn upon by modern writers. The following questions deal with some of the points of the story that are frequently mentioned.

1. Who was the mother of Hercules?
2. What goddess wished to destroy him? What did she do?
3. What sort of creatures were the centaurs?
4. What oracle did Hercules consult after the murder of his children?
5. How did the oracle direct him to atone for his crime?
6. What was the Hydra?
7. How did Hercules clean the Augean stables?
8. Why was it difficult to reach the Stymphalian birds?
9. Who were the Amazons?
10. Of what city was Laomedon king?
11. What gods had built the walls of Laomedon's city?
12. Where did the giant Cacus live?
13. Who helped Hercules obtain the apples of the Hesperides?
14. What was the name of the three-headed dog which Hercules brought from the underworld?
15. Who was Charon?
16. How did Hercules meet his end?

ROGUM SUMMĀ CELERITĀTE EXTRŪXIT

QUESTIONS ON GRAMMAR

1. Give the English meanings of some verbs that govern the dative. (Gr. S., 61.) 2. How is place to which expressed in Latin with names of cities and with **domus?** (Gr. S., 70.) With other words? (Gr. S., 70, *a*.)

A TEMPLE DEDICATED TO HERCULES

In this temple at Cori, Italy, Hercules was worshiped as one of the immortals.

3. What kind of ablative is used in the following sentence? **Linguā inter sē differunt.** Explain this use. (Gr. S., 86.) 4. How is place from which expressed with names of cities and with **domus?** (Gr. S., 75.) 5. Give all the active infinitives of **expectō, videō,** and **mittō.** (See p. 77.) 6. Give the passive infinitives of **rogō, videō, dīcō,** and **audiō.** (See p. 79.) 7. Give the infinitives of **mīror** and **proficīscor.** (See p. 79.) 8. Explain the use of the locative case. (Gr. S., 91.) 9. How are the tenses of the infinitive used in indirect discourse? (See p. 83.) 10. How is the imperfect subjunctive formed? (See p. 85.) 11. Conjugate **putō** in the imperfect subjunctive active, and **mittō** in the imperfect subjunctive passive. (Gr. S., 33, 36.) 12. What is the tense sign of the past perfect subjunctive active? On what stem is it formed? (See p. 95.) 13. Name four classes of subordinate clauses in which the verb is in the subjunctive. (See pp. 85, 89, 93, 95.) 14. What two cases may be used to describe a person or thing? (See p. 87.)

WORD STUDY II

English Words from Latin

Some English words have been borrowed from Latin without change in spelling, though not always with exactly the same meaning as in Latin.

campus, Latin **campus,** *field*   pastor, Latin **pāstor,** *shepherd*
vacuum, Latin **vacuus,** *empty*

In certain other words, a slight change in spelling appears, often the substitution of an English vowel for a Latin diphthong.

premium, Latin **praemium,** *reward*   tedium, Latin **taedium,** *weariness*

Some words are formed with a Latin suffix meaning "one who does."

narrator, from **nārrāre,** *tell*   monitor, from **moneō,** *advise*

The following words illustrate still other methods of derivation.

sanitarium, from **sānō,** *heal*   status, from **stō,** *stand*
aborigine, from **ab,** *from,* + **orīgine,** *the beginning*

EXERCISES

1. Give the Latin words from which the following English words come: benefactor, data, event, maximum, solarium, victor.

Idioms and Phrases

The following expressions appear in the text read and should be thoroughly learned.

> **contrā omnium opīniōnem,** *contrary to the expectation of all*
> **hōc cōnātū dēstitit,** *he gave up this attempt*
> **īrā commōtus,** *thoroughly angry*
> **ob hanc causam,** *for this reason*
> **paulō post,** *a little later*
> **summā (cum) difficultāte,** *with the greatest difficulty*

Vocabulary Review

The following words, which appear frequently in this book, are important in second-year work. Their meanings should be thoroughly learned.

acūtus	cōnsūmō	honor	offerō	quaerō
alter	dēpōnō	ignōrō	opera	quisquam
animadvertō	dēspērō	impōnō	opportūnus	rēgīna
atque, ac	difficultās	intrā	pābulum	sentiō
attingō	diū	līberō	pecus, -oris	servitūs
beneficium	ēgregius	manus	perdūcō	simul
celeritās	ēnūntiō	mīror	placeō	solvō
cernō	exerceō	mīrus	poscō	studeō
circumdō	extruō	mora	praebeō	suspīciō
colloquium	fīgō	neuter	praeda	tegō
committō	fossa	ob	praestō	vestis
cōnsuēscō	glōria	occāsus	procul	vīvus

THE ARGONAUTS FIGHT
A BATTLE IN THE AIR

A GREEK SHIP

THE ARGONAUTS

Her prow hath drunk the sea. . . . . . .
Out from the shore she strains—she swings—
And lifts, oh, gallantly!

WILLIAM ROSE BENÉT: THE ARGO'S CHANTEY

The Wicked Uncle

ERANT ōlim in Thessaliā duo frātrēs, quōrum alter Aesōn, alter Peliās appellātus est. Hōrum Aesōn prīmus rēgnum obtinuerat. 5 At post paucōs annōs Peliās, cupiditāte rēgnī adductus,[1] nōn modo frātrem suum expulit, sed etiam in animō habēbat Jāsonem, Aesonis fīlium, interficere.

10 Quīdam tamen ex amīcīs[2] Aesonis, ubi sententiam Peliae intellēxērunt, puerum ē tantō perīculō ēripere cōnstituērunt. Noctū igitur Jāsonem ex urbe abstulērunt, et cum posterō diē ad rēgem rediissent,[3] eī renūntiāvērunt puerum 15 mortuum esse. Peliās, cum haec audīvisset, etsī rē vērā[4] magnum gaudium percipiēbat, speciem tamen dolōris praebuit et causam 20 mortis quaesīvit. Illī tamen, cum bene intellegerent dolōrem ejus falsum esse, nesciō quam fābulam[5] dē morte puerī fīnxērunt.

[1] *influenced by a desire for royal power.*
[2] See page 85, note 4.
[3] In this paragraph two uses of the subjunctive appear: with **cum** meaning *when*, here and in line 18, and with **cum** meaning *although*, in line 22. These have been explained on pages 85 and 95.
[4] *really, in fact.*
[5] *some story or other*; literally, *I know not what story.*

101

A Mysterious Warning

SED Peliās, quī rēgnum tantā vī et fraude occupāverat, perīculum veritus est, et amīcum quendam Delphōs[1] ad ōrāculum
5 mīsit.

Ille igitur quam celerrimē Delphōs sē contulit et quam ob causam[2] vēnisset[3] dēmōnstrāvit.

Ōrāculum hoc respōnsum ad rē-
10 gem mīsit: "Nūllum est in praesentiā (*for the present*) perīculum. Sed hominem ūnum calceum gerentem cavē."

Post paucōs annōs Peliās mag-
15 num sacrificium facere volēbat. Nūntiōs in omnēs partēs dīmīsit et certum diem conveniendī[4] dīxit. Diē cōnstitūtō magnus numerus

WHERE THE ORACLE SPOKE
This is a reconstruction of the sacred inclosure at Delphi.

hominum undique ex agrīs convēnit; inter aliōs vēnit Jāsōn, quī ā 20 puerō apud Centaurum quendam vīxerat. Dum in itinere quoddam flūmen trānsit, ūnum calceum forte āmīsit.

The Golden Fleece

JĀSŌN igitur, cum[5] calceum āmissum nūllō modō recipere posset, ūnum calceum gerēns pervēnit. Quem cum[6] vīdisset, Peliās subitō timōre affectus est; intellēxit enim
30 hunc esse hominem quem ōrāculum dēmōnstrāvisset.[7]

Hoc igitur iniit cōnsilium. Rēx erat quīdam, nōmine Aeētēs, quī rēgnum Colchidis illō tempore obtinēbat. Huic commissum erat 35 vellus illud aureum quod Phrixus[8] ōlim ibi relīquerat. Cōnstituit igitur Peliās Jāsonem ad eum rēgem

---

[1] Accusative of place to which. We should say in English, *to the oracle at Delphi.* For Delphi, see map, page 116.

[2] *for what reason.*

[3] This use of the subjunctive is explained on page 103.

[4] *for the people to assemble;* literally, *of assembling.*

[5] Here **cum** has causal force; hence the subjunctive.

[6] Translate as if **cum eum.**

[7] Subjunctive in a subordinate clause in indirect discourse.

[8] The story was that Phrixus (frik'sus), with his sister Helle (hel'ē), had to flee from his stepmother, Ino (ī'nō). Phrixus and Helle were carried through the air on the back of a ram with a golden fleece, sent by the god Hermes (hĕr'mēz). Helle fell into the sea which was thereafter called the Hellespont (hel'es-pont). Phrixus arrived safely in Colchis, where he sacrificed the ram to Zeus (Zūs) and gave the fleece to King Aeētes. The king hung the fleece on an oak in the grove of Ares (ā'rēz), where it was guarded by a dragon.

ONE SHOE MISSING

INDIRECT QUESTIONS

A direct question is one which repeats the exact words of the speaker.

He asked, "Who is that man?"

The exact words of the speaker are inclosed in quotation marks.

An indirect question is one which repeats the thought, but not the exact words, of the speaker.

He asked who that man was.

Indirect questions depend on words of *asking, knowing, perceiving,* and the like.

In Latin an indirect question has its verb in the subjunctive. The subjunctive in indirect questions is usually translated in the same manner as the indicative.

Quaesīvī quis ille vir esset, *I asked who that man was.*

Dēmōnstrāvit quam ob causam vēnisset, *He made known for what reason he had come.*

mittere ut hoc vellus postulāret.[1]
Cum enim rēs esset magnī perīculī,
spērābat eum in itinere peritūrum
esse. Jāsonem igitur ad sē arces- sīvit et quid fierī[2] vellet[3] dēmōn- 5
strāvit. Jāsōn autem, etsī bene
intellegēbat rem esse difficillimam,
negōtium libenter suscēpit.

The Building of the Good Ship Argo

CUM tamen Colchis multōrum
diērum iter[4] ab eō locō abesset,
nōluit Jāsōn sōlus proficīscī. Dīmīsit igitur nūntiōs in omnēs partēs,
quī causam itineris docēbant et
diem certum conveniendī dīcēbant.
15　　Nāvem aedificārī jussit, et Argus quīdam, quī summam scientiam
rērum nauticārum[5] habēbat, huic
negōtiō[6] praefectus est. In hīs rēbus circiter decem diēs cōn-
sūmptī sunt; Argus enim tantam 20
dīligentiam praebēbat ut nē nocturnum quidem tempus ad labōrem
intermitteret.[7] Ut multitūdō hominum trānsportārētur, nāvis paulō
lātior erat quam quae fierī solitae 25
erant, atque tōta ē rōbore (*oak*)
facta est ut vim tempestātum
perferre posset.

The Anchor Is Weighed

INTEREĀ ea diēs[8] appetēbat quam
Jāsōn per nūntiōs ēdīxerat,
et ex omnibus regiōnibus Grae-
ciae multī quōs aut reī novitās
(*novelty*) aut spēs glōriae movēbat
undique conveniēbant. Trādunt[9]
35 in hōc numerō fuisse Herculem (dē
quō ante multa perscrīpsimus),
Orpheum,[10] citharoedum[11] praeclā-
rissimum (*very famous*), Thēse-
um,[12] Castorem,[13] et multōs aliōs quōrum nōmina nōtissima sunt. 40
Ex hīs Jāsōn, quōs[14] arbitrātus est
ad omnia perīcula parātissimōs
esse, eōs ad numerum quīnquāgintā
(*fifty*) dēlēgit et sociōs sibi adjūnxit.
　　Tum, paucōs diēs commorātus 45
ut ad omnēs cāsūs subsidia com-
parāret,[15] nāvem dēdūxit et, tempestātem[16] ad nāvigandum idōneam
nactus, magnō cum plausū (*applause*) omnium solvit. 50

---

[1] A clause of purpose. See page 105.
[2] *to be done.* In line 25 the same word
means *to be made.* The forms of fīō
will be explained later.
[3] For the imperfect subjunctive of
volō, see Gr. S., 45.
[4] An accusative of extent, further defined by the genitive of measure,
multōrum diērum.
[5] *of the science of navigation;* literally,
of nautical things.
[6] The dative is explained on page 105.
[7] The ut clause is one of result.
[8] Here feminine—usually masculine.
[9] *they say,* or *it is commonly reported.*
What is the literal meaning of the word?

[10] *Orpheus* (ôr'fūs—see pronunciation
key, p. 410), a mythical musician and
poet.
[11] *player of the cithara,* a stringed instrument.
[12] *Theseus* (thē'sūs), a Greek hero.
[13] *Castor,* a Greek hero, brother of
Pollux and of Helen of Troy.
[14] Subject of **esse**. Its antecedent is
eōs. A relative clause in Latin often pre-
cedes the antecedent; English idiom requires that the antecedent be translated
first.
[15] The ut clause is one of purpose. See
page 105.
[16] Not *tempest* or *storm.*

EXPRESSIONS OF PURPOSE

In English we express purpose in different ways.

I went to hear the music. *I went in order to hear the music.*

I went that (in order that) I might hear the music.

In the first example the infinitive *to hear* tells the speaker's purpose. In the second example the phrase *in order to hear* tells the purpose. The third example uses a subordinate clause to express purpose.

SUBJUNCTIVE IN A CLAUSE OF PURPOSE

In Latin, purpose may be expressed by a subordinate clause with its verb in the subjunctive. Such a clause is usually introduced by ut.

Vēnī ut tē vidērem, *I came to see* (literally, *that I might see) you.*

Jāsonem in Colchida mittere cōnstituit ut hoc vellus postulāret, *He decided to send Jason into Colchis to demand* (literally, *that he might demand) this fleece.*

Sometimes a relative pronoun introduces a purpose clause.

Crassum mīsit quī cōpiās dūceret, *He sent Crassus to lead the troops.*

Nūntium igitur ad nāvem mīsit quī Jāsonem sociōsque ad rēgiam vocāret, *Therefore he sent a messenger to the ship to call Jason and his comrades to the palace.*

The Latin infinitive is not used to express purpose. The sentence *I went to see the fire* is translated as if it read *I went that I might see the fire;* the sentence *I stayed in order to hear the music* is translated as if it read *I stayed that I might hear the music.*

To introduce a negative clause of purpose, **nē** is used.

Mīlitēs missī sunt nē urbs caperētur, *Soldiers were sent that the city might not be captured.*

DATIVE WITH COMPOUNDS

Many compound verbs which are formed from a verb and a prefix take a dependent noun or pronoun in the dative case. The most important prefixes whose compounds take the dative are **ante, ob, prae,** and **sub.**

Centuriō legiōnī praeest, *The centurion is in command of the legion.*

Argus quīdam huic negōtiō praefectus est, *A certain Argus (A certain man named Argus) was placed in charge of this task.*

In the examples above, **legiōnī** and **negōtiō** are in the dative case because they are dependent on verbs which are compounds of **prae.**

Other prefixes whose compounds sometimes take the dative are **ad, circum, com-, in, inter, post, prō, super.**

If the simple verb is transitive, the compound may have both an accusative and a dative.

Rōmānī Gallis bellum īnferunt, *The Romans make war on the Gauls.*

A Fatal Mistake

Haud multō post Argonautae[1] (ita enim appellātī sunt quī in istā nāve vehēbantur) īnsulam quandam nōmine Cyzicum[2] attigē-
5 runt et, ē nāve ēgressī, ā rēge illīus regiōnis hospitiō exceptī sunt.

Paucās hōrās ibi commorātī, ad sōlis occāsum rūrsus solvērunt. At, postquam pauca mīlia passuum
10 prōgressī sunt,[3] tanta tempestās subitō coorta est ut cursum tenēre nōn possent,[4] et in eandem partem īnsulae unde nūper profectī erant magnō cum perīculō dējiceren-
15 tur.

Incolae tamen, cum nox esset obscūra, Argonautās nōn agnōscē-bant (*did not recognize*), et nāvem inimīcam vēnisse arbitrātī, arma rapuērunt et eōs ēgredī prohibē- 20 bant. Ācriter in lītore pugnātum est,[5] et rēx ipse, quī cum aliīs dēcucurrerat, ab Argonautīs occī-sus est.

Mox tamen, cum jam dīlūcēsce- 25 ret (*it was growing light*), sēnsē-runt incolae sē errāre et arma ab-jēcērunt. Argonautae autem, cum vidērent rēgem occīsum esse, mag-num dolōrem percēpērunt. 30

A Comrade Wanders Away

Postrīdiē ejus diēī[6] Jāsōn, tem-pestātem satis idōneam esse arbitrātus (summa enim tranquilli-tās[7] jam cōnsecūta erat), ancorās
35 sustulit et, pauca mīlia passuum prōgressus, ante noctem Mȳsiam[8] attigit.

Ibi paucās hōrās in ancorīs[9] ex-pectāvit; ā nautīs enim cognōverat
40 aquae cōpiam quam sēcum habē-rent jam dēficere.[10] Quam ob causam quīdam ex Argonautīs in terram ēgressī aquam quaerēbant.

Hōrum in numerō erat Hylās[11]
45 quīdam, puer fōrmā praestantis-simā; quī[12] dum fontem quaerit,

ā comitibus paulum sēcesserat. Nymphae autem quae fontem co-lēbant, cum juvenem vīdissent, eī persuādēre cōnātae sunt ut 50 sēcum manēret,[13] et cum ille negā-ret[14] sē hoc factūrum esse, puerum vī abstulērunt.

Comitēs ejus, postquam Hylam[11] āmissum esse sēnsērunt, magnō 55 dolōre affectī, diū frūstrā quaerē-bant.

Herculēs autem et Polyphēmus, quī vēstīgia puerī longius secūtī erant, ubi tandem ad lītus red- 60 iērunt, Jāsonem solvisse cognōvē-runt.

Dining Made Difficult

Post haec Argonautae ad Thrā-ciam[15] cursum tenuērunt, et
65 postquam ad oppidum Salmydes-sum[16] nāvem appulerant, in terram

ēgressī sunt. Ibi, cum ab incolīs quaesīvissent quis rēgnum ejus regiōnis obtinēret, certiōrēs fac-tī sunt[17] Phīneum quendam tum 70

A GREEK DAGGER

NOUN CLAUSES OF DESIRE

The subjunctive is sometimes used in clauses introduced by **ut,** to express desire.

Lēgātus hortātus est <u>ut auxilium statim mitterētur</u>, *The envoy urged that aid be sent at once.*

In the English sentence above, the clause *that aid be sent at once* is the object of the verb *urged*. Such a clause is called a *noun clause*. Noun clauses of desire are used as subjects or objects of verbs meaning *to persuade, urge, direct, command, wish,* and *decide*.

When these clauses are negative, they are introduced by **nē** instead of **ut,** and they do not contain **nōn**.

Amīcī nostrī hortābantur <u>nē in urbe manērēmus</u>, *Our friends urged that we should not remain in the city.*

The subjunctive in a clause of desire introduced by **ut** or **nē** is commonly translated by an English infinitive.

Eī persuādēre cōnātae sunt <u>ut sēcum manēret</u>, *They tried to persuade him to remain with them.*

NOTES ON THE TEXT

[1] The word means *the sailors of the Argo;* we have Anglicized it as *Argonauts.*

[2] *Cyzicus* (siz'i-kus—see pronunciation key, p. 410), a city on the Sea of Marmora.

[3] A perfect with **postquam** is often to be translated as past perfect.

[4] The clause **ut . . . nōn possent** is a negative clause of result.

[5] Certain intransitive verbs may be used impersonally in the passive, the subject of such a passive being suggested by the meaning of the verb itself. Here, with **Ācriter**—*a fierce battle was fought.* Compare page 81, note 1.

[6] The words **ejus diēī** are, strictly speaking, unnecessary, since **Postrīdiē** alone means *the next day.* The use of the full phrase is common, however.

[7] *a calm.*

[8] *Mysia* (mizh'iä), an ancient district of Asia Minor. See map, page 116.

[9] *at anchor.*

[10] Indirect discourse.

[11] *Hylas* (hī'las).

[12] A relative at the beginning of an independent clause is translated by a personal pronoun.

[13] This use of the subjunctive is explained above.

[14] The verb **negō** is the normal Latin for *say (that) not.*

[15] *Thrace,* an ancient country of eastern Europe. See map, page 116.

[16] *Salmydessus* (sal-mi-des'us). See map, page 116.

[17] *were informed.* The phrase is followed by indirect discourse.

regem esse. Cognōvērunt etiam hunc caecum esse et dīrō quōdam suppliciō afficī, quod ōlim sē crūdēlissimum in fīliōs suōs prae-
5 buisset.

Cujus supplicii hoc erat genus. Missa erant ā Jove mōnstra quaedam, speciē horribilī, quae capita virginum, corpora volucrum
10 habēbant. Hae volucrēs, quae Harpyiae appellābantur, Phīneō summam molestiam (*annoyance*) afferēbant; quotiēns enim ille ac-cubuerat,[1] veniēbant et cibum ap-
15 positum[2] statim auferēbant. Quae cum ita essent,[3] Phīneus famē[4] paene mortuus est.

JUPITER, KING OF THE GODS

Fighting in the Air

Rēs igitur in hōc locō erant, cum Argonautae nāvem ap-
20 pulērunt. Phīneus autem, adventū eōrum audītō,[5] magnopere gāvīsus[6] est; sciēbat enim quantam[7] opī-niōnem[8] virtūtis Argonautae habē-rent, nec dubitābat quīn sibi auxi-
25 lium ferrent.[9]

Nūntium igitur ad nāvem mīsit quī Jāsonem sociōsque ad rēgiam vocāret. Eō cum vēnissent, Phī-neus dēmōnstrāvit quantō in perī-culō suae rēs essent, et prōmīsit sē 30 magna praemia datūrum esse sī illī remedium (*remedy*) repperissent.[10]

Argonautae negōtium libenter suscēpērunt, et ubi hōra vēnit, cum rēge accubuērunt.[1] At simul 35 ac cēna apposita est (*was served*), Harpyiae cēnāculum (*dining-room*) intrāvērunt et cibum auferre cōnā-bantur. Argonautae prīmum ēn-sibus volucrēs petīvērunt. Cum 40 tamen vidērent hoc nihil[11] prōdesse,

---

[1] *took a place* (*reclined*) *at table.* The Roman custom of assuming a half-reclining position at table is here at-tributed to a much earlier period.

[2] *as soon as it was served.*

[3] A very common expression; literally, *since these things were so;* better, *in consequence,* or *in view of these facts.*

[4] The ablative of this word has the ending of a fifth-declension noun, al-though its other forms belong to the third declension.

[5] The ablative is explained on page 109.

[6] From **gaudeō**. See Gr. S., 38, page 380.

[7] This word may be either a relative (with **tantus**) or an interrogative; the subjunctive **habērent** shows it to be an interrogative introducing an indirect question.

[8] The word sometimes means *opinion;* here it means *reputation.*

[9] *that they were coming to his rescue.* The use of **quīn** with the subjunctive is explained in Gr. S., 116.

[10] Translate with the auxiliary *would.*

[11] With **prōdesse**—*availed nothing,* i.e., *had no effect.*

THE INDEPENDENT PARTICIPIAL CONSTRUCTION

A phrase consisting of a noun or pronoun and a participle is sometimes used in a sentence without being closely connected with any other word in the sentence.

A new leader having been chosen, we may expect better results.

In this sentence the phrase *A new leader having been chosen* is not directly connected with any word in the rest of the sentence. Such a phrase is said to be independent of the rest of the sentence.

THE ABLATIVE ABSOLUTE

The case which is used in Latin for such independent constructions is the ablative. In the sentence given above as an example the word for *leader* would be put in the ablative in Latin and the participle for *having been chosen* would agree with it in case as well as in gender and number. This use of the ablative is called the *ablative absolute*.

Fīliīs meīs laudātīs, laetus sum, *My sons having been praised, I am happy.*[1]

Adventū eōrum audītō, Phīneus gāvīsus est, *Their arrival having been heard of, Phineas rejoiced.*

Often an adjective or another noun is used, instead of a participle, as the second part of the ablative absolute.

Amīcō meō aegrō, nōn manēbō, *My friend (being) sick, I shall not remain.*

Sextō duce, mīlitēs semper fortiter pugnābant, *Sextus (being) leader, the soldiers always fought bravely.*

In translating an ablative absolute of which the second part is an adjective or a noun, we often supply the participle *being*, as in the examples above.

FREE TRANSLATION OF THE ABLATIVE ABSOLUTE

In English, independent phrases which correspond to the literal translation of the ablative absolute are not often used. It is therefore frequently necessary to translate the ablative absolute by a dependent clause introduced by *when, after, if, since,* or *although,* as the sense of the independent clause may suggest.

duce captō, *after the leader had been captured*

adventū eōrum audītō, *when their arrival had been heard of,* or *when he had heard of their arrival*

Sometimes prepositional phrases are used in translating this ablative.

Sextō cōnsule, *in the consulship of Sextus*

Caesare duce, *under the leadership of Caesar*

[1] The original force of the ablative in this construction may be seen if the preposition *with* is used in the translation of these phrases: *with my sons (having been) praised, with their arrival (having been) heard of.*

Zētus[1] et Calais,[2] quī ālīs īnstrūctī erant, in āera[3] sē sublevāvērunt ut dēsuper (*from above*) impetum facerent. Quod cum[4] sēnsissent Har- pyiae, reī novitāte (*by the strangeness*) perterritae, statim aufūgērunt (*they fled*), neque posteā umquam rediērunt.

The Clashing Rocks

Hōc factō,[5] Phīneus, ut prō tantō beneficiō meritam grātiam referret, Jāsonī dēmōnstrāvit quā ratiōne Symplēgadēs vītāre posset. Symplēgadēs autem duae erant rūpēs ingentī magnitūdine, quae ā Jove positae erant eō cōnsiliō,[6] nē quis[7] ad Colchida pervenīret. Hae parvō intervāllō in marī natābant (*were floating*), et sī quid[8] in medium spatium vēnerat, incrēdibilī celeritāte concurrēbant.

Postquam igitur ā Phīneō dē hīs rēbus certior factus est, Jāsōn, sublātīs ancorīs,[9] nāvem solvit et, lēnī ventō prōvectus (*propelled*), mox ad Symplēgadēs appropinquā- vit. Tum in prōrā (*the prow*) stāns columbam (*dove*) quam in manū tenēbat ēmīsit. Illa rēctā viā[10] per medium spatium volāvit, et priusquam rūpēs cōnflīxērunt, incolumis ēvāsit, caudā (*tail*) tantum āmissā.

Tum rūpēs utrimque (*on both sides*) discessērunt. Argonautae, bene intellegentēs omnem spem salūtis in celeritāte positam esse, summā vī rēmīs contendērunt et nāvem incolumem perdūxērunt. Hōc factō, dīs grātiās libenter ēgērunt, quōrum auxiliō ē tantō perīculō ēreptī essent;[11] bene enim sciēbant nōn sine auxiliō deōrum rem ita. fēlīciter ēvēnisse.

A Heavy Task

Brevī intermissō spatiō,[12] Argonautae ad flūmen Phāsim[13] vēnērunt, quod in fīnibus Colchōrum erat. Ibi, cum nāvem appulissent et in terram ēgressī essent, statim ad rēgem Aeētem sē contulērunt et ab eō postulāvērunt ut vellus aureum sibi trāderētur.

Ille, cum audīvisset quam ob causam Argonautae vēnissent, īrā commōtus est et diū negāvit sē vellus trāditūrum esse. Tandem tamen, quod sciēbat Jāsonem nōn sine auxiliō deōrum hoc negōtium suscēpisse, mūtātā sententiā, prō- mīsit sē vellus trāditūrum sī Jāson labōrēs duōs difficillimōs prius perfēcisset; et cum is dīxisset sē ad omnia perīcula parātum esse, rēx quid fierī[14] vellet ostendit.

Prīmum Jāsonī[15] jungendī[16] erant duo taurī speciē horribilī, quī flammās ex ōre ēdēbant. Tum, hīs jūnctīs, ager quīdam arandus erat, et dentēs dracōnis serendī (*were to be sown*). Hīs audītīs, Jāsōn, etsī rem esse summī perīculī intellegēbat, tamen, sine ūllā morā rēgī respondit sē negōtium suscipere atque haec omnia cōnficere parātum esse.

FUTURE PASSIVE PARTICIPLE

Three Latin participles have previously been explained.

Present Active: **portāns,** *carrying*
Perfect Passive: **portātus,** *having been carried*
Future Active: **portātūrus,** *about to carry*

In addition, the Latin verb has also a future passive participle.

I	II	III	IV
portandus, -a, -um	monendus, -a, -um	dūcendus, -a, -um	audiendus, -a, -um
		capiendus, -a, -um	

This participle is formed on the present stem and has the endings **-ndus, -nda, -ndum** in the nominative singular. It is declined like **bonus.**

In **-iō**-verbs of the third conjugation and in verbs of the fourth conjugation, the present stem has **-ie-** in the future passive participle, just as in the present active participle: **capiēns, capiendus; audiēns, audiendus.**

The future passive participle is often used with forms of the verb **sum** to denote an act which must be done or ought to be done.

Auxilium <u>mittendum</u> est, *Help must be sent* (or *ought to be sent*).
<u>Jungendī</u> erant duo taurī, *Two bulls had to be yoked.*

DATIVE OF AGENT

With the future passive participle, the word denoting the person by whom the act must be done or ought to be done is regularly in the dative.

Epistula <u>mihi</u> mittenda est, *A letter ought to be sent by me.*
<u>Jāsonī</u> jungendī erant duo taurī, *Two bulls had to be yoked by Jason.*

Expressions which contain a future passive participle are often best translated by changing the verb to the active voice. The Latin dative of agent is then represented in English by the subject of the active verb.

<u>Jāsonī</u> jungendī erant duo taurī, *<u>Jason</u> had to yoke two bulls.*

NOTES ON THE TEXT

[1] *Zetus* (zē'tus—see pronunciation key, p. 410).

[2] *Calais* (kal'ā̆-is).

[3] *air.* Greek accusative form; the word is masculine.

[4] Do not translate *which when.*

[5] Ablative absolute, to be translated by a clause with *when.*

[6] *with this design* (*purpose*); explained by the clause which follows.

[7] *that no one.* Here **quis** is the indefinite pronoun, not the interrogative. In this use it most frequently follows **sī** or **nē.**

[8] *if anything;* for use of **quid** see the previous note.

[9] Ablative absolute.

[10] Translate the phrase **rēctā viā,** *straight;* how, literally? This is an ablative of route.

[11] The subjunctive is due to the informal indirect discourse (Gr. S., 119); that is, while no verb of saying is employed, one is implied in **grātiās ēgērunt,** *they thanked the gods,* by whose help (as they said), etc.

[12] Ablative absolute. The three words mean *after a short time;* literally, *a short time having elapsed.*

[13] *Phasis* (fā'sis). See map, page 116.

[14] *done* (*to be done*). The forms of **fīō** will be explained later.

[15] Dative of agent, explained above.

[16] This form is explained above.

The Magic Ointment

AT MĒDĒA, rēgis fīlia, Jāsonem adamāvit (*fell in love with*), et ubi audīvit eum tantum perīculum subitūrum esse, rem aegrē
5 ferēbat.[1] Intellegēbat enim patrem suum hunc labōrem prōposuisse eō ipsō cōnsiliō, ut Jāsōn morerētur.

Quae cum ita essent, Mēdēa,
10 quae summam perītiam medicīnae (*skill in the use of drugs*) habēbat, hoc cōnsilium iniit. Mediā nocte, īnsciente patre,[2] ex urbe ēvāsit; et postquam in montēs fīnitimōs vē-
15 nit, herbās quāsdam carpsit (*she picked*). Tum, sūcō expressō,[3] un-guentum parāvit quod vī suā corpus aleret[4] nervōsque (*and sinews*) cōnfirmāret.[4]

Hōc factō, Jāsonī unguentum 20 dedit; praecēpit autem ut eō diē quō istī labōrēs cōnficiendī essent,[5] corpus suum et arma māne (*in the morning*) oblineret (*he should smear*). 25

Jāsōn, etsī paene omnibus magnitūdine et vīribus corporis praestābat (vīta enim omnis in vēnātiōnibus[6] atque in studiīs reī mīlitāris cōnstiterat[7]), cēnsēbat ta- 30 men hoc cōnsilium nōn neglegendum esse.

Sowing the Dragon's Teeth

Mox is diēs vēnit quem rēx ad arandum agrum[8] ēdīxerat.
35 Jāsōn, nē occāsiōnem reī bene gerendae āmitteret, ortā lūce,[9] cum sociīs ad locum cōnstitūtum sē contulit. Ibi stabulum ingēns repperit, in quō taurī inclūsī erant. Tum, portīs apertīs, taurōs in 40

JASON YOKING THE BULLS

THE GERUNDIVE

As we have seen on page 57, the gerund is a verbal noun.

cupidus discēdendī, *desirous of departing*

The future passive participle is often used as a verbal adjective (*gerundive*) in a phrase which has the same meaning as a gerund with an object.

Gerund: **spēs urbem capiendī,** *hope of capturing the city*

Gerundive: **spēs urbis capiendae,** *hope of capturing the city*

The word **capiendae** is a verbal adjective, or gerundive. A gerundive agrees with its noun or pronoun in gender, number, and case. When the gerundive is used, the word it modifies is in the same case as the gerund would have been if it had been used.

The case uses of the gerundive construction are in general the same as those of the gerund.

Genitive: **cupidus oppidī expugnandī,** *desirous of storming the town*
auxiliī ferendī causā, *for the purpose (sake) of bringing aid*

Accusative: **ad eās rēs cōnficiendās,** *for accomplishing these things* (or *to accomplish these things*)

Ablative: **dē auxiliō mittendō,** *about sending aid*
lapidibus portandīs, *by carrying stones*

The Romans often used the gerundive construction where English usage would lead us to expect a gerund.

DISTINCTIONS BETWEEN GERUND AND GERUNDIVE

The following distinctions between the gerund and gerundive are to be observed:

GERUND	GERUNDIVE
A noun	A participle
Active	Passive
Neuter gender	All genders
Used only in the singular	Both numbers
No nominative	All cases

NOTES ON THE TEXT

[1] *was deeply grieved;* literally, *bore the thing with distress.*

[2] *without her father's knowledge;* ablative absolute.

[3] *having pressed out the juice.*

[4] A relative clause of purpose.

[5] *were to be performed.*

[6] *hunting.*

[7] *had consisted;* from **cōnstō.** What are its principal parts?

[8] *for plowing the field.* The gerundive construction is explained above.

[9] *at daybreak.*

lūcem trāxit et summā cum difficultāte jugum imposuit.

At Aeētēs, cum vidēret taurōs nihil[1] contrā Jāsonem valēre, magnopere mīrātus est; nesciēbat enim fīliam suam auxilium eī dedisse.

Tum Jāsōn, omnibus aspicientibus, arāre coepit. In agrō arandō magnam dīligentiam praebuit, et ante merīdiem tōtum opus cōnfēcit. 10 Hōc factō, ad locum ubi rēx sedēbat adiit et dentēs dracōnis postulāvit; quōs ubi accēpit, in agrum quem arāverat magnā cum dīligentiā sparsit. Hōrum autem dentium 15 nātūra erat tālis ut in eō locō ubi sparsī essent virī armātī mīrō quōdam modō gignerentur.

A Strange Crop

Nōndum tamen Jāsōn tōtum opus cōnfēcerat; imperāverat enim eī Aeētēs ut armātōs virōs quī ē dentibus gignerentur sōlus[2] interficeret.[3] Postquam omnēs dentēs in agrum sparsit, Jāsōn, lassitūdine (*by weariness*) exanimātus, quiētī sē trādidit dum virī istī gignerentur.[4]

Paucās hōrās dormiēbat. Sub[5] vesperum, tamen, ē somnō subitō excitātus, rem ita ēvēnisse ut[6] praedictum erat (*had been foretold*) cognōvit; nam in omnibus agrī partibus virī ingentī magnitūdine corporis, ēnsibus galeīsque armātī, mīrum in modum[7] ē terrā oriēbantur. Hōc cognitō, Jāsōn cōnsilium quod dederat Mēdēa nōn omittendum esse[8] putābat. Saxum igitur ingēns (ita enim praecēperat Mēdēa) in mediōs virōs conjēcit. 40

Illī undique ad locum concurrērunt, et cum quisque sibi id saxum (nesciō cūr[9]) habēre vellet, magna contrōversia orta est.

Mox, strictīs (*having been drawn*) 45 ēnsibus, inter sē[10] pugnāre coepērunt, et cum hōc modō plūrimī occīsī essent, reliquī vulneribus cōnfectī ā Jāsone nūllō negōtiō interfectī sunt. 50

Flight from Home

At rēx Aeētēs, ubi cognōvit Jāsonem labōrem prōpositum cōnfēcisse, īrā graviter commōtus est; intellegēbat enim id per dolum factum esse, nec dubitābat quīn 55 Mēdēa auxilium eī tulisset.[11]

---

[1] With **valēre**—*had no power.*

[2] That is, without assistance.

[3] With **ut**—*to kill.* A noun clause with its verb in the active, when used as the object of a verb of commanding, persuading, or warning, is usually to be translated by an infinitive.

[4] This use of the subjunctive is explained on page 115.

[5] *toward.*

[6] With the indicative this word means *as* or *when;* in the sense of *as,* it may be correlative with **ita** or **sīc.**

[7] The prepositional phrase **mīrum in modum** is equivalent to **mīrō modō.**

[8] Supply **sibi** as dative of agent.

[9] *for some reason or other;* compare page 101, note 5.

[10] *one another;* a phrase of frequent occurrence.

[11] Subjunctive with **quīn** and a verb of doubting. See Gr. S., 116.

A TRICK THAT WORKED

Jason has flung the stone into the midst of the warriors and stands ready to draw his sword if necessary.
But Medea's plan is succeeding—the warriors are slaughtering each other.

ANTICIPATORY SUBJUNCTIVE

The subjunctive may be used in subordinate clauses to denote an act which is anticipated, or expected.

Expectābam dum frāter <u>redīret,</u> *I was waiting until my brother should return*
(or *for my brother to return*).

Jāsōn quiētī sē trādidit dum virī istī gignerentur, *Jason rested (gave himself up to rest) until those men should spring up.*

In the first example the verb **redīret** denotes an act which is expected; hence the subjunctive. In the second example the verb **gignerentur** also denotes an act that is expected and is likewise in the subjunctive.

The *anticipatory subjunctive* is most frequently used with conjunctions meaning *until* or *before*. Observe that in both examples above, the conjunction **dum** is used with the meaning *until.*

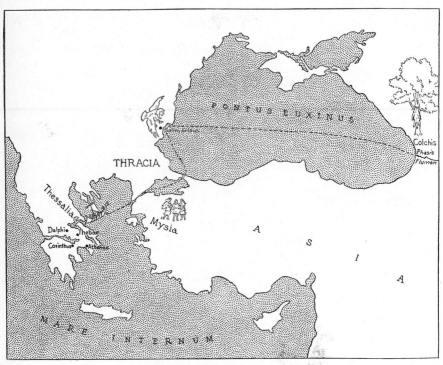

THE VOYAGE OF THE ARGO

Though the story of Jason is legendary, we are able to associate it with real places. The line of dashes shows the course of his voyage. Starting from Thessaly, he crossed the Aegean Sea, and passed through the Sea of Marmora. Then after he had successfully evaded the Symplegades, or Clashing Rocks, at the entrance to the Black Sea, he sailed to Salmydessus. There was still a long and arduous voyage for the little *Argo*, but the ship carried Jason safely all the way to Colchis.

Mēdēa autem, cum intellegeret sē in magnō fore[1] perīculō sī in rēgiā mānsisset, fugā salūtem petere cōnstituit.

5 Omnibus[2] igitur ad fugam parātīs, mediā nocte, īnsciente (*not knowing*) patre, cum frātre Absyrtō ēvāsit, et quam celerrimē ad locum ubi Argō[3] subducta[4] erat 10 sē contulit.

Eō cum vēnisset, ad pedēs Jāsonis sē prōjēcit, et multīs cum lacrimīs obsecrāvit (*begged*) eum nē[5] in tantō discrīmine mulierem dēsereret quae eī tantum prō- 15 fuisset.

Ille, quod memoriā tenēbat sē per ejus auxilium ē magnō perīculō ēvāsisse, libenter eam excēpit, et postquam causam veniendī 20

---

[1] Future infinitive of **sum,** a form often employed instead of **futūrus esse.** The subject is the reflexive pronoun **sē.**

[2] Translate the ablative absolute **omnibus parātīs** by a clause with *when.*

[3] *the ship Argo.*

[4] The comparatively small size of ancient ships made it possible to draw them up on the beach when a landing was made.

[5] With **dēsereret**—*not to desert.* The subjunctive in this clause is explained on page 107.

THE FLIGHT OF MEDEA

In this painting by a modern artist, the Argonauts push off, while Medea awaits the moment of departure. Her brother, Absyrtus, unaware of the terrible fate that awaits him, trustingly holds her hand.

audīvit, hortātus est nē patris īram timēret. Prōmīsit autem sē quam prīmum[1] eam in nāve suā āvectūrum.[2]

The Task Accomplished

POSTRĪDIĒ ejus diēī Jāsōn cum sociīs suīs, ortā lūce, nāvem dēdūxit et, tempestātem idōneam nactī, ad eum locum rēmīs contendērunt, quō in locō[3] Mēdēa 10 vellus cēlātum esse dēmōnstrāvit.

Eō cum vēnissent, Jāsōn in terram ēgressus est et, sociīs ad mare relictīs, ipse cum Mēdēā in 15 silvās viam cēpit. Pauca mīlia passuum per silvam prōgressus, vellus quod quaerēbat ex arbore suspēnsum (*suspended*) vīdit.

Id tamen auferre rēs erat summae 20 mae difficultātis; nōn modo enim locus ipse ēgregiē (*excellently*) et nātūrā et arte mūnītus erat, sed etiam dracō quīdam, speciē terribilī, arborem custōdiēbat.

At Mēdēa, quae, ut suprā dē- 25 mōnstrāvimus, artis medicae summam scientiam habuit, rāmum (*branch*) quem ex arbore proximā dēripuerat (*had taken*) venēnō īnfēcit. 30

Hōc factō, ad locum appropinquāvit, et dracōnem, quī faucibus apertīs[4] adventum expectābat, venēnō sparsit. Proinde, dum dracō somnō oppressus dormit, Jāsōn vel- 35 lus aureum ex arbore dēripuit (*took down*) et cum Mēdēā quam celerrimē pedem rettulit.[5]

---

[1] *as soon as possible.*
[2] For **āvectūrum esse.**
[3] Equivalent to **ubi.**

[4] *with open jaws.*
[5] For this form, see the verb **referō** in the Vocabulary.

Back to the Argo

Dum tamen ea geruntur, Argonautae, quī praesidiō[1] nāvī[1] ad mare relictī erant, animō ānxiō reditum Jāsonis expectābant; bene
5 enim intellegēbant id negōtium summī esse perīculī. Postquam igitur ad occāsum sōlis frūstrā expectāverant, dē ejus salūte dēspērāre coepērunt, nec dubitābant
10 quīn aliquī cāsus accidisset.

Quae cum ita essent, mātūrandum[2] sibi cēnsuērunt ut auxilium ducī ferrent. At, dum proficīscī parant, lūmen quoddam subitō cōnspiciunt, mīrum in modum in- 15 ter silvās refulgēns (*shining*), et magnopere mīrātī quae causa esset ejus reī, ad locum concurrunt. Quō cum[3] vēnissent, Jāsonī et Mēdēae advenientibus occurrērunt, et vel- 20 lus aureum lūminis ejus causam esse cognōvērunt.

Omnī timōre sublātō, magnō cum gaudiō ducem suum excēpērunt, et dīs grātiās libenter ēgē- 25 runt, quod rēs ita fēlīciter ēvēnisset.

Pursued by an Angry Father

Hīs rēbus gestīs, omnēs sine morā nāvem rūrsus cōnscendērunt et, sublātīs ancorīs, prī-
30 mā vigiliā[4] solvērunt; neque enim satis tūtum esse arbitrātī sunt in eō locō manēre.

At rēx Aeētēs, quī jam ante inimīcō in eōs fuerat animō,[5] ubi
35 cognōvit fīliam suam nōn modo ad Argonautās sē recēpisse, sed etiam ad vellus auferendum auxilium tulisse, hōc dolōre[6] gravius exārsit (*was enraged*).
40 Nāvem longam[7] quam celerrimē dēdūcī jussit et, mīlitibus imposi- tīs, fugientēs[8] īnsecūtus est. Argonautae, quī bene sciēbant rem in discrīmine esse, summīs vīribus rēmīs contendēbant.[9] Cum tamen 45 nāvis quā[10] vehēbantur ingentī esset magnitūdine, nōn eādem celeritāte quā Colchī prōgredī poterant. Quae cum ita essent, ā Colchīs sequentibus paene captī sunt; neque 50 enim longius intererat quam quō tēlum adjicī posset.[11]

At Mēdēa, cum vīdisset quō in locō rēs essent, paene omnī spē dēpositā, īnfandum hoc cōnsilium 55 cēpit.

A Fearful Expedient

Erat in nāve Argonautārum fīlius quīdam rēgis Aeētae, nōmine Absyrtus, quem, ut suprā
60 dēmōnstrāvimus, Mēdēa, ex urbe fugiēns, sēcum abdūxerat.

Hunc puerum Mēdēa cōnstituit interficere eō cōnsiliō ut, membrīs ejus in mare conjectīs, cursum Colchōrum impedīret; prō certō 65 enim sciēbat[12] Aeētem, cum mem-

DATIVE OF PURPOSE

Sometimes a noun in the dative is used to denote the purpose which something serves or is intended to serve.

Hunc librum dōnō mīsī, *I sent this book as a gift* (literally, *for a gift*).

Hī nautae praesidiō relictī sunt, *These sailors were left as a guard* (literally, *for a guard*).

The dative of purpose is sometimes employed where the English usage would require a predicate nominative.

Haec fāma auxiliō erit, *This reputation will be a help.*

DATIVE OF REFERENCE

The dative is sometimes used to denote the person or thing with reference to whom or to which an act is done or a situation exists.

Legiō equitātuī auxiliō missa est, *The legion was sent as aid* (literally, *for aid*) *to the cavalry.*

Argonautae, quī praesidiō nāvī relictī erant, reditum Jāsonis expectābant, *The Argonauts, who had been left as a guard* (literally, *for a guard*) *to* (or *for*) *the ship, awaited Jason's return.*

This use is especially important in expressions which contain also a dative of purpose, such as **auxiliō** and **praesidiō** in the two preceding examples.

NOTES ON THE TEXT

[1] The two datives **praesidiō** and **nāvī** are explained above.

[2] *that they ought to make haste;* impersonal use of the passive of an intransitive verb; **sibi** is a dative of agent. English idiom requires a personal construction in the active.

[3] Translate as if **eō cum.**

[4] For the purpose of reckoning time the Romans divided the night from sunset to sunrise into four equal "watches." The first watch began at sunset, the third at midnight. In this story the Roman usage is thought of as having been employed in the time of the Argonauts.

[5] The phrase **inimīcō animō** and the intervening words may be translated, *had entertained hostile feelings toward them;* **animō** is a descriptive ablative in the predicate.

[6] For **hujus reī dolōre,** *in resentment at this;* literally, *because of this resentment.*

[7] *a war-ship.*

[8] *fugitives;* the present participle used as a noun.

[9] *plied* (literally, *strove with*) *the oars with all their might;* **vīribus** is an ablative of manner; **rēmīs,** an ablative of means.

[10] *in which;* an ablative of means.

[11] Translate the clause beginning with **neque**—*for the distance between them was not greater than a javelin's throw;* literally, *greater than to which a javelin could be thrown.*

[12] With **prō certō**—*she felt certain;* literally, *knew for certain.*

THE VICTOR BRINGS BACK THE GOLDEN TROPHY

bra fīliī vīdisset, nōn longius prō-
secūtūrum esse; neque opīniō eam
fefellit.[1]

    Omnia enim ita ēvēnērunt ut
5 Mēdēa spērāverat. Aeētēs, ubi
prīmum[2] membra vīdit, ad ea col-
ligenda nāvem statuī jussit. Dum
tamen ea geruntur, Argonautae,
nōn intermissō rēmigandī labōre,[3]
mox (quod[4] necesse fuit) ē cōn- 10
spectū hostium remōtī sunt, neque
prius[5] fugere dēstitērunt quam ad
flūmen Ēridanum[6] pervēnērunt.

    At Aeētēs, nihil sibi prōfutūrum
esse arbitrātus sī longius prōgressus 15
esset,[7] animō dēmissō[8] domum re-
vertit ut fīliī corpus ad sepultūram
daret.

The Reward Postponed

TANDEM post multa perīcula
Jāsōn in eundem locum pervēnit unde ōlim profectus erat.
Tum ē nāve ēgressus, ad rēgem
Peliam, quī rēgnum adhūc obtinēbat, statim sē contulit et, vellere
25 aureō mōnstrātō, ab eō postulāvit
ut rēgnum sibi trāderētur. Peliās
enim pollicitus erat, sī Jāsōn vellus
rettulisset,[9] sē rēgnum eī trāditūrum.[10]

    Postquam Jāsōn quid fierī[11] vel- 30
let ostendit, Peliās prīmum nihil
respondit, sed diū in eādem trīstitiā (*sadness*) tacitus (*silent*) per-
mānsit. Tandem ita locūtus est:
"Cum videās mē aetāte jam cōn- 35
fectum esse, bene scīs rēgnum

PRESENT SUBJUNCTIVE

The tense sign of the present subjunctive in the first conjugation is -ē-, which replaces the characteristic letter of the conjugation (-ā-).

In the second, third, and fourth conjugations the sign of the present subjunctive is -ā-. In verbs of the second conjugation the tense sign is preceded by -e-, and in -iō-verbs of the third conjugation and all verbs of the fourth conjugation, it is preceded by -i-.

I	II	III		IV
		ACTIVE		
		SINGULAR		
portem	moneam	dūcam	capiam	audiam
portēs	moneās	dūcās	capiās	audiās
portet	moneat	dūcat	capiat	audiat
		PLURAL		
portēmus	moneāmus	dūcāmus	capiāmus	audiāmus
portētis	moneātis	dūcātis	capiātis	audiātis
portent	moneant	dūcant	capiant	audiant
		PASSIVE		
		SINGULAR		
porter	monear	dūcar	capiar	audiar
portēris	moneāris	dūcāris	capiāris	audiāris
portētur	moneātur	dūcātur	capiātur	audiātur
		PLURAL		
portēmur	moneāmur	dūcāmur	capiāmur	audiāmur
portēminī	moneāminī	dūcāminī	capiāminī	audiāminī
portentur	moneantur	dūcantur	capiantur	audiantur

The present subjunctive forms of **sum** and **possum** are as follows:

SINGULAR	PLURAL	SINGULAR	PLURAL
sim	sīmus	possim	possīmus
sīs	sītis	possīs	possītis
sit	sint	possit	possint

NOTES ON THE TEXT

[1] *and she was not mistaken;* literally, *the expectation did not deceive her.* From what verb does **fefellit** come?

[2] A phrase with the same meaning as **simul ac.** The phrase **cum prīmum** is more common.

[3] *by uninterrupted 'labor at the oars;* literally, *with the labor of rowing not interrupted.* Ablative absolute.

[4] Neuter, because reference is made to the following statement of fact.

[5] To be translated with **quam**—*before;* the two are often written as one word.

[6] *Eridanus* (ē-rid′a̰-nus—see pronunciation key, p. 410), sometimes thought to be the Po River.

[7] Translate, *it would do him no good to go farther.* The clause introduced by **sī** is in form a condition, but in thought it is the subject of **prōfutūrum esse.**

[8] Translate the phrase **animō dēmissō,** *dejected.*

[9] *should bring back.*

[10] For **trāditūrum esse;** the future infinitive frequently omits **esse.**

[11] *to do* (literally, *to be done*). The forms of **fīō** will be explained later.

mox tuum futūrum esse. Petō ut paulisper mihi hanc potentiam relinquās."

Hāc ōrātiōne adductus, Jāsōn respondit sē id factūrum quod ille rogāsset.[1]

A Magical Transformation

Hīs rēbus cognitīs, Mēdēa rem aegrē tulit[2] et, cupiditāte rēgnī adducta, cōnstituit mortem rēgī per dolum īnferre.[3]

Hōc cōnstitūtō, ad fīliās rēgis vēnit atque ita locūta est: "Vidētis patrem vestrum aetāte jam esse cōnfectum, neque ad labōrem rēgnandī perferendum satis valēre. Vultisne[4] eum rūrsus juvenem fierī[5]?"

Tum fīliae rēgis ita respondērunt: "Num[6] hoc fierī potest? Quis umquam ē sene juvenis factus est?"

At Mēdēa respondit, "Scītis mē artis medicae summam habēre scientiam. Nunc igitur vōbīs dēmōnstrābō quō modō haec rēs fierī possit."

Hīs dictīs, cum arietem aetāte jam cōnfectum interfēcisset, membra ejus in vāse aēneō posuit et, igne suppositō,[7] in aquam herbās quāsdam īnfūdit. Tum, dum aqua effervēsceret,[8] carmen (*song*) magicum cantābat (*she chanted*). Post breve tempus ariēs ē vāse exiluit (*leaped out*) et, vīribus refectīs, per agrōs currēbat.

A Dangerous Experiment

Dum fīliae rēgis hoc mīrāculum (*marvel*) stupentēs (*speechless*) intuentur (*gazed at*), Mēdēa ita locūta est: "Cum vīderītis[9] quantum valeat ars medica, sī vultis patrem vestrum in adulēscentiam (*youth*) redūcere, id quod fēcī ipsae faciētis. Vōs patris membra in vās conjicite. Ego herbās magicās praebēbō quās in vās īnfundātis.[10]"

Fīliae rēgis cōnsilium quod dederat Mēdēa nōn omittendum putāvērunt.

Patrem igitur Peliam necāvērunt, et membra ejus in vās aēneum conjēcērunt; nihil[11] enim dubitābant quīn hoc maximē eī prōfutūrum esset.[12]

At rēs omnīnō aliter ēvēnit ac[13] spērāverant; Mēdēa enim nōn eāsdem herbās dedit, quās ipsa in aquam cum membrīs arietis anteā īnfūderat. Itaque, postquam diū frūstrā expectāvērunt, patrem suum rē vērā[14] mortuum esse intellēxērunt.

Hīs rēbus gestīs, Mēdēa spērābat sē cum conjuge suō rēgnum acceptūram esse.[15] At cīvēs, cum intellegerent quō modō Peliās periisset, tantum scelus aegrē tulērunt[16] atque Jāsonem et Mēdēam ē rēgnō expulērunt.

PERFECT SUBJUNCTIVE

The perfect subjunctive, active, is formed on the perfect stem with the tense sign **-erī-**.

I	II	III	IV
		SINGULAR	
portāverim	monuerim	dūxerim	audīverim
portāverīs	monuerīs	dūxerīs	audīverīs
portāverit	monuerit	dūxerit	audīverit
		PLURAL	
portāverīmus	monuerīmus	dūxerīmus	audīverīmus
portāverītis	monuerītis	dūxerītis	audīverītis
portāverint	monuerint	dūxerint	audīverint

The perfect subjunctive of **sum** is formed in the same manner on the stem **fu-: fuerim, fuerīs,** etc.

The perfect subjunctive, passive, is made up of the perfect participle and the present subjunctive of **sum**.

I	II	III	IV
portātus sim	monitus sim	ductus sim	audītus sim
etc.	etc.	etc.	etc.

SEQUENCE OF TENSES

When the main verb denotes present or future time, a subjunctive in a subordinate clause is regularly present or perfect. When the main verb denotes past time, the subjunctive in a subordinate clause is regularly imperfect or past perfect.

If the main verb is a perfect which is equivalent to an English present perfect, i.e., translated with *have* or *has*, a dependent subjunctive is sometimes in the present and sometimes in the imperfect.

A result clause sometimes has its verb in the perfect after a main verb denoting past time.

NOTES ON THE TEXT

[1] A shortened form of the past perfect **rogāvisset.** Perfects in **-āvī, -ēvī,** and **-īvī,** with the forms derived from them, may drop the **-ve-** or **-vi-** before endings beginning with **-r-** or **-s-**.

[2] For **rem aegrē tulit** see page 113, note 1.

[3] *to cause the death of the king.* What is the literal translation of the phrase **mortem rēgī īnferre?** The dative **rēgī** depends on the compound verb **īnferre.**

[4] The **-ne** does not indicate whether a positive or a negative answer is expected.

[5] *to be made* or *to become.* In lines 19 and 25 **fierī** means *to be done.* The forms of **fīō** will be explained later.

[6] **Num** indicates that "no" is the expected answer: "This cannot be done, can it?"

[7] *having put fire under it.*

[8] *boiled.* Anticipatory subjunctive with **dum,** *until.* See page 115.

[9] This form is explained above.

[10] *for you to pour into the dish.*

[11] *not at all;* a stronger negative than **nōn.**

[12] *would benefit.*

[13] After **aliter** and similar words **ac** is translated *than.*

[14] See page 101, note 4.

[15] The infinitive with subject accusative is used after **spērō.**

[16] *were angry at.*

A Fatal Gift

Post haec Jāsōn et Mēdēa, ē Thessaliā expulsī, ad urbem Corinthum[1] vēnērunt, cujus urbis Creōn[2] quīdam rēgnum tum ob-
5 tinēbat.

Erat autem Creontī fīlia ūna,[3] nōmine Glaucē; quam cum vīdisset, Jāsōn cōnstituit Mēdēam uxōrem suam repudiāre (*to divorce*) eō
10 cōnsiliō, ut Glaucēn[4] in mātri-mōnium dūceret.

At Mēdēa, ubi intellēxit quae ille in animō habēret, īrā graviter com-mōta, jūre jūrandō cōnfirmāvit sē
15 tantam injūriam ultūram.

Hoc igitur cōnsilium cēpit. Ves-tem parāvit summā arte contextam (*woven*) et variīs colōribus (*colors*) tīnctam (*dyed*). Hanc dīrō quōdam
20 īnfēcit venēnō, cujus vīs tālis erat ut, sī quis eam vestem[5] in-

AT THE SITE OF ANCIENT CORINTH
These walls and pillars suggest the grandeur of this famous Greek city.

duisset, corpus ejus quasi igne ūrerētur.

Hōc factō, vestem Glaucae mīsit. Illa autem, nihil malī suspicāns, 25 dōnum libenter accēpit, et vestem novam (*mōre fēminārum*) statim induit.

A Tragic End

Vix vestem induerat Glaucē, cum dolōrem gravem per om-nia membra sēnsit, et post paulum dīrō cruciātū affecta ē vītā excessit.

Hīs rēbus gestīs, Mēdēa, furōre atque āmentiā (*madness*) impulsa,
35 fīliōs suōs necāvit. Tum ex Thes-saliā fugere cōnstituit, quod timē-bat nē in magnō perīculō esset[6] sī in eā regiōne manēret.

Hōc cōnstitūtō, Sōlem ōrāvit ut
40 in tantō perīculō auxilium sibi praebēret. Sōl autem, hīs precibus commōtus, currum mīsit, cui dra-cōnēs, ālīs īnstrūctī, jūnctī erant.

Mēdēa, nōn omittendam tantam occāsiōnem arbitrāta, currum cōn- 45 scendit, itaque per āera (*air*) vecta incolumis ad urbem Athēnās per-vēnit.

Jāsōn autem post breve tempus mīrō modō occīsus est. Ille enim 50 (sīve cāsū sīve cōnsiliō deōrum) sub umbrā (*shadow*) nāvis suae, quae in lītus subducta erat, ōlim dormiēbat. At nāvis, quae adhūc ērēcta steterat, in eam partem 55 ubi Jāsōn jacēbat subitō dēlāpsa (*falling over*), virum īnfēlīcem op-pressit.

CLAUSES OF FEAR

With verbs of fearing, as well as with other expressions of fear, a dependent clause with its verb in the subjunctive may be used to tell what one fears will happen. Such clauses are introduced by **nē** meaning *that* or by **ut** meaning *that . . . not.* (Occasionally **nē . . . nōn** is used instead of **ut.**)

With English expressions of fear the conjunction *that* is sometimes omitted.

I am afraid he will not arrive today.

In Latin the conjunction **nē** or **ut** is always used.

Remember that with other subjunctive clauses **ut** means *that* and **nē** means *that . . . not,* while in clauses of fear the translations are exactly reversed.

Verēmur ut fortis sīs, *We are afraid that you are not brave.*

Mēdēa timēbat nē in perīculō esset, *Medea feared that she would be in danger.*

The English future tense in a clause of fear is translated by the Latin present subjunctive.

I am afraid that he will not arrive today, **Timeō ut hodiē perveniat.**

NOTES ON THE TEXT

[1] *Corinth,* a city of ancient Greece. See map, page 116.

[2] *Creon* (krē′ọn — see pronunciation key, p. 410).

[3] The clause **Erat . . . ūna** is equivalent to **Creōn fīliam ūnam habēbat. Creontī** is dative. This use of the dative will be explained later.

[4] Accusative.

[5] Like the robe dipped in the blood of Nessus, in the story of Hercules.

[6] This subjunctive is explained above.

COMPREHENSION QUESTIONS

The answers to the questions below will recall the main events in the story of the Argonauts.

1. In what country did Jason's father live?
2. What warning was given to Pelias by the oracle of Delphi?
3. What task did Pelias give Jason?
4. Where was Colchis? (See map, p. 116.)
5. What was the name of Jason's ship?
6. What sort of creatures were the Harpies?
7. How did Jason succeed in passing between the Clashing Rocks?
8. What tasks did the King of Colchis require Jason to perform in order to win the golden fleece?
9. Who helped Jason obtain the fleece?
10. Why did the daughters of Pelias kill their father?
11. In what way did Medea bring about the death of Creon's daughter?
12. How did Medea escape after the death of her children?
13. What was the manner of Jason's death?

QUESTIONS ON GRAMMAR

1. What is an indirect question? Give an example in English. In what mood is the verb of an indirect question in Latin? (Gr. S, 117.) 2. What mood is used in a clause denoting purpose? What words introduce clauses of purpose? (Gr. S., 104.) 3. What are the most important prefixes whose compounds take the dative? (Gr. S., 65.) 4. Give an example of a noun clause of desire in English. What would be the mood of the verb in such a clause in Latin? (Gr. S., 107.) 5. Explain the ablative absolute construction. Give some forms of free translations which may be used for the ablative absolute. (Gr. S., 85.) 6. Explain the use of the future passive participle. (See p. 111.) With this participle, what case is commonly used to denote the person who does the act? (Gr. S., 66.) 7. What form of the verb is **arandō** in the phrase **in agrō arandō?** (Gr. S., 138.) 8. Give the present active subjunctive of **laudō** and **habeō.** (Gr. S., 33, 35.) 9. Give the present passive subjunctive of **mittō** and **audiō.** (Gr. S., 36.)

WORD STUDY III

Words Derived from Latin

The source of many a common English word is often unsuspected because changes in spelling or in meaning tend to conceal its origin. A number of words which come directly from Latin, but in which the Latin elements are not readily apparent, are listed below.

ANTIC, from **antīquus,** *old, old-fashioned.* Hence, an old-fashioned or quaint act.

BISCUIT, from **bis,** *twice,* and **coctus,** past participle of **coquere,** *to cook.* Originally a thin, crisp cake. In England biscuits correspond to our crackers.

COMBINE, from **com-,** *together,* and **bīnī,** *two by two.* At first, to put things together two by two; then, merely to put them together.

DEXTERITY, from **dextra (manus),** *the right hand.* Since most persons can use the right hand more skilfully than the left, a skilful way of doing things.

GLAND, from **glāns, glandis,** *acorn.* Certain glands are shaped like an acorn.

INFANT, from **in-,** *not,* and **fāns, fantis,** present participle of **for, fārī,** *speak.* Hence, a child unable to talk, a child in the first period of life.

KENNEL, from the stem of **canis,** *dog,* and (probably) the suffix **-ālis,** *pertaining to.* Hence, a house for a dog.

MAXIM, short for **maxima sententia,** *a most important idea.* Hence, a rule of conduct, a proverb.

SINISTER, from **sinister,** *left, left-hand.* The ancient (and modern) idea of bad luck associated with this word has given it its present meaning of *evil, threatening.*

USHER, from **ōstium,** *door.* Hence, a doorkeeper, and from that, one who escorts a person from the door to a seat in a church or auditorium.

1. Tell how each of the following English words is connected in meaning with the Latin word from which it is derived: insignia, minus, neuter, plus.

2. Give the meaning of each of the following English words: circumvent, dominate, multilateral, sinecure.

3. What Latin words can you find in each of the English words in Question 2?

Idioms and Phrases

The idioms and phrases listed below occur frequently in the text read. Learning them thoroughly will be of great help in reading.

auctōritāte ejus adductus, *prevailed on by his influence*
cum prīmum, *as soon as possible*
mātūrandum (esse) sibi cēnsuērunt, *they thought they must hurry*
nihil respondēre, *to make no reply*
quam celerrimē, *as quickly as possible*
quam ob causam, *for this reason, accordingly*

Vocabulary Review

The following words, which appear frequently in this book, are important in second-year work. Their meanings should be thoroughly learned.

aetās	difficilis	iste	num	removeō
alō	ēdō	jungō	omnīnō	semper
ancora	ēripiō	lēnis	ōrātiō	sī quis
apertus	etsī	lītus	pereō	subdūcō
at	famēs	merīdiēs	permaneō	supplicium
cēnseō	fōrma	modus	persuādeō	tardus
certus	frūstrā	mōs	perterreō	tempestās
cibus	fugiō	necesse	postrīdiē	tollō
commoror	īnferō	negō	praesidium	valeō
cruciātus	īnstitūtum	nē . . .	praesum	vehō
currō	intellegō	quidem	prex	ventus
dēns	intereā	nōn modo . . .	prōjiciō	
dēserō	intermittō	sed etiam	quisque	

CONSPECTUS OF SECOND-YEAR FORMS

SUBJUNCTIVE MOOD OF VERBS, ACTIVE VOICE

PRESENT SYSTEM

PRESENT

I	II	III (*-ō-verbs*)	III (*-iō-verbs*)	IV
porte-m	monea-m	dūca-m	capia-m	audia-m
portē-s	moneā-s	dūcā-s	capiā-s	audiā-s
porte-t	monea-t	dūca-t	capia-t	audia-t
portē-mus	moneā-mus	dūcā-mus	capiā-mus	audiā-mus
portē-tis	moneā-tis	dūcā-tis	capiā-tis	audiā-tis
porte-nt	monea-nt	dūca-nt	capia-nt	audia-nt

IMPERFECT

I	II	III (*-ō-verbs*)	III (*-iō-verbs*)	IV
portā-re-m	monē-re-m	dūce-re-m	cape-re-m	audī-re-m
portā-rē-s	monē-rē-s	dūce-rē-s	cape-rē-s	audī-rē-s
portā-re-t	monē-re-t	dūce-re-t	cape-re-t	audī-re-t
portā-rē-mus	monē-rē-mus	dūce-rē-mus	cape-rē-mus	audī-rē-mus
portā-rē-tis	monē-rē-tis	dūce-rē-tis	cape-rē-tis	audī-rē-tis
portā-re-nt	monē-re-nt	dūce-re-nt	cape-re-nt	audī-re-nt

PERFECT SYSTEM

PERFECT

I	II	III (*-ō-verbs*)	III (*-iō-verbs*)	IV
portāv-eri-m	monu-eri-m	dūx-eri-m	cēp-eri-m	audīv-eri-m
portāv-erī-s	monu-erī-s	dūx-erī-s	cēp-erī-s	audīv-erī-s
portāv-eri-t	monu-eri-t	dūx-eri-t	cēp-eri-t	audīv-eri-t
portāv-erī-mus	monu-erī-mus	dūx-erī-mus	cēp-erī-mus	audīv-erī-mus
portāv-erī-tis	monu-erī-tis	dūx-erī-tis	cēp-erī-tis	audīv-erī-tis
portāv-eri-nt	monu-eri-nt	dūx-eri-nt	cēp-eri-nt	audīv-eri-nt

PAST PERFECT

I	II	III (*-ō-verbs*)	III (*-iō-verbs*)	IV
portāv-isse-m	monu-isse-m	dūx-isse-m	cēp-isse-m	audīv-isse-m
portāv-issē-s	monu-issē-s	dūx-issē-s	cēp-issē-s	audīv-issē-s
portāv-isse-t	monu-isse-t	dūx-isse-t	cēp-isse-t	audīv-isse-t
portāv-issē-mus	monu-issē-mus	dūx-issē-mus	cēp-issē-mus	audīv-issē-mus
portāv-issē-tis	monu-issē-tis	dūx-issē-tis	cēp-issē-tis	audīv-issē-tis
portāv-isse-nt	monu-isse-nt	dūx-isse-nt	cēp-isse-nt	audīv-isse-nt

SUBJUNCTIVE MOOD OF VERBS, PASSIVE VOICE

PRESENT SYSTEM

PRESENT

I	II	III (*-ō-verbs*)	III (*-iō-verbs*)	IV
porte-r	monea-r	dūca-r	capia-r	audia-r
portē-ris	moneā-ris	dūcā-ris	capiā-ris	audiā-ris
portē-tur	moneā-tur	dūcā-tur	capiā-tur	audiā-tur
portē-mur	moneā-mur	dūcā-mur	capiā-mur	audiā-mur
portē-minī	moneā-minī	dūcā-minī	capiā-minī	audiā-minī
porte-ntur	monea-ntur	dūca-ntur	capia-ntur	audia-ntur

IMPERFECT

I	II	III (*-ō-verbs*)	III (*-iō-verbs*)	IV
portā-re-r	monē-re-r	dūce-re-r	cape-re-r	audī-re-r
portā-rē-ris	monē-rē-ris	dūce-rē-ris	cape-rē-ris	audī-rē-ris
portā-rē-tur	monē-rē-tur	dūce-rē-tur	cape-rē-tur	audī-rē-tur
portā-rē-mur	monē-rē-mur	dūce-rē-mur	cape-rē-mur	audī-rē-mur
portā-rē-minī	monē-rē-minī	dūce-rē-minī	cape-rē-minī	audī-rē-minī
portā-re-ntur	monē-re-ntur	dūce-re-ntur	cape-re-ntur	audī-re-ntur

PERFECT SYSTEM

PERFECT

portātus sim	portātī sīmus	portātus essem	portātī essēmus
portātus sīs	portātī sītis	portātus essēs	portātī essētis
portātus sit	portātī sint	portātus esset	portātī essent
monitus sim	monitī sīmus	monitus essem	monitī essēmus
monitus sīs	monitī sītis	monitus essēs	monitī essētis
monitus sit	monitī sint	monitus esset	monitī essent
ductus sim	ductī sīmus	ductus essem	ductī essēmus
ductus sīs	ductī sītis	ductus essēs	ductī essētis
ductus sit	ductī sint	ductus esset	ductī essent
captus sim	captī sīmus	captus essem	captī essēmus
captus sīs	captī sītis	captus essēs	captī essētis
captus sit	captī sint	captus esset	captī essent
audītus sim	audītī sīmus	audītus essem	audītī essēmus
audītus sīs	audītī sītis	audītus essēs	audītī essētis
audītus sit	audītī sint	audītus esset	audītī essent

PAST PERFECT

SUBJUNCTIVE MOOD OF IRREGULAR VERBS

PRESENT SYSTEM

PRESENT

(sum)	(possum)	(volō)	(eō)	(fīō)
sim	possim	velim	eam	fīam
sīs	possīs	velīs	eās	fīās
sit	possit	velit	eat	fīat
sīmus	possīmus	velīmus	eāmus	fīāmus
sītis	possītis	velītis	eātis	fīātis
sint	possint	velint	eant	fīant

IMPERFECT

essem	possem	vellem	īrem	fierem
essēs	possēs	vellēs	īrēs	fierēs
esset	posset	vellet	īret	fieret
essēmus	possēmus	vellēmus	īrēmus	fierēmus
essētis	possētis	vellētis	īrētis	fierētis
essent	possent	vellent	īrent	fierent

PERFECT SYSTEM

PERFECT

fu-eri-m	potu-eri-m	volu-eri-m	i-eri-m	factus sim
fu-erī-s	potu-erī-s	volu-erī-s	i-erī-s	factus sīs
fu-eri-t	potu-eri-t	volu-eri-t	i-eri-t	factus sit
fu-erī-mus	potu-erī-mus	volu-erī-mus	i-erī-mus	factī sīmus
fu-erī-tis	potu-erī-tis	volu-erī-tis	i-erī-tis	factī sītis
fu-eri-nt	potu-eri-nt	volu-eri-nt	i-eri-nt	factī sint

PAST PERFECT

fu-isse-m	potu-isse-m	volu-isse-m	īsse-m	factus essem
fu-issē-s	potu-issē-s	volu-issē-s	īssē-s	factus essēs
fu-isse-t	potu-isse-t	volu-isse-t	īsse-t	factus esset
fu-issē-mus	potu-issē-mus	volu-issē-mus	īssē-mus	factī essēmus
fu-issē-tis	potu-issē-tis	volu-issē-tis	īssē-tis	factī essētis
fu-isse-nt	potu-isse-nt	volu-isse-nt	īsse-nt	factī essent

INFINITIVE

ACTIVE

	I	II	III	IV
Pres.	portāre	monēre	dūcere	audīre
Perf.	portāvisse	monuisse	dūxisse	audīvisse
Fut.	portātūrus esse	monitūrus esse	ductūrus esse	audītūrus esse

PASSIVE

	I	II	III	IV
Pres.	portārī	monērī	dūcī	audīrī
Perf.	portātus esse	monitus esse	ductus esse	audītus esse
Fut.	portātum īrī	monitum īrī	ductum īrī	audītum īrī

OF IRREGULAR VERBS

	(sum)	(possum)	(volō)	(eō)	(fīō)
Pres.	esse	posse	velle	īre	fierī
Perf.	fuisse	potuisse	voluisse	īsse (iisse)	factus esse
Fut.	futūrus esse	————	————	itūrus esse	factum īrī

PARTICIPLE

ACTIVE

	I	II	III	IV
Pres.	portāns	monēns	dūcēns	audiēns
Fut.	portātūrus	monitūrus	ductūrus	audītūrus

PASSIVE

	I	II	III	IV
Perf.	portātus	monitus	ductus	audītus
Fut.	portandus	monendus	dūcendus	audiendus

GERUND

I	II	III	IV
portandī	monendī	dūcendī	audiendī
portandō	monendō	dūcendō	audiendō
portandum	monendum	dūcendum	audiendum
portandō	monendō	dūcendō	audiendō

LIFE IN ANCIENT GAUL

THE story of the conquest of Gaul, written by the commander of the conquering army, Julius Caesar, is one of the most famous works of ancient history. Gaul later became one of the richest and most important parts of the Roman Empire, and in spite of the many changes which the centuries have brought to this region, the influence of Roman civilization still lives on.

As is shown in the map on page 137, Gaul included an extensive territory. When Caesar was writing his account of the war, Cisalpine Gaul — northern Italy—had already been a Roman province for more than a century. In Transalpine Gaul—the southern part of present-day France—Roman authority had been established for sixty years.

But beyond Transalpine Gaul, which was usually referred to simply as "the Province," lay territory that had never been brought under Roman control. This included the rest of present-day France, Belgium, Holland, Luxemburg, and parts of Germany and Switzerland. The Gauls of this region, like those in the two Roman provinces, were fair-haired and blue-eyed, tall, and strong. Though their civilization was not so advanced as that of the Romans, they were a people of intelligence and energy and were far from being savages. The Gauls were divided into numerous independent tribes, each with its chief town. These

A GALLIC HELMET

towns were usually strong fortresses, and they also served as political capitals and business centers.

For the most part the Gauls lived in wooden houses, often with cone-shaped roofs that were shingled or thatched. The home of a rich noble was a large building with a number of rooms, including a great banquet hall for the many feasts which he gave. The house of a very poor family, on the other hand, was a mere one-room hut.

Outside the towns the Gauls dwelt on their farmlands, though some of the more backward tribes had their homes in the woods and rather inaccessible swampy regions. Then, as now, much of France was a fertile agricultural country, and the inhabitants raised grain from which to make bread. On their tables pork, cheese, and cider were also found. When the Roman soldiers penetrated into northern Gaul, they were much surprised to find that olive-oil, their common table fat, was unknown, and that butter was used instead—butter, which the Roman writer Pliny once referred to as "the luxury of barbarian tables." Game of various kinds—bison, deer, bear, reindeer, wild boar, and antelope—might also be on the menu, for the nobles took great pleasure in hunting the wild animals of the forests.

When the chiefs were not hunting, they were engaged in the more serious business of fighting or in politics. They might direct certain affairs of business, but manual labor was beneath them. The common people worked in the fields, prepared the food, and made the clothing.

Most clothes were made of wool, for sheep were raised on the farms. The chiefs and rich men had fine clothes and delighted in wearing jewelry — heavy rings, bracelets, armlets, and necklaces of bronze or gold.

Each tribe had a definite political organization and was governed by a chieftain, who was usually elected by the nobility, though in some instances there appear to have been hereditary kings. The chieftain was assisted by a council of the chiefs of the tribe, and was responsible to assemblies composed of the upper classes of people, for there was a distinct division into classes. The common people had no political rights, but were usually under the protection of some nobleman. The members of the tribe worshiped the same gods, used the same temples and other places of worship, and bought and sold in a central market.

A CHIEF

The territory of each nation appears to have been rather clearly marked, with definite boundaries. Sometimes there were customhouses at these boundaries, for the Gauls carried on a great deal of trade.

Caesar refers to the tribes as parts of larger groups differing from each other in language, customs, and laws. These larger groups, however, had no common government or union of any sort.

Of the various peoples, the Haeduans were probably the most advanced. Their capital, Bibracte, was the most important city in independent Gaul. Like many other large Gallic towns, it was fortified with walls and trenches, and its position, on a hill, made it difficult to attack. Since the Gauls built their towns largely of wood, few traces of their ancient cities are left, and the site of the great Bibracte is marked now only by grass-grown mounds.

At one time many roads must have led from this town to the various parts of the Haeduan territory as well as to other regions of Gaul. In the stout Gallic carts, drawn by oxen, farmers brought their products to market and traders carried their merchandise. Business was conducted in the Gallic language, of which little is now known. Since there was no Gallic alphabet, business and public documents were written in Greek characters, learned from the early Greek traders who had settled in southern Gaul. Since the language of the Gauls died out after the Roman conquest, practically no traces of it remain in modern French, which comes chiefly from the Latin.

A great deal of money circulated among the Gauls, and many tribes had their own coinage. Indeed, Gaul was second only to Spain in its mineral wealth. An ancient writer asserts that gold was abundant in Gaul. Silver was somewhat less plentiful. Tin and copper were used extensively to make bronze for tools, armor, and weapons—spear-heads, dart-heads, swords, and scabbards. The ability of the Gauls in metal-working is shown by many articles that have been unearthed.

Remains have been found, too,

A GALLIC GODDESS

of many statues and temples, which were often made of stone. Various gods were worshiped, of which some were common to all of the Gauls, while others were only local deities. The worship was in the hands of priests called Druids, who were very highly honored.

Boys from the noblest families were taken under the care of the Druids and trained to become priests in their turn. These pupils had to learn a great number of verses which embodied the wisdom of the Druids and which were always handed down orally.

The Druids foretold the future, and from their study of the sun, moon, and stars they were able to make a crude calendar.

In war the Gauls were brave, but they were undisciplined in comparison with the Roman armies. They had little knowledge of military tactics—and in Caesar

THE ROMANS HAD PLACES OF AMUSEMENT IN PARIS

Today French children play in this little Roman amphitheater, where their Gallic ancestors watched the bloody spectacles of the arena.

they faced one of the greatest generals of all time.

Unfortunately for them, the various tribes frequently quarreled among themselves, and these conflicts kept them from uniting successfully when danger from outside threatened. If they had all joined in facing Caesar and his legions, their very numbers might have brought defeat to the Roman general. In that case the history of western Europe would have been very different.

Caesar was successful in establishing Roman authority in Gaul. His stern punishment of those who defied the power of Rome frightened the nobles into submission. After his death there were some scattered outbreaks, but Roman authority and civilization were gradually accepted.

Eventually the Gauls were given many of the privileges of Roman citizens. Roman roads and towns were built, and agriculture and industry were encouraged. The Roman traders and officials brought with them their language and customs. In time the Gauls spoke Latin and adopted the ways of their conquerors.

The natural wealth of Gaul and the adaptability of its people made it a great prize. In this vast province, industries and civilization developed to such an extent that it became one of Rome's greatest sources of strength. The possession of Gaul helped the Romans to conquer and to Romanize Britain. And the Gauls helped hold back the German barbarians, thus prolonging the life of the Empire.

THE GALLIC WAR

BY GAIUS JULIUS CAESAR

Truly a wonderful man was Gaius Julius Caesar.
You are a writer and I am a fighter; but here was a fellow
Who could both write and fight, and in both was equally skilful.

LONGFELLOW: THE COURTSHIP OF MILES STANDISH

CAESAR AND THE HELVETIANS

Gaul and Its People

GALLIA est omnis[1] dīvīsa[2] in partēs trēs; ūnam partem incolunt Belgae, aliam Aquītānī,[3] tertiam Celtae,[4] quī ā nōbīs Gallī
5 appellantur. Hī omnēs linguā,[5] īnstitūtīs, lēgibus inter sē[6] differunt. Gallōs ab Aquītānīs[3] Garunna flūmen, ā Belgīs Matrona et Sēquana dīvidit.[7]
10 Hōrum omnium fortissimī sunt Belgae, proptereā quod ā cultū atque hūmānitāte prōvinciae[8] longissimē absunt; minimēque[9] ad eōs mercātōrēs saepe commeant,[10] quī
15 ea important (*bring in*) quae ad effēminandōs[11] animōs pertinent;

praetereā sunt proximī Germānīs,[12] quī trāns Rhēnum incolunt, quibuscum continenter bellum gerunt.

Quā dē causā Helvētiī quoque
20 reliquōs Gallōs virtūte praecēdunt, quod ferē cotīdiānīs proeliīs cum Germānīs contendunt, cum aut suīs fīnibus[13] eōs prohibent, aut ipsī in eōrum fīnibus bellum gerunt.
25

Eōrum[14] ūna pars, quam Gallī[15] obtinent, initium capit ā flūmine Rhodanō; continētur Garunnā flūmine, Ōceanō, fīnibus Belgārum; attingit etiam ab[16] Sēquanīs et Hel-
30 vētiīs flūmen Rhēnum; vergit (*it faces*) ad septentriōnēs.

---

[1] *as a whole;* including the three parts mentioned in lines 2-4.

[2] *is divided.* The present of the Latin verb would mean *is being divided.* The perfect here denotes a situation.

[3] *the Aquitanians.*

[4] *the Celts.*

[5] Ablative of respect, as are also **īnstitūtīs** and **lēgibus.**

[6] *from one another.*

[7] Singular, because the two rivers are thought of as one boundary.

[8] Rome's province of Transalpine Gaul in southern France is meant.

[9] To be taken with **saepe.**

[10] With **ad**—*visit.*

[11] The gerundive in a prepositional phrase; translate **ad . . . pertinent**—*tend to break down character.*

[12] Dative with **proximī.**

[13] Ablative of separation.

[14] We should expect the name of the country, **Galliae,** rather than a pronoun referring to the people.

[15] Those who in the Gallic language were called Celts; see line 4.

[16] *on the side of.*

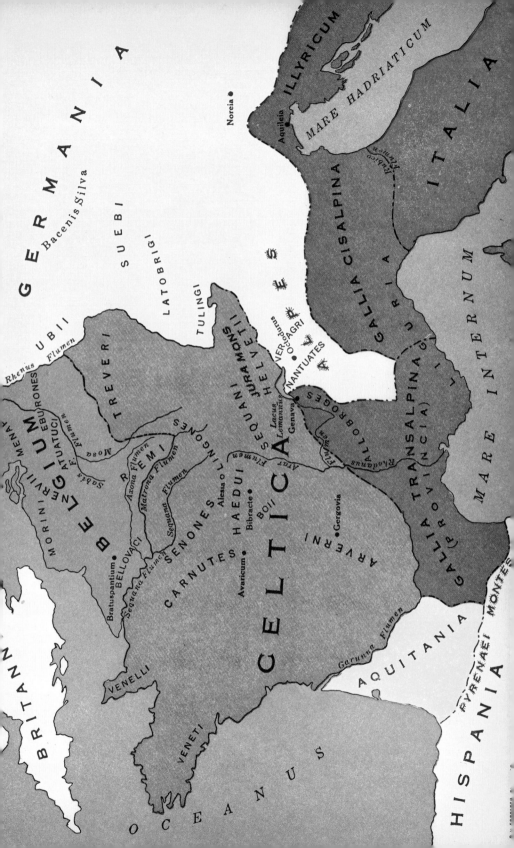

LACUS LEMANNUS — NOW CALLED LAKE GENEVA

The Latin name of this famous body of water still survives; for poets even today write of Lake Leman and also of Helvetia, meaning Switzerland.

Belgae ab extrēmīs Galliae[1] fīnibus oriuntur; pertinent ad īnferiōrem partem flūminis Rhēnī; spectant in septentriōnēs et orientem 5 sōlem.

Aquītānia[2] ā Garunnā flūmine ad Pȳrēnaeōs (*Pyrenees*) montēs et eam partem Ōceanī quae est ad[3] Hispāniam pertinet; spectat inter occāsum sōlis et septentriōnēs. 10

An Ambitious Leader

APUD Helvētiōs longē nōbilissimus fuit et dītissimus Orgetorīx. Is, M. Messālā, M. Pīsōne cōnsulibus,[4] rēgnī cupiditāte induc-15 tus, conjūrātiōnem nōbilitātis fēcit et cīvibus persuāsit ut dē fīnibus suīs cum omnibus cōpiīs exīrent.[5] "Perfacile est,[6]" inquit, "cum virtūte omnibus praestēmus, tōtīus 20 Galliae imperiō[7] potīrī."

Id hōc facilius[8] eīs persuāsit[9] quod undique locī nātūrā Helvētiī continentur; ūnā ex parte[10] flūmine Rhēnō lātissimō atque altissimō, 25 quī agrum Helvētium ā Germānīs dīvidit, alterā ex parte monte Jūrā

altissimō, quī est inter Sēquanōs et Helvētiōs, tertiā ex parte lacū Lemannō et flūmine Rhodanō, quī prōvinciam nostram ab Helvētiīs 30 dīvidit.

Itaque fīēbat ut minus lātē vagārentur[11] et minus facile fīnitimīs[12] bellum īnferre possent; quā dē causā hominēs bellandī cupidī mag-35 nō dolōre afficiēbantur. Prō[13] multitūdine autem hominum et prō glōriā bellī atque fortitūdinis (*of bravery*) angustōs sē fīnēs habēre arbitrābantur, quī in longitūdinem 40 (*length*) mīlia passuum CCXL, in lātitūdinem CLXXX patēbant.

THE IRREGULAR VERB *FIŌ*

The verb **faciō** has no passive forms in the present system. The missing passive is replaced by the irregular verb **fīō**, *I become, I am made*. The principal parts are: **fīō, fierī, factus sum.**

INDICATIVE

PRESENT		IMPERFECT		FUTURE	
fīō	——	fīēbam	fīēbāmus	fīam	fīēmus
fīs	——	fīēbās	fīēbātis	fīēs	fīētis
fit	fīunt	fīēbat	fīēbant	fīet	fīent

SUBJUNCTIVE

PRESENT		IMPERFECT	
fīam	fīāmus	fierem	fierēmus
fīās	fīātis	fierēs	fierētis
fīat	fīant	fieret	fierent

The perfect system of **faciō** in the passive is formed regularly: **factus sum, factus eram,** etc.

NOUN CLAUSES OF FACT

The third person singular of **fīō** is often translated *it results* (freely, *the result is*). A verb meaning *it happens, it results, it comes about* may have as subject a clause introduced by **ut** with its verb in the subjunctive. Such a clause is called a *noun clause of fact*. The subjunctive in clauses of this kind is translated in the same manner as the indicative.

> **Saepe accidit ut frātrem tuum in urbe videam,** *It often happens that I see your brother in the city.*

> **Fīēbat ut minus lātē vagārentur,** *It resulted that they roamed less widely.*

A clause of this kind may be used as the object of a verb meaning *to bring about, to make, to cause.*

> **Hoc effēcit ut castra tūta essent,** *This fact brought it about that the camp was safe* (i.e., *made the camp safe*).

NOTES ON THE TEXT

[1] Central, or Celtic, Gaul is meant, as described on page 136, lines 26-32.

[2] *Aquitania* (ak-wi-tā′ni-ạ), one of the three divisions of Gaul. See map, page 137.

[3] *next to.*

[4] *in the consulship of,* etc.; ablative absolute. The year was 61 B.C.

[5] The clause introduced by **ut** is a noun clause, used as object of **persuāsit,** to be translated by an infinitive.

[6] The subject of this verb is the infinitive **potīrī.**

[7] Ablative with **potīrī.** See Gr. S., 89.

[8] *the more easily;* **hōc** is ablative of degree of difference. It also carries an idea of cause in anticipation of the causal clause, **quod . . . continentur.**

[9] *he persuaded them to this.* Here the object of **persuāsit** is the pronoun **Id;** in line 16 the object was a clause.

[10] *on one side.*

[11] The use of the subjunctive in a noun clause of fact is explained above.

[12] *on their neighbors;* dative with the compound verb **īnferre,** which as a transitive verb takes also the direct object **bellum.**

[13] *in proportion to.*

THE HELVETIANS PLAN THEIR MIGRATION

Two Years of Preparation

Hīs rēbus adductī et auctōritāte Orgetorīgis permōtī, cōnstituērunt ea quae ad proficīscendum pertinērent comparāre, jūmentōrum 5 (*of pack animals*) et carrōrum quam maximum numerum coëmere,[1] sēmentēs (*sowings*) quam maximās facere ut in itinere cōpia frūmentī suppeteret (*might be available*), 10 cum proximīs cīvitātibus[2] pācem et amīcitiam cōnfirmāre. Ad eās rēs cōnficiendās[3] biennium (*two years*) sibi satis esse dūxērunt;[4] in tertium annum profectiōnem 15 lēge cōnfirmant.

Orgetorīx dux dēligitur. Is lēgātiōnem ad cīvitātēs suscipit. In eō itinere persuādet Casticō (*Casticus*), Sēquanō, ut rēgnum in cīvitāte suā occupāret; pater enim 20 ejus rēgnum in Sēquanīs multōs annōs obtinuerat et ā senātū populī Rōmānī[5] amīcus appellātus erat; itemque Dumnorīgī Haeduō, quī eō tempore prīncipātum in cīvitāte 25 obtinēbat ac maximē plēbī acceptus erat, ut idem cōnārētur persuādet, eīque fīliam suam in mātrimōnium dat.

"Perfacile factū[6] est," inquit, 30

[1] *to buy up the greatest number possible.*

[2] The Sequani and the Haeduans were the most important of these.

[3] *for the accomplishment of these things;* the gerundive in a prepositional phrase expressing purpose.

[4] Here used in the sense of *regarded, thought.*

[5] The genitive **populī Rōmānī** is to be taken with **senātū.**

[6] *to do;* the supine, ablative of respect. See Gr. S., 141.

"cōnāta (*undertakings*) perficere, proptereā quod ipse meae cīvitātis imperium obtentūrus sum. Nōn est dubium quīn[1] tōtīus Galliae plūrimum Helvētiī possint.[2] Meīs cōpiīs meōque exercitū vōbīs rēgna conciliābō." Hāc ōrātiōne adductī inter sē fidem et jūs jūrandum dant[3] et, rēgnō occupātō, per trēs potentissimōs ac firmissimōs populōs tōtīus Galliae[4] sēsē potīrī posse spērant.

The End of Orgetorix

EA RĒS est Helvētiīs per indicium[5] ēnūntiāta. Mōribus suīs Orgetorīgem ex vinculīs[6] causam dīcere coēgērunt.[7] Sī damnārētur (*he should be convicted*), igne eum cremātūrī erant (*they were going to burn*). Diē cōnstitūtā causae[8] dictiōnis, Orgetorīx ad jūdicium omnem suam familiam, ad[9] hominum mīlia decem, undique coēgit, et omnēs clientēs obaerātōsque (*and debtors*) suōs, quōrum magnum numerum habēbat, eōdem condūxit; per eōs, nē causam dīceret, sē ēripuit.

Cum cīvitās, ob eam rem incitāta, armīs jūs suum exequī (*to enforce*) cōnārētur multitūdinemque hominum ex agrīs magistrātūs cōgerent, Orgetorīx mortuus est. Multī ex Helvētiīs arbitrantur ipsum sibi mortem cōnscīvisse.[10]

A Desolated Homeland

POST ejus mortem nihilō minus Helvētiī ē fīnibus suīs exīre cōnantur. Ubi jam sē ad eam rem parātōs esse arbitrātī sunt, oppida sua omnia numerō[11] ad[12] duodecim, vīcōs ad quadringentōs, reliqua prīvāta aedificia incendunt; frūmentum omne, praeter quod sēcum portātūrī erant, combūrunt (*they burned*). Haec fēcērunt ut, domum reditiōnis (*of returning*) spē sublāta,[13] parātiōrēs ad omnia perīcula subeunda[14] essent. Trium mēnsium[15] molita cibāria[16] sibi quemque domō efferre jubent.

Persuādent Rauracīs[17] et Tu-

[1] *that;* regularly used with the subjunctive after expressions of doubt when these are accompanied by a negative.

[2] With **plūrimum**—*are the strongest (people)*.

[3] *they exchange.* The phrase **inter sē** denotes reciprocal action, as on page 136, line 6.

[4] With **potīrī**, which sometimes governs the genitive instead of the ablative.

[5] Translate as if **indicēs**, *informers.*

[6] *in chains.* How would this be translated literally?

[7] *they compelled.* In lines 23 and 32 the same verb means *collected.*

[8] Objective genitive with **dictiōnis**, which in turn depends on **Diē**.

[9] Used adverbially, *about.*

[10] Translate the last four words, *that he committed suicide.*

[11] Ablative of respect.

[12] See note 9.

[13] *by destroying the hope;* ablative absolute. What are the principal parts of **tollō**?

[14] *to undergo all dangers.*

[15] *for three months;* genitive of measure.

[16] The words **molita cibāria** mean *meal.*

[17] *the Rauraci* (râ′ra̤-sī), a tribe of Celtic Gaul.

THE PASS BETWEEN THE LANDS OF THE HELVETIANS AND THE SEQUANI

lingīs et Latobrīgīs, fīnitimīs, ut, oppidīs suīs vīcīsque exustīs (*having been burned*), ūnā cum eīs proficīscantur.

Boiōs,[1] quī trāns Rhēnum incoluerant et in agrum Nōricum[2] trānsierant Nōreiamque[3] oppugnābant, ad sē sociōs recipiunt.[4]

Two Possible Routes

Erant omnīnō itinera duo quibus itineribus domō exīre possent;[5] ūnum per Sēquanōs, angustum et difficile, inter montem Jūram et flūmen Rhodanum, vix quā singulī carrī dūcerentur;[6] mōns autem altissimus[7] impendēbat (*overhung*) ut facile perpaucī (*very few*) prohibēre[8] possent;[9] alterum per prōvinciam nostram, multō facilius atque expedītius, proptereā quod inter fīnēs Helvētiōrum et Allobrogum Rhodanus fluit, isque nōnnūllīs locīs vadō trānsitur.[10]

Extrēmum oppidum Allobrogum est proximumque Helvētiōrum fīnibus Genava. Ex eō oppidō pōns ad Helvētiōs pertinet.

Cōnsilium erat Helvētiōrum vel persuādēre Allobrogibus, quī nūper pācātī erant et nōndum bonō animō[11] in populum Rōmānum vidēbantur, vel vī cōgere ut per suōs fīnēs iter darent.[12]

---

[1] The word **Boiī** survives in the modern name *Bohemia*.

[2] *of Noricum.* See map, page 277.

[3] *and . . . Noreia* (nō-rē′ȧ). Noreia was a town of Noricum. See map, page 137.

[4] *they admit to their numbers as allies.*

[5] A relative clause of description; hence the subjunctive. See Gr. S., 112.

[6] *could be drawn.* The clause **vix quā . . . dūcerentur** is somewhat different

from the clause in lines 10-11, in that it suggests the idea of possibility.

[7] *very high.*

[8] Supply **eōs** as object.

[9] Subjunctive in a clause of result.

[10] *is crossed by fording.*

[11] *kindly disposed;* ablative of description in the predicate with **vidēbantur.**

[12] A noun clause, object of **persuādēre** and **cōgere.**

Omnibus rēbus ad profectiōnem comparātīs, diem dīcunt quā diē ad rīpam Rhodanī omnēs conveniant.[1] Is diēs erat a. d. v Kal. Apr.,[2] L. Pīsōne, A. Gabīniō[3] cōnsulibus.

Enter Caesar

CAESARĪ cum id[4] nūntiātum esset eōs per prōvinciam nostram iter facere cōnārī, mātūrat ab urbe proficīscī et quam maximīs potest itineribus[5] in Galliam ulteriōrem[6] contendit et ad[7] Genavam pervenit.

Prōvinciae tōtī[8] quam maximum potest mīlitum numerum imperat[9] (erat omnīnō in Galliā ulteriōre legiō ūna); pontem quī erat ad[10] Genavam jubet rescindī (*to be broken down*).

Ubi dē ejus adventū Helvētiī certiōrēs factī sunt, lēgātōs ad eum mittunt, nōbilissimōs cīvitātis. Hī dīxērunt Helvētiōs habēre in animō sine ūllō maleficiō iter per prōvinciam facere, proptereā quod aliud iter habērent nūllum; rogāvērunt ut ejus voluntāte[11] id sibi facere licēret.

Caesar memoriā tenēbat L. Cassium cōnsulem occīsum[12] exercitumque ejus ab Helvētiīs pulsum et

A YOUNG GAUL

This portrait bust probably represents the type of young men who fought against Caesar in the armies of the Gauls. His features could belong to a soldier of today.

sub jugum missum; concēdendum[13] igitur nōn putābat; neque hominēs inimīcō animō temperātūrōs (*would refrain*) ab injūriā et maleficiō exīstimābat.

[1] With **quā diē**—*on which (day) they are all to assemble;* a relative clause of purpose. In translation, **diē** should be omitted.

[2] Abbreviation for **ante diem quīntum Kalendās Aprīlēs**, *five days before the Kalends* (or *first*) *of April*, i.e., March 28. See page 408.

[3] *Aulus Gabinius* (â'lus ga̤-bin'i-us), consul in 58 B.C.

[4] *it*; explained by the indirect discourse following (**eōs ... cōnārī**).

[5] *by the longest journeys possible.* The plural **itineribus** is employed with reference to the daily distance; **quam** and a superlative alone might express the highest degree possible. See page 140, note 1.

[6] The Roman Province.

[7] Perhaps meaning *in the neighborhood of.*

[8] *on the entire province.* For the form **tōtī** see the declension of **sōlus**, Gr. S., 15. The list of adjectives with the genitive in **-īus** should be learned.

[9] *he levied.*

[10] *near*, or *at.*

[11] *with his approval.*

[12] In 107 B.C.

[13] *the privilege should be granted.* The verb is used impersonally; see page 107, note 5.

Tamen, quod mīlitēs quōs imperāverat nōndum convēnerant, lēgātīs respondit diem[1] sē ad dēlīberandum (*deliberate*) sūmptūrum; sī quid vellent, ad Īd. Apr.[2] reverterentur.[3]

"They Shall Not Pass"

INTEREĀ ā lacū Lemannō ad montem Jūram, mīlia passuum XIX, mūrum[4] in altitūdinem pedum sēdecim fossamque perdūcit. Eō opere perfectō, praesidia dispōnit (*he distributed*), castella commūnit (*fortified*), quō[5] facilius, sī sē invītō trānsīre cōnārentur, prohibēre posset.

Ubi lēgātī ad eum diē cōnstitūtō revertērunt, negat[6] sē mōre et exemplō populī Rōmānī posse iter ūllī per prōvinciam dare et, sī vim facere cōnentur, prohibitūrum[7] ostendit.

Helvētiī eā spē dējectī[8] nōn numquam interdiū (*by day*), saepius noctū, perrumpere[9] cōnātī sunt. Eōrum aliī nāvēs jūnxerant ratēsque (*and rafts*) complūrēs fēcerant; aliī vadīs Rhodanī, quā minima altitūdō flūminis erat, trānsīre cōnābantur.

Sed operis mūnītiōne et mīlitum concursū (*the attack*) et tēlīs repulsī hōc cōnātū dēstitērunt.

A Successful Negotiator

ŪNA[10] per Sēquanōs via relinquēbātur, quā Sēquanīs invītīs[11] propter angustiās[12] īre nōn poterant. Hīs cum[13] suā sponte persuādēre nōn possent, lēgātōs ad Dumnorīgem Haeduum mittunt ut eō dēprecātōre[14] ā Sēquanīs impetrārent.

Dumnorīx grātiā et largītiōne[15] apud Sēquanōs plūrimum poterat[16] et Helvētiīs erat amīcus, quod ex eā cīvitāte Orgetorīgis fīliam in mātrimōnium dūxerat; et cupiditāte rēgnī adductus novīs rēbus[17] studēbat et quam plūrimās cīvitātēs suō

---

[1] *time.*

[2] *by April 13.* See page 408.

[3] *let them return;* a subjunctive of indirect discourse, representing an imperative of the direct.

[4] Not a stone wall, but an earthwork made in great part by cutting down the top of the river bank so as to leave a steep front.

[5] This word is used to introduce a clause of purpose in connection with a comparative.

[6] The usual Latin for *say . . . not,* as has before been pointed out. In translating, take the negative with **posse.**

[7] The full expression would be **sē eōs prohibitūrum esse.**

[8] *disappointed in that hope;* **spē** is ablative of separation, as is also **cōnātū,** line 32.

[9] *to force a passage.*

[10] To be taken with **via**—*only the road.*

[11] *against the wish of the Sequani;* an ablative absolute.

[12] The narrow passage along the bank of the Rhone, which is described on page 142, lines 11-17 and 20-22.

[13] *since.*

[14] *through his intercession.*

[15] *because of his popularity and liberality.*

[16] *had the greatest influence.* The adverb **plūrimum** is in reality the accusative neuter of **plūrimus.**

[17] *revolution;* dative with **studēbat.**

Caesar and the Helvetians   145

beneficiō habēre obstrictās[1] volēbat. Itaque rem suscipit et ā Sēquanīs impetrat[2] ut per fīnēs suōs Helvētiōs īre patiantur, obsidēsque utī inter sēsē dent perficit—Sēquanī, nē itinere Helvētiōs prohibeant; Helvētiī, ut sine maleficiō et injūriā trānseant.

Caesar Enrolls Additional Forces

CAESARĪ nūntiātur Helvētiōs habēre in animō per agrum Sēquanōrum et Haeduōrum iter in Santonum[3] fīnēs facere; hī nōn longē ā Tolōsātium[4] finibus absunt, quae cīvitās est in prōvinciā. Id sī fieret,[5] hominēs bellicōsī (*warlike*), populī Rōmānī inimīcī, partī prōvinciae patentī (*open*) maximēque frūmentāriae finitimī futūrī erant.[6] Ob eās causās eī mūnītiōnī[7] quam fēcerat T. Labiēnum lēgātum praeficit. Ipse in Ītaliam magnīs itineribus contendit duāsque ibi legiōnēs cōnscrībit, et trēs, quae circum Aquileiam hiemābant, ex hībernīs ēdūcit, et proximō itinere in ulteriōrem Galliam per Alpēs cum hīs quīnque legiōnibus īre contendit.

Ibi Ceutronēs[8] et Graiocelī[8] et Caturīgēs,[8] locīs superiōribus occupātīs, itinere[9] exercitum prohibēre cōnantur.

Complūribus[10] hīs proeliīs pulsīs, ab Ocelō,[11] quod est oppidum citeriōris prōvinciae[12] extrēmum, in fīnēs Vocontiōrum[13] ulteriōris prōvinciae diē septimō pervenit; inde in Allobrogum fīnēs, ab Allobrogibus in Segusiāvōs[14] exercitum dūcit. Hī sunt extrā prōvinciam trāns Rhodanum prīmī.

An Appeal for Roman Protection

HELVĒTIĪ jam per angustiās et fīnēs Sēquanōrum suās cōpiās trādūxerant et in Haeduōrum fīnēs pervēnerant eōrumque agrōs populābantur.

Haeduī, cum sē suaque ab eīs dēfendere nōn possent, lēgātōs ad Caesarem mittunt rogātum[15] auxilium. "Ita nōs," inquiunt, "omnī tempore dē populō Rōmānō meritī sumus[16] ut paene in cōnspectū exercitūs vestrī agrī vāstārī, līberī in

[1] *bound (to him).*
[2] *prevailed upon the Sequani.* The object of **impetrat** is the noun clause ut . . . **patiantur,** *to allow,* etc.
[3] *of the Santoni* (san'tō-nī), a tribe of Celtic Gaul.
[4] *of the Tolosates* (tol-ō̱-sā'tēz), the people of Tolosa (modern Toulouse).
[5] *if this should be done.*
[6] *would be.*
[7] Dative with the compound **praeficit,** which has **Labiēnum** as direct object.
[8] *the Ceutrones* (sū'trō-nēz), *the Graioceli* (grā-yos'ē̱-lī), *the Caturiges* (kat-ū-rī'jēz), Gallic tribes.
[9] Ablative of separation, with **prohibēre.**
[10] With **proeliīs,** while **hīs** and **pulsīs** together are an ablative absolute.
[11] *Ocelum* (os'ē̱-lum).
[12] The Roman province in northern Italy, also called **Gallia Cisalpīna.** See map, page 137.
[13] *of the Vocontii* (vō̱-kon'shi-ī).
[14] *the Segusiavi* (seg'ū-shi-ā'vī).
[15] *to beg;* the accusative of the supine, expressing purpose; **auxilium** is its object. See Gr. S., 140.
[16] Translate with **Ita nōs,** etc.—*we have always so deserved of the Roman people.*

servitūtem abdūcī, oppida expug-
nārī nōn dēbuerint."

Eōdem tempore Ambarrī,[1] neces-
sāriī et cōnsanguineī Haeduōrum,
5 Caesarem certiōrem faciunt sēsē,
dēpopulātīs[2] agrīs, nōn facile ab
oppidīs vim hostium prohibēre.
Item Allobrogēs, quibus[3] trāns Rhodanum vīcī possessiōnēsque erant,
fugā sē ad Caesarem recipiunt et 10
dēmōnstrant sē praeter agrī solum
(*soil*) nihil habēre reliquum.

Quibus rēbus adductus Caesar
nōn expectāre statuit dum, omnibus fortūnīs sociōrum cōnsūmptīs, 15
in Santonōs[4] Helvētiī pervenīrent.[5]

Disaster at the River

Flūmen est Arar, quod per fīnēs
Haeduōrum et Sēquanōrum in
Rhodanum īnfluit (*flows*) incrēdi-
20 bilī lēnitāte[6] (*slowness*) ita ut oculīs in utram partem fluat[7] jūdicārī
nōn possit. Id Helvētiī ratibus
(*by means of rafts*) ac lintribus
jūnctīs trānsībant, trēsque jam
25 partēs cōpiārum trādūxerant.

Caesar dē tertiā vigiliā[8] cum
legiōnibus tribus ē castrīs profectus
ad eam partem pervēnit quae nōndum flūmen trānsierat. Eōs im-
30 pedītōs et inopīnantēs (*off their
guard*) aggressus[9] magnam partem
eōrum concīdit; reliquī sēsē fugae
mandārunt[10] atque in proximās
silvās[11] abdidērunt.

35   Is pāgus appellābātur Tigurī-
nus;[12] nam omnis cīvitās Helvētia
in quattuor pāgōs dīvīsa est.

Hic pāgus ūnus, cum domō exīsset patrum nostrōrum memoriā,[13]
L. Cassium cōnsulem interfēcerat 40
et ejus exercitum sub jugum mīserat. Ita sīve cāsū sīve cōnsiliō
deōrum immortālium, quae pars[14]
cīvitātis Helvētiae īnsignem calamitātem populō Rōmānō intule- 45
rat,[15] ea prīnceps[16] poenās persol-
vit.[17]

Quā in rē Caesar nōn sōlum
pūblicās, sed etiam prīvātās injūriās ultus est; nam Tigurīnī[18] in- 50
terfēcerant L. Pīsōnem lēgātum,
avum L. Pīsōnis, socerī (*father-in-
law*) Caesaris, eōdem proeliō quō
Cassium.

---

[1] *the Ambarri* (am-bär′ī), a tribe of
Celtic Gaul.

[2] Although deponent verbs are regularly active in meaning, the perfect participle may be used as a passive, as here.

[3] The dative of possession is explained
on page 147.

[4] See page 145, note 3.

[5] *should come;* an anticipatory subjunctive with **dum**, *until.*

[6] Ablative of description.

[7] Subjunctive, because in an indirect
question.

[8] *in the third watch.*

[9] Active in meaning, agreeing with
the subject of **concīdit**.

[10] A form contracted from **mandāvē-
runt**. See page 123, note 1.

[11] The accusative with **in** is used instead of the ablative, because of the
motion implied in **abdidērunt**.

[12] *Tigurinus* (tig-ū̆-rī′nus).

[13] Ablative denoting the time when.

[14] Translate as if **ea pars quae.**

[15] With such a word as **calamitās** or
injūria as object this verb means *inflict
. . . on.* Why the dative **populō**?

[16] *first.*

[17] *paid the penalty.*

[18] *the Tigurini* (tig-ū̆-rī′nī).

A MODERN PONTOON BRIDGE

This bridge on boats is in use today in northern Italy. The pontoon bridges over which Caesar's soldiers marched were similar in construction.

DATIVE OF POSSESSION

The possessor of something may be denoted by a noun or pronoun in the dative case. The word denoting the thing possessed is then in the nominative as the subject of a form of **sum.**

Sunt <u>mihi</u> multī librī, *I have many books.*

Allobrogēs, <u>quibus</u> trāns <u>Rhodanum</u> vīcī possessiōnēsque erant, ad Caesarem vēnērunt, *The Allobroges, who had villages and possessions across the Rhone, came to Caesar.*

The dative of possession emphasizes the fact of ownership rather than the owner.

Caesar and the Helvetian Ambassadors

IN ORDER to pursue the rest of the Helvetians, Caesar had a bridge of boats constructed across the Saône[1] River. Over this his army marched in one day.

The Helvetians, who had taken twenty days to cross, were frightened by Caesar's speed, and they sent a delegation to him to discuss the question of peace.

Through Divico, who was the leader of the delegation, they offered to settle in any region Caesar assigned them if he would cease hostilities. But Divico's speech was by no means humble in its tone. He told Caesar that if

the Romans continued the war, they would take a great risk in doing so, since the Helvetians were well-trained soldiers and were not afraid to fight. He asserted that his people had beaten the Romans before and might do so again.

In his reply Caesar reminded Divico that the Helvetian victory which he mentioned was due to the Romans' being taken off their guard. If the Helvetians continued to be defiant, they might expect a costly final reckoning. He ordered them to repay the other tribes for the damage they had done on their march. To make sure that they would carry out their

[1] The ancient Arar.

promises, he insisted on having hostages.

Divico answered haughtily that the Helvetians were in the habit of receiving hostages, but not of giving them, and that the Romans were quite well aware of this fact. With that, he left the Roman camp.

A Cavalry Battle

Postero diē castra ex eō locō movent. Idem facit Caesar, equitātumque omnem ad numerum quattuor mīlium, quem ex omnī 5 prōvinciā et Haeduīs atque eōrum sociīs coāctum habēbat,[1] praemittit quī videant[2] quās in partēs hostēs iter faciant.[3] Quī, cupidius (*too eagerly*) novissimum agmen īn- 10 secūtī, aliēnō locō cum equitātū Helvētiōrum proelium committunt, et paucī dē nostrīs cadunt.

Quō proeliō sublātī Helvētiī, quod quīngentīs equitibus tantam multitūdinem equitum prōpule- 15 rant, audācius subsistere (*to stand their ground*) nōn numquam et novissimō agmine[4] proeliō nostrōs lacessere coepērunt.

Caesar suōs ā proeliō continēbat 20 ac satis habēbat in praesentiā (*for the present*) hostem rapīnīs populātiōnibusque[5] prohibēre.[6] Ita diēs circiter xv iter fēcērunt ut inter novissimum hostium agmen et nos- 25 trum prīmum[7] nōn amplius quīnīs (*five*) aut sēnīs (*six*) mīlibus passuum interesset.[8]

The Need for Supplies

Interim cotīdiē Caesar frūmentum quod Haeduī essent[9] pūblicē pollicitī flāgitābat.

Nam propter frīgora (*cold*), quod Gallia sub septentriōnibus posita[10] est, nōn modo frūmenta in agrīs 35 mātūra nōn erant, sed nē pābulī quidem satis magna cōpia suppetēbat.[11] Eō autem frūmentō[12] quod flūmine Ararī[13] nāvibus subvexerat (*he had conveyed*), proptereā[14] 40 ūtī minus poterat, quod iter ab Ararī Helvētiī āverterant, ā quibus discēdere nōlēbat.

Diem ex diē[15] dūcunt[16] Haeduī; cōnferrī, comportārī, adesse[17] dī- 45 cunt.

Ubi sē diūtius[18] dūcī intellēxit et diem īnstāre, quō diē frūmentum mīlitibus mētīrī oportēret, convocāvit eōrum prīncipēs, quōrum magnam cōpiam in castrīs habē- 50 bat.

In hīs erant Dīviciācus et Liscus,[19] quī summō magistrātuī[20] praeerat, quem vergobretum[21] appellant Haeduī, quī creātur annuus 55 (*annually*) et vītae necisque in suōs[22] habet potestātem.

Tum Caesar graviter eōs accūsat (*accused*), quod, cum frūmentum neque emī neque ex agrīs sūmī 60 possit, hostibus tam propinquīs,[23] ab eīs nōn sublevētur,[24] praesertim cum magnā ex parte[25] eōrum precibus adductus bellum suscēperit.

Influential Agitators

TUM dēmum Liscus[19] ōrātiōne Caesaris adductus quod[26] anteā tacuerat prōpōnit: "Sunt nōnnūllī quōrum auctōritās apud plēbem plūrimum valeat, quī prīvātim (*as private citizens*) plūs possint[27] quam ipsī magistrātūs.

"Propter hōrum sēditiōsam (*seditious*) atque improbam (*disloyal*) ōrātiōnem multitūdō frūmentum nōn cōnferunt quod dēbent.

" 'Praestat,[28]' inquiunt,[29] 'sī jam prīncipātum Galliae obtinēre nōn possumus, Gallōrum quam Rōmānōrum imperia perferre; sī Helvētiōs superāverint Rōmānī, ūnā cum reliquā Galliā Haeduīs[30] lībertātem sine dubiō ēripient.'

ABLATIVE WITH CERTAIN DEPONENT VERBS

The deponent verbs **ūtor, fruor, fungor, potior**, and **vēscor** and their compounds take their objects in the ablative case.

Eō **frūmento ūtī** nōn poterat, *He could not use this grain.*

Rōmānī **castrīs** Gallōrum **potītī sunt**, *The Romans gained possession of the camp of the Gauls.*

NOTES ON THE TEXT

[1] *had collected.* The participle **coāctum** agrees with **quem** in line 4. The combination of the participle with the imperfect **habēbat**, although translated in the same way as **coēgerat**, past perfect of **cōgō**, was not quite identical in the thought of the Romans.

[2] A clause of purpose.

[3] Subjunctive in an indirect question.

[4] *from their rear line.*

[5] *from plundering and devastation.* Ablative of separation.

[6] With **satis habēbat**—*regarded it as sufficient to prevent.*

[7] Supply **agmen.**

[8] *there was a distance of not more than five or six miles.*

[9] Subjunctive of informal indirect discourse. The verb **flāgitābat**, *was demanding*, implies a statement. See Gr. S., 119.

[10] *situated.* See page 136, note 2.

[11] *was not available.*

[12] The use of the ablative with **ūtor** is explained above.

[13] Ablative of the way or route.

[14] Take with **quod**—*for the reason that.*

[15] *day after day.*

[16] *put off;* **eum** is to be understood as object.

[17] Supply **frūmentum** as subject of these infinitives.

[18] *too long.*

[19] *Liscus* (lis'kus).

[20] Dative with the compound verb **praeerat.**

[21] *vergobret* (vėr'gō-bret), the title of the chief magistrate of the Haeduans.

[22] *over his fellow-citizens.*

[23] *with the enemy so near.*

[24] The same explanation applies to the subjunctive here as in note 9.

[25] *to a great extent.*

[26] For **id quod.**

[27] *have more influence.*

[28] The subject is the infinitive **perferre**, line 15.

[29] The subject is *they*, referring to the trouble-makers of the preceding lines.

[30] *from the Haeduans;* dative of separation depending on **ēripient.**

"Ab eīsdem tua cōnsilia quaeque in castrīs geruntur hostibus ēnūntiantur; hōs coërcēre (*restrain*) nōn possum. Quīn etiam[1] intellegō quantō cum perīculō hanc necessāriam rem tibi ēnūntiāverim, et ob eam causam quam diū potuī[2] tacuī." 5

Two Brothers

CAESAR knew that Liscus was referring to Dumnorix, the brother of Diviciacus. So he dismissed the council, but asked Liscus to remain. Liscus then admitted that he meant Dumnorix and told Caesar more about him.

What Liscus said was later corroborated by others. Dumnorix had for years bought up the contracts for collecting taxes and had thus become wealthy. He had made himself popular by the free use of money, and his riches enabled him to keep a hired troop of cavalry to defend him. He had strengthened his friendship with the neighboring tribes of the Helvetians by marrying the daughter of a prominent Helvetian. In addition, he had brought about the marriage of his sister to a powerful noble of another tribe.

He hated the Romans because their coming interfered with his plans. Against Caesar he had a special grudge, because through him Diviciacus had been restored to a position of influence. Dumnorix still had hopes of becoming king if the Romans could be driven out. Caesar learned, also, that in the recent unsuccessful cavalry fight Dumnorix had been in command of the Haeduan cavalry, and that it was he who had begun the retreat.

Caesar now had evidence enough to condemn and punish Dumnorix, but he wished to avoid this for fear of offending Diviciacus, who seemed to be devoted to the Romans.

Caesar therefore sent for Diviciacus and with the aid of an interpreter laid the situation before him. He asked that suitable measures be taken for the punishment of the trouble-maker.

Diviciacus wept and admitted his brother's guilt. He begged Caesar not to punish him, however, explaining that he had two reasons for this appeal. First, he was still fond of his younger brother. Second, he felt sure that if punishment should be inflicted, the Gauls would blame the older brother and turn against him. Consequently Diviciacus would lose his popularity and influence with his people.

This appeal brought from Caesar the reply that he valued the friendship of Diviciacus so highly that he would overlook what had happened.

Later, however, he called in Dumnorix and told him in the presence of Diviciacus that he knew what had been going on and that he was disregarding past offenses out of regard for his brother. He warned Dumnorix to avoid ground for suspicion in the future. Then he arranged to have Dumnorix watched and a report made on all that he said and did.

---

[1] *nay more*, or *more than that.*

[2] *as long as I could.*

Caesar Plans a Surprise Attack

Eōdem diē ab explōrātōribus certior factus[1] hostēs sub monte cōnsēdisse mīlia passuum ab ipsīus castrīs octō, quālis (*what*) esset nātūra montis et quālis in circuitū[2] ascēnsus (*ascent*) quī cognōscerent[3] mīsit. Renūntiātum est facilem esse. Dē tertiā vigiliā T. Labiēnum, lēgātum prō praetōre,[4] cum duābus legiōnibus et eīs ducibus quī iter cognōverant summum jugum montis ascendere jubet; quid suī cōnsiliī sit[5] ostendit.

Ipse dē quārtā vigiliā eōdem itinere quō hostēs ierant ad eōs contendit equitātumque omnem ante sē mittit.

P. Cōnsidius, quī reī mīlitāris[6] perītissimus habēbātur et in exercitū L. Sullae[7] et posteā in M. Crassī[8] fuerat, cum explōrātōribus praemittitur.

An Officer's Mistake

Prīmā lūce summus mōns[9] ā Labiēnō tenēbātur. Ipse ab hostium castrīs nōn longius mīlle et quīngentīs passibus aberat, neque,[10] ut[11] posteā ex captīvīs comperit, aut ipsīus adventus aut Labiēnī cognitus erat.

Tum Cōnsidius equō admissō[12] ad eum accurrit atque dīcit montem quem ā Labiēnō occupārī voluerit ab hostibus tenērī; id sē ā Gallicīs armīs atque īnsignibus cognōvisse. Caesar suās cōpiās in proximum collem subdūcit et aciem īnstruit.

Labiēnus monte occupātō nostrōs expectābat proeliōque abstinēbat (*refrained from*); Caesar enim eum adventum suum expectāre jusserat ut undique ūnō tempore in hostēs impetus fieret.

Multō dēnique diē[13] per explōrātōrēs Caesar cognōvit et montem ā suīs tenērī et Helvētiōs castra mōvisse et Cōnsidium timōre perterritum quod[14] nōn vīdisset prō vīsō[15] sibi renūntiāsse.

Eō diē quō cōnsuērat intervāllō[16] hostēs sequitur et mīlia passuum tria ab eōrum castrīs castra pōnit.

[1] Remember that this phrase takes indirect discourse.

[2] *on all sides.*

[3] A relative clause of purpose. Supply **explōrātōrēs** as antecedent of **quī**. The verb has for object the indirect question **quālis esset**, etc. (ll. 4-6).

[4] *with praetorian rank.* Labienus, Caesar's most trusted lieutenant, had been assigned to Caesar's staff with the honorary designation **prō praetōre**, as if he had held the office of praetor.

[5] *what his plan was.*

[6] *in military affairs.* The genitive is dependent on the adjective **perītissimus**.

[7] Lucius Cornelius Sulla, consul in 88 B.C.; later, dictator.

[8] Supply **exercitū**.

[9] *the top of the mountain; the highest mountain* would be **mōns altissimus**.

[10] Take with **aut . . . aut**—*and neither . . . nor.*

[11] *as.*

[12] *with his horse at a gallop.* Ablative absolute.

[13] *well on in the day*, but this need not imply anything more than "well on into the morning."

[14] For **id quod.**

[15] *as seen.*

[16] *at the customary interval.*

AN IMPORTANT GALLIC TOWN ONCE STOOD ON THIS HEIGHT
Few traces remain of Bibracte, which was built on Mont Beuvray, shown in the background.

A Shortage of Food Supplies

POSTRĪDIĒ ejus diēī,[1] quod omnīnō bīduī frūmentum[2] supererat, reī frūmentāriae[3] prōspiciendum exīstimāns, iter ab Helvētiīs āvertit, ac Bibracte, oppidum Haeduōrum, īre contendit. Nam hoc oppidum longē maximum et cōpiōsissimum (*best supplied*) erat atque nōn amplius mīlibus passuum XVIII aberat. Ea rēs per fugitīvōs (*runaway slaves*) L. Aemiliī,[4] decuriōnis[5] equitum Gallōrum, hostibus nūntiātur. Helvētiī, commūtātō cōnsiliō atque itinere conversō, nostrōs ā novissimō agmine[6] īnsequī ac lacessere coepērunt.

Preparations for Battle

POSTQUAM id animum advertit,[7] cōpiās suās Caesar in proximum collem subdūxit equitātumque quī sustinēret hostium impetum mīsit. Ipse interim in colle mediō[8] triplicem aciem[9] īnstrūxit legiōnum quattuor veterānārum;[10] in summō jugō duās legiōnēs quās in Galliā citeriōre proximē cōnscrīpserat et

[1] In translation omit **ejus diēī**.

[2] *a two days' supply of grain.*

[3] Dative with **prōspiciendum (esse)**, *he must look out for.* The verb is used impersonally.

[4] *of Lucius Aemilius* (ē-mil'i-us).

[5] *decurion*, commander of a group of ten horsemen.

[6] *on the rear line.* The Helvetians were now following the Roman army.

[7] The phrase **animum advertit** is equivalent to **animadvertit** and takes **id** as a direct object.

[8] *half-way up the hill.* **Medius**, like **summus**, is one of the adjectives denoting a part.

[9] Each of the three lines consisted of about eight ranks.

[10] *veteran*, an adjective modifying **legiōnum**.

omnia auxilia collocāvit; impedīmenta sarcināsque[1] in ūnum locum
cōnferrī et eum[2] ab hīs quī in
superiōre aciē cōnstiterant mūnīrī
5 jussit. Helvētiī cum omnibus suīs
carrīs secūtī impedīmenta in ūnum
locum contulērunt; ipsī, cōnfertissi-
mā aciē, rejectō nostrō equitātū,
phalange[3] factā, sub prīmam nostram aciem successērunt. 10

Incidents of the Battle

Caesar prīmum suum[4] deinde
omnium[5] ex cōnspectū remōvit equōs ut aequātō omnium perīculō spem fugae tolleret. Cohortā-
15 tus inde suōs proelium commīsit.

Mīlitēs, ē locō superiōre pīlīs
missīs, facile hostium phalangem
perfrēgērunt (*broke up*). Eā dis-
jectā,[6] gladiīs dēstrictīs (*drawn*),
20 in eōs impetum fēcērunt.

Gallīs magnō ad pugnam erat
impedīmentō[7] quod plūra[8] eōrum
scūta ūnō ictū pīlōrum trānsfīxa et
colligāta (*fastened together*) erant;
25 nam cum ferrum sē īnflexisset,[9]
neque id ēvellere (*pull out*) neque
sinistrā impedītā satis commodē
pugnāre poterant. Multī igitur,
diū jactātō bracchiō,[10] praeoptāvē-
30 runt (*preferred*) scūtum manū ēmit-
tere et nūdō corpore[11] pugnāre.

Tandem vulneribus dēfessī et
pedem referre et, quod mōns sub-

A ROMAN CAVALRYMAN
This soldier was photographed in Hollywood.

erat (*was close by*) circiter mīlle
passuum spatiō, eō[12] sē recipere 35
coepērunt.

Captō[13] monte et succēdentibus
nostrīs, Boiī et Tulingī, quī hominum mīlibus circiter xv agmen
hostium claudēbant et novissimīs 40

[1] *and packs.*
[2] Supply **locum.**
[3] A close formation of infantry, in which the men of each rank were pro-tected by the shields of the men in front of them as well as by their own shields.
[4] Supply **equum.**
[5] The officers only.
[6] *when that was dispersed.*
[7] *it was a great hindrance to the Gauls in the battle;* **impedīmentō** is a dative of purpose or end. The subject of **erat** is the noun clause following, **quod . . . colligāta erant**—*that*, etc.
[8] *in many cases.* In the phalanx formation the shields overlapped, thus making it possible for a javelin to pierce two shields at one time.
[9] *when the iron had bent (itself).* This refers to the iron head of the javelin, the neck of which was of softer metal than the tip.
[10] *after tossing their arms about.* Abla-tive absolute.
[11] *with unprotected bodies.*
[12] An adverb.
[13] The verb is here used in the sense of "reach, gain."

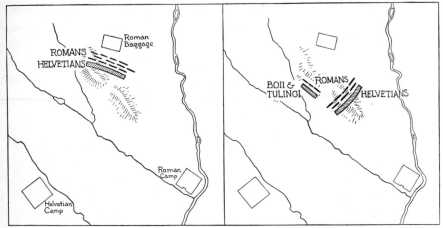

TWO STAGES OF THE BATTLE

praesidiō[1] erant, ex itinere[2] nostrōs ab[3] latere apertō aggressī circumveniēbant. Id cōnspicātī Helvētiī, quī in montem sēsē recēperant, 5 rūrsus īnstāre et proelium redintegrāre (*to renew*) coepērunt. Rōmānī signa bipertītō intulērunt;[4] prīma et secunda aciēs ut victīs ac summōtīs[5] resisteret; tertia, ut venientēs sustinēret. 10

Victory for the Romans

ITA ancipitī proeliō diū atque ācriter pugnātum est.[6] Diūtius cum sustinēre nostrōrum impetūs nōn possent, alterī[7] sē, ut coepe-15 rant, in montem recēpērunt; alterī[7] ad impedīmenta et carrōs suōs sē contulērunt. Nam hōc tōtō proeliō, cum[8] ab hōrā septimā ad vesperum pugnātum sit, āversum hos-20 tem[9] vidēre nēmō potuit.

Ad multam noctem[10] etiam ad impedīmenta pugnātum est, prop-terea quod prō vāllō[11] carrōs objēcerant et ē locō superiōre in nostrōs venientēs tēla conjiciē- 25 bant, et nōnnūllī inter carrōs raedāsque (*and carriages*) matarās (*javelins*) ac trāgulās subjiciēbant nostrōsque vulnerābant.

Diū cum esset pugnātum, im- 30 pedīmentīs castrīsque nostrī potītī sunt. Ibi Orgetorīgis fīlia atque ūnus ē fīliīs captus est. Ex eō proeliō circiter hominum mīlia

<hr/>

[1] *as a rear guard;* this word and **novissimīs**, page 153, line 40, are two datives, one of reference, the other of purpose.

[2] *forthwith, at once;* literally, *from their march*, i.e., without waiting to effect the usual battle formation.

[3] *on.*

[4] *advanced in two divisions.*

[5] Referring to the Helvetians, while **venientēs** refers to the Boii and the Tulingi.

[6] *they fought a long and stubborn double battle.*

[7] The words **alterī . . . alterī** may be translated *one party . . . the other*, referring respectively to the Helvetians and to the Boii and Tulingi.

[8] *although.*

[9] *an enemy in flight*, or *the back of an enemy.*

[10] *till the night was well advanced.*

[11] *as a rampart.*

cxxx superfuērunt eāque tōtā nocte continenter iērunt. In fīnēs Lingonum diē quārtō pervēnērunt,
cum et propter vulnera mīlitum
5 et propter sepultūram occīsōrum[1]
nostrī eōs sequī nōn potuissent.

Caesar ad Lingonēs litterās nūntiōsque mīsit, nē eōs frūmentō nēve[2]
aliā rē juvārent;[3] aliter sē eōs eōdem locō quō[4] Helvētiōs habitū- 10
rum.[5] Ipse, trīduō intermissō, cum
omnibus cōpiīs eōs sequī coepit.

The Helvetians Surrender

HELVĒTIĪ omnium rērum inopiā adductī lēgātōs dē dēdi-
15 tiōne ad eum mīsērunt. Quī cum[6]
eum in itinere convēnissent,[7] sē ad
pedēs prōjēcērunt suppliciterque
(*and humbly*) locūtī flentēs pācem
petīvērunt. Caesar eōs in eō locō
20 quō tum essent suum adventum
expectāre jussit. Eō[8] postquam

pervēnit, obsidēs, arma, servōs quī
ad eōs perfūgissent, poposcit.

Dum ea[9] conquīruntur[10] et cōn-
feruntur, circiter hominum mīlia 25
VI ejus pāgī quī Verbigenus[11] appellātur prīmā nocte[12] ē castrīs
Helvētiōrum ēgressī ad Rhēnum
fīnēsque Germānōrum contendērunt. 30

The Terms of Peace

QUOD[13] ubi Caesar resciit (*discovered*), quōrum per fīnēs
ierant, hīs[14] ut conquīrerent et
redūcerent,[15] sī sibi pūrgātī esse
35 vellent,[16] imperāvit; reductōs[17] in
hostium numerō habuit;[18] reliquōs
omnēs, obsidibus, armīs, perfugīs
trāditīs, in dēditiōnem accēpit.
Helvētiōs, Tulingōs, Latobrīgōs

in fīnēs suōs, unde erant profectī, 40
revertī jussit et, quod omnibus
frūgibus āmissīs,[19] domī nihil erat
quō famem tolerārent (*might withstand*), Allobrogibus imperāvit ut
eīs frūmentī cōpiam facerent. Ip- 45
sōs oppida vīcōsque quōs incen-
derant restituere jussit.

Id eā maximē ratiōne[20] fēcit,

---

[1] *of the slain.*
[2] Here translated *or.*
[3] *not to assist;* a noun clause (introduced by **nē**) depending on the idea of
command in **litterās nūntiōsque mīsit.**
[4] *in the same position as.*
[5] Indirect discourse.
[6] Translate as if **cum eī.**
[7] Usually intransitive, but transitive
here with **eum** as direct object.
[8] An adverb.
[9] Neuter, because its antecedents are
of different gender, one of them, **arma**,
being neuter.
[10] *while these were being hunted up.*
[11] *Verbigenus* (vėr-bij'ē̯-nus), one of the
four divisions of the Helvetians.
[12] *at nightfall.*

[13] *this.*
[14] Translate in the order **hīs per fīnēs
quōrum.**
[15] Supply as object **eōs.**
[16] *if they wished to be free from guilt
before him;* **sibi** is dative of reference.
[17] Agreeing with **eōs** (to be supplied).
[18] *treated them as enemies;* i.e., he either
put them to death or sold them as
slaves.
[19] *all the crops having been lost.* They
had burned all the grain except what
they were going to take with them. See
page 141, lines 41-43.
[20] *for this reason;* explained by the
noun clause **quod nōluit**, etc. (p. 156,
ll. 1-3), *that he did not wish*, etc.

quod nōluit eum locum unde Helvētiī discesserant vacāre (*to be*
unoccupied) nē[1] propter bonitātem
(*fertility*) agrōrum Germānī, quī
5 trāns Rhēnum incolunt, ex suīs
fīnibus in Helvētiōrum fīnēs trānsīrent et fīnitimī Galliae, prōvinciae,[2]

Allobrogibusque essent. Boiōs in
fīnibus Haeduōrum collocāvit; id
enim petēbant Haeduī, quī Boiōs 10
ēgregiā virtūte[3] esse cognōverant;
posteā eōs in parem jūris lībertā-
tisque condiciōnem atque[4] ipsī
erant recēpērunt.

The Muster Rolls

IN CASTRĪS Helvētiōrum tabulae
(*lists*) repertae sunt litterīs
Graecīs[5] cōnfectae et ad Caesarem
relātae, quibus in tabulīs (*lists*)
nōminātim ratiō[6] cōnfecta erat,
20 quī numerus domō exīsset[7] eōrum
quī arma ferre possent,[8] et item
sēparātim (*separately*) quot (*how*
many) puerī, senēs, mulierēsque.

Quārum omnium ratiōnum sum-
25 ma erat capitum[9] Helvētiōrum mī-

lium CCLXIII, Tulingōrum mīlium
XXXVI, Latobrīgōrum XIV, Rau-
racōrum[10] XXIII, Boiōrum XXXII;
ex hīs, quī arma ferre possent, ad[11]
mīlia nōnāgintā (*ninety*) duo. 30
Summa omnium fuērunt ad mīlia
CCCLXVIII.

Eōrum quī domum rediērunt
cēnsū habitō, ut Caesar imperāverat, repertus est numerus mīlium 35
c et x.

[1] *for fear that;* introducing a clause of
purpose.
[2] In apposition with **Galliae.**
[3] Ablative of description.
[4] With **parem**—*the same as.* With
words meaning "like" or "unlike,"
atque (ac) may mean *as* or *than.*
[5] *in the Greek alphabet.* The Gauls had
devised no alphabet of their own, but
they had learned the Greek alphabet
from Greek traders who had visited
Gaul. The language of the records was,
of course, Gallic.

[6] The words **nōminātim ratiō** mean
detailed list or *record.*
[7] The indirect question introduced by
quī (l. 20) depends on **ratiō.**
[8] Subjunctive in a relative descriptive
clause. See Gr. S., 112.
[9] *of persons.* The word may be
omitted in translation. Compare our
use of "head" in speaking of cattle.
[10] *of the Rauraci* (râ′ra̤-sī), a tribe of
Celtic Gaul.
[11] *about;* used adverbially here and in
line 31.

COMPREHENSION QUESTIONS

The answers to the following questions will bring to mind the main
points of Caesar's narrative of the campaign against the Helvetians.
Reread if necessary to find answers to some of the questions.

1. What were the three divisions of the Gauls?
2. To which of these did the Helvetians belong?   (See map, p. 137.)
3. Why did they wish to migrate from their country?
4. What was the plot of Orgetorix?
5. How did his death affect the original plans of the Helvetians?

THE CONQUEROR

6. What were the two routes open to the Helvetians?

7. Why did they expect help from the Allobroges?

8. How many legions were there in Transalpine Gaul when Caesar first arrived?

9. Who secured from the Sequani permission for the Helvetians to pass through their country?

10. How many new legions did Caesar enlist, and how many did he bring from the region about Aquileia?

11. At what river did Caesar's first attack on the Helvetians take place?

12. Why did Caesar have difficulty in getting supplies from the Haeduans?

13. Who was Diviciacus?

14. How had Dumnorix obtained his wealth?

15. Why did Caesar's plan for an attack on the Helvetians fail?

16. What was the name of the city of the Haeduans where Caesar hoped to get supplies?

17. Why did Caesar send away his horse and the horses of the other officers at the beginning of the battle with the Helvetians?

18. What is a phalanx?

19. What difficulty was caused for the Gauls by the fact that they were in very close array?

20. What indication of heavy losses on the part of the Romans is there in the chapter called "Victory for the Romans," which begins on page 154?

21. What were the final terms of peace?

22. In what alphabet were the Helvetian records written? Why?

QUESTIONS ON GRAMMAR

1. What verb is used to replace the missing passive of **faciō** in the present system? Conjugate this verb in the present indicative and the imperfect subjunctive. (See p. 139.)   2. What mood is used in noun clauses of fact? (Gr. S., 108.)   3. How does the declension of **nūllus** differ from that of **bonus?** (Gr. S., 15.)   4. What other adjectives are declined like **nūllus?** 5. Decline **ūllus.**   6. What mood is used in a subordinate clause in indirect discourse? (Gr. S., 131.)   7. Explain the use of the dative of possession. (Gr. S., 62.)   8. What verbs take their objects in the ablative case? (Gr. S., 89.)   9. Decline the indefinite **quīdam.** (Gr. S., 32.)   10. Decline the indefinite **quisque,** both as a pronoun and as an adjective, and give its meanings. (Gr. S., 32.)   11. Give the principal parts of **nōlō** and **volō.** (Gr. S., 45.)

ROMAN SOLDIERS CROSSING A PONTOON BRIDGE

WORD STUDY IV

English Words Coming from Latin through Other Languages

In addition to the English words which have been taken directly from Latin a great many Latin words have come into our language through French. A small number also have come by way of other Romance languages (that is, languages derived from Latin), chiefly Spanish, Italian, and Portuguese.

Words Coming from Italian through French

ALARM, French **alarme**, Italian **all'arme**, from the Latin words **ad illa arma**, a call to arms. Hence, any sudden warning.

CAVALRY, from **caballārius,** *horseman.* (**Caballus** at first meant a nag or cart-horse; then, any horse.) Hence, cavalry means soldiers on horseback.

COLONEL, from the word for a little column (of soldiers), derived from Latin **columna,** *pillar.* Hence, an officer in charge of such a column.

SALAD, from Italian **salata,** which was derived from Latin **sal,** *salt.* Hence, a salted or seasoned dish.

Words Coming through Italian

INCOGNITO, from **in-,** *not,* and **cognitus,** *known.* Hence, with identity concealed.

ISOLATE, from **īnsula,** *island.* Hence, to make an island of, to separate from other persons or places.

MADONNA, from **mea domina,** *my lady,* often used in referring to the Virgin Mary.

SCAMPER, from **ex,** *out of,* and **campus,** *field.* Hence, to get out of a place; then, to run quickly.

SOLO, from **sōlus,** *alone.* Hence, a song by one person.

Words Coming through Spanish

ALLIGATOR, from Spanish **el** (*the*) **lagarto,** derived from Latin **ille** and **lacertus,** *lizard.*

MOSQUITO, from Spanish **mosca,** derived from Latin **musca** and a diminutive ending. Hence, a little fly.

Words Coming through Portuguese

MOLASSES, from Latin **mel,** *honey,* and an ending meaning *like.*

MARMALADE, from **marmelo,** *quince,* derived from Latin **melimēlum,** *honey apple.* In Portugal marmalade was originally made of quinces.

IN THE ROMAN SENATE

EXERCISES

Find, by consulting a large dictionary, from what language each of the following English words comes:

albino	cork	lava	royal
ambuscade	desperado	malaria	tornado
cargo	fetish	parade	umbrella
chance	gentle	parcel	
chef	influenza	quartet	

Idioms and Phrases

The idioms and phrases listed below occur in the text read.   Learning them thoroughly will be of great help in reading.

ad omnia perīcula subeunda, *to face all dangers*
diū et ācriter pugnātum est, *the fight was long and fierce*
ē locō superiōre, *from a higher position*
hīs rēbus adductus, *influenced by these facts*
memoriā tenēbat, *he remembered*
quae cum ita essent, *since this was so, therefore*

Vocabulary Review

The following words, which appear frequently in this book, are important in second-year work.   Their meanings should be thoroughly learned.

abdō	convertō	incitō	paene	septimus
advertō	cupiditās	īnferior, īnfimus	pār	singulī
aggredior	deinde	intervāllum	perfugiō	sīve, seu
an	dēmōnstrō	jugum	posterus	statuō
angustiae	dīmittō	lacessō	praemittō	supersum
audācter	emō	lātitūdō	praetereā	trīduum
captīvus	eōdem	maleficium	pūblicus	unde
carrus	ferrum	mētior	quārtus	ut, utī
citerior	fleō	nēve, neu	quīntus	vadum
claudō	frūmentārius	nōndum	renūntiō	vagor
comperiō	hūmānitās	novus	rēs mīlitāris	vel
concīdō	imperō	pācō	scūtum	vinculum

JULIUS CAESAR—THE RISE OF A POLITICAL LEADER

PERHAPS the most famous name in Roman history is that of Gaius Julius Caesar—writer, orator, general, and statesman—who finally became the supreme power in the Roman State and thus master of the western world.

When Caesar was born, about 100 B.C., Rome was still a republic, but political conditions were in an unsettled state. The common people were struggling for greater rights, but the wealthy class—largely represented in the Senate—was determined to retain the privileges it had and to keep the common people in check. Thus there came to be two distinct political parties, the popular party and the senatorial, or aristocratic, party.

Caesar, though an aristocrat by birth, was from an early age attracted to the party of the people —very probably influenced by his uncle, the famous general, Marius. This great soldier was not only the popular hero of the day, but one of the leaders in political activities. When Caesar married, his connections with the popular party were further strengthened through his wife, Cornelia, daughter of the other great popular leader, Cinna.

But in 82 B.C. the aristocratic party gained control of the government, and it became a dangerous thing to be a supporter of the popular party. Sulla, the leader of the senatorial party, established a dictatorship and began a wholesale slaughter of his political enemies. Caesar was naturally among

SULLA, A RUTHLESS DICTATOR

those doomed. He could have secured his safety by divorcing the daughter of Cinna, but this he refused to do.

Instead, he fled to the hills east of the Tiber, where a number of times he barely escaped capture. Finally, at the pleas of Caesar's family and of the Vestal Virgins, Sulla pardoned him. "I let him live," said the dictator, "but there is many a Marius in this boy."

Although his life had been spared, Caesar knew that Rome was not really safe for him so long as Sulla remained in power. Therefore he joined the army in Asia Minor, where the legions of Rome were crushing the last resistance to Roman rule.

In 78 B.C. the dictator Sulla died, and Rome was again safe for Julius Caesar. He returned to the city and took a prominent part in the prosecution of two dishonest provincial governors. Although he distinguished himself by his ability in handling the cases, he lost them and decided to leave public life for a time. He then went to the Greek island of Rhodes to study public speaking.

In a few years Caesar was back in Rome, even more ambitious to achieve success in politics. According to Roman law, a man had to hold certain lower offices before he could become a candidate for the higher offices in the State. Caesar climbed from one office to another almost as rapidly as legal requirements permitted.

One of these offices was that of quaestor. In this position Caesar was chief assistant to the military governor of Spain. He next became curule aedile, an official who not only had charge of public works, public markets, and the policing of the city, but also superintended the public games.

This was not an office which it was necessary for Caesar to hold, but like most young Romans who were ambitious for a political career, he wanted it because it gave him a great opportunity to win popularity with the voters of Rome. As aedile he did all that he could to gain the favor of the people by presenting elaborate games. In one of these he exhibited three hundred twenty pairs of gladiators, all of whom are said to have worn gilded armor. He also had the Forum and various public buildings decorated with statues and paintings. But as Caesar's popularity increased, his funds decreased, for the curule aedile received no salary.

JULIUS CAESAR

This statue of the great general was found at the scene of one of his victories in Gaul.

After his term as curule aedile, Caesar became Pontifex Maximus, or chief priest. This position, unlike the other offices he had filled, was held for life and did not prevent its holder from being elected to other offices at the same time.

Next he was elected as one of the eight praetors who presided over the courts of Rome. It was customary for a praetor, after his term of office was over, to be appointed governor of a province. Accordingly, Caesar next became governor of the province of Farther Spain.

All these offices Caesar had held

POMPEY

But Caesar's colleague in the consulship, a man named Bibulus, was a person of no great ability, and Caesar assumed so much power that the last part of his year as consul was jokingly referred to as the year of Julius and Caesar, instead of that of Caesar and Bibulus in accordance with the Roman custom.

It was usual for a consul also to become governor of a province at the end of his term, but Caesar's opponents tried to get him into an unimportant position in Italy instead. This arrangement was overthrown by popular vote, and Caesar was made governor of three provinces: Illyricum, on the northeastern coast of the Adriatic; Cisalpine Gaul, which now is a part of Italy; and Transalpine Gaul, or "The Province."

as a representative of the party which presumably supported government by the people. Nevertheless, in 60 B.C. he joined two other political leaders in planning to control the state by a sort of "boss" rule. These two were Pompey, the noted general, and Crassus, the wealthiest man in Rome. The combination, called a triumvirate, was merely a private arrangement for the benefit of the men who composed it.

As a result of a private agreement made by the three, Caesar was elected to the highest office in the Roman Republic—that of consul. In some ways this office resembled that of president in this country. However, there were two consuls, and their term of office was only one year. They were supposed to work in harmony, each serving in turn for a certain period of time.

At this time there was a dangerous situation in Gaul, and the safety of "The Province" was thought to be threatened. Caesar, clever politician as he was, saw plainly that his chance to distinguish himself was in Gaul, where if he could conquer the independent tribes, he would gain new resources for Rome and win glory for himself.

With the ending of his consulship, Caesar left Rome to take up his duties as governor. He seized the opportunity which the situation offered, and for ten years devoted himself to the warfare and conquest which he describes in *The Gallic War* and which made him famous as one of the world's great generals.

THE WAR WITH ARIOVISTUS

Pride goeth before destruction, and an haughty spirit before a fall.
PROVERBS

A Threat to Gallic Civilization

AT THE close of the war with the Helvetians a group of prominent Gauls came to Caesar as representatives of their states. They offered him their congratulations and said that they were pleased with the outcome of the war. The Helvetian migration, they declared, had threatened all Gaul, since the Helvetians had intended to select the most desirable locations, make their homes there, and rule the whole country. The Gauls then asked whether they might call a general council to discuss some important matters.

After this council was over, the Gallic leaders who had previously visited Caesar returned and asked to talk with him privately. In this interview they told Caesar the story of their troubles, weeping as they did so. Their spokesman was Diviciacus, the Haeduan.

Diviciacus said that the Gallic tribes had been divided into two factions, each a sort of loose alliance, headed by the stronger nations. The leaders of one faction had been the Haeduans; of the other, the Sequani and the Arverni. For a long time the Haeduan faction had been successful in the struggle for leadership. Their opponents had finally hired fifteen thousand German soldiers from across the Rhine, and with the aid of these had crushed the Haeduans. But the Germans had found Gaul more attractive than their own country, and the number originally brought across the river had been increased from time to time.

Now there were one hundred twenty thousand Germans on the Gallic side of the Rhine. The former allies of the Sequani had become their masters. The German king, Ariovistus, had already seized one-third of the territory of the Sequani, and recently he had ordered half the remaining area vacated to make room for more Germans. He was an arrogant tyrant, harsh and brutal, and the situation was unbearable. Unless the Gauls could get the help of the Romans, they would be compelled to leave their homeland and migrate to some other country.

The Haeduans, after their defeat, had been compelled to give hostages to the Germans. If the Gauls attempted to revolt, these hostages would be in grave danger. Furthermore, the Haeduans had been forced to promise on oath that they would not appeal to the Romans for help. By leaving the country and going to Rome, Diviciacus had avoided giving his children as hostages. But the hostages given by the other Gauls were now at the mercy of Ariovistus, and their lives depended on this appeal to Caesar being kept secret.

Diviciacus ended by declaring that Caesar's influence and that of Rome could stop this invasion from Germany and protect the Gauls.

165

A Disastrous Alliance

Hāc ōrātiōne ab Dīviciācō habitā,[1] omnēs quī aderant magnō flētū[2] auxilium ā Caesare petere coepērunt. Animadvertit Caesar
5 ūnōs[3] ex omnibus Sēquanōs nihil eārum rērum facere quās cēterī facerent, sed trīstēs (*sad*), capite dēmissō,[4] terram intuērī (*look at*). Ejus reī quae causa esset mīrā-
10 tus,[5] ex ipsīs quaesīvit. Nihil Sēquanī respondērunt sed in eādem trīstitiā (*sadness*) tacitī permānsērunt.

Cum ab hīs saepius[6] quaereret
15 neque ūllam omnīnō vōcem ex- primere (*draw out*) posset, īdem[7] Dīviciācus Haeduus respondit: "Hōc[8] est miserior et gravior fortūna Sēquanōrum quam reli-
quōrum, quod sōlī nē in occultō 20 quidem querī neque auxilium implōrāre audent absentisque Ariovistī crūdēlitātem sīcut praesentis[9] horrent (*they dread*).

"Reliquīs enim Gallīs fugae fa- 25 cultās datur, Sēquanīs vērō, quī intrā fīnēs suōs Ariovistum recēpērunt, quōrum oppida omnia in potestāte ejus sunt, omnēs cruciātūs sunt perferendī.[10]" 30

Caesar's Decision

Hīs rēbus cognitīs, Caesar Gallōrum animōs verbīs cōnfirmāvit pollicitusque est sibi eam rem cūrae futūram[11]: magnam sē
35 habēre spem et beneficiō suō et auctōritāte adductum Ariovistum fīnem injūriīs factūrum. Hāc ōrātiōne habitā, concilium dīmīsit.

Secundum ea[12] multae rēs eum
40 hortābantur ad eam rem cōgitandam et suscipiendam: imprīmīs (*especially*), quod[13] Haeduī, frātrēs cōnsanguineīque saepenumerō (*very often*) ā senātū appellātī, in servitūte atque in diciōne (*power*) Ger- 45 mānōrum tenēbantur, eōrumque obsidēs apud Ariovistum ac Sēquanōs erant; quod[14] in tantō imperiō populī Rōmānī turpissimum sibi et reī pūblicae esse 50 arbitrābātur.

Paulātim autem Germānōs cōnsuēscere Rhēnum trānsīre et in Galliam magnam eōrum multitūdinem venīre populō Rōmānō perī- 55 culōsum[15] vidēbat; exīstimābat au-

[1] *having been delivered.*
[2] *with loud lamentation.*
[3] *alone.*
[4] Ablative absolute.
[5] Translate as present.
[6] *again and again.*
[7] *again;* literally, *the same* (*person*).
[8] For the case see page 139, note 8.
[9] *as if* (*he were*) *present.*
[10] *the Sequani have to submit to all cruelties.* Sēquanīs in line 26 is a dative of agent with perferendī, line 30.
[11] *that he would give attention to their*

case; **sibi** and **cūrae** are datives of reference and purpose, respectively.
[12] *in addition to these things,* i.e., the facts alleged by Diviciacus.
[13] *the fact that.*
[14] *a thing which;* relative pronoun— neuter because referring to the fact contained in the preceding sentence.
[15] A predicate adjective after **esse** (to be supplied). The subjects of **esse** are the infinitives with subject accusative preceding, **Germānōs cōnsuēscere** and **multitūdinem venīre.**

GERMAN SWORDS
With swords such as these, the warriors of Ariovistus went into battle.

tem hominēs ferōs ac barbarōs, omnī Galliā occupātā, ut[1] ante Cimbrī Teutonīque fēcissent, in prōvinciam atque inde in Italiam 5 exitūrōs esse, praesertim cum Sēquanōs ā prōvinciā nostrā Rho-danus[2] dīvideret; quibus rēbus quam mātūrrimē occurrendum putābat.[3] Ipse autem Ariovistus tantōs sibi spīritūs (*pride*), tantam 10 arrogantiam (*arrogance*) sūmpserat ut ferendus nōn vidērētur.

An Arrogant German King

Quam ob rem, lēgātīs ad Ariovistum missīs, ab eō pos-15 tulāvit ut aliquem locum medium utrīusque[4] colloquiō dēligeret: velle sēsē[5] dē rē pūblicā[6] et summīs utrīusque rēbus[7] cum eō agere.

Eī lēgātiōnī Ariovistus respondit: 20 "Sī quid mihi ā Caesare opus esset,[8] ad eum vēnissem; sī quid ille mē vult,[9] illum ad mē venīre oportet.

"Praetereā neque sine exercitū in eās partēs Galliae venīre audeō quās Caesar possidet, neque exer-25 citum sine magnō commeātū atque mōlīmentō (*trouble*) in ūnum locum contrahere possum.

"Mihi autem mīrum vidētur quid in meā Galliā, quam bellō vīcī, aut 30 Caesarī aut omnīnō populō Rōmānō negōtiī sit.[10]"

[1] *as;* the verb **fēcissent** is subjunctive in a subordinate clause in indirect discourse.

[2] *the Rhone* (*alone*). It had not been a serious barrier to the Helvetians.

[3] *this state of affairs he thought must be met as soon as possible;* **rēbus** is dative with the compound verb **occurrendum** (**esse**), which is itself used impersonally.

[4] *midway between them.*

[5] (he said that) *he wished.*

[6] *affairs of state.*

[7] *questions of the greatest interest to both;* **rēbus**, like **rē pūblicā**, depends on **dē**.

[8] Translate, *if I needed anything of Caesar, I should have come to him;* **quid** is subject; **opus** is predicate nominative.

[9] *if he wishes anything of me.*

[10] *what business Caesar has.* **Caesarī** is dative of possession, and **negōtiī** a genitive of the whole with **quid**.

A ROMAN FORTIFIED CAMP

This is a modern reproduction of a permanent Roman camp in Germany. The soldiers who lived behind the walls of the ancient fort helped hold the Germans in check.

Ariovistus Receives an Ultimatum

Hīs respōnsīs ad Caesarem re-
lātīs, iterum ad eum Caesar
lēgātōs cum hīs mandātīs mittit:
"Quoniam in cōnsulātū (*consulship*)
5 Caesaris rēx atque amīcus ā senātū
appellātus nunc in colloquium
venīre invītātus gravāris[1] atque dē
commūnī rē dīcere et cognōscere
nōn vīs, haec sunt quae ā tē postu-
10 lat: prīmum, nē quam multitūdinem hominum amplius trāns
Rhēnum in Galliam trādūcās;[2]
deinde ut obsidēs quōs habēs ab
Haeduīs reddās Sēquanīsque per-
mittās ut idem faciant; nēve Hae- 15
duōs injūriā lacessās nēve hīs
sociīsque eōrum bellum īnferās.

"Sī id ita fēceris, Caesarī[3] popu-
lōque Rōmānō perpetua grātia atque amīcitia tēcum erit; sī Caesar 20
nōn impetrāverit,[4] Haeduōrum injūriās nōn negleget.

"Nam ex senātūs cōnsultō, quod
paucīs ante annīs factum est, quīcumque Galliam prōvinciam ob- 25
tinet Haeduōs cēterōsque amīcōs populī Rōmānī dēfendere
dēbet."

[1] *you are unwilling.*
[2] *that you shall not lead,* etc. This clause and the two clauses which follow are noun clauses defining **haec**, line 9.

[3] This word and the next one are datives of possession.
[4] When used without an object, the verb **impetrāre** means *to gain one's request.*

A PRESENT-DAY SCENE ON THE RHINE

Defiance and a Challenge

AD HAEC Ariovistus respondit: "Jūs est bellī ut victōrēs victīs quem ad modum[1] velint[2] imperent. Item populus Rōmānus victīs nōn ad alterīus praescrīptum (*direction*), sed ad suum arbitrium (*judgment*) imperāre cōnsuēvit.

"Sī ego populum Rōmānum in ejus jūre nōn impediō, nōn oportet mē ā populō Rōmānō in meō jūre impedīrī. Haeduī, bellī fortūnā temptātā, superātī sunt mihique stīpendiāriī (*tributary*) sunt factī.

"Magnam Caesar injūriam facit, quī suō adventū vectīgālia (*revenues*) mihi dēteriōra (*less*) facit.

Haeduīs obsidēs nōn reddam, neque eīs neque eōrum sociīs injūriā[3] bellum īnferam, sī in eō manēbunt quod convēnit[4] stīpendiumque 20 quotannīs pendent; sī id nōn fēcerint, longē eīs frāternum nōmen populī Rōmānī aberit.[5]

"Quod[6] mihi Caesar dēnūntiat sē Haeduōrum injūriās nōn neglēctūrum, nēmō mēcum sine suā perniciē 25 (*destruction*) contendit. Cum volet, congrediātur.[7] Intelleget quid invictī (*unconquered*) Germānī, exercitātissimī (*thoroughly trained*) 30 in armīs, quī inter annōs XIV tēctum nōn subierint, virtūte possint."

[1] *as;* literally, *in what manner.*
[2] Subjunctive by attraction, since its clause depends upon another clause which has its verb in the subjunctive.
[3] *without reason, unjustly.*
[4] *if they abide by our agreement.*
[5] The clause beginning with **longē** means *the title of brothers of the Roman people will be of little value to them.*
[6] *as to the fact that;* with **dēnūntiat—** *as for Caesar's threat that,* etc.
[7] *let him come on;* subjunctive of desire, sometimes called volitive subjunctive. See Gr. S., 102.

More Appeals for Help

Haec eōdem tempore Caesarī mandāta referēbantur, et lē-

IN THE LAND OF THE TREVERI
These ruined walls were once part of magnificent baths in the Roman city *Augusta Trēverōrum.* Its modern name—Trier or Treves—is derived from that of the Gallic tribe, the Treveri.

gātī ab Haeduīs et ā Trēverīs veniēbant. Haeduī querēbantur, quod Harūdēs,[1] quī nūper in Galliam trānsportātī essent, fīnēs eōrum populārentur: sēsē nē, obsidibus quidem datīs,[2] pācem Ariovistī redimere potuisse.[3] Trēverī autem dīcēbant pāgōs centum Suēbōrum ad rīpās Rhēnī cōnsēdisse, quī Rhēnum trānsīre cōnārentur; hīs praeesse Nasuam et Cimberium[4] frātrēs.

Quibus rēbus Caesar vehementer commōtus mātūrandum sibi[5] exīstimāvit nē, sī nova manus Suēbōrum cum veteribus cōpiīs Ariovistī sēsē conjūnxisset, minus facile resistī posset.[6]

Itaque rē frūmentāriā quam celerrimē potuit comparātā, magnīs itineribus ad Ariovistum contendit.

The Race for Vesontio

Cum trīduī viam[7] prōcessisset, nūntiātum est eī Ariovistum cum suīs omnibus cōpiīs ad occupandum Vesontiōnem,[8] quod est oppidum maximum Sēquanōrum, contendere.

Id magnopere sibi praecavendum[9] Caesar exīstimābat. Namque omnium rērum quae ad bellum ūsuī[10] erant summa erat in eō oppidō facultās, idemque nātūrā locī sīc mūniēbātur ut magnam ad

[1] *the Harudes* (hä-rö′dēz), a German tribe.

[2] *by giving hostages;* ablative absolute.

[3] A verb of saying is implied in **querēbantur,** line 4.

[4] *Nasua* (nash′ū-ạ) *and Cimberius* (sim-bē′ri-us), leaders of the Suebi.

[5] *that he must make haste;* **sibi** is a dative of agent with the future passive participle.

[6] *resistance could be made less easily;* **resistī** is an impersonal use of the passive infinitive, depending on **posset.**

[7] Accusative of extent, further defined by the genitive of measure, **trīduī.**

[8] *Vesontio* (vē-son′shi-ō), a city of the Sequanians, now *Besançon* (be-zän-sôṅ).

[9] *must be forestalled.*

[10] *of use;* dative of purpose.

BESANÇON — SITE OF ANCIENT VESONTIO

dūcendum[1] bellum daret facultātem, proptereā quod flūmen
Dūbis,[2] ut circinō circumductum,[3]
paene tōtum oppidum cingit. Reli-
5 quum spatium, quod est nōn amplius pedum[4] DC, quā flūmen inter-
mittit, mōns continet magnā
altitūdine, ita ut rādīcēs (*base*)
montis ex utrāque parte rīpae
flūminis contingant. Hunc mūrus 10
circumdatus[5] arcem efficit et cum
oppidō conjungit.

Hūc Caesar magnīs nocturnīs
diurnīsque (*and by day*) itineribus
contendit occupātōque oppidō ibi 15
praesidium collocat.

Panic-stricken Soldiers

DUM paucōs diēs ad Veson-
tiōnem[6] reī frūmentāriae
commeātūsque causā morātur,
20 nostrī Gallōs ac mercātōrēs dē
Germānīs interrogant.

Illī ingentī magnitūdine[7] corporum Germānōs, incrēdibilī virtūte[7]
atque exercitātiōne[7] in armīs esse
praedicābant (saepenumerō[8] sēsē 25
cum hīs congressōs nē vultum
quidem atque aciem[9] oculōrum
dīcēbant ferre potuisse); quibus
ex vōcibus tantus subitō timor
omnem exercitum occupāvit ut 30
nōn mediocriter[10] omnium mentēs
animōsque perturbāret.

[1] Here **dūcere** means *prolong.*
[2] *Dubis* (dū´bis), now called the Doubs
(dö).
[3] *as if traced by a compass.*
[4] Genitive of measure in the predicate.
The comparative **amplius** is here used
without any effect on the case of the
words which follow. It may be translated as if it were **amplius quam.**

[5] *an encircling wall.*
[6] See page 170, note 8.
[7] Ablative of description, in the
predicate.
[8] *very often.*
[9] *fierce look.*
[10] Literally *not slightly;* hence, *to no
slight degree.*

Hic prīmum ortus est ā tribūnīs mīlitum,[1] praefectīs,[2] reliquīsque[3] quī ex urbe amīcitiae causā Caesarem secūtī nōn magnum in rē mīli-
5 tārī ūsum habēbant. Hī, variīs causīs domum proficīscendī illātīs,[4] petēbant ut ejus voluntāte discēdere licēret; nōnnūllī pudōre (*by shame*) adductī, ut timōris sus-
10 pīciōnem vītārent, remanēbant (*remained*).

Hī neque vultum fingere neque interdum lacrimās tenēre poterant; abditī in tabernāculīs aut suum fā-
15 tum querēbantur aut cum familiāribus suīs commūne perīculum miserābantur (*were deploring*). Vulgō (*everywhere*) tōtīs castrīs[5] testā-

menta obsignābantur (*wills were being sealed*). Hōrum vōcibus ac 20 timōre paulātim etiam eī quī magnum in castrīs ūsum habēbant, mīlitēs centuriōnēsque[6] quīque[7] equitātuī praeerant, perturbābantur. Quī sē ex hīs[8] minus 25 timidōs exīstimārī volēbant, dīcēbant: "Nōn hostem verēmur, sed angustiās itineris et magnitūdinem silvārum quae intercēdunt inter nōs atque Ariovistum; timēmus 30 etiam ut rēs frūmentāria satis commodē supportārī possit.[9]"

Nōnnūllī etiam Caesarī nūntiābant mīlitēs propter timōrem neque castra mōtūrōs neque signa 35 lātūrōs.

A Bold Decision

CAESAR then called his officers together, including the centurions, and addressed them.

"On a previous occasion Ariovistus made it clear that he desired the friendship of the Roman people," he said. "I feel sure that when he understands the fairness of the terms I propose, he will reject neither my friendship nor the friendship of Rome.

"But if he should be so foolish as to attack us, why should you be afraid? Can you not trust your own courage and my leadership? The Germans were defeated by Romans in the time of Marius. More recently a great number of slaves, with Roman arms and Roman training, were unable to face a Roman army. Even the Helvetians have defeated the Germans in the past; yet the Helvetians were no match for our army.

"The recent success of the Germans should not cause us any anxiety. For

---

[1] The military tribunes were officers in the army, and must not be confused with the tribunes of the people. They were less experienced than the **lēgātī**.

[2] The prefects were officers of auxiliary forces, some of them Romans, some of the same nationality as their troops.

[3] Sons of influential families who accompanied Caesar without performing military service.

[4] *offering various excuses.*

[5] *all through the camp.*

[6] The centurions were seasoned veterans who had been promoted from the ranks.

[7] For **et eī quī.**

[8] *such of them as.*

[9] *that grain supplies cannot be brought up to sufficiently good advantage.* What is the meaning of **nē** when used to introduce a clause with the subjunctive after a verb of fearing? See Gr. S., 109.

many months Ariovistus kept out of the way of the Gauls. Then he attacked when they did not expect a battle. Hence his victory was due to strategy rather than to courage.

"I am told that there are some who fear that the grain will give out or that the roads are too difficult. These are matters for the commander to look after. Three Gallic tribes have agreed to supply grain, and their wheat is already ripe in the fields.

"Still less am I troubled about the story that the army will refuse to march when ordered. When a commander is not obeyed, one of two things is true: either he is incompetent, or he is corrupt. My success against the Helvetians and my whole life disprove such suspicions in my case.

"I am therefore going to do immediately what I had planned to do later—we will start tomorrow morning. This will show whether fear or a sense of duty has the stronger hold on you.

"And if no others will go, I will start with only the tenth legion as a bodyguard. I have no doubts about the loyalty of that legion."

The Roman Army Advances

Hāc ōrātiōne habitā, mīrum in modum[1] conversae sunt omnium mentēs, summaque alacritās et cupiditās bellī gerendī innāta est 5 (*arose*); princepsque decima legiō per tribūnōs mīlitum eī grātiās ēgit, quod dē sē optimum jūdicium fēcisset, sēque esse ad bellum gerendum parātissimam cōnfirmāvit. 10 Deinde reliquae legiōnēs cum tribūnīs mīlitum et prīmōrum ōrdinum centuriōnibus ēgērunt[2] ut Caesarī satisfacerent: sē neque umquam dubitāsse neque timuisse neque dē summā bellī suum[3] jūdi- 15 cium, sed imperātōris esse exīstimāvisse. Caesar, eōrum satisfactiōne (*excuse*) acceptā et itinere exquīsītō[4] per Dīviciācum, quod ex Gallīs eī maximam fidem habēbat,[5] 20 dē quārtā vigiliā, ut dīxerat, profectus est. Septimō diē, cum iter nōn intermitteret,[6] ab explōrātōribus certior factus est Ariovistī cōpiās ā nostrīs mīlia passuum IV 25 et xx abesse.

A Soldier's Joke

Cognitō Caesaris adventū, Ariovistus per lēgātōs eī nūntiāvit sē jam in colloquium venīre 30 velle; quoniam Caesar propius accessisset, sē id sine perīculō facere posse exīstimāre.

Nōn respuit (*did not refuse*) condiciōnem Caesar jamque eum ad

---

[1] *in a marvelous manner.*

[2] *urged the tribunes and centurions.*

[3] In the predicate after **esse**—*was their own, and not the commander's.*

[4] *having been investigated.*

[5] Translate **ex . . . habēbat,** *of the Gauls, Caesar had the most confidence in him.*

[6] The clause means *after an unbroken march;* i.e., without taking a day for rest.

A SOLDIER OF THE LEGION

dēsistere arbitrābātur. Diēs colloquiō dictus est ex eō diē quīntus.

Interim saepe cum[1] lēgātī ultrō 5
citrōque inter eōs mitterentur,
Ariovistus dīxit sē īnsidiās verērī
postulāvitque ut uterque cum sōlō
equitātū ad colloquium venīret;
aliā ratiōne[2] sēsē nōn esse ventū- 10
rum.

Caesar, hāc condiciōne acceptā,
salūtem suam tamen Gallōrum
equitātuī[3] committere nōn audē-
bat. Itaque legiōnāriōs (*legionary*) 15
mīlitēs legiōnis decimae in equōs
Gallōrum equitum imposuit ut
praesidium quam amīcissimum habēret. Quod cum fieret, nōn irrī-
diculē (*without humor*) quīdam ex 20
mīlitibus decimae legiōnis dīxit:
"Plūs quam pollicitus est Caesar
facit. Pollicitus sē in cohortis
praetōriae[4] locō decimam legiōnem
habitūrum, ad equum rescrībit.[5]" 25

sānitātem (*sanity*) revertī perti-
nāciāque (*from his stubbornness*)

The Demands of Caesar

PLĀNITIĒS erat magna, et in eā
tumulus terrēnus (*earthen*) satis grandis (*large*). Hic locus ae-
quum ferē spatium ā castrīs utrīusque aberat. Eō, ut erat dictum, ad 30
colloquium vēnērunt. Legiōnem

Caesar quam equīs[6] dēvexerat (*had
brought*) passibus cc ab eō tumulō
cōnstituit.

Item equitēs Ariovistī parī in- 35
tervāllō cōnstitērunt. Ariovistus ex
equīs ut[7] colloquerentur et praeter

---

[1] Translate as if **cum saepe.**

[2] *otherwise;* literally, *on other terms.*

[3] Caesar's cavalry was composed at
various times of Gauls, Germans, or
Spaniards.

[4] The two words mean *a general's bodyguard.*

[5] *enroll.* The three words may have
two meanings: *is enrolling us among the
knights,* or *is enrolling us in the cavalry.*
The knights, **equitēs,** were a social and
semi-political order at Rome drawn
from the well-to-do middle class that at
an earlier period furnished the Roman
cavalry. Admission to their ranks
would be an honor. Now, however,
since the cavalry was furnished by non-
Romans, transfer to that branch of the
service was no mark of distinction.
Hence the pun on **equitēs.**

[6] *on horseback.*

[7] Twice in this sentence **ut** is out of
its normal place at the head of its
clause in order to emphasize other words,
ex equīs in one case and **praeter sē
dēnōs** in the other.

sē dēnōs (*ten men each*) ut ad colloquium addūcerent postulāvit.

Ubi eō ventum est,[1] Caesar initiō ōrātiōnis sua senātūsque in eum
5 beneficia commemorāvit, quod[2] rēx appellātus esset ā senātū, quod[2] amīcus,[3] quod[2] mūnera amplissimē missa.

"Haec rēs," inquit, "et paucīs
10 contigit et prō magnīs hominum officiīs cōnsuēvit tribuī. Tū, cum neque aditum neque causam postulandī jūstam habērēs, beneficiō ac līberālitāte (*generosity*) meā ac se-
15 nātūs ea praemia cōnsecūtus es.

"Veterēs jūstāsque causās necessitūdinis (*of alliance*) Rōmānī cum Haeduīs habent. Multa senātūs cōnsulta honōrifica (*honorable*) in eōs facta sunt. Omnī tempore tō-
20 tīus Galliae prīncipātum Haeduī tenuērunt, prius etiam quam nostram amīcitiam appetīvērunt.

"Populī Rōmānī haec est cōnsuētūdō,[4] ut sociōs atque amīcōs
25 nōn modo suī nihil[5] dēperdere (*should lose*), sed grātiā, dignitāte, honōre auctiōrēs velit esse; quod vērō ad amīcitiam populī Rōmānī attulērunt,[6] id eīs ēripī
30 quis patī potest?"

Postulāvit deinde eadem quae lēgātīs in mandātīs dederat: nē aut Haeduīs aut eōrum sociīs bellum īnferret;[7] obsidēs redderet; sī nūl-
35 lam partem Germānōrum domum remittere posset, at nē quōs[8] amplius Rhēnum trānsīre paterētur.

The Reply of Ariovistus

ARIOVISTUS ad postulāta (*demands*) Caesaris pauca respondit; dē suīs virtūtibus multa praedicāvit.

"Trānsiī Rhēnum," inquit, "nōn meā sponte, sed rogātus et arcessī-
45 tus ā Gallīs; nōn sine magnā spē magnīsque praemiīs domum propinquōsque relīquī. Sēdēs habeō in Galliā ab ipsīs[9] concessās, obsidēs ipsōrum voluntāte datōs. Stīpen-
50 dium capiō jūre bellī, quod victōrēs victīs impōnere cōnsuērunt.

"Nōn ego[10] Gallīs sed Gallī mihi bellum intulērunt. Omnēs Galliae cīvitātēs ad mē oppugnandum vēnērunt ac contrā mē castra habuē-
55 runt. Eae omnēs cōpiae ā mē ūnō proeliō pulsae ac superātae sunt.

"Sī iterum experīrī volunt, iterum parātus sum dēcertāre; sī pāce ūtī volunt, inīquum est dē stīpendiō
60 recūsāre, quod suā voluntāte ad hoc tempus pependērunt. Amīcitiam populī Rōmānī mihi ōrnāmentō et praesidiō,[11] nōn dētrī-

---

[1] *they had come;* impersonal passive.
[2] The **quod** clauses define **beneficia**.
[3] Supply **appellātus esset.**
[4] Explained by the clause **ut . . . velit**
—*to wish,* etc.
[5] *nothing that belongs to them;* **suī** is a genitive of the whole; literally, *of theirs.*
[6] *as for what they brought (with them)*

when they became friends of the Roman people. The antecedent of **quod** is the following **id.**
[7] *that he should not make war,* etc.
[8] *any.*
[9] Meaning the Gauls.
[10] Supply **bellum intulī.**
[11] *an honor and a safeguard;* datives of purpose.

ROMAN JAVELINS

mentō esse oportet, idque hāc spē petīvī.

"Sī per populum Rōmānum stīpendium remittētur et dēditīcii 5 (*captives*) subtrahentur (*are taken away*), nōn minus libenter recūsābō populī Rōmānī amīcitiam quam appetīvī. Quod[1] multitūdinem Germānōrum in Galliam trādūcō, id 10 meī mūniendī,[2] nōn Galliae oppugnandae causā faciō. Ejus reī testimōniō[3] est quod nisi rogātus nōn vēnī et quod bellum nōn intulī sed dēfendī.

15 "Ego prius in Galliam vēnī quam populus Rōmānus. Numquam ante hoc tempus exercitus populī Rōmānī Galliae prōvinciae finibus ēgressus est. Quid tibi vīs? Cūr in 20 meās possessiōnēs venīs? Prōvincia mea haec est Gallia,[4] sīcut illa vestra.[5]

"Ut mihi concēdī nōn oportēret[6] sī in vestrōs fīnēs impetum facerem, 25 sīc item vōs estis inīquī, quod in meō jūre mē interpellātis (*you hinder*).

"Quod frātrēs ā senātū Haeduōs appellātōs dīcis, neque bellō[7] Allobrogum proximō Haeduī Rōmānīs 30 auxilium tulērunt neque ipsī in hīs contentiōnibus (*struggles*) quās Haeduī mēcum et cum Sēquanīs habuērunt auxiliō populī Rōmānī ūsī sunt. Neque tam barbarus 35 neque tam imperītus sum rērum ut haec nōn sciam. Dēbeō suspicārī tē, simulātā amīcitiā, exercitum in Galliā meī opprimendī causā habēre. 40

"Nisi dēcēdēs atque exercitum dēdūcēs ex hīs regiōnibus, tē nōn prō amīcō sed prō hoste habēbō.[8] Quod sī[9] tē interfēcerō, multīs nōbilibus prīncipibusque populī Rō- 45 mānī grātum[10] fēcerō. Id ab ipsīs per eōrum nūntiōs compertum habeō,[11] quōrum omnium grātiam atque amīcitiam tuā morte redimere possum. 50

"Quod sī dēcesseris et līberam possessiōnem Galliae mihi trādideris, magnō tē praemiō remūnerābor (*I will repay*), et quaecumque bella gerī volēs sine ūllō tuō labōre et 55 perīculō cōnficiam."

---

[1] Not *because*. What does it mean?

[2] With the genitives of the pronouns **meī, tuī, suī, nostrī, vestrī**, the gerundive takes only the form in -endī without attempt to show actual gender or number; i.e., a woman speaking would say also **meī mūniendī causā** (not **meī mūniendae**).

[3] Predicate dative of purpose or end served. Translate, *the proof of this is, that*, etc.

[4] *this part of Gaul.*

[5] Used instead of **tua** to refer to the whole Roman nation, not to Caesar alone.

[6] *no concession should be made* (*me*); **concēdī** is an impersonal passive.

[7] This war occurred in 62-61 B.C.

[8] *I shall treat.*

[9] The words **quod sī** mean *but if.*

[10] *a welcome thing, a favor;* an adjective used as a noun.

[11] Translate **compertum habeō** as if **comperī**, and see page 149, note 1.

THE MEETING OF THE TWO COMMANDERS

The Basis for Roman Claims

Multa ā Caesare in eam sententiam dicta sunt, quārē[1] negōtiō dēsistere nōn posset.

"Neque mea," inquit, "neque populī Rōmānī cōnsuētūdō patitur ut optimē meritōs sociōs dēseram,[2] neque jūdicō Galliam potius esse tuam quam populī Rōmānī. Bellō[3] superātī sunt Arvernī et Rutēnī[4] ā Q. Fabiō Maximō;[5] quibus[6] populus Rōmānus ignōvit neque in prōvinciam redēgit neque stīpendium imposuit.

"Quod sī antīquissimum quodque tempus[7] spectārī oportet, populī Rōmānī jūstissimum est in Galliā imperium; sī jūdicium senātūs observārī (*to be observed*) oportet, lībera dēbet esse Gallia, quam bellō victam suīs lēgibus ūtī voluit."

A Treacherous Attack

Dum haec in colloquiō geruntur, Caesarī nūntiātum est equitēs Ariovistī propius tumulum[8] accēdere et ad nostrōs adequitāre[9]

[1] *to show why.*

[2] The verb **patior** may take either an infinitive with subject accusative or a noun clause.

[3] In 121 B.C.

[4] *the Ruteni* (rö-tē′nī), a Celtic tribe.

[5] *Quintus Fabius Maximus*, a Roman consul in 121 B.C.

[6] Dative with **ignōvit**, *pardoned.*

[7] *mere priority;* literally, *the time furthest back in each case.* Since the Roman conquest in this region went back as far as 121 B.C., Caesar argues that Roman claims were better founded than German.

[8] Accusative with the adverb **propius,** which may take an accusative.

[9] *were riding up* (*to*).

et lapidēs tēlaque in nostrōs conjicere. Caesar loquendī fīnem fēcit
sēque ad suōs recēpit suīsque imperāvit nē quod omnīnō tēlum in
5 hostēs rejicerent.

Nam etsī sine ūllō perīculō legiōnis dēlēctae cum equitātū proelium
fore vidēbat, tamen nōlēbat hostēs

dīcere posse, sī pulsī essent, sē ā
Rōmānīs per fidem[1] in colloquiō 10
circumventōs. Ita colloquium dī-
rēmptum est (*was broken off*).

Postquam mīlitēs dē hīs rēbus
certiōrēs factī sunt, multō major
alacritās studiumque pugnandī 15
majus exercituī injectum est.[2]

A Conference

TWO days later Ariovistus sent representatives to Caesar. He asked
that either a date be set for a second
interview with Caesar or that a Roman officer be sent to confer with him.
But Caesar felt that since the Germans
had treacherously attacked the Romans at the previous meeting, there
was little hope that another conference would do any good. Furthermore, he did not care to risk the life
of an officer by putting him in the
power of the treacherous German
king. Nevertheless, he sent two men

to confer with Ariovistus, one of them
a Gaul who could talk with him without an interpreter, since Ariovistus
knew the Gallic language.

When they reached the German
camp, they were at once arrested on
the pretext that they had come as
spies. Ariovistus then moved his
camp to a point nearer the Roman
army and attempted to prevent the
Haeduans and the Sequani from furnishing supplies to the Romans. He
avoided battle, however, although
Caesar repeatedly challenged him.

Caesar Divides His Forces

UBI eum castrīs sē tenēre
Caesar intellēxit, nē diūtius
commeātū prohibērētur, ultrā eum
20 locum, quō in locō Germānī cōn-
sēderant, circiter passūs DC ab hīs,
castrīs[3] idōneum locum dēlēgit aciē-
que triplicī īnstrūctā ad eum locum
vēnit. Prīmam et secundam aciem
25 in armīs esse, tertiam castra mūnīre jussit. Hic locus ab hoste
circiter passūs DC, ut dictum est,
aberat.

Eō circiter hominum XVI mīlia
expedīta[4] cum omnī equitātū Ario- 30
vistus mīsit quae cōpiae nostrōs
perterrērent et mūnītiōne prohibērent.[5] Nihilō sētius[6] Caesar, ut
ante cōnstituerat, duās aciēs hostem prōpulsāre (*to drive back*), ter- 35
tiam opus perficere jussit.

Mūnītīs castrīs, duās ibi legiōnēs
relīquit et partem auxiliōrum, quattuor reliquās in castra majōra redūxit.   40

---

[1] *through their faith in him;* i.e.,
treacherously.
[2] *was inspired in the army.*
[3] Dative, dependent on **idōneum.**
[4] The adjective limits **mīlia,** but should

be translated as if in agreement with
hominum.
[5] A relative clause of purpose.
[6] The words **Nihilō sētius** mean
nevertheless.

"No Battle before the New Moon"

Proximō diē, īnstitūtō suō Caesar ē castrīs utrīsque cōpiās suās ēdūxit paulumque ā majōribus castrīs prōgressus aciem īnstrūxit, hostibus pugnandī potestātem fēcit.

Ubi nē tum quidem eōs prōdīre (*come forth*) intellēxit, circiter merīdiem exercitum in castra redūxit.

Tum dēmum Ariovistus partem suārum cōpiārum quae castra minōra oppugnāret mīsit. Ācriter utrimque usque ad vesperum pugnātum est.[1] Sōlis occāsū suās cōpiās Ariovistus, multīs et illātīs et acceptīs vulneribus, in castra redūxit.

Cum ex captīvīs quaereret Caesar quam ob rem[2] Ariovistus proeliō nōn dēcertāret, illī respondērunt: "Apud Germānōs ea cōnsuētūdō est, ut mātrēs familiae eōrum sortibus et vāticinātiōnibus (*predictions*) dēclārent (*reveal*) utrum[3] proelium committī ex ūsū[4] sit necne (*or not*); eae ita dīcunt: 'Nōn est fās Germānōs superāre, sī ante novam lūnam proeliō contenderint.'"

The Romans Force a Battle

Postrīdiē ejus diēī Caesar praesidiō utrīsque castrīs[5] quod satis esse vīsum est relīquit. Omnēs ālāriōs (*auxiliaries*) in cōnspectū hostium prō castrīs minōribus cōnstituit, quod minus multitūdine mīlitum legiōnāriōrum prō[6] hostium numerō valēbat,[7] ut ad speciem ālāriīs (*auxiliaries*) ūterētur. Ipse, triplicī īnstrūctā aciē, usque ad castra hostium accessit.

Tum dēmum necessāriō (*necessarily*) Germānī suās cōpiās castrīs ēdūxērunt generātimque (*and by nations*) cōnstituērunt paribus intervāllīs, Harūdēs,[8] Marcomannōs,[9] Tribocōs, Vangionēs, Nemetēs, Sedusiōs, Suēbōs, omnemque aciem suam raedīs (*with wagons*) et carrīs circumdedērunt, nē qua spēs in fugā relinquerētur.

Eō[10] mulierēs imposuērunt, quae ad proelium proficīscentēs[11] mīlitēs passīs manibus flentēs implōrābant nē sē in servitūtem Rōmānīs trāderent.

[1] *both sides fought fiercely till evening;* **pugnātum est** is an impersonal passive.

[2] *why.*

[3] *whether,* introducing an indirect double question, that is, a question asking which of two alternatives is true.

[4] *of advantage.*

[5] *as a guard to both camps;* two datives, one of purpose, the other of reference.

[6] *in proportion to.*

[7] With **minus** . . . **legiōnāriōrum**—*he was not very strong in the number of his legionary soldiers.*

[8] See page 170, note 1.

[9] *the Marcomanni* (mär-kō-man′ī), *the Triboci* (trib′ō-sī), *the Vangiones* (van-jī′ō-nēz), *the Nemetes* (nem′ē-tēz), *the Sedusii* (sē-dö′si-ī).

[10] An adverb equivalent to **in raedās et carrōs.**

[11] Agreeing with **mīlitēs.**

GERMAN HUNTERS RETURN WITH THEIR KILL

Though little is known about details of home life among the people of Ariovistus, an artist has here given a general idea of what it may have been like.

Hand-to-Hand Fighting

CAESAR singulīs legiōnibus singulōs lēgātōs et quaestōrem[1] praefēcit ut eōs testēs suae quisque virtūtis habēret.

5 Ipse ā dextrō cornū, quod eam partem minimē firmam hostium esse animadverterat, proelium commīsit.

Et ita nostrī ācriter in hostēs 10 signō datō impetum fēcērunt, itaque[2] hostēs repente celeriterque prōcurrērunt (*rushed forward*) ut spatium pīla[3] in hostēs conjiciendī nōn darētur.

Prōjectīs pīlīs, comminus gladiīs 15 pugnātum est.[4] At Germānī, celeriter ex cōnsuētūdine suā phalange factā, impetūs gladiōrum excēpērunt. Repertī sunt complūrēs nostrī quī in phalangem īnsilīrent 20 (*leaped*) et scūta manibus revellerent (*tore away*) et dēsuper (*from above*) vulnerārent.[5]

Cum hostium aciēs ā sinistrō cornū pulsa atque in fugam conjecta esset, ā dextrō cornū vehementer multitūdine suōrum nostram aciem premēbant. Id cum

---

[1] Caesar had at this time six legions and one quaestor; five legions were therefore commanded by lieutenants.

[2] The word **itaque** is equivalent to **et ita**.

[3] Object of the gerund **conjiciendī**, which depends on **spatium**.

[4] The four words mean *they fought hand to hand with swords*.

[5] A relative descriptive clause.

animadvertisset P. Crassus[1] adulēscēns, quī equitātuī praeerat, quod
expedītior erat quam eī quī inter
aciem versābantur, tertiam aciem labōrantibus nostrīs subsidiō[2] 5
mīsit.

The Result of the Battle

ITA proelium restitūtum est, atque omnēs hostēs terga vertērunt neque prius[3] fugere dēstitē-
10 runt quam ad flūmen Rhēnum
mīlia passuum ex eō locō circiter
v pervēnērunt.

Ibi perpaucī (*very few*) aut vīribus[4] cōnfīsī trānāre (*to swim across*)
15 contendērunt aut lintribus inventīs
sibi salūtem reppererunt. In hīs fuit
Ariovistus, quī nāviculam (*small
boat*) dēligātam ad rīpam nactus
eā profūgit. Reliquōs omnēs cōn-
20 secūtī equitēs nostrī interfēcērunt.

Duae fuērunt Ariovistī uxōrēs,[5]
ūna Suēba nātiōne, quam domō
sēcum dūxerat, altera Nōrica,[6] rēgis
Vocciōnis[7] soror, quam in Galliā
25 dūxerat, ā frātre missam; utraque
in eā fugā periit. Fuērunt duae
fīliae; hārum altera occīsa, altera
capta est.

C. Valerius Procillus,[8] cum ā
custōdibus in fugā trīnīs (*triple*) 30
catēnīs vīnctus traherētur, in ipsum Caesarem hostēs equitātū
īnsequentem incidit.[9]

Quae quidem rēs Caesarī nōn
minōrem quam ipsa victōria volup- 35
tātem attulit, quod hominem ho-
nestissimum prōvinciae Galliae,
suum familiārem et hospitem,
ēreptum ē manibus hostium sibi
restitūtum vidēbat, neque[10] ejus 40
calamitāte dē tantā voluptāte et
grātulātiōne quicquam fortūna dē-
minuerat.[10]

Is sē praesente dē sē ter (*three
times*) sortibus cōnsultum[11] dīcēbat 45
utrum igne statim necārētur an in
aliud tempus reservārētur;[12] sor-
tium beneficiō sē esse incolumem.
Item M. Mētius[13] repertus et ad
eum reductus est. 50

[1] Son of the Marcus Crassus who was
an associate of Caesar and Pompey in
the First Triumvirate. Publius lost his
life in 53 B.C., in a battle in which the
army commanded by his father was
defeated by the Parthians, a people of
Asia. His father was also killed in this
battle.

[2] *to the relief of our men in distress.*

[3] Take with **quam.** The two are commonly written as one word.

[4] Ablative with **cōnfīsī,** *trusting in.*
Sometimes **cōnfīdō** takes the ablative
and sometimes the dative, but usually
the dative when referring to persons.

[5] Polygamy was not common among
the Germans, being restricted to the
chiefs.

[6] *a Norican,* from Noricum, the part
of Europe which is now Austria. See
map, page 277.

[7] *Voccio* (vok'shi-ō), king of Noricum.

[8] *Gaius Valerius Procillus* (gā'us vạ-lē'-
ri-us prō-sil'us), a Gallic friend of Caesar.

[9] *fell in with Caesar.*

[10] Translate freely, *and fortune had not
in any way diminished his great pleasure
and satisfaction* (over the victory) *by a
misfortune to Procillus.*

[11] Supply **esse.**

[12] *as to whether he should be put to
death with fire or reserved,* etc.

[13] *Marcus Metius* (mē'shius), envoy to
Ariovistus.

The End of the War

Hōc proeliō trāns Rhēnum nūntiātō, Suēbī, quī ad rīpās Rhēnī vēnerant, domum revertī coepērunt; ubi eī quī proximī Rhēnum[1] incolunt eōs perterritōs sēnsērunt, īnsecūtī magnum ex eīs numerum occīdērunt.

Caesar, ūnā aestāte duōbus maximīs bellīs cōnfectīs, mātūrius (*earlier*) paulō quam tempus annī postulābat in hīberna in Sēquanōs exercitum dēdūxit. Hībernīs Labiēnum praeposuit (*he placed in charge of*). Ipse in citeriōrem Galliam ad conventūs agendōs[2] profectus est.

[1] The accusative of a place name may be governed by the adjective **proximus.** On page 177, line 23, the accusative with the adverb **propius** occurred.

[2] *to hold the (provincial) courts.* It was part of his duty as governor of the province to hold these courts. He was supreme judge in them.

COMPREHENSION QUESTIONS

Find answers to the following questions in the narrative entitled "The War with Ariovistus."

1. Why did the Gallic envoys consider the defeat of the Helvetians a good thing for Gaul?

2. Why were the envoys of the Sequani afraid to join the others in the protest against Ariovistus?

3. What reasons did Caesar have for deciding to oppose further extension of German power in Gaul?

4. What was the substance of the reply of Ariovistus to Caesar's first request for a conference?

5. What favor had Ariovistus received from the Romans?

6. What were Caesar's demands?

7. How did Ariovistus reply to these demands?

8. What was the occasion for the embassy from the Haeduans and the Treveri?

9. What special advantage for defense had the town of Vesontio?

10. What was the reason for the panic which developed in Caesar's army?

11. In which legion did Caesar put most confidence?

12. In what way did Caesar provide for a bodyguard at the interview with Ariovistus?

13. Why was the interview broken off?

14. Why did Ariovistus encamp beyond Caesar's camp?

15. Why did the Germans so long delay battle?

16. In the chapter called "Hand-to-Hand Fighting," page 180, what comment does Caesar make on the swiftness of the attack?

17. How had Valerius Procillus escaped death?

18. Whom did Caesar put in charge of the winter quarters?

QUESTIONS ON GRAMMAR

1. Explain the use of the anticipatory subjunctive. (Gr. S., 110.) 2. Give an English sentence which if translated into Latin would take the dative of purpose. (Gr. S., 63.) 3. Explain the dative of reference. (Gr. S., 64.) 4. Conjugate **sum** and **possum** in the present and imperfect subjunctive. (Gr. S., 39, 40.) 5. What is the tense sign of the perfect subjunctive? With what stem is it used? (See p. 123.) 6. Conjugate **dīcō** in the perfect subjunctive active and **capiō** in the perfect subjunctive passive. (Gr. S., 35, 36.) 7. Give the principal parts of **mālō** and **nōlō**. (Gr. S., 45.) 8. Give a synopsis of each of the three verbs **volō, nōlō,** and **mālō** in the third person singular, indicative and subjunctive. (Gr. S., 45.) 9. Decline the pronoun **aliquis** and give its meaning. (Gr. S., 32.) 10. What is the difference between the endings of the adjective **aliquis** and the endings of the relative pronoun **quī** in the feminine nominative singular and in the neuter nominative and accusative plural? (Gr. S., 29, 32.)

WORD STUDY V

Personal Names of Latin Origin

Many of our given names come from Latin and had originally a definite meaning. The following list includes a number of familiar names of this kind.

AMANDA, from the gerundive of **amō.** Hence, *worthy of love, to be loved.*

BEATRICE, from **beātus,** *happy* (through Italian). Hence, *bearing happiness, making happy.*

CALVIN, from **calvus,** *bald.*

CLARENCE \
CLARA   ⟩ from **clārus,** *bright, illustrious.*

CLARIBEL, from **clārus,** *bright,* and **bellus,** *beautiful.*

CLEMENT   \
CLEMENTIA ⟩ from **clēmēns,** *merciful, kindly.*

FELIX   \
FELICIA ⟩ from **fēlīx,** *fortunate, happy.*

LAURENCE (LAWRENCE) ⟩ from **laurus,** *laurel.* Hence, *a victor,* since a victor in a \
LAURA   contest was crowned with laurel.

LEO (LEON), from **leō, leōnis,** *lion.*

MABEL (AMABEL), from **amābilis,** *lovable.*

MARTIN, from **Mārtīnus,** *belonging to Mars.* Hence, *warlike.*

MIRANDA, from the gerundive of **mīror.** Hence, *admirable, to be admired.*

OLIVER ⟩ from **olīva,** *olive.* Hence, *peaceful,* since the olive branch was a token of \
OLIVIA   peace.

PATRICK   \
PATRICIA ⟩ from **patricius,** *belonging to the aristocracy* (**patrēs**). Hence, *noble.*

VINCENT, from **vincēns, vincentis,** the present participle of **vincō.** Hence, *a conqueror.*

Exercises

1. Give the Latin words from which the following given names come: Benedict; Florence; Lily; Octavius, Octavia; Rose; Silvanus, Silas, Sylvester, Sylvia; Stella; Victor, Victoria.

Idioms and Phrases

The idioms and phrases listed below occur in the text read. Learning them thoroughly will be of great help in reading.

> **mē invītō,** *against my will*
> **mōribus suīs,** *in accordance with their customs*
> **nōn dubium erat quīn,** *there was no doubt that*
> **omnibus rēbus comparātīs,** *when everything was ready*
> **plūrimum possunt,** *they are the most (very) powerful*
> **proelium committere,** *to begin battle*

Vocabulary Review

The following words, which appear frequently in this book, are important in second-year work. Their meanings should be thoroughly learned.

aciēs	dētrīmentum	jūs	occultus	respōnsum
aedificium	et . . . et	lapis	octō	restituō
alius	ferus	līber, -a, -um	plānitiēs	rogō
amīcitia	fidēs, -eī	mandātum	praefectus	satisfaciō
amplius (*adv.*)	firmus	mātūrus	praesēns	significō
bīnī	grātia	medius	proptereā	simulō
condiciō	grātīs	mereō, mereor	quā	stīpendium
congredior	grātulātiō	mors	quidem	testis
conquīrō	impetrō	mulier	quod sī	tumulus
custōs	incidō	mūnītiō	ratiō	ultrā
decimus	īnsequor	neque . . . neque	regiō	vehementer
dēsistō	item	nōnnūllus	rēs pūblica	victor

CAESAR'S ARMY IN ACTION

BEFORE Caesar completed his conquest of the Gallic tribes, his legions must have marched many hundred miles, in rain and sun, in heat and cold.

From twelve to fifteen miles was the average day's march, but on a forced march a distance of twenty-four miles, or even more, might be covered. Though fifteen miles is not a very long day's march, the Roman soldier was burdened with a heavy load.

Swung over his shoulder on a stick, he carried a pack (*sarcina*), which contained his rations for a number of days, a cooking utensil, his cloak, tools for constructing fortifications, and usually one or two stakes to use in making defenses for the camp. In addition he also carried his weapons and armor.

The legions marching in column were protected by a vanguard (*prīmum agmen*) and a rear-guard (*novissimum agmen*), and each was followed by its baggage train (*impedīmenta*). The baggage, transported on pack animals or in wagons, included clothing, provisions, hand-mills for grinding grain, extra weapons and armor, tents, and other military stores, as well as feed for the cavalry horses and the animals of the baggage train.

When danger threatened, the heavy baggage was sometimes placed in the center of the column, where it could be defended on all sides and would not interfere with the movement of the troops.

In the first line of the marching legion appeared its standard — a pole topped by a silver or a bronze eagle (*aquila*) with wings spread wide. The divisions of the legions also carried standards of various forms. Sometimes these had decorations, in recognition of some exploit of the division.

AQUILA

The eagle, the patriotic symbol of America, was also the emblem of the Roman legion.

Roman soldiers were trained in hand-to-hand fighting, and their equipment was especially suited to this type of combat. The chief weapons were the javelin (*pīlum*) and the sword (*gladius*). The javelin, about six and a half feet long, consisted of a stout wooden shaft with a long iron head. It was really a light spear used for hurling at the enemy.

When the trumpeters sounded the charge, the Roman soldiers usually rushed forward, hurling their javelins into the ranks of the foe from a distance of forty or fifty feet. Then they flung themselves upon their opponents, who generally met them in a similar charge.

The sword, straight, pointed, and rather short, was used for stabbing in hand-to-hand fighting. Since the Roman soldier was made to feel that it was an extreme disgrace to hold back during a fight or to retreat without orders, the

A ROMAN FIRST-AID STATION

The Roman army was equipped with a kind of hospital unit, as can be seen from this ancient sculpture.

conflict was usually one to the death between individuals.

For protection against blows and missiles, the Roman soldier wore a leather or metal helmet (*galea*), somewhat like the helmet used by soldiers today. He also wore a coat of mail (*lōrīca*), composed of metal plates fastened on leather. Sometimes he wore greaves, a form of armor which protected his shins. On his left arm he carried a shield (*scūtum*) of wooden boards covered with cloth and leather.

Sometimes the soldiers advanced with the front rank holding their shields before them, while the others held their shields joined over their heads—a formation known as the *testūdō*.

In those far-away days there were no Red-Cross workers to give

first aid, and no emergency hospitals back of the lines. There were, however, crude dressing stations. Carved on an ancient memorial column in Rome is a representation of soldiers having their wounds bandaged in such a station.

Besides fighting many open battles in Gaul, Caesar also captured a number of fortified towns. There were three chief ways of taking a town: by quick assault (*oppugnātiō repentīna*), by siege (*oppugnātiō*), involving more or less continuous attack, or by blockade (*obsidiō*), cutting the inhabitants off from food supplies.

The blockade was used where neither of the two forms of siege was possible. Strong lines of entrenchment (*circumvāllātiō*) were constructed around the unfortunate town to cut off access from outside sources, thus starving the inhabitants into surrender.

If the walls of a town were not strong, it was usually taken by quick assault. Under such circumstances the ditch or trench around the walls was hurriedly filled with earth and other materials so that the soldiers could come close to the walls. This was also done in case of siege. Then the gates or walls were battered down. Often the walls were scaled with the help of ladders (*scālae*). During the attack the light-armed troops of the Roman army shot arrows and threw stones from slings at the defenders on the wall.

The siege, which was often difficult and prolonged, called for the use of artillery. The Romans, without gunpowder and steel, could not, of course, produce anything so deadly as our modern cannon.

Their artillery, however, was so effective that the strongly fortified cities of their opponents usually fell before the Roman attack. Instead of the power created by the explosion of gunpowder, the power used in these ancient machines was created by tightly twisted strands of rope or hair attached to the framework of the engine. These were suddenly released to produce the force necessary to propel stones or arrows. Because of the twisting, these machines were called *tormenta* (from *torqueō*, twist).

Of these, the *catapulta* and *scorpiō* were used for shooting darts and spears. On the same column in Rome which shows the dressing-station there is portrayed a small *catapulta* mounted on a cart drawn by horses. The most powerful *catapultae*, however, were

THE CANNON OF THE ROMANS

The *ballista* was an effective piece of artillery which could hurl large stones into the forces of the enemy.

much larger. The *scorpiō* seems to have been similar to the *catapulta*, but smaller.

The *ballista* was another type of missile-throwing machine mentioned by Caesar. It was used to hurl stones. A large *ballista* could fling huge stones weighing from sixty to four hundred pounds. It was so arranged that the stones could be flung at an angle, doing immense damage to the walls of a beleaguered city.

The battering-ram (*ariēs*) was a large beam which was swung back and forth against the walls, breaking them down with repeated blows. In its simplest form the ram was carried by the soldiers, who drove it against the wall as heavily as they could. The larger battering-rams, however, were headed with iron and suspended by machinery, and it sometimes required as many as a hundred men to operate one. Only the strong-

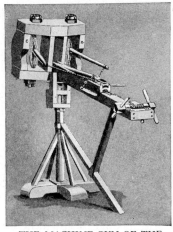

THE MACHINE-GUN OF THE ROMANS

A rain of darts and spears from a *catapulta* like this put many a barbarian force to flight.

WHAT HOPE FOR A GALLIC TOWN THUS BESIEGED?

est walls could resist the impact of these large rams.

Naturally the battering-rams and other engines of war were greatly feared by the defenders of the besieged town, who made every possible effort to destroy them. To protect their artillery the Romans sometimes built movable sheds. If all attempts from the wall failed, the defenders might tunnel under a ram or other device used in the attack.

Frequently in a prolonged siege the Romans used high towers which were moved on rollers close to the wall. Then they let down a bridge from the tower to the wall and tried to fight their way across. In these towers platforms were arranged, one above another, so that groups of soldiers might fight from different levels. The mere sight of such a tower before the stronghold of the Atuatuci so terrified its defenders that they begged for terms.

While the artillery was assailing the walls and the defenders of a town, men would sometimes tunnel under the walls. If they succeeded, soldiers would then creep through the tunnel, make their way to the gates, and throw them open.

In battle and on the march as well as while besieging towns, Caesar's legionaries showed the utmost strength, endurance, and daring. Although Caesar was one of the greatest military geniuses the world has ever known, he could not have achieved the conquest of Gaul if his men had not been trained and disciplined soldiers.

THE CRUSHING OF THE BELGIAN LEAGUE

You all do know this mantle; I remember
The first time ever Caesar put it on;
'Twas on a summer's evening, in his tent,
That day he overcame the Nervii.

SHAKESPEARE: JULIUS CAESAR.

War Clouds Gather in the North

CUM esset Caesar in citeriōre Galliā, ita utī[1] suprā dēmōnstrāvimus, crēbrī ad eum rūmōrēs afferēbantur litterīsque item Labiēnī certior fīēbat[2] omnēs Belgās, quam[3] tertiam esse Galliae partem dīxerāmus, contrā populum Rōmānum conjūrāre obsidēsque inter sē dare.

Conjūrandī hās esse causās[4]: prīmum, quod verērentur nē[5] omnī pācātā Galliā[6] ad eōs exercitus noster addūcerētur; deinde, quod ab nōnnūllīs Gallīs sollicitārentur. Ex hīs quīdam, ut[7] Germānōs diūtius in Galliā versārī nōluerant, ita[7] populī Rōmānī exercitum hiemāre atque inveterāscere (*become established*) in Galliā molestē ferēbant.[8] Nōnnūllī mōbilitāte (*on account of fickleness*) et levitāte (*lightness*) animī novīs imperiīs[9] studēbant. Ab aliīs quoque sollicitābantur quod in Galliā ā potentiōribus atque eīs quī ad condūcendōs hominēs[10] facultātēs habēbant vulgō (*commonly*) rēgna[11] occupābantur, quī minus facile eam rem imperiō nostrō[12] cōnsequī poterant.

---

[1] In place of the more usual **ut**. Notice that the indicative follows.

[2] *and also he was informed from time to time by letters from Labienus.* The imperfect is used here to denote repeated action.

[3] The antecedent is **Belgās,** but the pronoun is attracted into the gender and number of the predicate noun **partem**—*who, as we had said, constitute the third part of Gaul.*

[4] A continuation of the indirect discourse depending on **certior fīēbat,** line 5. Two reasons are given: (1) **prīmum, quod verērentur nē . . . addūcerētur;** and (2) **deinde, quod ab nōnnūllīs . . . sollicitārentur.**

[5] *that.* See Gr. S., 109.

[6] Here the word means Celtic Gaul, as described on page 136, lines 26-32.

[7] The words **ut** and **ita** are used to mean *as before . . . so now.*

[8] *resented it that . . . should winter.* The infinitives are in indirect discourse with **molestē ferēbant.**

[9] *a change of government;* dative case with **studēbant.** See Gr. S., 61.

[10] *for hiring mercenaries.*

[11] There was no hereditary monarchy in Gaul, but the stronger chiefs often assumed unlimited power. Caesar sometimes speaks of these leaders as kings.

[12] *under our sovereignty.*

189

Helpful Allies

Hīs nūntiīs litterīsque commōtus, Caesar duās legiōnēs in
citeriōre Galliā novās cōnscrīpsit,
et initā aestāte,[1] in ulteriōrem
5 Galliam[2] quī dēdūceret,[3] Q. Pedium[4]
lēgātum mīsit. Ipse, cum prīmum
pābulī[5] cōpia esse inciperet,[6] ad
exercitum vēnit. Dat negōtium
Senonibus[7] reliquīsque Gallīs quī
10 fīnitimī Belgīs erant utī ea quae
apud eōs gerantur cognōscant sēque
dē hīs rēbus certiōrem[8] faciant.
Hī cōnstanter (*continually*) omnēs
nūntiāvērunt manūs[9] cōgī, exercitum in ūnum locum condūcī. 15

Tum vērō dubitandum nōn exīstimāvit quīn ad eōs proficīscerētur.[10] Rē frūmentāriā prōvīsā castra movet, diēbusque circiter xv
ad fīnēs Belgārum pervenit. 20

Discretion Is the Better Part of Valor

A ROMAN ARCH IN RHEIMS
This city takes its name from the Remi.

Eō[11] cum dē imprōvīsō[12] celerius-
que omnium opīniōne[13] vēnisset, Rēmī, quī proximī Galliae[14] ex
Belgīs[15] sunt, ad eum lēgātōs Iccium
et Andebrogium,[16] prīmōs cīvitātis, 25
mīsērunt quī dīcerent sē suaque
omnia[17] in fidem atque potestātem
populī Rōmānī permittere,[18] neque
sē cum reliquīs Belgīs cōnsēnsisse
neque contrā populum Rōmānum 30
conjūrāsse, parātōsque esse et obsidēs dare et imperāta facere[19] et

[1] *at the beginning of summer;* ablative absolute. The year was 57 B.C.
[2] The phrase depends on **dēdūceret**.
[3] A relative clause of purpose, to be taken after the main clause.
[4] *Quintus Pedius* (pē'di-us), Julius Caesar's grandnephew.
[5] Food for the animals of the baggage train and for the cavalry horses.
[6] The usual construction with **cum prīmum**, *as soon as*, is the indicative, but here the clause is made a descriptive clause of situation.
[7] *the Senones* (sen'ō-nēz), a tribe of Celtic Gaul.
[8] In agreement with **sē**, the object of **faciant**. The corresponding passive construction occurs on page 189, line 5.
[9] Small bodies of troops, which made up the **exercitus**.

[10] *to set out* (literally, *but that he should set out*).
[11] Adverb, depending on **vēnisset**.
[12] The phrase means *unexpectedly*.
[13] *than anyone anticipated* (literally, *than the expectation of all*). For case see Gr. S., 77.
[14] Meaning Celtic Gaul; dative, depending on **proximī**.
[15] Translate like a genitive of the whole.
[16] *Andebrogius* (an-dē-brō'ji-us).
[17] *themselves and all their possessions;* object of **permittere**. The subject **sē** is omitted to avoid a repetition of the word.
[18] With **in fidem atque potestātem**— *put under the protection and sovereignty.*
[19] *to obey his orders* (literally, *to do the things commanded*).

oppidīs[1] recipere[2] et frūmentō cē-
terīsque rēbus juvāre.

Cōnfirmāvērunt reliquōs omnēs
Belgās in armīs esse, Germānōsque
5 quī cis (*on this side of*) Rhēnum in-
colant sēsē cum hīs conjūnxisse,
tantumque esse eōrum omnium fu-
rōrem ut nē Suessiōnēs[3] quidem,[4]
frātrēs cōnsanguineōsque suōs,
quī eōdem jūre[5] et eīsdem lēgi- 10
bus[6] ūtantur, ūnum imperium
ūnumque magistrātum cum ipsīs
habeant,[7] dēterrēre (*restrain*) potu-
erint[8] quīn cum hīs cōnsentīrent.[9]

The Gathering of the Clans

Cum ab eīs[10] quaereret quae
cīvitātēs quantaeque in armīs
essent et quid in bellō possent,[11] sīc
reperiēbat: plērōsque Belgās esse
ortōs ā Germānīs[12] Rhēnumque[13]
20 antīquitus trāductōs propter locī
fertilitātem (*fertility*) ibi cōnsēdisse,
Gallōsque[14] quī ea loca incolerent
expulisse, sōlōsque esse quī patrum
nostrōrum memoriā[15] omnī Galliā
25 vexātā[16] Teutonōs Cimbrōsque intrā suōs fīnēs ingredī prohibuerint;[17] quā ex rē fierī utī[18] eārum
rērum memoriā[19] magnam sibi auctōritātem magnōsque spīritūs in
rē mīlitārī sūmerent.[20]   30

Dē numerō eōrum omnia sē
habēre explōrāta Rēmī dīcēbant,
proptereā quod propinquitātibus
affīnitātibusque conjūnctī[21] quantam quisque multitūdinem in com- 35
mūnī Belgārum conciliō ad id
bellum pollicitus sit cognōverint.

Plūrimum inter eōs Bellovacōs
et virtūte[22] et auctōritāte[22] et hominum numerō[22] valēre;[23] hōs posse 40

[1] The ablative denotes both place and means.

[2] Supply eōs, i.e., Rōmānōs.

[3] Object of dēterrēre in line 13.

[4] The emphatic word stands between nē and quidem.

[5] *rights*.

[6] *laws*.

[7] Supply et quī before ūnum.

[8] The verb of the result clause, with ut, line 8.

[9] *from conspiring.* After words of hindering, preventing, and the like, the subjunctive with nē, quōminus, or quīn may be used.

[10] The envoys of the Remi.

[11] *what was their military strength.*

[12] Ablative of source or origin. With this kind of ablative ab is sometimes used, to denote remote origin, as here.

[13] Depends on the prefix (trāns) in trāductōs.

[14] Object of expulisse, which has the same subject as the other infinitives in lines 18-23.

[15] *in the time.*

[16] *having been overrun.* The Cimbri and the Teutons, German tribes from the shores of the Baltic, had overrun Celtic Gaul. They also had defeated several Roman armies, and were a constant menace to the safety of Rome itself till they were at last overthrown by Marius in the Battles of Aquae Sextiae (modern Aix, in France) and Vercellae (102, 101 B.C.).

[17] *prevented from entering.*

[18] *the result was that.* The subject of fierī is utī sūmerent.

[19] Ablative of cause. Contrast the meaning of this word in line 24.

[20] With magnōs spīritūs—*assumed great haughtiness.* Compare English "put on airs."

[21] *closely connected by ties of blood and by intermarriage.*

[22] Ablative of specification.

[23] With Plūrimum—*were the strongest.*

cōnficere armāta mīlia[1] centum; pollicitōs[2] ex eō numerō ēlēcta (*picked men*) mīlia LX, tōtīusque bellī imperium sibi postulāre.

5 Suessiōnēs suōs esse fīnitimōs; fīnēs lātissimōs ferācissimōsque agrōs possidēre. Apud eōs fuisse rēgem nostrā etiam memoriā Dīviciācum,[3] tōtīus Galliae poten- 10 tissimum, quī cum[4] magnae partis hārum regiōnum, tum[4] etiam Britanniae,[5] imperium obtinuerit; nunc esse rēgem Galbam; ad hunc propter jūstitiam prūdentiamque sum-

mam tōtīus bellī omnium volun- 15 tāte dēferrī; oppida habēre[6] numerō XII, pollicērī mīlia armāta L; totidem Nerviōs, quī maximē ferī inter ipsōs habeantur longissimēque absint;[7] xv mīlia Atrebātēs[8], Ambiā- 20 nōs x mīlia, Morinōs xxv mīlia, Menapiōs VII mīlia, Caletōs x mīlia, Veliocassēs et Viromanduōs totidem, Atuatucōs XIX mīlia; Condrūsōs,[9] Eburōnēs, Caerōsōs, 25 Caemānōs, quī ūnō nōmine Germānī appellantur, arbitrārī[10] ad XL mīlia.

Preparations to Meet the Foe

CAESAR, Rēmōs cohortātus līberāliterque ōrātiōne prōsecūtus,[11] omnem senātum[12] ad sē convenīre prīncipumque līberōs obsidēs[13] ad sē addūcī jussit. Quae omnia ab hīs dīligenter ad diem 35 facta sunt.

Ipse Dīviciācum Haeduum magnopere cohortātus docet quantō opere reī pūblicae[14] commūnisque salūtis intersit[15] manūs hostium distinērī, nē cum tantā multitūdine 40 ūnō tempore cōnflīgendum sit.[16] Id fierī posse, sī suās cōpiās Haeduī

[1] **armāta mīlia** is equivalent to **armātōrum mīlia;** so also **ēlēcta mīlia,** lines 2-3, is equivalent to **ēlēctōrum mīlia.**

[2] Supply **esse.**

[3] Not to be confused with the Haeduan of the same name who has previously been mentioned and is referred to in line 36 on this page.

[4] The words **cum** and **tum** are used to mean *not only . . . but also.*

[5] Probably only that part of the island nearest to Gaul.

[6] Supply **Suessiōnēs.**

[7] Meaning from the Province.

[8] All the tribes mentioned are of Belgic Gaul: *the Atrebates* (ạt're-bā'tēz); *the Ambiani* (am'bi-ā'nī); *the Morini* (mor'i-nī); *the Menapii* (mē-nā'pi-ī); *the Caleti* (kal'ē-tī);*the Veliocasses* (vē'li-ọ̄-kas'ēz); *the Viromandui* (vir'ọ̄-man'dū-ī); *the Atuatuci* (at'ū-at'ū-sī).

[9] The accusatives are subjects of **pollicērī** understood, the construction

depending on **arbitrārī,** line 27. These tribes are: *the Condrusi* (kọn-drö'sī); *the Eburones* (eb-ū-rō'nēz); *the Caerosi* (sē-rō'sī); *the Caemani* (sẹ-mā'nī).

[10] Supply **sē** (=**Rēmōs**) as subject.

[11] *addressing them with kindly words.*

[12] Caesar uses a Roman term to designate the Gallic council made up of the older and more influential men.

[13] Hostages were usually the chief men of a state or their children. They might be tortured or put to death if their tribe failed to keep its agreements.

[14] Meaning the Roman State. With forms of the impersonal verbs **interest** and **rēfert** the genitive of a noun may be used to denote the person or thing concerned.

[15] With **quantō opere**—*how greatly it concerned.* The subject of the verb is **manūs . . . distinērī.**

[16] *that they* (the Romans and their allies) *may not be compelled to fight.*

in fīnēs Bellovacōrum introdūxerint et eōrum agrōs populārī coeperint. Hīs datīs mandātīs, eum ā sē dīmittit.

5 Postquam omnēs Belgārum cōpiās in ūnum locum coāctās ad sē venīre vīdit, neque jam longē abesse ab eīs quōs mīserat explōrātōribus et ab Rēmīs cognōvit,[1] flūmen 10 Axonam, quod est in extrēmīs Rēmōrum fīnibus,[2] exercitum trādūcere mātūrāvit atque ibi castra posuit. Quae rēs[3] et[4] latus ūnum castrōrum rīpīs flūminis mūniēbat et,[4] post eum quae erant, tūta ab 15 hostibus reddēbat,[5] et[4] commeātūs ab Rēmīs reliquīsque cīvitātibus ut sine perīculō ad eum supportārī possent efficiēbat.[6]

In eō flūmine pōns erat. Ibi 20 praesidium pōnit et in alterā parte flūminis Q. Titūrium Sabīnum lēgātum cum sex cohortibus relinquit. Castra in altitūdinem pedum[7] XII vāllō fossāque duodēvīgintī 25 pedum[8] mūnīrī jubet.

"Help Us, or We Perish"

A B HĪS castrīs oppidum Rēmōrum nōmine[9] Bibrax aberat mīlia passuum VIII. Id ex 30 itinere[10] magnō impetū Belgae oppugnāre coepērunt. Aegrē eō diē sustentātum est.[11]

Gallōrum eadem atque Belgārum oppugnātiō est haec.[12] Ubi circum- jectā[13] multitūdine hominum tōtīs 35 moenibus, undique in mūrum lapidēs jacī coeptī sunt[14] mūrusque dēfēnsōribus[15] nūdātus est, testūdine factā, portās succēdunt mūrumque subruunt (*undermine*). 40

Quod tum[16] facile fīēbat. Nam cum tanta multitūdō lapidēs ac

---

[1] Translate in this order: **cognōvit ab eīs explōrātōribus quōs mīserat et ab Rēmīs [eās] nōn longē abesse (neque = et . . . nōn),** *and after he had learned from the scouts whom he had sent and from the Remi that they* (the forces of the Belgians) *were now not far distant.*

[2] *in the most remote part of the territory,* i.e., most remote from the Province.

[3] *this measure.*

[4] Correlative. Omit the first **et** in translation.

[5] *made (those places) which were behind him safe from the enemy.*

[6] A simpler order would be **efficiēbat ut commeātūs . . . possent.** For mood of **possent,** see Gr. S., 108.

[7] To be taken with **vāllō; pedum** is a descriptive genitive expressing measure.

[8] Meaning in width, measured at the top.

[9] Ablative of respect. We should say, *a town called Bibrax* (bib'raks).

[10] That is, without stopping to make the usual preparations for an assault.

[11] Translate by the personal construction, *they held out.*

[12] *(is) the same as (that) of the Belgians and is as follows.* With words meaning "like" or "unlike," **atque (ac)** may mean *as* or *than,* as explained on page 156, note 4.

[13] *having been stationed around.*

[14] The passive forms of this verb are commonly used when the dependent infinitive is passive.

[15] Ablative of separation.

[16] *on this occasion.* The description of a siege given above is general. Caesar now applies it to the particular siege of Bibrax.

tēla conjicerent,[1] in mūrō cōnsistendī potestās erat nūllī.[2] Cum fīnem oppugnandī nox fēcisset, Iccius Rēmus, summā nōbilitāte 5 et grātiā inter suōs, quī tum oppidō praeerat, ūnus ex eīs quī lēgātī[3] dē pāce ad Caesarem vēnerant, nūntiōs ad eum mittit: nisi subsidium sibi submittātur, sēsē diūtius sustinēre nōn posse.   10

Caesar to the Rescue

Eō[4] dē[5] mediā nocte Caesar, eīsdem ducibus[6] ūsus quī nūntiī ab Icciō vēnerant, Numidās[7] et Crētēs[8] sagittāriōs et funditōrēs 15 Baleārēs[9] subsidiō[10] oppidānīs[10] mittit; quōrum adventū et[11] Rēmīs cum spē dēfēnsiōnis (*of defense*) studium prōpugnandī[12] accessit,[13] et[14] hostibus eādem dē causā spēs 20 potiundī oppidī discessit.[13] Itaque paulisper apud oppidum morātī agrōsque Rēmōrum dēpopulātī, omnibus vīcīs aedificiīsque quō[15] adīre potuerant incēnsīs,[16] ad castra 25 Caesaris omnibus cōpiīs contendērunt et ā mīlibus[17] passuum minus[18] duōbus castra posuērunt;

From *The Roman Soldier*

AN ARCHER AND A SLINGER
The archers and slingers were not Romans, but auxiliary troops from the provinces.

[1] A causal clause. The verb is plural because it agrees in sense with **multitūdō,** page 193, line 42.

[2] *it was not possible for anyone to stand;* **nūllī** is a dative of possession. Caesar regularly uses this form for the dative of **nēmō.** The form **cōnsistendī** is genitive of the gerund, depending on **potestās.**

[3] *as envoys;* predicate appositive.

[4] To Bibrax.

[5] *immediately after.*

[6] *as guides;* predicate appositive. So also **nūntiī.**

[7] *the Numidians.* **Numidās** is used as a noun. The Numidians were auxiliary troops from one of the African provinces.

[8] *Cretan.* **Crētēs** is an adjective modifying **sagittāriōs.**

[9] *Balearic* (bal-ē-ar′ik), from the Balearic Islands in the Mediterranean, off the coast of Spain.

[10] The first dative is one of purpose; the second, one of reference. Translate freely, *to help the townspeople.*

[11] *on the one hand.*

[12] *an eagerness to take the offensive.* The forces under Iccius were so encouraged by the arrival of the reinforcements that they were eager to sally out and attack the besiegers.

[13] **accessit,** *was aroused in* (literally, *came to*); **discessit,** *left.* **Rēmīs** depends on **accessit; hostibus,** as dative of reference, on **discessit.**

[14] *on the other hand.*

[15] Equivalent to **ad quae** (i.e., **vīcōs aedificiaque**).

[16] Agrees with **vīcīs** and **aedificiīs** in the ablative absolute.

[17] Ablative of measure of difference, depending on **ā,** *off, away,* which is used adverbially.

[18] Here equivalent to **minus quam.**

quae castra, ut fūmō atque ignibus significābātur, amplius mīlibus[1] passuum VIII in lātitūdinem patēbant.

Just before the Battle

CAESAR prīmō et propter multitūdinem hostium et propter eximiam (*unusual*) opīniōnem virtūtis proeliō supersedēre (*to defer*) statuit. Cotīdiē tamen equestribus
10 proeliīs, quid hostis virtūte posset et quid nostrī audērent, perīclitābātur (*he was trying to find out*). In hīs proeliīs nostrōs nōn esse īnferiōrēs vidēbat.

15 Locus prō castrīs ad aciem īnstruendam nātūrā opportūnus atque idōneus erat, quod is collis ubi castra posita erant paulum ex plānitiē ēditus erat atque tantum[2]
20 adversus in lātitūdinem patēbat quantum locī aciēs īnstrūcta occupāre poterat. Ex utrāque parte[3] lateris dējectūs (*slopes*) habēbat et in fronte lēniter (*gradually*) fastīgātus (*sloping*) paulātim ad 25 plānitiem redībat.

Itaque ab utrōque latere ejus collis trānsversam[4] fossam obdūxit (*extended*) circiter passuum CD et ad extrēmās fossās castella cōnstituit. 30 Tormenta ibi collocāvit nē cum aciem īnstrūxisset, hostēs, quod tantum multitūdine poterant, ab lateribus[5] pugnantēs suōs circumvenīre possent. 35

Hōc factō, duābus legiōnibus quās proximē cōnscrīpserat in castrīs relictīs, ut, sī quō opus esset,[6] subsidiō dūcī possent, reliquās sex legiōnēs prō castrīs in aciē cōnstituit. Hostēs item suās cōpiās ex 40 castrīs ēductās īnstrūxērunt.

The Conflict Begins

PALŪS erat nōn magna inter nostrum[7] atque hostium exercitum.
45 Hanc sī nostrī trānsīrent,[8] hostēs expectābant. Nostrī autem, sī ab illīs initium trānseundī fieret, ut impedītōs[9] aggrederentur parātī in armīs erant.

Interim proeliō equestrī inter 50 duās aciēs contendēbātur. Ubi neutrī trānseundī initium faciunt, secundiōre equitum proeliō nostrīs,[10] Caesar suōs in castra redūxit.

Hostēs prōtinus ex eō locō ad 55 flūmen Axonam contendērunt,

---

[1] Ablative of comparison. See Gr. S., 77.

[2] Translate **tantum . . . poterat** freely, *was wide enough on the side facing the enemy to afford space for a battle-line.*

[3] *end.*

[4] *at right angles* (*to the hill*).

[5] *on the flanks.*

[6] *if there should be need* (*of their being led*) *anywhere.*

[7] Supply **exercitum.**

[8] *in case our men should cross,* or *to see if,* etc.

[9] By the crossing of the swamp, when they could not defend themselves effectively.

[10] *and when the cavalry battle had resulted favorably for our men;* ablative absolute suggesting cause; **nostrīs** is dative.

quod esse post nostra castra dēmōnstrātum est. Ibi vadīs reper-
tīs, partem suārum cōpiārum trādūcere cōnātī sunt eō cōnsiliō ut,
5 sī possent, castellum, cui praeerat
Q. Titūrius lēgātus, expugnārent
pontemque interscinderent (*might
cut down*); sī minus[1] potuissent,
agrōs Rēmōrum populārentur, quī
magnō nōbīs ūsuī ad bellum geren- 1c
dum erant, commeātūque nostrōs
prohibērent.[2]

Unavailing Valor

CAESAR certior factus ab Ti-
túriō omnem equitātum et
15 levis armātūrae Numidās,[3] funditōrēs sagittāriōsque ponte[4] trādūcit atque ad eōs contendit. Ācriter in eō locō pugnātum est. Hostēs
impedītōs nostrī[5] in flūmine ag-
20 gressī magnum eōrum numerum
occīdērunt; per eōrum corpora reliquōs audācissimē trānsīre cōnantēs
multitūdine tēlōrum reppulērunt,
prīmōsque, quī trānsierant, equi-
25 tātū circumventōs interfēcērunt.

Hostēs ubi et dē expugnandō oppidō et dē flūmine trānseundō spem
sē fefellisse[6] intellēxērunt neque
nostrōs in locum inīquiōrem prō-
30 gredī[7] pugnandī causā vīdērunt,
atque ipsōs[8] rēs frūmentāria dēficere coepit, conciliō convocātō, cōnstituērunt optimum esse[9] domum
suam quemque revertī et, quōrum[10]
in fīnēs prīmum Rōmānī exerci- 35
tum intrōdūxissent, ad eōs dē-
fendendōs undique convenīre ut
potius in suīs quam in aliēnīs fīnibus dēcertārent et domesticīs cōpiīs
reī frūmentāriae ūterentur. 40

Ad eam sententiam cum reliquīs
causīs haec quoque ratiō[11] eōs dēdūxit, quod[12] Dīviciācum atque
Haeduōs fīnibus[13] Bellovacōrum
appropinquāre cognōverant.[14] Hīs 45
persuādērī ut diūtius morārentur
neque suīs auxilium ferrent nōn
poterat.[15]

[1] *if . . . not.*
[2] In the same construction as **expugnārent**, line 6.
[3] *the Numidian light infantry.*
[4] Ablative of route.
[5] Subject of **occīdērunt**. Other acts of
the same subject are expressed by **reppulērunt**, line 23, and **interfēcērunt**,
line 25.
[6] *that they were deceived in their hope*
(literally, *that their hope had deceived
them*). Review the principal parts of
fallō.
[7] The phrase is equivalent to **et nostrōs nōn prōgredī** (vīdērunt).
[8] Meaning the enemy. The Gauls
had not learned the necessity of providing for an adequate food supply.

[9] The subject is **quemque revertī**.
[10] The antecedent of **quōrum** is **eōs**,
line 36.
[11] *this further consideration.* The adverb **quoque** emphasizes the word immediately preceding; **haec ratiō** is explained by the **quod** clause.
[12] When introducing a substantive
clause, **quod** is regularly translated *that*
or *the fact that.*
[13] Dative with **appropinquāre**.
[14] Translate as an imperfect (*they had
found out = they knew*). Similarly the
perfect, **cognōvī**, may be translated,
I know.
[15] With **Hīs persuādērī**—*these* (the
Bellovaci) *could not be persuaded* (literally, *it could not be persuaded to them*).

A CAVALRYMAN

A Disastrous Retreat

A ROMAN OF CAESAR'S TIME
To this Roman of the Republican era, Caesar's
campaigns in Gaul were probably absorbing
"current events."

Eā rē cōnstitūtā, secundā vigiliā magnō cum strepitū ac tumultū castrīs ēgressī[1] nūllō certō ōrdine neque imperiō,[2] cum sibi quisque prīmum itineris locum peteret et domum pervenīre properāret, fēcērunt ut cōnsimilis (*very like*) fugae profectiō vidērētur.[3]

Hāc rē statim Caesar per speculātōrēs (*scouts*) cognitā īnsidiās veritus, quod quā dē causā discēderent nōndum perspexerat, exercitum equitātumque castrīs continuit. Prīmā lūce, cōnfirmātā rē ab explōrātōribus, omnem equitātum, quī novissimum agmen[4] morārētur,[5] praemīsit.

Hīs Q. Pedium[6] et L. Aurunculeium Cottam lēgātōs praefēcit. T. Labiēnum lēgātum cum[7] legiōnibus tribus subsequī jussit.

Hī novissimōs adortī et multa mīlia passuum prōsecūtī magnam multitūdinem eōrum fugientium concīdērunt, cum ab extrēmō agmine ad quōs ventum erat[8] cōnsisterent fortiterque impetum nostrōrum mīlitum sustinērent; priōrēs,[9] quod abesse ā perīculō vidērentur[10] neque ūllā necessitāte (*by any need*) neque imperiō continērentur,[10] exaudītō (*having been heard*) clāmōre, perturbātīs ōrdinibus omnēs in fugā sibi praesidium pōnerent.

Ita sine ūllō perīculō tantam eōrum multitūdinem nostrī interfēcērunt quantum fuit diēī spatium.[11] Sub occāsum sōlis sequī dēstitērunt sēque in castra, ut erat imperātum, recēpērunt.

---

[1] The participle may be translated as if correlative with **fēcērunt,** line 7— *they set out . . . and.*

[2] *with no definite order or leadership.*

[3] *made their departure seem,* etc. For the use of the ut clause see Gr. S., 108.

[4] *the rear.*

[5] Subjunctive in a relative clause of purpose.

[6] See page 190, note 4.

[7] The preposition could not be omit-ted here, because the modifier is a numeral. See Gr. S., 80, *b.*

[8] With **cum ab extrēmō agmine,** etc., —*since those in the extreme rear, whom our men had overtaken;* **ventum erat** is an impersonal passive. The resistance of the scattered bands along the rear line could accomplish little against the Roman legionaries.

[9] (*while*) *those in front,* etc.

[10] For the subjunctive see Gr. S., 118.

[11] *as the length of the day allowed.*

SOISSONS, THE MODERN FRENCH CITY NAMED FOR THE SUESSIONES

Resistance Is Hopeless

Postrīdiē ejus diēī Caesar, priusquam sē hostēs ex terrōre ac fugā reciperent, in fīnēs Suessiōnum, quī proximī Rēmīs erant, exercitum dūxit et magnō itinere[1] ad oppidum Noviodūnum[2] contendit.

Id ex itinere oppugnāre cōnātus, quod vacuum ab dēfēnsōribus esse[3] audiēbat, propter lātitūdinem fossae mūrīque altitūdinem, paucīs dēfendentibus,[4] expugnāre nōn potuit.

Castrīs mūnītīs, vīneās agere[5] quaeque[6] ad oppugnandum ūsuī erant[7] comparāre coepit. Interim omnis ex fugā Suessiōnum multitūdō in oppidum proximā nocte convēnit.

Celeriter vīneīs ad oppidum āctīs, aggere jactō[8] turribusque cōnstitūtīs, magnitūdine operum, quae[9] neque vīderant ante Gallī neque audīverant, et celeritāte Rōmānōrum permōtī lēgātōs ad Caesarem dē dēditiōne mittunt et, petentibus Rēmīs[10] ut cōnservārentur,[11] impetrant.[12]

[1] *by a forced march*—from twenty-four to thirty miles. An ordinary day's march was about twelve to fifteen miles.

[2] *Noviodunum* (nō'vi-ọ-dö'num), a town of the Suessiones, near modern Soissons (swä-sôṅ).

[3] *was without defenders;* **dēfēnsōribus** is an ablative of separation.

[4] *although there were only a few defenders.*

[5] *to move up,* or *to advance.*

[6] The word is equivalent to **et (ea) quae.**

[7] *were necessary;* **ūsuī** is a dative of purpose.

[8] *after an earthwork had been constructed.*

[9] *such as.*

[10] *at the request of the Remi;* ablative absolute.

[11] Depends on **petentibus.**

[12] *they obtain their wish;* used absolutely.

PUERĪ MULIERĒSQUE PĀCEM AB RŌMĀNĪS PETĪVĒRUNT

A Plea for Mercy

CAESAR, obsidibus[1] acceptīs prīmīs[2] cīvitātis atque ipsīus Galbae rēgis duōbus fīliīs, armīsque omnibus ex oppidō trāditīs, in dē-
5 ditiōnem Suessiōnēs accipit exercitumque in Bellovacōs dūcit.

Quī cum sē suaque omnia in oppidum Bratuspantium[3] contulissent, atque ab eō oppidō Caesar
10 cum exercitū circiter mīlia passuum v abesset, omnēs majōrēs nātū[4] ex oppidō ēgressī manūs ad Caesarem tendere et vōce significāre coepērunt sēsē in ejus fidem ac potestātem venīre[5] neque contrā populum Rōmānum armīs contendere.

Item, cum ad oppidum accessisset castraque ibi pōneret, puerī[6] mulierēsque ex mūrō passīs[7] manibus suō mōre pācem ab Rōmānīs petīvērunt.

[1] *as hostages.*

[2] *the leading men;* see page 192, note 12.

[3] *Bratuspantium* (brat-us-pan'shium). See map, page 137.

[4] *the old men;* **nātū** is an ablative of respect.

[5] *gave themselves up to his protection and submitted to his authority.*

[6] *children.*

[7] The sense will make it possible to decide whether this participle comes from **pandō** or **patior.**

The Appeal of a Friend

PRŌ[1] hīs Dīviciācus (nam post discessum Belgārum dīmissīs Haeduōrum cōpiīs ad eum[2] reverterat) facit verba[3]: Bellovacōs omnī
5 tempore in fidē atque amīcitiā cīvitātis Haeduae fuisse; impulsōs[4] ab suīs prīncipibus, quī dīcerent Haeduōs ā Caesare in servitūtem redāctōs[5] omnēs indignitātēs contu-
10 mēliāsque perferre,[6] et ab Haeduīs dēfēcisse et populō Rōmānō bellum intulisse.

Quī[7] ejus cōnsiliī prīncipēs fuissent, quod intellegerent quantam calamitātem cīvitātī[8] intulissent, in 15 Britanniam profūgisse. Petere[9] nōn sōlum Bellovacōs sed etiam prō hīs Haeduōs ut suā[10] clēmentiā ac mānsuētūdine (*mercy*) in eōs[11] ūtātur. Quod sī fēcerit,[12] Haeduōrum auctō- 20 ritātem apud omnēs Belgās amplificātūrum,[13] quōrum auxiliīs atque opibus, sī qua bella inciderint, sustentāre cōnsuērint.[14]

Plain Living Makes Bold Fighters

CAESAR honōris Dīviciācī[15] atque Haeduōrum causā[16] sēsē eōs in fidem receptūrum[17] et cōnservātūrum dīxit; et quod erat cīvitās magnā inter Belgās auctō-
30 ritāte atque hominum multitūdine[18] praestābat, DC obsidēs poposcit.

Hīs trāditīs omnibusque armīs ex oppidō collātīs, ab eō locō in

fīnēs Ambiānōrum[19] pervēnit, quī sē 35 suaque omnia sine morā dēdidērunt.

Eōrum fīnēs Nerviī attingēbant; quōrum dē nātūrā mōribusque Caesar cum quaereret, sīc reperiēbat: 40 nūllum esse aditum ad eōs mercātōribus;[20] nihil patī[21] vīnī[22] reliquārumque rērum[22] ad lūxuriam (*luxury*) pertinentium īnferrī, quod hīs

[1] *in behalf of.*
[2] Caesar.
[3] *spoke as follows;* introducing indirect discourse.
[4] Participle, agreeing with **eōs**, which is to be supplied as subject of **dēfēcisse**, line 11, and **intulisse**, line 12.
[5] *having been reduced.*
[6] *were enduring.*
[7] Supply as antecedent **eōs**, the subject of **profūgisse**, line 16.
[8] Why dative?
[9] The subjects are **Bellovacōs** and **Haeduōs.**
[10] *his well-known.*
[11] Referring to **Bellovacōs.**
[12] *if he should do this.*
[13] *would increase.* Supply **eum** (i.e., **Caesarem**) as subject.
[14] Freely, *upon whose assistance and*

resources they always relied whenever any war broke out. The ablatives **auxiliīs** and **opibus** denote means.
[15] Objective genitive depending on **honōris.**
[16] The phrase **honōris causā** means *out of respect for.* It depends on the infinitives **receptūrum** and **cōnservātūrum** (**esse**).
[17] *would take under his protection.*
[18] *in numbers;* ablative of respect.
[19] *of the Ambiani.*
[20] *traders had;* **mercātōribus** is dative of possession. The Greek and Roman traders carried on a rather extensive commerce throughout Gaul and parts of Germany.
[21] *they allow.*
[22] Genitive of the whole, depending on **nihil.**

rēbus relanguēscere animōs et re-
mittī virtūtem[1] exīstimārent; esse
hominēs ferōs magnaeque virtūtis;
increpitāre (*they rebuked*) atque
5 incūsāre reliquōs Belgās, quī sē

populō Rōmānō dēdidissent pa-
triamque[2] virtūtem prōjēcissent;
cōnfirmāre[3] sēsē neque lēgātōs mis-
sūrōs neque ūllam condiciōnem
pācis acceptūrōs.   10

How Labienus Saved the Day

THE Nervii had prevailed on two other tribes, the Atrebates and the Viromandui, to join them in making a stand against the Romans. They had developed in their country a unique system of defense against cavalry raids from neighboring tribes, and they probably counted on this to cause difficulties for Caesar's army. Here and there they had made rows of hedges by slashing young trees and bending them over. From these saplings the branches had grown up, making a thicket. This had been reinforced by thorn bushes and briers planted thickly among the saplings.

With their combined forces, which greatly outnumbered Caesar's army, the Gauls took up a position on a wooded hill near the banks of the Sambre[4] River. Here they waited in hiding for the approach of Caesar's forces. When the first Roman detachment appeared on a hill across the valley, the Gauls swept down to the river and up the slope on the opposite side.

The Romans had selected a place on the hill as a site for a camp, and were just beginning to construct the usual defenses. When the attack occurred, some of the soldiers were strung out in marching order and some were busy with their shovels. The situation was one of confusion.

Luckily for Caesar the soldiers were veterans, who did not have to wait for orders. They fell into line wherever they happened to be, without stopping to hunt for the military unit to which they belonged. The commander rushed from one part of the battle-front to another, trying to make the customary appeal to the soldiers. But there was little time for conventional procedure. At one point where Caesar found the soldiers massed so closely that they could not use their weapons effectively, he snatched a shield from a soldier and pushed his way into the front ranks to reorganize the hard-pressed line.

On one flank, Labienus, the most efficient of Caesar's officers, drove the attacking force back across the valley and pursued them up the opposite slope. From this elevation he saw that the Gauls had broken through the Roman center and were in the camp. He promptly sent back one legion. The Gauls were apparently caught between two lines, and in spite of a desperate and heroic resistance they were routed.

After the battle a delegation from the Nervii came to plead for peace. Satisfied that they were sufficiently humbled, Caesar granted them generous terms.

[1] Freely, *the warlike spirit was weakened, and courage was diminished.*
[2] *inherited from their ancestors.*

[3] *they asserted that they would,* etc.
[4] Pronounced sän-br. This was the ancient Sabis. See map, page 137.

"Here We Take Our Stand"

ATUATUCĪ, dē quibus suprā[1] dīximus, cum omnibus cōpiīs auxiliō Nerviīs[2] venīrent, hāc pugnā nūntiātā, ex itinere domum reverterunt. Cūnctīs (*all*) oppidīs castellīsque dēsertīs, sua omnia in ūnum oppidum ēgregiē (*excellently*) nātūrā mūnītum contulērunt.

Quod cum[3] ex omnibus in circuitū partibus[4] altissimās rūpēs dējectūsque (*and descents*) habēret, ūnā ex parte lēniter acclīvis[5] aditus in lātitūdinem nōn amplius pedum[6] cc relinquēbātur, quem locum duplicī altissimō mūrō mūnierant; tum magnī ponderis saxa et praeacūtās trabēs in mūrō collocābant.

Ipsī erant ex Cimbrīs Teutonīsque prōgnātī (*descended*), quī, cum iter in prōvinciam nostram atque Ītaliam facerent, eīs impedīmentīs quae sēcum agere[7] ac portāre nōn poterant citrā (*on this side of*) flūmen Rhēnum dēpositīs, custōdiae[8] ac praesidiō[9] VI mīlia hominum ūnā[10] relīquerant. Hī post eōrum[11] obitum (*death*) multōs annōs ā fīnitimīs exagitātī (*having been harassed*), cum aliās[12] bellum īnferrent, aliās[12] illātum dēfenderent,[13] cōnsēnsū[14] eōrum omnium, pāce factā, hunc sibi domiciliō (*for a home*) locum dēlēgerant.

A Scornful Foe

AC PRĪMŌ adventū exercitūs[15] nostrī crēbrās ex oppidō excursiōnēs (*sallies*) faciēbant parvulīsque proeliīs[16] cum nostrīs contendēbant. Posteā vāllō pedum XII,[17] in circuitū xv mīlium[18] crēbrīsque castellīs circummūnītī[19] oppidō sēsē continēbant.

Ubi vīneīs āctīs, aggere extrūctō, turrim procul cōnstituī vīdērunt, prīmum irrīdēre[20] ex mūrō atque increpitāre[20] (*taunted*) vōcibus,

[1] The passage to which Caesar refers is not included in this book, since that portion of the *Gallic War* is summarized (p. 202).

[2] For construction see page 194, note 10.

[3] *although this,* or *while this.* The adversative **cum** as well as **cum** in a descriptive clause of situation may occasionally be translated, as here, *while.*

[4] *on all* (*the other*) *sides.*

[5] *gently sloping.*

[6] Genitive of measure depending on **aditus.** The construction is not affected by **amplius.**

[7] The **impedīmenta** included cattle as well as portable belongings.

[8] *as a guard,* who had the immediate care of the baggage. They were not necessarily of the soldier class.

[9] *a garrison,* to protect the place; **praesidiō** and **custōdiae** are datives of purpose.

[10] Adverb.

[11] *of the others*—their countrymen who had invaded Italy and the Province, and had been overwhelmingly defeated by Marius.

[12] For correlative use of **aliās** see Vocabulary.

[13] *waged defensive war* (literally, *warded off war waged against them*).

[14] Depends on **dēlēgerant.**

[15] *immediately after the arrival of our army;* **prīmō** is an adjective.

[16] *in skirmishes;* literally, *in small battles.*

[17] Meaning in height.

[18] Supply **pedum.**

[19] *having been fortified all around.*

[20] Historical infinitive. See Gr. S., 126.

quod tanta māchinātiō (*machine*) ā tantō spatiō[1] īnstituerētur: Quibusnam manibus[2] aut quibus vīribus[3] praesertim hominēs tan-
5 tulae statūrae (nam plērumque[4] omnibus Gallīs prae magnitūdine corporum suōrum brevitās nostra contemptuī est[5]) tantī oneris tur- rim in mūrō sēsē posse collocāre cōnfīderent[6]?   10

He Laughs Best Who Laughs Last

UBI vērō[7] movērī[8] et appropin- quāre mūrīs vīdērunt, novā atque inūsitātā speciē commōtī, lē-
15 gātōs ad Caesarem dē pāce mīsē- runt, quī ad hunc modum locūtī[9]: nōn sē exīstimāre Rōmānōs sine ope dīvīnā bellum gerere, quī tan- tae altitūdinis māchinātiōnēs (*ma- chines*) tantā celeritāte prōmovēre
20 (*move forward*) possent; sē suaque omnia eōrum potestātī permittere dīxērunt.

Ūnum petere[10] ac dēprecārī: sī forte prō[11] suā clēmentiā ac mān- suētūdine (*mercy*), quam ipsī ab 25 aliīs audīrent, statuisset Atuatucōs esse cōnservandōs, nē sē armīs[12] dēspoliāret (*he would not deprive*). Sibi omnēs ferē fīnitimōs esse ini- mīcōs ac suae virtūtī invidēre 30 (*envy*); ā quibus[13] sē dēfendere trāditīs armīs nōn possent.

Sibi praestāre,[14] sī in eum cāsum dēdūcerentur, quamvīs (*any*) for- tūnam ā populō Rōmānō patī 35 quam ab hīs per cruciātum[15] inter- ficī inter quōs dominārī (*to rule*) cōnsuēssent.

Terms of Surrender

AD HAEC Caesar respondit: sē magis cōnsuētūdine suā quam meritō eōrum[16] cīvitātem cōn- servātūrum, sī, priusquam mūrum aries attigisset, sē dēdidissent; sed dēditiōnis nūllam esse condiciōnem nisi armīs trāditīs. Sē id quod in 45 Nerviīs fēcisset factūrum fīnitimīs-

[1] *so far off.* For case see page 194, note 17.

[2] *with what hands, pray?* A touch of sarcasm is added to the question by the use of the suffix **-nam.**

[3] What is the nominative singular of this word? The nominative plural?

[4] Neuter accusative used as an ad- verb.

[5] *our short stature is an object of con- tempt;* **contemptuī** is a dative of purpose.

[6] The Gauls had no knowledge of movable towers, but knew only of such as were built upon walls; and so they naturally believed that this one, too, was to be placed on the wall.

[7] *however.*

[8] Supply **turrim** as subject.

[9] Governs the indirect discourse through **possent,** line 20. The rest of the sentence is governed by **dīxērunt,** line 22.

[10] More exactly defined by **dēprecārī.** Translate the two verbs, *they earnestly begged for.*

[11] *in accordance with,* i.e., as was to be expected from.

[12] Ablative of separation.

[13] *from them.*

[14] *that it was better for them.*

[15] *by torture;* almost equivalent to an ablative of means.

[16] Equivalent to a causal clause— *because they deserved it.*

que imperātūrum nē quam[1] dēditīciīs (*upon the captives*) populī Rōmānī injūriam īnferrent.[2]

Rē renūntiātā ad suōs, illī sē
5 quae imperārentur[3] facere dīxērunt. Armōrum magnā multitūdine dē mūrō in fossam quae erat ante oppidum[4] jactā, sīc ut prope summam mūrī aggerisque altitūdinem acervī armōrum adaequārent,[5] et tamen 10 circiter parte tertiā, ut posteā perspectum est, cēlātā atque in oppidō retentā, portīs patefactīs eō diē pāce sunt ūsī.[6]

Treachery and Its Punishment

SUB vesperum Caesar portās
claudī mīlitēsque ex oppidō exīre jussit, nē quam noctū oppidānī ā mīlitibus injūriam acciperent.

20 Illī ante initō, ut intellēctum est, cōnsiliō,[7] quod dēditiōne factā nostrōs praesidia dēductūrōs aut dēnique indīligentius (*somewhat carelessly*) servātūrōs crēdiderant, 25 partim cum[8] eīs quae retinuerant et cēlāverant armīs, partim scūtīs ex cortice (*bark*) factīs aut vīminibus[9] intextīs, quae subitō,[10] ut temporis exiguitās (*shortness*) postulābat, pellibus indūxerant, tertiā 30 vigiliā, quā[11] minimē arduus (*steep*) ad nostrās mūnītiōnēs[12] ascēnsus (*ascent*) vidēbātur, omnibus cōpiīs repente ex oppidō ēruptiōnem fēcērunt. 35

Celeriter, ut ante Caesar imperāverat, ignibus[13] significātiōne factā, ex proximīs castellīs eō concursum est,[14] pugnātumque ab hostibus ita ācriter est[14] ut ā virīs forti- 40 bus in extrēmā spē salūtis inīquō locō contrā eōs quī ex vāllō turribusque tēla jacerent pugnārī dēbuit,[15] cum in ūnā virtūte omnis spēs salūtis cōnsisteret. 45

Occīsīs ad[16] hominum mīlibus IV reliquī in oppidum rejectī sunt. Postrīdiē ejus diēī, refrāctīs (*having been broken down*) portīs, cum jam dēfenderet nēmō, atque intrōmissīs 50

[1] The indefinite adjective, modifying **injūriam**.

[2] With **nē**, etc., *not to inflict any injury*, etc.

[3] Subjunctive in a subordinate clause in indirect discourse; **quae** is a relative with an antecedent, **ea**, understood.

[4] We are told on page 203, lines 11-15, that the wall and ditch were about two hundred feet long.

[5] *so that the piles of weapons were almost on a level with the highest point of the wall and the earthworks.*

[6] *they remained peaceable.*

[7] *according to a prearranged plan* (literally, *a plan having previously been formed*).

[8] Governs **eīs armīs**, and also **scūtīs**.

[9] Ablative of means or material, depending on **intextīs** (supply **scūtīs**). Translate, *woven from osiers* (i.e., willows or other shrubs with pliant twigs).

[10] *hurriedly.*

[11] *where.*

[12] The surrounding siege-works built by the Romans, which were higher than the ground at the foot of the plateau on which the **oppidum** was situated.

[13] *signal fires.*

[14] Translate by a personal verb in the active voice.

[15] With **ā virīs fortibus**, lines 40-41. Translate freely, *as one should have expected brave men to fight.*

[16] *about.* The word **ad** is here an adverb.

(*having been admitted*) mīlitibus nostrīs sectiōnem[1] ejus oppidī ūniversam Caesar vēndidit (*sold*). Ab eīs quī ēmerant capitum (*of individuals*) numerus ad eum relātus est mīlium LIII.

The End of the Campaign

AT THE same time, Publius Crassus, who had been sent against the tribes living along the northwest coast of Gaul, reported their surrender. This apparently completed for the time the conquest of Gaul.

Caesar's fame and the prestige of Rome were now so great that delegations came from some of the German tribes which lived on the other side of the Rhine, promising to give hostages and agreeing to submit to Roman authority.

The Roman legions were stationed in winter quarters in the regions where they had been fighting, and their commander started to Italy.

The news of Caesar's victories had already reached Rome, and a public thanksgiving of fifteen days was decreed—an honor which no one had ever received before.

[1] *booty*. This was not merely the property belonging to the Atuatuci, but the people themselves, who were sold as slaves.

COMPREHENSION QUESTIONS

The main events described in Caesar's account of the crushing of the Belgian league are referred to in the following questions.

1. Where did Caesar spend the winter following the war with Ariovistus?
2. What were the reasons for the dissatisfaction among the Belgians?
3. Which one of the Belgian tribes first submitted to the Romans?
4. What was said to be the origin of most of the Belgian tribes?
5. How were the Haeduans directed to assist in breaking up the Belgian confederacy?
6. To what tribe did Bibrax belong? Where was Bibracte? (See map, p. 137.)
7. What was the result of the battle on the Aisne?
8. What plan did the Belgians adopt after the battle?
9. Why was Caesar unable to capture Noviodunum by the first assault?
10. Who interceded on behalf of the Suessiones?
11. What was the origin of the Atuatuci?
12. Who were the Cimbri and Teutons?
13. How did the Roman soldiers compare in size with the Gallic warriors?
14. What influenced the Atuatuci to surrender?
15. What secret preparations did the Atuatuci make for renewing the war?
16. From what material did they make shields to replace those which had been surrendered?
17. In what way did Caesar give the signal of danger to his troops?
18. What was done with the inhabitants of the town after its surrender?

WORD STUDY VI

Place Names of Latin Origin

Many place names in our own country and in other countries are derived from Latin words. As in the case of other derivatives, some of these have come through French, Spanish, or Italian.

ARGENTINA, from **argentum,** *silver.* The early explorers obtained silver ornaments from the Indians in this region.

AUGUSTA, feminine form of the adjective **augustus,** *majestic.* This word was given as an honorary title to the wife of the Emperor Augustus.

CHESTER, from **castra.** Hence, the place of a camp. Various forms of **castra** are seen in the place names "Lancaster," "Dorchester," "Worcester."

ECUADOR, the Spanish word for *equator,* from the Latin **aequātor,** *that which makes equal,* from **aequāre,** *to make equal.* Hence, the imaginary line which makes an equal division of the surface of the earth into northern and southern hemispheres is called the equator, and the Spanish-speaking country through which this line passes is called Ecuador.

NEVADA, a Spanish word from the Latin **nivāta,** which comes from **nix, nivis,** *snow.* Hence "Nevada" means "snowy," and the state is so named because of the snow-covered mountains on its western border.

PROVIDENCE, from **prōvidēre,** *to see beforehand,* or *to act with foresight.*

RIO GRANDE, two Spanish words, the first from the Latin **rīvus,** *stream,* and the second from **grandis,** *large.* Hence, the great river.

VERMONT, from French **vert,** *green* (Latin **viridis**), and **mont,** *mountain* (Latin **mōns, montis**). Hence, the Green Mountain State.

EXERCISES

1. Find Latin words in the following: Florida (through Spanish); Mediterranean; Montana; Montenegro (through Italian); Pennsylvania; Virginia.

2. Make a list of towns and cities with names derived from Latin words.

Vocabulary Review

The following words, which appear frequently in this book, are important in second-year work. Their meanings should be thoroughly learned.

accēdō	cōnflīgō	expediō	populor	tamen
addūcō	conjūrō	fors	possideō	tendō
aditus	cōnsentiō	frōns	potius	terror
agger	cōnsistō	funditor	prōtinus	totidem
aliēnus	contumēlia	impellō	quīdam	tōtus
altitūdō	cum . . . tum	īnsidiae	rēgnum	trabs
arbitror	dēcertō	īnstruō	repente	tumultus
autem	dēdō	interim	rēs frūmentāria	undique
castellum	dēfēnsor	nūllus	sagittārius	ūsus
collocō	ēditus	oppidānus	sōlus	vacuus
commeātus	efficiō	partim	speciēs	vērō
comparō	equester	permittō	subitō	vigilia

CONSTRUCTING A ROMAN CAMP

In this scene taken from the decorations on a Roman column, a foreman supervises two soldiers bringing up materials, while above, two soldiers lift a heavy stone into position.

CAESAR'S ARMY ENCAMPED

CAESAR'S forces never spent a night outside a fortified camp (*castra*). Even when they were on the march, their overnight camps were fortified carefully according to a set plan. This was, of course, a necessary measure of defense in a hostile country; but even when no danger threatened, the legionaries entrenched themselves for the night.

While the troops were still marching, men were sent ahead to find a suitable place for the camp. They searched for an open site, on high ground if possible, so that the enemy could not make a surprise attack on the camp. It was essential that they find a site with an abundant supply of water for men and animals, and also that there be woods near by where fuel could be cut.

When the main body of the troops reached camp, the soldiers set to work with spades and other entrenching tools to make the camp secure.

In constructing a camp the soldiers dug a trench (*fossa*), which was usually V-shaped and which formed part of the camp's defense. Often it was ten feet deep and from twelve to eighteen feet wide.

Out of the earth dug from this trench they built a rampart (*vāl-lum*), in which they drove stakes (*vāllī*) to form a stockade such as the early settlers in this country built around their forts for protection from the Indians. Inside the rampart was the rectangular camp with its leather-covered tents arranged in orderly rows along the passageways, or "streets."

On each of the four sides was a gate. The main gates were in the long side of the rectangle and were connected by the chief street of the camp (*via prīncipālis*), which was usually wide. Other passageways (*viae*) led to various parts of the camp.

The space in the camp was so systematically allotted that the various legions, cohorts, maniples, and centuries could easily find their quarters, even without the flags and standards which indicated them.

A century consisted theoretically of one hundred men, a maniple of two hundred. A maniple may be compared with a company in the United States army, which consists of approximately two hundred fifty men. Six centuries, or three maniples, made up a cohort. Ten cohorts formed a legion, a unit which is comparable to an American division.

At full strength a legion would have numbered six thousand soldiers, but none ever reached this count, for some men were always sick or disabled. It is estimated that during one of Caesar's campaigns his eleven legions had a total number of only about forty thousand, whereas the full strength would have been sixty-six thousand.

In addition to his infantry, Caesar's camp also sheltered a force of cavalry, which numbered from four to five thousand and was composed of men of Gallic, Span-

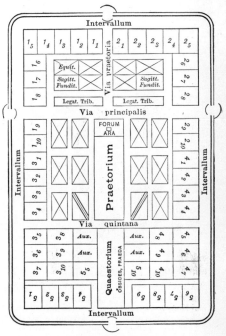

PLAN OF A CAMP

ish, and German birth. On the march it did scouting duty, and its divisions served as advance guards. When the enemy was routed, the cavalry pursued and cut down the panic-stricken fugitives. In battle the chief reliance was on the legions.

In the camp were also found light-armed infantry auxiliaries, among them slingers (*funditōrēs*) and archers (*sagittāriī*). These soldiers were enlisted from the provinces and from friendly tribes and were not Roman citizens. They were commanded by Roman officers.

To each legion was attached a band of carpenters and other workmen. They had charge of bridge-building and similar work. There

A CENTURION OF THE TWENTIETH
CENTURY
This Hollywood actor in the moving picture
Cleopatra impersonates a "captain" in the
Roman army.

cers. Caesar, as commander-in-chief (*dux* or *imperātor*), had under him subordinate officers commonly called lieutenants (*lēgātī*), military tribunes (*tribūnī mīlitum*), centurions (*centuriōnēs*), and prefects (*praefectī*). Of these officers the lieutenants were the most important. They were sometimes placed in command of divisions of the army or single legions. The tribunes, numbering six to a legion, were assigned various unimportant duties. The prefects were put in charge of the auxiliary troops and the engineers.

Corresponding in some ways to the captains in our army were the centurions, seasoned veterans who had been promoted from the ranks because of their courage and length of service.

Unceasing vigilance was maintained in guarding a camp when there was possibility of attack. Outposts of infantry and cavalry were placed before the gates, and sentries kept watch on the ramparts. Guard duty at night (*vigiliae*) was maintained with strictness. Four times during the night the guards were changed at the signal of the trumpet.

In the permanent and stationary camps there was a forum, used as a meeting-place for the soldiers. The storehouses and the paymaster's office were also near the center of the camp.

In the winter camp (*hīberna*) the leather tents used on the march were discarded, and the soldiers were sheltered from storm and cold by straw-thatched huts (*casae*). In

were also musicians with trumpets, which were used somewhat as are bugles in a modern army. In camp the trumpets were used to give the signals to change the detachments on guard, and very likely for reveille and taps. They were also used to give the signal for a charge at the beginning of a battle.

Near the center of Caesar's camp were the general's quarters (*praetōrium*). In front of headquarters there was an altar on which sacrifice was offered. On the right a mound was sometimes constructed from which the commander could address his troops and on which he was seated when acting as judge of a military court.

In the center of the camp were also the quarters of the other offia winter camp and in a stationary camp (*castra statīva*) towers (*turrēs*) were sometimes built at brief intervals along the rampart, while the intervening spaces were further protected by a roof.

Both in camp and on the march the Roman soldier wore a short-sleeved woolen tunic (*tunica*), extending nearly to the knees and fastened at the waist by a belt. He had no trim uniform such as the modern soldier wears. In rainy and cold weather he wore a woolen cloak (*sagum*), which also served as a blanket at night. His hobnailed shoes (*caligae*) had thick leather soles, usually with openwork uppers of leather strips.

For all their fighting and toil the legionaries received only the equivalent of from two to five dollars a month. Sometimes, however, part of the spoils of war was divided among them.

In the Roman army the quaestor not only acted as paymaster and had charge of supplies, but also attended to the sale of booty and prisoners. The duties of the quaestor who served in Caesar's army could not have been light, especially since it is asserted that nearly a million captured Gauls

From *The Roman Soldier*
A FULLY-EQUIPPED FOOT-SOLDIER

were sold into slavery as a result of his campaigns.

Many soldiers at the end of their terms settled in the small towns which grew up outside the walls of permanent camps and there went into business for themselves. There are in France today a number of towns and cities which began as small Roman settlements growing up under the protecting shadow of a camp. Thus these retired legionaries aided in Romanizing Gaul after they had helped to conquer it.

MARTIGNY, A MODERN SWISS TOWN ON THE SITE OF ANCIENT OCTODURUS

A SHORT CAMPAIGN IN THE ALPS

Exiguī numerō, sed bellō vīvida virtūs.
Few in number, but with a spirit bold for war.

VERGIL

Help for Harassed Traders

Cum in Ītaliam proficīscerētur Caesar, Ser. Galbam[1] cum legiōne XII et parte equitātūs in Nantuātēs, Veragrōs, Sedūnōsque[2] mīsit, quī ā fīnibus Allobrogum et lacū Lemannō et flūmine Rhodanō ad summās Alpēs pertinent.[3]

Causa mittendī fuit quod iter[4] per Alpēs, quō[5] magnō cum perīculō magnīsque cum portōriīs[6] mercātōrēs īre cōnsuērant, patefierī volēbat. Huic permīsit, sī opus esse arbitrārētur,[7] utī in hīs locīs legiōnem hiemandī causā collocāret.

Galba, secundīs aliquot proeliīs factīs, castellīsque[8] complūribus eōrum expugnātīs, missīs ad eum undique lēgātīs, obsidibusque datīs et pāce factā, cōnstituit cohortēs duās in Nantuātibus collocāre et ipse cum reliquīs ejus legiōnis cohortibus in vīcō Veragrōrum, quī appellātur Octodūrus,[9] hiemāre; quī vīcus positus in valle, nōn magnā

---

[1] Afterwards one of the assassins of Caesar. He was the great-grandfather of the Emperor Galba.

[2] *and the Seduni* (sē-dö′nī). The Seduni were a Gallic tribe.

[3] With **quī**. The meaning is *whose country extends.*

[4] Subject of **patefierī**, line 11.

[5] Referring to **iter.**

[6] *tolls*, collected by the natives on goods passing through their country.

[7] The clause means *if he thought that it was necessary.*

[8] *fortified villages.*

[9] *Octodurus* (ok-tō-dö′rus). See map, page 137.

adjectā plānitiē,[1] altissimīs montibus undique continētur.
Cum hic[2] in duās partēs flūmine
dīviderētur, alteram partem ejus
vīcī Gallīs concessit, alteram vacu- 5
am ab hīs relictam[3] cohortibus at-
tribuit. Eum locum vāllō fossāque
mūnīvit.

Hostile Mountaineers

Cum diēs[4] hībernōrum complūrēs trānsīssent frūmentumque
eō[5] comportārī jussisset, subitō per
explōrātōrēs certior factus est ex
eā parte vīcī quam Gallīs conces-
serat omnēs noctū discessisse, mon-
5 tēsque quī impendērent (*overhung*)
ā maximā multitūdine Sedūnōrum[6]
et Veragrōrum tenērī.

Id aliquot dē causīs acciderat, ut
subitō Gallī bellī renovandī legiō-
20 nisque opprimendae cōnsilium ca-
perent[7]: prīmum, quod legiōnem,
neque eam plēnissimam,[8] dētractīs[9]
cohortibus duābus et complūribus
singillātim,[10] quī commeātūs petendī causā missī erant, absenti- 25
bus, propter paucitātem dēspiciē-
bant. Tum etiam, quod propter in-
īquitātem (*unfavorableness*) locī,[11]
cum ipsī ex montibus in vallem dē-
currerent et tēla conjicerent, nē 30
prīmum quidem impetum suum
posse sustinērī exīstimābant.

Accēdēbat quod[12] suōs ab sē līberōs abstractōs[13] obsidum nōmine[14]
dolēbant et Rōmānōs nōn sōlum 35
itinerum causā sed etiam per-
petuae possessiōnis[15] culmina (*sum-
mits*) Alpium occupāre cōnārī et
ea loca fīnitimae prōvinciae[16] ad-
jungere sibi persuāsum habēbant.[17] 40

Galba Asks Advice

Hīs nūntiīs acceptīs Galba, cum
neque opus hībernōrum[18] mūnītiōnēsque[19] plēnē (*fully*) essent
perfectae neque dē frūmentō reliquō-
que commeātū satis esset prōvīsum,[20] 45
quod dēditiōne factā obsidibus-

---

[1] *with a small plain adjacent;* ablative
absolute.
[2] Supply **vīcus**.
[3] *left unoccupied by* (literally, *left free
from*).
[4] Nominative plural.
[5] Equivalent to in **hīberna**.
[6] *of the Seduni.*
[7] The ut clause explains **Id**.
[8] *and that, too, not at full strength.*
[9] This ablative absolute and the one
which follows (**complūribus . . . absen-
tibus**) explain why the legion was not
plēnissima.
[10] *individually,* as opposed to the detachments.
[11] The prepositional phrase with **propter** belongs with **impetum sustinērī**,
lines 31-32.
[12] *an additional reason was that.* The
quod clause is the subject of **Accēdēbat**.
[13] Supply **esse**, *had been carried away.*
The infinitive depends on **dolēbant**.
[14] The two words mean *as hostages.*
[15] Supply **causā**.
[16] Not genitive.
[17] *they had persuaded themselves.*
[18] Including marking off the ground
for the camp, erecting huts, etc.
[19] Referring to the wall and rampart;
see lines 7-8.
[20] With **neque**. The three words mean
and sufficient provision had not been made.

que acceptīs nihil dē bellō timendum exīstimāverat, cōnsiliō[1] celeriter convocātō sententiās exquīrere
(*to investigate*) coepit.

5 Quō in cōnsiliō, cum tantum re-
pentīnī perīculī[2] praeter opīniōnem accidisset ac jam omnia
ferē superiōra loca multitūdine armātōrum complēta cōnspiceren-
10 tur, neque subsidiō venīrī[3] neque
commeātūs supportārī interclūsīs

itineribus possent, prope jam
dēspērātā salūte nōnnūllae ejus
modī[4] sententiae dīcēbantur, ut
impedīmentīs relictīs, ēruptiōne 1
factā, eīsdem itineribus quibus eō
pervēnissent ad salūtem contenderent.

Majōrī tamen partī placuit,[5] hōc
reservātō[6] ad extrēmum cāsum cōn- 2
siliō, interim reī ēventum experīrī
et castra dēfendere.

A Desperate Situation

BREVĪ spatiō interjectō,[7] vix[8]
ut eīs rēbus quās cōnstituis-
25 sent collocandīs atque administran-
dīs[9] tempus darētur, hostēs ex
omnibus partibus signō datō dē-
currere,[10] lapidēs gaesaque (*and
javelins*) in vāllum conjicere.[10]

30 Nostrī prīmō, integrīs vīribus,[11]
fortiter prōpugnāre[10] (*fought*) neque
ūllum frūstrā tēlum ex locō superiōre[12] mittere,[10] et quaecumque pars
castrōrum nūdāta dēfēnsōribus

premī[13] vidēbātur, eō occurrere[14] 3
et auxilium ferre;[10] sed hōc superā-
rī,[15] quod diūturnitāte[16] pugnae hostēs dēfessī sī proeliō excēdēbant,
aliī integrīs vīribus[17] succēdēbant.

Quārum rērum ā nostrīs propter 4
paucitātem fierī nihil poterat, ac
nōn modo[18] dēfessō[19] ex pugnā
excēdendī, sed nē sauciō[19] (*to a
wounded man*) quidem ejus locī
ubi cōnstiterat relinquendī ac suī 4
recipiendī facultās dabātur.

[1] The council of war was usually composed of the tribunes, the centurions of
first rank, and the cavalry officers—
from fifteen to twenty men in all.
[2] Genitive of the whole with **tantum**.
[3] Impersonal. Supply **posset** from
the following **possent**, and translate, *and
neither could aid reach them*.
[4] *of this sort, to this effect*; a descriptive
genitive.
[5] *the majority thought it best*.
[6] The phrase is equivalent to **hoc cōnsilium . . . reservāre et.**
[7] *after an interval* (*so*) *short*.
[8] Placed first in its clause for emphasis.
[9] *for arranging and carrying out these
measures*. The dative of the gerundive
seldom occurs.
[10] Historical infinitive. See Gr. S., 126.

[11] *while their strength was fresh*; ablative
absolute.
[12] The phrase means **ex vāllō**. This,
of course, was higher than the plain
into which the enemy had descended.
[13] What are the principal parts of
premō?
[14] In a hostile sense—*they rushed up*,
or *would rush up*, to oppose the enemy.
The historical infinitive is here equivalent to an imperfect indicative of repeated action.
[15] *in this they were at a disadvantage;*
explained by **quod . . . succēdēbant.**
[16] *by the long continuance of the battle.*
[17] Descriptive ablative with **aliī.**
[18] Equivalent to **nōn modo nōn**—*not
only was the opportunity not given*, etc.
The second **nōn** is omitted only when
a negative follows.
[19] Dative with **dabātur,** line 46.

One Chance Left

Cum jam amplius hōrīs[1] sex continenter pugnārētur[2] ac nōn sōlum vīrēs, sed etiam tēla nostrōs dēficerent, atque hostēs ācrius īnstārent languidiōribusque nostrīs[3] vāllum scindere (*to tear down*) et fossās complēre coepissent rēsque esset jam ad extrēmum perducta cāsum, P. Sextius Baculus,[4] prīmī pīlī centuriō,[5] quem Nervicō proeliō[6] complūribus cōnfectum vulneribus dīximus,[7] et item C. Volusēnus,[8] tribūnus mīlitum, vir et cōnsiliī magnī et virtūtis, ad Galbam accurrunt atque ūnam esse spem salūtis docent,[9] sī, ēruptiōne factā, extrēmum auxilium experīrentur.[10] Itaque, convocātīs centuriōnibus, celeriter mīlitēs certiōrēs facit[11] paulisper intermitterent proelium ac tantummodo (*only*) tēla missa exciperent[12] sēque ex labōre reficerent, post[13] datō signō, ex castrīs ērumperent (*they should rush out*) atque omnem spem salūtis in virtūte pōnerent.

All's Well That Ends Well

Quod jussī sunt[14] faciunt, ac subitō omnibus portīs[15] ēruptiōne factā, neque cognōscendī[16] quid fieret neque suī colligendī[17] hostibus facultātem relinquunt.

Ita commūtātā fortūnā, eōs quī in spem potiundōrum castrōrum vēnerant[18] undique circumventōs intercipiunt, et ex hominum mīlibus amplius[19] xxx, quem numerum barbarōrum ad castra vēnisse cōnstābat,[20] plūs[19] tertiā parte interfectā reliquōs perterritōs in fugam conjiciunt ac nē in locīs quidem superiōribus cōnsistere patiuntur.

[1] The Romans counted twelve hours from sunrise to sunset, the length of the hour varying with the length of the day at different seasons of the year.
[2] Translate by a past perfect, *when the battle had been going on.*
[3] *and our men having become more faint;* ablative absolute, denoting cause.
[4] *Publius Sextius Baculus* (bak′ū-lus).
[5] Literally, *the centurion of the first maniple;* i.e., the chief centurion.
[6] *in the battle with the Nervii.* For the Nervii, see map, page 137.
[7] The story of this battle is told on page 202.
[8] "The only tribune of whom Caesar makes honorable mention." He was later a commander of cavalry in the civil war between Caesar and Pompey.
[9] *told him.*
[10] The clause is loosely used to explain **spem.**
[11] *he informed them (of his will that);* governing **intermitterent** and the other subjunctives which follow.
[12] The clause means that they were merely to protect themselves against the missiles of the enemy.
[13] An adverb.
[14] *as* (literally, *what*) *they were commanded.*
[15] Ablative of route.
[16] Depending on **facultātem.**
[17] *of rallying.*
[18] *had come to have hopes.*
[19] The adverb does not affect the construction.
[20] *the number of barbarians who were known to have taken part in the attack on the camp.*

ROMAN WAR-SHIPS

Sīc omnibus hostium cōpiīs fūsīs armīsque exūtīs,[1] sē intrā mūnītiōnēs suās recipiunt. Quō proeliō factō, quod saepius fortūnam temptāre Galba nōlēbat atque aliō sē in hīberna cōnsiliō[2] vēnisse meminerat (*remembered*), aliīs occurrisse rēbus vīderat,[3] maximē frūmentī inopiā permōtus, posterō diē omnibus ejus vīcī aedificiīs incēnsīs in prōvinciam revertī contendit ac, nūllō hoste prohibente aut iter dēmorante (*delaying*), incolumem legiōnem in Nantuātēs, inde in Allobrogēs perdūxit ibique hiemāvit.

A Naval Battle[4]

AS EARLY as possible in the spring, active war by land was begun in the country of the Veneti, who had been the leaders in an uprising. However, the Romans could accomplish little until their ships arrived. Whenever the enemy found that any town could no longer be defended, they took to their boats, with their forces intact, and sailed away to another town, leaving the Romans an empty victory.

Finally the Roman fleet appeared, and the Gauls sailed out to meet it.

---

[1] *stripped of their arms*, i.e., compelled to throw away their arms in flight; **exūtīs** agrees with **cōpiīs**; **armīs** is an ablative of separation depending on **exūtīs**.

[2] *with one plan.*

[3] (*but*) *saw that he had met a different state of affairs.*

[4] Galba's campaign was conducted in the winter of 57-56 B.C. The events here described occurred in 56 B.C.

The naval battle that followed was the first on the Atlantic in which Roman ships were ever engaged.

At the beginning of the battle, the Romans were at a disadvantage because the peculiar construction of the Gallic vessels made the usual Roman tactics almost impossible. The ships were too high to be caught with grappling hooks and too strongly built to be damaged when rammed by the bows of the Roman boats.

But the Gallic boats were propelled entirely by sails, while the Roman vessels were equipped with oars, and this fact gave the Romans an advantage which decided the outcome. Attaching hooks to long poles, the Romans tore away the sails of the Gallic boats, thus rendering them helpless. They then attacked them, two or three Roman boats assailing first one boat of the enemy, and then another.

A sudden calm made escape impossible for the enemy's vessels which were still uninjured, and the Romans sank almost the entire Gallic fleet. The survivors surrendered, but Caesar made an example of the Veneti by executing their leaders and selling the others as slaves.

COMPREHENSION QUESTIONS

Answer the following questions, which are based on the short selection from Caesar's *Gallic War* that has just been read.

1. What was the occasion for sending Galba into the country of the Alpine tribes?

2. What was the situation of Octodurus?

3. What did the Gauls believe to be the real purpose in establishing a Roman force in the region of the Alps?

4. What was the plan proposed by the minority group in the council which had been called by Galba?

5. How did the number of the Romans under Galba compare with the attacking force?

6. Who was Baculus?

7. What did Galba decide to do after the Gauls were routed?

8. Where was the country of the Veneti? (If necessary, see map, p. 137.)

WORD STUDY VII

Six Important Prefixes

Many Latin verbs have been formed by adding a prefix to a simple verb. Six prefixes thus used are given below with some compound verbs in which they occur.

ante, *before* (in time or place)

antecēdō, *go before, surpass*   **antepōnō,** *place before, prefer*

dis- (**dī-, dif-**[1]), *apart, not, opposite of*

discēdō, *go away, depart*   **dīmittō,** *send away*

differō, *carry* or *bear apart, put off, differ*

ob (**oc-, of-, op-**), *against, toward*

occurrō, *run against* or *toward, meet*   **offerō,** *bring* or *bear toward, offer*

opprimō, *press against, overpower*

re- (**red-**), *back, again*

renovō, *make new again, renew*   **reddō,** *give back, restore*

sē- (**sēd-**), *apart, aside*

sēcēdō, *go apart, withdraw*

trāns (**trā-**), *across, through, over, beyond*

trānsportō, *carry across, convey*   **trādūcō,** *lead across* or *over, transfer*

These same prefixes appear also in many English words, both verbs and other parts of speech. Some of these words have been derived from Latin compounds, others have been formed in English. Examples of such words in common use are given here.

antedate	disconnected	obstruct	recline	seclusion	transatlantic
antepenult	displease	offend	redeem	sedition	transpose
anteroom	diffuse	opponent	reject	separate	traverse

EXERCISES

1. Give some additional English words in which the prefixes **ante** and **dis-** occur.

2. Which of the six prefixes given in this lesson is used to form a compound of the English word *call?*

3. Find in a large English dictionary the origin of the word *transfer.*

4. What is the literal meaning of the English word *disperse* in accordance with its derivation?

5. Find from a large dictionary ten additional English words in which the prefix **sē-** appears.

6. What are the different forms taken by the prefix **ob?**

---

[1] The forms in parentheses are variant forms taken by the prefix before certain letters.

Idioms and Phrases

The idioms and phrases listed below occur frequently in the text read. Learning them thoroughly will be of great help in reading.

certior factus est, *he was informed*
cōnsilium inīre (cōnsilium capere), *to form a plan*
cupiditāte rēgnī adductus, *influenced by a desire for royal power*
hīs rēbus gestīs, *after these events*
pedem referre, *to withdraw, retreat*
tempestātem idōneam nactus, *finding suitable weather*

Vocabulary Review

The following words, which appear frequently in this book, are important in second-year work. Their meanings should be thoroughly learned.

adjiciō	cōnstituō	hiemō	occurrō	recēns
aequus	contineō	inopia	opīniō	reficiō
brevis	dēfessus	ita	opprimō	repentīnus
calamitās	dēspiciō	itaque	paulisper	subsidium
causa	doleō	modo	perficiō	supportō
causā	ēruptiō	nātūra	perpetuus	sustineō
commoveō	experior	nihil	plērīque	tēlum
complūrēs	expugnō	nisi	potior, -īrī	tribūnus
concilium	extrēmus	noceō	prīmō	vallēs
cōnficiō	fīnitimus	noctū	prīmum	vīcus
conjungō	fundō	nūdō	proficīscor	vix
cōnor	hīberna	obses	prōsequor	vulnus

A ROMAN AMPHITHEATER IN ARLES, FRANCE

UPRISINGS IN THE WEST AND SOUTH

Amidst the noise of endless wars—
MILTON: PARADISE LOST

A New Gallic Leader Appears

DUM haec in Venetīs geruntur, Q. Titūrius Sabīnus cum eīs cōpiīs quās ā Caesare accēperat in fīnēs Venellōrum pervēnit.

5 Hīs praeerat Viridovīx ac summam imperiī[1] tenēbat eārum omnium cīvitātum quae dēfēcerant, ex quibus exercitum coēgerat; atque hīs paucīs diēbus Aulercī Ebu-
10 rovīcēs[2] Lexoviīque,[3] senātū suō interfectō quod auctōrēs bellī esse nōlēbant,[4] portās clausērunt sēque cum Viridovīce conjūnxērunt; magnaque praetereā multitūdō undique
15 ex Galliā perditōrum (*desperate*) hominum latrōnumque convēnerat, et quōs[5] spēs praedandī (*of plundering*) studiumque bellandī ab agrīcultūrā et cotīdiānō labōre sēvocā-
20 bat (*called away*).

Sabīnus idōneō omnibus rēbus locō castrīs sē tenēbat, cum[6] Viridovīx contrā eum duōrum mīlium spatiō[7] cōnsēdisset cotīdiēque prōductīs cōpiīs pugnandī potestātem 25 faceret[8] ut jam nōn sōlum hostibus in contemptiōnem Sabīnus venīret,[9] sed etiam nostrōrum mīlitum vōcibus nōn nihil[10] carperētur (*was censured*); tantamque opīniōnem ti- 30 mōris praebuit[11] ut jam ad vāllum castrōrum hostēs accēdere audērent.

Id eā dē causā faciēbat, quod[12] cum tantā multitūdine hostium, 35 praesertim eō absente quī summam imperiī tenēret, nisi aequō locō aut opportūnitāte (*opportunity*) aliquā datā lēgātō[13] dīmicandum nōn ex- īstimābat.
40

---

[1] *the chief command.*

[2] *the Aulerci Eburovices* (â-lèr'sī eb'ū-rō̞-vī'sēz), that is, the Eburovices who were a branch of the Aulerci.

[3] *and the Lexovii* (lek-sō̞'vi-ī). Like the other tribe just mentioned, they were a people of Celtic Gaul.

[4] *were unwilling to sanction the war.* The subject is supplied from **senātū**, in line 10.

[5] The antecedent is an understood **hominum** (or **eōrum**).

[6] *while;* adversative.

[7] Ablative of measure of difference.

[8] *offered him an opportunity.*

[9] With **hostibus in contemptiōnem**— *came to be an object of contempt to the enemy.*

[10] *somewhat* (*not a little*).

[11] *inspired such a belief* (on the part of the enemy) *in his fear.*

[12] With **eā dē causā**—*for the reason that.* Sometimes forms of the demonstrative **is** are equivalent to the definite article. The definite article in the modern languages derived from Latin, however, is from **ille.**

[13] Dative of agent, with **dīmicandum (esse)**. Translate by a nominative as subject of the equivalent of **dīmicandum esse** in the active voice.

Successful Strategy

Hāc cōnfirmātā opīniōne timōris idōneum quendam homi-
nem et callidum dēligit, Gallum, ex
eīs quōs auxiliī causā sēcum habē-
5 bat. Huic magnīs praemiīs pollicitātiōnibusque (*and promises*) persuādet utī ad hostēs trānseat, et quid
fierī velit ēdocet.[1]

Quī ubi prō perfugā[2] ad eōs vēnit,
10 timōrem Rōmānōrum prōpōnit;
quibus angustiīs ipse Caesar ā
Venetīs premātur[3] docet, neque
longius[4] abesse quīn proximā nocte
Sabīnus clam ex castrīs exercitum
15 ēdūcat et ad Caesarem auxiliī ferendī causā proficīscātur. Quod ubi
audītum est, conclāmant omnēs
occāsiōnem negōtiī bene gerendī
āmittendam nōn esse; ad castra īrī

oportēre.[5] Multae rēs ad hoc cōn- 20
silium Gallōs hortābantur: superiōrum[6] diērum Sabīnī cūnctātiō
(*hesitation*), perfugae cōnfirmātiō
(*assurance*), inopia cibāriōrum, cui
reī parum dīligenter ab eīs erat 25
prōvīsum, spēs Veneticī bellī,[7] et
quod[8] ferē libenter hominēs id quod
volunt crēdunt.

Hīs rēbus adductī nōn prius
Viridovīcem reliquōsque ducēs ex 30
conciliō dīmittunt quam ab eīs sit
concessum[9] arma utī capiant et ad
castra contendant. Quā rē conces-
sā laetī, ut explōrātā victōriā,[10] sar-
mentīs virgultīsque (*fagots and* 35
brushwood) collēctīs quibus fossās
Rōmānōrum compleant, ad castra
pergunt (*advanced*).

More Bravery Than Judgment

Locus erat castrōrum ēditus et
paulātim ab īmō acclīvis (*sloping*) circiter passūs mīlle.[11] Hūc
magnō cursū contendērunt ut quam
minimum spatiī[12] ad sē colligendōs
armandōsque Rōmānīs darētur, ex-
45 animātīque pervēnērunt. Sabīnus

suōs hortātus cupientibus[13] signum
dat. Impedītīs hostibus propter
ea quae ferēbant onera,[14] subitō
duābus portīs ēruptiōnem fierī
jubet. 50

Factum est opportūnitāte (*from
the favorable situation*) locī, hostium

---

[1] *explained.*

[2] *as a deserter.*

[3] Like **abesse**, dependent on **docet.**

[4] *and that not later than the next night
Sabinus would lead out,* etc. (literally,
and it was no further distant, i.e., no
longer time intervened), etc.

[5] Translate by the personal construction—*they ought to advance;* **īrī**, the subject of **oportēre,** is the present passive
infinitive of **eō** used impersonally.

[6] *preceding.*

[7] *of the war with the Veneti.* They
had probably heard of Caesar's diffi-

culties in the early part of the campaign,
but they had not yet learned the results
of the war.

[8] *and the fact that.* The clause states a
general truth.

[9] *until they had given their consent.*
The subjunctive is anticipatory.

[10] *as if the victory were already assured;*
ablative absolute.

[11] Accusative of extent with **acclīvis.**

[12] *as little time as possible.*

[13] *as they eagerly desired;* dative.

[14] The brush and other material to
fill the Roman trenches.

A CAVALRYMAN IN THE ROMAN ARMY

ut nē prīmum quidem nostrōrum impetum ferrent ac statim terga verterent. 5

Quōs integrīs vīribus mīlitēs nostrī cōnsecūtī magnum numerum eōrum occīdērunt; reliquōs equitēs[2] cōnsectātī (*having pursued*) paucōs 10 quī ex fugā ēvāserant relīquērunt.

Sīc ūnō tempore et dē nāvālī (*naval*) pugnā Sabīnus et dē Sabīnī victōriā Caesar est certior factus, cīvitātēsque omnēs sē statim Ti- 15 tūriō[3] dēdidērunt. Nam ut ad bella suscipienda Gallōrum alacer ac prōmptus (*ready*) est animus, sīc mollis (*soft*) ac minimē resistēns ad calamitātēs ferendās mēns eō- 20 rum est.

inscientiā[1] ac dēfatīgātiōne (*exhaustion*), virtūte mīlitum et superiōrum pugnārum exercitātiōne,

A Siege

WHILE the campaigns against the coast tribes and the Venelli were going on, another Roman force was active in Aquitania, the southwestern part of Gaul. The natives of this region appear to have employed more skilful military tactics than most of the Gauls to the north.

One tribe, the Sotiates, lured the Romans into a valley where the greater part of the Gallic forces were concealed, and attacked them from ambush. Roman discipline saved the day, however, and the Gauls were finally routed.

When the Romans began a siege of the town to which the enemy had retreated, the Gauls drove mines to the Roman positions. Their efforts

to defend themselves or to cut their way through the Roman lines failed, and they finally surrendered to the Roman commander.

Next the Romans marched into the territories of two neighboring tribes. The defeat of the Sotiates and the capture of their town made it evident to these tribes that they were facing a desperate struggle. They called to their help a number of Spanish leaders from over the Pyrenees who had served under a Roman general and were familiar with Roman military usage. Under the direction of these leaders they chose their positions skilfully, fortified their camps according to Roman methods, and proceeded to cut the lines of com-

[1] *ignorance.* Opposed to **exercitātiōne.**
[2] Subject of the verb **relīquērunt,** line 11, which has **paucōs** as its object.

[3] Meaning Sabinus, who is mentioned in line 13; the full name of this officer was Quintus Titurius Sabinus.

munication by which the Romans were getting their supplies.

Although they outnumbered the Romans, they shrewdly avoided battle, believing they could compel the invaders to abandon the campaign through lack of supplies. When the Roman soldiers marched out in front of their camp as a challenge to fight, the Gauls made no move to leave their own defenses. To attack a fortified position with a force smaller than that of the defenders was a dangerous undertaking, but the Romans had no choice, unless they were willing to give up all hope of final success.

Learning from cavalry scouts that the Gallic fortifications at the rear of the camp were poorly constructed, the Roman commander sent a detachment to make an attack there. Meanwhile the main body of his forces was engaging the attention of the Gauls by a vigorous assault on the front. This move was successful, and the attacking force from the rear broke through the defenses and got into the camp. The Gauls were thrown into a panic by this unforeseen development, and the result was a complete victory for the Romans.

As a consequence of this battle almost all the remaining tribes of Aquitania submitted to the Romans.

COMPREHENSION QUESTIONS

The main incidents related in the account of the uprisings in the west and south are the basis of the questions that follow.

1. How did Sabinus lure the Venelli to attack his camp?
2. What preparations did the Gauls make for the attack?
3. Where was Aquitania?
4. How was the Gallic camp finally captured?

WORD STUDY VIII
Words of Interesting Derivation

Some English words coming directly from the Latin have an interesting history. Observe those given below.

AISLE, from āla, originally meaning *wing*, then *wing* of an army, later *wing* of a building. Afterwards the word came to mean a passage at the side, and then a passage between rows of seats.

ALIMONY, from alimōnia, *a means of support*, which comes from alō, *support*. Hence, the modern meaning of an allowance granted to a divorced person.

BIB, from bibō, *drink*. Hence, something worn to protect a child's clothing while drinking, or eating.

CAUTION, from caveō, *guard against*. Hence, anything serving as a warning.

CENSUS, from cēnseō, *estimate*. Hence, a counting of the people in a city or country.

CONFLICT, from cōnflīctus, past participle of cōnflīgō, *collide*. Hence, a conflict is an actual clash, as in war, or a figurative clash, as of ideas.

CORROBORATE, from corrōborātus, past participle of corrōborāre, from rōbur, *strength*. Hence, to strengthen, make more certain.

DILAPIDATED, from **dis-** and **lapis, lapidis,** *stone*. The Latin verb **dīlapidō** meant to scatter like stones. Hence, when we speak of something as dilapidated, we mean that it appears to be falling in ruins, like a stone structure, the stones of which have fallen apart.

ERUDITE, from the past participle of **ērudiō,** *instruct*. This verb is in turn from **ē** and **rudis,** *rude, untaught*. So an erudite person is instructed, learned.

MORSEL, from **morsus,** participle of **mordeō,** *bite*. Hence, a small bit of food, or small piece of anything.

PRECARIOUS, from **prex,** *prayer*, which gives the verb **precor,** *pray*. Hence, something is precarious when it depends on favor or is uncertain.

VALEDICTORY, from **valē,** *good-by*, and **dīcō,** *say*. Hence, a farewell address.

EXERCISES

1. What is the meaning of the word *pecuniary?* How is it connected in meaning with the Latin **pecus,** *cattle?*

2. Why are the characters used in writing numbers called *digits?*

3. Is there any connection in meaning between Latin **lūna** and English *lunatic?*

4. What are the three French words that have been combined to form *dandelion?* What are the Latin words from which these have come?

5. Why is the East sometimes referred to as the *Orient?*

Idioms and Phrases

The idioms and phrases listed below occur frequently in the text read. Learning them thoroughly will be of great help in reading.

> **ad eās rēs cōnficiendās,** *to carry out these plans*
> **eā spē dējectī,** *disappointed in this hope*
> **nāvem cōnscendit,** *he went on board a ship*
> **neque quisquam,** *and no one*
> **nōn bonō animō sunt,** *they do not have (are not in) a friendly attitude*
> **parātiōrēs esse,** *to be better prepared*

Vocabulary Review

The following words, which appear frequently in this book, are important in second-year work. Their meanings should be thoroughly learned.

aliquis	cum (*conj.*)	hortor	oportet	spēs
armō	cursus	impetus	paulātim	studium
auctor	dēficiō	integer	perferō	summa
circiter	dēligō, -ere	labor, -ōris	praesertim	superus,
clam	doceō	lēgātus	prōdūcō	superior
colligō, -ere	dum	mēns	prōpōnō	suscipiō
concēdō	eō (*adv.*)	multitūdō	reliquus	tantus
cōnfīdō	eō (*verb*)	nāvigō	saepe	timor
cōnsequor	exīstimō	negōtium	salūs	vetustus
contendō	facultās	nōlō	senātus	virtūs
contrā	ferō	occāsiō	sōlum (*adv.*)	vīs
cotīdiānus	fīō	onus	spatium	volō, velle

CAESAR CROSSING THE RUBICON IN DEFIANCE OF THE SENATE'S ORDER

CAESAR, THE DICTATOR

THE news that Caesar had won important victories in Gaul aroused great enthusiasm in Rome. The conqueror of Gaul was the hero of the day, and holidays were voted in recognition of his achievements. But in spite of this popular enthusiasm, the political situation was not altogether favorable to Caesar. The triumvirate had been broken up; Crassus was dead, and Pompey had been won over by Caesar's enemies.

Caesar wished to become a candidate for a second term as consul, and it had previously been arranged with Pompey and Crassus that he should run for office without leaving his province. Thus he would become consul when his term as governor ended.

His enemies were determined to prevent this, for the reason that if he returned to Rome as a private citizen before the election, he could be prosecuted on a trumped-up charge of misgovernment. Even though such a charge might have little basis, it would prevent his election as consul. His opponents in the Senate, with the support of Pompey, succeeded in having a law passed by which Caesar was ordered to give up his command and return to Rome.

At this time Caesar was in Cisalpine Gaul. When he received the Senate's order, he realized that to obey it meant the end of his public career. At once he made a stirring speech to his soldiers, and in defiance of the Senate he set out to meet the forces that had been collected to oppose him.

On the march Caesar had to cross the Rubicon, a small stream forming part of the boundary between Italy and his province.

There is a story that he hesitated for a short time, since to lead his army across this boundary meant that he was disobeying the orders of the government, and the only result could be civil war. But he decided to go on, and led his soldiers across, saying to his officers that this put an end to any chance of turning back. Hence, the phrase "crossing the Rubicon" is used to describe an act from which there can be no turning back.

The forces of the government were commanded by Caesar's old ally, Pompey—now his enemy. But Caesar's advance aroused so much enthusiasm throughout the country that Pompey in alarm abandoned Italy without attempting battle and immediately transported all his troops to Greece. There he planned to make a stand against his rival.

Within the next sixty days Caesar subdued Italy. This meant that he controlled Italy, Illyricum, and Gaul. Pompey's forces held Spain, Africa, Sicily, Greece, and the provinces of Asia. The whole Roman world was now drawn into the conflict. Before following Pompey to Greece, Caesar conducted a brief campaign in Spain, where he quickly defeated two of Pompey's officers.

Upon his return to Rome he was elected consul for 48 B.C. This victory in the election put him in a better position, since he was at the head of the government and his soldiers were no longer illegally in Italy. He was now ready to go to Greece in pursuit of his enemy.

A TRIUMPHAL PROCESSION
Roman eagles escort a victorious commander on a Hollywood production lot.

When Caesar faced Pompey and his army in the Battle of Pharsalus, Pompey's forces were crushed, and their commander fled to Egypt for refuge. As Pompey was disembarking from a small boat, he was treacherously slain by the Egyptians.

But his two sons and other leaders of the faction opposed to Caesar had strong forces. With these they were able to prolong the war, and it was not until three years after the Battle of Pharsalus that the last of the organized opposition to Caesar was crushed.

After the establishment of peace a series of elaborate triumphs was celebrated for his conquests in Gaul, in Egypt, in Asia Minor, and in Africa. During the celebration every Roman citizen received a sum of money, ten bushels of wheat, and ten pounds of oil, while the poor had no rent to pay for a year.

Caesar was then made dictator for life. During the period of his power he showed that he was a statesman as well as a great general. He introduced important reforms into the government of Rome, such as reorganizing the legal system in order to provide a better method of administering justice.

A large number of citizens had been supplied with grain at government expense. Caesar brought down by more than half the number of these people "on relief" by means of such measures as finding homes in other parts of the Roman world for some of the unemployed. To reduce unemployment still further, a law was passed requiring the owners of large estates to employ more free laborers. Farms were granted, as a form of pension, to soldiers who were mustered out of service.

One of Caesar's most useful achievements was his correction of the calendar, in which there was an error of three months. He ordered a new calendar to be adopted, making the year three hundred sixty-five days, with an additional day every fourth year, giving three hundred sixty-six days for leap year. This calendar was so nearly correct that after seventeen centuries it was only a few days in error. In honor of Julius Caesar the month which had been known as *Quintīlis*, or the fifth month, was changed to the month of *Jūlius*—July.

JULY WAS NAMED FOR JULIUS CAESAR

This versatile man not only was an author and a general, but also had many other interests. So well did he solve the problem of a correct calendar that after thousands of years we still use a calendar similar to the one he evolved.

With statesmanlike regard for the future, Caesar planned great public works. He proposed to drain the Pontine Marsh near Rome—a project which has actually been carried out only in the last few years. It was said that he contemplated changing the course of the Tiber River in order to remove the danger of floods at Rome.

He also wished to rebuild parts of Rome. In order that there might be more space for public business, the buildings were cleared away from a region near the Forum and a new forum was constructed, though it was not completed until

THE FORUM OF JULIUS CAESAR

The pillars in the foreground were once part of a structure as impressive as the modern monument which looms in the background.

after Caesar's death. Within the past few years the modern buildings which had been constructed on the site of Caesar's Forum have been removed, and the ancient pavement has been uncovered.

There were many Romans who did not believe the State should be ruled by one man, no matter how competent he might be. Roman citizens had a horror of the word "king," and when Caesar's enemies declared that he intended to take this title, the tide of popular favor turned against him. Whether or not he really had such an intention no one can say. However, a group of political leaders, claiming that they believed this to be the case, formed a plot against his life.

On the Ides (the fifteenth day) of March, 44 B.C., Caesar went to a meeting of the Senate. When he was seated, several senators approached, as though intending to ask favors of him. It was not uncommon for petitions to the dictator to be made in this manner.

Among those bringing a petition was Tullius Cimber. When it was refused, he clutched Caesar's toga as if to beg for a more favorable reply. Meanwhile, Casca, another plotter, who had stepped behind Caesar, suddenly drew a dagger and stabbed him.

Caesar sprang from his seat, but daggers flashed on all sides and blows rained down upon him. Legend says that when Caesar saw

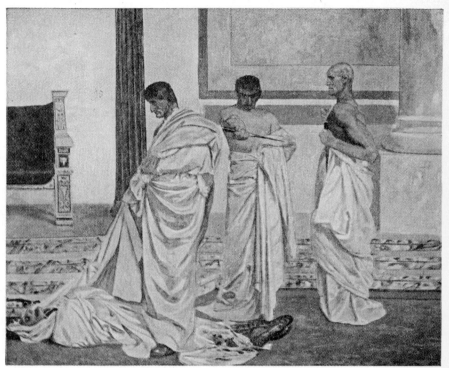

"O MIGHTY CAESAR, DOST THOU LIE SO LOW!"

Brutus, whom he especially loved and trusted, with dagger raised, he cried, "And you, too, Brutus!" and ceased to resist.

Thus a violent death ended the career of a dictator who had established his power through violence and civil wars. The law-abiding ideals characteristic of the Roman Republic had been forgotten, and force ruled.

But the assassins gained no profit from his death, nor was the cause of popular government furthered. Bitter civil warfare followed, which was ended when Octavianus, the grandnephew and adopted son of Caesar, won supreme power in the State. Though for a time the outward form of the Republic was maintained, Octavianus ruled under the name of Augustus as the first of a long line of emperors.

It became the custom for each emperor to call himself *Caesar*, and the title survived in modern times. "Czar," a word derived from *Caesar*, was the title of the emperor of Russia, and the monarch of Germany was called the Kaiser. Through the ages many a great man has borne this proud title, but never has there been one more famous than the first Caesar.

CAESAR IN BRITAIN

*Primus omnium Rōmānōrum dīvus Jūlius[1] cum exercitū Britanniam
ingressus . . . potest vidērī ostendisse posterīs, nōn trādidisse.*

Julius Caesar, who was the first of all the Romans to invade Great
Britain with an army, may seem to have pointed it out to later genera-
tions, rather than to have put it into their possession.

TACITUS: AGRICOLA

Trouble-Makers from over the Rhine

IN THE winter of 56 B. C. two German tribes which had been unable
to defend their territory against their
powerful neighbors, the Suebi, crossed
the lower Rhine. Here they proceeded
to establish themselves in the towns
of the Menapii, one of the Belgian
nations.

Fearing that this development might
lead to a combination of Gauls and
Germans against the Romans, Caesar
started with his army for the region
occupied by the invaders.

When Caesar approached, the Germans sent representatives to him,
saying that their intentions were
peaceful and asking him to assign
them lands in Gaul. They declared
somewhat insolently, however, that
they had no fear of any foe except
the Suebi. Caesar's answer was that
they must return to Germany. He
offered to secure lands for them among
the Ubii, a German tribe who were
also suffering from the depredations
of the Suebi.

Immediately after this conference,
a body of German horsemen attacked
the Roman cavalry, routing them
with serious loss on the part of the
Romans.

The next day a group of German
leaders came to Caesar's camp, either
to apologize for the unprovoked attack, or as Caesar asserts, to win
further delay, so that they might be
in better condition for a decisive
battle. Caesar promptly arrested the
envoys and immediately made an
attack on the German camp. The
Germans were completely routed, and
great numbers of them killed.

Caesar was severely criticized in the
Senate at Rome for what his political
opponents declared was an act of bad
faith in thus attacking the Germans
while they were attempting to nego-
tiate with him. It seems probable,
however, that he was justified in regarding the appeal of the Germans as
insincere.

After this battle Caesar decided to
invade Germany. In order to cross
the Rhine without relying on boats,
most of which he probably would have
had to secure from the Gauls, he
built a bridge, of which he gives an
elaborate account. The Germans withdrew at his approach, and no battles
were fought.

After laying waste the country for
the purpose of terrorizing the enemy,
Caesar returned to Gaul and destroyed
the bridge.

[1] After his death Caesar was commonly
referred to by Roman writers as **dīvus Jūlius**,
the deified Julius.

230

Looking across the Channel

EXIGUĀ parte aestātis reliquā,[1] Caesar, etsī in hīs locīs, quod omnis Gallia ad septentriōnēs vergit (*lies toward*), mātūrae sunt hie-
5 mēs, tamen in Britanniam proficīscī contendit, quod omnibus ferē Gallicīs bellīs hostibus[2] nostrīs inde subministrāta (*had been supplied*) auxilia[3] intellegēbat; et, sī
10 tempus annī ad bellum gerendum dēficeret, tamen magnō sibi ūsuī fore[4] arbitrābātur sī modo īnsulam adīsset,[5] genus hominum perspexisset, loca, portūs, aditūs cognō-
15 visset; quae omnia ferē Gallīs erant incognita.[6] Neque enim temere praeter mercātōrēs illō[7] adit quisquam,[8] neque hīs ipsīs quicquam praeter ōram maritimam atque eās regiōnēs quae sunt contrā Galliam 20 nōtum est.

Itaque vocātīs ad sē undique mercātōribus, neque quanta[9] esset īnsulae magnitūdō neque quae aut quantae nātiōnēs incolerent neque 25 quem ūsum bellī habērent aut quibus īnstitūtīs ūterentur neque quī essent ad majōrem nāvium multitūdinem idōneī portūs[10] reperīre poterat. 30

Prospects of a Peaceful Reception

AD HAEC cognōscenda,[11] priusquam perīculum faceret,[12] idōneum esse arbitrātus C. Volusēnum[13] cum nāve longā praemittit.
35 Huic mandat ut explōrātīs omnibus rēbus ad sē quam prīmum revertātur.

Ipse cum omnibus cōpiīs in Morinōs proficīscitur, quod inde erat
40 brevissimus in Britanniam trājectus (*passage*). Hūc nāvēs undique ex fīnitimīs regiōnibus et quam[14] superiōre aestāte ad Veneticum bellum[15] fēcerat classem jubet convenīre. 45

Interim, cōnsiliō ejus cognitō et per mercātōrēs perlātō ad Britannōs (*the Britons*), ā complūribus īnsulae cīvitātibus ad eum lēgātī veniunt quī polliceantur obsidēs 50 dare[16] atque imperiō populī Rōmānī obtemperāre (*to obey*). Qui-

[1] Ablative absolute, to be translated as a concessive clause coördinate with **etsī . . . sunt hiemēs.**

[2] Indirect object of **subministrāta.**

[3] Caesar hints at such aid (see p. 201, ll. 15-16) and mentions it definitely in his account of the war with the Veneti:

[4] *it would be of great advantage to him.*

[5] Caesar's thought was **mihi ūsuī erit, sī . . . adierō.**

[6] *unknown.* This statement is not quite accurate. The coast tribes, at least, had some knowledge of Britain.

[7] Adverb.

[8] With **Neque**—*for no one.*

[9] The indirect questions depend on **reperīre,** line 29.

[10] With **quī**—*which were suitable harbors.*

[11] To be taken with **praemittit,** line 34.

[12] *should incur any risk.*

[13] The clause is equivalent to **C. Volusēnum, quem idōneum** (*a suitable man*) **esse arbitrābātur.**

[14] The antecedent is **classem,** line 44.

[15] *the war with the Veneti.* For this tribe, see map, page 137.

[16] Instead of **sē datūrōs,** to emphasize the immediate and certain fulfillment of the promises.

LIFE IN ANCIENT BRITAIN

bus audītīs, līberāliter pollicitus[1] hortātusque ut in eā sententiā permanērent, eōs domum remittit et cum eīs ūnā Commium, quem ipse Atrebātibus[2] superātīs rēgem ibi[3] cōnstituerat, cujus et virtūtem et cōnsilium[4] probābat et quem sibi fidēlem esse arbitrābātur,[5] cujusque auctōritās in hīs regiōnibus magnī habēbātur,[6] mittit.

Huic imperat[7] quās possit adeat cīvitātēs hortēturque ut populī Rōmānī fidem sequantur,[8] sēque celeriter eō ventūrum nūntiet. Volusēnus perspectīs regiōnibus, quantum eī facultātis darī potuit[9] quī nāve ēgredī ac sē barbarīs committere nōn audēret, quīntō diē ad Caesarem revertitur quaeque ibi perspexisset renūntiat.

---

[1] *making liberal promises.*

[2] See page 192, note 8.

[3] Meaning among the Atrebates.

[4] *discretion.*

[5] But Commius later disappointed Caesar by heading a revolt in 52 B.C.

[6] *was highly regarded.*

[7] These orders are expressed in the subjunctives **adeat, hortētur, nūntiet,** which are in noun clauses of desire without **ut.**

[8] *put themselves under the protection.*

[9] *so far as opportunity could be given to one.* The word **facultātis** is genitive of the whole with **quantum.**

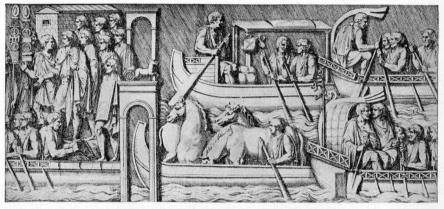

ARMY TRANSPORTS OF ROMAN TIMES

Even on the steamboats used today, travelers consider it an ordeal to cross the stormy English Channel. Caesar's troops must have had an uncomfortable crossing, since men, as well as horses and supplies, were carried in boats probably similar to these small craft manipulated by oars.

Making Ready for the Expedition

Dum in hīs locīs Caesar nāvium parandārum causā morātur, ex magnā parte Morinōrum ad eum lēgātī vēnērunt quī sē dē superiō-
5 ris temporis cōnsiliō[1] excūsārent (*to excuse*), quod hominēs[2] barbarī et nostrae cōnsuētūdinis[3] imperītī bellum populō Rōmānō fēcissent, sēque ea quae imperāsset factūrōs
10 pollicērentur.

Hoc sibi Caesar satis opportūnē accidisse arbitrātus, quod neque post tergum hostem relinquere volēbat neque bellī gerendī propter

annī tempus facultātem habēbat 15 neque hās tantulārum rērum occupātiōnēs Britanniae antepōnendās[4] jūdicābat, magnum eīs numerum obsidum imperat. Quibus adductīs eōs in fidem recipit. 20

Nāvibus circiter LXXX onerāriīs coāctīs, quot satis esse ad duās trānsportandās legiōnēs exīstimābat, quod praetereā nāvium longārum habēbat[5] quaestōrī, lēgātīs 25 praefectīsque distribuit. Hūc accēdēbant[6] XVIII onerāriae nāvēs, quae ex eō locō ā mīlibus passuum

[1] *for their attitude in the past;* explained by **quod . . . fēcissent.**

[2] In apposition with the unexpressed subject of **fēcissent.** Translate, *being men,* etc.

[3] The custom of sparing and protecting those who voluntarily surrender to the Romans. Caesar implies that they had expected to be slain or cast into slavery.

[4] Freely, *that these quite unimportant*

matters ought not to be given attention instead of the expedition to Britain. **Britanniae** is a dative with the compound of **ante.**

[5] *the additional war-ships which he* (Caesar) *had.* The noun **nāvium** is a genitive of the whole, and the entire **quod** clause serves as an object of the verb **distribuit.**

[6] With **Hūc**—*in addition to these, there were.*

VIII[1] ventō tenēbantur quōminus in eundem portum venīre possent;[2] hās equitibus tribuit.

Reliquum exercitum Q. Titūriō 5 Sabīnō et L. Aurunculeiō Cottae lēgātīs in Menapiōs atque in eōs pāgōs Morinōrum ā quibus ad eum lēgātī nōn vēnerant dūcendum dedit. P. Sulpicium Rūfum[3] lēgātum cum eō praesidiō quod satis 10 esse arbitrābātur portum tenēre jussit.

Roman Soldiers See Britain for the First Time

Hīs cōnstitūtīs rēbus nactus idōneam ad nāvigandum tem-15 pestātem tertiā ferē vigiliā solvit[4] equitēsque in ulteriōrem portum prōgredī et nāvēs cōnscendere et sē sequī jussit. Ā quibus cum paulō tardius esset administrātum,[5] ipse 20 hōrā diēī circiter quārtā[6] cum prīmīs nāvibus Britanniam attigit atque ibi in omnibus collibus expositās hostium cōpiās armātās cōnspexit. Cujus locī haec[7] erat 25 nātūra, atque ita montibus mare continēbātur[8] utī ex locīs superiōribus in lītus tēlum adigī posset.

Hunc ad ēgrediendum[9] nēquāquam (*in no way*) idōneum locum 30 arbitrātus, dum[10] reliquae nāvēs eō convenīrent, ad hōram nōnam in ancorīs expectāvit.

Interim lēgātīs tribūnīsque mīlitum convocātīs, et quae ex Volusēnō cognōvisset et quae fierī vellet 35 ostendit monuitque, ut[11] reī mīlitāris ratiō maximēque ut maritimae rēs postulārent,[12] ut,[13] cum celerem atque īnstabilem mōtum habērent,[14] ad nūtum (*at a nod*) et ad 40 tempus[15] omnēs rēs ab eīs administrārentur.

Hīs dīmissīs et ventum et aestum ūnō tempore nactus secundum, datō signō et sublātīs ancorīs circiter mīlia passuum VII ab eō locō 45 prōgressus apertō ac plānō (*level*) lītore nāvēs cōnstituit.

[1] *at a distance of eight miles.*

[2] *so that they could not.*

[3] *Publius Sulpicius Rufus* (pub'li-us sŭl-pish'ius rö'fus).

[4] *he set sail* (literally, *loosed*, i.e., the boats from the moorings).

[5] Perhaps best taken as an adversative clause loosely used; translate, *when they had proceeded to carry out these orders, though a little too slowly*—that is, too slowly to take advantage of the favoring winds that carried Caesar to Britain. A change of wind kept them in port for three days.

[6] The fourth hour would be about 10 A.M. The point sighted was near Dover, about 28 miles from Boulogne.

[7] *such.*

[8] Freely, *so narrow was the seashore below the cliffs* (literally, *the sea was hemmed in by the cliffs in such a way*).

[9] *for disembarking.*

[10] *until.*

[11] The *ut* clause means *as the rules of war and especially as naval operations demand.*

[12] Subjunctive by attraction. See Gr. S., 118.

[13] To be taken with the verb **administrārentur**, lines 41-42. The noun clause **ut . . . administrārentur** depends on **monuit**, line 36.

[14] The *cum* clause means *inasmuch as they have (to do with) rapid and irregular movements.*

[15] *on the instant.*

Through the Surf

AT BARBARĪ, cōnsiliō Rōmā-nōrum cognitō, praemissō[1] equitātū et essedāriīs (*charioteers*), quō plērumque genere[2] in proeliīs ūtī cōnsuērunt, reliquīs cōpiīs sub-secūtī nostrōs nāvibus ēgredī[3] pro-hibēbant.

Erat ob hās causās summa diffi-cultās, quod nāvēs propter magni-tūdinem nisi in altō[4] cōnstituī nōn poterant, mīlitibus autem ignōtīs locīs,[5] impedītīs manibus[6] magnō et gravī onere armōrum pressīs,[6] simul et dē nāvibus dēsiliendum[7] et in flūctibus cōnsistendum[8] et cum hostibus erat pugnandum, cum illī[9] aut ex āridō aut paulum in aquam prōgressī omnibus membrīs expedītīs, nōtissimīs locīs audācter tēla conjicerent et equōs īnsuēfac-tōs (*well-trained*) incitārent.

Quibus rēbus nostrī perterritī atque hujus omnīnō generis[10] pug-nae imperītī nōn eādem alacritāte ac studiō quō in pedestribus ūtī proeliīs cōnsuērant ūtēbantur.

"Follow the Flag"

QUOD ubi Caesar animadver-tit, nāvēs longās, quārum et speciēs erat barbarīs inūsitātior[11] et mōtus ad ūsum expedītior,[12] pau-lum removērī ab onerāriīs nāvibus et rēmīs incitārī et ad latus apertum hostium cōnstituī[13] atque inde fun-dīs (*by slings*), sagittīs, tormentīs hostēs prōpellī ac submovērī jus-sit;[14] quae rēs magnō ūsuī nostrīs fuit. Nam et nāvium figūrā (*by the shape*) et rēmōrum mōtū et in-ūsitātō genere tormentōrum per-mōtī barbarī cōnstitērunt ac pau-lum modo pedem rettulērunt.[15]

Atque nostrīs mīlitibus cūnctan-tibus (*delaying*), maximē propter altitūdinem maris, quī[16] x legiōnis aquilam ferēbat, obtestātus (*hav-ing called upon*) deōs, ut ea rēs le-giōnī fēliciter ēvenīret, "Dēsilīte," inquit, "commīlitōnēs (*comrades*),

[1] Translate as a verb in the active voice.

[2] *a kind of troops which.*

[3] See page 191, note 17, on **ingredī prohibuerint.**

[4] *in deep water.*

[5] Ablative absolute.

[6] Take with **mīlitibus**—*burdened as they were.*

[7] *the soldiers had to leap down;* **mīlitibus** in line 11 is dative of agent.

[8] *get a foothold.*

[9] *while the enemy.*

[10] For case see Gr. S., 55.

[11] *quite unfamiliar.* The large trading vessels that visited Britain were different in shape from the war-ships of the Romans and had no oars. The Britons themselves used small wicker boats covered with skins.

[12] *which were more easily managed* (lit-erally, *whose motion was less encumbered for management*).

[13] *should be stationed near the unpro-tected flank of the enemy,* i.e., on the right side.

[14] Governs five infinitives with ac-cusatives as subject—**nāvēs** of the first three, and **hostēs** of the last two.

[15] The usual expression for an orderly retreat is **pedem referre.**

[16] *the man who.*

"FOLLOW ME, COMRADES!"

nisi vultis[1] aquilam hostibus prō-
dere. Ego certē meum reī pūblicae
atque imperātōrī officium praesti-
terō.[2]"

5　Hoc cum vōce magnā dīxisset,
sē ex nāve prōjēcit atque in hostēs
aquilam ferre coepit.

Tum nostrī cohortātī inter sē[3]
nē tantum dēdecus (*disgrace*) ad-
mitterētur, ūniversī ex nāve dēsi- 10
luērunt.

Hōs item ex proximīs nāvibus
cum cōnspexissent,[4] subsecūtī hostibus appropinquāvērunt.

Rowboats to the Rescue

PUGNĀTUM est ab utrīsque ācriter. Nostrī tamen, quod neque
ōrdinēs servāre neque firmiter
īnsistere[5] neque signa subsequī
poterant, atque alius aliā ex nāve,[6]
20　quibuscumque signīs occurrerat
sē aggregābat,[7] magnopere perturbābantur.

Hostēs vērō, nōtīs omnibus vadīs,[8] ubi ex lītore aliquōs singulārēs
ex nāve ēgredientēs cōnspexerant, 20
incitātīs equīs impedītōs adoriē-
bantur, plūrēs paucōs circumsistē-
bant,[9] aliī ab latere apertō in ūni-
versōs tēla conjiciēbant.

Quod cum animadvertisset Cae- 30

---

[1] From **volō**.　See Gr. S., 45.
[2] Future perfect.
[3] *encouraging one another.*
[4] *also the soldiers from the nearest
ships, when they had seen these.*
[5] The two words mean *to stand firmly.*

[6] *men from different ships (one from
one ship, another from another).*
[7] *gathered about whatever standards they
happened upon.*
[8] Ablative absolute denoting cause.
[9] *large bands surrounded small groups.*

sar, scaphās[1] longārum nāvium, item speculātōria nāvigia[2] mīlitibus complērī jussit[3] et, quōs[4] labōrantēs cōnspexerat, hīs subsidia sub-
5 mittēbat.

Nostrī, simul[5] in āridō cōnstitērunt, suīs omnibus cōnsecūtīs in

hostēs impetum fēcērunt atque eōs in fugam dedērunt, neque[6] longius[7] prōsequī potuērunt, quod equitēs 10 cursum tenēre atque īnsulam capere nōn potuerant. Hoc ūnum[8] ad prīstinam fortūnam Caesarī dēfuit.

An Apology Accepted

Hostēs proeliō superātī, simul atque sē ex fugā recēpērunt, statim ad Caesarem lēgātōs dē pāce mīsērunt; obsidēs sēsē datūrōs quaeque imperāsset factūrōs polli-
20 citī sunt.

Ūnā cum hīs lēgātīs Commius Atrebās vēnit, quem suprā dēmōnstrāveram ā Caesare in Britanniam praemissum.

25 Hunc illī ē nāve ēgressum, cum ad eōs ōrātōris modō[9] Caesaris mandāta dēferret, comprehenderant atque in vincula conjēcerant. Tum proeliō factō remīsērunt et in
30 petendā pāce ejus reī culpam (*blame*) in multitūdinem[10] contulērunt et propter imprūdentiam[11] ut ignōscerētur[12] petīvērunt.

Caesar questus quod, cum ultrō
35 in continentem lēgātīs missīs pā-

BRITANNIA

cem ab sē petīssent, bellum sine causā intulissent, ignōscere[13] imprūdentiae[11] dīxit obsidēsque im-

---

[1] Small messenger boats belonging to the war-ships.

[2] *scouting boats*, light, swift-sailing vessels used in reconnoitering. They were painted green to escape observation, and the sailors were dressed in green for the same reason.

[3] Note the change in tense. The perfect denotes a single act; the past perfect and imperfect denote repeated acts.

[4] The antecedent is **hīs.**

[5] Equivalent to **simul atque.**

[6] *but . . . not.*

[7] *very far.*

[8] *In this alone did Caesar's usual good fortune fail him.*

[9] *in the character (of) an ambassador.*

[10] Probably the leaders had been equally responsible.

[11] *ignorance* (of the rights of envoys).

[12] *that they might be pardoned.* Verbs governing the dative are used impersonally in the passive, and the dative is usually retained.

[13] Supply **sē** as subject.

perāvit; quōrum illī partem statim dedērunt, partem ex longinquiō- ribus (*more distant*) locīs arcessī- tam paucīs diēbus sēsē datūrōs 5 dīxērunt.

Intereā suōs in agrōs remigrāre (*to return*) jussērunt, prīncipēsque undique convenīre et sē cīvitātēs- que suās Caesarī commendāre coe- pērunt.

Caught in a Storm

Hīs rēbus pāce cōnfirmātā post diem quārtum quam[1] est in Britanniam ventum nāvēs XVIII, dē quibus suprā dēmōnstrātum 15 est, quae equitēs sustulerant,[2] ex superiōre portū lēnī ventō sol- vērunt.[3] Quae cum appropinquā- rent Britanniae et ex castrīs vidē- rentur, tanta tempestās subitō co- 20 orta est ut nūlla eārum cursum

tenēre posset, sed aliae eōdem unde erant profectae referrentur, aliae ad īnferiōrem partem īnsulae, quae est propius[4] sōlis occāsum, magnō suō cum perīculō dējiceren- tur; quae tamen[5] ancorīs jactīs, cum flūctibus complērentur, neces- sāriō (*necessarily*) adversā nocte[6] in altum prōvectae continentem (*hav- ing set out*) petīvērunt.

A Dismal Outlook

Eādem nocte[7] accidit ut esset lūna plēna (*full*), quī diēs ma- ritimōs aestūs[8] maximōs in Ōceanō efficere cōnsuēvit;[9] nostrīsque id 35 erat incognitum (*unknown*).[10] Ita ūnō tempore et longās nāvēs, quās Caesar in āridum subdūxerat,[11] aestus complēbat, et onerāriās, quae ad ancorās erant dēligātae,

tempestās afflictābat (*damaged*), neque ūlla nostrīs facultās aut administrandī[12] aut auxiliandī (*of aiding*) dabātur.

Complūribus nāvibus frāctīs,[13] re- liquae cum essent, fūnibus (*ropes*), ancorīs, reliquīsque armāmentīs (*rigging*) āmissīs, ad nāvigandum inūtilēs (*useless*), magna,[14] id quod

[1] Equivalent to **quārtō diē postquam.**

[2] *had taken on board.* From what verb does this form come?

[3] *sailed;* with **nāvēs** as subject, used absolutely. Contrast with **solvit,** *he set sail,* in line 15 of page 234.

[4] This comparative adverb sometimes governs an accusative (here **occāsum**).

[5] With **ancorīs jactīs,** which may be translated by a principal clause—*never- theless* (in spite of the storm) *they cast anchor; but since the boats* (**quae**) *began to fill,* etc.

[6] *in the face of the night* (literally, *with the night against them*).

[7] According to astronomical calcula- tion, the night of August 30.

[8] The tides rise to the height of 19 feet at Dover and 25 feet at Boulogne.

[9] *a time which always causes.*

[10] The tides in the Mediterranean are so slight as to be hardly noticeable.

[11] The regular word for beaching ships, especially for the winter.

[12] Used absolutely—*of managing* (the ships).

[13] *wrecked.*

[14] Modifying **perturbātiō,** in line 2 of page 239.

necesse erat accidere, tōtīus exercitūs perturbātiō (*alarm*) facta est.

Neque[1] enim nāvēs erant aliae quibus reportārī possent, et omnia dēerant quae ad reficiendās nāvēs erant ūsuī, et, quod omnibus cōnstābat[2] hiemārī in Galliā oportēre, frūmentum in hīs locīs in hiemem prōvīsum nōn erat. 10

Hope for the Islanders

QUIBUS rēbus cognitīs, prīncipēs Britanniae, quī post proelium ad Caesarem convēnerant, inter sē collocūtī, cum et equitēs et nāvēs et frūmentum Rōmānīs dēesse[3] intellegerent et paucitātem mīlitum ex castrōrum exiguitāte (*the smallness*) cognōscerent,[4] quae hōc[5] erant etiam angustiōra, quod sine impedīmentīs Caesar legiōnēs trānsportāverat, optimum factū[6] esse dūxērunt[7] rebelliōne (*revolt*) factā frūmentō commeātūque nostrōs prohibēre et rem in hiemem prōdūcere, quod hīs superātīs aut[8] reditū interclūsīs nēminem posteā bellī īnferendī causā in Britanniam trānsitūrum cōnfīdēbant.

Itaque rūrsus conjūrātiōne factā 30 paulātim ex castrīs discēdere et suōs clam ex agrīs dēdūcere coepērunt.

FROM ANCIENT BRITAIN
These elaborately made bridle bits with their fine enamel decorations show beautiful workmanship.

Justifiable Suspicions

AT CAESAR, etsī nōndum eōrum cōnsilia cognōverat, tamen et ex ēventū[9] nāvium suārum et ex eō, quod[10] obsidēs dare intermīserant, fore id[11] quod accidit suspicābātur. Itaque ad omnēs cāsūs subsidia comparābat. Nam 40 et frūmentum ex agrīs cotīdiē in castra cōnferēbat et quae[12] gravissimē afflīctae erant (*had been*

[1] *for on the one hand there were no other ships*, etc. Translate et in line 5, *on the other hand*, and et in line 7, *then, too.*

[2] *it was evident to all.* The subject of cōnstābat is the infinitive oportēre.

[3] *that the Romans lacked.*

[4] Repeat the conjunction cum in translating.

[5] *on this account;* an ablative of measure of difference with an idea of cause.

[6] See Gr. S., 141.

[7] Equivalent to putāvērunt.

[8] *or at least.*

[9] The word has here the rarer meaning of *accident*, or *disaster.*

[10] *from the fact that.*

[11] The words fore id are equivalent to id futūrum esse.

[12] With nāvēs in line 1 on page 240. See note 1 on that page.

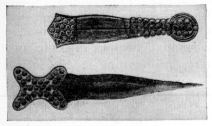

A BRITISH DAGGER AND SHEATH

damaged) nāvēs, eārum[1] māteriā atque aere ad reliquās reficiendās ūtēbātur et quae[2] ad eās rēs erant ūsuī ex continentī comparārī jubēbat.

Itaque, cum summō studiō ā 5 mīlitibus administrārētur, xii nāvibus āmissīs, reliquīs[3] ut nāvigārī satis commodē posset effēcit.[4]

Dangerous Harvesting

D<small>UM</small> ea geruntur, legiōne ex cōnsuētūdine ūnā frūmentātum[5] missā, quae appellābātur vii, neque ūllā ad id tempus bellī suspīciōne interpositā,[6] cum pars hominum in agrīs remanēret, pars 15 etiam in castra ventitāret (*were coming often*), eī quī prō portīs castrōrum in statiōne erant[7] Caesarī nūntiāvērunt pulverem majōrem quam cōnsuētūdō ferret[8] in eā 20 parte vidērī quam in partem legiō iter fēcisset.

Caesar, id quod erat[9] suspicātus, aliquid novī ā barbarīs initum cōnsiliī,[10] cohortēs quae in statiōnibus 25 erant sēcum in eam partem proficīscī, ex reliquīs duās in statiōnem succēdere, reliquās armārī[11] et cōnfestim sē subsequī jussit.

Cum paulō longius ā castrīs prōcessisset, suōs ab hostibus premī 30 atque aegrē sustinēre[12] et cōnfertā legiōne ex omnibus partibus tēla conjicī animadvertit.

Nam quod omnī ex reliquīs partibus dēmessō (*having been reaped*) 35 frūmentō pars ūna[13] erat reliqua, suspicātī hostēs hūc nostrōs esse ventūrōs noctū in silvīs dēlituerant (*had hidden*). Tum dispersōs dēpositīs armīs in metendō (*reaping*) 40 occupātōs subitō adortī paucīs interfectīs reliquōs incertīs ōrdinibus[14] perturbāverant, simul equitātū atque essedīs circumdederant.

---

[1] The words **quae . . . nāvēs, eārum** are equivalent to **eārum nāvium quae.**

[2] The antecedent is an understood **ea,** the subject of **comparārī.**

[3] Put ahead of its normal position for emphasis.

[4] *made it possible for them to sail tolerably well.*

[5] *to gather grain,* a supine. See Gr. S., 140.

[6] *without any suspicion having arisen.*

[7] Before each of the four gates a cohort was regularly placed on guard (**statiō**).

[8] *unusually large* (literally, *larger than custom brings*).

[9] The expression is explained by **aliquid . . . cōnsiliī**—*namely, that some new plot,* etc.

[10] Genitive of the whole, with **aliquid.**

[11] Equivalent to **sē armāre.**

[12] Used absolutely, *stood their ground.*

[13] *only one place* (from which grain could be obtained).

[14] *in disordered ranks.* The sudden attack of the enemy made the usual formation impossible.

BRITISH CHARIOTS DASHING INTO BATTLE

Cavalry on Wheels

Genus hoc est ex essedīs pugnae. Prīmō per omnēs partēs perequitant[1] et tēla conjiciunt atque ipsō terrōre equōrum et strepitū rotārum[2] ōrdinēs plērumque perturbant, et cum sē inter equitum turmās (*troops*) īnsinuāvērunt,[3] ex essedīs dēsiliunt et pedibus proeliantur (*fight*).

Aurīgae interim paulum ex proeliō excēdunt atque ita currūs collocant ut, sī illī[4] ā multitūdine hostium premantur, expedītum ad suōs receptum (*retreat*) habeant. Ita mōbilitātem (*agility*) equitum, stabilitātem (*steadiness*) peditum in proeliīs praestant,[5] ac tantum ūsū et cotīdiānā exercitātiōne efficiunt utī in dēclīvī ac praecipitī locō[6] incitātōs[7] equōs sustinēre[8] et brevī[9] moderārī (*to control*) ac flectere et per tēmōnem[10] percurrere (*to run*) et in jugō īnsistere (*to stand*) et sē inde in currūs citissimē recipere cōnsuērint.

[1] *they* (the Britons) *ride.*

[2] *by the mere terror which the horses inspire and by the rattling of the* (chariot) *wheels.*

[3] *they have pushed.* The charioteers drove into the spaces between their own troops of cavalry, where the men dismounted. The chariots then withdrew a short distance until they were needed.

[4] Meaning the dismounted charioteers.

[5] *they display.*

[6] *and even precipitous ground;* here the word **ac,** as often, adds a stronger expression.

[7] *when at full speed.*

[8] *to check;* a complementary infinitive with **cōnsuērint.**

[9] Equivalent to **celeriter.**

[10] The prepositional phrase means *along the pole.*

A Rescue in the Nick of Time

QUIBUS rēbus perturbātīs nostrīs[1] tempore opportūnissimō Caesar auxilium tulit; namque ejus adventū hostēs cōnstitērunt, nostrī
5 sē ex timōre recēpērunt.

Quō factō ad lacessendum hostem et committendum proelium aliēnum esse tempus arbitrātus suō[2] sē locō continuit et, brevī
10 tempore intermissō, in castra legiōnēs redūxit.

Dum haec geruntur, nostrīs omnibus occupātīs, quī erant in agrīs reliquī[3] discessērunt.

Secūtae sunt continuōs complū-
rēs diēs tempestātēs quae[4] et nostrōs in castrīs continērent et hostem ā pugnā prohibērent. Interim barbarī nūntiōs in omnēs partēs dīmīsērunt paucitātemque nostrōrum mīlitum suīs praedicāvērunt et quanta praedae faciendae atque in perpetuum suī līberandī facultās darētur sī Rōmānōs castrīs expulissent, dēmōnstrāvērunt.

Hīs rēbus[5] celeriter magnā multitūdine peditātūs equitātūsque coāctā ad castra vēnērunt.

Another Attack That Failed

CAESAR, etsī idem quod superiōribus diēbus acciderat fore vidēbat, ut,[6] sī essent hostēs pulsī,[7] celeritāte perīculum effugerent, tamen nactus equitēs circiter xxx, quōs Commius Atrebās, dē quō
35 ante[8] dictum est, sēcum trānsportāverat, legiōnēs in aciē prō castrīs cōnstituit.

Commissō proeliō, diūtius nostrōrum mīlitum impetum hostēs ferre nōn[9] potuērunt ac terga vertērunt. Quōs nostrī tantō[10] spatiō secūtī quantum cursū et vīribus efficere potuērunt,[11] complūrēs ex eīs occīdērunt; deinde omnibus longē lātēque aedificiīs incēnsīs sē in castra recēpērunt.

Back to Gaul

EŌDEM diē lēgātī ab hostibus missī ad Caesarem dē pāce vēnērunt. Hīs Caesar numerum

obsidum quem ante imperāverat duplicāvit[12] eōsque in continentem addūcī jussit, quod propinquā diē

---

[1] Dative with **auxilium tulit.**

[2] **suus**—*one's own, favorable,* as opposed to **aliēnus** is *another's, unfavorable.*

[3] The Britons mentioned in lines 13-14 of page 240.

[4] *of a sort that;* hence the subjunctive.

[5] *by such measures.*

[6] *namely* (*that*).

[7] In direct discourse we should have, instead of **essent pulsī,** the future perfect indicative.

[8] On page 232, line 4, and page 237, line 21.

[9] The words **diūtius nōn** mean *not very long.*

[10] With **quantum**—*as far as.*

[11] Freely, *as it was possible to continue the pursuit on foot* (literally, *as they could by running and by [their own] strength*). The cavalry were usually employed to pursue a retreating enemy.

[12] *demanded of them twice the number.*

aequinoctiī[1] īnfirmīs (*weakened*) nāvibus hiemī nāvigātiōnem subjiciendam[2] nōn exīstimābat.

Ipse idōneam tempestātem nactus paulō post mediam noctem nāvēs solvit; quae omnēs incolumēs ad continentem pervēnērunt, sed ex eīs onerāriae duae eōsdem portūs, quōs reliquae,[3] capere nōn potuērunt et paulō īnfrā[4] dēlātae sunt. 10

An Inhospitable Reception

QUIBUS ex nāvibus[5] cum essent expositī mīlitēs circiter ccc atque in castra[6] contenderent, Morinī, quōs Caesar in Britanniam proficīscēns pācātōs relīquerat, spē praedae adductī[7] prīmō[8] nōn ita[9] magnō suōrum numerō circumstetērunt[10] ac, sī sē interficī nōllent, arma pōnere[11] jussērunt.

Cum illī, orbe factō,[12] sēsē dēfenderent, celeriter ad clāmōrem hominum[13] circiter mīlia VI convēnērunt. Quā rē nūntiātā, Caesar omnem ex castrīs equitātum suīs auxiliō mīsit. 25

Interim nostrī mīlitēs impetum hostium sustinuērunt atque amplius hōrīs IV fortissimē pugnāvērunt et, paucīs vulneribus acceptīs,[14] complūrēs ex hīs occīdērunt. 30 Posteā vērō quam equitātus noster in cōnspectum vēnit, hostēs abjectīs armīs terga vertērunt, magnusque eōrum numerus est occīsus.

Driven into the Forest

CAESAR posterō diē T. Labiēnum lēgātum cum eīs legiōnibus quās ex Britanniā redūxerat in Morinōs, quī rebelliōnem fēcerant,[15] mīsit. Quī cum propter siccitātēs[16] palūdum, quō sē reciperent nōn habērent,[17] quō perfugiō superiōre annō erant ūsī,[18] omnēs ferē in potestātem Labiēnī vēnērunt.

At Q. Titūrius et L. Cotta lēgātī, quī in Menapiōrum fīnēs legiōnēs 45 dūxerant, omnibus eōrum agrīs

---

[1] With **quod propinquā diē** (p. 242, l. 52)—*as the time of the equinox was drawing near.* Severe storms often occur about this time of year.

[2] *the voyage should be exposed to stormy weather.*

[3] Supply **cēpērunt.**

[4] South of Boulogne.

[5] Referring to the two transports mentioned above, line 8.

[6] Made by Sulpicius Rufus at Boulogne. Caesar had already reached his camp.

[7] The attacking party was apparently an unorganized mob.

[8] An adverb.

[9] *not very.*

[10] The object of this verb and the subject of **pōnere** are easily supplied.

[11] *to lay down.*

[12] This formation presented a protected front against an enemy attacking in superior numbers on every side.

[13] Take with **mīlia.**

[14] Adversative—*while they themselves received only a few wounds.*

[15] *had revolted.*

[16] *dryness.* Plural because referring to several places.

[17] *had no place to which they could withdraw.*

[18] *which they had used as a place of refuge;* **quō** refers to **palūdum,** but is attracted into agreement with **perfugiō.**

vāstātīs, frūmentīs succīsīs (*having been cut*), aedificiīs incēnsīs, quod Menapiī sē omnēs in dēnsissimās silvās abdiderant, sē ad Caesarem recēpērunt.

Caesar in Belgīs omnium legiō-

num hīberna cōnstituit. Eō duae omnīnō cīvitātēs ex Britanniā obsidēs mīsērunt, reliquae neglēxērunt.[1] Hīs rēbus gestīs, ex litterīs Caesaris diērum xx supplicātiō ā senātū dēcrēta est.[2]

[1] Supply **hoc facere.**

[2] This thanksgiving, in spite of the opposition of Caesar's enemies at Rome, was made even longer than the previous one. The length of the thanksgiving shows the importance which the Romans attached to these campaigns and the influence of Caesar's political supporters.

COMPREHENSION QUESTIONS

Find answers to the following questions regarding Caesar's first invasion of Britain.

1. What reason does Caesar give for planning to invade Britain?
2. From whom did he attempt to obtain information regarding the island?
3. How many legions did he plan to take with him?
4. What was the character of the coast at the point which the Roman fleet first reached?
5. What class of troops did the Britons use which had not been mentioned in the account of the wars with the Gauls and the Germans?
6. What special difficulties were connected with the effort of the Romans to disembark?
7. What part of Caesar's forces had failed to arrive with the main body of the army?
8. What reason does Caesar give for not having anticipated danger from the high tides?
9. How were the Britons affected by the disaster to Caesar's fleet?
10. How did Caesar secure materials for repairing the damaged boats?
11. How did the Britons select the location in which to place an ambush for the Romans?
12. What was the method of chariot fighting?
13. What was the result of the attack of the Britons on Caesar's camp?
14. Which of the Gallic tribes attempted to renew the war when Caesar's troops returned from Britain?
15. How extensive a celebration at Rome was voted in honor of Caesar's campaigns of the year 55 B.C.?

WORD STUDY IX

Suffixes in Latin and in English

Numerous suffixes are employed in the formation of Latin words. Examples of words formed with some of the most common suffixes are given here.

Nouns Formed from Verbs

Latin nouns are frequently formed from verbs by the addition of the suffixes -iō, -tūra, -men, -mentum (*pl.* -menta).

conjūrātiō, *conspiracy*, from conjūrō, *conspire*
dēditiō, *surrender*, from dēdō, *surrender*
oppugnātiō, *attack*, from oppugnō, *attack*
profectiō, *departure*, from proficīscor, *set out*

agmen, *army*, from agō, *drive*
certāmen, *contest*, from certō, *struggle*
flūmen, *river*, from fluō, *flow*

cultūra, *cultivation*, from colō, *cultivate*
nātūra, *nature*, from nāscor, *be born*
sepultūra, *burial*, from sepeliō, *bury*
statūra, *stature*, from stō, *stand*

documentum, *proof*, from doceō, *teach*
impedīmenta, *baggage*, from impediō, *hinder*
monumentum, *monument*, from moneō, *remind*

These suffixes in modified form appear in English words: -iō as *-ion;* -tūra as *-ture;* -mentum as *-ment.*

legion	armature	impediment
oration	nature	monument
rebellion	stature	

Nouns Formed from Adjectives

Latin nouns are also made from adjectives.

audācia, *boldness*, from audāx, *bold*
clēmentia, *mercy*, from clēmēns, *mild*
grātia, *favor*, from grātus, *grateful*

jūstitia, *justice*, from jūstus, *just*
nōtitia, *fame*, from nōtus, *well-known*
vigilia, *watch*, from vigil, *watchful*

Adjectives Formed from Verbs

Latin adjectives are frequently derived from verbs by the addition of the suffixes -āx, -idus, -ilis, and -bilis.

audāx, *bold*, from audeō, *dare*
pugnāx, *warlike*, from pugnō, *fight*
rapāx, *grasping*, from rapiō, *seize*

cupidus, *eager*, from cupiō, *desire*
fluidus, *fluid*, from fluō, *flow*
timidus, *timid*, from timeō, *fear*

facilis, *easy*, from faciō, *do*
amābilis, *lovely*, from amō, *love*
horribilis, *horrible*, from horreō, *shudder*
stabilis, *stable*, from stō, *stand*

These suffixes appear in English in slightly changed form: -āx (with another suffix) as *-acious;* -idus as *-id;* -bilis as *-ble.*

audacious	rapid	amiable
capacious	valid	visible
loquacious	horrid	sensible

EXERCISES

1. Find at least three additional English words made with the suffixes given in the last paragraph of page 245.

Idioms and Phrases

The idioms and phrases listed below occur frequently in the text read. Learning them thoroughly will be of great help in reading.

agmen claudere, *to bring up the rear*
novissimīs praesidiō erant, *they served as rear guard*
quid fierī vellet ostendit, *he explained what he wanted to have done*
quō cōnsuērat intervāllō, *at the usual distance*
reī mīlitāris perītissimus, *thoroughly familiar with military affairs*
signa īnferre, *to advance to the attack*

Vocabulary Review

The following words, which appear frequently in this book, are important in second-year work. Their meanings should be thoroughly learned.

accidō	dēclīvis	nancīscor	priusquam	remittō
aestus	dēsum	nūntiō	prōgredior	sententia
aquila	effugiō	occidō	prohibeō	singulāris
celer	exercitātiō	occīdo	prope	statim
classis	expōnō	paulō	pulvis	statiō
commendō	incendō	paulum	quaestor	submittō
commūnicō	incolō	permoveō	quantus	subsequor
compleō	īnfrā	perspiciō	-que	suspicor
cōnfestim	latus, -eris	perturbō	quīcumque	temere
cōnscrībō	legiō	polliceor	quō	tergum
cōnspectus	magnitūdō	postulō	quōminus	tribuō
cotīdiē	mīlle	prīnceps	redigō	vāstō

THE ROMANS IN BRITAIN

THE island which the Romans knew as *Britannia* is today the busy and densely populated center of an empire far larger than the one ruled by ancient Rome. But when Caesar and his soldiers first crossed from the continent to the island, Britain was occupied for the most part by scattered barbaric tribes. To the civilized peoples of the Mediterranean region it was almost an unknown land.

The men who so fiercely disputed Caesar's landing were related to the Gauls, and their civilization was similar to that of their cousins across the Channel. Of the various tribes, those in the southeastern part of Britain were the most highly civilized. These were skilful in building ships, and they had long carried on a considerable trade with the Gauls, as well as with more distant peoples.

Even before Rome was founded, ships from Phoenicia, on the far-eastern coast of the Mediterranean, had made their way through the Strait of Gibraltar and up to Cornwall. There the traders exchanged their manufactured goods for cargoes of tin from the mines

BRONZE SHIELD

The Britons did very beautiful work in bronze, as can be seen from the fine ornamentation on this shield.

of Cornwall. By the fourth century B.C. there was also a regular trade in tin between Cornwall and *Massilia*, the modern Marseilles.

British craftsmen were expert in weaving cloth with tartan, or plaid, designs and in working with wood and metals. Their enamel and bronze work also showed much artistic ability. The Britons were sufficiently advanced so that they had used gold coins in their commerce for several centuries before Caesar's invasion, though in some parts of the island iron bars or rods served as currency. The forests had been cleared in many places; grain was grown, and stock raised.

Caesar did not succeed in adding Britain to Rome's possessions, and his immediate successors regarded the Channel as the outer boundary of the Empire. But when, about eighty-five years after Caesar's death, the Emperor Claudius led an army to Britain, the real conquest was begun. It was not an

BRITISH HELMET

The shape of this helmet is similar to those worn by the Gauls. Notice the beautiful workmanship and decorations.

easy task, since the Britons, like the Gauls, had always lived in freedom, and therefore made a valiant resistance.

PAN USED IN RELIGIOUS RITES
From this dish wine was poured out in distant Britain as an offering to Roman gods.

The more civilized tribes in the southeastern and central lowlands were first overcome. Here a beginning was made in the process of converting a conquered region into a Roman province. Many retired Roman veterans settled here. Towns were established and given the civic rights enjoyed by towns in Italy. Roman laws and customs were introduced.

Life in Britain came to be similar to that in any other part of the Roman Empire. The people who lived in the towns and came into contact with Roman soldiers began gradually to speak Latin. Even the people of some rural regions learned the language of the conquerors.

The tribes living in the hilly and mountainous regions of northern and western Britain—Scotland and Wales—were never really subdued, and for many years they waged an intermittent warfare. Peaceful occupation of these regions was not possible, but many forts were built in strategic places, in the same way that forts were constructed along our own frontier

to help keep the hostile Indians in check. Now and then the defenders of an outlying Roman fort were wiped out by an attacking band, just as were the garrisons of some isolated forts in the pioneer days of American history.

In the second century A.D. the Emperor Hadrian built the famous fortified wall which bore his name. It ran all the way across Britain—east and west over seventy miles. At every Roman mile along this wall was a small fort, and between every two forts were two signal towers. Although Hadrian's successor built a rampart still farther north, which was held for some years, the "Great Wall" was definitely accepted as marking the limit of Roman conquest on the north.

By the third century A.D. the Roman-British civilization in the lowlands was firmly established. Before this had been accomplished, there had been a series of uprisings, in one of which thousands of Romans were massacred and many

ROMAN BROOCHES FOUND IN BRITAIN

ON THE ROMAN WALL

towns sent up in flames. But now there were a number of flourishing towns. Londinium, on the site of modern London, had become a place of importance. It served as the financial headquarters of the province and was developing into a rich trading center.

British industries were thriving, and cloth and various artistic products were exported. In fact, the fame of the skilled British craftsmen was well established on the continent.

Great tracts of land were under cultivation, and British grain supplied the Roman armies holding the frontier along the Rhine and the Danube.

In spite of their prosperity, the towns of Britain were not very large, and none could boast of having public buildings of any great importance. Most towns had public baths, a forum surrounded by busy shops, and perhaps a small amphitheater outside the walls. In all Britain there have been found the remains of only one theater, and there seem to have been no public libraries. Temples were comparatively few, so far as can be judged by their remains.

It is true that in Aquae Sulis, the modern city of Bath, the ruins of fine public baths have been uncovered, proving that the place was a popular health resort in the days of the Roman occupation, even as it is today. There was also a richly adorned temple in

IN AQUAE SULIS TODAY

This picture shows a corner of the Roman bath at Bath.

Aquae Sulis. In general, however, as one writer has expressed it, the quality of Roman life was to be found in Britain, but the quantity was thin.

The country houses of the wealthy landowners were made comfortable with heating systems. Many of the homes were decorated with frescoes and mosaics and filled with valuable objects of art, but they did not compare in size and luxury with the Italian villas.

The land in the large country estates was usually worked by slave labor, although tracts might be parceled off into small farms, which were handed over to tenants.

Britain never became a profitable province, for the expense of maintaining Roman rule there far exceeded the income which it afforded the Empire. When the frontiers of the Empire began to crumble under the onslaught of the barbarians, this relatively unimportant and remote province was gradually abandoned. Rome, fighting for its existence, could not defend it. Troops were withdrawn from their stations and from the "Great Wall" itself. The half-savage tribes of the North then swarmed down on the defenseless people, while the equally uncivilized Angles and Saxons—Teutonic tribes from whom the Britons had implored aid—seized the coast region, and later overran all the southern part of the island.

There are today many reminders of Roman rule in Britain. The "-chester," "-caster," and "-cester" in which the names of a number of English towns end, such as Winchester, Lancaster, and Leicester, show that these towns developed around Roman camps (*castra*). The ruins of Hadrian's Wall and of other structures, the highways which follow Roman roads, and the many relics of domestic, military, and industrial life which have been unearthed all bear witness to the days when the inhabitants of ancient Britain were brought into direct contact with the Roman Empire.

A ROMAN CAMP BESIEGED

They fought like brave men, long and well.
HALLECK: MARCO BOZZARIS

Success in Britain; Disaster on the Continent

APPARENTLY feeling that his first campaign in Britain had not sufficiently convinced the islanders of the power of Rome, Caesar planned a second expedition for the summer of 54 B. C. In order to guard against any uprising in Gaul during his absence, he decided to take with him to Britain several Gallic leaders whom he felt he could not fully trust.

Among these was Dumnorix, the Haeduan. Shortly before time for sailing, Dumnorix left the camp with a group of followers and attempted to escape. He was at once pursued by a detachment of cavalry, and on refusing to surrender, he was killed.

Labienus was left in Gaul with three legions, to see that Roman authority was maintained, while Caesar sailed for Britain with the rest of the army. The landing was made without difficulty. The Britons, overawed by the great array of ships carrying the Roman forces, offered no resistance.

In the course of the summer a considerable number of tribes in the southeastern part of the island were compelled to recognize the authority of the Romans. When Caesar returned to Gaul in the autumn, he took with him a group of hostages and left instructions as to the amount of tribute to be paid by the tribes he had conquered. The army was then distributed in winter quarters in different parts of Gaul.

Shortly after the troops had reached their respective winter camps, an unexpected attack on one of the camps was made by the Eburones, led by Ambiorix. The officers in command of this camp were Sabinus and Cotta. The attack was beaten off, and the Gauls then asked for a conference.

In this conference Ambiorix asserted that the attack had not been made because he wished it, but as a result of the hostile attitude of his nation as a whole toward the Romans—an attitude which he was unable to resist. Pretending personal friendship for the Romans, he urged them to abandon the camp and join one of the other divisions.

In the Roman council which was held after this conference, Sabinus urged that the advice of Ambiorix be taken. Cotta opposed, but after a prolonged and heated argument the plan of Sabinus was adopted. When the Romans marched out of camp the next morning, they were attacked by the Gauls from ambush, and almost the entire force, including the two commanders, was slaughtered.

The Gauls, in high spirits over the success of this attempt, hurried on to the camp of another division of the army. This was in charge of Quintus Cicero, the younger brother of the great orator. Here they were repulsed, though the Eburones had been joined by several other tribes.

The Letters That Never Arrived

Mᴵᵀᵀᵁᴺᵀᵁᴿ ad Caesarem cōnfestim ā Cicerōne litterae,
magnīs prōpositīs praemiīs sī per-
tulissent.[1] Obsessīs omnibus viīs
5 missī[2] intercipiuntur. Noctū ex eā
māteriā quam mūnītiōnis causā
comportāverant turrēs admodum
cxx excitantur; incrēdibilī celeritāte quae dēesse operī[3] vidēbantur
10 perficiuntur.

Hostēs posterō diē multō majōribus coāctīs cōpiīs castra oppugnant; fossam complent. Ā nostrīs
eādem ratiōne quā prīdiē resisti-
15 tur.[4] Hoc idem reliquīs deinceps
fit diēbus.

Nūlla pars nocturnī temporis ad
labōrem intermittitur; nōn aegrīs,
nōn vulnerātīs facultās quiētis
datur.   20

Quaecumque ad proximī diēī op-
pugnātiōnem opus sunt, noctū com-
parantur; multae praeustae sudēs,[5]
magnus mūrālium pīlōrum[6] numerus īnstituitur; turrēs contabulan- 25
tur;[7] pinnae lōrīcaeque[8] ex crāti-
bus (*wickerwork*) attexuntur (*are
woven*).

Ipse Cicerō, cum tenuissimā
valētūdine[9] esset, nē nocturnum 30
quidem sibi tempus ad quiētem
relinquēbat, ut ultrō mīlitum concursū (*from the thronging*) ac vōcibus sibi parcere cōgerētur.

A Treacherous Appeal

Tᵁᴹ ducēs prīncipēsque Nerviōrum, quī aliquem sermōnis
aditum[10] causamque amīcitiae cum
Cicerōne habēbant, colloquī sēsē
velle dīcunt.

40 Factā potestāte, eadem quae
Ambiorīx cum Titūriō ēgerat com-
memorant: omnem Galliam esse in
armīs; Germānōs Rhēnum trāns-
isse; Caesaris reliquōrumque hīberna oppugnārī.   45

Addunt etiam dē Sabīnī morte;
Ambiorīgem ostentant (*they show*)
fideī faciendae causā.

Errāre eōs[11] dīcunt, sī quicquam ab eīs[12] praesidiī spērent 50
quī suīs rēbus diffīdant (*distrust*);
sēsē tamen hōc esse in Cicerōnem

---

[1] The subject refers to the messengers
to whom the letters were intrusted.

[2] *the messengers.*

[3] The regular defenses of the camp,
consisting of the ditch and the rampart
of earth, with a row of palisades on top.

[4] Impersonal. Translate by an active
form in the plural.

[5] *stakes burned at the end,* i.e., sharpened and hardened by fire. These were to
serve as missile weapons in place of javelins, the supply of which was giving out.

[6] *of wall-javelins,* i.e., large pikes
hurled from the walls.

[7] *were built by stories.* Platforms were
arranged one above another so that
groups of soldiers might fight from different levels.

[8] *battlements and breastworks;* **lōrīca**
usually means *a coat of mail.*

[9] *in very delicate health,* an ablative of
description.

[10] *grounds on which to ask an interview.*
Just what the special basis of acquaintance between Cicero and the Nervii was
we are not told.

[11] The Romans in the camp.

[12] The soldiers in the other camps.

A ROMAN ATTACK ON A TOWN

The Nervii were clever enough to imitate Roman machines they had seen and use them against their originators.

populumque Rōmānum animō ut nihil nisi hīberna recūsent atque hanc inveterāscere (*to become established*) cōnsuētūdinem nōlint; licēre illīs per sē[1] incolumibus ex hībernīs discēdere et quāscumque in partēs velint sine metū proficīscī.

Cicerō ad haec ūnum modo respondet: nōn esse cōnsuētūdinem populī Rōmānī accipere ab 10 hoste armātō condiciōnem; sī ab armīs discēdere[2] velint, sē adjūtōre ūtantur[3] lēgātōsque ad Caesarem mittant; spērāre sē prō ejus jūsti- 15 tiā quae petīverint impetrātūrōs.

Substitutes for Shovels

AB HĀC spē[4] repulsī Nerviī vāllō pedum x et fossā pedum xv hīberna cingunt. Haec et[5] superiōrum annōrum cōnsuētūdine ā nōbīs cognōverant et, quōsdam dē exercitū nactī captīvōs, ab hīs docēbantur; sed, nūllā ferrāmentōrum (*of iron tools*) cōpiā[6] quae

essent ad hunc ūsum idōnea, gla- 25 diīs caespitēs (*sod*) circumcīdere (*to cut*), manibus sagulīsque (*in cloaks*) terram exhaurīre (*to take out*) cōgēbantur.

Quā quidem ex rē hominum 30 multitūdō cognōscī potuit; nam minus hōrīs tribus mīlium passuum

[1] *so far as they were concerned.*
[2] *to lay down their arms.*
[3] *they might rely on him as their advocate.*

[4] Hope of trapping Cicero.
[5] Correlative with **et** of line 21; omit in translation.
[6] Ablative absolute.

A MECHANICAL STONE-THROWER
Such machines were used to hurl large stones at a high angle.

III in circuitū mūnītiōnem perfēcē-
runt. Reliquīs diēbus turrēs ad[1]
altitūdinem vāllī, falcēs (*hooks*)
testūdinēsque, quās eīdem captīvī
docuerant, parāre ac facere coepē- 5
runt.

Fire As a Weapon

Septimō oppugnātiōnis diē maximō coortō ventō ferventēs
fūsilī ex argillā glandēs[2] fundīs
10 (*with slings*) et fervefacta jacula
(*heated javelins*) in casās (*huts*),
quae mōre Gallicō strāmentīs (*with
straw*) erant tēctae, jacere coepērunt. Hae celeriter ignem com-
15 prehendērunt et ventī magnitūdine
in omnem locum castrōrum distulē-
runt.[3] Hostēs maximō clāmōre,
sīcutī partā jam atque explōrātā
victōriā,[4] turrēs[5] testūdinēsque agere et scālīs (*with ladders*) vāllum 20
ascendere coepērunt.

At tanta mīlitum virtūs atque
ea[6] praesentia animī fuit ut, cum
undique flammā torrērentur (*they
were scorched*) maximāque tēlōrum 25
multitūdine premerentur suaque
omnia impedīmenta atque omnēs
fortūnās cōnflagrāre intellegerent,
nōn modo dē vāllō dēcēderet nēmō,
sed paene nē respiceret quidem 30

---

[1] *proportioned to.*
[2] *hot balls of molded clay.* It has been
found by experiment that heated balls
of clay will retain enough heat to set
fire to straw. The suggestion has been
made that the slings from which these
balls were thrown must have been lined
with metal.

[3] The word **ignem** is the object of this
verb as well as of **comprehendērunt** in
lines 14-15.
[4] Translate **sīcutī . . . victōriā**, *as if
victory were at hand and assured.*
[5] Apparently the Gauls had learned
Roman methods of attack.
[6] About equivalent to **tanta**.

quisquam,[1] ac tum omnēs ācerrimē fortissimēque pugnārent.

Hic diēs nostrīs longē gravissimus fuit; sed tamen hunc habuit ēventum, ut[2] eō diē maximus numerus hostium vulnerārētur atque interficerētur, ut sē sub ipsō vāllō cōnstīpāverant recessumque prīmīs[3] ultimī[4] nōn dabant.

Paulum quidem intermissā flammā et quōdam locō turrī adāctā et contingente vāllum, tertiae cohortis centuriōnēs ex eō quō stābant locō recessērunt[5] suōsque omnēs remōvērunt.

Nūtū (by nod) vōcibusque hostēs, sī introīre vellent, vocāre coepērunt;[6] quōrum prōgredī ausus est nēmō.

Tum ex omnī parte lapidibus conjectīs dēturbātī,[7] turrisque succēnsa est (was set on fire).

And They Never Did Settle the Question

ERANT in eā legiōne fortissimī virī, centuriōnēs, quī jam prīmīs ōrdinibus appropinquārent, T. Pullō et L. Vorēnus. Hī perpetuās inter sē contrōversiās habēbant uter alterī anteferrētur,[8] omnibusque annīs dē locō summīs simultātibus (with the greatest rivalry) contendēbant.

Ex hīs Pullō, cum ācerrimē ad mūnītiōnēs pugnārētur,[9] "Quid dubitās," inquit, "Vorēne, aut quem locum tuae probandae virtūtis expectās? Hic diēs dē nostrīs contrōversiīs jūdicābit."

Haec cum dīxisset, prōcēdit extrā mūnītiōnēs, quaeque pars hostium cōnfertissima est vīsa,[10] in eam irrumpit. Nē Vorēnus quidem sēsē tum vāllō continet, sed omnium veritus exīstimātiōnem (opinion) subsequitur.

Mediocrī spatiō relictō Pullō pīlum in hostēs immittit (hurls) atque ūnum ex multitūdine prōcurrentem (running forward) trājicit; quō percussō et exanimātō, hunc scūtīs prōtegunt (protect) hostēs, in illum[11] ūniversī tēla conjiciunt neque dant prōgrediendī facultātem.

Trānsfigitur scūtum Pullōnī,[12] et verūtum (javelin) in balteō dēfīgitur (is fastened). Āvertit hic cāsus vāgīnam (scabbard) et gladium ēdūcere cōnantī[13] dextram morātur manum, impedītumque hostēs circumsistunt.

[1] scarcely anyone even looked back.
[2] What does the mood of the verb tell as to the meaning of ut?
[3] to those in front.
[4] those in the rear.
[5] retired.
[6] When battle was largely a matter of individual combat, the challenge to "come on if you dare" was a natural incident.
[7] Supply sunt—were driven off.
[8] as to which was the better man (literally, which should be preferred to the other); an indirect deliberative question.
[9] Impersonal.
[10] The words quaeque pars est vīsa are equivalent to in eam partem quae vīsa est.
[11] Referring to Pullo.
[12] A dative of reference, to be translated like a genitive.
[13] when he tried; agreeing with eī understood, which is in the same construction as Pullōnī, line 54.

AT THE MERCY OF THE ENEMY

Pullo—with a force of Gauls rushing upon him—is unable to draw his sword.   The story below tells
what happened next.

Succurrit (*runs to help*) inimīcus illī[1] Vorēnus et labōrantī[1] subvenit (*brings aid*).   Ad hunc sē cōnfestim ā Pullōne omnis multitūdō convertit; illum verūtō (*by the javelin*) trānsfīxum arbitrantur. Vorēnus gladiō rem comminus gerit[2] atque ūnō interfectō reliquōs paulum prōpellit; dum cupidius (*more eagerly*) īnstat, in locum dēlātus īnferiōrem[3] concidit (*he falls*).

Huic rūrsus circumventō fert subsidium Pullō, atque ambō incolumēs complūribus interfectīs summā cum laude sēsē intrā mūnītiōnēs recipiunt.

Sīc fortūna in contentiōne (*strife*) et certāmine utrumque versāvit ut alter alterī inimīcus[4] auxiliō salūtīque esset, neque dījūdicārī (*be decided*) posset uter utrī virtūte anteferendus (*to be preferred*) vidērētur.

[1] Dative with a compound of **sub**.

[2] *fights at close range* (literally, *carries on the affair hand to hand*).

[3] *stepping into a low place.*

[4] The words **alter inimīcus** may be translated *each of the two rivals.*

A Relief Expedition

DAILY the siege grew worse. Many of the soldiers were wounded, so that there were scarcely enough able-bodied men to defend the camp.

Cicero continued sending messengers in the hope of informing Caesar of the situation, but his messengers, one after another, were captured.

Finally Vertico, a friendly Gaul, offered a great reward to one of his slaves if he succeeded in getting through to Caesar. The slave carried a letter bound around a javelin, so that it escaped notice.

Caesar promptly ordered the troops from the nearest camps to join him, and started immediately to relieve Cicero.

Labienus, who was among those directed to participate in the relief expedition, found the situation so threatening in the region in which he was located that he did not dare attempt to leave his camp.

Hold the Fort, for I Am Coming

CAESAR, cōnsiliō ejus probātō, etsī opīniōne trium legiōnum dējectus[1] ad duās reciderat,[2] tamen ūnum commūnī salūtī auxilium in celeritāte pōnēbat.

Venit magnīs itineribus in Nerviōrum fīnēs. Ibi ex captīvīs cognōscit quae apud Cicerōnem gerantur quantōque in perīculō rēs sit. Tum cuidam ex equitibus Gallīs magnīs praemiīs persuādet utī ad Cicerōnem epistulam dēferat.

Hanc Graecīs cōnscrīptam litterīs[3] mittit nē, interceptā epistulā, nostra ab hostibus cōnsilia cognōscantur. Sī adīre[4] nōn possit, monet ut trāgulam cum epistulā ad amentum (*thong*) dēligātā intrā mūnītiōnēs castrōrum abjiciat.

In litterīs scrībit sē cum legiōnibus profectum celeriter affore;[5] hortātur ut prīstinam virtūtem retineat. Gallus perīculum veritus, ut erat praeceptum, trāgulam mittit.

Haec cāsū ad turrim adhaesit (*stuck*) neque ā nostrīs bīduō animadversa tertiō diē ā quōdam mīlite cōnspicitur; dēmpta (*having been taken down*) ad Cicerōnem dēfertur. Ille perlēctam[6] in conventū (*meeting*) mīlitum recitat (*reads aloud*) maximāque omnēs laetitiā afficit.[7]

Tum fūmī incendiōrum (*of the fires*) procul vidēbantur; quae rēs omnem dubitātiōnem (*doubt*) adventūs legiōnum expulit.

---

[1] *disappointed in his expectation;* opīniōne is an ablative of separation.

[2] *had been reduced.*

[3] The Helvetians had used Greek characters in their muster rolls, as stated on page 156. On the other hand, Caesar apparently had reason to believe that the forces under Ambiorix were more familiar with the Latin alphabet than the Greek.

[4] Supply **Cicerōnem** (or **ad Cicerōnem**).

[5] Future infinitive of **adsum**, equivalent to **affutūrum esse.**

[6] *having read it (himself).*

[7] *all were greatly delighted.*

To Meet the Approaching Romans

GALLĪ, rē cognitā per explōrā-tōrēs, obsidiōnem relinquunt;[1] ad Caesarem omnibus cōpiīs contendunt. Haec erant armāta cir-
5 citer mīlia LX.[2]

Cicerō, datā facultāte, Gallum alium ab eōdem Verticōne[3] quem suprā dēmōnstrāvimus repetit (*requests*) quī litterās ad Caesarem
10 dēferat. Hunc admonet iter[4] cautē (*cautiously*) dīligenterque faciat. Perscrībit in litterīs hostēs ab sē discessisse omnemque ad eum multitūdinem convertisse.

15 Quibus litterīs circiter mediā nocte Caesar allātīs suōs facit certiōrēs eōsque ad dīmicandum animō cōnfirmat.[5]

Posterō diē lūce prīmā movet
20 castra et circiter mīlia passuum quattuor prōgressus trāns vallem magnam et rīvum (*stream*) multitūdinem hostium cōnspicātur.

Erat magnī perīculī rēs tantulīs cōpiīs inīquō locō dīmicāre. Tum, 25 quoniam obsidiōne līberātum Cicerōnem sciēbat, aequō animō remittendum dē celeritāte[6] exīstimābat.

Cōnsīdit et quam aequissimō po- 30 test locō castra commūnit (*fortifies*), atque haec, etsī erant exigua per sē, vix hominum mīlium septem, praesertim nūllīs cum impedīmentīs, tamen angustiīs viārum 35 quam maximē potest contrahit eō cōnsiliō, ut in summam contemptiōnem (*contempt*) hostibus veniat.

Interim, speculātōribus (*scouts*) in omnēs partēs dīmissīs, explōrat 40 quō commodissimē itinere vallem trānsīre possit.

Successful Roman Strategy

AFTER some skirmishes of cavalry, Caesar fortified his camp more strongly. Then by a pretense of fear he lured the Gauls to make an assault with all their forces.

Falling into the trap, the enemy pressed the attack, for they supposed the Romans to be too panic-stricken to do more than remain behind their defenses. Then Caesar ordered a sudden charge from the camp. The infantry, with all the cavalry, dashed out. The Gauls—taken by surprise— were completely routed. Many were slain, and all the others deprived of their arms.

---

[1] If they had continued the siege, they would have been caught between the advancing Roman army and the garrison in the camp.

[2] Caesar had scarcely seven thousand men to meet this formidable number of Gauls.

[3] *Vertico*. Mentioned in the third paragraph of page 257.

[4] The clause **iter . . . faciat** is object of **admonet** (*reminds*); **ut** might have been used to introduce **faciat**.

[5] *encouraged them for the battle;* **animō eōs cōnfirmat** is, literally, *strengthened them in spirit.*

[6] **aequō . . . celeritāte,** *that he might slacken the speed of his advance without any apprehension.*

The Commander-in-Chief Approves

Longius prōsequī veritus, quod silvae palūdēsque[1] intercēdēbant, omnibus suīs incolumibus, eōdem diē ad Cicerōnem pervenit.

Īnstitūtās turrēs, testūdinēs, mūnītiōnēsque hostium admīrātur; prōductā legiōne, cognōscit nōn decimum quemque[2] esse reliquum mīlitem sine vulnere; ex hīs omnibus jūdicat rēbus quantō cum perīculō et quantā cum virtūte rēs sint administrātae.

Cicerōnem prō ejus meritō legiōnemque collaudat (*he praises highly*); centuriōnēs singillātim (*individually*) tribūnōsque mīlitum appellat, quōrum ēgregiam fuisse virtūtem testimōniō (*by the testimony*) Cicerōnis cognōverat. 20

Dē cāsū Sabīnī et Cottae certius ex captīvīs cognōscit.

Posterō diē, cōntiōne (*public assembly*) habitā, rem gestam prōpōnit; mīlitēs cōnsōlātur (*he 25 consoles*) et cōnfirmat; quod dētrīmentum[3] culpā (*by the fault*) et temeritāte (*rashness*) lēgātī[4] sit acceptum, hōc aequiōre animō ferendum docet, quod beneficiō deōrum 30 immortālium et virtūte eōrum expiātō incommodō,[5] neque hostibus diūtina laetitia (*happiness*) neque ipsīs longior dolor relinquātur.

A Troublesome Enemy Removed

The failure of the attack on Cicero's camp halted the military activities of the hostile tribes for a short time, but the spirit of unrest continued to exist.

The Treveri, under the leadership of Indutiomarus, attempted to induce some of the German tribes to join them in a war against the Romans. Though they were unsuccessful with the Germans, they were supported by some of the other Gallic nations.

Having assembled his forces, Indutiomarus with his cavalry advanced on the camp of Labienus. Imitating the tactics of Caesar, Labienus held his men in camp while the Gauls rode about the fortifications, taunting the Romans and challenging them to come out and fight.

One evening, as the Gauls were withdrawing, Labienus sent out his cavalry with orders to attack the enemy, and to make a special point of singling out Indutiomarus and killing him. The order was carried out, and the Gallic leader killed in the fighting. Without their leader the Gauls abandoned the campaign, and for a time Gaul was quiet.

[1] The appearance of the landscape in France now is very different from what it was when Caesar saw it.

[2] *not one man in ten.*

[3] Equivalent to **id dētrīmentum quod.**

[4] Referring to Sabinus. His associate, Cotta, had opposed the adoption of the plan which led to the disaster.

[5] An ablative absolute expressing cause.

COMPREHENSION QUESTIONS

One of the most interesting stories in the entire history of Caesar's wars in Gaul is that of the siege of Cicero's camp. The following questions deal with incidents of this story.

1. What relation was Cicero, the officer in Caesar's army, to Cicero the famous orator? What were the first names of these two men?
2. How did Cicero attempt to inform Caesar of the danger in which the camp was involved?
3. What were some of the weapons used by the Romans in defense of the camp?
4. How did the Gauls try to set fire to the buildings in the Roman camp?
5. Tell the story of the rivalry between Pullo and Vorenus.
6. Who finally succeeded in carrying a message to Cicero?
7. Tell how Caesar's reply came into Cicero's hands.
8. What was Caesar's opinion of the manner in which Cicero had conducted the defense of the camp?

WORD STUDY X

Latin Words with Numerous Derivatives

Often a single Latin word furnishes a rather long list of English derivatives. Some important words of this sort, with some of their English derivatives, are given below.

currō (cursum)	nāscor (nātus)	tangō (tāctum)	emō (ēmptum)
currency	nascent	tangent	exempt
current	natal	tangible	peremptory
curriculum	nation	tact	preëmpt
cursory	nationality	tactile	redeem
corridor*	native	intact	redemption
courier*	naïve*	attain*	ransom*
concur	nature	contingent	
discourse	cognate	contact	**patior (passus)**
excursion	innate	contagion*	patience
incur	international	integer	passion*
occur	renaissance*		passive
precursor		**valeō**	compatible
recur	**sequor (secūtus)**	valentine*	compassion
	sequel	valiant*	impatient
	sequence	valid	
loquor (locūtus)	sect	invalid	**spērō (spērātum)**
loquacious	sue*	valor*	despair
circumlocution	suit*	value	desperate
colloquial	consequence	avail	prosper
elocution	consecutive	convalescence	prosperity
eloquence	ensue*	equivalent	
soliloquy	persecute	invaluable	
ventriloquist	prosecute	prevalent	

* These words have come through French, some of them through Old-French forms.

Exercises

1. Find additional English derivatives from **currō**, **sequor**, and **spērō**.

Idioms and Phrases

The idioms and phrases listed below occur frequently in the text read. Learning them thoroughly will be of great help in reading.

> **maximā laetitiā affectus est,** *he was very greatly delighted*
> **rēs erat magnī perīculī,** *it was a very dangerous undertaking*

Vocabulary Review

The following words, which appear frequently in this book, are important in second-year work. Their meanings should be thoroughly learned.

administrō	circumsistō	ēventus	māteria	prīstinus
admīror	clāmor	exiguus	mediocris	prōcēdō
admodum	cognōscō	explōrātor	nocturnus	quiēs
adversus (*adj.*)	colloquor	explōrō	obsidiō	rūrsus
adversus (*prep.*)	commemorō	genus	oppugnātiō	sīcut
aeger	commodus	humilis	oppugnō	suprā
afferō	comprehendō	inquam	ōrdō	turris
afficiō	cōnfertus	īnstō	palūs	ultrō
bīduum	cōnspicor	intercēdō	pīlum	ūniversus
bis	contrōversia	laus	praecipiō	uter
cāsus	dīmicō	licet	praedicō, -āre	vāllum
centuriō	dubitō	majōrēs	prīdiē	versor

A COURTYARD IN POMPEII RESTORED TO ITS FORMER BEAUTY

TRACES OF THE ROMANS ARE FOUND IN RUSSIA
On the northern shore of the Black Sea are these remains of a seaport which was once thronged with
Roman ships.

THE ROMAN EMPIRE AND ITS TRADE

IN THE days of the Roman Empire, every known land — on three continents — was drawn on to supply the needs of Rome and its provinces. The various provinces—north, south, east, west— all traded with each other and with Italy.

Huge transport wagons, heavily loaded, rolled along the straight, well-paved roads of the Empire. Where there were no roads, pack animals were used.

In addition, a large amount of commerce was borne by water. A famous Roman poet of the early Empire said that there were as many men on sea as on land. Over the sea lanes of the Mediterranean, boats constantly sailed from one port to another. Most of the merchant ships of that time would seem very small and inadequate today, but some of those ships even sailed out on the Atlantic, in order to make trips along the coast.

Rome itself was not a seaport, for the Tiber was too swift and too shallow for large ships, but the ancient city used two harbors. As early as 212 B.C. the thriving port of Puteoli, located some distance to the south, was receiving large quantities of goods for Rome. The cargoes were unloaded and sent on by land.

Because of its nearness Ostia, at the mouth of the Tiber, was Rome's natural port. Originally, however, the harbor there was unsatisfactory because it was poorly protected from the southwest gales. It was not until the early days of the Empire that the harbor was improved and reached its full usefulness.

Magnificent docks were built at Ostia. The warehouses constructed there by the Emperor Trajan were nearly three miles long. They were fine buildings and were ornamented with statues. At Rome there were about three hundred public warehouses. Those which held the grain shipped from foreign lands occupied one large section. Each year vast quantities of wheat were stored in these warehouses to help feed the people of Rome.

With the conquest of its provinces Rome had come into possession of mines, quarries, farmlands, forests, and fisheries at various distances from Italy. Spain, for instance, was the source of copper, lead, gold and silver, timber, hides, and fur. The provinces along the Danube produced gold, iron, and salt. Many of the provinces, especially those in the eastern part of the Mediterranean world, were noted for their manufactures. These natural resources were developed by the Romans.

Italy, with its large population, was a rich market, receiving far more goods than it sent out. Grain was one of the chief imports, since the people of Italy did not raise enough to feed themselves. In the time of Augustus one-third of the grain came from Egypt, and large amounts were imported from Sicily.

Of all the cities of the Empire, Rome was the greatest market, not only for goods from the provinces, but also for foreign goods—especially luxuries. Long caravans, toiling through the heat of the desert, bore merchandise from the interior of Africa to the coast. Products of the Far East came by caravan along the familiar trade routes. Carpets and fine leather were brought from Persia; ivory, rare marbles and woods from Africa; spices and all kinds of precious stones from India; tortoise-shell from the shores of the distant Indian Ocean; silk and silk yarn from China; table delicacies from all parts of the known world. All these things and many more were shown in the shops of the city. Conditions had indeed changed since the simple days when the settlers on the seven hills went down to the Tiber and bartered their grain and cattle for the metal goods which the early traders brought.

But Italy was not only a market for goods from the provinces and from abroad; it carried on an extensive export trade as well. Even countries remote from the boundaries of the Empire shared in the commerce. Weapons and utensils of Roman make, undoubtedly imported from the Empire, have been found in the region of the Baltic Sea, and Roman coins have been found even in China.

In nearly every part of what was once the Roman Empire, there have been found lamps manufactured in Italy during the Age of Augustus. Roman glassware has been discovered in graves of south Russia. Ancient bronze dishes

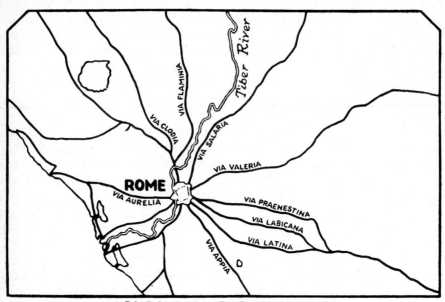

A ROAD MAP OF THE METROPOLITAN AREA

Just as each of our large cities is the center of a network of railroads and truck lines, so Rome was the heart of a highly efficient and well-organized transportation system.

stamped with the name of an Italian manufacturer have been found in such distant places as Switzerland, northern Germany, England, and Scotland.

Some Italian-manufactured goods dominated the markets, and certain cities were distinguished for special articles of manufacture. For instance, Aquileia specialized in the manufacture of amber toilet articles—the material for which was brought from the shores of the Baltic Sea. One city turned out a famous red-glazed pottery, while another was renowned for the pro-.duction of fine bronze articles.

Since it was the policy of Rome to encourage and protect trade.

there was little interference with the individual trader, who was usually enterprising and courageous. Long before Caesar conquered Gaul, traders had penetrated far into that country. Later, when these merchants were harshly treated by local tribes and made to pay heavy tolls, Caesar took measures to insure their safety, just as a modern government often uses military force to protect foreign trade. It was the individual achievements of the merchants and traders of the Roman world—whether in Asia, Africa, or Europe—that helped make possible the amazing prosperity of the Roman Empire.

THE CUSTOMS OF THE GAULS

The different ways that different things are done.
KIPLING: SESTINA OF THE TRAMP ROYAL

Hostilities in Various Regions

THE attack on Cicero's camp had resulted in failure, and Indutiomarus, the chief of the Treveri, was dead. In spite of these facts, there were unmistakable signs that the Gauls were planning to renew hostilities early in the year 53 B. C.

Without waiting for their plans to be carried out, Caesar advanced into the territory of the Nervii. He captured a large number of prisoners, laid waste the country, and compelled the Nervii to give hostages for their future good behavior. In like manner the Senones and Menapii soon submitted.

Labienus lured the Treveri to at-* tack his forces, with the result that their army was badly defeated and scattered. Caesar now determined to make a second crossing into Germany with his legions.

Trouble in the Rhineland

CAESAR, postquam ex Menapiis in Trēverōs vēnit, duābus dē causīs Rhēnum trānsīre cōnstituit; quārum ūna erat quod
5 Germānī auxilia contrā sē Trēverīs mīserant, altera, nē ad eōs Ambiorīx receptum[1] habēret.[2]

His cōnstitūtīs rēbus, paulō suprā eum locum quō ante exercitum
10 trādūxerat facere pontem īnstituit. Nōtā atque īnstitūtā ratiōne,[3] magnō mīlitum studiō paucīs diēbus opus efficitur.

Firmō in Trēverīs ad pontem
15 praesidiō relictō nē quis ab hīs subitō mōtus orīrētur, reliquās cōpiās equitātumque trādūcit.

Ubiī, quī ante obsidēs dederant atque in dēditiōnem vēnerant, pūrgandī suī causā ad eum lēgātōs 20 mittunt quī doceant neque ex suā cīvitāte auxilia in Trēverōs missa neque ab sē fidem laesam.[4]

Petunt atque ōrant ut sibi[5] parcat, nē commūnī odiō Germā- 25 nōrum[6] innocentēs (*the innocent*) prō nocentibus poenās pendant. Sī amplius obsidum velit darī, pollicentur.

Cognitā Caesar causā reperit ab 30 Suēbīs auxilia missa esse. Ubiōrum satisfactiōnem (*the excuse*) accipit, aditūs viāsque in Suēbōs perquīrit (*carefully seeks out*).

[1] *way of retreat;* a noun of the fourth declension.

[2] A substantive clause of desire, explaining altera (**causa**).

[3] Freely, *since the plan was familiar as already drawn up.* The bridge was exactly like the one built two years

before; hence Caesar's engineers had the plans at hand.

[4] *nor had they broken their word.*

[5] Dative with **parcat.** See Gr. S., 61.

[6] *in his hatred of the Germans in general;* literally, *in common hatred of the Germans.*

265

Taking to the Woods

INTERIM paucīs post diēbus fit ab Ubiīs certior Suēbōs omnēs[1] in ūnum locum cōpiās cōgere atque eīs nātiōnibus quae sub eōrum sint
5 imperiō dēnūntiāre[2] ut auxilia peditātūs equitātūsque mittant.

His cognitīs rēbus, rem frūmentāriam prōvidet; castrīs idōneum locum dēligit; Ubiīs imperat ut
10 pecora dēdūcant suaque omnia ex agrīs in oppida cōnferant, spērāns barbarōs atque imperītōs hominēs inopiā cibāriōrum ad inīquam pugnandī condiciōnem posse dēdūcī.
15 Mandat ut crēbrōs explōrātōrēs in Suēbōs mittant[3] quaeque apud eōs gerantur cognōscant. Illī impe-

rāta faciunt et, paucīs diēbus intermissīs, referunt[4]: Suēbōs omnēs, posteāquam certiōrēs nūntiī dē 20 exercitū Rōmānōrum vēnerint, cum omnibus suīs sociōrumque cōpiīs quās coēgissent, penitus (*all the way*) ad extrēmōs[5] fīnēs sē recēpisse; silvam ibi esse īnfīnītā 25 (*vast*) magnitūdine, quae appellētur Bacēnis;[6] hanc longē intrōrsus (*into the interior*) pertinēre et prō nātīvō mūrō[7] objectam Chēruscōs[8] ab Suēbōrum Suēbōsque ab Chē- 30 ruscōrum[8] injūriīs incursiōnibusque (*and raids*) prohibēre; ad ejus silvae initium Suēbōs adventum Rōmānōrum expectāre cōnstituisse.

Feudal Lords of Long Ago

QUONIAM ad hunc locum[9] perventum est, nōn aliēnum esse vidētur dē Galliae Germāniaeque mōribus et quō differant hae nātiōnēs inter sēsē prōpōnere.[10]
40   In Galliā nōn sōlum in omnibus cīvitātibus atque in omnibus pāgīs, sed paene etiam in singulīs domibus factiōnēs sunt, eārumque

factiōnum prīncipēs sunt quī summam auctōritātem eōrum[11] jūdiciō 45 habēre exīstimantur, quōrum[12] ad arbitrium[13] jūdiciumque summa[14] omnium rērum cōnsiliōrumque redeat.[15] Idque ejus reī causā antīquitus īnstitūtum vidētur, nē quis 50 ex plēbe contrā potentiōrem auxiliī[16] egēret;[17] suōs enim quisque

---

[1] With **cōpiās**.

[2] *were ordering.* The word implies a threat accompanying the command.

[3] Scouts from the Ubii would be more familiar with the country and would more easily escape detection than scouts sent by Caesar.

[4] Equivalent to **renūntiant.**

[5] *the farthest part of,* i.e., farthest from the Rhine.

[6] *Bacenis* (ba̤-sē′nis), a forest in Germany. See map, page 137.

[7] *as a natural wall.* With their primitive tools it was not easy for the Germans to cut roads through the forest

which would afford an easy passage for their armies.

[8] *the Cherusci* (kḛ-rus′ī), a German tribe.

[9] *point* (in the narrative).

[10] *to give a description of.*

[11] Meaning **Gallōrum.**

[12] Like **quī**, referring to **prīncipēs.**

[13] *discretion.*

[14] *the final decision.*

[15] *is referred.*

[16] Genitive with **egeō**, which more commonly takes the ablative.

[17] *should lack.* This clause explains **ejus reī causā,** line 49.

opprimī et circumvenīrī[1] nōn patitur, neque, aliter sī faciat, ūllam inter suōs habeat auctōritātem.

Haec eadem ratiō est in summā tōtīus Galliae;[2] namque omnēs cī- 5 vitātēs dīvīsae sunt in duās partēs.

Civil Strife

CUM Caesar in Galliam vēnit, alterīus factiōnis prīncipēs erant Haeduī, alterīus Sēquanī. Hī[3] cum per sē minus valērent, quod summa auctōritās antīquitus erat in Haeduīs magnaeque eōrum erant clientēlae, Germānōs atque Ariovistum sibi adjūnxerant eōsque ad sē magnīs jactūrīs pollicitātiōnibusque[4] perdūxerant.

Proeliīs vērō complūribus factīs secundīs atque omnī nōbilitāte Haeduōrum interfectā, tantum potentiā antecesserant ut magnam partem clientium ab Haeduīs ad sē trādūcerent obsidēsque ab hīs prīncipum fīliōs acciperent et pūblicē jūrāre[5] cōgerent nihil sē contrā Sēquanōs cōnsiliī initūrōs, et partem fīnitimī agrī per vim occupātam possidērent Galliaeque tōtīus prīncipātum obtinērent.

Quā necessitāte (*by this necessity*) adductus, Dīviciācus auxiliī petendī causā Rōmam ad senātum profectus īnfectā rē[6] redierat. Adventū Caesaris factā commū-

tātiōne rērum, obsidibus Haeduīs 35 redditīs, veteribus clientēlīs restitūtīs, novīs per Caesarem comparātīs,

A GALLIC STANDARD

Roman soldiers who followed the eagle into battle met Gallic standard-bearers carrying a variety of emblems. This boar, which served as the top of a standard, probably was used in many a bloody battle.

quod eī quī sē ad eōrum[7] amīcitiam aggregāverant (*had joined*) meliōre condiciōne atque aequiōre 40 imperiō sē ūtī[8] vidēbant, reliquīs rēbus[9] eōrum grātiā dignitāteque amplificātā (*having been increased*), Sēquanī prīncipātum dīmīserant.[10]

In eōrum locum Rēmī successe- 45 rant; quōs[11] quod adaequāre apud Caesarem grātiā intellegēbātur, eī quī propter veterēs inimīcitiās (*enmities*) nūllō modō cum Haeduīs conjungī poterant sē Rēmīs in 50 clientēlam dicābant.[12]

---

[1] *to be harmed.*

[2] *this same policy exists generally* (**in summā**) *throughout the whole of Gaul.* The phrase **tōtīus Galliae** depends on **ratiō.**

[3] *the latter.*

[4] The three words mean *by great sacrifices and promises.*

[5] Supply **prīncipēs** as subject.

[6] *without accomplishing his purpose.*

[7] Meaning **Haeduōrum.**

[8] *were enjoying.*

[9] *by all other means.*

[10] *had been compelled to give up.*

[11] Subject of **adaequāre,** *equaled.* Supply **Haeduōs** as object.

[12] *placed themselves under the protection of the Remi.*

THE DRUIDS OF ANCIENT GAUL.

Hōs illī dīligenter tuēbantur; ita novam et repente collēctam[1] auctōritātem tenēbant. Eō tamen statū[2] rēs erat ut longē prīncipēs Haeduī habērentur, secundum locum dignitātis Rēmī obtinērent. 5

The Priests of the Mistletoe

IN OMNĪ Galliā eōrum hominum quī aliquō sunt numerō[3] atque honōre genera sunt duo; nam plēbēs paene servōrum habētur locō,[4] quae nihil audet per sē, nūllī adhibētur cōnsiliō.

Plērīque, cum aut aere aliēnō aut magnitūdine tribūtōrum (*of the tributes*) aut injūriā potentiōrum premuntur, sēsē in servitūtem dicant nōbilibus; quibus in hōs eadem omnia sunt jūra quae dominīs in servōs.

Sed dē hīs duōbus generibus alterum est druidum, alterum equitum. Illī rēbus dīvīnīs intersunt,[5] sacrificia pūblica ac prīvāta prōcūrant (*attend to*), religiōnēs[6] interpretantur (*interpret*); ad eōs magnus adulēscentium numerus disciplīnae causā[7] concurrit, magnōque hī[8] sunt apud eōs[9] honōre.

[1] *acquired.*
[2] With **Eō**—*in that state,* or *condition.*
[3] *are of any account,* or *importance.*
[4] *are regarded as slaves.*
[5] *have charge of sacred rites.* The Druid priests wore a distinguishing dress of white. They held the oak-tree and the mistletoe in the greatest reverence, and performed their sacrifices in oak-groves.
[6] Denoting everything connected with matters of religious belief.
[7] The phrase is equivalent to **discendī causā.**
[8] The Druids.
[9] The Gauls.

Nam ferē dē omnibus contrōversiīs pūblicīs prīvātīsque cōnstituunt; et, sī quod est facinus admissum, sī caedēs facta, sī dē hērēditāte 5 (*inheritance*), dē fīnibus contrōversia est, eīdem dēcernunt, praemia poenāsque cōnstituunt; sī quī aut prīvātus aut populus eōrum dēcrētō nōn stetit,[1] sacrificiīs inter- 10 dīcunt.[2]

Haec poena apud eōs est gravissima. Quibus ita est interdictum,[3] hī numerō impiōrum (*of the wicked*) ac scelerātōrum habentur; hīs om- 15 nēs dēcēdunt,[4] aditum eōrum sermōnemque dēfugiunt (*flee from*) nē quid ex contāgiōne (*contact*) incommodī accipiant, neque eīs petentibus jūs redditur neque ho- 20 nōs ūllus commūnicātur.

Hīs autem omnibus druidibus praeest ūnus, quī summam inter eōs habet auctōritātem. Hōc mortuō, aut, sī quī[5] ex reliquīs excellit 25 (*excels*) dignitāte, succēdit, aut, sī sunt plūrēs parēs, suffrāgiō (*by vote*) druidum, nōn numquam etiam armīs dē prīncipātū contendunt.

Hī certō annī tempore in fīnibus Carnutum, quae regiō tōtīus Gal- 30 liae media[6] habētur, cōnsīdunt[7] in locō cōnsecrātō (*consecrated*). Hūc omnēs undique quī contrōversiās habent conveniunt eōrumque dēcrētīs (*decisions*) jūdiciīsque pā- 35 rent.

Disciplīna[8] in Britanniā[9] reperta atque inde in Galliam trānslāta esse[10] exīstimātur, et nunc[11] quī dīligentius eam rem cognōscere volunt 40 plērumque illō[12] discendī causā proficīscuntur.

What It Meant to Be a Druid

DRUIDĒS ā bellō abesse cōnsuērunt neque tribūta (*trib-* 45 *ute*) ūnā cum reliquīs pendunt. Tantīs excitātī praemiīs et suā sponte multī in disciplīnam conveniunt[13] et ā parentibus propinquīsque mittuntur.

Magnum ibi numerum versuum[14] 50 ēdiscere (*to memorize*) dīcuntur. Itaque annōs nōnnullī xx in disciplīnā permanent. Neque fās esse exīstimant ea[15] litterīs mandāre, cum[16] in reliquīs ferē rēbus, 55 pūblicīs prīvātīsque ratiōnibus,[17]

[1] *does not abide by their decisions.*

[2] *they forbid.* Supply **eī; interdīcere** takes a dative of the person, and an ablative of the place or action forbidden.

[3] Impersonal verb: literally, *to whom it is thus forbidden;* i.e., whoever is kept from the sacrifices.

[4] *avoid.*

[5] Translate **sī quī,** *whoever.*

[6] *the center* (*of*).

[7] *hold their meetings.*

[8] *the system.*

[9] It is more probable that the Britons had originally received the Druidical

system from the continent, but little is positively known about Druidism.

[10] *to have been transferred.*

[11] *and so even now.*

[12] *there,* an adverb; equivalent to **in Britanniam.**

[13] Used with the same meaning as **disciplīnae causā concurrit,** page 268, line 27.

[14] *of verses,* lines of poetry containing the substance of the Druidical teaching.

[15] Meaning **quae discunt.**

[16] *although.*

[17] *accounts.*

Graecīs litterīs[1] utantur. Id mihi duābus dē causīs īnstituisse videntur, quod neque in vulgus disciplīnam efferrī velint, neque eōs quī discant litterīs cōnfisōs[2] minus memoriae studēre;[3] quod ferē plērīsque accidit, ut praesidiō[4] litterārum dīligentiam in perdiscendō (*learning thoroughly*) ac memoriam remittant.

Imprīmīs hoc volunt persuādēre, nōn interīre animās (*souls*), sed ab aliīs post mortem trānsīre ad aliōs;[5] atque hōc maximē ad virtūtem excitārī putant, metū mortis neglēctō. Multa praetereā dē sīderibus (*stars*) atque eōrum mōtū, dē mundī ac terrārum[6] magnitūdine, dē rērum nātūrā, dē deōrum immortālium vī ac potestāte disputant (*they discuss*) et juventūtī (*to the youths*) trādunt.[7]

What It Meant to Be a Knight

ALTERUM genus est equitum. Hī, cum est ūsus[8] atque aliquod bellum incidit (quod[9] ferē ante Caesaris adventum quotannīs accidere solēbat, utī aut ipsī injūriās īnferrent aut illātās prōpulsārent[10]), omnēs in bellō versantur, atque eōrum ut quisque[11] est genere cōpiīsque amplissimus, ita plūrimōs circum sē ambactōs (*dependents*) clientēsque habet. Hanc ūnam grātiam potentiamque nōvērunt.

Human Victims for Sacrifice

NĀTIŌ est omnis Gallōrum admodum dēdita[12] religiōnibus, atque ob eam causam quī sunt affectī graviōribus morbīs (*with diseases*) quīque in proeliīs perīculīsque versantur aut prō victimīs hominēs[13] immolant aut sē immolātūrōs vovent, administrīsque (*and as assistants*) ad ea sacrificia druidibus ūtuntur, quod, prō vītā hominis nisi hominis vīta[14] reddātur, nōn posse deōrum immortālium nūmen (*divine will*) plācārī arbitrantur; pūblicēque ejusdem generis habent īnstitūta sacrificia.

Aliī immānī (*immense*) magnitūdine simulācra[15] habent, quōrum contexta vīminibus[16] membra vīvīs

---

[1] The language was Gallic.

[2] *relying on writing.*

[3] *pay less attention to the memory.*

[4] Equivalent to **auxiliō.**

[5] *pass from one body to another.* The belief in the transmigration of souls was common among the ancients, and it appears even yet in some Oriental religions.

[6] *the universe and the earth.*

[7] Equivalent to **docent.**

[8] *need.*

[9] Explained by the **utī** clause. Compare lines 3-22 above.

[10] *repelled.*

[11] Translate **ut quisque,** etc., *the more distinguished a man is . . . the more,* etc.

[12] *given over,* or *devoted.*

[13] Object of **immolant** and **immolātūrōs.**

[14] Observe the reversal of word order, known as "chiasmus."

[15] *images.* Supply **hominum.**

[16] *woven of willow shoots.*

hominibus complent; quibus suc-
cēnsīs (*having been set on fire*),
circumventī flammā exanimantur
hominēs.

5 Supplicia eōrum quī in fūrtō
(*theft*) aut in latrōciniō (*robbery*)

aut in aliquā[1] noxiā (*crime*) sint
comprehēnsī grātiōra[2] dīs immor-
tālibus esse arbitrantur; sed cum
ejus generis cōpia dēficit, etiam 10
ad innocentium[3] supplicia dēscendunt.

The Gods of the Gauls

Dᴇōʀᴜᴍ[4] maximē Mercurium
colunt; hujus sunt plūrima
15 simulācra (*images*); hunc omnium
inventōrem (*inventor*) artium ferunt;[5] hunc viārum atque itinerum ducem; hunc ad quaestūs[6]
pecūniae mercātūrāsque (*and
20 trade*) habēre vim maximam arbitrantur.

Post hunc Apollinem et Mārtem
et Jovem et Minervam. Dē hīs
eandem ferē quam reliquae gentēs
25 habent opīniōnem: Apollinem mor-
bōs dēpellere,[7] Minervam operum[8]
atque artificiōrum[9] initia trādere,[10]
Jovem imperium caelestium te-

nēre, Mārtem bella regere. Huic,
cum proeliō dīmicāre cōnstituē- 30
runt, ea quae bellō cēperint plērumque dēvovent.[11] Cum superāvē-
runt, animālia capta immolant
reliquāsque rēs in ūnum locum
cōnferunt. 35

Multīs in cīvitātibus hārum rērum extrūctōs cumulōs (*mounds*)
locīs cōnsecrātīs (*consecrated*) cōn-
spicārī licet; neque saepe accidit
ut neglēctā quispiam (*anyone*) re- 40
ligiōne aut capta apud sē occultāre
aut posita[12] tollere audēret, gravis-
simumque eī reī supplicium cum
cruciātū cōnstitūtum est.

Some Strange Customs

Gᴀʟʟī sē omnēs ab Dīte[13] patre[14]
prōgnātōs[15] praedicant idque

ab druidibus prōditum dīcunt. Ob 47
eam causam spatia omnis temporis

---

[1] Here equivalent to **aliā aliquā.**

[2] *especially pleasing.*

[3] *of the innocent.* Similarly, it is said
that when the supply of criminals to
be thrown to the beasts in the Roman
arena ran short, men were sometimes
condemned on trumped-up charges.

[4] With **maximē.** Caesar gives the
names of Roman gods to the Gallic
gods who resembled them. He identi-
fies Mercury with the Gallic god Woden.

[5] *they call.*

[6] *gain.* The plural denotes the different kinds of money-making and business.

[7] *drives away diseases.*

[8] *handicrafts.*

[9] *trades.*

[10] Used with the same meaning as
trādunt, on page 270, line 22.

[11] *they vow.* Compare **sē immolātūrōs
(esse) vovent,** on page 270, lines 41-42.

[12] Supply **in cumulīs.**

[13] A name of *Pluto,* god of the underworld.

[14] *as a father;* predicate.

[15] *descended.* They asserted that they
were aborigines, i.e., that they were not
descendants of immigrants from any
other region.

nōn numerō diērum sed noctium[1] fīniunt;[2] diēs nātālēs (*birthdays*) et mēnsium et annōrum initia sīc observant (*observe*) ut noctem diēs subsequātur.

In reliquīs vītae īnstitūtīs hōc ferē ab reliquīs differunt, quod suōs līberōs, nisi cum adolēvērunt ut[3] mūnus mīlitiae (*of military service*) sustinēre possint, palam ad sē adīre nōn patiuntur; fīliumque puerīlī aetāte[4] in pūblicō in cōnspectū patris assistere[5] turpe dūcunt.

The Head of the Family

VIRĪ, quantās pecūniās[6] ab uxōribus dōtis nōmine accēpērunt, tantās ex suīs bonīs aestimātiōne (*an estimate*) factā cum dōtibus commūnicant. Hujus omnis pecūniae conjūnctim ratiō habētur,[7] frūctūsque[8] servantur. Uter eōrum vītā superāvit, ad eum pars utrīusque cum frūctibus superiōrum temporum pervenit.

Virī in uxōrēs, sīcutī in līberōs, vītae necisque habent potestātem; et cum pater familiae[9] illūstriōre (*more illustrious*) locō nātus dēcessit, ejus propinquī conveniunt et, dē morte sī rēs in suspīciōnem vēnit,[10] dē uxōribus[11] in servīlem modum quaestiōnem[12] habent et, sī compertum est,[13] ignī[14] atque omnibus tormentīs excruciātās (*tortured*) interficiunt.

Fūnera (*funerals*) sunt prō cultū Gallōrum magnifica et sūmptuōsa (*expensive*); omniaque quae vīvīs cordī fuisse (*to have been dear*) arbitrantur in ignem īnferunt, etiam animālia; ac paulō suprā hanc memoriam[15] servī et clientēs quōs ab eīs dīlēctōs esse (*to have been beloved*) cōnstābat, jūstīs[16] fūnebribus (*funeral rites*) cōnfectīs, ūnā cremābantur (*were burned*).

Too Much Talk Makes Trouble

QUAE cīvitātēs commodius suam rem pūblicam administrāre exīstimantur habent lēgibus sānctum,[17] sī quis quid dē rē

---

[1] The English "fortnight" (fourteen nights) and "sennight" (seven nights) illustrate the practice of reckoning time by nights instead of days.

[2] *mark off*, or *measure.*

[3] *so that.*

[4] *youthful age.* Descriptive ablative.

[5] *to appear at his father's side.*

[6] Plural, on account of the plural **Virī.** So also **dōtibus,** line 18.

[7] *an account is kept jointly.*

[8] *income*, or *interest.*

[9] More commonly, **pater familiās.**

[10] Meaning if the circumstances of his

death were such as to bring the wives under suspicion.

[11] From this it would seem that polygamy was practiced among the Gauls, though probably only by the nobility.

[12] *an inquiry after the slave manner.* At Rome, only in the case of slaves could torture be used to force a confession.

[13] *if proof of guilt is discovered.*

[14] The ablative of **ignis** often ends in ī.

[15] *before our time.*

[16] *regular, proper.*

[17] *have a legal enactment.*

Let Latin be a stimulating reading experience'

with   LATIN   BOOK   TWO

Thorough functional review of first-year forms and vocabulary in the ten travel stories insures a firm foundation for second-year reading.

Provision for growing mastery is as careful in LATIN
BOOK TWO as in LATIN BOOK ONE. The recurrence of every
word and form in the book was charted to control the
rate of introduction and repetition of vocabulary and
grammar concepts. The use of visible vocabulary (see
the preface) relieves the student of the traditional
second-year burden of looking up many new words he won't
use again. Result: increased reading interest and reading fluency.

Complete correlation of grammar with reading makes reading more efficient and grammar a recognizable reading
tool. New grammatical constructions are presented func-
tionally in a reading selection; on the opposite page
they are fully explained and their use is illustrated in
English and Latin.

A balanced reading program builds reading skills and
motivates interest by its diversity. Caesar, presented
as readable first-hand history, becomes meaningful for
students who begin classical Latin with a solid fund of
language and word knowledge. (Read the preface, page 4,
before examining the interesting presentation of the
Gallic War.)

Illustrations and English essays not only are intrin-
sically interesting but are closely integrated with
the reading. They enrich the student's general background, and deepen his understanding of Roman civilization and its significance for America today.

LATIN BOOK ONE, $1.11 Net   LATIN BOOK TWO, $1.26 Net

pūblicā ā fīnitimīs rūmōre[1] ac fāmā[2] accēperit, utī ad magistrātum dēferat nēve cum quō aliō commūnicet, quod saepe hominēs temerāriōs atque imperītōs falsīs rūmōribus terrērī et ad facinus impellī et dē summīs rēbus cōnsilium capere cognitum est. Magistrātūs quae vīsa sunt[3] occultant, quae esse ex ūsū jūdicāvērunt multitūdinī prōdunt. Dē rē pūblicā nisi per concilium loquī nōn concēditur.

German Religion

GERMĀNĪ multum ab hāc cōnsuētūdine differunt; nam neque druidēs[4] habent quī rēbus dīvīnīs praesint, neque sacrificiīs student.[5] Deōrum numerō eōs sōlōs dūcunt quōs cernunt et quōrum apertē (*obviously*) opibus juvantur, Sōlem et Vulcānum et Lūnam. Reliquōs nē fāmā quidem accēpērunt.[6]

Vīta omnis in vēnātiōnibus atque in studiīs reī mīlitāris cōnsistit. Ā parvīs[7] labōrī ac dūritiae (*hardship*) student.

Public Ownership of Land

AGRICULTŪRAE nōn student, majorque pars eōrum vīctūs (*food*) in lacte (*milk*), cāseō (*cheese*), carne cōnsistit.

Neque quisquam agrī modum certum aut fīnēs habet propriōs; sed magistrātūs ac prīncipēs in annōs singulōs gentibus cognātiōnibusque hominum[8] quīque[9] ūnā coiērunt (*have united*) quantum et quō locō vīsum est[10] agrī[11] attribuunt, atque annō post aliō[12] trānsīre cōgunt.

Ejus reī multās afferunt causās[13]: nē assiduā cōnsuētūdine captī studium bellī gerendī agricultūrā[14] commūtent; nē lātōs fīnēs parāre studeant potentiōrēs atque humiliōrēs possessiōnibus expellant; nē accūrātius[15] ad frīgora[16] atque aestūs vītandōs aedificent; nē qua oriātur pecūniae cupiditās, quā ex rē factiōnēs dissēnsiōnēsque nāscuntur; ut animī aequitāte[17] plēbem contineant, cum suās quisque opēs cum potentissimīs aequārī videat.

[1] *by gossip,* or *hearsay.*
[2] *by current report,* which may be true.
[3] *what seems best.*
[4] The Germans had no exclusive priestly class as the Gauls had, but they had priests and priestesses for sacrificing, taking the omens, etc.
[5] *lay stress on,* or *attach importance to.*
[6] *have heard of.*
[7] *from childhood.*
[8] *to families and kinsmen.*
[9] Individuals and small groups of men who did not belong to the same stock united themselves for this purpose.
[10] The meaning is the same here as in line 9.
[11] With **quantum.** Translate *as much land as.*
[12] *to another place,* an adverb equivalent to **alium in locum.**
[13] Four reasons are each introduced by **nē,** and a fifth by **ut.**
[14] *for agriculture;* a special use of the ablative of means.
[15] *with more care.*
[16] *cold.*
[17] *in a contented frame of mind*—viewed as the means by which the common people are kept in order.

War a Popular Employment

CĪVITĀTIBUS maxima laus est
quam lātissimē circum sē vāstātīs fīnibus sōlitūdinēs (*wilder-
nesses*) habēre. Hoc[1] proprium
5 virtūtis exīstimant, expulsōs agrīs
fīnitimōs cēdere neque quemquam
prope sē audēre cōnsistere. Simul
hōc[2] sē fore tūtiōrēs arbitrantur,
repentīnae incursiōnis (*raid*) ti-
10 mōre sublātō.

Cum bellum cīvitās aut illātum
dēfendit aut īnfert, magistrātūs
quī eī bellō praesint et vītae necisque habeant potestātem dēligun-
15 tur. In pāce nūllus est commūnis
magistrātus, sed prīncipēs regiōnum atque pāgōrum inter suōs jūs
dīcunt contrōversiāsque minuunt.[3]

Latrōcinia (*robberies*) nūllam ha-
20 bent īnfāmiam (*disgrace*) quae extrā fīnēs cujusque cīvitātis fīunt,
atque ea juventūtis (*the youths*)
exercendae ac dēsidiae (*idleness*)
minuendae causā fierī praedicant.
Atque ubi quis ex prīncipibus in 25
conciliō dīxit sē ducem fore, quī
sequī velint profiteantur,[4] cōnsur-
gunt (*rise up*) eī quī et causam
et hominem probant, suumque
auxilium pollicentur, atque ā mul- 30
titūdine collaudantur (*are highly
praised*); quī ex hīs secūtī nōn sunt
in dēsertōrum ac prōditōrum (*of
traitors*) numerō dūcuntur, om-
niumque hīs rērum posteā fidēs 35
dērogātur.[5]

Hospitem violāre fās nōn putant;
quī[6] quācumque dē causā ad eōs
vēnērunt ab injūriā prohibent sānc-
tōsque habent; hīsque omnium 40
domūs patent, vīctusque (*and food*)
commūnicātur.[7]

Trouble for the Eburones

RETURNING to Gaul, Caesar demol-
ished the part of the bridge next
to the German bank of the river.
The part connected with the Gallic
side was left standing as a mute re-
minder that his return might be
expected.

Next he turned his attention to
Ambiorix and the Eburones. By a
hurried march he surprised and routed
their army, although Ambiorix escaped.

Following this, guerrilla warfare was
maintained for some time. Caesar in-
vited the neighboring tribes to plunder
the country of the Eburones—an
invitation which they readily accepted. A considerable body of Germans also joined the Gauls in pillaging
the villages and countryside in the
land of the Eburones.

While they were thus engaged, news
reached them that a Roman detachment in charge of Cicero was so situat-

[1] Explained by **expulsōs . . . cōnsistere.**
[2] Explained by **timōre sublātō.**
[3] *settle.*
[4] *let them volunteer.* The subjunctive
represents a command in direct discourse.
[5] *all confidence is taken away.*
[6] *those who.*
[7] Supply **cum hīs.**

ed that it might readily be captured. Since the booty promised to be much more valuable than what could be found in the country of the Eburones, the Germans started for Cicero's camp. They reached it at a time when that officer, contrary to Caesar's orders, had permitted part of his troops to go outside the defenses. With some difficulty Cicero repulsed them. After being beaten off, the Germans gathered the plunder which they had secured from the Eburones and went back across the Rhine.

COMPREHENSION QUESTIONS

In addition to an account of a second invasion of Germany, the part of Caesar's *Gallic War* which you have just read gives information about the customs and social organization of the Gauls and Germans. The questions that follow are based upon the most important parts of this selection.

1. What tribes were the leaders of the two factions in Gaul at the time of Caesar's arrival?

2. From what source had the Sequani secured help in their contest with the Haeduans?

3. What Haeduan leader had gone to Rome to appeal for help?

4. How had the situation changed after the arrival of Caesar?

5. Tell what you can of the Druids.

6. Which Roman gods does Caesar say were worshiped by the Gauls?

7. How much authority did Gallic men have over their wives and children?

8. What were some of the main features of German life and customs as Caesar describes them?

9. What was the attitude of the Germans toward robbery and brigandage?

A ROMAN AMPHITHEATER IN A GERMAN CITY

WORD STUDY XI

More Latin Words with Numerous Derivatives

In Word Study X, page 260, some Latin words, each with a large number of English derivatives, were seen. Other words of this kind, together with some of their English derivatives, follow.

cadō (cāsūrus)	regō (rēctum)	pendō (pēnsum)	vertō (versum)
cadence	regent*	pension	verse
case	regal	pensive	version
casual	régime*	compensate	vertebra
casually	regiment	dispense	vertical
accident	rectangle	expand	vertigo
coincidence	realm*	expensive	adverse
deciduous	royal*	recompense	anniversary
incident	dirigible		aversion
occasion	direct	**teneō**	controversy
occident	director	tenacious	convert
chance*		tenant	reverse
		tenement	traverse*
	videō (vīsum)	tenure	universal
eō (itum)	visible*	abstain*	
ambition	visor	continent	**cernō (crētum or certum)**
circuit	evident	detain*	certain
initial	provident	entertain*	certify
initiative	provision	lieutenant*	concern
uninitiated	review*	maintain*	discern
perish*	supervise	obtain*	discretion
sedition	survey*	retain*	discreet
transit		sustain*	decree*

EXERCISES

1. Find additional English derivatives from **eō**, **teneō**, and **vertō**.

Vocabulary Review

The following words, which appear frequently in this book, are important in second-year work. Their meanings should be thoroughly learned.

adhibeō	dividō	jūstus	nōscō	prīvātus
admittō	equitātus	littera	nūntius	prōdō
aliter	exanimō	loquor	objiciō	referō
amplus	factiō	magistrātus	occultō	sīc
cēdō	familia	mīlitāris	onerārius	succēdō
cliēns	ferē	mōtus	ops	tormentum
crēber	fīdūcia	mūnus	orior	trādō
dēditiō	ignis	mūrus	pāgus	tūtus
dēdūcō	initium	namque	parum	ūllus
dēferō	intereō	nāscor	pendō	unā
dignitās	jūdicō	nātiō	plērumque	vetus
disciplīna	jūrō	nōbilitās	prīncipātus	vulgus

* These have come through French, some of them through Old French forms.

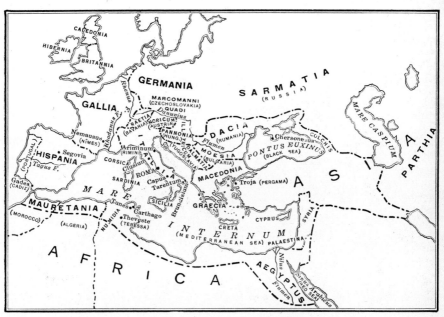

ROME AND ITS VAST DOMAIN

The heavy line of dots and dashes shows the outermost boundaries of the Empire.

ROME AND ITS PROVINCES

IN THE days of its glory Rome governed about forty provinces. This vast domain reached three thousand miles from east to west, and two thousand miles from north to south. It occupied parts of three continents and included within its boundaries many races of people.

From the provinces Rome drew great wealth; not only were they heavily taxed, but their products also poured into Rome. The capital developed and protected the provinces, but the provinces also enriched the city.

The Roman province first organized was the island of Sicily, taken from Carthage in 241 B.C.; the one acquired last—about four hundred fifty years later—was Nu-midia, in Africa. The best known province was Gaul, which became one of the most important parts of the Empire; and the most remote one was Britain.

With few other provinces did Rome, the greatest market in the world, carry on so extensive a commerce as with Spain. A constant procession of merchant ships bore through the Mediterranean the metals, wine, oil, linen, and wool produced in Spain. Most of Rome's silver came from Spanish mines, for so great is the mineral wealth of this land that it has been referred to as one solid block of metal.

The contribution of Greece to the Roman world was largely cultural. So far as material advantages were

THE RUINS OF A ROMAN FORTRESS IN CZECHOSLOVAKIA
Remains of the Roman stronghold that occupied this splendid site on the Danube are still to be seen.

concerned, Greece was poor, for it was devastated during the wars in which it was brought under Roman control and also in the civil wars. From then on, its population declined, and it fell into gradual decay. Because of their admiration for Greek culture, the Romans gave unusual privileges to many of the cities of Greece, Athens being especially favored.

Across central Europe, reaching from Gaul to the Black Sea, stretched the provinces of Raetia —corresponding roughly to what is now Bavaria, or southwest Germany; Noricum—present-day Austria; Pannonia—modern Hungary; and Moesia—a region which is included in Bulgaria today. These were frontier provinces, forming a barrier between the Roman world and the restless Germanic tribes to the north, as well as the hordes from the plains of Russia. In those provinces camps and forts were more common than cities and towns.

North of Moesia, in what is now Rumania, lived the Dacians, a fierce people. There still stands in Rome a tall column covered with carved reliefs which tell the story of the conquest of Dacia.

Across the Adriatic Sea from Italy lay Dalmatia. From the harbors of the beautiful Dalmatian coast sailed pirates who preyed on Roman merchant ships, and even on the shores of Italy, until they were driven from the seas by the Roman fleet. The capture of the pirates' retreats and hiding-places gave Rome a foothold on the eastern coast of the Adriatic. Dalmatia, one of the first of the provinces, in time became highly Romanized.

From east to west—from the Red Sea to the Pillars of Hercules—the entire northern coast of Africa finally came under Roman control. The shifting sands of the Sahara prevented advance to the south.

The most western of the African provinces was Mauretania, extending across land now occupied by Morocco and Algeria. In Mauretania, Numidia, and the other African provinces there were many flourishing Roman cities and many large villas. Ruins of harbors, reservoirs, roads, baths, amphitheaters, temples, and other public works reveal the vigor of Roman life in Africa.

The most important province of Africa was Egypt, with a remarkable civilization, older than that of the Romans by thousands of years. It came under the control of the Romans with the downfall of Cleopatra, the famous Egyptian queen. The special value of Egypt was as the granary of the Empire; from it came each year about one-third of the grain which fed the people of Rome. Linen cloth and glassware made by skilful Egyptian craftsmen were distributed throughout the Empire.

Since practically all the papyrus used in the ancient world for books and writing material was made from plants which grew along the Nile, Caesar undoubtedly wrote his *Gallic War* on sheets of papyrus from Egypt.

In the East, between the Black Sea and the Red Sea, were a large number of small kingdoms and city states. Many of these cities had been founded by the Greeks long before Rome existed. No uniformity of administration could be enforced on them, as was done in Gaul and Britain. The various principalities were balanced against each other and given numerous privileges.

One of the most prosperous of the eastern provinces was Syria, long famous for the production of purple dye and dyed cloth. South of Syria, and once a part of it, was Palestine, from which spread the Christian faith.

Beyond the Roman provinces in Asia was the powerful kingdom of Parthia. For centuries the Parthians withstood all Rome's efforts to extend its eastern boundary. What temporary advances the Romans made were gained at great cost of life.

In the days of the Republic the policy of the Roman government toward the provinces was in general unsatisfactory, for there was no uniformity and much abuse in their administration. The fact that the governor was not paid a salary, but had to depend for his income on fees and requisitions, encouraged graft and bribery. Moreover, he could not be called to account during his term of office.

Most governors took office with the intention of making a fortune. The career of Verres in Sicily is an outstanding example of a Roman governor at his worst. Verres sold offices and judicial decisions, enforced ruinous taxes, and appropriated whatever precious works of art struck his fancy. It took Sicily a long time to recover from the evil effects of his administration.

The Emperor Augustus reorganized the administration of the provinces, permitting the people as much freedom as possible in the management of local affairs. He fixed definitely the total of the taxes, and permitted only two direct taxes to be levied—the land tax and the head tax. Great amounts of money, however, were brought in by the tariffs and other tolls. Much of the income from a province was spent within its boundaries in keeping up the army, paying salaries, and constructing public works.

In general the Romans respected the customs and religion of a conquered people. Their tolerance was extraordinary for the times. But generous as the Romans were in the treatment of their provincial subjects, they were reluctant at times to grant them the rights of Roman citizens. It was only as a mark of special favor that certain classes of provincials or the inhabitants of a selected city were admitted to citizenship. Not until the beginning of the third century A.D. was the entire free population of the Empire given Roman citizenship.

IN ROMAN AFRICA
These storage houses were built by the Romans in one of their African provinces. Probably they were used for feed.

In the general peace which prevailed throughout the Empire under Augustus and his immediate successors, the provinces prospered exceedingly. Good roads connected them. Industry and commerce increased, swelling the vast volume of trade already carried on among them and with Italy.

The Roman ruins now found in the various regions once included in the Empire bear witness not only to its great extent, but also to the thoroughness with which the provinces were Romanized.

The advance of the legions meant also the advance of Roman civilization, and a peaceful conquest always followed one of force. As Seneca, an ancient Roman philosopher, once wrote, "Wherever a Roman has conquered, there he also lives."

A GREAT GALLIC LEADER ARISES

Alpibus Ītaliam mūnierat anteā nātūra, non sine aliquō dīvīnō nūmine ...
Quae jam licet cōnsidant.
Nature, not without some divine purpose, had formerly protected Italy by means of the Alps. Now they may sink down.   CICERO[1]

In Union There Is Hope

FOR six years the Gauls had been meeting with disaster in their efforts to beat back the Roman threat to their independence. But they had failed to learn the lesson that their only hope lay in unity of action. The seventh year brought the first widespread movement toward a real union of their forces. Further, it brought to the front a leader of outstanding ability.

A considerable number of tribes were resentful toward Roman authority, which seemed to be growing ever stronger throughout Gaul, and they felt that at this time conditions were especially favorable for successful resistance. In Italy the political situation was one of great disorder. Reports of this condition had doubtless come to the Gauls, and they may have had reason to believe that a revolution was probable. Such an event would either recall Caesar to the capital or at any rate interfere with his securing the support needed to maintain himself in Gaul.

Among the tribes active in the revolt were the Arvernians, a powerful people of central Gaul. Their leader was Vercingetorix, who was soon recognized as the most able among the

VERCINGETORIX
This statue of the Gallic chief stands in the modern French town that is on the site of Alesia, the scene of his last stand.

chieftains of the tribes in the newly-organized coalition. On being chosen as commander-in-chief of the Gallic forces, he at once set about preparing for active warfare with a vigor and a shrewdness which justified his selection as leader.

At this time Caesar was engaged in administrative duties in northern Italy. Learning of the uprising, he at once started for Gaul and began hostilities against the tribes involved in the revolt. He captured three of their towns and with the help of his German horsemen routed the cavalry

---

[1] Cicero is praising Caesar's conquest of Gaul, which has made the Alps no longer a necessary defense for Italy against invasion by the Gauls.

281

of Vercingetorix, who was marching to the aid of his allies.

Vercingetorix, seeing that his forces were not able to face the Romans in open battle, adopted the plan of laying waste the country, burning the towns, and wearing down the Romans by cutting off their supplies.

The Bituriges begged him to spare Avaricum, their chief town, from destruction. Vercingetorix unwillingly assented to their plea and began to make preparations for a stand in this place.

A long siege followed, but the town was finally captured, and the Roman soldiers took savage vengeance for their losses and sufferings during the siege.

Caesar next marched on Gergovia, the chief town of the Arvernians.

Here he met his most serious reverse in the campaign, the only unsuccessful operation of the entire war where he was personally in command. His forces were beaten back, and as a result of their rashness in disregarding orders, suffered heavy losses.

The siege was abandoned, and the Romans marched into the country of the Senones.

Meanwhile Labienus, with a detachment of the army, had been carrying on the war in central Gaul along the Seine River near the site of the modern city of Paris. After some rather successful activities he rejoined Caesar. The spirit of the Gauls was still high, and they had now been joined by the Haeduans, who through the preceding campaigns had remained loyal to the Romans.

The Fires of Revolt Burn Higher

DĒFECTIŌNE (*revolt*) Haeduōrum cognitā bellum augētur. Lēgātiōnēs in omnēs partēs circummittuntur (*are sent around*); quan-
5 tum[1] grātiā, auctōritāte, pecūniā valent, ad sollicitandās cīvitātēs nītuntur (*they strive*). Nactī obsidēs quōs Caesar apud eōs dēposuerat, hōrum suppliciō dubitantēs
10 territant (*they terrify*).

Petunt ā Vercingetorīge Haeduī ut ad sē veniat ratiōnēsque bellī gerendī commūnicet. Rē impetrātā, contendunt ut ipsīs summa imperiī trādātur; et rē in contrōversiam[2] dēductā tōtīus Galliae concilium Bibracte indīcitur.

Conveniunt undique frequentēs (*in great numbers*). Multitūdinis suffrāgiīs (*to the votes*) rēs per- 20 mittitur; ad ūnum omnēs Vercingetorīgem probant imperātōrem.

Ab hōc conciliō Rēmī, Lingonēs, Trēverī āfuērunt: illī,[3] quod amīcitiam Rōmānōrum sequēbantur; 25 Trēverī, quod aberant longius et ā Germānīs premēbantur, quae fuit causa quārē tōtō abessent bellō et neutrīs auxilia mitterent.

Magnō dolōre Haeduī ferunt sē 30 dējectōs prīncipātū. Queruntur fortūnae commūtātiōnem et Caesaris indulgentiam (*indulgence*) in sē requīrunt (*miss*), neque tamen

---

[1] With **valent**—*so far as they can do so.*
[2] Naturally Vercingetorix would not be at all inclined to admit the claim of

the Haeduans to the leadership of the war.
[3] The Remi and the Lingones.

suscepto bello suum consilium ab reliquis separare (*to separate*) audent.

Inviti summae spei adulescentes, Eporedorix et Viridomarus,[1] Vercingetorigi parent.

Victory Is Worth Any Cost

ILLE[2] imperat reliquis civitatibus obsides, diemque ei rei constituit. Omnes equites, quindecim milia numero, celeriter convenire jubet. Peditatu quem antea habuerit se fore contentum dicit neque fortunam temptaturum aut acie dimicaturum. Sed, quoniam abundet[3] equitatu, perfacile esse factu Romanos deterrere (*to hinder*) ne pabulentur; aequo modo animo sua ipsi frumenta corrumpant[4] aedificiaque incendant, qua rei familiaris jactura perpetuum imperium libertatemque se consequi videant. His constitutis rebus Haeduis Segusiavisque,[5] qui sunt finitimi provinciae, decem milia peditum imperat; huc addit equites DCCC. His praeficit fratrem Eporedorigis bellumque inferre Allobrogibus jubet.

Altera ex parte Gabalos[6] proximosque pagos Arvernorum in Helvios,[6] item Rutenos[6] Cadurcosque[6] ad fines Volcarum Arecomicorum[6] depopulandos mittit. Nihilo minus clandestinis (*secret*) nuntiis legationibusque Allobroges sollicitat, quorum mentes nondum ab superiore bello resedisse (*had settled down*) sperabat. Horum principibus pecunias, civitati autem imperium totius provinciae pollicetur.

Loyal Allies of the Romans

AD HOS omnes casus[7] provisa erant praesidia cohortium duarum et viginti, quae ex ipsa coacta provincia ab L. Caesare[8] legato ad omnes partes opponebantur.[9]

Helvii,[6] sua sponte cum finitimis proelio congressi, pelluntur; et C. Valerio Domnotauro,[10] Caburi[11] filio, principe civitatis, compluribusque aliis interfectis intra oppida murosque compelluntur. Allobroges, crebris ad Rhodanum dispositis (*having been placed*) praesidiis, magna cura et diligentia suos fines tuentur.

Caesar, quod hostes equitatu superiores esse intellegebat et in-

---

[1] *Eporedorix* (ep'ọ-red'ọ-rix) *and Viridomarus* (vir'i-dọ-mā'rus), Haeduans.

[2] Vercingetorix.

[3] *he was well supplied with.*

[4] *they must not hesitate to destroy their own crops;* **corrumpant** and **incendant** represent commands in the direct form, the utterance of Vercingetorix.

[5] *and the Segusiavi* (sē'gö-si-ā'vī), a Celtic tribe.

[6] *the Gabali* (gab'a̤-lī), *the Helvii* (hel'- vi-ī), *the Ruteni* (rö-tē'nī), *the Cadurci* (ka̤-dẹr'sī), *the Volcae Arecomici* (vol'sē ar-ẹ-kom'i-sī), tribes of Gaul.

[7] *to meet all these dangers.*

[8] A distant relative of the commander.

[9] *were opposed to the enemy.*

[10] *Gaius Valerius Domnotaurus* (va̤-lē'ri-us dom-nọ-tâ'rus), a Gaul, whose father had received Roman citizenship.

[11] *Caburus* (ka̤-bū'rus), a leader of the Helvii.

terclūsīs omnibus itineribus nūllā rē ex prōvinciā atque Ītaliā sub-levārī poterat, trāns Rhēnum in Germāniam mittit ad eās cīvitā-tēs quās superiōribus annīs pācā-verat, equitēsque ab hīs arcessit et levis armātūrae peditēs[1] quī inter eōs proeliārī (*to fight*) cōnsuērant. Eōrum adventū, quod minus idōneīs equīs ūtēbantur, ā tribūnīs mīlitum reliquīsque equitibus Rō-mānīs atque ēvocātīs (*veterans*) equōs sūmit Germānīsque distri-buit.

Ready for Battle

INTEREĀ, dum haec geruntur, hostium cōpiae ex Arvernīs equi-tēsque quī tōtī Galliae erant im-perātī conveniunt. Magnō hōrum coāctō numerō, cum Caesar in Sēquanōs per extrēmōs Lingonum fīnēs iter faceret quō facilius sub-sidium prōvinciae ferre posset, cir-citer mīlia passuum decem ab Rōmānīs trīnīs[2] castrīs Vercinge-torīx cōnsīdit; convocātīsque ad cōnsilium praefectīs equitum, vē-nisse tempus victōriae dēmōnstrat: fugere in prōvinciam Rōmānōs Galliāque excēdere. Id sibi ad praesentem obtinendam lībertātem satis esse; ad reliquī temporis pā-cem atque ōtium parum prōficī; majōribus enim coāctīs cōpiīs re-versūrōs[3] neque fīnem bellandī fac-tūrōs.[3]

Proinde in agmine impedītōs adoriantur.[4] Sī peditēs suīs auxi-lium ferant atque in eō morentur, iter facere nōn posse; sī, id quod magis futūrum cōnfīdat, relictīs impedīmentīs suae salūtī cōnsulant, et ūsū rērum necessāriārum et dig-nitāte spoliātum īrī;[5] nam dē equi-tibus hostium, quīn nēmō eōrum prōgredī modo[6] extrā agmen au-deat, nē ipsōs quidem dēbēre du-bitāre. Id quō majōre faciant animō, cōpiās sē omnēs prō castrīs habitūrum et terrōrī hostibus fu-tūrum.

Conclāmant equitēs sānctissimō jūre jūrandō cōnfirmārī oportēre nē tēctō recipiātur, nē ad līberōs, ad parentēs, ad uxōrem aditum habeat quī nōn bis per agmen hostium perequitārit.[7]

High Hopes Prove Vain

PROBĀTĀ rē atque omnibus ad jūs jūrandum adāctīs,[8] posterō diē in trēs partēs distribūtō equi-tātū, duae sē aciēs ab duōbus la-teribus ostendunt; ūna ā prīmō agmine iter impedīre coepit. Quā

---

[1] The words **levis armātūrae peditēs** mean *light infantry*.

[2] With nouns that are plural in form but singular in meaning, such as **castra**, the distributive numerals are used in-stead of the cardinals (here **trīnīs**, *three*, instead of **tribus**).

[3] The subject refers to the Romans.

[4] For a subjunctive expressing an ex-hortation in the direct form ("let us attack").

[5] The infrequently used future passive infinitive—*they would lose both their property and their prestige.*

[6] Adverb.

[7] *had not ridden*, instead of **perequitā-verit**, a perfect subjunctive.

[8] *bound by oath.*

rē nūntiātā, Caesar suum quoque equitātum tripertītō (*into three parts*) dīvīsum contrā hostem īre jubet. Pugnātur ūnā[1] omnibus in partibus. Cōnsistit agmen; impedīmenta intrā legiōnēs recipiuntur.

Sī quā in parte nostrī labōrāre aut gravius premī vidēbantur, eō signa īnferrī Caesar aciemque convertī jubēbat; quae rēs et hostēs ad īnsequendum tardābat et nostrōs spē auxiliī cōnfirmābat.

Tandem Germānī[2] ab dextrō latere summum jugum nactī hostēs locō dēpellunt (*drive away*); fugientēs usque ad flūmen, ubi Vercingetorīx cum pedestribus cōpiīs cōnsēderat, persequuntur complūrēsque interficiunt. Quā rē animadversā reliquī, nē circumvenīrentur veritī, sē fugae mandant. Omnibus locīs fit caedēs.

Trēs nōbilissimī Haeduī captī ad Caesarem perdūcuntur: Cotus,[3] praefectus equitum, quī contrōversiam cum Convictolitāve[3] proximīs comitiīs[4] habuerat, et Cavarillus,[3] quī post dēfectiōnem (*revolt*) Litaviccī[3] pedestribus cōpiīs praefuerat, et Eporēdorīx, quō duce ante adventum Caesaris Haeduī cum Sēquanīs bellō contenderant.[5]

Toward the Last Stand

FUGĀTŌ (*having been routed*) omnī equitātū, Vercingetorīx cōpiās suās, ut prō castrīs collocāverat, redūxit prōtinusque Alesiam, quod[6] est oppidum Mandubiōrum,[7] iter facere coepit; celeriterque impedīmenta ex castrīs ēdūcī et sē subsequī jussit. Caesar, impedīmentīs in proximum collem ductīs, duābus legiōnibus praesidiō relictīs, secūtus hostēs quantum diēī tempus est passum, circiter tribus mīlibus ex novissimō agmine interfectīs, alterō diē ad Alesiam castra fēcit. Perspectō urbis sitū perterritīsque hostibus, quod equitātū, quā maximē parte[8] exercitūs cōnfīdēbant, erant pulsī, adhortātus (*having encouraged*) ad labōrem mīlitēs Alesiam circumvāllāre[9] īnstituit.

The Siege of Alesia

CAESAR first constructed a line of fortifications around the city of Alesia to prevent the escape of the army of Vercingetorix.

He then took measures to protect his own army against attack by a force which might assemble to relieve the besieged Gauls. For this purpose he prepared a second line of earthworks back of the position he occu-

---

[1] Equivalent to **ūnō tempore**.

[2] Auxiliaries in the Roman army.

[3] *Cotus* (kō'tus), *Convictolitavis* (kon-vik'tol-i-tā'vis), *Cavarillus* (kav-a̯-ril'-us), *Litaviccus* (lit-a̯-vik'us).

[4] *in the late* (*recent*) *elections.*

[5] As told on page 165.

[6] Another example of the relative

agreeing in gender with a predicate noun (here **oppidum**), instead of with its antecedent.

[7] *of the Mandubii* (man-dö'bi-ī), a Gallic tribe.

[8] Ablative with **cōnfīdō**, which is oftener used with the dative, especially to refer to persons.

[9] *to surround with a wall.*

pied. The Romans were thus inclosed between two parallel lines of fortifications that encircled the town.

The outer line of defense was of an unusually elaborate character, including rows of pits with sharpened stakes at the bottom, iron hooks, and other devices intended especially to hinder cavalry action.

Vercingetorix sent out messengers, urging that an army be raised at once for the relief of Alesia. The Gauls were slow in responding to his call, and supplies in the besieged town began to run short. In order to save the food for the soldiers, the non-combatants were expelled from the city.

Caesar refused to allow these unfortunate refugees to pass through his lines, and they starved to death between friends and foes.

Finally the forces which had been collected in response to the plea of Vercingetorix appeared, and a series of battles followed. So skilfully had the Roman defenses been constructed, and so courageously did Caesar's soldiers meet every attack of the enemy, that the Gauls were everywhere defeated. The army which was attempting to relieve the town was routed.

Vercingetorix, seeing that the situation was hopeless, surrendered with all his surviving forces. He was sent to

IN WAR, NO MERCY

In this modern French painting Vercingetorix is shown on the wall of Alesia. Before him Gallic women and children, who have been expelled from the town, plead for food.

Rome and thrown into prison. Seven years later he was led in Caesar's triumphal procession, and then executed.

The fall of Alesia marked the end of the most thoroughly organized effort the Gauls ever made to free themselves from the power of Rome. Some uprisings occurred later, but they did not involve large numbers of tribes. Caesar's work of conquest was virtually done, and the Romanizing of Gaul was the result.

COMPREHENSION QUESTIONS

The great revolt of 52 B.C. came near being a success. The following questions deal with the organization and the outcome of this last Gallic stand for freedom.

1. What was the name of the leader of the Gallic revolt in the year 52 B.C.?
2. To what tribe did he belong?
3. Name one of the tribes which remained loyal to the Romans at this time.
4. What measures did Vercingetorix take to hinder the Romans from securing supplies?

CAESAR'S FORTIFICATIONS BEFORE ALESIA
Our modern instruments of warfare are hardly more diabolical than the means by which Caesar planned
to stop the enemy.

5. From what source did Caesar secure cavalry?
6. What place did Vercingetorix select for his last stand?
7. What kind of defenses did Caesar prepare back of his lines?
8. Tell what you can of the outcome of the great revolt and of the fate of
Vercingetorix.

WORD STUDY XII
English Words of Interesting Derivation

Our word ROSTRUM has an interesting history. It is the same as the Latin
word for *the beak of a bird*, and was also applied by the Romans to the curved
end of the prow of a ship. The Romans decorated the platform in the Forum
from which public speeches were made with the *beaks* (**rōstra**) of captured
vessels. Later the platform itself came to be called **rōstra** from the decorations
upon it. From this word, in its singular form, **rōstrum,** comes the word which
is now used for any stage, platform, or pulpit from which public addresses
may be made.

INAUGURATE, a word which means install formally in office, is derived from
the Latin word **augur,** *prophet, soothsayer.* The Romans never undertook
anything of significance without first having an augur observe and interpret
the omens, so that no unfavorable signs might attend their undertaking.

CONTEMPLATE, meaning meditate or consider thoughtfully, goes back to the
Latin word **templum,** which, in its original use, meant *a space for observation
marked out by the augur.*

CARNIVAL, which we think of as a time of general gayety and merrymaking,
is derived from two Latin words, **carō (carnis),** *flesh,* and **levāre,** *to take away;*
hence, the putting away of meat. In ancient times it was a season of revelry
and feasting which preceded a period of fasting.

AVIATOR is derived from the Latin word **avis,** *bird.* We keep this idea in the name "The Bird Man," which is applied to a modern statue of a man in the ordinary costume of an aviator, but having wings.

ARENA today means a place of public contest or exertion. By the Romans in classical antiquity it was applied to that part of the amphitheater in which games and combats took place. The word itself, **arēna** (more frequently spelled **harēna**), meant *sand,* as the place in which the gladiators fought was usually covered with sand to absorb the blood.

DEAN was originally the word for the chief (**decānus**) in charge of ten (**decem**) soldiers. Later it was applied to the chief of ten monks. The word is no longer used in the military world, but is common in both religious and educational institutions, as we speak of "the dean of the law school," meaning the head of that institution.

CEILING is derived from **caelum,** the Latin word for *sky* or *arched covering.* Now it means that which is overhead in a room.

TANTALIZE, tease or torment, is a word derived from the name of a mythical king, Tantalus. In the lower world this king was punished by being placed in the middle of a lake whose waters reached to his chin, but receded whenever he attempted to quench his thirst, while over his head hung branches laden with fruit which likewise receded whenever he attempted to grasp them.

NOON comes from **nōna hōra,** the ninth hour of the day according to the Roman reckoning. This was about three in the afternoon by our time (see p. 409), but it has come to mean midday.

SALARY is derived from the Latin word **sāl,** *salt.* In ancient times a sum of money called **salārium,** *salt money,* was given to the soldiers. Later the word came to mean payment in general for services.

EQUINOX, from the Latin **aequus,** *equal,* and **nox,** *night,* is used to denote the times in the year in which days and nights are of equal length—about March 21 and September 22. The former is the vernal (Latin **vēr,** *spring*) equinox; the latter the autumnal (Latin **autumnus,** *autumn*) equinox.

Vocabulary Review

The meanings of the following words should be thoroughly learned.

adigō	compellō	fortūna	obtineō	recipiō
adorior	cōnfirmō	impedīmentum	pābulor	revertō,
agmen	cōnsīdō	impediō	pedes	revertor
anteā	cōnsulō	indīcō, -ere	pedester	sequor
arcessō	cūra	interclūdō	persequor	sinister
auctōritās	dēcernō	invītus	praeficiō	sollicitō
augeō	dexter	jūs jūrandum	prior	sponte suā
caedēs	distribuō	lēgātiō	prōficiō	sūmō
cīvitās	eques	lībertās	queror	tardō
cōgō	excēdō	mandō, -āre	quīn	tueor
cohors	extrā	moror	quoniam	usque
collis	familiāris	necessārius	quoque	vereor

THE CONQUEST OF GAUL—THE STORY IN BRIEF

EVENTS OF 58 B.C.

The Helvetians decide to abandon their country and establish themselves in another part of Gaul.

They attempt to pass through the Roman Province, but are beaten back by Roman soldiers at the banks of the Rhone.

In passing through the territory of the Haeduans, the Helvetians plunder the country, and the Haeduans appeal to Caesar for help.

Caesar follows the Helvetians with his army and attacks them at the Saône River, almost destroying one of the four divisions of the tribe.

The Helvetians ask for peace, but refuse to give hostages, and hostilities are continued.

After following the Helvetians for some time, Caesar turns aside in order to secure supplies for his army.

The Helvetians change their course and follow the Romans, making attacks on their rear line.

A general battle is fought, in which the Helvetians are completely defeated.

Caesar orders the survivors to return to their own country.

After the defeat of the Helvetians, a deputation from a number of Gallic tribes calls on Caesar, asking for protection against the German king, Ariovistus.

Caesar advances toward the region occupied by the forces of Ariovistus.

An interview between Caesar and Ariovistus is broken off by the hostile action of the German cavalry.

The Germans avoid battle for a time, but Caesar compels them to fight by advancing on their camp.

The Germans are routed, and many of them are killed or captured. Ariovistus and some of his followers escape across the Rhine.

EVENTS OF 57 B.C.

The Belgian tribes form a league to oppose further extension of Roman power in Gaul.

The Belgian forces are repulsed at the River Aisne.

They decide to return home; but as they are withdrawing, they are attacked by the Romans, and many of them are killed.

The Nervii make a surprise attack on the Romans at the River Sambre.

The Romans narrowly escape disaster, but the Nervii are finally routed with heavy loss.

289

The Atuatuci, after agreeing to surrender their town, make a treacherous attack on the Romans.

The town of the Atuatuci is captured, and the surviving inhabitants are sold as slaves.

Servius Galba is sent with a body of troops to prevent the Alpine tribes from interfering with traders passing through their country.

The Gauls attack Galba's camp and are driven off with difficulty.

Galba abandons the plan to winter in the Alps.

EVENTS OF 56 B.C.

The tribes along the northwestern coast of Gaul provoke hostilities with the Romans.

A naval battle is fought in which the Romans are victorious and the fleet of the Gauls is destroyed.

Sabinus is sent into the country of the Venelli, where he wins a decisive victory.

Crassus conducts a successful campaign in Aquitania.

Caesar attempts to subdue the Morini and Menapii, but his campaign is stopped by unfavorable weather.

EVENTS OF 55 B.C.

Two German tribes cross into Gaul near the mouth of the Rhine.

Caesar orders them to return to their own country.

A surprise attack on Caesar's cavalry is made by the German cavalry.

Caesar attacks the camp of the Germans and kills a large number of them.

Caesar constructs a bridge over the Rhine, and crosses into Germany.

The Ubii, who are friendly to the Romans, are relieved from the oppression of the Suebi.

After the country of the Suebi has been laid waste, the Roman army is led back into Gaul, and the bridge is broken down.

Caesar crosses to Britain with two legions.

The Britons attempt to prevent his landing, but are unsuccessful.

A storm damages the Roman fleet on the beach.

The Britons attack Caesar's camp but are routed.

After this defeat, the Britons promise to give hostages, and Caesar returns to the continent with his forces.

EVENTS OF 54 B.C.

Caesar leads a second expedition to Britain.

The Britons organize a league to oppose the Romans, and make Cassivellaunus commander of their forces.

They attack the Romans and are routed with difficulty.

The Romans advance inland and capture the stronghold of Cassivellaunus.

An attack on the Roman camp at the seashore is beaten off, and Cassivellaunus submits to the Romans.

Caesar returns to Gaul and distributes his army for the winter in six camps, some distance apart.

One of these camps, under command of Sabinus and Cotta, is attacked by the Gauls.

The Romans repulse the enemy, but decide to abandon the camp and join one of the other divisions of the army.

They are attacked from ambush, and almost the entire force is slaughtered.

The Gauls attack another camp, which is under the command of Quintus Cicero.

The Romans defend themselves with difficulty, but are saved by the approach of Caesar's forces.

The camp of Labienus is unsuccessfully attacked by the Treveri.

EVENTS OF 53 B.C.

Caesar enlarges his army, fearing a general uprising.

He invades the country of the Nervii and compels them to give hostages.

A number of other tribes, among them the Menapii, are compelled to submit.

The Treveri attack Labienus, but are defeated.

Caesar again constructs a bridge across the Rhine, and invades Germany a second time.

The hostile Suebi retreat into the forests and avoid battle.

Caesar returns to Gaul and breaks down part of the bridge, leaving the part next to the Gallic bank standing.

A body of Germans who have been plundering the country of the Eburones suddenly attack a Roman camp, which is in charge of Quintus Cicero, and are driven off with difficulty.

The Romans pursue Ambiorix, the leader of the hostile Eburones, but are unable to capture him.

EVENTS OF 52 B.C.

A number of Gallic tribes plan to begin war for the purpose of freeing themselves from Roman control.

The Carnutes kill the Roman citizens at Cenabum and seize their property.

Vercingetorix is chosen commander-in-chief of the forces of the tribes involved in the revolt.

He attacks a town of the Boii, who are loyal to the Romans.

Caesar advances to the relief of the Boii, capturing several towns of the Gauls on his march.

Vercingetorix adopts a policy of laying waste the country and burning the towns in order to deprive the Roman army of supplies.

Avaricum is spared in this policy of devastation, and the Gauls attempt to defend the town.

Avaricum is captured and destroyed by the Romans.

Caesar besieges the town of Gergovia, but meets with heavy losses and is compelled to abandon the siege.

The Haeduans, who have heretofore been loyal to the Romans, join the forces of Vercingetorix.

The Gallic army occupies the town of Alesia, and Caesar begins the siege of this town.

The Gauls in Alesia attack the besieging force unsuccessfully.

The Gallic tribes organize another army and attempt to relieve Alesia.

Both the relieving force and the army in the town are defeated by the Romans.

Vercingetorix surrenders with the rest of his army.

HOW CAESAR BESIEGED AVARICUM

ROMAN BRIDGES AND AQUEDUCTS

THE Romans were the most famous bridge-makers of antiquity. In fact, our modern bridge-builders owe much to the skill of the Roman engineers, whose methods were but little improved until iron and steel came into use. So well did the Romans build, that after nearly two thousand years many of their bridges are still standing. In fact some of them are even bearing modern traffic. In southern France, for instance, two of the bridges which carry automobile traffic of the twentieth century were built by the Romans and are almost perfectly preserved.

Roman bridges were supported by arches. Since the span of the stone arch had to be short, it was necessary to use a series of arches in carrying a bridge across a wide stream. Our modern bridges of steel construction nat-urally have a much greater span. The George Washington Bridge, which crosses the Hudson River not far above its mouth, has a gigantic span of thirty-five hundred feet, whereas the arch in a Roman bridge did not usually span more than fifty feet.

One of the most famous of ancient Roman bridges was the *Pons Mulvius*, which crossed the Tiber River north of Rome. The great highway known as *Via Flaminia* was carried out from the city over this bridge. We do not know exactly when the *Pons Mulvius* was built, but it must have been erected before 223 B.C., the year when the highway was constructed. This bridge has been repaired a number of times; of its six arches, four are ancient.

The Flavian Bridge in southern France is another interesting old

THE MULVIAN BRIDGE

Some of the arches of this bridge belong to the ancient structure, across which passed Romans of two thousand years ago, on foot, on horseback, in litters, or in elegant carriages.

THE ROMANS BUILT WELL

These sturdy arches have survived their builders by about two thousand years. They are a section of the *Aniō Vetus*, an aqueduct one hundred fifty miles long that carried water to ancient Rome.

supplied with water brought by carefully planned and constructed aqueducts.

Rome itself required a vast amount of water for its fountains, private homes, and great public baths. Local springs and wells could by no means supply such quantities of water, and it had to be brought from a distance.

The pioneer in providing Rome with a good water supply was Appius Claudius, an able and public-spirited official. In 312 B.C. he constructed an aqueduct which brought water from hillside springs east of the city. This was called the Appian Aqueduct in his honor. It was ten and a half miles long, and for almost all its length was a tunnel of masonry.

Another aqueduct, four times as long as the Appian, was built forty years later. It carried water to Rome from the upper part of the Anio River in the Apennine Mountains, and was known as the *Aniō Vetus*. In the centuries which followed, many other aqueducts were built to serve the growing city on its seven hills. At the present time Rome is supplied by four aqueducts, which use the original channels in certain parts of their courses.

While in an ancient aqueduct the water flowed for most of the way through an underground channel of masonry lined with cement, sometimes the aqueduct was carried across a valley or a marsh on great stone arches. Since there were no powerful pumping stations

one. Built during the reign of Augustus, it is a fine structure with an imposing arch at each end. There is also a well-preserved bridge at Rimini on the east coast of Italy. Still another splendid example of the Roman engineer's skill is the bridge which crosses the Tagus River in Spain. It also is in use today.

Even more than these ancient bridges, the ruins of the great aqueducts which brought water down from the hills and mountains to cities throughout the Empire give evidence of the genius of the Roman engineer. Every important town in Italy, as well as many a city in the provinces, was in those days, it was necessary for the water to flow from high places down to the city served.

Lead pipes were used to conduct the water from the mains to homes as well as to public fountains and baths. These pipes were made from strips of sheet lead, which were folded over and welded. Many pieces of pipe bearing the names of ancient owners of houses have been found in Rome. By these marked pipes it has been possible to locate sites where certain Roman citizens of long ago had their homes.

The poor people of Rome, who could not afford to have water piped to their houses, drew what they needed from the public fountains. Since there were many hundreds of these fountains scattered throughout the city, people did not usually have to walk far with their heavy pitchers.

Remains of Roman aqueducts are found in France, Spain, Africa, and other regions which were once Roman provinces, as well as in Italy. One of the most remarkable is the aqueduct at Segovia in Spain, which is still in use after two thousand years. It is built of granite blocks laid without cement and is twenty-seven hundred feet long and nearly a hundred feet high where it crosses a valley.

Another aqueduct, part of which is now known as the *Pont du Gard*, once brought water to the Roman colony located where the city of Nîmes now stands, in southern France. Three tiers of stately arches support it over the River Gard, but the rest of the aqueduct has almost entirely disappeared. The height of the topmost series of arches is one hundred sixty feet above the river. One can now walk through the lofty water-channel which is supported by the arches.

The Claudian Aqueduct, which was finished A.D. 52, was one of the most magnificent ever erected. The arches which supported it for part of its course near Rome are still an interesting feature of the landscape. These mighty ruins rise against the Italian skies as a constant memorial to Roman achievement.

ARCHES OF THE CLAUDIAN AQUEDUCT

STORIES FROM ROMAN HISTORY

Rome ruled in all her matchless pride,
Queen of the world, an empire state;
Her eagles conquered far and wide,
Her word was law, her will was fate.

ARTHUR CHAMBERLAIN

The Pilgrim Fathers of Rome

OLIM in Asiā erat urbs antīqua, quae Trōja appellāta est. Eam urbem Graecī decem annōs obsēdērunt tandemque cēpērunt. Priamō rēge fīliīsque ejus interfec-
tīs, urbem dēlēvērunt. Sed Aenēās,[1] quī inter clārissimōs dēfensōrēs urbis fuerat, cum paucīs comitibus ex urbe effūgit. Cum profugōs ex omnibus partibus coēgisset, in Ītaliam migrāre cōnstituit.

Post septem annōs vēnit in eam partem Ītaliae ubi erat urbs Laurentum.[2] Ibi cum Trōjānī praedam[3] ex agrīs agerent, Latīnus,[4] rēx, Aborīginēsque,[5] quī tum ea loca tenēbant, agrōs dēfendere parāvērunt. Sed Latīnus, postquam in colloquiō orīginem (*origin*) multitūdinis ducisque cognōvit, pācem cum Aenēā fēcit atque posteā eī Lāvīniam fīliam in mātrimōnium dedit. Trōjānī urbem condidērunt, quam Aenēās ab nōmine uxōris Lāvīnium appellāvit.

Deinde Turnus, rēx Rutulōrum, cui Lāvīnia ante adventum Aenēae dēspōnsa erat, bellō Latīnum Trōjānōsque aggressus est. Victī sunt Rutulī, sed victōrēs ducem Latīnum ā̆misērunt. Inde Turnus auxilium petīvit ab Etrūscīs,[6] quī tōtam Ītaliam fāmā nōminis suī implēverant. Illī metuentēs novam urbem multitūdine opibusque crēscentem laetī[7] auxilium tulērunt.

Aenēās in tantō discrīmine, ut Aborīginēs Trōjānōsque sub eōdem jūre atque nōmine habēret, Latīnōs utramque gentem appellāvit.[8] Cum[9]

---

[1] A Greek noun adapted to the Latin first declension. Its forms are as follows: *nom.* Aenēās, *gen.* and *dat.* Aenēae, *acc.* Aenēān or Aenēam, *abl.* Aenēā.

[2] *Laurentum* (lâ-ren'tum), a town of ancient Italy. See map, page 305.

[3] Since booty consisted largely of cattle, agō, *drive*, is an appropriate verb. In English, *collect, carry off* are the usual terms.

[4] The king's name. See Vocabulary.

[5] *and the Aborigines* (ab-ọ-rij'i-nēz). They were the first inhabitants, ancestors of the Romans.

[6] The Etruscans were a people whose origin is unknown. They were not of the same racial stock as the Romans and other peoples of Italy. They attained a high degree of civilization and exercised a marked influence on Roman civilization.

[7] To be translated by an adverb.

[8] *called both nations Latins;* two accusatives with the active of a verb of naming; likewise in lines 24-25.

[9] The fact that the conjunction is concessive (*although*) is shown by **tamen** (p. 297, l. 2) in the principal clause.

AENĒĀS EX URBE TRŌJĀ EFFŪGIT

adversus Etrūscōs sē moenibus dēfendere posset,[1] tamen in aciem cōpiās ēdūxit. Etrūscī victī sunt; victōrēs tamen ducem ut anteā āmīsērunt; post pugnam enim [5] Aenēam reperīre nōn potuērunt. Multī igitur eum ad deōs trānsīsse[2] crēdidērunt.

A New Settlement

LĀVĪNIA inde rēgnāvit, quoad Ascanius,[3] Aenēae fīlius, adolēvit. Tum ille propter abundantem Lāvīniī multitūdinem mātrī urbem relīquit. Ipse novam aliam urbem sub Albānō monte condidit, [15] quae Alba Longa[4] appellāta est. Multī rēgēs post Ascanium[3] imperium Albānum gessērunt.

Quīdam ex hīs, cui[5] nōmen Proca erat, duōs fīliōs, Numitōrem atque Amūlium, habuit. Numitōrī, quī [20] major[6] erat, rēgnum relīquit. Pulsō tamen frātre, Amūlius rēgnāvit. Fīlium frātris necāvit; fīliam, quae Rhēa Silvia[7] appellābātur, per speciem honōris sacerdōtem Vestae[8] [25] lēgit.

[1] *could have defended.*

[2] Since, according to legend, Aeneas was the son of the goddess Venus, it was not unnatural to represent his disappearance as a "translation" to the ranks of the gods.

[3] *Ascanius* (as-kā′ni-us).

[4] *Alba Longa.* See map, page 305.

[5] *whose name was Proca;* **cui** is a dative of possession.

[6] *older;* a frequent meaning, the full expression being **major nātū** (literally, *greater by birth*).

[7] *Rhea Silvia* (rē′ȧ sil′vi-ȧ).

[8] *Vesta*, Roman goddess of the hearth of each home, but also worshiped by the State. In the Roman Forum stood the small round temple which was the seat of the State cult. Here a never-dying fire was tended by the Vestal Virgins.

The Royal Twins

EX HĀC fīliā nātī sunt duo fīliī, Rōmulus et Remus. Pater eōrum, ut fāma est,[1] Mārs deus erat. Sed nec dī nec hominēs
5 mātrem et puerōs ā crūdēlitāte rēgiā dēfendērunt. Sacerdōs in custōdiam[2] data est; puerōs rēx in Tiberim injicī (*to be thrown*) jussit. Forte Tiberis abundāverat, ne-
10 que eī quī puerōs ferēbant adīre ad altam aquam poterant. Itaque puerōs in alveō (*trough*) posuērunt atque in tenuī (*shallow*) aquā relīquērunt.[3] Sed alveus (*trough*) in
15 siccō sēdit.[4] Deinde lupa (*wolf*) sitiēns (*thirsty*)—sīc enim est trāditum—ex montibus quī circā (*near by*) sunt ad puerōrum vāgītum (*wailing*) cursum flexit.
20 Faustulus,[5] pāstor rēgius, eam invēnit puerōs nūtrientem (*nursing*). Ab eō atque Lārentiā[6] uxōre puerī ēducātī[7] sunt. Cum prīmum adolēvērunt, vēnārī (*to hunt*)
25 coepērunt, et in latrōnēs praedā onustōs (*loaded*) impetūs facere pāstōribusque[8] praedam dīvidere.

Dum quoddam lūdicrum celebrātur (*game was being celebrated*), latrōnēs īrātī ob praedam āmissam[9] 30 impetum in Rōmulum et Remum fēcērunt. Captum Remum rēgī Amūliō trādidērunt. Puerōs praedam ex agrīs Numitōris ēgisse incūsābant.[10] Sīc ad supplicium 35 Numitōrī Remus dēditur.

Jam prīdem Faustulus[5] crēdiderat puerōs jussū (*by order*) rēgis expositōs[11] apud[12] sē ēducārī. Tum perīculō Remī mōtus rem Rōmulō 40 aperit. Forte Numitor quoque audīverat frātrēs geminōs esse; tum comparāns et aetātem eōrum et nōbilem animum Remī nepōtem agnōvit (*recognized*). 45

Rōmulus cum manū pāstōrum in rēgem Amūlium impetum facit. Remus aliā parātā manū adjuvat. Ita rēx interfectus est. Imperium Albānum Numitōrī avō ab juveni- 50 bus restitūtum est. Deinde Rōmulus et Remus in eīs locīs ubi expositī ubique ēducātī erant urbem condere cōnstituērunt.

Fatal Strife between Brothers

UTERQUE juvenis nōmen novae urbī dare eamque regere cupiēbat. Sed quod geminī erant, nec rēs aetāte dēcernī poterat,

---

[1] *according to tradition* (literally, *as the report is*).

[2] *custody.*

[3] Supply **eōs** as object.

[4] *drifted ashore* (literally, *settled on dry ground*).

[5] *Faustulus* (fâs'tū-lus).

[6] *Larentia* (lạ-ren'shiä).

[7] This word should regularly be translated *rear*, *bring up*, although "educate"

is derived from it. What is the difference between **ēducō** and **ēdūcō?**

[8] Dative of indirect object, although we say "among" with the verb "divide."

[9] *loss of.*

[10] *brought as an accusation;* with dependent indirect discourse, **Puerōs . . . ēgisse;** better, *accused the boys of,* etc.

[11] *who had been abandoned.*

[12] *at his house,* or *in his home.*

auguriīs ūsī sunt.[1] Ā Remō prius
vīsī sunt sex vulturēs (*vultures*).
Rōmulō posteā duodecim sēsē os-
tendērunt. Uterque ab amīcīs rēx
5 appellātus est atque rēgnum postulābat. Cum īrātī arma rapuis-
sent, in pugnā Remus cecidit.

Ex aliā fāmā Remus illūdēns
(*making fun of*) frātrem novōs mū-
10 rōs urbis trānsiluit (*jumped over*).
Inde interfectus est ab īrātō Rōmulō, quī haec verba quoque
addidit: "Sīc deinde pereat[2] quīcumque alius trānsiliet (*shall leap
15 over*) moenia mea."

Ita sōlus potītus est imperiō
Rōmulus; conditam[3] urbem ā suō
nōmine Rōmam appellāvit.
Palātium[4] prīmum, in quō ipse
erat ēducātus, mūnīvit. Vocātā 20
ad concilium multitūdine, jūra dedit.[5] Īnsignia quoque imperiī, sel-
lam curūlem[6] togamque praetex-
tam,[7] et duodecim līctōrēs[8] sūmpsit. Asȳlum aperuit in monte 25
Capitōlīnō,[9] quō[10] multī ex fīnitimīs populīs profūgērunt.
Creāvit etiam centum senātōrēs,
quī honōris causā[11] patrēs appellātī sunt. 30

Unwilling Brides

JAM rēs Rōmāna[12] firma et fīnitimīs cīvitātibus[13] bellō pār erat.
Sed Rōmānī neque uxōrēs neque
cum fīnitimīs jūs cōnūbiī habēbant.
35 Tum Rōmulus quōsdam ex patribus lēgātōs in vīcīnās gentēs mīsit
quī societātem cōnūbiumque novō
populō peterent. Nusquam benignē lēgātī audītī sunt; nam fīni-
40 timī nōn sōlum Rōmānōs spernē-

bant, sed etiam tantam in mediō
crēscentem urbem metuēbant. Itaque īrātī Rōmānī vī ūtī statuērunt.

Ad eam rem Rōmulus, lūdīs
parātīs, fīnitimōs ad spectāculum 45
invītāvit. Multī convēnērunt ut
et lūdōs spectārent et novam urbem vidērent. Sabīnōrum omnis
multitūdō inermis cum līberīs ac
conjugibus vēnit. 50

[1] *they resorted to.*
[2] *so perish;* optative subjunctive. See
Gr. S., 103.
[3] Equivalent to a relative clause, as
in line 39, page 298.
[4] *the Palatine Hill.* This hill was
doubtless the location of the earliest
settlement made on the site of Rome.
Its isolated position and considerable
area made it the natural situation for a
fortified town. See map, page 39.
[5] *he gave them laws.*
[6] *curule chair*, an ivory stool without
back, with curved legs, and with a seat
of plaited leather straps.
[7] The **toga praetexta** (*bordered toga*),
worn by boys and curule magistrates,
had a scarlet border. See picture, page

160. The toga of the Roman citizen
who was not a magistrate was white.
[8] *lictors.* They were attendants upon
the Roman kings; later upon certain
magistrates of the Republic.
[9] The Capitoline had two peaks. The
depression between them is thought to
have been the site of the asȳlum—*place
of refuge.*
[10] An adverb.
[11] *as a mark of distinction.* Remember
that the ablatives **causā** and **grātiā**,
meaning *for the sake of,* stand after the
dependent genitive.
[12] This is virtually equivalent to the
phrase **rēs pūblica Rōmāna**—*the Roman
State.*
[13] Dative depending on **pār**.

SABĪNAE MULIERĒS AUSAE SUNT SĒ INTER TĒLA VOLANTIA ĪNFERRE

Ubi spectāculī tempus vēnit omnēsque intentī in lūdōs[1] erant, tum, signō datō, Rōmānī rapere virginēs coepērunt. Parentēs virginum profūgērunt clāmantēs Rōmānōs hospitium violāvisse. Nec raptae virginēs aut spem dē sē meliōrem aut indignātiōnem minōrem habēbant. Sed ipse Rōmulus circumībat (*went about*) ostendēbatque id patrum superbiā[2] factum esse. "Quamquam vī captae estis," inquit, "omnia jūra Rōmānōrum habēbitis."

Wives and Daughters As Peacemakers

JAM multō minus perturbātī animī raptārum[3] erant. At parentēs eārum cīvitātēs fīnitimās, ad quās ejus injūriae pars pertinēbat, ad arma concitābant. Hae cīvitātēs omnēs ā Rōmulō victae sunt.

Novissimum bellum ab Sabīnīs ortum est, quod multō maximum fuit. Sabīnī arcem Rōmānam in monte Capitōlīnō dolō cēpērunt.

Rōmānī posterō diē arcem recuperāre cōnātī sunt. Ubi Hostius Hostīlius, dux exercitūs Rōmānī, cecidit, cōnfestim aciēs Rōmāna pulsa est.

At Rōmulus templum vōvit Jovī Statōrī[4] ōrāvitque auxilium. Tum crēdēns precēs suās audītās esse "Hinc (*from here*)," inquit, "Rōmānī, Juppiter optimus maximus[5]

---

[1] *on the games.*
[2] *because of the haughtiness.*
[3] *of the captured women.*
[4] *the Stayer.*

[5] A set phrase applied to Jupiter. When the phrase is translated into English, it is necessary to insert *and* between the adjectives.

nōs resistere[1] ac renovāre pugnam jubet." Restitērunt[2] Rōmānī tamquam caelestī vōce jussī.

Tum Sabīnae mulierēs ausae 5 sunt sē inter tēla volantia īnferre[3] ut pācem ā patribus virīsque implōrārent. Ducēs eā rē mōtī nōn modo pācem sed etiam cīvitātem ūnam ex duābus faciunt. Rēgnum 10 quoque cōnsociant (*united*) atque Rōmam faciunt sēdem imperiī.

Multitūdō ita aucta novō nōmine Quirītēs[4] appellāta est ex Curibus, quae urbs[5] caput Sabīnō- 15 rum erat. Deinde Rōmulus, populō in cūriās trīgintā dīvīsō, nōmina mulierum raptārum cūriīs dedit.

Post aliquot annōs Tatius[6] ab Laurentibus[7] interfectus est. Rō- 20 mulus posteā sōlus rēgnāvit. Annīs sequentibus bella secunda[8] cum Fidēnātibus Veientibusque, populīs Etrūscīs, gesta sunt.

Dum Rōmulus quōdam tempore exercitum in Campō Mārtiō re- 25 cēnset (*was reviewing*), tempestās subitō coorta eum nimbō operuit.[9] Patrēs quī proximī steterant prōnūntiāvērunt rēgem sublīmem[10] raptum esse. Deinde ūniversī clā- 30 mant: "Salvē, deus deō nāte.[11]"

Rōmulus dīcitur posteā cuidam cīvī sē ostendisse et eum hīs verbīs allocūtus esse: "Nūntiā Rōmānīs deōs velle meam Rōmam caput 35 orbis terrārum esse. Proinde rēs mīlitāris colenda est; nam nūllae opēs hūmānae armīs Rōmānīs resistere possunt."

Posteā nōmen Quirīnus[12] Rōmulō 40 additum est. Rēgnāvit septem et trīgintā annōs.

A Peaceful King

CERTĀMEN inde dē rēgnō inter factiōnēs ortum est. Sabīnī 45 rēgem suae factiōnis creārī cupiēbant. Rōmānī veterēs peregrīnum rēgem recūsābant. Interrēgnō[13] se- cūtō, senātus imperium gessit. Deinde plēbs clāmāre coepit multōs dominōs prō ūnō factōs esse. Op- 50 timum igitur vīsum est sine morā rēgem creāre.

[1] Here in the less frequent meaning, *make a stand.*

[2] Emphatic by its position.

[3] With sē—*to rush in.*

[4] *Quirites* (kwi-rī'tēz), a name applied to Roman citizens.

[5] We say *a city which*, putting *city* in apposition with the name.

[6] *Tatius* (tā'shius), a Sabine king. He was killed in revenge for ill treatment inflicted by certain of his relatives upon envoys from Laurentum.

[7] *the Laurentines* (lâ-ren'tīnz), people of Laurentum. See map, page 305.

[8] Derived from **sequor**—*follow.* From one point of view that which *follows* is second; from another, that which *follows* or *goes with you* is *favorable, successful.* Which meaning is appropriate here?

[9] *concealed him by a cloud.* There was another legend to the effect that Romulus was killed by the senators.

[10] Predicate adjective with **raptum esse**; translate, *had been carried away on high.*

[11] *"Hail to thee, thou god, son of a god."*

[12] *Quirinus* (kwi-rī'nus).

[13] *interregnum.* This word was applied originally to the time intervening between the death of one king and the accession of another. In modern times it may mean any period marked by a lapse in governmental authority.

JANUS, THE TWO-FACED GOD

Habitābat eō tempore Curibus[1]
Numa Pompilius, vir jūstissimus
perītusque omnis dīvīnī atque hūmānī jūris.[2] Rēgnum eī omnium
5 cōnsēnsū dēlātum est. Is urbem
novam, quae ā Rōmulō armīs condita erat, jūre lēgibusque firmāvit
(*he strengthened*).

Arcum portīs īnstrūctum fēcit,
10 quī arcus Jānī[3] appellātus est.
Apertus bellī index (*sign*) erat,
clausus pācis. Per omne rēgnum
Numae clausus fuit. Pāx cum
cīvitātibus fīnitimīs societāte ac
15 foederibus facta est.

Rēx inde ad mōrēs populī cul-
tumque deōrum animum convertit. Ut populī fidem conciliāret,
simulāvit sē cum deā Ēgeriā[4] con-
20 gressūs habēre et monitū (*by ad-*

vice) ejus sacra īnstituere sacerdō-
tēsque legere. Annum ad cursum
lūnae[5] in duodecim mēnsēs dīscrīpsit (*he divided*). Quōsdam diēs ne-
fāstōs[6] fēcit, per quōs diēs comitia 25
(*assemblies*) nōn habēbantur. Virginēs Vestālēs[7] lēgit, quās caeri-
mōniīs quibusdam sānctās fēcit.

Multa etiam alia ā rēge īnstitūta
sunt: rītūs (*rites*), caerimōniae, sa- 30
cerdōtia (*priesthoods*). Multitūdō
hīs rēbus ā vī et armīs conversa
rēgis mōrēs imitābātur. Fīnitimī
populī cīvitātem Rōmānam tōtam
in cultum deōrum versam violāre 35
nōlēbant.

Ita duo deinceps rēgēs, Rōmulus
bellō, Numa pāce, cīvitātem auxē-
runt. Numa annōs trēs et quadrāgintā rēgnāvit. 40

A VESTAL VIRGIN

---

[1] A locative. See Gr. S., 91.
[2] An objective genitive with **perītus**;
we say *skilled in* or *familiar with*.
[3] *of Janus* (jā′nus). Janus was the
god of beginnings and of entrances.
[4] *Egeria* (ē-jē′ri-ạ), a nymph.
[5] *according to*, etc. This old lunar

year of 355 days stood as the official
year until Julius Caesar reformed the
calendar in 46 B.C. See page 408.
[6] *inauspicious*, i.e., not open to the
transaction of public business.
[7] *Vestal Virgins*, priestesses of Vesta,
goddess of the hearth and household.

A Warlike King

NUMĀ mortuō, interrēgnum ut anteā secūtum est. Inde Tullus Hostīlius, nepōs Hostīliī quī Rōmulō rēgnante[1] pugnāns ad-
5 versus Sabīnōs ceciderat, rēx creātus est. Hic ferōcior etiam quam Rōmulus fuit. Quod cīvitās torpēre (*to be growing spiritless*) ōtiō vidēbātur, causās undique bellī
10 quaerēbat.

Bellum cum Albānīs prīmum ortum est. Albānī priōrēs magnō exercitū in agrum Rōmānum impetum fēcērunt. Ibi Cluilius,[2] Al-
15 bānus rēx, moritur. Albānī dictātōrem[3] Mettium Fufetium creant. Ubi is ab Tullō colloquium petīvit, rēx Rōmānus nōn recūsāvit.

Mettius sīc locūtus est: "Uterque
20 populus sē bellum gerere propter injūriās dīcit. Rē vērā cupīdō (*a desire*) imperiī duōs cognātōs (*re-*

lated) vīcīnōsque populōs ad arma concitat. Sed potius metuere dēbēmus Etruscōs quī, cum dēfes- 25 sī cōnfectīque erimus, simul victōrem ac victum aggredientur. Certāmen igitur dē imperiō paucōrum proeliō potius dēcernāmus.[4]" 30

Tullus cōnsilium probāvit, quamquam magnam spem victōriae habēbat.

Forte in utrōque exercitū erant trigeminī frātrēs,[5] nec aetāte nec 35 vīribus disparēs, Horātiī et Cūriātiī. Hī Albānī erant; illī Rōmānī. Frātrēs, ad hanc pugnam dēlēctī (*having been selected*), arma capiunt et in medium inter duās aciēs 40 prōcēdunt. Duo exercitūs, ērēctī (*alert*) ānxiīque, in spectāculum animōs intendunt. Signō datō, ternī[6] juvenēs concurrunt.

Three against Three

PRĪMŌ congressū duo Rōmānī interfectī sunt, et trēs Albānī vulnerātī.[7] Eum quī integer fuit trēs Cūriātiī circumsistere cōnātī sunt. Cum jam Rōmānus paulum
50 fūgisset, respexit atque vīdit trēs Cūriātiōs magnīs intervāllīs sequentēs. Subitō cōnstitit et in proximum Cūriātium impetum facit.

Dum exercitus Albānus Cūriātiōs 55 obsecrat (*was entreating*) ut frātrī auxilium ferant, Horātius eum interfēcit. Deinde victor secundum frātrem petit.

Tum magnō clāmōre Rōmānī 60 adjuvant mīlitem suum, et ille cōnficere proelium properat. Priusquam cōnsecūtus est tertius, Horātius alterum Cūriātium cōnficit.

---

[1] *in the reign of Romulus.*

[2] *Cluilius* (klö-il′i-us).

[3] During the Republic the Romans sometimes replaced the consuls by a dictator, in order better to conduct a war. The Albans are represented as using a dictatorship to fill an interregnum.

[4] For form of translation see Gr. S., 102. The people whose champions were victorious would rule the other people.

[5] *three brothers who were triplets.*

[6] *the three on each side.* A distributive numeral.

[7] Supply **sunt.**

THE OATH OF THE HORATII
The three heroic brothers make their vow, while the women of the family grieve at the prospect of death.

Jamque singulī supererant, sed nec spē nec vīribus parēs. Alter integer et ferōx superiōribus victōriīs erat; alter dēfessus vulnere, animō frāc-
5 tus, in certāmen vēnit. Nec illud proelium fuit. Cūriātium vix sustinentem arma Horātius caedit et jacentem spoliat.

Ad sepultūram inde suōrum Rō-
10 mānī atque Albānī, nēquāquam (*in no way*) paribus animīs, vertuntur,[1] alterī[2] victōrēs, alterī[2] victī. Exercitūs domōs[3] abductī sunt.

Horātiī soror, quae ūnī ex Cūriā-
15 tiīs dēspōnsa erat, cognōvit inter spolia (*booty*) palūdāmentum (*military cloak*) spōnsī, quod ipsa cōnfēcerat. Solvit[4] crīnēs (*hair*) et multīs cum lacrimīs spōnsum mortuum appellat.[5] Frāter, īrātus 20 propter maerōrem (*sorrow*) sorōris in victōriā suā tantōque pūblicō gaudiō, gladiō eam interfēcit.

Rēs ad populum relāta est. Hominēs vehementer mōtī sunt in eō 25 jūdiciō, Pūbliō Horātiō patre clāmante fīliam jūre caesam esse. Sed magis admīrātiōne[6] virtūtis quam jūre causae juvenem absolvērunt (*they acquitted*). 30

---

[1] *turn;* the passive voice in a reflexive sense. See page 81, note 6.

[2] The singular forms **alter . . . alter** mean *the one* (*person*) *. . . the other.* The plural is here employed to mean *the one people . . . the other.*

[3] The accusative plural of this noun, like the accusative singular, **domum,** may be used without a preposition to denote the place to which.

[4] Loosening the hair was a common sign of mourning in antiquity.

[5] Here in the sense of *call upon.*

[6] *from admiration.*

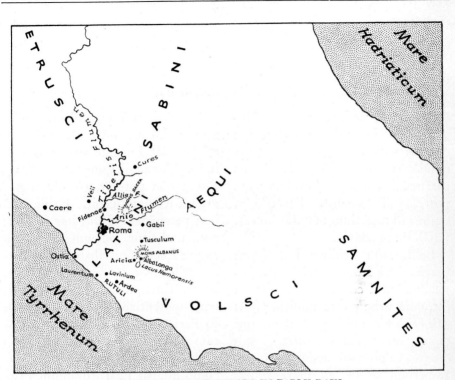

ROME AND ITS NEIGHBORS IN EARLY DAYS
All around the young town were hostile cities and peoples.

The End of Alba Longa

POPULUS Albānus īrā ārdēbat, quod Mettius tribus mīlitibus fortūnam pūblicam commīserat. Is igitur prāvō (*dishonest*) cōnsiliō foedera rumpere cōnātus est; nam pollicitus est adjuvāre Fidēnātēs Veientēsque, quī bellum adversus Rōmānōs parābant. Bellō inceptō, Mettius, quī in aciē contrā Fidēnātēs positus erat, ad collēs proximōs sine certāmine Albānōs abdūxit.

Tullus, simulāns sē id jussisse, clārā vōce clāmāvit Mettium exercitum Fidēnātium ā tergō oppugnātūrum esse. Fidēnātēs, quī Latīnē sciēbant,[1] hanc vōcem audīvērunt et fūgērunt. Veientēs quoque pulsī sunt. Proeliō factō,[2] rēx Mettium interficī propter prōditiōnem (*treason*) jussit. Populō omnī Albānō Rōmam trāductō, cīvitās plēbī data est, et prīncipēs Albānōrum in patrēs lēctī sunt.

Posteā pestilentia (*plague*) gravis in urbem incidit, quā rēx quoque affectus est. Hāc calamitāte frāctus sacrīs[3] posteā animum dedit.

---

[1] *understood Latin.* English idiom requires a noun instead of an adverb.

[2] *after the battle was over.*

[3] *to religious observances.*

Postrēmō, quia sacrum quoddam nōn rīte (*properly*) fēcerat — ita fāma est — Tullus fulmine (*by lightning*) percussus cum domō cōn- flagrāvit. Rēgnāvit annōs[1] duōs et trīgintā. 5

A Period of Expansion

Ancus Mārcius, nepōs[2] Nu- mae Pompiliī, quārtus rēx creātus est. Ut Numa in pāce religiōnēs īnstituerat, sīc Ancus caerimōniās īnstituit, quibus bella posteā indicta sunt. Sacerdōtēs, quibus id negōtium mandātum est, fētiālēs[3] appellāvit. 10

Bellīs cum urbibus Latīnōrum gestīs, cīvēs Rōmam trādūxit. Jā- niculum, quī collis[4] trāns Tiberim est, cum urbe ponte subliciō (*by a pile bridge*) conjūnxit. Carcer,[5] quī etiam nunc extat (*exists*), sub monte Capitōlīnō aedificātus est. Imperium usque ad mare prōlā- tum est, et in ōre Tiberis Ōstia[6] urbs condita. 15 20

Ancō rēgnante, vir quīdam, nō- mine Lucumō, habitābat Tarqui- niīs,[7] quae urbs Etrūsca erat. Pater ejus erat Dēmarātus,[8] profugus Co- rinthius (*Corinthian*). Lucumō in mātrimōnium Tanaquīlem, mulie- rem nōbilem, dūxerat. Etrūscī spernēbant Lucumōnem, exulis fī- lium. Tanaquil, quae ferre indigni- tātem nōn poterat, cōnsilium mi- grandī Rōmam[9] cēpit. Facile con- jugī persuādet. Dum iter faciunt, aquila dīcitur pilleum (*cap*) ab capite Lucumōnis abstulisse et rūr- sus reposuisse (*to have replaced it*). Laeta Tanaquil accēpit id auguri- um[10] potentiae futūrae (*future*); Etrūscī enim caelestium prōdigiō- rum (*omens*) perītī erant. 25 30 35 40

Postquam Rōmam vēnērunt, Lu- cumō nōmen L. Tarquinium Prīs- cum sibi sūmpsit. Ibi paulātim īnsignis factus est dīvitiīs aliīsque rēbus. Postrēmō in amīcitiam rē- gis receptus, tūtor (*guardian*) lībe- rōrum rēgis testāmentō (*by the will*) īnstitūtus est. Ancus annōs quattuor et vīgintī rēgnāvit. 45 50

An Ambitious Ruler

Jam fīliī Ancī prope adultī erant. Sed Tarquinius ipse rēx creārī cupiēbat. Is prīmus palam rēg- num petīvit,[11] memorāns (*mention- ing*) officia prīvāta ac pūblica et benignitātem (*kindness*) in omnēs. Magnō cōnsēnsū populus Rōmā- nus eum rēgnāre jussit. 55 60

---

[1] Why accusative?

[2] He was the son of Numa's daughter.

[3] *fetial priests.* A fetial priest was one employed in making declarations of war and treaties of peace.

[4] *a hill which.*

[5] A small stone structure.

[6] *Ostia* (os'ti-ạ). See map, page 305.

It was about fifteen miles from Rome; extensive remains exist.

[7] *at Tarquinii* (tär-kwin'i-ī). Locative.

[8] *Demaratus* (dem-ạ-rā'tus).

[9] Place to which.

[10] *this as a token.*

[11] With **prīmus**—*was the first to canvass for.*

Tarquinius, Latīnīs bellō victīs, lūdōs magnificōs fēcit. Tum prīmum locus circō,[1] quī Maximus dīcitur, dēsignātus est. Lūdī sol-
5 lemnēs[2] mānsērunt, Rōmānī[3] aut magnī appellātī.

Magna quoque opera ā rēge in- cepta sunt ut populus nōn quiētior[4] in pāce quam in bellō esset. Mūrō lapideō (*of stone*) urbem cingere 10 parāvit, et loca circā (*around*) Forum aliāsque convallēs cloācīs siccāvit.[5] Fundāmenta aedis Jovis in Capitōliō jēcit.[6]

A Strange Omen

Eō FERĒ tempore in rēgiā prōdigium (*omen*) mīrābile fuit. Caput puerī dormientis, cui Servius Tullius fuit nōmen, multōrum in cōnspectū ārsit. Servī, quī aquam
20 ad restinguendam (*put out*) flammam ferēbant, ab rēgīnā retentī sunt. Mox cum puer ē somnō excitātus esset, flamma abiit.

Tum, abductō in sēcrētum virō,[7] Tanaquil "Vidēsne tū hunc pue- 25 rum," inquit, "quem tam humilī cultū[8] ēducāmus? Lūmen profectō portendit[9] eum aliquandō (*some day*) nōbīs praesidiō futūrum esse.[10] Proinde artibus līberālibus (*worthy* 30 *of a freeman*) ērudiendus est.[11]"

Ingenium juvenis vērē (*truly*) rēgium erat. Tarquinius igitur eī fīliam suam dēspondit.

The Murder of a King

Etsī Ancī fīliī duo anteā īrātī fuerant quod peregrīnus Rōmae rēgnābat, tum major erat indignātiō, quoniam servō jam rēgnum patēre vidēbātur. Rēgem
40 igitur interficere rēgnumque occupāre cōnstituērunt. Ex pāstōribus duo ferōcissimī ad facinus dēlēctī in vēstibulō (*the entrance*) rēgiae speciē rixae (*of a quarrel*) in sē omnēs appāritōrēs rēgiōs conver- 45 tērunt.

Inde vocātī ad rēgem dīcere in vicem (*turn*) jussī sunt. Ūnus rem expōnit. Dum intentus in eum sē rēx tōtus āvertit, alter ēlātam 50 secūrim in caput rēgis dējēcit;[12] relictō in vulnere tēlō, ambō forās (*out of doors*) fugiunt. Tarquinium moribundum (*dying*) appāritōrēs

[1] Dative of purpose with **dēsignātus est**, *was marked out.* The Circus Maximus lay between the Palatine and the Aventine Hills. See map, page 39.

[2] Translate the adjective, *a fixed event.*

[3] The "Roman games" were celebrated in September of each year.

[4] *just as busy.* The clause ut . . . esset is one of purpose, **nōn** going closely with **quiētior**.

[5] *drained with sewers.* The low-lying area of the Forum was originally swampy.

[6] *laid the foundation of the temple.* The temple was completed and dedicated by his son.

[7] *taking her husband aside.* Frequently **vir** means *husband.*

[8] *manner of life, station.*

[9] *surely foretells.*

[10] *will be a support to us.*

[11] *must be educated.*

[12] With **ēlātam**—*raised and brought down.* Latin frequently employs a perfect passive participle in agreement with an object where we use coördinate verbs. The object of **dējēcit** is **secūrim**, *ax*, an accusative ending in **-im**.

ROMAN SENATORS WEARING THEIR TOGAS
According to tradition, the Senate in the early days of Rome was the most dignified and honorable
assembly in the world.

excipiunt; illōs fugientēs līctōrēs[1] comprehendunt. Magnus sequitur populī tumultus, inter quem Tanaquil claudī rēgiam jubet.

5 Serviō inde celeriter ad sē vocātō, auxilium ōrāvit. "Tuum est rēgnum," inquit, "Servī, sī vir es, nōn eōrum quī aliēnīs manibus pessimum facinus fēcērunt. Ērige 10 tē deōsque ducēs[2] sequere,[3] quī dīvīnā flammā hoc caput clārum futūrum esse portendērunt (*have indicated*). Nōlī perturbārī quod peregrīnus es. Etiam nōs pere-15 grīnī rēgnāvimus. Sī propter subitam (*sudden*) rem cōnsilia fingere

nōn potes, mea tamen cōnsilia sequere." Cum jam clāmor multitūdinis vix sustinērī posset, Tanaquil ex superiōre parte rēgiae popu-20 lum ita allocūta est: "Cum vulnus rēgis grave sit, jam tamen ad sē redit; brevī tempore rēgem ipsum vidēbitis. Interim vult Servium Tullium rem pūblicam adminis-25 trāre." Itaque Servius per aliquot diēs, cum Tarquinius jam mortuus esset, suās opēs firmāvit (*strengthened*). Tum dēmum mors rēgis nūntiāta est. Servius, praesidiō 30 firmō mūnītus, prīmus injussū populī voluntāte patrum[4] rēgnāvit.

---

[1] See page 299, note 8.
[2] In apposition with **deōs**. We may translate, *the guidance of the gods.*

[3] Imperative.
[4] *of the senate.* As often, **patrēs** is used for **patrēs cōnscrīptī.**

THE PALATINE HILL
Once the site of temples and palaces, it has only ruins now.

Seeking Prestige for Rome

SERVIUS prīmum[1] cēnsum īnstituit et populum in classēs prō opibus dīscrīpsit (*divided*). Ex[2] cēnsū posteā officia bellī pācisque tribūta sunt. Ad multitūdinem crēscentem duo collēs, Quirīnālis Vīminālisque,[3] ad urbem additī sunt. Imperium quoque hōc cōnsiliō auctum est. Fānum (*temple*) erat nōbile Diānae Ephesiae,[4] quod commūniter (*in common*) ā cīvitātibus Asiae factum esse dīcēbātur. Servius, inter prīncipēs Latīnōrum eō cōnsēnsū cīvitātum Asiāticārum (*of Asia*) vehementer laudātō,

tandem populīs Latīnīs persuāsit ut Rōmae cum populō Rōmānō fānum (*temple*) Diānae facerent. Ea erat cōnfessiō caput rērum Rōmam[5] esse, dē quō totiēns (*so many times*) certātum erat.[6]

Lūcius Tarquinius, Prīscī fīlius, interdum querēbātur quod Servius injussū populī rēgnāret. Servius igitur prius agrum captum ex hostibus virītim (*among all the men*) dīvīsit.

Hōc modō voluntātem plēbis conciliāvit. Populus deinde maximō cōnsēnsū eum rēgnāre jussit.[7]

---

[1] An adverb.
[2] *in accordance with.*
[3] *the Quirinal* (kwir′i-nạl) *and the Viminal* (vim′i-nạl). See map, page 39.
[4] *of Ephesus* (ef′e-sus), a city in Asia Minor. See map, page 61.

[5] *that Rome,* etc. The infinitive (**esse**) with subject accusative depends on **cōnfessiō,** *acknowledgment.*
[6] *there had been a contest;* impersonal.
[7] Their action merely ratified the authority which he already held.

A Cruel Daughter

Rēx duās fīliās Lūciō atque Arruntī Tarquiniīs, Prīscī fīliīs, in mātrimōnium dederat. Mōrēs hōrum disparēs erant. Nam 5 Arrūns Tarquinius mītis (*gentle*) erat, L. Tarquinius ferōx et vehemēns nātūrā. Duae Tulliae item disparēs erant. Forte Arrūns ferōcem Tulliam in mātrimōnium dūx- 10 erat. Similitūdō (*similarity*) celeriter L. Tarquinium et ferōcem Tulliam contrahit. Cum prope continuīs[1] caedibus domōs vacuās fēcissent, juguntur nūptiīs (*in mar-* 15 *riage*).

Paulātim inde mulier conjugem ad caedem Serviī excitat. Itaque Tarquinius prius omnibus rēbus cīvēs et maximē patrēs conciliāvit. 20 Postrēmō, ubi jam tempus agendī[2] vīsum est, stīpātus (*accompanied*) armātīs[3] in forum irrūpit.

Inde in rēgiā sēde prō cūriā sedēns patrēs in cūriam per prae- 25 cōnem (*herald*) ad rēgem Tarquinium vocārī jussit. Ibi incūsābat rēgem, quod rēgnum muliebrī (*of a woman*) dōnō jam prīdem

occupāvisset; querēbātur item dē cōnsiliīs populāribus (*democratic*), 30 dē agrō plēbī dīvīsō, dē cēnsū īnstitūtō; prōnūntiāvit sē rēgem esse.

Dum loquitur, Servius intervēnit (*came in*) et ā vēstibulō (*entrance*) cūriae magnā vōce "Quid 35 tibi vīs,[4]" inquit, "Tarquinī? Quā audāciā tū, mē vīvō, vocāre patrēs aut in sēde meā cōnsīdere ausus es?"

Tarquinius ferōciter (*fiercely*) re- 40 spondit sē sēdem patris suī tenēre, sē rēgnī hērēdem[5] esse. Tum medium[6] arripit (*he seized*) Servium, ēlātumque[7] ē cūriā per gradūs[8] dējicit; inde in cūriam redit. 45 Appāritōrēs rēgis fugiunt.

Rēx ipse ā servīs Tarquiniī interficitur. Tullia carpentō in forum invecta (*riding*) conjugem ēvocāvit[9] rēgemque prīma appellāvit. Dum 50 domum redit, dīcitur patrem in viā jacentem invēnisse et per corpus carpentum ēgisse. Hic locus posteā vīcus scelerātus[10] vocātus est.

Servius Tullius rēgnāvit annōs 55 quattuor et quadrāgintā.

The Reign of a Tyrant

Inde L. Tarquinius rēgnāre coepit, cui propter facta cognōmen Superbus datum est. Prīncipēs patrum, quī Servium dīlēxerant 60 (*had been devoted to*), interfēcit. Suum corpus armātīs circumsaep-

---

[1] *almost without an interval between.*
[2] *for action.*
[3] A participle used as a noun.
[4] *What do you mean?* How, literally?
[5] *heir.* The king had been elected. Here, as in the case of the sons of Ancus, was an attempt to create a dynasty.
[6] *around the waist.*

[7] In agreement with **eum,** to be supplied; a perfect participle for a coördinate verb, as on page 307, line 50. Translate, *carried him out and hurled.*
[8] *down the steps.* In line 52 **per** means *over.*
[9] *summoned.*
[10] *the accursed street.*

sit (*surrounded*). Jūdicia capitā-
lium rērum[1] sine cōnsiliīs per sē
sōlus exercēbat. Ita poterat occīdere, in exilium agere, bonīs[2]
5 spoliāre omnēs quōs cupiēbat.

Etsī rēgēs superiōrēs senātum dē
omnibus rēbus cōnsulere solitī
erant, Tarquinius domesticīs cōnsiliīs[3] rem pūblicam administrāvit.
10 Bellum, pācem, foedera, societātēs
per sē ipse fēcit. Latīnōrum gentem sibi maximē conciliābat. Oc-
tāviō Mamiliō[4] Tusculānō[5] — is
longē nōbilissimus Latīnōrum erat
15 — fīliam in mātrimōnium dat.

Cum jam magna Tarquiniī auctōritās inter Latīnōrum prīncipēs
esset, concilium in certam diem
convocāvit. Conveniunt frequen-
20 tēs (*in great numbers*) prīmā lūce.
Ipse Tarquinius diem quidem servāvit, sed paulō ante sōlis occāsum
vēnit.

Turnus Herdonius Arīcīnus[6] ferō-
25 citer (*fiercely*) absentem Tarquinium accūsāverat (*had criticized*).
Dīxit Tarquinium patientiam (*pa-
tience*) Latīnōrum temptāre et af-
fectāre (*was aspiring to*) imperium
30 in eōs.

Rēx, hōc cognitō, quia prō imperiō palam Turnum interficere
nōn poterat, cōnfestim statuit falsō

crīmine (*by an accusation*) eum
opprimere. Proximā igitur nocte, 35
auctōre Tarquiniō,[7] quīdam Arīcī-
nī,[6] Turnō[8] inimīcī, in dēversōrium
ejus magnum numerum gladiōrum
clam intulērunt.

Tarquinius paulō ante lūcem ad 40
sē prīncipēs Latīnōrum vocāvit
certiōrēsque dē gladiīs cēlātīs fēcit.
"Cognōvī," inquit, "Turnum cupere Latīnōrum sōlum imperium
tenēre, et jam necem omnium 45
parāre." Dūxit deinde eōs ad
dēversōrium.

Ubi gladiī ex omnibus locīs dē-
versōriī prōlātī sunt, manifesta
(*clear*) vīsa est perfidia, Turnusque 50
in catēnās conjectus est.

Cōnfestim concilium Latīnōrum
convocātur. Ibi magna indignātiō
oritur, gladiīs in mediō positīs.
Itaque Turnus, indictā causā,[9] in 55
aquam Ferentīnam[10] mersus est.

Rēx, auctōritāte inter Latīnōs
ita auctā, cum eīs renovāvit foedus
quod ā Tullō rēge anteā factum
erat. Latīnī nōn repugnāvērunt 60
(*did not refuse*), quamquam in eō
foedere rēm Rōmānam superiō-
rem esse vīdērunt. Mors enim
Turnī docēbat potentiam Tarquiniī ac perīculum eōrum quī resis- 65
tēbant.

---

[1] *trials in capital cases.*

[2] Ablative of separation.

[3] Tarquin was the first king to rely
for advice solely upon personal friends
instead of senatorial or official advisers.

[4] *to Octavius Mamilius* (ok-tā′vi-us
ma-mil′i-us).

[5] *of Tusculum.* See map, page 305.

[6] *of Aricia* (a-rish′iä). Aricia was a

town of ancient Italy. See map, page
305.

[7] *at the instigation of Tarquin.*

[8] Dative with **inimīcī**, but to be translated as if genitive.

[9] *without a trial;* literally, *his case un-
pleaded.* Caesar uses **causam dīcere**
with the meaning *to plead a case*, page
141, lines 15-16.

[10] *the Ferentine Marsh.*

Victory through Treachery

A GREAT DRAINAGE PROJECT

One can still see the mouth of the *Cloāca Maxima*, or great sewer of Rome, which, according to legend, was built in the reign of Tarquin the Proud.

TARQUINIUS, quamquam injūstus (*unjust*) in pāce rēx fuit, ducem bellī tamen nōn prāvum (*incompetent*) sē praebuit. Is prīmus cum Volscīs bellum gessit et magnam praedam cēpit. In aliō bellō, cum Gabiōs, vīcīnam urbem, vī capere nōn posset, fraude ac dolō aggressus est.[1]

Sextus enim, fīlius Tarquiniī, quī minimus[2] ex tribus erat, trānsiit Gabiōs, crūdēlitātem intolerābilem (*intolerable*) patris vehementer querēns atque sē inimīcum eī prōnūntiāns. Benignē ā Gabīnīs exceptus in cōnsilia pūblica adhibē-

tur, et dēnique dux legitur. Proelia parva inter Rōmam Gabiōsque facta sunt, quibus Gabīnī superiōrēs erant. Gabīnī Sextum Tarquinium dōnō deōrum sibi missum esse ducem crēdidērunt.

Inde Sextus ūnum ex suīs Rōmam mīsit quī mandāta patris peteret.[3] Rēx nihil vōce respondit, sed tamquam rem dēlīberāns (*deliberating*) in hortum aedium (*of the palace*) trānsiit, sequente nūntiō fīliī. Ibi inambulāns (*walking up and down*) tacitus (*silently*) summa papāverum (*of the poppies*) capita baculō dējēcit. Nūntius, dēfessus interrogandō[4] expectandōque respōnsum, redit Gabiōs remque mīram refert.

Sextus intellēxit quid pater fierī vellet. Prīncipēs igitur cīvitātis variīs crīminibus (*on various charges*) necāvit. Rēs[5] Gabīna ita spoliāta cōnsiliō auxiliōque rēgī Rōmānō sine certāmine gravī trāditur.

Gabiīs receptīs, Tarquinius ad negōtia urbāna (*in the city*) animum convertit. Prīmum templum in monte Tarpeiō[6] aedificāre tōtumque montem Jovī dēdicāre (*to consecrate*) cōnstituit. Hoc templum pater jam anteā vōverat.

Ad hoc opus fabrīs Etrūscīs et

---

[1] **eam** (**urbem**) is to be supplied as object.

[2] *youngest.*

[3] A relative clause of purpose.

[4] The ablative of the gerund may be employed to express cause. Observe

that **expectandō** has a direct object, **respōnsum.**

[5] **Rēs** is here equivalent to the phrase **rēs pūblica.**

[6] *the Tarpeian* (tär-pē′an) *Rock*, on the Capitoline Hill. See map, page 39.

operāriīs (*laborers*) ex plēbe Rōmā-
nā ūsus est. Plēbs etiam ad alia
opera trāducta[1] forōs (*seats*) in
circō fēcit cloācamque maximam[2]
sub terram ēgit, quam etiam nunc 5
vidēmus. Multī quoque ex plēbe
colōnī[3] Signiam[4] Circeiōsque[5] missī sunt quī praesidia urbī essent.

A Portent and Its Interpretation

Dum haec aguntur, portentum
(*sign*) terribile vīsum est:
anguis (*a snake*) ex columnā ligneā
ēlāpsus (*gliding*) terrōrem fugam-
que in rēgiā fēcit atque ipsīus rēgis
pectus ānxiīs cūrīs implēvit.
15 Itaque Tarquinius filiōs, Titum
(*Titus*) et Arruntem, Delphōs ad
clārissimum in terrīs ōrāculum mittere statuit. Comes eīs additus
est L. Jūnius Brūtus, ex Tar-
20 quiniā,[6] sorōre rēgis, nātus. Cognōmen ejus hōc modō parātum
erat: rēx eōs prīncipēs cīvitātis
quōs timēbat interficere solēbat,
in quibus frātrem Brūtī interfēcit.
25 Hic,[7] ut crūdēlitātem rēgis vītāret,
cōnsultō (*purposely*) stultitiam imi-
tātus bona sua rēgem spoliāre
passus est neque cognōmen Brūtī[8]
recūsāvit.
30 Is tum igitur ab Tarquiniīs duc-
tus est Delphōs, lūdibrium (*object
of ridicule*) vērius quam comes.
Tulit tamen dōnum Apollinī aureum baculum inclūsum in baculō
35 corneō (*of cornel-wood*), tamquam
effigiem (*representation*) ingeniī suī.
Postquam juvenēs Delphōs vē-

AN ETRUSCAN CHARIOT

nērunt patrisque mandāta cōnfē-
cērunt, statuērunt quaerere ex
ōrāculō ad quem eōrum[9] rēgnum 40
esset[10] ventūrum.
   Vōx reddita est: "Imperium summum Rōmae habēbit quī vestrum[9]
prīmus, Ō juvenēs, mātrem oscu-
lābitur."   45
   Tarquiniī, Brūtum contemnentēs,
ipsī inter sē jūs mātris ōsculandae[11]

---

[1] *transferred.*
[2] *and the great sewer.*
[3] *as colonists.*
[4] *to Signia* (sig'ni-ä). Signia was a town
of ancient Italy. See map, page 305.
[5] *and to Circeii* (ser-sē'ī). Circeii was a
town of ancient Italy. See map, page 305.

[6] *Tarquinia* (tär-kwin'i-ä).
[7] *the latter.*
[8] The word is properly an adjective, *dull.*
[9] A genitive of the whole.
[10] With **ad quem,** an indirect question
—*was destined to come.*
[11] A gerundive construction.

JUVENĒS DELPHŌS VĒNĒRUNT

Rōmae sortī permittunt. Brūtus, quī aliō modō ōrāculum interpretātus erat (*had interpreted*), cecidit terramque ōsculātus est, scīlicet (*of course*) quod ea commūnis māter est omnium mortālium (*of mortals*). Rediērunt inde juvenēs Rōmam.

Revolution

PAULŌ post Rōmānī, quī jam dūdum superbiam (*tyranny*) Tarquiniī rēgis atque fīliōrum aegrē ferēbant, ita scelere quōdam Sextī Tarquiniī concitātī sunt ut rēgiam familiam in exilium pellere statue-
15 rent. Tum prīmum vērum ingenium Brūtī apertum est; eō enim duce populus jūrāvit sē nec Tarquinium nec alium quemquam rēgnāre Rōmae passūrum esse.

20 Brūtus inde in castra profectus est, ubi exercitus Rōmānus Ardeam, caput Rutulōrum, obsidē-
bat. Tulliam rēgīnam domō profugientem omnēs virī mulierēsque execrātī sunt (*cursed*).
Ubi nūntiī hārum rērum in castra perlātī sunt, rēx Rōmam perrēxit (*proceeded*). Brūtus adventum rēgis sēnsit flexitque viam. Ita eōdem ferē tempore dīversīs itineribus Brūtus Ardeam, Tarquinius Rōmam vēnērunt.
Hic portās clausās invēnit; Brūtum līberātōrem (*as liberator*) urbis laeta castra accēpērunt exāctīque sunt (*were driven out*) līberī

rēgis; duo patrem secūtī exulēs Caere,[1] quae urbs Etrūsca erat. Sextus Tarquinius Gabiōs, tamquam in suum rēgnum, profectus ab ultōribus (*avengers*) veterum injūriārum quās ipse intulerat interfectus est. Vīta ejus hunc exitum habuit. L. Tarquinius Superbus rēgnāvit annōs quīnque et vīgintī. Rēgnum Rōmae annōs ducentōs quadrāgintā dūrāverat (*had lasted*). Duo cōnsulēs inde creātī sunt, L. Jūnius Brūtus et L. Tarquinius Collātīnus.

The People Demand Rights

PRĪMĪS temporibus reī pūblicae līberae[2] magna dissēnsiō orta est inter patrēs et plēbem propter aes aliēnum,[3] quō paene tōta plēbs premēbantur; crēditōrī (*the creditor*) enim licēbat dēbitōrem (*the debtor*) etiam in servitūtem dūcere. Praetereā jūs reddēbātur[4] ā cōnsulibus, quī magistrātus tantum patribus patēbat.[5]

Cum jam plēbs auxilium ā cōnsulibus postulārent,[6] Latīnī equitēs nūntiāvērunt Volscōs ad urbem oppugnandam venīre.

Plēbs exultābant (*exulted*) gaudiō atque inter sē hortābantur nē nōmina darent.[7] At ūnus ē cōnsulibus, plēbe convocātā, pollicitus est jūdicia intermittere quoad mīlites in castrīs essent; bellō cōnfectō, senātum plēbī[8] cōnsultūrum esse. Eō modō plēbī persuāsit ut nōmina darent. Volscī aliīque populī fīnitimī victī sunt.

Posteā tamen jūs[9] dē crēditīs[10] pecūniīs crūdēliter (*cruelly*), ut anteā, dictum est. Tandem plēbs, cum exercitus, aliō bellō coortō, in armīs esset, dēspērātō cōnsulum senātūsque auxiliō, in sacrum montem sēcessērunt.

Hic mōns trāns Aniēnem[11] flūmen est, tria ab urbe mīlia passuum. Patrēs arbitrātī nūllam spem nisi in concordiā cīvium reliquam esse ad plēbem mīsērunt Menēnium Agrippam, ipsum plēbeium (*a plebeian*) et plēbī cārum.

---

[1] *Caere* (sē′rē). See map, page 305. **Caere**, neuter, is the antecedent of **quae**; but the relative agrees in gender with the predicate noun **urbs** instead of with the antecedent.

[2] The phrase **rēs pūblica** means *State* or *commonwealth* and implies nothing as to form of government. **Rēs pūblica lībera** means *republic* or *free commonwealth*.

[3] Literally, *another's money*. This is a striking way of denoting *debt*.

[4] *justice was administered.*

[5] *an office which was open only to patricians.* In the change from monarchy to free government the patricians had secured for themselves alone the privilege of office-holding, although the plebeians possessed the right to vote.

[6] A collective noun sometimes takes a plural verb.

[7] *not to enlist.*

[8] When **cōnsulō** means *consult the interest of*, it takes a dative. When it means *consult, ask the advice of*, it takes an accusative.

[9] For the meaning of **jūs dictum est,** see note 4.

[10] *loaned.*

[11] *the Anio* (an′i-ō), a river near Rome. See map, page 305.

Menenius Agrippa and His Fable

MENĒNIUS hoc nārrāsse fertur[1]: "Ōlim reliquae partēs corporis hūmānī indignābantur (*were indignant*) quod suā cūrā, suō labōre ac ministeriō[2] ventrī omnia quaererentur, venter in mediō quiētus datīs voluptātibus fruerētur (*enjoyed*). Itaque conjūrāvērunt inde nē[3] manūs ad ōs cibum umquam ferrent, nēve[4] ōs datum cibum acciperet, nēve dentēs cōnficerent.[5]

"Sed dum ventrem famē domāre (*to subdue*) volunt, ipsa membra tōtumque corpus paene periērunt. Inde sēnsērunt ventris quoque ministerium[2] haud iners (*unimportant*) esse."

Ostendit Menēnius deinde dissēnsiōnem inter partēs corporis similem esse īrae plēbis in[6] patrēs et omnium interesse concordiam habēre.

Concordiā reconciliātā (*having been restored*), plēbī permissum est suōs magistrātūs[7] creāre tribūnōs plēbeiōs (*of the plebeians*), quī auxilium plēbī adversus cōnsulēs ferrent.

A Farmer to the Rescue

POSTEĀ, dum tribūnī imperium cōnsulāre lēgibus dēfīnīre[8] cōnantur, L. Quīnctius Cincinnātus cōnsul factus est. Ut[9] magistrātum iniit, reprehendit (*he rebuked*) et senātum et plēbem, quod eīdem tribūnī etiam atque etiam creātī cīvitātem turbārent. Senātus igitur dēcrēvit magistrātūs continuārī[10] contrā rem pūblicam[11] esse.

Plēbs tamen eōsdem, quōs anteā, tribūnōs creāvērunt. Patrēs quoque, nē quid cēderent plēbī,[12] Lūcium Quīnctium cōnsulem fēcē-

runt. At is "Minimē mīrum est," inquit, "sī nihil auctōritātis, patrēs cōnscrīptī, habētis apud plēbem. Vōs eam minuitis, quī in continuandīs (*reëlecting*) magistrātibus plēbem imitāminī. Ego mē contrā senātūs cōnsultum cōnsulem reficī nōn patiar." Alius igitur cōnsul factus est.

Post paucōs annōs Aequī[13] exercitum Rōmānum mūnītiōnibus clausum obsidēbant. Cum hoc Rōmam nūntiātum esset, L. Quīnctius cōnsēnsū omnium dictātor

---

[1] *is said;* a frequent meaning.

[2] *service.*

[3] The noun clauses give the substance of the oath, *that the hands should not*, etc.

[4] This word is the negative conjunction regularly employed between subjunctives denoting an idea of wish or desire, **neque** being used between indicatives.

[5] *chew.*

[6] *toward.*

[7] *as magistrates of their own.*

[8] *to limit.* The laws had not hitherto been put into written form. This fact gave an advantage to the patrician magistrates.

[9] Here in a temporal sense, *when.*

[10] The English idiom is "for magistrates to be reëlected." The subject of **esse** is **continuārī**.

[11] *the general interest, public policy.*

[12] *not to yield anything to the plebeians,* i.e., not to be outdone by the plebeians; a clause of purpose.

[13] *the Aequi* (ē'kwī), a people of ancient Italy. See map, page 305.

LĒGĀTĪ CINCINNĀTUM AGRUM COLENTEM INVĒNĒRUNT

dictus est. Lēgātī ā senātū missī eum invēnērunt trāns Tiberim agrum quattuor jūgerum colentem atque in opus intentum. Rogāvē-runt ut togātus (*clad in his toga*) mandāta senātūs audīret. Quīnctius admīrātus jubet uxōrem togam properē (*quickly*) ē tuguriō (*cottage*) prōferre. Cum, abstersō sūdōre (*the sweat having been wiped away*), togā vēlātus (*clad*) prō-cessisset, dictātōrem eum lēgātī salūtant (*greeted*) atque in urbem vocant; quī[1] terror sit in exercitū expōnunt.

Quīnctius exercitum obsessum celeriter līberāvit et hostēs sub jugum[2] mīsit. Triumphāns[3] urbem iniit sextōque decimō diē dictātūram (*dictatorship*) in sex mēnsēs acceptam dēposuit. Magnā laude dignus exīstimātus est.

How the Geese Saved Rome

OLIM lēgātī ab Clūsīnīs[4] Rōmam vēnērunt auxilium pe-tentēs adversus Senonēs,[5] gentem Gallicam. Tum Rōmānī mīsērunt

[1] Interrogative adjective.
[2] The yoke consisted of two spears set upright in the ground with a cross-spear high enough to let the conquered troops pass under.
[3] *in triumph.* In case of an important victory the Roman Senate might grant the successful general the privilege of entering the city in triumphal procession. The general rode in a special triumphal car drawn by four white horses.
[4] *the people of Clusium*, a city of ancient Italy.
[5] *the Senones* (sen′ọ̄-nēz). See map, page 137.

AN ATTACK ON A FORTIFIED TOWN

lēgātōs quī monērent Gallōs nē[1] amīcōs populī Rōmānī oppugnārent. Proeliō tamen commissō, lēgātī Rōmānī contrā jūs gentium[2] arma cēpērunt auxiliumque Clūsīnīs[3] tulērunt.

Gallī posteā ā senātū Rōmānō postulāvērunt ut prō[4] jūre gentium ita violātō lēgātī Rōmānī dēderentur. Hōc negātō, exercitus Gallicus Rōmam profectus est.

Rōmānī, quī nihil ad tantum perīculum idōneum parāverant, apud flūmen Alliam superātī sunt. Diem quō hoc proelium factum est Rōmānī posteā Alliēnsem[5] appellāvērunt. Magna pars exercitūs incolumis Veiōs perfūgit. Cēterī Rōmam petīvērunt et nē clausīs quidem[6] portīs urbis in arcem Capitōliumque cum conjugibus et līberīs sē contulērunt.

Gallī ingressī urbem nēminī parcunt, dīripiunt incenduntque tēcta. Post aliquot diēs, testūdine factā, impetum in arcem[7] fēcērunt. At Rōmānī mediō ferē colle[8] restitērunt, atque inde ex locō superiōre, impetū factō, Gallōs pepulērunt. Obsidiō inde ā Gallīs parāta est. Pars exercitūs Gallicī dīmissa est ad frūmentum cōnferendum ex

---

[1] With **oppugnārent**—*not to attack;* a noun clause, object of **monērent**.

[2] The ancient equivalent of our international law.

[3] See page 317, note 4.

[4] *in return for,* or *in satisfaction of.*

[5] *the day of the Allia.* This day was always regarded as one of ill omen, on which no official assemblies of the people were held.

[6] *without even closing.*

[7] The citadel was on the Capitoline Hill. See map, page 39.

[8] *about the middle of the hill.*

agrīs populōrum fīnitimōrum. Hōs fortūna ipsa dūxit Ardeam, ubi Camillus,[1] imperātor clārissimus, in exiliō vīvēbat.

5 Ardeātēs[2] eō duce castra Gallōrum nocte oppugnant et solūtōs somnō[3] trucīdant (*massacred*). Veiīs[4] interim nōn animī[5] sōlum in diēs[6] sed etiam vīrēs crēscēbant. 10 Nam praeter Rōmānōs, quī ex pugnā Alliēnsī (*of the Allia*) eō perfūgerant, voluntāriī (*volunteers*) ex Latiō[7] conveniēbant. Hī jam cōnstituērunt Rōmam hostibus lī-15 berāre. Omnibus placuit Camillum arcessī, sed anteā senātum cōnsulī.[8] Ad eam rem Pontius Cominius,[9] audāx juvenis, sublevātus cortice[10] secundō Tiberī[11] ad urbem dēfer-20 tur. Senātū probante, Camillus dictātor dictus est.

Interim arx Rōmae Capitōliumque in ingentī perīculō fuit.[12] Nocte enim Gallī, praemissō mīlite quī 25 viam temptāret, tantō silentiō in summum ēvāsērunt[13] ut[14] nōn sōlum custōdēs fallerent, sed nē canēs quidem excitārent. Ānserēs (*geese*) nōn fefellērunt, quī avēs Jūnōnis

sacrae erant. Nam M. Mānlius, 30 vir bellō ēgregius, clangōre eōrum (*by their noise*) ālārumque crepitū (*the flapping*) excitātus, dējēcit Gallum quī jam in summō cōnstiterat. Jamque aliī Rōmānī tēlīs 35 saxīsque hostēs prōpellunt, tōtaque aciēs Gallōrum praeceps (*headlong*) dēfertur.

Sed famēs jam utrumque exercitum urgēbat (*was distressing*), Gal-40 lōs pestilentia (*plague*) etiam. Diem ex diē[15] Rōmānī frūstrā auxilium ab dictātōre expectābant. Postrēmō mīlle pondō aurī[16] cum Gallīs pactī sunt (*bargained*) ut 45 obsidiōnem relinquerent. Huic reī, per sē turpissimae, indignitās addita est; nam pondera[17] ab Gallīs allāta sunt inīqua.

Rōmānīs recūsantibus gladius ā 50 Brennō (*Brennus*), rēge Gallōrum, ponderī additus est cum hīs verbīs, "vae victīs.[18]" Sed priusquam rēs perfecta est, dictātor pervēnit auferrīque aurum dē mediō et 55 Gallōs summovērī jussit. Cum illī dīcerent sē pactōs esse (*had made a bargain*), negat eam pactiō-

---

[1] He had previously taken the Etruscan city of Veii after a long siege, but had subsequently been exiled from Rome on the charge of having unfairly divided the spoils of Veii.
[2] *the Ardeates* (ar-dē̯-ā'tēz), the people of Ardea, a city of the Rutuli. See map, page 305.
[3] *while sleeping*. How, literally?
[4] A locative.
[5] Plural. Compare the English "their spirits."
[6] *day by day*.
[7] *Latium* (lā'shium), a district of west central Italy.
[8] Passive infinitive.

[9] *Pontius Cominius* (pon'ti-us kọ-min'-i-us), a Roman youth.
[10] *on* (*a float made of*) *bark*.
[11] *down the Tiber*. See map, page 305.
[12] The verb agrees in number with the nearer part of its subject.
[13] *made their way up*.
[14] Introducing a clause of result.
[15] *day after day*.
[16] *a thousand pounds of gold*. Translate, *they bargained with the Gauls for a thousand pounds of gold that they should abandon the siege*.
[17] *weights* (for the scales).
[18] *woe to the vanquished*.

THE SACRED GEESE—AND
MANLIUS—SAVE ROME

nem (*bargain*) valēre, quae, postquam ipse dictātor creātus esset,
injussū suō facta esset. Tum dēnūntiat Gallīs ut sē ad proelium
5 parent.

Gallī et in urbe et alterō proeliō
viā Gabīnā[1] superātī sunt. Cōpiae
eōrum fugātae (*having been routed*)
in omnēs partēs dispersae sunt.
10 Dictātor triumphāns[2] in urbem
rediit. Deinde servātam in bellō
patriam iterum in pāce servāvit.
Cum enim tribūnī plēbem agitārent

ut relictīs ruīnīs Veiōs migrārent,[3]
Camillus ōrātiōne ācrī cīvibus per- 15
suāsit ut Rōmam restituerent.

Centuriō quoque populum mōvit[4]
vōce opportūnē (*opportunely*) ēmis-
sā, quī cum cohortibus Forum
trānsiēns clāmāvit: "Signum sta- 20
tue, signifer (*standard-bearer*); hīc
manēbimus optimē." Quā vōce
audītā, et[5] senātus ē cūriā ēgressus
ōmen (*omen*) accipere sē conclāmā-
vit, et plēbs circumfūsa (*crowding* 25
around) probāvērunt.

The Honor of a Roman

RŌMĀNĪ ā Pyrrhō, rēge Ēpīrī,[6]
proeliō superātī lēgātōs Tarentum[7] ad eum dē redimendīs cap-
30 tīvīs mīsērunt. Inter lēgātōs Rōmānōs erat C. Fābricius, vir bonus
et bellō ēgregius, sed admodum
pauper (*poor*). Pyrrhus, quī cum
Rōmānīs pācem facere volēbat,
35 lēgātīs magna dōna obtulit sī
Rōmānīs pācem suādērent.[8] Quamquam haec omnia sprēta sunt, rēx
tamen captīvōs dīcitur sine pretiō
(*ransom*) Rōmam mīsisse.

40 Pyrrhus Fābriciī virtūtem admīrātus illī sēcrētō (*secretly*) quār-
tam etiam rēgnī suī partem obtulit
sī patriam dēsereret sēcumque vī-
veret; cui Fābricius ita respondit:

"Sī mē virum bonum jūdicās, cūr 45
mē vīs corrumpere (*to corrupt*)?
Sīn vērō malum, cūr meam amīcitiam cupis?"

Annō interjectō (*having intervened*), omnī spē pācis inter Pyr- 50
rhum et Rōmānōs conciliandae ab-
lātā, Fābricius cōnsul factus contrā
eum missus est. Cumque vīcīna
castra ipse et rēx habērent, medicus
rēgis nocte ad Fābricium vēnit 55
eīque pollicitus est, sī praemium
sibi prōposuisset, sē Pyrrhum venēnō necātūrum.[9]

Hunc Fābricius vīnctum ad
Pyrrhum remīsit atque eum cer- 60
tiōrem fēcit quae medicus pollicitus esset. Tum rēx admīrātus eum

---

[1] *on the road to Gabii.* For Gabii, see
map, page 305.
[2] See page 317, note 3.
[3] *were inciting the people to migrate;*
migrārent takes a subject supplied from
plēbem. Why is the verb plural?
[4] This incident illustrates the very
common tendency of the Romans to
find omens in ordinary remarks.
[5] With **et** of line 25—*both . . . and.*
[6] *of Epirus* (ē-pī′rus). Epirus was a
district of Greece. See map, page 61.

[7] *to Tarentum* (tȧ-ren′tum), a city in
southern Italy. See map, page 277.
Now Taranto (tä-rän′tō).
[8] *if they would urge peace upon the
Romans.* The subjunctive is due to the
informal indirect discourse (*Pyrrhus
said that he would make large presents,
if,* etc.).
[9] A verb meaning "promise" may take
either a future infinitive with subject
accusative, as here, or simply a present
infinitive without subject.

dīxisse fertur: "Ille est Fābricius, quī difficilius (*with greater difficulty*) ab honestāte (*honor*) quam sōl ā suō cursū potest āvertī."

5 Fābricius cum apud Pyrrhum rēgem lēgātus esset, cum Cīneā,[1] lēgātō Pyrrhī, sermōnem contulit.[2]

Hic[3] dīxit quendam philosophum 10 (*philosopher*) esse Athēnīs, quī dīceret omnia quae facerēmus ad voluptātem[4] esse referenda. Tum Fābricium exclāmāsse ferunt: "Utinam (*O that*) id hostibus nostrīs 15 persuādeāmus,[5] quō facilius vincī possint, cum sē voluptātibus dederint!"

Nihil magis ab ejus vītā[6] aliēnum erat quam voluptās et lūxus (*lux-* 20 *ury*). Tōta ejus supellex argentea ex salīnō ūnō cōnstābat[7] et ex patellā (*a small dish*) ad ūsum sacrōrum, quae corneō pediculō (*by a pedestal of horn*) sustinēbā- 25 tur.

Cēnābat ad focum (*fireplace*) rādīcēs (*radishes*) et herbās, cum lēgātī Samnītium[8] ad eum vēnērunt magnamque eī pecūniam obtulērunt; quibus sīc respondit: 30 "Quamdiū (*as long as*) cupiditātibus imperāre poterō, nihil mihi dēerit; vōs autem pecūniam eīs quī eam cupiunt dōnāte (*give*)." 35

Fābricius omnem vītam in glōriōsā paupertāte (*honored poverty*) exēgit (*spent*), adeōque inops (*poor*) dēcessit ut unde[9] dōs fīliārum darētur nōn relinqueret. 40

Senātus patris sibi partēs sūmpsit et, datīs ex aerāriō (*treasury*) dōtibus, fīliās collocāvit pecūniā pūblicā.

Giving All for His Native Land

Cum prīmō Pūnicō (*Punic*) bellō Rōmānī contrā Carthāginiēnsēs dē imperiō Siciliae contenderent, M. Atīlius Rēgulus, cōnsul Rōmānus, nāvālī (*naval*) 50 pugnā classem Pūnicam (*Carthaginian*) superāvit. Proeliō factō, Hannō, dux Carthāginiēnsis, ad eum vēnit simulāns sē velle dē pāce agere, rē vērā ut tempus extraheret (*he might gain*), dum 55 novae cōpiae ex Āfricā advenīrent.

Mīlitēs Rōmānī clāmāre coepērunt Rēgulum idem facere opor-

---

[1] *Cineas* (sin'ē̆-äs). See the declension of **Aenēās**, page 296, note 1. Cineas was famed for his powers of persuasion and was Pyrrhus' favorite adviser. The king was reported to have said that he had taken more cities through the eloquence of Cineas than he had won by force of arms.

[2] *engaged in conversation.*

[3] *the latter.*

[4] *to the standard of pleasure;* contrasted with a theory of life based on duty or obligation.

[5] *would that we might persuade* (*I wish we might persuade*) *our enemies of this.* The subjunctive **persuādeāmus** and the clause of purpose following are explained in Gr. S., 103 and 104.

[6] With **aliēnum**. In English we say *foreign to.*

[7] *all his silverware consisted of one salt-cellar.*

[8] *of the Samnites* (sam'nīts). The Samnites were a people living in central Italy. See map, page 305.

[9] *the means from which.* The idea of possibility is involved in the subjunctive **darētur**—*could be furnished.*

tēre[1] quod Carthāginiēnsēs paucīs ante annīs in cōnsule quōdam fēcissent. Is enim tamquam in colloquium per fraudem vocātus ā Poenīs[2] comprehēnsus erat et in catēnās conjectus. Jam Hannō timēre incipiēbat, sed perīculum respōnsō callidō reppulit. "Sī hoc fēceritis," inquit, "nihilō eritis Poenīs meliōrēs."

Cōnsul tacēre jussit eōs quī pār parī[3] referrī volēbant, et conveniēns (*appropriate*) gravitātī Rōmānae (*to Roman dignity*) respōnsum dedit: "Istō tē metū, Hannō, fidēs Rōmāna līberat." Dē pāce, quia Poenus ex animō[4] nōn agēbat et cōnsul bellum gerere quam pācem facere mālēbat, nōn convēnit.[5]

Deinde Rēgulus et collēga (*colleague*), L. Mānlius Vulsō, in Āfricam prīmī Rōmānōrum ducum trānsiērunt. Ibi, multīs castellīs expugnātīs magnāque praedā captā, Tūnētem[6] occupāvērunt, quae urbs decem tantum mīlibus[7] passuum ā Carthāgine aberat.

Vulsō in Ītaliam cum parte mīlitum rediit, collēgā (*colleague*) ad agrōs vāstandōs relictō.

Dum Rēgulus ita hiemem in Āfricā agit, vīlicus in agellō (*little farm*) septem jūgerum, quem Rēgulus cōnsul habēbat, mortuus est. Occāsiōnem nactus mercēnnārius (*the hired servant*), ablātō rūsticō īnstrūmentō (*the farm tools*), aufūgit (*ran away*); ita perīculum erat nē, dēsertō agrō, alimenta (*food*) uxōrī Rēgulī ac līberīs dēessent.[8]

Dīcitur litterīs ā cōnsulibus petīsse ut sibi successor (*successor*) mitterētur. At senātus cōnstituit reī pūblicae interesse eum in Āfricā manēre atque agrum colī pūblicē et alimenta (*food*) conjugī ejus ac līberīs praebērī jussit.

Īnsequentī (*in the following*) annō Rēgulus, arbitrātus Carthāginiēnsēs jam sē dēdere parātōs esse, ad colloquium eōs invītāvit. Laetī vēnērunt, ut dē pāce agerent. Sed, cum postulāta (*the demands*) Rēgulī audīvissent, cōnstituērunt condiciōnēs tam dūrās recūsāre bellumque renovāre.

Eō ferē tempore Lacedaemonius[9] quīdam, nōmine Xanthippus,[10] reī[11] mīlitāris perītissimus, Carthāginem cum conductīs (*mercenaries*) vēnit. Carthāginiēnsibus celeriter persuāsit ut sē ducem facerent. Quō factō, fortūna mūtāta est; nam nōn sōlum exercitum Rōmānum

---

[1] The infinitive is due to the indirect discourse. Its subject is another infinitive with subject accusative, **Rēgulum . . . facere.**

[2] **Poenīs** and **Carthāginiēnsēs** are used of the same people, the former referring to their Phoenician origin, the latter derived from the name of their chief city.

[3] *like for like.*

[4] *sincerely* (literally, *from his heart*).

[5] Impersonal; *no agreement was reached.*

[6] *Tunis.* See **Tunes** on map, page 277.

[7] Ablative of degree or measure of difference. What part of speech is the plural of **mīlle?**

[8] The noun clause is used with **perīculum erat** exactly as with a verb of fearing. See Gr. S., 109 *b.*

[9] *Lacedaemonian* (las'ę-dē-mō′ni-ạn), a man from Lacedaemon, or Sparta.

[10] *Xanthippus* (zan-tip′us), a general.

[11] Objective genitive with **perītissimus.**

vīcērunt, sed etiam Rēgulum im-perātōrem cēpērunt.

Paucīs post annīs,[1] cum iterum dē pāce agere cōnstituissent, Rēgu-lum cum lēgātīs Rōmam mīsērunt quī Rōmānīs pācem suādēret et dē commūtandīs captīvīs ageret.

Jūre jūrandō autem adstrictus est ut, nisi dē captīvīs im-petrāret, redīret[2] ipse Carthā-ginem.

Is, cum Rōmam vēnisset, ēgit aliter ac[3] Poenī mandāverant; nam senātuī suāsit nē pāx cum Poenīs fieret; illōs enim frāctōs tot cāsibus spem nūllam habēre.[4] Reddī captī-vōs negāvit esse ūtile; adulēscentēs esse et bonōs ducēs, sē jam cōnfec-tum senectūte (*by old age*). Dīxit etiam malum exemplum[5] futūrum esse, sī captīvī Rōmānī redime-rentur.

Senātus eō auctōre[6] pācem recū-sāvit Poenōsque captīvōs retinuit. Rēgulus ut captīvus[7] conjugem par-vōsque nātōs ā sē remōvit[8] Carthā-ginemque rediit. Ibi crūdēlissimīs suppliciīs necātus esse dīcitur.

[1] An ablative of degree of difference with **post**. We have also had **post paucōs annōs**. See Gr. S., 84.

[2] *bound himself by an oath to return;* because of the implied indirect dis-course (*he said he would return*), the subordinate clause, **nisi . . . impetrāret**, has the subjunctive.

[3] *than;* a meaning explained on page 123, note 11.

[4] The infinitive with subject accusa-tive depends on a verb of saying implied in the preceding sentence.

[5] A Roman soldier was expected to fight to the death rather than be taken prisoner.

[6] *by his advice;* ablative absolute.

[7] *as a prisoner;* and so not the equal of free Romans.

[8] *shunned.*

COMPREHENSION QUESTIONS

1. Who was Aeneas?

2. What was the cause of the war between the Trojans and the Rutulians?

3. What was the name of the city founded by Ascanius? Where was it located?

4. What was the name of the shepherd who rescued Romulus and Remus?

5. How was the decision made as to whether Romulus or Remus should give his name to the new city?

6. How did the Romans obtain wives?

7. What was the story of the death of Romulus?

8. Who was the second king of Rome? What was his character?

9. How was the war between the Romans and the Albans decided?

10. How many kings of Rome were there? Who was the last of these?

11. Who was the leader of the Romans in the expulsion of the last king?

12. What was the cause of dissension between the plebeians and the pa-tricians?

13. From what class in Roman society were the tribunes elected? What was their duty?

14. Who was Cincinnatus? What was he doing when notified of his election as dictator?

15. How was Rome saved from capture by the Gauls?

16. Who was Pyrrhus? How did he try to bribe Fabricius?

17. Why did Regulus advise the Romans not to make peace with the Carthaginians?

18. What was the result of his advice?

WORD STUDY XIII

Abbreviations of Latin Words and Phrases

The abbreviations found in the following list are often used in English. They represent Latin words, and it is easier to remember their meanings if the words they stand for are known.

A.B. *or* B.A.—**Artium Baccalaureus,** *Bachelor of Arts*

A.D.—**Annō Dominī,** *in the year of Our Lord*

ad lib.—**ad libitum,** *at pleasure,* or *as much as one wishes*

A.M.—**ante merīdiem,** *before noon*

A.M. *or* M.A.—**Artium Magister,** *Master of Arts*

A.U.C.—**ab urbe conditā,** *from the founding of the city* (Rome)

d.—**dēnārius,** *penny* (in British money)

D.G.—**Deī grātiā,** *by the grace of God*

D.O.M.—**Deō Optimō Maximō,** *to God, the Best, the Greatest*

D.V.—**Deō volente,** *God willing*

e.g.—**exemplī grātiā,** *for example*

et al.—**et aliī,** *and others,* or **et alibī,** *and elsewhere*

etc.—**et cētera,** *and the rest,* or *and so forth*

et seq.—**et sequēns** or **sequentia,** *and the following*

ibid.—**ibīdem,** *in the same place*

id.—**idem,** *the same*

i.e.—**id est,** *that is*

I.N.R.I.—**Iēsus (Jēsus) Nazarēnus, Rēx Iūdaeōrum (Jūdaeōrum),** *Jesus of Nazareth, King of the Jews*

J.D.—**Jūrum Doctor,** *Doctor of Laws*

£—the first letter of **lībra,** *pound,* with a line drawn through it to show that it is an abbreviation. It means *a pound* in British money.

lb.—**lībra,** *a pound* (in weight)

l.c.—**locō citātō,** *in the place cited*

Lit.D. *or* Litt.D.—**Litterārum Doctor,** *Doctor of Letters* (Literature)

LL.D.—**Lēgum Doctor,** *Doctor of Laws*

M.—**merīdiēs,** *noon*

M.D.—**Medicīnae Doctor,** *Doctor of Medicine*

n.b.—**nōtā bene,** *note well,* or *take notice*

no.—**numerō** (abl. sing.), *in number*

Ph.D.—**Philosophiae Doctor,** *Doctor of Philosophy*

P.M.—**post merīdiem,** *after noon*

P.S.—**post scrīptum,** *written afterwards*

pro tem.—**prō tempore,** *for the time,* or *temporarily*

prox.—**proximō,** for **proximō mēnse,** *in the next month*

R.I.P.—**Requiēscat in pāce,** *May he (she) rest in peace*

scil.—**scīlicet,** *namely*

S.P.Q.R.—**Senātus Populusque Rōmānus,** *the Senate and People of Rome*

s.v.—**sub verbō,** *under the word*

vid.—**vidē,** *see*

viz.—**vidēlicet,** *namely*

ult.—**ultimō,** for **ultimō mēnse,** *in the preceding month*

EXERCISES

1. What connection is there between Latin **candidus,** *white,* and the English word *candidate?*
2. What is the literal meaning of *exaggerate* as shown by its derivation?
3. What is the meaning of *accident?* What is the source of the word?
4. What is a *peninsula?* Why is it so called?

Idioms and Phrases

The idioms and phrases listed below occur frequently in the text read.

> **dum ea geruntur,** *while this was going on, in the meantime*
> **in dēditiōnem eōs accipere,** *to grant them terms of surrender*
> **inimīcō animō erat,** *he was unfriendly (of an unfriendly attitude)*
> **inter sē differunt,** *they differ from one another*
> **postrīdiē ejus diēī,** *the next day*
> **sub vesperum,** *toward evening*
> **unā ex parte,** *on one side*

Vocabulary Review

The following words, which appear frequently in this book, are important in second-year work. Their meanings should be thoroughly learned.

adeō (*adv.*)	exitus	mālō	prōnūntiō	sublevō
adeō (*verb*)	factum	metus	prūdēns	toga
aes	fallō	minuō	quiētus	tot
audāx	gēns	nōnus	recuperō	trānseō
cadō	incolumis	novem	recūsō	turpis
campus	indūcō	octāvus	reddō	umquam
centum	ineō	opus	regō	uterque
contemnō	inermis	ōrō	rēmus	ūtilis
continuus	īnstituō	parcō	religiō	ūtor
dignus	interest	patior	reperiō	vehemēns
dīripiō	interrogō	perfidia	rumpō	verbum
dispergō	jam prīdem	pertineō	saxum	vīgintī
dīversus	līberī	plēbs	stō	vīvō

ROMAN HISTORY IN BRIEF

B.C

Founding of Rome (see pp. 298-299) 753

Rome, the Kingdom

Period of the kings 753-509
    Conquest of the towns near Rome (see pp. 303-304)
    Destruction of the ancient city of Alba Longa (see p. 305)
    Founding of Ostia, the seaport of Rome (see p. 306)
    Building of the Servian Wall to inclose the entire city

Rome, the Republic

Establishment of the Republic (see p. 315) 509
Battle of Lake Regillus, in which the Romans defeated the Etruscans, their
    traditional rivals for power 496
First secession of the plebeians, or common people (see p. 315) 494
Establishment of the office of tribune, an official selected to protect the interests
    of the plebeians (see p. 316) 493
Publication of the Twelve Tables of Law, the first written code 449
Second secession of the plebeians 449
Capture of Rome by the Gauls (see pp. 318-319) 390
Battle of the Caudine Forks, in which the Romans were defeated by the
    Samnites, a people of central Italy 321
Construction of the Appian Way, the most important Roman road (see pp.
    24-25, 29) 312
War with Pyrrhus, the king called upon by the Greek cities of Italy to protect
    them from the Romans 281-272
First Punic War, which ended in a Roman victory (see p. 322) 264-241
    Surrender of Sicily to Rome by Carthage and its annexation as the first
        Roman province (see p. 16) 241
Second Punic War 218-201
    Battle of Cannae, in which the Romans were defeated by Hannibal, the
        great Carthaginian general 216
    Battle of Zama, in which Carthage was defeated and Rome made supreme
        in the Western world 202
Third Macedonian War, which resulted in the annexation of the northern
    part of the Balkan peninsula as a Roman province 171-167
Third Punic War 149-146
    Destruction of Carthage 146
Capture and destruction of the important Greek city of Corinth 146
Tribunate of Tiberius Gracchus, who attempted to aid the poor by redistribu-
    tion of public lands 133
Tribunate of Gaius Gracchus, who introduced unwise reforms which led to
    the dependence of the poor upon the State 123
War in Africa, led by Marius, ending with the downfall of Jugurtha, usurper
    of Roman authority in Africa 112-105
Birth of Cicero, the great orator and statesman 106
Victory of Marius, as consul, over two Germanic tribes, the Teutones and
    Cimbri, who invaded Italy 102-101

B. C.

Birth of Julius Caesar (see p. 162) 100

*War against the Italian tribes allied with Rome, with the final result that
they were granted Roman citizenship* 90-88

*Civil war between Marius and Sulla, resulting in the downfall of Marius
(see p. 162)* 87-82

*Dictatorship of Sulla, during which the authority of the Senate was increased
and the powers of the tribunes lessened (see p. 162)* 82-79

*Third Mithridatic War, in which Pompey defeated Mithridates, ruler of the
Asiatic kingdom of Pontus* 74-63

*War with the gladiator Spartacus—leader of the slaves who revolted against
Rome—ending in his defeat* 73-71

Birth of Vergil, greatest of Roman poets 70

Consulship of Cicero 63

*Formation of the first triumvirate, in which the control of public affairs was
seized by three leaders, Caesar, Crassus, and Pompey (see p. 164)* 60

Consulship of Caesar (see p. 164) 59

Caesar's campaigns in Gaul (see pp. 136 ff.) 58-50

*Civil war between Caesar and Pompey for supremacy in Rome, ending with
the success of Caesar (see p. 226)* 49-45

Assassination of Caesar (see pp. 26, 228-229) 44

Assassination of Cicero 43

*Battle of Actium, between Mark Antony and Octavius, who were struggling
to succeed Caesar in power—culminating in the victory of Octavius,
grand-nephew of Caesar* 31

Rome, the Empire

Octavius becomes emperor and is given the name Augustus (see p. 229) 27

Death of Vergil 19

A. D.

Death of Augustus 14

*Reign of Nero, marked by cruel persecution of the Christians and the destruc-
tion of more than half of Rome by fire* 54-68

*Destruction of the Italian cities, Pompeii and Herculaneum, by the eruption of
Mount Vesuvius* 79

Building of Aurelian's Wall . . . . .about 275

*Reign of Diocletian, marked by vitality in government and by the last perse-
cution of the Christians* 284-305

*Battle of the Mulvian Bridge, in which Constantine defeated Maxentius,
another candidate for emperor, and adopted the Christian cross as a war
standard* 312

*Reign of Constantine, during which Christianity was established as the State
religion* 324-337

First separation of the Eastern and Western Roman Empires 364

Fall of Rome 476

THE REPUBLIC AND THE EMPIRE

A ROMAN KING

In this painting by Andrea Mantegna, a famous Italian artist of the fifteenth century, Tarquin is shown consulting the oracle at Cumae.

WHEN in 509 B.C. Tarquin, the last of the ancient Roman kings, was driven into exile, the Republic was established. The tyranny of this ruler had so affronted the Romans that they swore solemnly never again to endure a monarchy. The common people soon found, however, that they had merely exchanged one form of tyranny for another, for the patricians, or nobles, now controlled the government.

During the first two centuries of the Republic the plebeians, or common people, struggled continually to gain certain rights. But in spite of many concessions to the people, the Roman government never became a democratic one like our own.

At the head of the Republic were two consuls, who were invested with the powers once held by the kings. They were patricians, elected in an assembly controlled by patricians. The other important magistrates were likewise patricians, who naturally furthered the interests of their own class.

In an effort to protect themselves, the plebeians met in an assembly of their own and elected officials, called tribunes, to defend their rights. These tribunes were given power to veto all acts contrary to public interest. Later, their powers were increased until they exceeded those of the consuls.

In the days of the monarchy the king had been advised by a "council of old men." This became the famous Roman Senate, which differed from our Congress in having administrative, as well as legislative, powers. Its legislative powers, however, were not so complete as those of our Congress, for the laws proposed and discussed in the Roman Senate had to be voted on by the people.

For many years during the Republic the Senate was at the head of the state, guiding it through a number of critical wars. The Senate of this period has been declared the greatest body of rulers of the ancient world and perhaps of all time.

The attitude of the early Roman citizen toward his city-state was one of devotion and loyalty. In times of war he fought valiantly for it; in times of peace he continued to serve it. His life at home was of the utmost simplicity. Even in the houses of the nobles there

AMID THE LUXURY OF IMPERIAL GARDENS
The gardens of the Villa d'Este in Italy are world famous. They were made in the sixteenth century
as a copy of Roman imperial gardens.

was little display of wealth. Family life was faithfully preserved, and children were carefully trained in the duties of citizenship.

As Rome's conquests were extended, vast riches began to pour in, and an enormous import trade brought luxuries from the provinces. A new moneyed class sprang up.

Moreover, the conquest of Greece in the second century B.C. brought the Romans in contact with the ancient and highly developed Greek civilization. Little by little the simplicity of family and social life disappeared.

With the increase in wealth came the growth of large estates in the country and the gradual disappearance of the small farm and of the independent life of its owner. Slaves did the work on the estates, and the free farmer, deprived of his livelihood, drifted to Rome. After a while there were so many discontented, unemployed people in Rome that the free grain distributed to them became a serious item of public expenditure.

The Roman politician now sought office for selfish motives and freely gave and accepted bribes. He courted popularity by sponsoring cruel gladiatorial combats.

By the time of Julius Caesar the social and political disorder was great. Caesar took all power into his own hands and, without assuming the title, became an emperor in fact. "The word of Caesar stood against the world."

Augustus, the successor of Caesar, was careful to maintain the outward forms of the old Republic. Aside from *imperātor*, which was his title as commander-in-chief of the army, his chief title was *prīnceps*, the first citizen. The senators and the republican magistrates, however, were nearly all his nominees or his appointees. And the Senate, without the control of the army, could not oppose him in his quiet seizure of power.

Augustus was one of the great administrators of Rome, devoting himself to the reorganization of the government and of the provinces. In general he used his powers in an attempt to build up the state.

For many years the Roman emperors continued, to a certain extent, to preserve the forms and names of the old republican government, but eventually these were forever discarded. The assemblies disappeared, the magistrates became mere figureheads, and the Senate was finally charged with nothing more important than the municipal affairs of Rome. The emperors became open despots.

There never was a hereditary monarchy in Rome, although in settled times an emperor often named his son as his successor. In many cases the emperor was chosen by the army, which, unlike the army of the Republic, was filled with soldiers from many different lands.

In the period from A.D. 192 to 284 all the emperors were elected by the army and were known as the "barracks" emperors. In this pe-

AUGUSTUS, THE FIRST EMPEROR

riod of less than a hundred years there were twenty-five emperors, all of whom except four came to a violent end; for if the soldiers could raise a favorite to the purple, they could also make away with him when he failed to please them. Once the soldiers actually sold the office of emperor to the highest bidder, who reigned for only sixty-five days.

In the long succession of emperors who ruled over the Roman world, there were some who used their absolute powers wisely, but more who used them foolishly or harshly.

One of the finest emperors was Marcus Aurelius (A.D. 161-180). He strove to attain perfection of character and believed he could not do so without continual service to mankind. The people were his family, not his prey. He protected

MARCUS AURELIUS AS A YOUNG MAN

the weak, aided the poor, and tempered justice with mercy. This enlightened man was one of the few ancient rulers who believed that the criminal should be reformed, not merely punished. But even Marcus Aurelius, while deferring outwardly to the Senate, did not neglect to increase his regal powers.

One of the worst emperors was Caligula (A.D. 37-41), who tortured and killed for pleasure. At the end of his brief reign there was no great family in Rome not in mourning. His extravagances and follies soon emptied the public treasuries—he made away with the equivalent of half a million dollars in a day—and private fortunes were seized and taxes levied without warning. Caligula insulted every institution and tradition of Rome. He had himself worshiped as a god in the Forum and made his favorite horse a consul. That the Empire did not crash under him was doubtless due to the solid foundation laid by Augustus.

Up to the time of Elagabalus (A.D. 218-222) all the emperors had had something of the Roman character. But Elagabalus, who was raised to power by an eastern garrison, was an Oriental, a priest of the Syrian sun god. He brought with him to Rome the shapeless black stone which was the image of this god and installed it in a temple on the Palatine, where it was worshiped as representing the supreme deity of the state. Romans were treated to the spectacle of an emperor who made his favorite barbers and dancers high magistrates. After four years the rule of Elagabalus came to a violent end, and his body was thrown into the Tiber.

A despotic and unstable monarchy controlled by a greedy and barbarous soldiery did not promote the welfare of the Empire. Taxes became so heavy that the people were impoverished. Wars, plagues, and general wretchedness decreased the population, and from all sides the barbarians began to crowd in on an empire already shattered from within. And so, Rome finally fell! The glorious Empire which the Romans had built, they themselves destroyed, for they had lost forever the spirit of the ancient Romans who "in Rome's quarrel spared neither land nor gold, nor son nor wife, nor limb nor life."

TRŌJA CAPTA

PERSŌNAE (*Characters*)

Scaena Prīma

AENĒĀS ⎫
HYPANIS ⎪
DYMĀS ⎬ *Trōjānī*
PANTHŪS ⎪
THYMOETĒS⎪
CAPYS ⎭
IŪLUS, *fīlius Aenēae*
PRIAMUS, *rēx Trōjānōrum*
LĀOCOŌN, *sacerdōs*
SINŌN, *Graecus*
PĀSTŌRĒS, *Trōjānī*
CASSANDRA, *fīlia Priamī*

Scaena Secunda

SINŌN ⎫
MACHĀŌN[1] ⎪
THESSANDRUS[1]⎪
STHENELUS[1] ⎬*Graecī*
ACAMĀS[1] ⎪
THOĀS[1] ⎪
PYRRHUS ⎭
MENELĀUS, *rēx*
ULIXĒS, *rēx*
EPĒUS, *fabricātor* (maker)
equī
CASSANDRA

Scaena Tertia

PRIAMUS
HECUBA, *uxor Priamī*
POLĪTĒS, *fīlius Priamī*
PYRRHUS
AENĒĀS
ANCILLAE HECUBAE

Scaena Quārta

AENĒĀS
ANCHĪSĒS, *pater Aenēae*
CREŪSA, *uxor Aenēae*
IŪLUS

SCAENA PRĪMA. IN LĪTORE

Haud procul ā tergō stat urbs Trōja.
Ā sinistrā stat ingēns equus, mā-
china (structure) *lignea.* TRŌ-
JĀNĪ *laetīs clāmōribus in lītus*
5 *dēscendunt.*

AENĒĀS [*quī* IŪLUM *dūcit*]. Hīc
Achillēs, vir saevus, tabernāculum pōnēbat.
IŪLUS. Ubi nunc sunt Graecī, mī[2]
10 pater?
AENĒĀS. Domum rediērunt, quia
nōs vincere nōn poterant.
HYPANIS. Hīc Agamemnōn sedēbat ā ducibus cīnctus.
15 DYMĀS. Gaudeō, quia jam Mycē-
nās[3] rediit.
IŪLUS. Ōlim Agamemnonem, dum
Graecōs in moenia dūcit, ego
vīdī.
20 AENĒĀS. Cum vir factus eris, contrā eum tū ipse fortasse pugnā-
bis.

IŪLUS. Hoc spērō.
PANTHŪS. Hīc aciē certāre (*to fight*)
solēbāmus.   25
HYPANIS. Multōs amīcōs hīc occī-
sōs perdidī (*I have lost*).
PANTHŪS. Quia nōn jam impetum
gladiīs strictīs[4] faciēmus, valdē
(*very much*) doleō.   30
AENĒĀS. Immō vērō[5] gaudē, quia
pācem diū optātam (*wished for*)
habēmus. [IŪLŌ.] Hīc nāvēs
jacēbant, quibus nunc Graecī
procul āvehuntur.   35
PANTHŪS. Mox, cum vīrēs refēce-
rimus, in Graeciam nōs invādēmus.
IŪLUS. Hūc venī, pater. Hoc mōnstrum spectā! Quid est? Unde 40
venit?
OMNĒS. Mīrābile est.
DYMĀS. Graecī sine dubiō hanc
māchinam (*structure*) fabrī fēcē-
runt.   45

---

[1] All these names are spelled the same
in English as in Latin, and pronounced
as follows: (mạ-kā′on), (the-san′drus),
(sthen′ẹ-lus), (ak′ạ-mus), (thō′ạs).

[2] Vocative of **meus.**
[3] *to Mycenae* (mī-sē′nẹ), a Greek city.
[4] *with drawn swords.*
[5] The two words mean *rather.*

AENĒĀS. Dōnum potest esse quod nostrae deae offerunt.

HYPANIS. Dōnō opus est Minervam plācandī causā.

5 THYMOETĒS. Rēctē[1] dīcitis. Certē Minervae hoc dedērunt. Equus intrā mūrōs dūcendus et in arce ante templum Minervae pōnendus est. Operam date, comitēs!

10 CAPYS. Festīnā lentē,[2] Thymoetēs. Nōlī imprūdenter (*unwisely*) agere.

THYMOETĒS [*gladiō equum ferit*[3]]. Ligneus est equus; lignum nōn 15 est timendum.

CAPYS. Nesciō quae īnsidiae hae sunt Graecōrum. Jacite, comitēs, in mare equum aut subjectīs flammīs ūrite, aut latebrās (*hid-* 20 *ing-places*) saltem (*at least*) explōrāte!

LĀOCOŌN [*ab arce dēcurrit; Priamus longē sequitur*].

Ō miserī, quae tanta īnsānia (*mad-*
25   *ness*), cīvēs?
Crēditis āvectōs hostēs? Aut ūlla
        putātis
Dōna carēre (*are free from*) dolīs
        Danaum? Sīc nōtus Ulīxēs?
30 Quidquid (*whatever*) id est, timeō
        Danaōs—et dōna ferentēs!

[*In latus equī hastam contorquet.*[4]]

CAPYS. Armōrum audiō clangōrem (*sound*). Fortasse . . .

35 [*Subitō intrant trēs* PĀSTŌRĒS, *quī captīvum vīnctum dūcunt* SINŌNEM.]

PĀSTŌRĒS. Graecum afferimus captīvum.

[TRŌJĀNĪ *circum captīvum ruunt*.] 40

HYPANIS. Ubi eum cēpistis, Ō pāstōrēs?

DYMĀS. Ubi latēbat?

AENĒĀS. Armātusne erat?

PANTHŪS. Explōrātor est.   45

OMNĒS. Occīdendus est.

PANTHŪS. Ex arce eum dējicite!

OMNĒS. In arcem dūcite captīvum!

PRIAMUS. Manēte, cīvēs! Multa captīvus, sī vult, nōbīs nārrāre 50 potest.

OMNĒS. Loquere, captīve. Rēx Priamus tē jubet loquī.

PRIAMUS. Unde venīs, captīve? Cūr inermis es?   55

SINŌN.

Heu (*alas*), quae nunc tellūs (*land*),
Ō rēx, quae mē aequora (*seas*) possunt
Accipere? Aut quid jam miserō mihi 60
    dēnique restat (*is left*),
Cui neque apud Danaōs usquam
    (*anywhere*) locus, et super[5] ipsī
Trōjānī īnfēnsī (*enraged*) poenās cum
    sanguine poscunt?   65

OMNĒS. Sanguinem istīus poscimus.

PRIAMUS. Dēsistite, juvenēs. Audiendus est captīvus. Loquere! Quis es? Quōmodo (*how*) hūc vēnistī?   70

SINŌN. Omnia tibi dīcam, Ō rēx, vēra. Sinōn vocor, quī magnum inter Danaōs nōmen quondam habēbam. At perfidus Ulīxēs . . .

OMNĒS. Ō perfidum Ulīxem!   75

SINŌN. Hic perfidus Ulīxēs, quī mē ōderat, in hōc lītore mē relinquī jussit. Occīde mē, rēx, sī id tibi placet; nōlō enim jam vīvere.

---

[1] *you are right;* literally, *you speak rightly.*

[2] *make haste slowly.*

[3] From **feriō, -īre**, *strike.*

[4] *hurls.*

[5] An adverb, meaning *besides.*

PRIAMUS. Sī nōbīs omnia dīcēs, tibi parcam. Quō Graecī iērunt? Cūr ā nostrā terrā discessērunt? Quō cōnsiliō hoc mōnstrum in 5 lītore relīquērunt?

OMNĒS. Respondē, Sinōn; nisi vērum dīcēs, membra tua dīlaniābimus (*we will tear to pieces*).

SINŌN. Domum rediērunt Graecī, 10 quia urbem vestram neque vī neque īnsidiīs capere potuērunt. At deam vestram timent; itaque hoc dōnum relīquērunt eam plācandī causā. Sī equō ligneō 15 nocēbis, Ō rēx Trōjānōrum, magnum exitium (*destruction*) erit imperiō tuō; sīn equum in summā arce pōnēs, Trōjānī Graecōs vincent.

20 LĀOCOŌN. Nōlīte, cīvēs, Graecō crēdere.

DYMĀS. Favē (*guard*) linguā, Lāocoōn. Impia (*wicked*) verba loqueris.

25 PANTHŪS. Nōnne Graecōs vincere vīs?

HYPANIS. Vīsne deae īram in nōs vertere?

LĀOCOŌN. Ō rēx, prūdēns es! Nōlī 30 Graecō crēdere.

THYMOETĒS. Timidus es, Lāocoōn, quia sacerdōs es. Quid equus ligneus nōbīs nocēre potest?

PRIAMUS. Ō Trōjānī, Graecum au- 35 dīvistis. Utrum vōbīs placet facere? Estne dūcendus in urbem equus annōn (*or not*)?

OMNĒS. Dūcendus.

[CASSANDRA *in medium ruit.*]

CASSANDRA. Cavēte, Ō Trōjānī, 40 cavēte! Hāc nocte Trōja cadet. Sanguis uxōrum līberōrumque per viās fluet. Senēs puerīque caedentur.

IŪLUS. Pater, dēfende mē. Quid 45 haec dīcit?

CASSANDRA. Quid videō? Sanguinem, cadāvera (*dead bodies*), flammās, cinerēs (*ashes*).

IŪLUS [*lacrimat*]. Īnsāna (*mad*) est. 50 Mē occīdere vult.

CASSANDRA. Ecce, domūs nostrae flammīs ūruntur. Rēgia domus ruit. Priamus gladiō occīditur. Vae nōbīs! 55

PRIAMUS. Īnsānīs (*you are mad*), Cassandra. Saepe haec et alia dīxistī, neque rēs male nōbīs ēvēnit. Dēmentem (*the mad woman*) removēte. 60

[TRŌJĀNĪ CASSANDRAM ē cōnspectū PRIAMĪ *trahunt.*]

Equum in arcem dūcite.

OMNĒS. Iō triumphe (*hurrah*)!

[*Magnīs clāmōribus equum in mū-* 65 *rōs urbis trahunt.*]

SCAENA SECUNDA. IN ARCE

Equus ligneus ante templum Minervae stat. SINŌN *post columnam latet* (is hiding).

70 SINŌN [*ex latebrīs*[1] *prōdit*]. Graecī ex classe flammās nōndum os-

[1] *from his hiding-place.*

tendērunt. Signum nostrōrum ducum expectō. Sed venit aliquis. Mē in umbrīs (*shadows*) cēlābō.

[*Intrat* CASSANDRA.] 75

CASSANDRA. Vae victīs! Ante oculōs meōs Trōja ruit; sanguinem

Priamī fīliōrumque ejus humī (*on the ground*) effūsum (*poured out*) videō. Expergīsciminī (*awake*), Ō Trōjānī; Graecī in mediā urbe sunt. [*Exit.*]

5 SINŌN. Gaudeō quod nēmō huic īnsānae (*mad woman*) crēdere vult. Ad mare iterum prōspiciam (*I shall look out*). Flamma 10 oritur. Signum ab Agamemnone datur. Statim claustra (*bars*) lignea revellam (*I shall remove*). [*Portam aperit.*] Trōjānī dormiunt. Jam, jam dēscendite, 15 Graecī.

[*Dēscendunt silentiō* MACHĀON,[1] THESSANDRUS, STHENELUS, ACAMĀS, THOĀS, PYRRHUS, MENELĀUS, ULĪXĒS, EPĒUS.]

MENELĀUS. Tibi, Ō Ulīxēs, grā- 20 tiās agimus, quia hoc cōnsilium audāx excōgitāvistī (*you devised*), et Epēō, quia equum ligneum fabricāvit (*he made*). Prīmō ad portam maritimam tendēmus; 25 cum vigilēs occīderimus et portam reclūserimus (*we have opened*), in Trōjānōs dormientēs invādēmus. Silentiō prōgrediminī! Ad portam maritimam! 30

SCAENA TERTIA. IN ĀTRIŌ RĒGIŌ

Āra in mediā aulā (a court) *stat. Ā tergō stat* PRIAMUS *senex; circum rēgem ancillae lacrimant.*

PRIAMUS. Arma mihi date, an- 35 cillae. [*Alia lōrīcam, alia galeam, alia ocreās[2] ferunt.*] Aptāte (*adjust*) lōrīcam, fīgite ocreās,[2] galeam in capite impōnite. Festīnāte (*hasten*)! Nōnne hostēs 40 meam in urbem invāsērunt? Nōnne meōs fīliōs et comitēs et amīcōs caedunt? Sī ego meōs dūcam, etiam nunc dī nōbīs victōriam dabunt.

45 [*Intrat* HECUBA.]

HECUBA. Quid facis, miserrime vir? Cūr tē hīs armīs cingis?

PRIAMUS. Rēx sum; Trōjānōs ad victōriam dūcam. Clipeum me- 50 um mihi date et gladium.

HECUBA. Quō ruis?

[PRIAMUS *gladium clipeumque sūmit.*]

Nōn tālī auxiliō, nec dēfēnsōribus istīs, 55
Tempus eget (*does need*).

PRIAMUS [*gladium tractāre[3] cōnātur*]. Senex nōn possum id facere quod faciēbam juvenis.

HECUBA. Āra auxiliō erit nōbīs; 60 āra nōs omnēs dēfendet, aut ante āram simul moriēmur.

[*Intrat*, PYRRHŌ *īnsequente*, POLĪTĒS, *ūnus ē fīliīs* PRIAMĪ. PYRRHUS POLĪTEM *hastā trāns-* 65 *figit*.]

POLĪTĒS [*cadit*]. Ō meum patrem! Ō Trōjam dēvictam (*vanquished*)!

PRIAMUS. Tibi, quī fīlium ante oculōs patris occīdistī, dī meri- 70 tum praemium dabunt. Pater tuus, Achillēs, nōn contrā senēs

---

[1] For the pronunciation of these names see page 333, note 1.

[2] *greaves*, pieces of armor for the shin.
[3] *to draw.*

et puerōs pugnābat. [*Tēlum in*
Pyrrhum *conjicit, quod ille clipeō*
repellit.]

Pyrrhus. Ad Achillem patrem
5 meum nūntius ībis; illī mea
trīstia (*deplorable*) facta nārrā-
bis. Morere! [*Senem ad āram*
trahit et gladiō occīdit. Exit.]

Hecuba. Lacrimāte, ancillae! Vir
10 meus mortuus est; cecidit rēx
Trōjānōrum. [*Fēminae lacri-*
mant.] Servae (*slaves*) erimus
Graecīs; Agamemnōn nōs vīnc-
tās dēdūcet procul ā nostrā
15 terrā. Ēheu (*alas*)! Ēheu!
[*Intrat* Aenēās.]

Aenēās.
Haec fīnis Priamī fātōrum; hic exi-
tus illum
Sorte tulit, Trōjam incēnsam et prō- 20
lāpsa (*fallen*) videntem
Pergama,[1] tot quondam populīs ter-
rīsque superbum
Rēgnātōrem (*ruler*) Asiae.

Nunc vērō dēvicta est (*is over-* 25
thrown) Trōja. Nōn jam Graecīs
resistere possumus. Jam tempus est mihi et meīs dē salūte
cōnsulere. Senex Anchīsēs et ux-
or mea, Creūsa, et Iūlus domī 30
manent trementēs (*trembling*).
Illūc[2] quam prīmum redībō.
[*Exit.*]

SCAENA QUĀRTA. APUD AENĒAM

Anchīsēs *senex in sellā* (a chair),
35 *capite dēmissō, sedet. Jūxtā*
(near) *eum* Creūsa Iūlum *am-*
plectitur (is embracing). *Omnēs*
ad jānuam spectant.

Creūsa. Vīvitne adhūc Aenēās?

40 Anchīsēs. Graecī sine dubiō meum fīlium occīdērunt; mox hūc
venient nōs caedendī causā.

Creūsa. Nōnne suam uxōrem et
suum fīlium meminit (*does re-*
45 *member*) Aenēās?

Anchīsēs. Cum dē Trōjā agitur,
Aenēam decet[3] suōrum oblīvīscī.[4]

Iūlus. Māter, sonitum (*sound*)
audiō pedum.

50 Anchīsēs. Mors advenit. Nimis
(*too long*) jam vīxī.
[*Jānua pulsātur.*]

Creūsa [*magnō clāmōre*]. Ō! Mortem timeō.

Aenēās [*audītur*]. Ego Aenēās ad- 55
sum. Relaxāte claustra (*release*
the bars).
[Iūlus *jānuam aperiendī causā*
currit.]

Creūsa. Ō vir, gaudeō quod vīvus 60
es.

Iūlus [*laetus*]. Pater vīvus est;
nunc nōs servābit. Nōlī jam
lacrimāre, māter. Nōnne audīs,
ave? Pater nōs omnēs servābit. 65

Anchīsēs. Trōja ruit. Jam vīvere nōlō.

Aenēās. Noster rēx mortuus est.
Corpus inanimum (*lifeless*) ejus
hīs oculīs vīdī. Nihil ā nōbīs hīc 70
fierī potest. Nihil praeter fugam

---

[1] *Pergama* (pėr'ga̤-ma̤), another name
for Troy. See map, page 277.
[2] *there.*

[3] Impersonal verb, *it is fitting.*
[4] With the genitive suōrum—*to forget*
his own family.

nōbīs restat (*is left*). Vōs pa-
rāte, dum tempus habēmus.
Caecum exitum ex urbe nōvī,
quō ex urbe effugere poterimus
5 et usque ad dēsertum Cereris[1]
templum pervenīre.

ANCHĪSĒS. Rēx mortuus est, Trōjānī victī, urbs dēlēta; nōn jam
superesse volō. Discēdite, vōs;
10 mē relinquite. Mortem manū
ipse meā inveniam.

AENĒĀS. Dēdecet[2] patrem suum
relinquere. Nisi tū nōbīscum
fugere volēs, in media arma redī-
15 bō. Valēte, ad mortem eō.

CREŪSA [*ad genua virō*[3] *sē jacit*].
Nōlī nōs relinquere. Ecce, genua
(*knees*) tua amplector (*I em-
brace*); abīre sine mē nōn potes.
20 Aspice fīlium tuum! [IŪLUM *ante*
AENĒAM *pōnit*.] Parce illī!

Sī peritūrus abīs, et nōs rape in omnia
    tēcum;
Sīn aliquam expertus sūmptīs spem
25   pōnis in armīs,
Hanc prīmum tūtāre (*protect*) domum.
    Cui parvus Iūlus,[4]
Cui, pater,[4] et conjūnx quondam tua
    dicta relinquor?

30 AENĒĀS. Apage (*away*), fēmina!
Virī est prō patriā morī.

¹ *of Ceres* (sē'rēz), goddess of agriculture.
² An impersonal verb, *it is shameful.*
³ *at her husband's knees.*
⁴ Supply **relinquitur.**
⁵ With **cervīcī**—*on my shoulders;* here
nostrae is equivalent to **meae.**

CREŪSA. Aspicite caput nostrī fīliī! Flamma ex capite ejus orīrī
vidētur. Quid significat? Hoc
signum nōn nisi rēgiō in capite 35
appāret (*appears*). Rēx erit noster fīlius. Hoc dī signō haud
incertō (*uncertain*) mōnstrāvē-
runt. Nōnne nunc Iūlum vīs
servāre?   40

ANCHĪSĒS. Imperāvērunt dī. Nōbīs faciendum est id quod dī
imperāvērunt.

Jam, jam nūlla mora est; sequor
    et, quā dūcitis, adsum.   45
Dī patriī (*ancestral*), servāte domum,
    servāte nepōtem!
Vestrum hoc augurium, vestrōque
    in nūmine (*divine power*) Trōja est.
Cēdō equidem (*for my part*) nec, 50
    nāte, tibi comes īre recūsō.

AENĒĀS. Ergō (*then*), age, cāre
pater, cervīcī impōnere nostrae.[5]
[*Sē submittit.*]

Ipse subībō umerīs [*patrem in umerōs* 55
    sublevat et surgit[6]], nec mē labor
    iste gravābit;[7]
Quō rēs cumque[8] cadent, ūnum et
    commūne perīclum,[9]
Ūna salūs ambōbus[10] erit.   60

[*Dextram* IŪLĪ *sinistrā prehendit et,*
CREŪSĀ *sequente, exit.*]

⁶ *rises.*
⁷ *will burden.*
⁸ **quō cumque**, *however*, is ordinarily
written as one word.
⁹ For **perīculum.**
¹⁰ Declined like **duo, duae, duo.** See
Gr. S., 22.

EXERCISES

PART ONE

The following exercises may be used at any time after the class has studied page 41 of this book.

I

A. READING:

1. Ōlim cīvēs Rōmānī mūnera pūblica grātīs suscēpērunt. 2. Cōnsul dīxit avum suum in eō proeliō occidisse. 3. Quod explōrātōrēs renūntiāvērunt nūlla frūmenta mātūra in agrīs esse, exercitus in castrīs mānsit. 4. Tempora vetustissima saepe apud nōs laudantur. 5. Neque frūmenta mātūra neque pābulum eō tempore reperīre poterāmus. 6. Ex opīniōne vetustissimā majōrēs Etrūscōrum ōlim in Asiā habitāvērunt. 7. In hōc bellō multī cīvēs occident, et in urbe erit dolor. 8. In eā īnsulā hiemēs sunt mātūrae, aestātēs brevēs. 9. Nōmina eōrum hominum quī hīc occidērunt semper in honōre erunt. 10. Id dōnum mihi grātīs datum est, neque pretium (*price*) postulātum est.

B. TRANSLATION:

1. The enemy despised our small army, but they were soon routed. 2. In that island iron and copper are found. 3. The Belgians, who are brave soldiers, are farthest distant from the refinement of the Province.

PART TWO

The following exercises provide additional drill on the grammatical points which have been taught in the reading on pages 47 ff.

I

(*To be used after* **ferō, volō,** *and* **nōlō** *have been studied. See p. 49.*)

A. READING:

1. Quid vīs, vigil? Cūr tantum clāmōrem tollis? 2. Hostēs appropinquāre videō, et omnēs cīvēs excitāre volō. 3. Puer frātrem quī dormiēbat excitāre volēbat. 4. Dux noster cibum fert, et mox cēnam parābimus. 5. Mīlitēs ex lītore ligna cōnferunt et ignem incendunt. 6. Puerī ex casā arma ferunt et haec arma patrī suō dant. 7. Cīvēs sē fortiter dēfendunt, et auxilium ā mīlitibus fertur. 8. Nēmō in hōc locō diūtius manēre vult. 9. Putāmus vōs inermēs in hōc locō diūtius manēre nōlle.

B. TRANSLATION:

1. The king wishes to return to (**in**) his native land. 2. The soldier brings money from (**ā**) the centurion's father. 3. We are unwilling to send money to these men. 4. The horsemen wish to return to the camp at once. 5. A letter is brought by the slave.

II

(To be used after deponent verbs of the first and second conjugations have been studied. See p. 51.)

A. READING:

1. Hī hominēs auxilium pollicentur.
2. Ille rēx urbem dēfendere nōn cōnātus est. 3. Herculem magnopere mīrantur quod semper fortis est. 4. Herculēs leōnem nōn veritus est. 5. Illī barbarī lātē vagābantur et agrōs gentium fīnitimārum vāstābant. 6. Ōlim Herculēs magnum leōnem necāvit quī in silvā vagābātur. 7. Incōlae ejus regiōnis leōnem magnopere verēbantur. 8. Magnum praemium quod pollicitī erant Herculī dedērunt.

B. TRANSLATION:

1. The man does not try to defend his brother. 2. We cannot promise aid. 3. The Gauls feared punishment because they had killed the lieutenant. 4. The Etruscans wondered at the courage of Horatius. 5. The boys are wandering through the forest.

III

(To be used after deponent verbs of the third and fourth conjugations have been studied. See p. 53.)

A. READING:

1. Hunc cibum partiēmur quod amīcī nostrī ēsuriunt *(are hungry)*. 2. Parvus puer patrem diūtius sequī nōn potest. 3. Tum dux Rōmānus ad collem cum equitibus prōgressus est. 4. In Eurōpam cum amīcīs proficīscimur, et duōs annōs ibi manēbimus. 5. Duo centuriōnēs ex castrīs prōgrediuntur et cum hostibus pugnant. 6. Tē sequēmur quod cōnsilium tuum semper bonum fuit. 7. Herculēs usque ad eum collem prōgressus est ubi Rōma posteā condita est. 8. Equitēs in castrīs mānsērunt, sed aliī mīlitēs profectī sunt. 9. Pācem nōbīs pollicitus es, sed pācem nōn habēmus.

B. TRANSLATION:

1. The cavalry were following the enemy, who had fled from the camp. 2. We shall not advance far from the camp. 3. The leader shares this honor with the soldiers. 4. The Romans set out into the region where the barbarians were laying waste the fields. 5. Many wondered at the courage of Hercules. 6. The leader promised money to the scouts who had set out with the army.

IV

(To be used after active participles have been studied. See pp. 55 and 57.)

A. READING:

1. Puer per agrōs ambulāns serpentem vīdit. 2. Hic sonus īnfantem dormientem excitāvit. 3. Herculēs arcum et sagittās rapuit et animal necātūrus erat. 4. Māter clāmōrem īnfantium in cūnīs *(cradle)* cubantium *(lying)* audīvit et marītum suum excitāvit. 5. Marītus ejus lūmen accēnsūrus erat. 6. Epistulam dē hīs rēbus mox missūrus sum. 7. Hostēs legiōnem venientem vīdērunt et statim fūgērunt. 8.

Haec urbs nōbīs nōn grāta est, et mox ad alium locum cum amīcīs profectūrī sumus.

B. Translation:

Translate the italicized words in the following sentences:

1. We saw the *ship coming* to the land. 2. We hear the voices *of the sail-ors demanding* food. 3. The consul is the brother *of the man standing* on the bridge. 4. I saw a *deer running* through the forest. 5. The *scouts fleeing* from the enemy crossed this river. 6. Your *friends are going to remain* in Europe. 7. The *man is going to kill* the snake. 8. I am *going to send* you money soon.

V

(To be used after the gerund has been studied. See p. 57.)

A. Reading:

1. Tum cupidus manendī in eā urbe cum amīcīs eram. 2. Spem effugiendī nōn habēbāmus. 3. Cōnsul cōpiās coēgit et omnia ad proficīscendum parāvit. 4. In quaerendō repperimus epistulam in mēnsā esse. 5. Hostēs spem vincendī āmīsērunt, et lēgātōs mittent. 6. Multī ex omnibus partibus resistendī causā convēnērunt. 7. Fēmina epistulam legere vult quam fīlius suus mīsit. 8. Dux Rōmānus Gallīs bellum īnfert quod oppida sociōrum expugnāre cōnantur. 9. Centuriō nūntiāvit hostēs in castrīs esse. 10. Hic servus in omnibus rēbus est dīligēns. 11. Nōnō diē omnēs convenient. 12. Dīligēns es, sed tardus es ad discendum. 13. Mārcus cum amīcīs lūdendī cupidus est.

B. Translation:

1. Everything is now prepared for setting out, and the citizens will assemble tomorrow (**crās**). 2. The barbarians, who had no hope of resisting, withdrew into the mountains. 3. These boys have come for the purpose of learning. 4. Why do you (*singular*) wish to go with your friend at this time? 5. We are not desirous of remaining.

VI

(To be used after the dative with special verbs has been studied. See p. 69.)

A. Reading:

1. Herculēs semper glōriae studēbat neque ūlla perīcula timēbat. 2. Haec gēns quae semper bellō studuit mox pācem habēre cupiet. 3. Puerō persuāsī, sed patrī ejus persuādēre nōn potuī. 4. Cūr epistula mea tibi nōn placet? 5. Mīlitēs fortiter hostibus resistēbant et pontem dēfendēbant. 6. Rōmānī Horātiō pārēbunt et in urbem redībunt. 7. Gallīs resistēmus et patriam dēfendēmus. 8. Hoc cōnsilium mihi nōn placet, sed multī probant. 9. Ūna legiō exercituī barbarōrum restitit, neque eōs pābulārī passa est.

B. Translation:

1. This story greatly pleased the men. 2. The boy obeyed his father

and remained in the town.   3. Why
have the Etruscans not resisted the
Romans?   4. Our nation has always
been devoted to peace.   5. You have
persuaded my friends, but you cannot
persuade me.

VII

(To be used after the ablative of respect has been studied.   See p. 73.)

A. Reading:

1. Herculēs, quī rēgem Thēbārum
virtūte praecessit, hostēs nōn timēbat.
2. Incolae ejus terrae ā nōbīs linguā
et īnstitūtīs differunt.   3. Ille vir dux
nōmine erat, sed nūllam potestātem
habēbat.   4. Ulīxēs, quī reliquōs Graecōs sapientiā praecēdit, multa perīcula
effugiet.   5. Incolae inermēs ex omnibus partibus audiendī causā convēnērunt.   6. Ille rēx crūdēlis Herculem
immolātūrus erat.   7. Hostēs in nostrōs mīlitēs ex castrīs prōcēdentēs
impetum fēcērunt.   8. Illī virī quōs
laudātis semper sapientiae studuērunt.
9. Dux noster reliquōs ducēs prūdentiā
et virtūte praecēdit.   10. In colle ad-
versō hostēs aciem īnstrūxerant et
nōstrōs ibi expectābant.

B. Translation:

1. Ulysses surpassed his companions
in wisdom, and he saved them from
many dangers.   2. These men are
good citizens, but they differ in courage.   3. The Alps, which surpass the
other mountains of Europe in height,
can be seen from this place.   4. The
inhabitants of this region waged many
wars with nations which desired (**studēre**) peace.   5. The scouts standing
on the hill saw the enemy, who were
fortifying a camp.   6. The legion
wishes to follow the enemy at once.

VIII

(To be used after infinitives have been studied.   See pp. 77 and 79.)

A. Reading:

1. Invītārī; invītāvisse; invītātus
esse.   2. Audītūrus esse; audīvisse;
audīrī.   3. Cēpisse; dūxisse; mūnīvisse.
4. Mittī; mīsisse; missus esse.   5.
Monērī; monitūrus esse; monuisse.
6. Dīcī; dīxisse; dictūrus esse.   7. Pos-
tulārī; timērī; petī; interficī; mūnīrī.
8. Jūvisse; relīquisse; fūgisse.   9. Da-
tūrus esse; mānsūrus esse; mūnītūrus
esse.   10. Stetisse; dedisse; jēcisse.

B. Translation:

1. To defend; to be defended; to
have defended.   2. To order; to have
ordered; to have been ordered.   3. To
take; to be taken; to be going to take.
4. To have feared; to have been left;
to have been led.   5. To be destroyed;
to have been destroyed; to have destroyed.   6. To have been killed; to
have killed; to have been received.
7. To have called; to be called.

IX

(To be used after place constructions have been studied.   See pp. 71 and 81.)

A. Reading:

1. Legiōnēs nōna et octāva statim
Aquileiā profectae sunt.   2. Cōnsul
post proelium Rōmam cum frātre
vēnit.   3. Herculēs, postquam avēs
interfēcit, Stymphālī nōn diū mānsit.

4. Ulīxēs in Graeciam cum comitibus redīre volēbat. 5. Legiōnēs magnō cum gaudiō ex Galliā discessērunt. 6. Multa bella in Ītaliā gesta sunt, et multae urbēs expugnātae sunt. 7. Priamus, quī Trōjae rēgnābat, multōs fīliōs habēbat. 8. Herculēs aurēs (*ears*) nūntiōrum quī Thēbās missī sunt abscīdit. 9. Fīlius cōnsulis Rōmānī Athēnīs cum comitibus discessit et domum rediit.

B. Translation:

1. My brother has remained in Rome, but his friend has gone to Geneva. 2. The Greeks returned from Troy after the war. 3. I came to the city because I did not wish to remain in Gaul. 4. The consul set out from Italy for Carthage. 5. Our friends wish to return to Athens. 6. The soldiers who had crossed the river did not hear the sound of the trumpet.

X

(*To be used after tense of infinitives in indirect discourse has been studied. See p. 83.*)

A. Reading:

1. Cīvēs putābant Perseum mōnstrum interfectūrum esse. 2. Rēx vidēbat fīliam suam servātam esse. 3. Servus dīxit arcam (*chest*) ad lītus appulsam esse. 4. Poētae dīcunt rēgem mātrem Perseī benignē excēpisse. 5. Scīmus Minervam viam dēmōnstrāvisse. 6. Audīvimus hanc fābulam ā magnō poētā scrīptam esse. 7. Herculēs crēdidit sē leōnem sagittīs necātūrum esse. 8. Māter Perseī dīxit

sē rēgem magnopere timēre. 9. Vīdimus hostēs magnās cōpiās habēre.

B. Translation:

1. Romulus believed that he had founded a great city. 2. The citizens thought that the army would defend the town. 3. We had heard that Horatius defended the bridge bravely. 4. The soldier said that his brother would send the money at once. 5. The sailor announced that he had found food on the island.

XI

(*To be used after the subjunctive in* cum *concessive clauses has been studied. See p. 85.*)

A. Reading:

1. Cum frāter tuus vir honestus esset, tamen paucōs amīcōs habēbat. 2. Cum urbem nōn expugnārēmus, tamen agrōs vāstāvimus. 3. Cum viātor viam nōn facile reperīre posset, tamen sine timōre prōcēdēbat. 4. Putābāmus Helvētiōs sine injūriā trānsitūrōs esse. 5. Herculēs intellēxit perīculum in eō locō esse magnum. 6. Nūntiātum est hostēs cōpiās suās ex

castrīs ēdūxisse. 7. Nūntius dīxit hanc esse causam veniendī. 8. Multās hōrās in legendō cōnsūmpsī. 9. Cum haec regiō longē abesset, tamen sine timōre octāvō diē profectī sumus.

B. Translation:

1. Although I often warned you, still you remained in this dangerous place. 2. Although the legion was able to defend the city, the citizens

were frightened. 3. We are not desirous of setting out with the messenger. 4. Although the barbarians were few, still they fought bravely. 5. We are going to send money to our allies.

XII

(To be used after the ablative and genitive of description have been studied. See p. 87.)

A. Reading:

1. Fīliae Atlantis erant praestantissimā fōrmā. 2. Hic centuriō erat magnā auctōritāte apud mīlitēs. 3. Mūrus erat magnā altitūdine, et oppidum tūtum erat. 4. Mīlitēs, quī iter sex diērum fēcerant, dēfessī erant. 5. Ille dux erat magnā audāciā, et hostēs eum timēbant. 6. Ulīxēs, dē quō multa scrīpta sunt, erat vir summae prūdentiae. 7. Legiōnēs nostrae in eō proeliō magnā virtūte pugnāvērunt. 8. Herculēs et comitēs ejus diū expectābant, sed Amāzones impetum nōn fēcērunt. 9. Jāsōn, quī erat vir summā virtūte, statim negōtium suscēpit. 10. Atlās, quī caelum umerīs sustinēbat, erat vir ingentī magnitūdine corporis. 11. Eratne ille rēx fortis an ignāvus?

B. Translation:

1. The task which Jason undertook was (one) of great difficulty. 2. We know that we have a leader of the greatest wisdom. 3. The king of Thessaly was a man of great cruelty. 4. The Roman centurions were always men of great courage. 5. The queen of the Amazons was (a woman) of great boldness. 6. Although the mountains were high, Hercules decided to cross. 7. The king thought that this task would be very difficult.

XIII

*(To be used after **cum** causal clauses have been studied. See p. 89.)*

A. Reading:

1. Cum magnae cōpiae hostium venīrent, ex eō locō discessimus. 2. Cum legiō ā fortī centuriōne dūcerētur, hostēs repulsī sunt. 3. Cum (see p. 85) perīculum esset tantum, tamen nēmō in hīs locīs tēla gerēbat. 4. Hic puer īrātus est et saxa in (*at*) aliōs puerōs jactūrus est. 5. Cum nōn bene regerēs, ex urbe expulsus es. 6. Cum pāstor nūlla tēla gereret, sē dēfendere nōn poterat. 7. Reliquī hostēs fūgērunt quod crūdēlitātem Rōmānōrum timēbant. 8. Cūr hī captīvī tantam fīdūciam habent? 9. Sagitta in scūtō centuriōnis fīxa est. 10. Mīlitēs statim discēdendī ex eō locō cupidī erant. 11. Gigās nōn arbitrātus est Herculem flūmen trānsitūrum esse.

B. Translation:

1. Since we desired peace, we sent envoys. 2. Since the soldiers were assembling from all sides, we did not fear the enemy. 3. Since you had many companions, you were safe. 4. Since the wall was high, the enemy did not dare to attack the city. 5. Although you saw our danger, still you did not send aid. 6. We know that we have a leader of great courage.

XIV

(To be used after clauses of result have been studied.   See p. 93.)

A. READING:

1. Ille vir erat tam benignus ut omnēs eum amārent.   2. Exercitus noster erat tantus ut hostēs nōn timērēmus.   3. Stultitia ejus hominis erat tanta ut nūllōs amīcōs habēret. 4. Ille mōns erat tam altus ut ab urbe nostrā facile vidērētur.   5. Eōdem diē nūntiī ad rēgem rediērunt et dīxērunt exercitum in magnō perīculō esse. 6. Nūntius dīxit sē tōtam rem expositūrum esse.   7. Sciō vōs hunc virum saepe vīdisse.   8. Īnstitūta lēgēsque Rōmānōrum laudāta sunt.   9. Puer tam prūdēns erat ut ab omnibus laudārētur.   10. Graecī cum mīlle nāvibus Trōjam profectī sunt.   11.

Cum puer patrī nōn pāreat, nūllum praemium eī datum est.

B. TRANSLATION:

1. The picture was so beautiful that it was praised by all.   2. The river was so wide that we did not dare to cross.   3. The danger was so great that the citizens remained in the city. 4. Our allies had so great an army that they did not fear the enemy.   5. Perseus was a man of great boldness. 6. Since Atlas was the father of the nymphs, he thought that he would easily persuade them.   7. Although the giant was strong, still he could not resist me.

XV

(To be used after descriptive clauses of situation have been studied.   See p. 95.)

A. READING:

1. Cum pāstor pecudēs suās in montēs ēgisset, latrōnēs eum aggressī sunt.   2. Cum latrō praedam peteret, ā mīlitibus captus est.   3. Cum Rōmulus urbem suam condidisset, multī ad eum locum vēnērunt.   4. Cum puer nāvem vīdisset, ad urbem properāvit.   5. Pater tuus tam benignus erat ut multōs amīcōs habēret.   6. Cum hostēs audīrēmus, statim ad mūrōs properāvimus.   7. Haec animālia tam fera erant ut nōn facile caperentur.   8. Cum frāter tuus multōs librōs habēret, tamen nōn saepe legere

cupiēbat.   9. Ille vir rēx factus est cum frātrem suum expulisset.

B. TRANSLATION:

1. When the robber had seen the shepherds, he called his companions. 2. When we had withdrawn from the town, the enemy made an attack. 3. Romulus was so brave that he did not fear the robbers.   4. Although the enemy had been seen in this place, still the farmers did not leave their fields.   5. Since this city had a high wall, we were not able to capture it easily.

XVI

(To be used after indirect questions have been studied.   See p. 103.)

A. READING:

1. Avus Rōmulī quaesīvit ubi pāstor eōs puerōs invēnisset.   2. Ignōrābā-

mus quis in eō locō hanc pecūniam relīquisset.   3. Cum multās terrās pulchrās vīdissēmus, tamen in patriam redīre volēbāmus. 4. Quaesīvistī cūr in eō locō manērēmus. 5. Cum Rōmulus in Palātiō stāret, duodecim vulturēs (*vultures*) vīdit. 6. Rēx tam crūdēlis erat ut īnfantēs interficere cuperet. 7. Intellēximus ā quō illa epistula missa esset. 8. Cum ea urbs ab hostibus capta esset, multae fēminae et multī virī interfectī sunt. 9. Multī in eō locō interiērunt.

B. TRANSLATION:

1. The citizens asked why the consul had not sent soldiers. 2. We did not know (**ignōrō**) by whom this town had been founded. 3. When I was on the hill, I saw a fire in the forest. 4. Since your friend had often praised this picture, I gave it to him. 5. We knew who had given a name to this city.

XVII

(To be used after expressions of purpose have been studied. See p. 105.)

A. READING:

1. Perseus ad īnsulam rediit ut mātrem reperīret. 2. Herculēs exercitum condūxit ut cum hostibus bellum gereret. 3. Rōmulus novam urbem mūnīvit nē ab hostibus expugnārētur. 4. Patrēs nostrī mare trānsiērunt ut in terrā līberā habitārent. 5. Cum castra mūnīrentur, Gallī cōpiās nostrās aggressī sunt. 6. Legiō ita celeriter appropinquāvit ut barbarī cōpiās condūcere nōn possent. 7. Hī virī mare nōn trānsiērunt ut dīvitiās reperīrent. 8. In urbem vestram nōn vēnimus ut injūriās acciperēmus. 9. Vīgintī mīlitēs relictī sunt quī captīvōs custōdīrent. 10. Explōrātōrēs bīnī ex castrīs profectī sunt.

B. TRANSLATION:

1. The Gauls collected an army to defend (that they might defend) their native country. 2. We fled that we might not be captured. 3. Other legions were sent that the town might be defended. 4. The barbarians crossed the river that they might lay waste our fields. 5. We had so few friends in that city that we were not happy.

XVIII

(To be used after the dative with compounds has been studied. See p. 105.)

A. READING:

1. Dux quī oppidō praeest prūdēns est. 2. Cīvēs alium ducem exercituī praeficient. 3. Vir callidus huic negōtiō praefectus erat. 4. Rōmānīs bellum nōn īnferimus, sed nōbīs Rōmānī bellum īnferunt. 5. Sextus equitibus praeest quī hostēs sequuntur. 6. Omnēs eum ducem ōderant quī Siciliae praefectus erat. 7. Peliās fīlium frātris ex urbe mīsit ut is vītam āmitteret. 8. Mēdēa dēmōnstrāvit quō in locō Jāsōn vellus aureum invenīret. 9. Bellum huic gentī īnferēmus quod agrī nostrī vāstātī sunt. 10. Germānī sociīs Rōmānōrum bellum intulērunt, sed victī sunt et in patriam redīre coāctī sunt.

B. TRANSLATION:

1. The lieutenant who has been placed in command of the ships is a

brave man. 2. Jason, who was in command of the Argonauts, was a prudent leader. 3. We do not wish to make war on your allies. 4. We have heard that the Amazons made war on the inhabitants of that region. 5. Jason set out into the forest with Medea. 6. Medea knew that the golden fleece was guarded by a dragon, but she did not fear the dragon.

XIX

(To be used after noun clauses of desire have been studied. See p. 107.)

A. READING:

1. Cōnsul hortātus est ut major exercitus mitterētur. 2. Cōnsul plēbī persuāsit ut iste homō propter perfidiam interficerētur. 3. Imperātor mīlitēs hortātus est nē hostēs timērent. 4. Centuriō mīlitibus imperāvit nē sine armīs extrā mūnītiōnēs īrent. 5. Quaesīvī quis mēcum flūmen trānsīre vellet. 6. Cum explōrātor montem trānsīret, equitēs hostium vīdit. 7. Quis huic legiōnī praeest?

B. TRANSLATION:

1. The general commanded the soldiers (*dative*) to remain (that they remain) in camp. 2. No one could persuade me to go (*not infinitive*) outside the fortifications. 3. I urged you not to fear the common people. 4. When you wished to destroy the city, you found that there was a brave consul. 5. The leader persuaded the citizens not to surrender (that they should not surrender) their arms.

XX

(To be used after the ablative absolute has been studied. See p. 109.)

A. READING:

1. Hīs labōribus cōnfectīs, Herculēs in Graeciam rediit. 2. Hostibus victīs, exercitus in urbem reductus est. 3. Cōnsul, exercitū coāctō, cum hostibus bellum gessit. 4. Epistulā acceptā, puer statim domum profectus est. 5. Rēx tam ignāvus erat ut urbem contrā hostēs dēfendere nōn audēret. 6. Cum Graecī ex Asiā profectī essent, magna tempestās coorta est. 7. Omnibus rēbus comparātīs, Jāsōn cum comitibus ā portū discessit. 8. Dux paucōs diēs morātus est ut sociōs condūceret. 9. Cum magna tempestās coorta esset, tamen nautae in portum redīre nōlēbant. 10. Dux cīvibus persuādēre ut in urbe manērent nōn poterat. 11. Hasta tua brevis nōn est ūtilis.

B. TRANSLATION:

1. Collecting soldiers (Soldiers having been collected), Hercules defeated the enemy. 2. After the capture of the city (The city having been captured), the king was killed. 3. On seeing the enemy (The enemy having been seen), the soldiers seized their arms. 4. Hearing the sound (The sound having been heard), the soldiers ran to the gates of the city. 5. After the founding of the city, a king was elected.

XXI

(To be used after the future passive participle and the dative of agent have been studied. See p. 111.)

A. READING:

1. Conditor (*founder*) urbis nostrae nōbīs laudandus est. 2. Dīvitiās habēre vīs, sed labor tibi nōn vītandus est. 3. Remus frātrī suō nōn interficiendus erat. 4. Ponte ruptō, flūmen lātum trānsīre nōn poterāmus. 5. Eum ducem multōs comitēs arcessere oportēbat. 6. Jāsōn rēgī in Asiam nōn mittendus erat. 7. Cum in eō locō morārentur, ūnum ē comitibus āmīsērunt. 8. Is quī oppidō praeerat nūntiōs ad Caesarem bis mīsit. 9. Ille rēx bene intellēxit cūr Jāsōn vēnisset.

B. TRANSLATION:

1. The city ought to be defended by the citizens. 2. This book ought to be read by boys and girls. 3. The ships ought to be sent to this harbor. 4. We know that your companions have undertaken this task. 5. We did not know why they had undertaken this task.

XXII

(To be used after the gerundive has been studied. See p. 113.)

A. READING:

1. Haec fēmina spem fīliae suae videndae habet. 2. Ad eās rēs cōnficiendās hominēs missī sunt. 3. Barbarī lapidibus jaciendīs multōs vulnerāvērunt. 4. Sabīnī pācis petendae causā lēgātōs mīsērunt. 5. Fratrem tuum domum redīre vult. 6. Lēgātus diūtius Genavae (Gr. S., 91) manēre nōlēbat. 7. Agrī nostrī nōn vāstandī sunt. 8. Taurīs jūnctīs, Jāsōn agrum arāre coepit. 9. Bellī gerendī semper cupidī fuistis. 10. Hae gentēs īnstitūtīs lēgibusque (Gr. S., 86) differunt, sed sociī sunt. 11. Cum hoc negōtium difficile sit, tamen nōbīs suscipiendum est. 12. Caesar bīna castra mūnīvit et vigilēs posuit. 13. In oppidō dīripiendō mīlitēs tardātī sunt.

B. TRANSLATION:

1. By throwing javelins the Romans drove back the enemy. 2. The cohort was left for the purpose of defending the bridge. 3. A leader has been chosen for accomplishing these things. 4. We have no hope of defending the city.

XXIII

(To be used after the anticipatory subjunctive has been studied. See p. 115.)

A. READING:

1. Legiōnēs pervēnērunt priusquam oppidum caperētur. 2. Caesar expectāre cōnstituit dum reliquae nāvēs appropinquārent. 3. Cum frātrem meum offendissēs (*you had offended*), tamen pecūniam ad tē mīsit. 4. Castrīs captīs, cōpiae hostium dispersae sunt. 5. Iter in fīnēs hostium fēcimus priusquam cōpiās condūxissent. 6. Multī vēnērunt novae urbis videndae causā. 7. Equitēs profectī sunt ad

frūmentum petendum. 8. Explōrātōrēs quō in locō hostēs castra pōnerent
nūntiāvērunt. 9. Comitēs Jāsonis
tardī erant et diū in silvā vagātī sunt.

B. TRANSLATION:

1. The slaves escaped from this
place before the legions arrived (should

arrive). 2. We waited until the cavalry crossed (should cross) the river.
3. We fortified the camp before the
Gauls made (should make) an attack.
4. I warned you not to remain in that
dangerous place. 5. Caesar did not
wait until the lands (fields) of the
allies were (should be) laid waste.

XXIV

*(To be used after the dative of purpose and the dative of reference have
been studied. See p. 119.)*

A. READING:

1. Hic liber mihi dōnō missus est.
2. Caesar statim legiōnem subsidiō
oppidānīs mīsit. 3. Cōnsilium tuum
nōbīs semper auxiliō fuit. 4. Lēgātus
duās cohortēs castrīs praesidiō relīquit.
5. Explōrātor tam callidus erat ut
hostēs eum nōn vidērent. 6. In silvā
manēbāmus nē hostēs nōs vidērent.
7. Cum flūmen lātum et altum esset,
in hōc locō trānsīre nōn cōnātī sunt.
8. Duābus legiōnibus cōnscrīptīs; Caesar montēs trānsiit. 9. Lēgātī ex
multīs terrīs Genavam profectī sunt.

10. Propter lātitūdinem flūminis, hostēs trānsīre nōn poterant.

B. TRANSLATION:

1. Labienus at once sent the cavalry
as aid (for aid) to the town. 2. The
eighth and ninth legions were sent
as aid to our allies, whose towns were
being burned. 3. We have come as
reinforcements to you, because your
nation ought not to be defeated.
4. The friendship of the Romans was
(for) a great help to this leader. 5.
We knew who wrote this letter.

XXV

(To be used after clauses of fear have been studied. See p. 125.)

A. READING:

1. Senex timēbat nē fīlius suus vulnerārētur. 2. Verēmur nē bellum inter hās gentēs oriātur. 3. Cīvēs verēbantur ut dux satis magnās cōpiās
habēret. 4. Cum omnia (*all things*)
jam parāta sint, ancorās tollēmus.
5. Hic puer inter tālēs hominēs nōn
ēducandus est. 6. Quaerō quis meum
librum in hōc locō relīquerit. 7. Cum
nūllum auxilium missum sit, castra
diūtius dēfendere nōn possumus. 8.
Cum arma habeātis, cūr illōs hostēs

timētis? 9. Rēx nūntium mīsit quī
Jāsonem ad rēgiam vocāret.

B. TRANSLATION:

1. The Gauls were afraid the Roman
army would remain in that part of
Gaul. 2. The general feared that his
army would be defeated by the barbarians. 3. Do you know who sent
this letter? 4. The Germans were
afraid the Gauls would cross the river
with the Romans. 5. Labienus sent
one legion as reinforcements to the
camp.

XXVI

(To be used at any time after p. 125.)

A. Reading:

1. Mīlitēs bīna pīla ferēbant, neque temere ad hostēs appropinquābant. 2. Barbarī, quī hastīs longīs et acūtīs pugnābant, gladiōs et scūta nostrōrum contemnēbant. 3. Ē nāvibus in eō locō ēgredī nōn commodum vidēbātur, quod hostēs locum ēditum occupāverant, quī nōn longē aberat. 4. Praefectus nōn dignus est quī praemium accipiat. 5. Legiō nōna in Gallōs impetum fēcit et eōs dispersit. 6. Exitum occultum ex oppidō invēnimus. 7. Helvētiī respondērunt majōrēs suōs numquam obsidēs dedisse; hujus reī Rōmānōs esse testēs. 8. Virtūs mīlitum singulāris erat, neque quisquam propter altitūdinem aquae tardus erat. 9. Ille rēx adeō erat crūdēlis et vehemēns ut nūllōs amīcōs habēret. 10. Inter patrēs hōrum hominum erat hospitium vetustum. 11. Hoc tibi grātīs pollicitus sum.

B. Translation:

1. The deer was swift, but Hercules at last captured it. 2. Caesar noticed the dust, and he feared that the enemy had made an attack on the legion. 3. The Romans and the Germans had set out to the same place, but the Romans were delayed on account of the storms. 4. On account of the recent battle the townspeople were frightened, and they entrusted themselves and their possessions to Caesar. 5. The Germans were unwilling either to make reparation to the Gauls or (**vel . . . vel**) to restore the hostages. 6. The city was safe because the magistrates were brave and careful.

PART THREE

The following exercises, which are based on the vocabulary and constructions of the Latin text in this book, may be used from time to time as the teacher may direct.

I

1. The kinsmen of Regulus urged him to remain (urged that he remain) at Rome. 2. The king persuaded his son-in-law (**gener, -ī**) to send (that he send) archers and slingers. 3. It happened that we had no horses. 4. It resulted that the scouts were not able to approach the gate (*dative*) of the town. 5. The messengers entreated that aid be sent at once. 6. It happened that the general had come without a shield. 7. The river was so wide that we did not try to cross. 8. The cohort withdrew when the Belgians had made an attack. 9. The citizens did not think this man was brave. 10. The Etruscans tried to regain the hill and the camp.

II

1. There was no one in the city who did not fear war. (Gr. S., 112.) 2. There were some (**nōnnūllī**) who wished to move the camp at once.

(Gr. S., 112.) 3. The women feared that their children would wander in the forest. 4. We are afraid that our country does not have a sufficiently large army. 5. There were many who trusted this leader. (Gr. S., 112.) 6. I am afraid that the boy is ill.

7. We urge that you open the gate. 8. It happened that there were no old men in this town. 9. I do not think your friend is worthy of trust. 10. I do not understand why this place is not safe. 11. Will the leader send infantry or cavalry to the allies?

III

1. The enemy sent messengers, some in one direction (**pars**), others in another.* 2. Some birds are found in one region, others in another. 3. Some praised one tribune, others another. 4. The ships of the enemy were injured because they could not flee. 5. We were persuaded to buy (Gr. S., 107) a large number of horses. 6. The leaders are young men, but they will be obeyed. 7. There are some who do not see these crimes. 8. The camp-followers were afraid that the soldiers would close the gates. 9. The scout said that his faithful dog was his only companion.

IV

1. Do you not see the rampart by which the camp is fortified? 2. Did the soldiers hear the shouting of the enemy who were ascending the hill? 3. The cavalry and the camp-followers were about to cross the river. 4. I wish to see my friends every day, because I am about to depart from the city. 5. This victory does not seem incredible, does it? 6. I am about to announce to you a great loss. 7. On account of our recent victory, the enemy has come to seek peace. 8. When the army had crossed the river, a storm arose. 9. On account of the nature of the place, the soldiers did not dare to remain outside the rampart.

V

1. This country (land) was called Gaul. 2. Orgetorix had been chosen leader of the Helvetians. 3. The centurion was killed by an arrow. 4. I shall defend the leader with a sword. 5. The soldiers will defend the centurion with weapons. 6. The Helvetians killed our soldiers with arrows. 7. The leader of the Helvetians was killed by the weapons of the soldiers. 8. The Germans fought with swords and arrows. 9. The centurion was chosen leader of the soldiers. 10. The brave centurion killed the leader of the Germans with a sword.

VI

1. The friend of Marcus the consul was a brave man. 2. The city which you see is Rome. 3. The father of this centurion was called Marcus. 4. The Germans have killed the brave centurion, the leader of the soldiers.

* See page 236, note 7.

5. The city in which you live is a beautiful city.   6. I shall be called the father of my country (**patria**) because I have defended the citizens. 7. The father of this citizen who has been elected consul is a brave man.

8. The soldiers whose leader you see will defend the city with weapons. 9. The citizen who was killed by the arrow of the Helvetian was a friend of the centurion. 10. The gate of the camp was defended (**mūnīre**) by a large beam.

VII

1. In our country (**patria**) are many beautiful towns and cities.   2. The Romans founded cities in Africa and in Asia.   3. The Greeks waged wars in Sicily and captured cities in that island. 4. Wars were waged by the Romans in Gaul and in Spain.   5. Many Gauls were captured by the soldiers whom the centurion led.   6. The consul, by whom the army was led, was a brave man.   7. The city will be defended by the Gauls, who have a brave leader. 8. I shall remain in the island in which my friends live. 9. We saw many cities of Spain, your native country.

VIII

1. The leader returned from Spain with the army. 2. The consul's father remained in Italy with the citizens. 3. The Romans surpassed the Gauls in knowledge of war.   4. These nations differ from each other (**inter sē**) in language and in customs.   5. The language of the Gauls and the language of the Germans were not the same.   6. The customs of the Gauls were sometimes praised by the Romans.   7. The citizens will be defended by the soldiers who have remained in the city.   8. The Gauls do not surpass our soldiers in courage. 9. The citizens praised the courage of the soldiers who had defended the city.

IX

1. The Gauls used long swords and large shields.   2. The Romans gained possession of the camp of the enemy, but many Romans were killed.   3. We returned by the same road, and we crossed the river with the soldiers. 4. The legion will set out by this road and will avoid the enemy.   5. The leader of the enemy did not surpass the consul in knowledge of war.   6. The Romans waged war with the Gauls and the Germans.   7. The Gauls and Romans did not use the same weapons. 8. The road by which the Helvetians set out was not easy.   9. We remained in the town, but our friends set out to (**ad**) the army.   10. We had been with our friends in the forest the day before.

X

1. After the consul had been killed (The consul having been killed), the army fled.   2. In the same year my brother and your father were in Spain. 3. When the city had been captured (The city having been captured), the

citizens did not defend themselves.
4. We were in great danger on that
day. 5. The soldiers who had been
sent crossed the river by a bridge.
6. The sword which the leader of the
enemy used was long and heavy.
7. We shall not return to your city
this year. 8. Another letter was sent
on the same day. 9. After sending a
messenger (A messenger having been
sent), the consul returned to (into)
the camp. 10. It is of importance that
you remain. 11. The leader decided
to measure out grain to the soldiers.

XI

1. A river separates your country
from Gaul, but this river has many
bridges. 2. The messenger saw the
danger and returned with great speed.
3. The mountains which separate Spain
from Gaul are high. 4. The enemy
defended their country with great
courage, but they were defeated by
the Romans. 5. On receiving your
letter (Your letter having been received), I set out at once. 6. The
river is wide, but we shall cross without
danger. 7. The wide sea separates our
country from our enemies. 8. On
hearing the shout (The shout having
been heard), I returned without delay.
9. Caesar set out into Gaul by another road.

XII

1. The Gauls gave hostages to the
Romans. 2. Hostages were given the
Romans by the Gauls. 3. The arrival of Caesar's army was not pleasing to the Helvetians. 4. Why did
you say this (*pl.*) to your brother?
5. This leader of the Gauls was
friendly to the Romans. 6. After the
bridge was made (*abl. abs.*), the
legion was led across. 7. Because the
enemy fight with great courage, we
cannot capture the city. 8. We were
not able to gain possession of the
baggage. 9. I shall show this letter
to your father. 10. The captive whom
we were leading into camp shed tears.

XIII

1. The letter that you sent will not
please your father. 2. We did not
try to persuade these men. 3. I have
many friends, and I am happy in
this town. 4. The army did not
have a large supply of grain. 5. The
enemy were brave, but they could
not resist our army. 6. Our leader is
wise, and we shall obey him. 7. You
do not dare to say this to your father.
8. This man has great influence in the
city. 9. The country (**patria**) is dear
to all the citizens. 10. The camp had
been placed on a downward-sloping hill.

XIV

1. The cavalry had been sent as
aid (for aid) to the town. 2. Our
army set out as reinforcements (for
reinforcements) to the Gauls. 3. The
friendship of his brother was a protection for this man. 4. The cohorts

were sent as a protection for the bridge. 5. Many Gauls favored the Romans and helped them. 6. The victory of the army pleased the citizens. 7. This man has four sons and two daughters. 8. When the town had been burned (*abl. abs.*), the citizens fled. 9. The Helvetians will resist the Germans bravely and will defend their native country. 10. The consul set out from Rome with the army. 11. The Helvetians were foraging and laying waste the lands of the Haeduans.

XV

1. This mountain ought to be seized by the soldiers. 2. The camp ought to be moved by the Romans. 3. Vercingetorix was then in command of the Gauls. 4. Who had been in command of the cavalry? 5. The men ought to change their plans. 6. Caesar placed the lieutenant in command of the legion. 7. The cavalry were not an aid (for an aid) to the Romans. 8. This plan did not please the citizens who had remained in the city. 9. The king of the Germans had one son. 10. Catching sight of the men (*abl. abs.*) on the mountain, I fled with great speed.

XVI

1. Part of the enemy bravely withstood the attack of our men. 2. Many of the Gauls were killed in flight on that day. 3. The swords of the Romans were not long. 4. Your father, who is the wisest of our citizens, wrote this letter. 5. This boy ought not to ask for money (Money ought not to be asked for, etc.). 6. We were not able to gain possession of the town because the Gauls had large forces. 7. The large shield was a hindrance (*dative*) to the soldier in flight. 8. The Gauls did not make war on the Romans. 9. The lieutenant was in command of the legion which had remained in camp. 10. You have been placed in command of this province. 11. This poet never praises the common people.

XVII

1. We have no fear of treachery, and we shall remain in the town. 2. The Helvetians do not wish to wage war, but they have no hope of peace. 3. Our allies were (men) of great courage, who gave us aid. 4. The consul's brother was then (a man) of great influence in the city. 5. I had no hope of a large reward. 6. My friend has found part of the money which you lost. 7. The brave soldier did not ask for a reward of this kind. 8. The lieutenant ought to leave the legion in this town. 9. The Gauls had long spears. 10. The consul received our congratulations.

XVIII

1. One of your friends has been in Italy this year. 2. Two of the Helvetians came into our camp in the night. 3. Three thousand soldiers were sent into Gaul with the general. 4. Part of the hostages remained in

the city with my friends. 5. Two thousand Gauls escaped from that battle, but many were captured. 6. The Gauls were (men) of great stature, and they scorned the Romans. 7. The storm injured the bridge which the enemy had made. 8. After this war many thousand slaves were sent to Italy. 9. We are desirous of peace, but we will defend our country.

XIX

1. We waged war with the enemy for six years. 2. The boy has walked many miles, and he seems tired. 3. I shall remain with my sister in the town four months. 4. The centurion led the soldiers across the River Aisne. 5. Our forces were led* across the Rhone by the tribune of the soldiers. 6. Two of the scouts were captured by the enemy. 7. Many thousand Belgians were in arms, and a large army was being collected. 8. Dumnorix was a man of great influence in that part of Gaul. 9. This nation is desirous of war on account of the folly of its leader.

XX

1. The whole army will hasten to our camp. 2. Two new legions have been sent into Gaul. 3. My friend wishes to return to Rome this summer. 4. The general set out to the province with our army. 5. After the war all the soldiers returned home. 6. The Greeks set out to Troy with large forces. 7. Two cohorts of the third legion were led across the Rhine by the lieutenant. 8. The camp of our allies extended for many miles. 9. One of the centurions was wounded twice by arrows. 10. The embassy will return to Geneva in the winter, but they will accomplish nothing.

XXI

1. The Romans who are returning from Britain will not delay at Marseilles. 2. We remained at home to-day on account of the storm. 3. The Gauls set out from Rome at night, but they were arrested by the praetors. 4. Caesar returned from Aquileia with three legions. 5. Many who lived in Rome had never seen an enemy. 6. This king had no authority in the kingdom, but he had loyal friends. 7. He set out from Saguntum in the third watch with part of the army. 8. The soldiers who are in Saguntum will not surrender their arms. 9. The rest of the soldiers delayed in the camp four days. 10. Ariovistus was a violent and cruel king.

XXII

1. The citizens had no hope of escaping, because the city was surrounded. 2. The Helvetians prepared everything for (ad) departure (for departing). 3. The Romans were desirous of destroying the town because the inhabitants were treacherous. 4. In crossing the river we lost a few

men. 5. We did not come into Gaul for the purpose of (**causā**) plundering. 6. These envoys have come for the purpose of seeking peace. 7. You will not avoid danger by delaying.

8. Sextus returned from Marseilles to Italy with a few companions. 9. We shall remain in Geneva a few days with friends. 10. This king has no hope of returning to the city.

XXIII

1. Having encouraged the soldiers, Caesar gave the signal. 2. The scouts returned to the camp with great speed. 3. The enemy, having crossed (**trāns-gredior**) the river, made an attack on the legion. 4. For these reasons (**dē** *with abl.*) we cannot remain longer in your city. 5. Having followed the enemy for three days, the soldiers were tired. 6. We have lost hope of conquering, and we shall return home.

7. The barbarians fought with great courage and withstood our attack for a long time. 8. Having set out with great hope, the Helvetians were unwilling to return to their own territories. 9. All my friends have now departed, and I am not desirous of remaining. 10. We heard the voices of the enemy, and we were frightened. 11. This river is deep and wide, and the man does not dare to cross.

XXIV

1. The soldiers defended themselves, but many were killed. 2. The Gauls who came to Rome brought (**addūcere**) with them an interpreter. 3. The soldier who jumped down from the wall injured himself (see p. 69) with his sword. 4. My book is new, but your book is old. 5. Our cities have many beautiful buildings, which you will see. 6. Your arrival will be a pleasure

(see p. 69) to your father and to your friends. 7. The ships, having set out from Gaul, could not find a good harbor. 8. Our ancestors crossed the sea with great danger. 9. They came to this land because they were desirous of finding liberty. 10. Many have come to our country (**patria**) from other lands, because they also love liberty.

XXV

1. The scout said that the enemy were fleeing from their towns and villages. 2. A messenger reported that the cavalry of the Belgians were in sight. 3. Your friends believe you will be safe in this city. 4. I knew the letter had not been sent. 5. You say that Rome had many famous writers. 6. This poet says that part of the Trojans came from Asia into Italy after the overthrow of Troy. 7. We have heard that a city was

founded in Africa by the Phoenicians. 8. Wise men are praised by others, but they do not praise themselves. 9. My friends will never be your friends. 10. No one believed you would come, because your brother reported that you were ill. 11. The queen could not persuade the leader of the Trojans to remain longer in Africa. 12. Will the leader send infantry or cavalry? 13. This place has many conveniences.

XXVI

1. Since we can accomplish nothing here, we will return home. 2. Since you often praise this picture, I will give it to you. 3. The river is so deep that the men do not dare to cross. 4. The wall was so strong that the enemy did not try to capture the city. 5. We have heard that our ancestors founded a small town here. 6. The consul knew that the Gauls would set out in the night. 7. Since you are happy in this city, why do you not remain here? 8. The noise in the street was so great that I did not hear your voice. 9. The number of the enemy is so large that we have no hope of resisting. 10. The consul was praised with very generous words.

XXVII

1. When the enemy had surrendered their arms, they could not defend themselves. 2. Although I remained in Italy three months, I· never saw the king. 3. When we arrived in the city, we sent a messenger to your sister. 4. Although I have received your letter, I have not read it. 5. Since the soldiers had set out without weapons, they were in great danger. 6. The town was so large that we could not easily find our friend's house. 7. When I had crossed the lake, I arrived at a small village. 8. Although the praetor was an honorable man, still few praised him. 9. I think the citizens will assemble if it is convenient.

XXVIII

1. We walked so many miles yesterday that we were tired. 2. When the lieutenant had received the letter, he hastened to the camp at once. 3. Since your mother does not wish to go, I will invite your sister. 4. We did not know that the city had been taken. 5. Although the enemy fled into the swamps, they were finally captured. 6. The towns of Gaul were sometimes destroyed by the Romans. 7. The night is so dark that we cannot see the way. 8. The tribune who was in command of the legion was not a good leader. 9. The man said that he could send the money at once.

XXIX

1. Our ancestors did not cross the sea to find (that they might find) wealth. 2. They left their native country that they might not lose their liberty. 3. Caesar sent one cohort to fortify (which should fortify) this hill. 4. The boy worked energetically (**ācriter**) that he might not lose a reward. 5. A scout was sent to watch (who should watch) the camp of the enemy. 6. We have returned in order to see our friends again. 7. The messenger said he had seen the enemy on the top of the mountain. 8. When the ships had been built (made), the soldiers set out to the harbor. 9. One of the soldiers had left his helmet and shield in his tent.

XXX

1. Caesar returned to (**in**) Italy in order to collect a larger army.   2. I asked why the letter had not been sent.   3. The Romans made a bridge in order that they might cross the river more quickly.   4. The scouts will be able to see in what direction (part) the Gauls are marching (making a march).   5. One cohort was left in camp to defend the baggage.

6. The soldiers jumped down from the ships that they might not be thought cowardly.   7. Although your city is large, it does not have many good citizens.   8. The soldiers were so crowded that they could not use their swords.   9. Will this cohort follow the enemy or remain in camp?   10. On account of his insults, this man was driven from the city.

GRAMMATICAL SUMMARY

NOUNS

FIRST AND SECOND DECLENSIONS

1. ā-stems | **2.** o-stems

SINGULAR					SINGULAR
Nom. rosa	amīcus	puer	ager	vir	templum
Gen. rosae	amīcī	puerī	agrī	virī	templī
Dat. rosae	amīcō	puerō	agrō	virō	templō
Acc. rosam	amīcum	puerum	agrum	virum	templum
Abl. rosā	amīcō	puerō	agrō	virō	templō

PLURAL					PLURAL
Nom. rosae	amīcī	puerī	agrī	virī	templa
Gen. rosārum	amīcōrum	puerōrum	agrōrum	virōrum	templōrum
Dat. rosīs	amīcīs	puerīs	agrīs	virīs	templīs
Acc. rosās	amīcōs	puerōs	agrōs	virōs	templa
Abl. rosīs	amīcīs	puerīs	agrīs	virīs	templīs

The vocative singular of -us nouns ends in -e: amīce. The vocative singular (and sometimes the genitive singular) of **fīlius** and of proper nouns in -ius ends in ī: fīlī.

All nouns ending in -um in the nominative singular are neuter.

The accusative singular of a neuter noun has the same form as the nominative singular, and the accusative plural has the same form as the nominative plural. The nominative and accusative plural always end in -a.

THIRD DECLENSION

3. MASCULINE AND FEMININE CONSONANT STEMS

SINGULAR			
Nom. lēx	mīles	frāter	homō
Gen. lēgis	mīlitis	frātris	hominis
Dat. lēgī	mīlitī	frātrī	hominī
Acc. lēgem	mīlitem	frātrem	hominem
Abl. lēge	mīlite	frātre	homine

PLURAL			
Nom. lēgēs	mīlitēs	frātrēs	hominēs
Gen. lēgum	mīlitum	frātrum	hominum
Dat. lēgibus	mīlitibus	frātribus	hominibus
Acc. lēgēs	mīlitēs	frātrēs	hominēs
Abl. lēgibus	mīlitibus	frātribus	hominibus

Some masculine and feminine nouns of the third declension have the nominative ending -s. If the stem ends in -c or -g, the combination of the final -c or -g of the stem with -s gives -x: **dux**, nominative from the stem **duc-**; **lēx**, nominative from the stem **lēg-**.   If the stem ends in -d or -t, the final consonant is dropped before -s: **laus**, nominative from the stem **laud-**.

In words of more than one syllable, short **e** of the final syllable of the nominative regularly appears as **i** in the other cases: nominative **mīles**, genitive **mīlitis**; **prīnceps, prīncipis.**

Nouns with stems ending in -tr have the nominative ending in -ter: **frāter** from the stem **frātr-**; **māter** from the stem **mātr-**.

Nouns with stems ending in -din and -gin replace -in of the stem by -ō in the nominative: **virgō** from the stem **virgin-**; **multitūdō** from the stem **multitūdin-**. The nominative **homō** is also formed by replacing -in of the stem by -ō.

4.   NEUTER CONSONANT STEMS

SINGULAR

Nom.	flūmen	caput	corpus	iter
Gen.	flūminis	capitis	corporis	itineris
Dat.	flūminī	capitī	corporī	itinerī
Acc.	flūmen	caput	corpus	iter
Abl.	flūmine	capite	corpore	itinere

PLURAL

Nom.	flūmina	capita	corpora	itinera
Gen.	flūminum	capitum	corporum	itinerum
Dat.	flūminibus	capitibus	corporibus	itineribus
Acc.	flūmina	capita	corpora	itinera
Abl.	flūminibus	capitibus	corporibus	itineribus

5.   I-STEMS AND MIXED STEMS

SINGULAR

	MASCULINE AND FEMININE			NEUTER		
Nom.	collis	nūbēs	nox	īnsigne	exemplar	animal
Gen.	collis	nūbis	noctis	īnsignis	exemplāris	animālis
Dat.	collī	nūbī	noctī	īnsignī	exemplārī	animālī
Acc.	collem	nūbem	noctem	īnsigne	exemplar	animal
Abl.	colle	nūbe	nocte	īnsignī	exemplārī	animālī

PLURAL

Nom.	collēs	nūbēs	noctēs	īnsignia	exemplāria	animālia
Gen.	collium	nūbium	noctium	īnsignium	exemplārium	animālium
Dat.	collibus	nūbibus	noctibus	īnsignibus	exemplāribus	animālibus
Acc.	collēs, -īs	nūbēs, -īs	noctēs, -īs	īnsignia	exemplāria	animālia
Abl.	collibus	nūbibus	noctibus	īnsignibus	exemplāribus	animālibus

Masculine and feminine i-stems and mixed stems include two classes: (1) nouns having the same number of syllables in the genitive as in the nominative; (2) nouns having two consonants before the ending of the genitive singular.   Exceptions are: **pāter, māter, frāter.**

The ablative singular of **turris** and sometimes of **ignis** and a few other words ends in -ī instead of -e.   The accusative singular of **turris** is **turrim.**

Neuter i-stems end in -e, -al, or -ar.

6. FOURTH DECLENSION, u-stems   **7.** FIFTH DECLENSION, ē-stems

	MASC. AND FEM.		NEUT.		MASC. AND FEM.			
	SING.	PLU.	SING.	PLU.	SING.	PLU.	SING.	PLU.
Nom.	exercitus	exercitūs	cornū	cornua	diēs	diēs	rēs	rēs
Gen.	exercitūs	exercituum	cornūs	cornuum	diēī	diērum	reī	rērum
Dat.	exercituī, -ū	exercitibus	cornū	cornibus	diēī	diēbus	reī	rēbus
Acc.	exercitum	exercitūs	cornū	cornua	diem	diēs	rem	rēs
Abl.	exercitū	exercitibus	cornū	cornibus	diē	diēbus	rē	rēbus

8. IRREGULAR NOUNS

	MASCULINE		MASC. AND FEM.	
	SINGULAR	PLURAL	SINGULAR	PLURAL
Nom.	vīs	vīrēs	bōs	bovēs
Gen.	—	vīrium	bovis	boum
Dat.	—	vīribus	bovī	būbus, bōbus
Acc.	vim	vīrēs, -īs	bovem	bovēs
Abl.	vī	vīribus	bove	būbus, bōbus

The noun **domus** has forms of both the second and the fourth declensions.

	FEMININE	
	SINGULAR	PLURAL
Nom.	domus	domūs
Gen.	domūs	domuum, domōrum
Dat.	domuī, domō	domibus
Acc.	domum	domōs, domūs
Abl.	domū, domō	domibus
Loc.	domī	

ADJECTIVES

9. FIRST AND SECOND DECLENSION

	SINGULAR			PLURAL		
	MASC.	FEM.	NEUT.	MASC.	FEM.	NEUT.
Nom.	bonus	bona	bonum	bonī	bonae	bona
Gen.	bonī	bonae	bonī	bonōrum	bonārum	bonōrum
Dat.	bonō	bonae	bonō	bonīs	bonīs	bonīs
Acc.	bonum	bonam	bonum	bonōs	bonās	bona
Abl.	bonō	bonā	bonō	bonīs	bonīs	bonīs
Nom.	miser	misera	miserum	miserī	miserae	misera
Gen.	miserī	miserae	miserī	miserōrum	miserārum	miserōrum
Dat.	miserō	miserae	miserō	miserīs	miserīs	miserīs
Acc.	miserum	miseram	miserum	miserōs	miserās	misera
Abl.	miserō	miserā	miserō	miserīs	miserīs	miserīs
Nom.	pulcher	pulchra	pulchrum	pulchrī	pulchrae	pulchra
Gen.	pulchrī	pulchrae	pulchrī	pulchrōrum	pulchrārum	pulchrōrum
Dat.	pulchrō	pulchrae	pulchrō	pulchrīs	pulchrīs	pulchrīs
Acc.	pulchrum	pulchram	pulchrum	pulchrōs	pulchrās	pulchra
Abl.	pulchrō	pulchrā	pulchrō	pulchrīs	pulchrīs	pulchrīs

THIRD DECLENSION

10.   THREE TERMINATIONS—I-STEMS

	SINGULAR			PLURAL	
MASC.	FEM.	NEUT.	MASC.	FEM.	NEUT.
Nom. ācer	ācris	ācre	ācrēs	ācrēs	ācria
Gen. ācris	ācris	ācris	ācrium	ācrium	ācrium
Dat. ācrī	ācrī	ācrī	ācribus	ācribus	ācribus
Acc. ācrem	ācrem	ācre	ācrēs, -īs	ācrēs, -īs	ācria
Abl. ācrī	ācrī	ācrī	ācribus	ācribus	ācribus

11.   TWO TERMINATIONS—I-STEMS

SINGULAR		PLURAL	
MASC. AND FEM.	NEUT.	MASC. AND FEM.	NEUT.
Nom. omnis	omne	omnēs	omnia
Gen. omnis	omnis	omnium	omnium
Dat. omnī	omnī	omnibus	omnibus
Acc. omnem	omne	omnēs, -īs	omnia
Abl. omnī	omnī	omnibus	omnibus

12.   ONE TERMINATION—I-STEMS

SINGULAR

MASC. AND FEM.	NEUT.	MASC. AND FEM.	NEUT.
Nom. fēlīx	fēlīx	potēns	potēns
Gen. fēlīcis	fēlīcis	potentis	potentis
Dat. fēlīcī	fēlīcī	potentī	potentī
Acc. fēlīcem	fēlīx	potentem	potēns
Abl. fēlīcī	fēlīcī	potentī, -e	potentī, -e

PLURAL

MASC. AND FEM.	NEUT.	MASC. AND FEM.	NEUT.
Nom. fēlīcēs	fēlīcia	potentēs	potentia
Gen. fēlīcium	fēlīcium	potentium	potentium
Dat. fēlīcibus	fēlīcibus	potentibus	potentibus
Acc. fēlīcēs, -īs	fēlīcia	potentēs, -īs	potentia
Abl. fēlīcibus	fēlīcibus	potentibus	potentibus

13.   ONE TERMINATION—CONSONANT STEM

SINGULAR		PLURAL	
MASC. AND FEM.	NEUT.	MASC. AND FEM.	NEUT.
Nom. vetus	vetus	veterēs	vetera
Gen. veteris	veteris	veterum	veterum
Dat. veterī	veterī	veteribus	veteribus
Acc. veterem	vetus	veterēs	vetera
Abl. vetere	vetere	veteribus	veteribus

14.   PRESENT PARTICIPLES

SINGULAR		PLURAL	
MASC. AND FEM.	NEUT.	MASC. AND FEM.	NEUT.
Nom. portāns	portāns	portantēs	portantia
Gen. portantis	portantis	portantium	portantium
Dat. portantī	portantī	portantibus	portantibus
Acc. portantem	portāns	portantēs, -īs	portantia
Abl. portante, -ī	portante, -ī	portantibus	portantibus

15. IRREGULAR ADJECTIVES

alius, -a, -ud
sōlus, -a, -um
ūllus, -a, -um
ūnus, -a, -um
tōtus, -a, -um

nūllus, -a, -um

alter, -era, -erum
neuter, -tra, -trum
uter, -tra, -trum

SINGULAR

	MASC.	FEM.	NEUT.	MASC.	FEM.	NEUT.
Nom.	sōlus	sōla	sōlum	uter	utra	utrum
Gen.	sōlīus	sōlīus	sōlīus	utrīus	utrīus	utrīus
Dat.	sōlī	sōlī	sōlī	utrī	utrī	utrī
Acc.	sōlum	sōlam	sōlum	utrum	utram	utrum
Abl.	sōlō	sōlā	sōlō	utrō	utrā	utrō

The plurals are like those of **bonus** and **pulcher.**

16. REGULAR COMPARISON OF ADJECTIVES

POSITIVE	COMPARATIVE	SUPERLATIVE
lātus	lātior, lātius	lātissimus, -a, -um
fortis	fortior, fortius	fortissimus, -a, -um
fēlīx	fēlīcior, fēlīcius	fēlīcissimus, -a, -um
miser	miserior, miserius	miserrimus, -a, -um
facilis	facilior, facilius	facillimus, -a, -um

17. IRREGULAR COMPARISON OF ADJECTIVES

POSITIVE	COMPARATIVE	SUPERLATIVE
bonus	melior, melius	optimus, -a, -um
malus	pejor, pejus	pessimus, -a, -um
magnus	major, majus	maximus, -a, -um
parvus	minor, minus	minimus, -a, -um
multus	——, plūs	plūrimus, -a, -um

18. DECLENSION OF COMPARATIVES

	SINGULAR		PLURAL
	MASC. AND FEM.	NEUT.	MASC. AND FEM.	NEUT.
Nom.	lātior	lātius	lātiōrēs	lātiōra
Gen.	lātiōris	lātiōris	lātiōrum	lātiōrum
Dat.	lātiōrī	lātiōrī	lātiōribus	lātiōribus
Acc.	lātiōrem	lātius	lātiōrēs, -īs	lātiōra
Abl.	lātiōre	lātiōre	lātiōribus	lātiōribus
Nom.	——	plūs[1]	plūrēs	plūra
Gen.	——	plūris	plūrium	plūrium
Dat.	——	——	plūribus	plūribus
Acc.	——	plūs	plūrēs, -īs	plūra
Abl.	——	plūre	plūribus	plūribus

[1]Used in singular as noun only.

ADVERBS

19. REGULAR COMPARISON **20.** IRREGULAR COMPARISON

POSITIVE	COMPARATIVE	SUPERLATIVE	POSITIVE	COMPARATIVE	SUPERLATIVE
lātē	lātius	lātissimē	bene	melius	optimē
fortiter	fortius	fortissimē	male	pejus	pessimē
ācriter	ācrius	ācerrimē	magnopere	magis	maximē
facile	facilius	facillimē	multum	plūs	plūrimum
			parum	minus	minimē
			prope	propius	proximē
			saepe	saepius	saepissimē
			diū	diūtius	diūtissimē

NUMERALS

21. LIST OF NUMBERS

ROMAN NUMERALS	CARDINALS	ORDINALS	DISTRIBUTIVES
I	ūnus, -a, -um	prīmus, -a, -um	singulī, -ae, -a
II	duo, duae, duo	secundus, alter	bīnī
III	trēs, tria	tertius	ternī, trīnī
IV	quattuor	quārtus	quaternī
V	quīnque	quīntus	quīnī
VI	sex	sextus	sēnī
VII	septem	septimus	septēnī
VIII	octō	octāvus	octōnī
IX	novem	nōnus	novēnī
X	decem	decimus	dēnī
XI	ūndecim	ūndecimus	ūndēnī
XII	duodecim	duodecimus	duodēnī
XIII	tredecim	tertius decimus	ternī dēnī
XIV	quattuordecim	quārtus decimus	quaternī dēnī
XV	quīndecim	quīntus decimus	quīnī dēnī
XVI	sēdecim	sextus decimus	sēnī dēnī
XVII	septendecim	septimus decimus	septēnī dēnī
XVIII	duodēvīgintī	duodēvīcēsimus	duodēvīcēnī
XIX	ūndēvīgintī	ūndēvīcēsimus	ūndēvīcēnī
XX	vīgintī	vīcēsimus	vīcēnī
XXI	ūnus et vīgintī, vīgintī ūnus	vīcēsimus prīmus	vīcēnī singulī
XXVIII	duodētrīgintā	duodētrīcēsimus	duodētrīcēnī
XXIX	ūndētrīgintā	ūndētrīcēsimus	ūndētrīcēnī
XXX	trīgintā	trīcēsimus	trīcēnī
XL	quadrāgintā	quadrāgēsimus	quadrāgēnī
L	quīnquāgintā	quīnquāgēsimus	quīnquāgēnī
LX	sexāgintā	sexāgēsimus	sexāgēnī
LXX	septuāgintā	septuāgēsimus	septuāgēnī
LXXX	octōgintā	octōgēsimus	octōgēnī
XC	nōnāgintā	nōnāgēsimus	nōnāgēnī
C	centum	centēsimus	centēnī

ROMAN NUMERALS	CARDINALS	ORDINALS	DISTRIBUTIVES
CI	centum (et) ūnus	centēsimus (et) prīmus	centēnī singulī
CC	ducentī, -ae, -a	ducentēsimus	ducēnī
CCC	trecentī, -ae, -a	trecentēsimus	trecēnī
CCCC	quadringentī	quadringentēsimus	quadringēnī
D	quīngentī	quīngentēsimus	quīngēnī
DC	sescentī	sescentēsimus	sescēnī
DCC	septingentī	septingentēsimus	septingēnī
DCCC	octingentī	octingentēsimus	octingēnī
DCCCC	nōngentī	nōngentēsimus	nōngēnī
M	mīlle	mīllēsimus	singula mīlia
MM	duo mīlia	bis mīllēsimus	bīna mīlia

The ordinal numerals often end in **-ēnsimus** instead of **-ēsimus**.

22. DECLENSION OF *DUO*, *TRĒS*, AND *MĪLIA*

	MASC.	FEM.	NEUT.	MASC. AND FEM.	NEUT.	NEUT.
Nom.	duo	duae	duo	trēs	tria	mīlia
Gen.	duōrum	duārum	duōrum	trium	trium	mīlium
Dat.	duōbus	duābus	duōbus	tribus	tribus	mīlibus
Acc.	duōs, duo	duās	duo	trēs, trīs	tria	mīlia
Abl.	duōbus	duābus	duōbus	tribus	tribus	mīlibus

In the singular, **mīlle**, *thousand*, is an indeclinable adjective. In the plural it is a neuter noun, and is modified by the genitive of the noun denoting the persons or things which are numbered.

PRONOUNS

23. PERSONAL

	FIRST PERSON		SECOND PERSON	
	SINGULAR	PLURAL	SINGULAR	PLURAL
Nom.	ego	nōs	tū	vōs
Gen.	meī	nostrum, nostrī	tuī	vestrum, vestrī
Dat.	mihi	nōbīs	tibi	vōbīs
Acc.	mē	nōs	tē	vōs
Abl.	mē	nōbīs	tē	vōbīs

There is no personal pronoun of the third person. Its place is taken either by a demonstrative pronoun (usually **is**, *he*, **ea**, *she*, **id**, *it*) or, if the antecedent is the subject of the sentence or clause, by a reflexive pronoun.

24. REFLEXIVE

	FIRST PERSON		SECOND PERSON		THIRD PERSON	
	SING.	PLU.	SING.	PLU.	SING.	PLU.
Gen.	meī	nostrī	tuī	vestrī	suī	suī
Dat.	mihi	nōbīs	tibi	vōbīs	sibi	sibi
Acc.	mē	nōs	tē	vōs	sē, sēsē	sē, sēsē
Abl.	mē	nōbīs	tē	vōbīs	sē, sēsē	sē, sēsē

25.   POSSESSIVES

REFERRING TO SINGULAR ANTECEDENT

1st pers.   **meus, -a, -um,** *my*
2d pers.   **tuus, -a, -um,** *your* (of one person)
3d pers.   {**suus, -a, -um,** *his, her, its* (reflexive)
            {**ejus** (gen. sing. of **is**), *his, her, its* (not reflexive)

REFERRING TO PLURAL ANTECEDENT

1st pers.   **noster, -tra, -trum,** *our*
2d pers.   **vester, -tra, -trum,** *your* (of more than one person)
3d pers.   {**suus, -a, -um,** *their* (reflexive)
            {**eōrum, eārum, eōrum** (gen. pl. of **is**), *their* (not reflexive)

The vocative singular masculine of **meus** is **mī.**
Meus, tuus, suus, noster, vester are used as adjectives, agreeing with the thing possessed.

26.   DEMONSTRATIVES

	SINGULAR			PLURAL		
	MASC.	FEM.	NEUT.	MASC.	FEM.	NEUT.
Nom.	hic	haec	hoc	hī	hae	haec
Gen.	hujus	hujus	hujus	hōrum	hārum	hōrum
Dat.	huic	huic	huic	hīs	hīs	hīs
Acc.	hunc	hanc	hoc	hōs	hās	haec
Abl.	hōc	hāc	hōc	hīs	hīs	hīs
Nom.	ille	illa	illud	illī	illae	illa
Gen.	illīus	illīus	illīus	illōrum	illārum	illōrum
Dat.	illī	illī	illī	illīs	illīs	illīs
Acc.	illum	illam	illud	illōs	illās	illa
Abl.	illō	illā	illō	illīs	illīs	illīs
Nom.	is	ea	id	eī, iī	eae	ea
Gen.	ejus	ejus	ejus	eōrum	eārum	eōrum
Dat.	eī	eī	eī	eīs, iīs	eīs, iīs	eīs, iīs
Acc.	eum	eam	id	eōs	eās	ea
Abl.	eō	eā	eō	eīs, iīs	eīs, iīs	eīs, iīs

The demonstrative **iste** is declined like **ille.**
The demonstratives are used either as pronouns or as adjectives.

WORDS USED AS PRONOUNS OR ADJECTIVES

27.   THE IDENTIFYING PRONOUN

SINGULAR

	MASC.	FEM.	NEUT.
Nom.	īdem	eadem	idem
Gen.	ejusdem	ejusdem	ejusdem
Dat.	eīdem	eīdem	eīdem
Acc.	eundem	eandem	idem
Abl.	eōdem	eādem	eōdem

PLURAL

	MASC.	FEM.	NEUT.
Nom.	eīdem, īdem	eaedem	eadem
Gen.	eōrundem	eārundem	eōrundem
Dat.	eīsdem, īsdem	eīsdem, īsdem	eīsdem, īsdem
Acc.	eōsdem	eāsdem	eadem
Abl.	eīsdem, īsdem	eīsdem, īsdem	eīsdem, īsdem

The nominative plural of the masculine is sometimes spelled **iīdem,** and the dative and ablative plurals are sometimes spelled **iīsdem.**

28. THE INTENSIVE

	SINGULAR			PLURAL		
	MASC.	FEM.	NEUT.	MASC.	FEM.	NEUT.
Nom.	ipse	ipsa	ipsum	ipsī	ipsae	ipsa
Gen.	ipsīus	ipsīus	ipsīus	ipsōrum	ipsārum	ipsōrum
Dat.	ipsī	ipsī	ipsī	ipsīs	ipsīs	ipsīs
Acc.	ipsum	ipsam	ipsum	ipsōs	ipsās	ipsa
Abl.	ipsō	ipsā	ipsō	ipsīs	ipsīs	ipsīs

29. THE RELATIVE

	SINGULAR			PLURAL		
	MASC.	FEM.	NEUT.	MASC.	FEM.	NEUT.
Nom.	quī	quae	quod	quī	quae	quae
Gen.	cujus	cujus	cujus	quōrum	quārum	quōrum
Dat.	cui	cui	cui	quibus	quibus	quibus
Acc.	quem	quam	quod	quōs	quās	quae
Abl.	quō	quā	quō	quibus	quibus	quibus

30. INTERROGATIVES

	SINGULAR		PLURAL		
	MASC. AND FEM.	NEUT.	MASC.	FEM.	NEUT.
Nom.	quis	quid	quī	quae	quae
Gen.	cujus	cujus	quōrum	quārum	quōrum
Dat.	cui	cui	quibus	quibus	quibus
Acc.	quem	quid	quōs	quās	quae
Abl.	quō	quō	quibus	quibus	quibus

31.

The interrogative adjective in the singular is the same as the relative pronoun (Section 29), except that the nominative masculine may be either **quis** or **quī.** The plural of the interrogative adjective is the same as that of the interrogative pronoun (Section 30).

32.   INDEFINITES

	PRONOUNS			ADJECTIVES	
		SINGULAR			
	MASC. AND FEM.	NEUT.	MASC.	FEM.	NEUT.
Nom.	quisque	quidque	quisque	quaeque	quodque
Gen.	cujusque	cujusque	cujusque	cujusque	cujusque
Dat.	cuique	cuique	cuique	cuique	cuique
Acc.	quemque	quidque	quemque	quamque	quodque
Abl.	quōque	quōque	quōque	quāque	quōque

The plural is seldom used.

		SINGULAR			
Nom.	aliquis	aliquid	aliquī	aliqua	aliquod
Gen.	alicujus	alicujus	alicujus	alicujus	alicujus
Dat.	alicui	alicui	alicui	alicui	alicui
Acc	aliquem	aliquid	aliquem	aliquam	aliquod
Abl.	aliquō	aliquō	aliquō	aliquā	aliquō

		PLURAL			
Nom.	aliquī	aliqua	aliquī	aliquae	aliqua
Gen.	aliquōrum	aliquōrum	aliquōrum	aliquārum	aliquōrum
Dat.	aliquibus	aliquibus	aliquibus	aliquibus	aliquibus
Acc.	aliquōs	aliqua	aliquōs	aliquās	aliqua
Abl.	aliquibus	aliquibus	aliquibus	aliquibus	aliquibus

	SINGULAR		
	MASC.	FEM.	NEUT.
Nom.	quīdam	quaedam	quiddam (quoddam)
Gen.	cujusdam	cujusdam	cujusdam
Dat.	cuidam	cuidam	cuidam
Acc.	quendam	quandam	quiddam (quoddam)
Abl.	quōdam	quādam	quōdam

	PLURAL		
Nom.	quīdam	quaedam	quaedam
Gen.	quōrundam	quārundam	quōrundam
Dat.	quibusdam	quibusdam	quibusdam
Acc.	quōsdam	quāsdam	quaedam
Abl.	quibusdam	quibusdam	quibusdam

The forms in parentheses are used as adjectives.

	SINGULAR	
	MASC. AND FEM.	NEUT.
Nom.	quisquam	quicquam, quidquam
Gen.	cujusquam	cujusquam
Dat.	cuiquam	cuiquam
Acc.	quemquam	quicquam, quidquam
Abl.	quōquam	quōquam

The plural is not found.

VERBS

FIRST CONJUGATION

Principal parts: **portō, portāre, portāvī, portātum**

33.

ACTIVE

INDICATIVE	SUBJUNCTIVE

PRESENT
SINGULAR

portō, *I carry*	portem
portās, *you carry*	portēs
portat, *he carries*	portet

PLURAL

portāmus, *we carry*	portēmus
portātis, *you carry*	portētis
portant, *they carry*	portent

IMPERFECT
SINGULAR

portābam, *I was carrying*	portārem
portābās, *you were carrying*	portārēs
portābat, *he was carrying*	portāret

PLURAL

portābāmus, *we were carrying*	portārēmus
portābātis, *you were carrying*	portārētis
portābant, *they were carrying*	portārent

FUTURE
SINGULAR

portābō, *I shall carry*	(None.)
portābis, *you will carry*	
portābit, *he will carry*	

PLURAL

portābimus, *we shall carry*
portābitis, *you will carry*
portābunt, *they will carry*

PERFECT
SINGULAR

portāvī, *I have carried, I carried*	portāverim
portāvistī, *you have carried*, etc.	portāverīs
portāvit, *he has carried*, etc.	portāverit

PLURAL

portāvimus, *we have carried*, etc.	portāverīmus
portāvistis, *you have carried*, etc.	portāverītis
portāvērunt, -ēre, *they have carried*, etc.	portāverint

INDICATIVE	SUBJUNCTIVE

PAST PERFECT

SINGULAR

portāveram, *I had carried*	portāvissem
portāverās, *you had carried*	portāvissēs
portāverat, *he had carried*	portāvisset

PLURAL

portāverāmus, *we had carried*	portāvissēmus
portāverātis, *you had carried*	portāvissētis
portāverant, *they had carried*	portāvissent

FUTURE PERFECT

SINGULAR

portāverō, *I shall have carried*	(None.)
portāveris, *you will have carried*	
portāverit, *he will have carried*	

PLURAL

portāverimus, *we shall have carried*
portāveritis, *you will have carried*
portāverint, *they will have carried*

IMPERATIVE

PRESENT	FUTURE
Sing. portā, *carry*	*Sing.* 2. portātō, *you shall carry*
Plu. portāte, *carry*	3. portātō, *he shall carry*
	Plu. 2. portātōte, *you shall carry*
	3. portantō, *they shall carry*

INFINITIVE	PARTICIPLE
Pres. portāre, *to carry*	*Pres.* portāns, *carrying*
Perf. portāvisse, *to have carried*	*Fut.* portātūrus, *going to carry*
Fut. portātūrus esse, *to be going to carry*	

GERUND	SUPINE
Gen. portandī, *of carrying*	*Acc.* portātum, *to carry*
Dat. portandō, *to, for carrying*	*Abl.* portātū, *to carry*
Acc. portandum, *carrying*	
Abl. portandō, *from, by carrying*	

34. *PASSIVE*

INDICATIVE	SUBJUNCTIVE

PRESENT

SINGULAR

portor, *I am (being) carried*	porter
portāris, -re, *you are (being) carried*	portēris, -re
portātur, *he is (being) carried*	portētur

INDICATIVE

SUBJUNCTIVE

PLURAL

portāmur, *we are (being) carried*   portēmur
portāminī, *you are (being) carried*   portēminī
portantur, *they are (being) carried*   portentur

IMPERFECT

SINGULAR

portābar, *I was (being) carried*   portārer
portābāris, -re, *you were (being) carried*   portārēris, -re
portābātur, *he was (being) carried*   portārētur

PLURAL

portābāmur, *we were (being) carried*   portārēmur
portābāminī, *you were (being) carried*   portārēminī
portābantur, *they were (being) carried*   portārentur

FUTURE

SINGULAR

portābor, *I shall be carried*   (None.)
portāberis, -re, *you will be carried*
portābitur, *he will be carried*

PLURAL

portābimur, *we shall be carried*
portābiminī, *you will be carried*
portābuntur, *they will be carried*

PERFECT

SINGULAR

portātus sum, *I have been carried*   portātus sim
portātus es, *you have been carried*   portātus sīs
portātus est, *he has been carried*   portātus sit

PLURAL

portātī sumus, *we have been carried*   portātī sīmus
portātī estis, *you have been carried*   portātī sītis
portātī sunt, *they have been carried*   portātī sint

PAST PERFECT

SINGULAR

portātus eram, *I had been carried*   portātus essem
portātus erās, *you had been carried*   portātus essēs
portātus erat, *he had been carried*   portātus esset

PLURAL

portātī erāmus, *we had been carried*   portātī essēmus
portātī erātis, *you had been carried*   portātī essētis
portātī erant, *they had been carried*   portātī essent

INDICATIVE   SUBJUNCTIVE

FUTURE PERFECT

SINGULAR

portātus erō, *I shall have been carried*   (None.)
portātus eris, *you will have been carried*
portātus erit, *he will have been carried*

PLURAL

portātī erimus, *we shall have been carried*
portātī eritis, *you will have been carried*
portātī erunt, *they will have been carried*

IMPERATIVE

PRESENT

Sing. **portāre,** *be carried*
Plu. **portāminī,** *be carried*

FUTURE

Sing. 2. **portātor,** *you shall be carried*
     3. **portātor,** *he shall be carried*
Plu. 2. ———
     3. **portantor,** *they shall be carried*

INFINITIVE

Pres. **portārī,** *to be carried*
Perf. **portātus esse,** *to have been carried*
Fut. **portātum īrī,** *to be about to be carried*

PARTICIPLE

Perf. **portātus,** *having been carried*
Fut. **portandus,** *to be carried*

SECOND, THIRD, AND FOURTH CONJUGATIONS

Principal parts: **moneō, monēre, monuī, monitum**
                 dūcō, dūcere, dūxī, ductum
                 capiō, capere, cēpī, captum
                 audiō, audīre, audīvī, audītum

INDICATIVE

ACTIVE

PRESENT

SINGULAR

35.

moneō	dūcō	capiō	audiō
monēs	dūcis	capis	audīs
monet	dūcit	capit	audit

PLURAL

monēmus	dūcimus	capimus	audīmus
monētis	dūcitis	capitis	audītis
monent	dūcunt	capiunt	audiunt

IMPERFECT

SINGULAR

monēbam	dūcēbam	capiēbam	audiēbam
monēbās	dūcēbās	capiēbās	audiēbās
monēbat	dūcēbat	capiēbat	audiēbat

PLURAL

monēbāmus	dūcēbāmus	capiēbāmus	audiēbāmus
monēbātis	dūcēbātis	capiēbātis	audiēbātis
monēbant	dūcēbant	capiēbant	audiēbant

FUTURE

SINGULAR

monēbō	dūcam	capiam	audiam
monēbis	dūcēs	capiēs	audiēs
monēbit	dūcet	capiet	audiet

PLURAL

monēbimus	dūcēmus	capiēmus	audiēmus
monēbitis	dūcētis	capiētis	audiētis
monēbunt	dūcent	capient	audient

PERFECT

SINGULAR

monuī	dūxī	cēpī	audīvī
monuistī	dūxistī	cēpistī	audīvistī
monuit	dūxit	cēpit	audīvit

PLURAL

monuimus	dūximus	cēpimus	audīvimus
monuistis	dūxistis	cēpistis	audīvistis
monuērunt, -ēre	dūxērunt, -ēre	cēpērunt, -ēre	audīvērunt, -ēre

PAST PERFECT

SINGULAR

monueram	dūxeram	cēperam	audīveram
monuerās	dūxerās	cēperās	audīverās
monuerat	dūxerat	cēperat	audīverat

PLURAL

monuerāmus	dūxerāmus	cēperāmus	audīverāmus
monuerātis	dūxerātis	cēperātis	audīverātis
monuerant	dūxerant	cēperant	audīverant

FUTURE PERFECT

SINGULAR

monuerō	dūxerō	cēperō	audīverō
monueris	dūxeris	cēperis	audīveris
monuerit	dūxerit	cēperit	audīverit

PLURAL

monuerimus	dūxerimus	cēperimus	audīverimus
monueritis	dūxeritis	cēperitis	audīveritis
monuerint	dūxerint	cēperint	audīverint

SUBJUNCTIVE

PRESENT

SINGULAR

moneam	dūcam	capiam	audiam
moneās	dūcās	capiās	audiās
moneat	dūcat	capiat	audiat

PLURAL

moneāmus	dūcāmus	capiāmus	audiāmus
moneātis	dūcātis	capiātis	audiātis
moneant	dūcant	capiant	audiant

IMPERFECT

SINGULAR

monērem	dūcerem	caperem	audīrem
monērēs	dūcerēs	caperēs	audīrēs
monēret	dūceret	caperet	audīret

PLURAL

monērēmus	dūcerēmus	caperēmus	audīrēmus
monērētis	dūcerētis	caperētis	audīrētis
monērent	dūcerent	caperent	audīrent

PERFECT

monuerim, etc.	dūxerim, etc.	cēperim, etc.	audīverim, etc.

PAST PERFECT

monuissem, etc.	dūxissem, etc.	cēpissem, etc.	audīvissem, etc.

IMPERATIVE

PRESENT

SINGULAR

monē	dūc[1]	cape	audī

PLURAL

monēte	dūcite	capite	audīte

FUTURE

SINGULAR

2. monētō	dūcitō	capitō	audītō
3. monētō	dūcitō	capitō	audītō

PLURAL

2. monētōte	dūcitōte	capitōte	audītōte
3. monentō	dūcuntō	capiuntō	audiuntō

---

[1] This is an irregular form. The imperative forms of **mittō** are **mitte, mittite,** etc., which illustrate the regular formation in the third conjugation.

PARTICIPLE
PRESENT
monēns	dūcēns	capiēns	audiēns

FUTURE
monitūrus	ductūrus	captūrus	audītūrus

INFINITIVE
PRESENT
monēre	dūcere	capere	audīre

PERFECT
monuisse	dūxisse	cēpisse	audīvisse

FUTURE
monitūrus esse	ductūrus esse	captūrus esse	audītūrus esse

GERUND
monendī	dūcendī	capiendī	audiendī
monendō	dūcendō	capiendō	audiendō
etc.	etc.	etc.	etc.

SUPINE
Acc.	monitum	ductum	captum	audītum
Abl.	monitū	ductū	captū	audītū

36. *PASSIVE*
PRESENT
SINGULAR
moneor	dūcor	capior	audior
monēris, -re	dūceris, -re	caperis, -re	audīris, -re
monētur	dūcitur	capitur	audītur

PLURAL
monēmur	dūcimur	capimur	audīmur
monēminī	dūciminī	capiminī	audīminī
monentur	dūcuntur	capiuntur	audiuntur

IMPERFECT
SINGULAR
monēbar	dūcēbar	capiēbar	audiēbar
monēbāris, -re	dūcēbāris, -re	capiēbāris, -re	audiēbāris, -re
monēbātur	dūcēbātur	capiēbātur	audiēbātur

PLURAL
monēbāmur	dūcēbāmur	capiēbāmur	audiēbāmur
monēbāminī	dūcēbāminī	capiēbāminī	audiēbāminī
monēbantur	dūcēbantur	capiēbantur	audiēbantur

FUTURE

SINGULAR

monēbor	dūcar	capiar	audiar
monēberis, -re	dūcēris, -re	capiēris, -re	audiēris, -re
monēbitur	dūcētur	capiētur	audiētur

PLURAL

monēbimur	dūcēmur	capiēmur	audiēmur
monēbiminī	dūcēminī	capiēminī	audiēminī
monēbuntur	dūcentur	capientur	audientur

PERFECT

SINGULAR

monitus sum	ductus sum	captus sum	audītus sum
monitus es	ductus es	captus es	audītus es
monitus est	ductus est	captus est	audītus est

PLURAL

monitī sumus	ductī sumus	captī sumus	audītī sumus
monitī estis	ductī estis	captī estis	audītī estis
monitī sunt	ductī sunt	captī sunt	audītī sunt

PAST PERFECT

SINGULAR

monitus eram	ductus eram	captus eram	audītus eram
monitus erās	ductus erās	captus erās	audītus erās
monitus erat	ductus erat	captus erat	audītus erat

PLURAL

monitī erāmus	ductī erāmus	captī erāmus	audītī erāmus
monitī erātis	ductī erātis	captī erātis	audītī erātis
monitī erant	ductī erant	captī erant	audītī erant

FUTURE PERFECT

SINGULAR

monitus erō	ductus erō	captus erō	audītus erō
monitus eris	ductus eris	captus eris	audītus eris
monitus erit	ductus erit	captus erit	audītus erit

PLURAL

monitī erimus	ductī erimus	captī erimus	audītī erimus
monitī eritis	ductī eritis	captī eritis	audītī eritis
monitī erunt	ductī erunt	captī erunt	audītī erunt

SUBJUNCTIVE

PRESENT

SINGULAR

monear	dūcar	capiar	audiar
moneāris, -re	dūcāris, -re	capiāris, -re	audiāris, -re
moneātur	dūcātur	capiātur	audiātur

PLURAL

moneāmur	dūcāmur	capiāmur	audiāmur
moneāminī	dūcāminī	capiāminī	audiāminī
moneantur	dūcantur	capiantur	audiantur

IMPERFECT

SINGULAR

monērer	dūcerer	caperer	audīrer
monērēris, -re	dūcerēris, -re	caperēris, -re	audīrēris, -re
monērētur	dūcerētur	caperētur	audīrētur

PLURAL

monērēmur	dūcerēmur	caperēmur	audīrēmur
monērēminī	dūcerēminī	caperēminī	audīrēminī
monērentur	dūcerentur	caperentur	audīrentur

PERFECT

SINGULAR

monitus sim, etc.	ductus sim, etc.	captus sim, etc.	audītus sim, etc.

PLURAL

monitī sīmus, etc.	ductī sīmus, etc.	captī sīmus, etc.	audītī sīmus, etc.

PAST PERFECT

SINGULAR

monitus essem, etc.	ductus essem, etc.	captus essem, etc.	audītus essem, etc.

PLURAL

monitī essēmus, etc.	ductī essēmus, etc.	captī essēmus, etc.	audītī essēmus, etc.

IMPERATIVE

PRESENT

SINGULAR

monēre	dūcere	capere	audīre

PLURAL

monēminī	dūciminī	capiminī	audīminī

FUTURE

SINGULAR

2. monētor	dūcitor	capitor	audītor
3. monētor	dūcitor	capitor	audītor

PLURAL

2. ———	———	———	———
3. monentor	dūcuntor	capiuntor	audiuntor

PARTICIPLE

PERFECT

monitus	ductus	captus	audītus

FUTURE

monendus	dūcendus	capiendus	audiendus

INFINITIVE

PRESENT

| monērī | dūcī | capī | audīrī |

PERFECT

| monitus esse | ductus esse | captus esse | audītus esse |

FUTURE

| monitum īrī | ductum īrī | captum īrī | audītum īrī |

37.   SYNOPSIS OF VERBS

A group of forms representing one person and number of a verb in all the tenses is called a synopsis. The synopsis of **portō** in the first person singular of the indicative and subjunctive, active and passive, is as follows:

ACTIVE

	INDICATIVE	SUBJUNCTIVE
Pres.	portō	portem
Imperf.	portābam	portārem
Fut.	portābō	———
Perf.	portāvī	portāverim
P. Pf.	portāveram	portāvissem
F. Pf.	portāverō	———

PASSIVE

Pres.	portor	porter
Imperf.	portābar	portārer
Fut.	portābor	———
Perf.	portātus sum	portātus sim
P. Pf.	portātus eram	portātus essem
F. Pf.	portātus erō	———

38.   DEPONENT VERBS

Principal parts: cōnor, cōnārī, cōnātus sum
                  polliceor, pollicērī, pollicitus sum
                  sequor, sequī, secūtus sum
                  partior, partīrī, partītus sum

INDICATIVE

| I | II | III | IV |

PRESENT

SINGULAR

cōnor	polliceor	sequor	partior
cōnāris, -re	pollicēris, -re	sequeris, -re	partīris, -re
cōnātur	pollicētur	sequitur	partītur

PLURAL

cōnāmur	pollicēmur	sequimur	partīmur
cōnāminī	pollicēminī	sequiminī	partīminī
cōnantur	pollicentur	sequuntur	partiuntur

IMPERFECT

cōnābar, etc.   pollicēbar, etc.   sequēbar, etc.   partiēbar, etc.

FUTURE

cōnābor, etc.   pollicēbor, etc.   sequar, etc.   partiar, etc.

PERFECT

cōnātus sum, etc.   pollicitus sum, etc.   secūtus sum, etc.   partītus sum, etc.

PAST PERFECT

cōnātus eram, etc.   pollicitus eram, etc.   secūtus eram, etc.   partītus eram, etc.

FUTURE PERFECT

cōnātus erō, etc.   pollicitus erō, etc.   secūtus erō, etc.   partītus erō, etc.

SUBJUNCTIVE
PRESENT

cōner, etc.   pollicear, etc.   sequar, etc.   partiar, etc.

IMPERFECT

cōnārer, etc.   pollicērer, etc.   sequerer, etc.   partīrer, etc.

PERFECT

cōnātus sim, etc.   pollicitus sim, etc.   secūtus sim, etc.   partītus sim, etc.

PAST PERFECT

cōnātus essem, etc.   pollicitus essem, etc.   secūtus essem, etc.   partītus essem, etc.

IMPERATIVE
PRESENT

cōnāre   pollicēre   sequere   partīre

FUTURE

cōnātor   pollicētor   sequitor   partītor

INFINITIVE
PRESENT

cōnārī   pollicērī   sequī   partīrī

PERFECT

cōnātus esse   pollicitus esse   secūtus esse   partītus esse

FUTURE

cōnātūrus esse   pollicitūrus esse   secūtūrus esse   partītūrus esse

PARTICIPLE
PRESENT

cōnāns	pollicēns	sequēns	partiēns

PERFECT

cōnātus	pollicitus	secūtus	partītus

FUTURE ACTIVE

cōnātūrus	pollicitūrus	secūtūrus	partītūrus

FUTURE PASSIVE

cōnandus	pollicendus	sequendus	partiendus

GERUND

cōnandī, etc.	pollicendī, etc.	sequendī, etc.	partiendī, etc.

SUPINE

Acc.	cōnātum	pollicitum	secūtum	partītum
Abl.	cōnātū	pollicitū	secūtū	partītū

The following verbs are semi-deponent. The present system is active, and the perfect system is passive:

> audeō, audēre, ausus sum, *dare*
> gaudeō, gaudēre, gāvīsus sum, *rejoice*
> soleō, solēre, solitus sum, *be accustomed*
> fīdō, fīdere, fīsus sum, *trust*

IRREGULAR VERBS

39.   *CONJUGATION OF SUM*

Principal parts: **sum, esse, fuī, futūrus**

INDICATIVE

PRESENT		IMPERFECT	
SINGULAR	PLURAL	SINGULAR	PLURAL
sum, *I am*	sumus, *we are*	eram, *I was*	erāmus, *we were*
es, *you are*	estis, *you are*	erās, *you were*	erātis, *you were*
est, *he is*	sunt, *they are*	erat, *he was*	erant, *they were*

FUTURE

SINGULAR	PLURAL
erō, *I shall be*	erimus, *we shall be*
eris, *you will be*	eritis, *you will be*
erit, *he will be*	erunt, *they will be*

PERFECT

fuī, *I was, I have been*	fuimus, *we were, we have been*
fuistī, *you were, you have been*	fuistis, *you were, you have been*
fuit, *he was, he has been*	fuērunt, -ēre, *they were, they have been*

PAST PERFECT

SINGULAR	PLURAL
fueram, *I had been*	fuerāmus, *we had been*
fuerās, *you had been*	fuerātis, *you had been*
fuerat, *he had been*	fuerant, *they had been*

FUTURE PERFECT

fuerō, *I shall have been*	fuerimus, *we shall have been*
fueris, *you will have been*	fueritis, *you will have been*
fuerit, *he will have been*	fuerint, *they will have been*

SUBJUNCTIVE

PRESENT		IMPERFECT	
SINGULAR	PLURAL	SINGULAR	PLURAL
sim	sīmus	essem	essēmus
sīs	sītis	essēs	essētis
sit	sint	esset	essent

PERFECT		PAST PERFECT	
fuerim	fuerīmus	fuissem	fuissēmus
fuerīs	fuerītis	fuissēs	fuissētis
fuerit	fuerint	fuisset	fuissent

IMPERATIVE
PRESENT

SINGULAR	PLURAL
es, *be*	este, *be*

FUTURE

SINGULAR	PLURAL
2. estō, *be, you shall be*	estōte, *be, you shall be*
3. estō, *let him be, he shall be*	suntō, *let them be, they shall be*

PARTICIPLE
Fut. futūrus, *about to be*

INFINITIVE
Pres. esse, *to be*
Perf. fuisse, *to have been*
Fut. futūrus esse or fore, *to be about to be*

40.   *CONJUGATION OF POSSUM*

Principal parts: **possum, posse, potuī**

INDICATIVE		SUBJUNCTIVE	
	PRESENT		
SINGULAR	PLURAL	SINGULAR	PLURAL
possum	possumus	possim	possīmus
potes	potestis	possīs	possītis
potest	possunt	possit	possint

INDICATIVE		SUBJUNCTIVE	
	IMPERFECT		
SINGULAR	PLURAL	SINGULAR	PLURAL
poteram	poterāmus	possem	possēmus
poterās	poterātis	possēs	possētis
poterat	poterant	posset	possent

	FUTURE		
poterō, etc.	poterimus, etc.	(None.)	

	PERFECT		
potuī, etc.	potuimus, etc.	potuerim, etc.	potuerīmus, etc.

	PAST PERFECT		
potueram, etc.	potuerāmus, etc.	potuissem, etc.	potuissēmus, etc.

	FUTURE PERFECT		
potuerō, etc.	potuerimus, etc.	(None.)	

INFINITIVE

Pres. posse   *Perf.* potuisse

41.   *CONJUGATION OF PRŌSUM*

Principal parts: **prōsum, prōdesse, prōfuī**

INDICATIVE		SUBJUNCTIVE	
	PRESENT		
SINGULAR	PLURAL	SINGULAR	PLURAL
prōsum	prōsumus	prōsim	prōsīmus
prōdes	prōdestis	prōsīs	prōsītis
prōdest	prōsunt	prōsit	prōsint

The remaining forms of the present system are conjugated like **sum,** with the prefix **prōd-.** The perfect system is regularly formed with the stem **prōfu-.**

42.   *CONJUGATION OF FERŌ*

Principal parts: **ferō, ferre, tulī, lātum**

INDICATIVE

PRESENT

Active		*Passive*	
SINGULAR	PLURAL	SINGULAR	PLURAL
ferō	ferimus	feror	ferimur
fers	fertis	ferris, -re	feriminī
fert	ferunt	fertur	feruntur

IMPERFECT

ferēbam, etc.	ferēbāmus, etc.	ferēbar, etc.	ferēbāmur, etc.

Active			*Passive*
		FUTURE	
SINGULAR	PLURAL	SINGULAR	PLURAL
feram, etc.	ferēmus, etc.	ferar, etc.	ferēmur, etc.

PERFECT

tulī, etc.	tulimus, etc.	lātus sum, etc.	lātī sumus, etc.

PAST PERFECT

tuleram, etc.	tulerāmus, etc.	lātus eram, etc.	lātī erāmus, etc.

FUTURE PERFECT

tulerō, etc.	tulerimus, etc.	lātus erō, etc.	lātī erimus, etc.

SUBJUNCTIVE

PRESENT

feram, etc.	ferāmus, etc.	ferar, etc.	ferāmur, etc.

IMPERFECT

ferrem, etc.	ferrēmus, etc.	ferrer, etc.	ferrēmur, etc.

PERFECT

tulerim, etc.	tulerīmus, etc.	lātus sim, etc.	lātī sīmus, etc.

PAST PERFECT

tulissem, etc.	tulissēmus, etc.	lātus essem, etc.	lātī essēmus, etc.

IMPERATIVE

PRESENT

fer	ferte	ferre	feriminī

FUTURE

2. fertō	fertōte	fertor	————
3. fertō	feruntō	fertor	feruntor

INFINITIVE

ACTIVE	PASSIVE
Pres. ferre	ferrī
Perf. tulisse	lātus esse
Fut. lātūrus esse	lātum īrī

PARTICIPLE

ACTIVE	PASSIVE
Pres. ferēns	*Perf.* lātus
Fut. lātūrus	*Fut.* ferendus

GERUND	SUPINE
ferendī, etc.	*Acc.* lātum *Abl.* lātū

43. *CONJUGATION OF EŌ*

Principal parts: **eō, īre, iī (īvī), itum**

INDICATIVE		SUBJUNCTIVE	
		PRESENT	
SINGULAR	PLURAL	SINGULAR	PLURAL
eō	īmus	eam	eāmus
īs	ītis	eās	eātis
it	eunt	eat	eant

IMPERFECT

ībam, etc.	ībāmus, etc.	īrem, etc.	īrēmus, etc.

FUTURE

ībō, etc.	ībimus, etc.	(None.)

PERFECT

iī, īvī etc.	iimus, īvimus etc.	ierim, īverim etc.	ierīmus, īverīmus etc.

PAST PERFECT

ieram, īveram etc.	ierāmus, īverāmus etc.	īssem, īvissem etc.	īssēmus, īvissēmus etc.

FUTURE PERFECT

ierō, īverō etc.	ierimus, īverimus etc.

IMPERATIVE		INFINITIVE	PARTICIPLE
Pres. ī	īte	*Pres.* īre	*Pres.* iēns (*gen.* euntis)
Fut. 2. ītō	ītōte	*Perf.* īsse, iisse	*Fut.* itūrus
3. ītō	euntō	*Fut.* itūrus esse	

GERUND

eundī, etc.

44. *CONJUGATION OF FĪŌ*

Principal parts: **fīō, fierī, factus sum**

INDICATIVE		SUBJUNCTIVE	
		PRESENT	
SINGULAR	PLURAL	SINGULAR	PLURAL
fīō	——	fīam	fīāmus
fīs	——	fīās	fīātis
fit	fīunt	fīat	fīant

IMPERFECT

fīēbam	fīēbāmus	fierem	fierēmus

FUTURE

fīam	fīēmus	(None.)

INDICATIVE		SUBJUNCTIVE	
	PERFECT		
SINGULAR	PLURAL	SINGULAR	PLURAL
factus sum, etc.	factī sumus, etc.	factus sim, etc.	factī sīmus, etc.

PAST PERFECT

factus eram, etc.	factī erāmus, etc.	factus essem, etc.	factī essēmus, etc.

FUTURE PERFECT

factus erō, etc.	factī erimus, etc.	(None.)

IMPERATIVE	INFINITIVE	PARTICIPLE
Pres. fī fīte	*Pres.* fierī	*Perf.* factus
	Perf. factus esse	*Fut.* faciendus
	Fut. factum īrī	

45.   *CONJUGATION OF **VOLŌ** AND ITS COMPOUNDS*

Principal parts: volō, velle, voluī
nōlō, nōlle, nōluī
mālō, mālle, māluī

INDICATIVE

PRESENT

SINGULAR

volō	nōlō	mālō
vīs	nōn vīs	māvīs
vult	nōn vult	māvult

PLURAL

volumus	nōlumus	mālumus
vultis	nōn vultis	māvultis
volunt	nōlunt	mālunt

IMPERFECT

volēbam, etc.	nōlēbam, etc.	mālēbam, etc.

FUTURE

volam, etc.	nōlam, etc.	mālam, etc.

PERFECT

voluī, etc.	nōluī, etc.	māluī, etc.

PAST PERFECT

volueram, etc.	nōlueram, etc.	mālueram, etc.

FUTURE PERFECT

voluerō, etc.	nōluerō, etc.	māluerō, etc.

SUBJUNCTIVE
PRESENT

velim, etc.	nōlim, etc.	mālim, etc.

IMPERFECT

vellem, etc.	nōllem, etc.	māllem, etc.

PERFECT

voluerim, etc.	nōluerim, etc.	māluerim, etc.

PAST PERFECT

voluissem, etc.	nōluissem, etc.	māluissem, etc.

IMPERATIVE

	SINGULAR	PLURAL
Pres.	nōlī	nōlīte
Fut. 2.	nōlītō	nōlītōte
3.	nōlītō	nōluntō

INFINITIVE

Pres.	velle	nōlle	mālle
Perf.	voluisse	nōluisse	māluisse

PARTICIPLE

Pres.	volēns	nōlēns

46.   DEFECTIVE VERBS

A few verbs are defective, that is, they lack some forms which are found in the conjugation of other verbs. The most important are **aiō**, *I say, I assent;* **inquam,** *I say;* **coepī,** *I began;* **meminī,** *I remember;* **ōdī,** *I hate.*

(1) The forms of **aiō** most commonly used are found in the present indicative, and are as follows:

	SINGULAR	PLURAL
1.	aiō	———
2.	aïs	———
3.	aït	aïunt

A few other forms, including the whole of the imperfect indicative and the second and third persons singular of the present subjunctive, are sometimes found.

(2) The only forms of **inquam** in common use are found in the present indicative. They are as follows:

	SINGULAR	PLURAL
1.	inquam	———
2.	inquis	———
3.	inquit	inquiunt

(3) The three verbs **coepī, meminī,** and **ōdī** have no present, imperfect, or future forms. The perfects of **meminī** and **ōdī** are used with present meanings, the past perfects with imperfect meanings, and the future perfects with future meanings. The tenses of **coepī** have their regular meanings. The present, imperfect, and future of **coepī** are supplied by the forms of **incipiō**.

SYNTAX

The grammatical principles presented in the following pages are those which are especially important for the work of the second year. The mood and case uses treated are limited almost entirely to those which are found in the reading or exercises of this book.

AGREEMENT

47.   OF ADJECTIVES AND PARTICIPLES

An adjective or a participle agrees with its noun in gender, number, and case.

magna urbs, *a great city*   **magnae** partis, *of a great part*

magnīs perīculīs, *in great dangers*

48.   OF RELATIVE PRONOUNS

A relative pronoun agrees with its antecedent in gender and number, but its case depends on its use in its own clause.

Homō **quem** vidēs amīcus meus est, *The man whom you see is my friend.*

49.   OF APPOSITIVES

A noun in apposition is in the same case as the noun which it explains.

Agricola, **vir** benignus, puerōs laudat, *The farmer, a kind man, praises the boys.*

50.   OF VERBS

A verb agrees with its subject in person and number.

Puer **labōrat**, *The boy works.*   Puerī **labōrant**, *The boys work.*

NOUNS

51.   THE NOMINATIVE CASE

The nominative is the case of the subject or of the predicate noun used with a finite[1] verb.

Puella canit, *The girl sings.*

Frāter tuus est agricola, *Your brother is a farmer.*

(*a*) The predicate nominative is used with the verb **sum** and with the passive voice of verbs meaning *to name, call, appoint, choose*, and the like.

Is rēx tyrannus appellātus est, *This king was called a tyrant.*

THE GENITIVE CASE

52.   GENITIVE OF POSSESSION

The genitive is used to denote the possessor.

Liber puerī repertus est, *The boy's book has been found.*

53.   GENITIVE OF THE WHOLE (PARTITIVE GENITIVE)

With words denoting a part, a dependent genitive is used to name the whole to which the part belongs.

Multī amīcōrum meōrum in eā urbe habitant, *Many of my friends live in that city.*

---

[1] That is, any verb form which denotes person and number.

(*a*) The ablative with **dē** or **ex** is sometimes used in place of the genitive of the whole, regularly so with cardinal numerals and **quīdam.**

ūnus ē fīliīs tuīs, *one of your sons*

54.   GENITIVE OF DESCRIPTION

The genitive, modified by an adjective, may be used to describe a person or thing.

homō **magnae virtūtis,** *a man of great courage*

(*a*) The genitive is sometimes employed in this construction to denote measure.

mūrus **quattuor pedum,** *a four-foot wall* (*a wall of four feet*)

55.   OBJECTIVE GENITIVE

Nouns and adjectives which denote action sometimes take a genitive which shows the object of the action.

timor **perīculī,** *fear of danger*   **causae** dictiōnis, *of pleading the case*

56.   SUBJECTIVE GENITIVE

Nouns which denote action sometimes take a genitive to indicate the person who does the act.

adventus **Caesaris,** *the arrival of Caesar*

57.   GENITIVE OF MATERIAL OR COMPOSITION

The genitive may be used to denote the material of which something is composed, or the persons or objects making up a collective noun.

exercitus **virōrum** fortium, *an army of brave men*

58.   GENITIVE WITH VERBS

The verbs **meminī** and **reminīscor,** *remember*, and **oblīvīscor,** *forget*, frequently take a genitive as object.

Virtūtis vestrae nōn oblīvīscor, *I do not forget your courage.*

(*a*) If the object of these verbs is a neuter pronoun or a neuter adjective used as a noun, it is always in the accusative.

Rōmānī **haec** semper meminerint, *The Romans will always remember these things.*

THE DATIVE CASE

59.   DATIVE OF INDIRECT OBJECT

The indirect object is in the dative.

Fēmina **puerō** epistulam dat, *The woman gives the boy a letter.*

60. DATIVE WITH ADJECTIVES

The dative is used in dependence on adjectives meaning *kind, friendly, dear, pleasing, hostile, near,* and some others.

Fīlius tuus <u>sorōribus</u> benignus est, *Your son is kind to (his) sisters.*

61. DATIVE WITH SPECIAL VERBS

Most verbs meaning *to please, displease, trust, distrust, believe, persuade, serve, obey, favor, resist, envy, threaten, pardon,* and *spare* govern the dative.

Illīs <u>barbarīs</u> nēmō nunc cōnfīdit, *No one now trusts those barbarians.*

62. DATIVE OF POSSESSION

The possessor of something may be denoted by a noun or pronoun in the dative, with the word denoting the thing possessed in the nominative as the subject of a form of **sum.**

<u>Puerō</u> gladius est, *The boy has a sword.*

63. DATIVE OF PURPOSE

A noun in the dative is sometimes used to denote the purpose which something serves or is intended to serve.

Hunc librum <u>dōnō</u> mīsī, *I sent this book as a gift* (literally, *for a gift*).

64. DATIVE OF REFERENCE

The dative is sometimes used to denote the person with reference to whom an act is done or a situation exists. This use is especially common in expressions which contain a dative of purpose.

Legiō <u>equitātuī</u> auxiliō missa est, *The legion was sent as aid* (literally, *for aid*) to the cavalry.

65. DATIVE WITH COMPOUNDS

Verbs compounded with **ante, ob, prae,** and **sub** frequently have a dependent noun or pronoun in the dative case. This construction is sometimes found also with compounds of **ad, circum, com-, in, inter, post, prō,** and **super.**

<u>Legiōnī</u> praeest, *He is in command of the legion.*

(*a*) If the simple verb from which the compound is formed is a transitive verb, the compound may take both the accusative and the dative.

Labiēnum <u>castrīs</u> praefēcit, *He placed Labienus in charge of the camp.*

66. DATIVE OF AGENT

With the future passive participle, the person by whom the act must be done or ought to be done is regularly denoted by the dative.

Epistula <u>mihi</u> mittenda est, *A letter ought to be sent by me.*

(*a*) With a verb which has a dependent dative of some other kind, the dative of agent is sometimes replaced by the ablative of agent (**76**) to avoid confusion in the meaning of the sentence.

THE ACCUSATIVE CASE

67.   ACCUSATIVE OF DIRECT OBJECT

The direct object of a verb is in the accusative.

Silvam vidēmus, *We see the forest.*

68.   ACCUSATIVE OF DURATION OF TIME

The accusative without a preposition is used to tell how long an act or a situation continues.

Multās hōrās in īnsulā mānsī, *I remained many hours on the island.*

69.   ACCUSATIVE OF EXTENT IN SPACE

The accusative without a preposition is used to express extent in space.

Puer quīnque mīlia passuum ambulāvit, *The boy walked five miles.*

70.   ACCUSATIVE OF PLACE TO WHICH

The accusative of **domus** and of names of cities, towns, and small islands is used without a preposition to denote place to which.

Exercitus Rōmam redībit, *The army will return to Rome.*

(*a*) With other words in this construction, a preposition, **ad** or **in,** is used.

Exercitus in urbem redībit, *The army will return to the city.*

71.   ACCUSATIVE WITH PREPOSITIONS

Certain prepositions have their objects in the accusative case. Among the most important of these are **ad, ante, apud, circum, contrā, inter, ob, per, post, praeter, propter, trāns.** (See also **153-154.**)

Is poēta inter barbarōs diū habitāvit, *This poet lived a long time among barbarians.*

72.   ACCUSATIVE AS SUBJECT OF INFINITIVE

The accusative is used as the subject of the infinitive.

Explōrātor dīxit urbem incēnsam esse, *The scout said the city had been burned.*

73.   TWO ACCUSATIVES

Verbs of *naming, calling, appointing, thinking,* and the like may have, in addition to the direct object, a second accusative telling what the person or thing denoted by the object is named, called, appointed, etc.

Frātrem tuum praetōrem creāvimus, *We have elected your brother praetor.*

(*a*) Compounds of **trāns** sometimes take two objects, one governed by **trāns,** the other by the simple verb.

Legiōnem flūmen trādūxī, *I led the legion across the river.*

With the passive of such verbs the object governed by the preposition may be retained.

Legiō flūmen trāducta est, *The legion was led across the river.*

THE ABLATIVE

74. ABLATIVE OF SEPARATION

Verbs meaning *to separate, remove, deprive of, be absent,* and the like, take the ablative of separation, often with **ab** or **ex.**

Hī montēs Galliam <u>ab Hispāniā</u> dīvidunt, *These mountains separate Gaul from Spain.*

75. ABLATIVE OF PLACE FROM WHICH

The ablative of **domus** and of names of cities, towns, and small islands is used without a preposition to express the idea of place from which.

Lēgātus <u>Genavā</u> profectus est, *The envoy set out from Geneva.*

(*a*) With other words in this construction a preposition, **ab, dē,** or **ex,** is used.

Lēgātus <u>ex oppidō</u> profectus est, *The lieutenant set out from the town.*

76. ABLATIVE OF AGENT

With passive verbs the noun or pronoun which denotes the person by whom the act is done is in the ablative with **ā** or **ab.**

Explōrātor ā <u>mīlitibus</u> captus est, *The scout was captured by the soldiers.*

77. ABLATIVE OF COMPARISON

With the comparative form of an adjective (occasionally of an adverb), if **quam** is omitted, the noun or pronoun denoting the person or thing with which comparison is made is in the ablative without a preposition.

Puella altior <u>puerō</u> est, *The girl is taller than the boy.*

(*a*) If **quam** is used, the word denoting the person or thing with which comparison is made is in the same case as the thing compared.

Puella est altior quam <u>puer</u>, *The girl is taller than the boy.*

78. ABLATIVE OF PLACE

The ablative with **in** denotes the place where something is or where some act occurs. (But see also **91.**)

<u>In</u> eīs <u>montibus</u> multa animālia reperiuntur, *Many animals are found in these mountains.*

79. ABLATIVE OF TIME

The time at which or within which an act takes place is regularly expressed by a noun or pronoun in the ablative case without a preposition.

Eō <u>annō</u> pater meus tēctum novum aedificāvit, *My father built a new house that year.*

80. ABLATIVE OF ACCOMPANIMENT

The ablative with the preposition **cum** is used to denote the person with whom one is associated in doing an act.

<u>Cum amīcō</u> ambulō, *I walk with a friend.*

(*a*) The ablative of accompaniment also denotes the person with whom one is contending.

Cum Germānīs bellum gessērunt, *They waged war with the Germans.*

(*b*) The preposition **cum** may be omitted in military expressions, if the noun in the ablative is modified by an adjective other than a numeral.

Multīs mīlitibus flūmen trānsiī, *I crossed the river with many soldiers.*

Cum tribus legiōnibus flūmen trānsiī, *I crossed the river with three legions.*

81.   ABLATIVE OF MANNER

The ablative, frequently with the preposition **cum,** is used to express manner.

Magnā cum cūrā (*or* **Magnā cūrā**) **omnia parāvimus,** *We have prepared everything with great care.*

(*a*) Some words of frequent occurrence have no preposition in this construction. Among these are **jūre,** *justly* (*with justice*), **injūriā,** *unjustly* (*with injustice*), **meritō,** *deservedly* (*with merit*), **cāsū,** *accidentally* (*by chance*).

82.   ABLATIVE OF MEANS

A word which denotes the means used to accomplish an act is in the ablative without a preposition.

Gallī gladiīs pugnābant, *The Gauls fought with swords.*

83.   ABLATIVE OF ROUTE

The route by which one goes may be denoted by the ablative without a preposition.

Breviōre itinere rediimus, *We returned by a shorter route.*

84.   ABLATIVE OF DEGREE OF DIFFERENCE

The ablative without a preposition is used to express the degree of difference between two things.

Arbor decem pedibus altior mūrō (*or* **quam mūrus**) **est,** *The tree is ten feet higher than the wall.*

85.   ABLATIVE ABSOLUTE

A noun or pronoun in the ablative, together with an adjective, a participle, or another noun in agreement, may be used to denote some circumstance or event loosely connected with the rest of the sentence.

Duce captō, hostēs fūgērunt, *The leader having been captured, the enemy fled.*

(*a*) An ablative absolute is frequently translated by a clause introduced by *when, after, if, since, although,* or by a prepositional phrase. Thus, the ablative absolute in the preceding example may be translated, *When the leader had been captured* or *After the capture of the leader.*

86. Ablative of Respect

The ablative without a preposition is used to indicate in what respect a statement is true.

Helvētiī reliquōs Gallōs <u>virtūte</u> praecēdunt, *The Helvetians surpass the rest of the Gauls in courage.*

87. Ablative of Description

The ablative modified by an adjective may be used to describe a person or thing.

homō <u>magnā virtūte</u>, *a man of great courage*

(*a*) In many phrases, such as the example above, either the ablative or the genitive of description (**54**) may be used. But physical characteristics are usually expressed by the ablative, and measure always by the genitive.

88. Ablative of Cause

The ablative is sometimes used to express cause.

Hostēs <u>timōre</u> fugere coepērunt, *The enemy began to flee on account of fear.*

(*a*) Sometimes a preposition (**ab, dē,** or **ex**) is used with the ablative of cause.

Ex <u>commūtātiōne</u> rērum dolent, *They grieve because of the change of circumstances.*

(*b*) Cause is frequently expressed by **propter** or **ob** with the accusative.

propter <u>timōrem</u>, *on account of fear*

89. Ablative with *Ūtor*, etc.

The deponents **ūtor,** *use,* **fruor,** *enjoy,* **fungor,** *perform,* **potior,** *gain possession of,* and **vēscor,** *feed upon,* take their objects in the ablative.

Mīlitēs nostrī <u>hastīs</u> nōn ūtuntur, *Our soldiers do not use spears.*

(*a*) Occasionally the genitive is used with **potior** instead of the ablative.

<u>Urbis</u> potīrī cupiunt, *They wish to gain possession of the city.*

90. The Vocative

The vocative denotes the person addressed.

Ubi, <u>Mārce</u>, pater tuus est? *Marcus, where is your father?*

(*a*) The vocative regularly stands after one or more words of the sentence.

91. The Locative

With names of cities, towns, and small islands and with **domus,** place where is denoted by the locative case. The locative has the same form as the genitive in the singular of nouns of the first and second declensions. In the singular of nouns of the third declension and in all plural nouns it has the same form as the ablative.

Rōmae, *at Rome*   **domī,** *at home*   **Athēnīs,** *at Athens*

ADJECTIVES

92.   ADHERENT ADJECTIVES

An adjective which is directly connected with the noun which it modifies is called an adherent adjective.

vir **fortis**, *a brave man*   arbor **alta**, *a tall tree*

93.   PREDICATE ADJECTIVES

An adjective which is connected with its noun by some form of the verb meaning *to be* is called a predicate adjective.

Vir fortis est, *The man is brave.*

94.   SUBSTANTIVE USE OF ADJECTIVES

Adjectives and participles are sometimes used as substantives (nouns or pronouns). Words meaning *many, all, others, few,* and the like are especially common in this use. The masculine refers to men, or to persons in general, the feminine to women, and the neuter to things.

Multī tē laudant, *Many praise you.*

Omnia parāta sunt, *All things are prepared.*

In military expressions **nostrī** is used to mean *our men* or *our soldiers.* Other possessives are sometimes used with a similar meaning, as **tuī** or **vestrī,** *your men, your soldiers.*

95.   ADJECTIVES DENOTING A PART

There are a few adjectives which tell what part of an object is meant instead of telling what kind. Among the most important are **summus, medius, extrēmus,** and **īmus.**

> **summus** mōns, *the highest part of the mountain, the mountain top*
> **medius** collis, *the middle of the hill*
> **mediō** colle, *half-way up the hill* (*on the middle of the hill*)

96.   ADJECTIVES WITH ADVERBIAL FORCE

Sometimes an adjective modifying the subject or object is best translated by an adverb.

Invītī vēnērunt, *They came unwillingly.*

97.   TRANSLATION OF THE COMPARATIVE AND SUPERLATIVE

The comparative and superlative forms of adjectives and adverbs are commonly translated by the corresponding English forms. But sometimes the comparative is translated by a positive form preceded by *too* or *rather,* and the superlative by a positive form preceded by *very.*

altior, *rather high*   **altissimus,** *very high*

VERBS

INDICATIVE MOOD

98. INDICATIVE IN MAIN CLAUSES

The indicative is used in statements of fact and in questions which imply that the answer expected is a statement of fact.

Caesar aciem īnstrūxit, *Caesar drew up a line of battle.*

Quid Cōnsidius dīxit? *What did Considius say?*

99. INDICATIVE AFTER CERTAIN CONJUNCTIONS

The indicative is used in subordinate clauses after the conjunctions **quamquam,** *although*, **postquam,** *after*, **ubi,** *when*, and some others.

100. RELATIVE CLAUSES

A clause introduced by a relative pronoun commonly takes its verb in the indicative, except in the special uses described later. (See especially **104,** *a*, and **112.**)

101. NOUN (OR SUBSTANTIVE) CLAUSES WITH *QUOD*

A clause introduced by **quod** meaning *that*, with its verb in the indicative, is sometimes used as the subject or object of a verb, or in apposition with a noun or pronoun.

(*a*) Sometimes **quod** is translated *as to the fact that*, and the clause it introduces then serves as an adverbial modifier, loosely connected with the rest of the sentence.

SUBJUNCTIVE MOOD

102. SUBJUNCTIVE OF DESIRE

The subjunctive is used to express an act as willed by some person. This is sometimes called the volitive subjunctive.

Epistulās statim mittāmus, *Let us send the letters at once.*

(*a*) The negative used with the volitive subjunctive is **nē.**

Nē diūtius maneāmus, *Let us not remain longer.*

103.

The subjunctive, commonly with **utinam,** is used to express a wish. This is sometimes called the optative subjunctive. The use of tenses is as follows:

(1) A wish that something had been true in the past has the past perfect subjunctive.

Utinam hunc locum numquam vīdissem, *Would that I had never seen this place* (*I wish I had never seen this place*).

(2) A wish that something were true in the present has the imperfect subjunctive.

Utinam meliōrem ducem habērēmus, *Would that we had a better leader* (*I wish that we had a better leader*).

(3) A wish relating to the future has the present subjunctive.

(Utinam) frāter tuus salvus redeat, *May your brother return safely* (*I hope your brother may return safely*).

(*a*) The negative used with wishes is sometimes **nē** and sometimes **nōn**.

104.   CLAUSES OF PURPOSE

A subordinate clause which expresses purpose has its verb in the subjunctive. Such a clause is commonly introduced by **ut** or (if negative) by **nē**.

Vēnī ut tē vidērem, *I came to see you* (literally, *that I might see you*).
Mīlitēs missī sunt nē urbs caperētur, *Soldiers were sent that the city might not be captured.*

(*a*) Sometimes a purpose clause is introduced by a relative pronoun. This form of purpose clause is found chiefly after **mittō** and its compounds, and after **relinquō** and a few other verbs.

Puerum mittam quī tē adjuvet, *I will send a boy to help you* (literally, *who shall help you*).

(*b*) The clause of purpose may be translated by a simple infinitive, by an infinitive with *in order*, or by a clause with *that* or *in order that*. The following translations are possible for the sentence **Vēnī ut tē vidērem**:

> *I came to see you.*
> *I came in order to see you.*
> *I came that I might see you.*
> *I came in order that I might see you.*

105.

A purpose clause which contains a comparative form of an adjective or adverb is usually introduced by **quō** instead of **ut**.

Pontem faciunt quō facilius trānseant, *They are making a bridge that they may cross more easily.*

106.   CLAUSES OF RESULT

A subordinate clause which expresses result has its verb in the subjunctive. Such a clause is introduced by **ut,** or occasionally by a relative pronoun. The negative is **nōn**.

Mīlitēs tam fortiter restitērunt ut hostēs repellerentur, *The soldiers resisted so bravely that the enemy were driven back.*

Est nēmō tam sapiēns quī numquam erret, *There is no one so wise that he never errs.*

Tempestātēs tantae erant ut ex portū proficīscī nōn audērēmus, *The storms were so great that we did not dare to set out from the harbor.*

107. NOUN (OR SUBSTANTIVE) CLAUSES OF DESIRE

Verbs expressing an idea of desire, such as those meaning *to command*, *urge*, *persuade*, *request*, and the like, may take as object (or as subject in the passive) a clause introduced by **ut** or **nē** with its verb in the subjunctive.

Helvētiīs persuāsit ut exīrent, *He persuaded the Helvetians to emigrate.*

Mīlitibus imperāvit nē saxa jacerent, *He ordered the soldiers not to throw stones.*

(*a*) These clauses are frequently translated by an infinitive with a subject, as in the examples above.

(*b*) Such expressions as **jūs est,** *there is a law*, and **cōnsilium est,** *the plan is*, may be followed by a substantive clause telling what the law or plan is to which reference is made.

(*c*) The verbs **jubeō,** *order*, and **vetō,** *forbid*, regularly take an infinitive with subject accusative, instead of a clause with the subjunctive. Verbs meaning *to wish* sometimes take the infinitive with subject accusative.

Legiōnem flūmen trānsīre jussit, *He ordered the legion to cross the river.*

108. NOUN (OR SUBSTANTIVE) CLAUSES OF FACT

Verbs meaning *to accomplish* and impersonal verbs meaning *it happens*, *it results*, *it remains*, and the like take a dependent clause with the subjunctive, introduced by **ut.** The negative is **nōn.**

Accidit ut duae cohortēs ante castra essent, *It happened that there were two cohorts in front of the camp.*

(*a*) Such expressions as **mōs est,** *the custom is*, may be followed by a substantive clause with **ut,** telling what the custom is to which reference is made.

109. CLAUSES OF FEAR

Verbs and other expressions of fear may take a dependent clause with the subjunctive, introduced by **nē** translated *that* or **ut** translated *that . . . not.*

Verēbantur nē exercitus noster in Galliā manēret, *They feared that our army would remain in Gaul.*

Timeō ut sē fortiter dēfendat, *I fear that he will not defend himself bravely.*

(*a*) Sometimes **nē . . . nōn** is used instead of **ut** with words of fear.

Timeō nē sē nōn dēfendat, *I fear that he will not defend himself.*

(*b*) Such expressions as **perīculum est** may take the same construction as that used with words of fear.

Perīculum est nē cohors capiātur, *There is danger that the cohort will be captured.*

(*c*) The present subjunctive in clauses depending on words of fear is often translated by the English future indicative.

110.   ANTICIPATORY SUBJUNCTIVE

The subjunctive may be used in subordinate clauses to denote an act which is anticipated or expected.

Expectābam dum frāter redīret, *I was waiting until my brother should return (or for my brother to return).*

(*a*) The anticipatory subjunctive is used mainly after words meaning *until* or *before* (**dum, antequam, priusquam**). Occasionally this use is found after **cum** meaning *when.*

(*b*) Sometimes the indicative is used after words meaning *until* or *before,* to state a new fact which is of importance in the narrative or to represent an actual event as looked back upon.

111.   CLAUSES OF PROVISO

The conjunctions **dum, modo,** and **dummodo,** when meaning *provided, provided that,* or *if only,* take the subjunctive.

Urbs salva erit, dum tū exeās, *The city will be safe, provided you withdraw.*

112.   SUBJUNCTIVE IN RELATIVE CLAUSES OF DESCRIPTION

A relative clause with its verb in the subjunctive is sometimes used to describe the antecedent of the relative.

Paucī erant quī arma ferre nōn possent, *There were a few who could not bear arms.*

(*a*) Such clauses are used when the antecedents are indefinite or negative and with expressions of existence and non-existence, such as **sunt quī,** *there are those who,* **est nēmō quī,** *there is no one who.*

(*b*) A clause of description which is parenthetical in character or which has a personal pronoun or a proper noun as antecedent takes the indicative.

113.   *CUM* CAUSAL CLAUSES

A subordinate clause introduced by **cum** meaning *since* has its verb in the subjunctive.

Cum nūlla nāvis in cōnspectū sit, domum revertar, *Since there is no ship in sight, I shall return home.*

(*a*) Sometimes a causal clause with its verb in the subjunctive is introduced by a relative pronoun.

Fēlīx es quī tot amīcōs habeās, *You are fortunate, since you have* (literally, *who have*) *so many friends.*

114.   *CUM* CONCESSIVE CLAUSES

A subordinate clause introduced by **cum** meaning *although* has its verb in the subjunctive.

Cum ea urbs parva esset, tamen magnam glōriam habēbat, *Although that city was small, nevertheless it had great fame.*

(*a*) The principal clause with which a concessive clause is connected frequently, but not always, contains the adverb **tamen.**

(*b*) A concessive clause is sometimes introduced by a form of the relative pronoun.

Tum Cethēgus, quī paulō ante aliquid respondisset, repente conticuit, *Then Cethegus, although he* (literally, *who*) *had made some reply a little before, suddenly became silent.*

115. CUM DESCRIPTIVE CLAUSES OF SITUATION

The imperfect or past perfect subjunctive is often used in a clause introduced by **cum** meaning *when.* Such a clause describes the situation at the time of the main act.

Cum pōns factus esset, exercitus trāductus est, *When the bridge had been made, the army was led across.*

(*a*) If the clause with **cum** is used to make definite the time denoted by the adverb **tum** or any other word of time, it takes the indicative.

Tum cum hostēs impetum faciēbant, auxilium nōn missum est, *At the time when the enemy were making an attack, help was not sent.*

(*b*) If the verb of the **cum** clause denotes repeated action, it is commonly in the indicative. In such clauses **cum** is sometimes translated *whenever.*

Cum nāvem hostium vīderant, ad eam properābant, *Whenever they saw a ship of the enemy, they hurried toward it.*

(*c*) The present or future indicative, and occasionally the perfect indicative, may be used with **cum** meaning *when.*

116. CLAUSES WITH QUĪN, QUŌMINUS, ETC.

(1) Words and phrases of doubt, when accompanied by a negative, are followed by **quīn** and the subjunctive.

Nōn dubitō quīn Belgae fortēs sint, *I do not doubt that the Belgians are brave.*

Nōn est dubium quīn hoc fēcerit, *There is no doubt that he did this.*

(2) Verbs of hindrance, prevention, and check are followed by a subjunctive clause introduced by **quīn, quōminus,** or **nē.** **Quīn** is used only after a negative, **nē** only after an affirmative clause, and **quōminus** after either an affirmative or a negative.

Hostēs impedīvimus nē (or **quōminus**) **trānsīrent,** *We prevented the enemy from crossing.*

Hostēs nōn impedīvimus quīn (or **quōminus**) **trānsīre t,** *We did not prevent the enemy from crossing.*

117.   INDIRECT QUESTIONS

An indirect question has its verb in the subjunctive.

Dux quaesīvit in quō locō hostēs castra posuissent, *The leader asked where (in what place) the enemy had pitched camp.*

118.   SUBJUNCTIVE BY ATTRACTION

Sometimes a subordinate clause which would otherwise have its verb in the indicative takes the subjunctive because it is closely dependent on a subjunctive or an infinitive.

Ita ācriter pugnāvērunt ut omnēs hostēs quī flūmen trānsīssent celeriter repellerentur, *They fought so fiercely that all the enemy who had crossed the river were quickly driven back.*

119.   IMPLIED (OR INFORMAL) INDIRECT DISCOURSE

The subjunctive may be used in a subordinate clause to indicate that it is a quotation, although no main clause of indirect discourse stands in the context.

Servōs quī ad eōs perfūgissent poposcit, *He demanded the slaves who had fled to them (who he said had fled to them).*

120.   CAUSAL CLAUSES WITH *QUOD, QUIA,* AND *QUONIAM*

Clauses of reason introduced by **quod, quia,** and **quoniam** take the indicative to denote a reason given directly by the speaker or writer.   Such clauses, however, take the subjunctive if the reason is given as a quotation from someone else or from the thought or utterance of the writer or speaker at another time.

Profectus est quod verēbātur, *He set out because he was afraid.*

Grātiās cōnsulī ēgērunt quod rem pūblicam servāvisset, *They thanked the consul because (as they said) he had saved the state.*

121.   IMPERATIVE MOOD

The imperative mood is used to express commands.

Dēsilīte, commīlitōnēs, *Jump down, comrades.*

(*a*) While the English imperative is used only in the present tense and in the second person, the Latin imperative has a future as well as a present.   The future has the second and third persons; the present has only the second person.

122.   NEGATIVE COMMANDS

Negative commands (prohibitions) in the second person are commonly expressed by the imperative of **nōlō (nōlī, nōlīte)** with the infinitive of the verb denoting the act forbidden.

Nōlī hīc manēre, *Do not remain here.*

(*a*) Sometimes the perfect subjunctive with **nē** is used to express a negative command.

Nē hīc mānserīs, *Do not remain here.*

INFINITIVE

123. COMPLEMENTARY INFINITIVE

An infinitive is sometimes used to complete the meaning of another verb. When thus used, it denotes another action of the same subject as that of the verb on which it depends.

Omnēs redīre volunt, *All wish to return.*

124. INFINITIVE AS SUBJECT

The infinitive, with or without subject accusative, may be used as the subject of many impersonal verbs and also of **est** with a predicate adjective or noun. **Eum manēre oportet,** *He ought to stay.*

Mē īre necesse est, *I must go.*

(*a*) The subjunctive is sometimes used with **necesse est** and with a few verbs which commonly take the infinitive.

125. INFINITIVE WITH SUBJECT ACCUSATIVE

(1) The infinitive with subject accusative is used with words of *saying, hearing, knowing, thinking, believing, seeing,* and the like (Indirect Discourse).

Caesar dīcit Belgās omnium Gallōrum fortissimōs esse, *Caesar says the Belgians are the bravest of all the Gauls.*

(2) The infinitive with subject accusative is regularly used with **jubeō,** *order,* **vetō,** *forbid,* and sometimes with **patior,** *permit,* **cōgō,** *compel,* **volō,** *wish,* **nōlō,** *be unwilling,* **mālō,** *prefer.*

Dux mīlitēs impetum facere jussit, *The leader ordered the soldiers to make an attack.*

126. HISTORICAL INFINITIVE

Occasionally the infinitive is used in narration as the equivalent of the imperfect indicative or of the perfect denoting a simple past act.

Nostrī prīmō fortiter pugnāre, *At first our men fought bravely.*

(*a*) The subject of the historical infinitive is in the nominative case.

CONDITIONAL SENTENCES

127. NON-COMMITTAL CONDITIONAL SENTENCES

A conditional sentence which does not imply that the condition is either true or false has both verbs in the indicative.

Sī puerī in silvā errant, in perīculō sunt, *If the boys are wandering in the forest, they are in danger.*

Sī hostēs tūtī effūgērunt, nostrī eōs capere nōn cōnātī sunt, *If the enemy have escaped safely* (literally, *safe*), *our men did not try to capture them.*

(*a*) Sometimes an imperative or a subjunctive expressing *will* is used in the conclusion of a conditional sentence of this type instead of an indicative.

Sī pācem cupitis, arma trādite, *If you wish peace, surrender your arms.*

128.   FUTURE MORE VIVID CONDITIONAL SENTENCES

A future more vivid conditional sentence refers to future time and gives no indication as to the attitude of the speaker or writer toward the fulfillment of the condition.   The verbs are in the future (or future perfect) tense.

Sī auxilium **mittētur**, oppidum **dēfendētur**, *If aid is* (literally, *shall be*) *sent, the town will be defended.*

(*a*) The verb of the condition in a sentence of this type is commonly translated by the present indicative with future meaning, as in the example above. Sometimes the future with *shall* is used.

(*b*) The future perfect may be used in either clause to represent an act as occurring before some expressed or implied future time.

(*c*) The future more vivid conditional sentence is merely a non-committal conditional sentence in future time.

129.   FUTURE LESS VIVID CONDITIONAL SENTENCES

A future less vivid conditional sentence refers to future time, and implies doubt on the part of the writer or speaker as to the fulfillment of the condition. The conclusion refers to a future act or situation as conceivable or imaginable without asserting that it will take place or be realized.   The verbs are in the present (or perfect) subjunctive.

Sī mīlitēs flūmen **trānseant**, multī **interficiantur**, *If the soldiers should cross the river, many would be killed.*

(*a*) The perfect may be used in either clause to show that an act, if occurring, would take place before some expressed or implied future time.

130.   CONDITIONAL SENTENCES CONTRARY TO FACT

A conditional sentence which implies that the condition is not true has its verbs in the imperfect or past perfect subjunctive, the imperfect to refer to present time and the past perfect to refer to past time.

Sī Haeduī majōrēs cōpiās **habērent**, oppida **dēfenderent**, *If the Haeduans had larger forces, they would defend the towns.*

Sī Haeduī majōrēs cōpiās **habuissent**, oppida **dēfendissent**, *If the Haeduans had had larger forces, they would have defended the towns.*

Commonly the tense of the verbs in the two clauses is the same, but the imperfect may be used in one clause and the past perfect in the other, if the sense requires.

131.   INDIRECT DISCOURSE

Indirect discourse is used with words of *saying, hearing, knowing, thinking, believing,* and the like.   The use of moods is as follows:

(1) A main clause expressing a statement has its verb in the infinitive with subject accusative.

(2) A main clause expressing a command has its verb in the subjunctive.

(3) All subordinate clauses have their verbs in the subjunctive.

Eā condiciōne quae ā Caesare ferrētur sē ūsūrōs esse ostendēbant; sibi trīduī spatium daret, *They stated* (literally, *showed*) *that they would accept the terms which were offered by Caesar; let him give them the space of three days.*

132. PARTICIPLES

The Latin verb has four participles: present active, perfect passive, future active, and future passive.

(*a*) Deponent verbs have the same number of participles as other verbs. The perfect participle of a deponent is usually active in meaning, but it is occasionally used as a passive.

133. PRESENT PARTICIPLE

The present active participle denotes an act taking place at the same time as the main verb. It is less frequently used than the English present participle. Its declension is given in section **14.**

Nostrī in hostēs advenientēs impetum fēcērunt, *Our men made an attack on the enemy coming up* (i.e., *as they were coming up*).

(*a*) The English present participle is often used with a form of *to be* to make the progressive form of the verb. Thus, *he is marching, we were standing.* The Latin present participle is never so used.

134. PERFECT PARTICIPLE

The perfect passive participle denotes an act which took place before the time of the main verb. It is declined like **bonus,** section **9.**

Legiō ā Caesare praemissa castra mūniēbat, *The legion, having been sent ahead by Caesar, was fortifying the camp.*

135. FUTURE ACTIVE PARTICIPLE

The future active participle is used chiefly with forms of **sum** to denote an act which someone intends to do or is about to do. It is declined like **bonus.**

Bellum cum Gallīs gestūrī erant, *They intended to* (or *were about to*) *wage war with the Gauls.*

136. FUTURE PASSIVE PARTICIPLE

The future passive participle is used chiefly with forms of **sum** to denote an act which ought to be done or must be done by someone. It is declined like **bonus.**

Epistula mihi mittenda est, *A letter ought to be sent by me.*

(*a*) The future passive participle of a deponent verb is passive in meaning.

137.   GERUND

The gerund is a verbal noun of the second declension, used only in the genitive, dative, accusative, and ablative of the singular number.

(*a*) The genitive of the gerund is used chiefly as an objective genitive with an adjective or noun.   With the ablative **causā** it expresses purpose.

> **cupidus bellandī,** *desirous of engaging in war*
>
> **resistendī causā,** *for the purpose (sake) of resisting*

(*b*) The dative of the gerund is rarely used.

(*c*) The accusative of the gerund is frequently used as the object of the preposition **ad** to express purpose.   It is never used as a direct object.

> **ad oppugnandum,** *for attacking, to attack*

(*d*) The ablative of the gerund is used to express means or cause, or as object of the prepositions **ab, dē, ex, in.**

> **pugnandō,** *by fighting*   **in quaerendō,** *on inquiring*

The infinitive is used to supply the place of the missing nominative of the gerund.   The infinitive is also used instead of the gerund as an accusative of direct object.

138.   GERUNDIVE

The future passive participle is often used as a verbal adjective in a phrase which has the same meaning as a gerund with an object.   Such a verbal adjective is called a gerundive.

> **spēs urbis capiendae,** *hope of capturing the city*

(*a*) The case uses of the gerundive are in general the same as those of the gerund.

> **cupidus oppidī expugnandī,** *desirous of storming the town*
>
> **auxiliī ferendī causā,** *for the purpose (sake) of bringing aid*
>
> **ad eās rēs cōnficiendās,** *for accomplishing these things*
>
> **dē auxiliō mittendō,** *about (concerning) sending aid*
>
> **lapidibus portandīs,** *by carrying stones*

139.

The following distinctions between the gerund and the gerundive are to be observed:

GERUND	GERUNDIVE
A noun	An adjective
Active in meaning	Passive in meaning
Neuter gender	All genders
Used only in the singular	Both numbers
No nominative	All cases

(*a*) The genitive of the gerund, and also the ablative, when used without a preposition, sometimes take a direct object.   But no form of the gerund standing as the object of a preposition can have a direct object.   The gerundive must be used instead.

140.   SUPINE

The supine is a verbal noun of the fourth declension, used only in the accusative and ablative. The accusative is used to express purpose in clauses in which the finite verb expresses motion.

> **Lēgātōs pācem <u>petītum</u> mīsērunt,** *They sent envoys to ask peace.*

(*a*) The supine of a transitive verb may take a direct object.

141.

The ablative of the supine is used with a few adjectives as an ablative of respect. It is usually translated by the English present infinitive.

> **optimum <u>factū</u>,** *best to do* (*the best thing to do*)

142.   TENSES

The tenses of the Latin indicative are the present, imperfect, future, perfect, past perfect, and future perfect.   In the subjunctive only the present, imperfect, perfect, and past perfect are found.

143.   PRESENT

The present tense, as in English, is used to denote present time.

(*a*) In a narrative of past events the present indicative is sometimes used to present the situation more vividly to the reader or the hearer. This is called the historical present.

(*b*) The present subjunctive is sometimes used with future force. This is especially common in clauses of fear.

144.

A clause introduced by **dum** meaning *while* takes its verb in the present indicative.

> <u>**Dum** haec geruntur</u>, **ex urbe profectus sum,** *While this was going on, I set out from the city.*

(*a*) **Dum** meaning *as long as* may take any tense of the indicative which the sense requires.

145.   IMPERFECT

The imperfect tense represents a past act in progress or a past situation continuing.

(*a*) The imperfect indicative is sometimes used to denote a customary act or one of frequent occurrence in past time.

(*b*) The imperfect indicative is often translated by the progressive form of the English past tense—*was praising, was warning,* etc., but sometimes the simple English past is used as its equivalent.

(*c*) The imperfect subjunctive is sometimes used to express action which was at a past time thought of as future.

146. FUTURE

The future tense, as in English, denotes future time.

(*a*) When used with conjunctions meaning *if* or *when*, the future tense is regularly translated by the English present.

147. PERFECT

The perfect tense has two uses.

(1) It may be equivalent in meaning to an English present perfect (translated with the auxiliary verbs *have* or *has*).

(2) It may be equivalent to the English past tense, referring to an indefinite past act.

(*a*) In future less vivid conditional sentences the perfect subjunctive is sometimes used to refer to a future act which, if occurring, would take place before some expressed or implied future time.

148. PAST PERFECT

The past perfect is used to represent an act as having occurred before some expressed or implied past time.

(*a*) The past perfect subjunctive is sometimes used to refer to an act which was thought of in the past as likely to occur before some expressed or implied future time.

(*b*) The past perfect is sometimes used in subordinate clauses to denote repeated action.

149. FUTURE PERFECT

The future perfect is used to show that an act will occur before some expressed or implied future time.

(*a*) The future perfect is used more frequently in Latin than in English.

150. SEQUENCE OF TENSES

The tense of the subjunctive in a dependent clause usually bears a definite relation to the tense in the principal clause. This relation is called the sequence of tenses.

(1) If the main verb is present, future, or future perfect, the dependent subjunctive is present or perfect.

(2) If the main verb is imperfect, perfect, or past perfect, the dependent subjunctive is imperfect or past perfect.

A perfect indicative which is translated by an English present perfect may be followed by a present or perfect subjunctive.

151.

Exceptions to the rule for the sequence of tenses are sometimes found:

(1) In a clause of result a perfect subjunctive is sometimes used where ordinary sequence of tenses would demand an imperfect.

(2) The historical present may be followed either by the tenses which would follow a perfect or by the tenses which would follow a present.

(3) Sometimes a strongly marked difference between the time ideas of the subordinate clause and the main clause leads to a seeming disregard of the sequence of tenses.

152. **PREPOSITIONS**

The following prepositions take their objects in the ablative case: **ā (ab), cum, dē, ē (ex), prae, prō, sine.**

Cum is attached to the end of the following words: **mē, tē, sē, nōbīs,** and **vōbīs.** This is called the enclitic use of **cum.** The word is commonly also used as an enclitic with **quō, quā,** and **quibus.**

mēcum, *with me*   **tēcum,** *with you*   **quibuscum,** *with whom*

153.

The prepositions **in** and **sub** are used with the ablative in expressions denoting existence or continuance in a place; they are used with the accusative in expressions denoting motion toward a place.

In <u>urbe</u> **mānsī,** *I remained in the city.*   In <u>urbem</u> **vēnī,** *I came into the city.*

154.

All prepositions found in this book except those given above take their objects in the accusative.

155.

When the object of a monosyllabic preposition is a noun modified by an adjective, the preposition sometimes stands between the adjective and the noun.

magnō <u>cum</u> perīculō, *with great danger*

THE ROMAN CALENDAR

Our calendar is a modification of the calendar which was introduced into Rome in 45 B.C. by Julius Caesar. This was called the Julian calendar, and it continued in use unchanged throughout Europe until its correction by Pope Gregory XIII in 1582. In certain countries the Gregorian calendar, which is now in general use, did not displace the Julian calendar until the early part of the twentieth century.

Before Caesar's changes, the Roman calendar was based on the lunar month, i.e., the interval between one new moon and the next. But no lunar calendar can be made to fit the solar year exactly, because twelve lunar months make only about 355 days, whereas the solar year has about 365¼ days.

The Romans had made up this deficiency by adding days after the twenty-third of February in certain years. Caesar established a year of 365 days with a day added to every fourth year—like our leap year.

In Caesar's time the Roman months were named *Jānuārius, Februārius, Mārtius, Aprīlis, Maius, Jūnius, Quintīlis, Sextīlis, September, Octōber, November,* and *December.* Afterwards the name of *Quintīlis* was changed to *Jūlius* in honor of Julius Caesar's correction of the calendar, and later the name of *Sextīlis* was changed to *Augustus,* in honor of the first emperor.

In giving dates the Romans counted the days backward from three points in each month: *Kalendae* (the Kalends), *Nōnae* (the Nones), and *Īdūs* (the Ides).

The first day of each month was called the Kalends; the first of January, for example, was known as *Kalendae Jānuāriae* (usually abbreviated *Kal. Jān.*).

The Ides were the thirteenth day of every month except March, May, July, and October. In these months the Ides were the fifteenth. Thus, the thirteenth day of April was *Īdūs Aprīlēs (Īd. Apr.),* and the fifteenth of March was *Īdūs Mārtiae (Īd. Mār.).*

The Nones, as the name indicates, were nine days before the Ides. Since the Romans counted both the first and last days, the Nones, or ninth day before the Ides, would be the eighth day by our method of reckoning. Therefore, in those months on which the Ides were the thirteenth, the Nones were the fifth; similarly when the Ides were the fifteenth, the Nones were the seventh.

The day before each date-point was designated as *prīdiē.* So March 6 was *pr. Nōn. Mār.;* April 12 was *pr. Īd. Apr.;* December 31 was *pr. Kal. Jān.* Though December 31 was designated in reference to a January date-point, it was considered as a part of the month of December, as were all other "days before the Kalends."

The following table shows the designation of the days of each month:[1]

Mar., May, July, Oct.	Jan., Feb., Apr., June, Aug., Sept., Nov., Dec.		
1. Kal.	Kal.		
2. a.d. vi Nōn.[2]	a.d. iv Nōn.		
3. a.d. v Nōn.	a.d. iii Nōn.		
4. a.d. iv Nōn.	pr. Nōn.		
5. a.d. iii Nōn.	Nōn.		
6. pr. Nōn.	a.d. viii Īd.		
7. Nōn.	a.d. vii Īd.		
8. a.d. viii Īd.	a.d. vi Īd.		
9. a.d. vii Īd.	a.d. v Īd.		
10. a.d. vi Īd.	a.d. iv Īd.		
11. a.d. v Īd.	a.d. iii Īd.		
12. a.d. iv Īd.	pr. Īd.		
13. a.d. iii Īd.	Īdūs		
	Jan., Aug., Dec. 31 days	Apr., June, Sept., Nov. 30 days	Feb. 28 days
14. pr. Īd.	a.d. xix Kal.	a.d. xviii Kal.	a.d. xvi Kal.
15. Īdūs	a.d. xviii Kal.	a.d. xvii Kal.	a.d. xv Kal.
16. a.d. xvii Kal.	a.d. xvii Kal.	a.d. xvi Kal.	a.d. xiv Kal.
17. a.d. xvi Kal., etc.	a.d. xvi Kal., etc.	a.d. xv Kal., etc.	a.d. xiii Kal., etc.

In Roman times the daylight itself was divided into twelve hours, but the length of the hour varied at different times of the year. Each hour was always one-twelfth of the time between sunrise and sunset.

Thus in June, when the days are longest, the Roman hours were longest —a *hōra* was then about an hour and fifteen minutes. But in December the shortest *hōra* was only about forty-five minutes long.

A simple way to calculate the hours of the day is according to the old couplet:

The English hour you may fix
If to the Latin you add six.

The night was divided into four parts of equal length, each called a *vigilia*, or "watch."

[1] The method of calculating dates which is here given applies only to the years after 46 B.C.
[2] *ante diem* vi *Nōnae*, six days before the Nones.

NOTES ON THE VOCABULARY

The Vocabulary beginning on page 411 includes the basic words of *Latin Book Two*—those which occur frequently in the reading. Words which are needed to tell the story, but which are used only once or twice, are translated on the page, either in parentheses or in footnotes. The words of this "visible vocabulary" are not included in the following list, since they are not needed as a permanent part of the Latin vocabulary at this time. Attention of both pupil and teacher can thus be concentrated on acquisition of the basic vocabulary listed in the following pages.

The pronunciation of the English form of many proper names is given in the Vocabulary in parentheses after the name. The following key will help in pronouncing these words.

PRONUNCIATION KEY

a at, can	e end, bend	o on, not	u up, but
ā came, face	ē equal, be	ō more, open	ū use, pure
ä far, father	ė her, certain	ö move, to	u̇ full, put
â all, ball	ẹ prudent, towel	ô off, song	ụ̄ nature, picture
à ask		ǫ actor, second	
ã care, dare	i it, pin		ṅ as in French
ạ alone, company	ī line, mine		bon
ä̤ beggar, opera			zh azure, measure

A single dot under ā, ē, ō, ö, or ū means that the sound is a little shorter, as in cottạ̄ge, rẹ̄duce, demǫcrat, intọ̈, ụ̄nited.

A

ā, ab, *prep. with abl.: of place or source,* from, away from, from the vicinity of; *of position,* at, on, on the side of; *of time,* from, since, after; *of agency,* by; *adverbially with expressions of distance,* away, off, at a distance of.

ab-dō, -dere, -didī, -ditum, put away, hide, conceal.

ab-dūcō, -dūcere, -dūxī, -ductum, lead *or* take away, bring away; take aside.

ab-eō, -īre, -iī, -itum, go away, depart, retire; vanish.

abjiciō, -jicere, -jēcī, -jectum [ab+ jaciō], throw *or* cast away, throw aside, throw down; hurl, throw.

ablātus, -a, -um, *see* **auferō.**

abscīdō, -cīdere, -cīdī, -cīsum [abs+ caedō], cut off *or* away, tear off *or* away.

absēns, *gen.* **-entis,** *adj.* [absum], absent, away.

ab-sum, -esse, āfuī, āfutūrus, be away, be distant, be absent; refrain from, take no part in; be wanting *or* lacking.

Absyrtus, -ī, *m.,* Absyrtus (ab-sèr'tus), *brother of Medea.*

ab-undō, -āre, -āvī, — [unda, wave], overflow; abound; **abundāns,** *gen.* **-antis,** *pres. part.,* overflowing, superabundant.

ac, *see* **atque.**

accēdō, -cēdere, -cessī, -cessum [ad+ cēdō], come near *or* to, approach; be added, be in addition; be inspired in.

accendō, -cendere, -cendī, -cēnsum [ad+candeō, glitter], set fire to, kindle, light; inflame, excite.

acceptus, -a, -um, *adj.* [pf. part. of **accipiō**], acceptable, pleasing, popular.

accidō, -cidere, -cidī, — [ad+cadō], fall to *or* upon, fall; happen, come about, occur; happen to.

accipiō, -cipere, -cēpī, -ceptum [ad+ capiō], take, take in, receive, accept; learn, hear; endure, suffer.

accurrō, -currere, -currī, -cursum [ad+currō], run to, hasten to, come up hurriedly.

ācer, ācris, ācre, *adj.,* sharp, keen; harsh, severe, spirited, bold, eager, fierce.

Achillēs, Achillis, *m.,* Achilles (a-kil'ēz), *a famous Greek hero.*

aciēs, -ēī, *f.,* tip, point, sharp edge; line of battle, battle-line, battle array; encounter, battle; flash (*of the eye*).

ācriter, *adv.* [ācer], sharply, vigorously, fiercely, severely, bravely.

acūtus, -a, -um, *adj.* [pf. part. of **acuō,** sharpen], sharpened, sharp, pointed.

ad, *prep. with acc.: with verbs of motion,* to, up to, toward, to the vicinity of; *of position,* at, near; *to express purpose,* for, to; *of time,* up to, until, on; *with expressions of number or amount,* about, toward; *in other relations,* at, according to, up to, among, in the eyes of; *used adverbially with numerals,* about.

ad-dō, -dere, -didī, -ditum, add, join to, attach; give.

ad-dūcō, -dūcere, -dūxī, -ductum, lead *or* bring to, lead against, conduct, bring; draw to, pull taut, draw tight; induce, influence.

ad-eō, -īre, -iī, -itum, go *or* come up to, come up, approach; visit.

ad-eō, *adv.,* to such an extent *or* degree, so, so much; indeed, in fact.

adhibeō, -ēre, -uī, -itum [ad+habeō], apply; summon, admit, invite; use, employ; have on hand; supply.

ad-hūc, *adv.,* until now, heretofore, as yet; yet, still.

adigō, -igere, -ēgī, -āctum [ad+agō], drive (to), compel, urge; hurl, send *or* drive home (*a weapon*), thrust; drive down, ram in *or* down; bind, obligate; haul, move.

aditus, -ūs, *m.* [adeō, -īre], way of approach, approach, entrance; access; means, right.

adjiciō, -jicere, -jēcī, -jectum [ad+jaciō], hurl toward *or* upon, hurl, throw; add, add to; say in addition.

ad-jungō, -jungere, -jūnxī, -jūnctum, join to, attach, add; associate.

ad-juvō, -āre, -jūvī, -jūtum, aid, help, assist; support, sustain.

ad-ministrō, -āre, -āvī, -ātum, manage, administer, attend to, superintend, direct, govern.

ad-mīror, -ārī, -ātus sum, be astonished at, admire; wonder, wonder at, be surprised.

ad-mittō, -mittere, -mīsī, -missum, admit, receive; let go, give reins to; commit.

ad-modum, *adv.,* to the limit; fully, very, quite, very much.

adolēscō, -ere, adolēvī, adultum, grow up, grow to maturity.

ad-orior, -orīrī, -ortus sum, rise against; fall upon, attack, assail.

ad-sum, -esse, -fuī, -futūrus, be at hand, be present, be here, be near; attend, assist, support.

adulēscēns, *gen.* **-entis,** *adj.* [*pres. part. of* adolēscō], youthful, young; *m. and f. as noun,* **adulēscēns, -entis,** a young man *or* woman, a youth; the younger, junior.

ad-veniō, -venīre, -vēnī, -ventum, come to, come up, approach, arrive.

adventus, -ūs, *m.* [adveniō], approach, coming, arrival.

adversus, -a, -um, *adj.* [*pf. part. of* advertō], turned toward, facing, in front, opposite; in the face of; unfavorable, adverse, hostile.

adversus, *prep. with acc.,* against, opposed to; opposite, facing.

ad-vertō, -vertere, -vertī, -versum, turn to, direct to; proceed against; **animum advertere,** observe, notice.

aedificium, -ī, *n.* [aedificō], a building, structure.

aedificō, -āre, -āvī, -ātum [aedēs, building+faciō], build, construct.

Aeētēs, -ae, *m.,* Aeëtes (ē-ē′tēz), *a king of Colchis* (*see map, p. 116*).

aeger, -gra, -grum, *adj.,* ill, sick, feeble.

aegrē, *adv.* [aeger], painfully; with difficulty, hardly; with grief; with resentment; **aegrē ferre,** be indignant, resent.

Aenēās, -ae, *m.,* Aeneas (ē-nē′ạs), *a Trojan hero who settled in Italy.*

aēneus, -a, -um, *adj.* [aes], of copper, of bronze.

Aeolus, -ī, *m.,* Aeolus (ē′ọ̄-lus), *the god of the winds.*

aequō, -āre, -āvī, -ātum [aequus], make even *or* equal, equalize; be equal to, equal.

aequus, -a, -um, *adj.,* even, level, smooth, flat; equal; just, fair, favorable; calm, composed; kindly.

aes, aeris, *n.,* copper, bronze; money; **aes aliēnum,** (another's money), debt.

Aesōn, -onis, *m.,* Aeson (ē′sọn), *the father of Jason.*

aestās, -ātis, *f.,* summer; **initā aestāte,** at the beginning of summer.

aestus, -ūs, *m.,* boiling, heat; tide, breakers.

aetās, -ātis, *f.,* time of life, age; lifetime, generation.

afferō, -ferre, attulī, allātum [ad+ferō], bring *or* carry to, bring; bring forward, allege; bring news, report.

afficiō, -ficere, -fēcī, -fectum [ad+faciō], do to; affect, treat; visit with, afflict; reward, honor; cause, occasion; **magnō dolōre afficere,** annoy greatly.

Āfrica, -ae, *f.,* Africa.

Agamemnōn, -onis, *m.,* Agamemnon (ag-ạ-mem'non), *the leader of the Greeks in the Trojan War.*

ager, agrī, *m.,* field, land, farm; country, territory, district.

agger, -eris, *m.* [ad+gerō], mound, siege-mound, rampart, earthwork, dike; materials for a siege-mound, materials for a rampart.

aggredior, -gredī, -gressus sum [ad+ **gradior,** step], advance against, attack; begin, undertake; approach.

agmen, -inis, *n.* [agō], a marching army, a column, a marching column; army; **agmen claudere,** to bring up the rear; **novissimum agmen,** the rear, rear line *or* column.

agō, -ere, ēgī, āctum, drive; bring up; do, act, transact, perform, attend to; spend, pass; hold, preside over (*courts, assemblies*); treat, deal, confer; move up; construct, make.

agricola, -ae, *m.* [ager+colō], farmer.

agricultūra, -ae, *f.,* agriculture.

Agrippa, -ae, *m.,* Menenius Agrippa (mẹ-nē'ni-us a-grip'ạ), *a prominent Roman of the early Republic.*

aiō, *defective verb,* say, affirm.

āla, -ae, *f.,* wing (*of a bird*); wing (*of an army*); squadron (*of cavalry*).

alacer, -cris, -cre, *adj.,* active, spirited, eager, keen, ready, cheerful.

alacritās, -ātis, *f.* [alacer], activity, energy, eagerness, readiness.

Albānus, -a, -um, *adj.,* Alban, of Alba Longa (*see map, p. 305*); *m. pl. as noun,* **Albānī, -ōrum,** the Albans, the people of Alba Longa.

albus, -a, -um, *adj.,* white.

Alcmēna, -ae, *f.,* Alcmene (alk-mē'nē), *the mother of Hercules.*

Alesia, -ae, *f.,* Alesia (ạ-lē'zhyạ), *a Gallic town, the scene of the final stand made by Vercingetorix against the Romans. See map, page 137.*

aliēnus, -a, -um, *adj.* [alius], of another, another's, of others, others, alien, foreign, strange; out of place; out of harmony; inappropriate; unfavorable; **aes aliēnum** (another's money), debt.

aliquī, aliqua, aliquod, *adj.,* some, any.

aliquis, aliquid, *pron.,* someone, somebody, anyone, anything, something.

aliquot, *indecl. adj.,* several, some, a small number of.

aliter, *adv.* [alius], otherwise, in another way, differently; on any other conditions; **aliter ac,** otherwise than, differently from what.

alius, -a, -ud, *adj.,* another, other; different, else; **alius . . . alius,** one . . . another; *pl.,* **aliī . . . aliī,** some . . . others.

Allia, -ae, *f.,* the Allia (al'i-ạ), *a small river near Rome. See map, page 305.*

Allobrogēs, -um, *m. pl.,* the Allobroges (a-lob'rọ-jēz), *a Gallic tribe in the Roman province of Transalpine Gaul. See map, page 137.*

alloquor, -loquī, -locūtus sum [ad+ **loquor**], speak to, address, greet.

alō, -ere, aluī, altum, nourish, feed, support; keep, rear; sustain, increase.

Alpēs, -ium, *f. pl.,* the Alps. *See map, page 137.*

alter, altera, alterum, *adj.,* one of two, the other, a second, another; **alter . . . alter,** the one . . . the other.

altitūdō, -inis, *f.* [altus], height, altitude, depth.

altus, -a, -um, *adj.* [*pf. part.* of alō], nourished, well-grown; high, lofty; deep; profound; *n. as noun,* **altum, -ī,** deep water; the deep, the sea.

Amāzones, -um, *f. pl.,* the Amazons, *a fabulous race of women warriors.*

Ambiorīx, -īgis, *m.,* Ambiorix (am-bĭ'ọ-riks), *a king of the Eburones, a tribe of Belgic Gaul (see map, p. 137).*

ambō, -ae, -ō, *num. adj.,* both.

ambulō, -āre, -āvī, -ātum, walk.

amīcitia, -ae, *f.* [amīcus], friendship.

amīcus, -a, -um, *adj.* [amō], friendly, loving, kind; *m. as noun,* a friend.

ā-mittō, -mittere, -mīsī, -missum, lose; let slip, miss; send away.

amō, -āre, -āvī, -ātum, love.

ā-moveō, -movēre, -mōvī, -mōtum, move away, remove.

amphitheātrum, -ī, *n.,* amphitheater.

amplius, *compar. adv.,* more, in addition; *n.* **amplius, -ī,** more, a greater amount.

amplus, -a, -um, *adj.,* large, of great extent, great, spacious, noted, renowned, honorable, splendid, magnificent, generous.

Amūlius, -ī, *m.,* Amulius (a-mū'li-us), *a king of Alba Longa* (*see map, p. 305*).

an, *conj., used in double questions,* or; **utrum . . . an,** whether . . . or; *used alone, introducing a question,* or is it that? can it be that?

Anchīsēs, -ae, *m.,* Anchises (an-kī'-sēz), *the father of Aeneas.*

ancilla, -ae, *f.,* maid-servant.

ancora, -ae, *f.,* anchor; **ancoram tollere,** weigh anchor, set sail.

Ancus Mārcius, *m.,* Ancus Marcius (ang'kus mär'shius), *the fourth king of Rome.*

angustia, -ae, *f.* [angustus], narrowness; *usually pl.,* a narrow place *or* pass, difficulties.

angustus, -a, -um, *adj.,* narrow, confined.

animadvertō, -vertere, -vertī, -versum [animus+advertō], turn *or* direct the mind to, observe, notice.

animal, animālis, -ium, *n.,* a living being, an animal.

animus, -ī, *m.,* soul, mind, courage, spirit; feeling, heart, disposition, nature; high spirit, arrogance; **animum advertere,** observe, notice.

annus, -ī, *m.,* year.

ante, *prep. with acc., and adv.: as prep.,* before, in front of; *as adv.,* before, formerly, previously, ago.

anteā, *adv.,* formerly, previously, before, first.

ante-cēdō, -cēdere, -cessī, -cessum, precede, go ahead; surpass, excel, go before.

ante-quam *or* **ante quam,** *conj.,* before.

antīquitus, *adv.* [antīquus], from early times, in former times, long ago.

antīquus, -a, -um, *adj.,* old, former, ancient, of long ago; *m. pl. as noun,* **antīquī, -ōrum,** the ancients.

antrum, -ī, *n.,* cave, grotto, cavern.

ānxius, -a, -um, *adj.,* anxious, apprehensive, troubled.

aperiō, -īre, aperuī, apertum, open, open up, make accessible; establish; reveal, disclose, make known.

apertus, -a, -um, *adj.* [*pf. part. of* **aperiō**], open, exposed, unprotected; plain, evident; frank, candid.

Apollō, Apollinis, *m.,* Apollo (a-pol'ō), *the god of archery, prophecy, music, poetry, and medicine.*

appāritor, -ōris, *m.,* servant, attendant.

appellō, -āre, -āvī, -ātum, call by name, address, call to, greet, salute; call upon, appeal to; give name to, name, call.

appellō, -pellere, -pulī, -pulsum [ad+pellō], drive to, bring to; *with or without* **nāvem,** bring to land, bring up, come to land, land, put ashore.

appetō, -petere, -petīvī, -petītum [ad+petō], strive after, seek; approach, be at hand.

appropinquō, -āre, -āvī, -ātum [ad+propinquō, draw near], approach.

apud, *prep. with acc.,* at, near, before; among, in, with; to; in the vicinity of; at the house of; in the possession of; in the opinion of; on the bank of.

aqua, -ae, *f.,* water.

aquila, -ae, *f.,* eagle; the eagle (*of metal, as standard of a Roman legion*).

Aquileia, -ae, *f.,* Aquileia (ä-kwē-lē'-yä), *a city of Cisalpine Gaul. See map, page 137.*

āra, -ae, *f.,* altar.

Arar, -aris, *m.,* the Arar (ā'rär), *a river in Celtic Gaul, now called the Saône* (sōn). *See map, page 137.*

arbitror, -ārī, -ātus sum [arbiter, judge], judge, think, believe, suppose, consider.

arbor, -oris, *f.,* tree.

arcessō, -ere, arcessīvī, arcessītum, send for, summon, call, invite, seek.

arcus, -ūs, *m.,* bow, arch.

Ardea, -ae, *f.,* Ardea (är'dē-ạ), *a town of the Rutuli. See map, page 305.*

ārdeō, -ēre, ārsī, ārsūrus, be on fire, blaze, burn, burn up, be consumed; be inflamed (*with emotion*); **ārdēns,** *gen.* **ārdentis,** *pres. part.,* burning, blazing.

Argonautae, -ārum, *m. pl.,* the crew of the *Argo,* the Argonauts.

Argus, -ī, *m.,* Argus (är'gus), *the builder of the Argo.*

āridus, -a, -um, *adj.* [āreō, be dry], parched, arid; *n. as noun,* **āridum, -ī,** dry land.

ariēs, -etis, *m.,* ram; a battering-ram; a buttress.

Ariovistus, -ī, *m.,* Ariovistus (ā'ri-ọ-vis'tus), *a king of the Germans.*

arma, -ōrum, *n. pl.,* arms, weapons, accoutrements, implements, equipment.

armātus, -a, -um, *adj.* [*pf. part. of* **armō**], armed, equipped, in arms; *m. pl. as noun,* **armātī, -ōrum,** armed men, troops, soldiers.

armō, -āre, -āvī, -ātum [arma], arm, equip, fit out.

arō, -āre, -āvī, -ātum, plow, till.

Arrūns, -untis, *m.,* Arrūns Tarquinius, Arruns Tarquinius (ar'unz tärkwin'i-us), (*1*) *a son of Tarquinius Priscus;* (*2*) *a grandson of Tarquinius Priscus and nephew of* (*1*).

ars, artis, -ium, *f.,* skill, art; business, calling, profession; art; branch of study, study; quality, gift; artifice, craft, cunning.

Arvernī, -ōrum, *m. pl.,* the Arverni (är-ver'nĭ), *a tribe of Celtic Gaul. See map, page 137.*

arx, arcis, -ium, *f.,* citadel, fortress, stronghold.

ascendō, -scendere, -scendī, -scēnsum [ad+scandō, climb], ascend, climb, mount; go aboard.

Asia, -ae, *f.,* Asia.

aspiciō, -spicere, aspexī, aspectum [ad+speciō, look], look at, behold, look on; inspect, examine.

assiduus, -a, -um, *adj.,* close at hand; continual, constant.

at, *conj.* (*used to contradict or introduce objections*), but, yet, at least; but (you say).

Athēnae, -ārum, *f. pl.,* Athens. *See map, page 61.*

Atīlius, -ī, *m.,* M. Atīlius Rēgulus, Marcus Atilius Regulus (ạ-til'i-us reg'ū-lus), *a consul in 256 B.C.*

Atlās, -antis, *m.,* Atlas, *a giant who held up the heavens on his shoulders.*

atque (*before consonants* **ac**), *conj.* [ad+-que], and; and also, and even, and especially; *after words of likeness and unlikeness,* as, than, from; **simul atque,** as soon as.

Atrebās, -ātis, *m.,* one of the Atrebates (at-rē-bā'tēz), an Atrebatian; *pl.,* the Atrebates, Atrebatians, *a tribe of Belgic Gaul.*

ātrium, -ī, *n.,* atrium, *the principal room or hall of a Roman house.*

attingō, -tingere, -tigī, -tāctum [ad+tangō], touch, reach, attain; border *or* touch upon, adjoin; arrive at.

attribuō, -tribuere, -tribuī, -tribūtum [ad+tribuō], allot, assign, hand over; ascribe, attribute.

Atuatucī, -ōrum, *m. pl.,* the Atuatuci (at-ū-at'ū-sī), *a tribe of Belgic Gaul, descended from the Teutones and Cimbri. See map, page 137.*

auctor, -ōris, *m.* [augeō], promoter, instigator, originator, leader, author, cause; supporter.

auctōritās, -ātis, *f.* [auctor], influence, authority, prestige, dignity, standing.

auctus, -a, -um, *adj.* [*pf. part. of* augeō], increased; abundant, ample.

audācia, -ae, *f.* [audāx], daring, boldness; audacity, presumption.

audācter, *adv.* [audāx], boldly, bravely, fiercely.

audāx, *gen.* **-ācis,** *adj.*, daring, bold; presumptuous.

audeō, -ēre, ausus sum, *semi-deponent,* dare, venture; be daring *or* courageous.

audiō, -īre, -īvī, -ītum, hear, listen to; hear of; learn.

auferō, -ferre, abstulī, ablātum [ab+ ferō], carry away, carry off, remove; make way with, destroy.

augeō, -ēre, auxī, auctum, enlarge, make grow, increase.

augurium, -ī, *n.* [augur, augur], augury, divination, omen.

Augustus, -ī, *m.,* Octavius Caesar Augustus, *the first Roman emperor.*

Aulus, -ī, *m.,* Aulus (â'lus), *a Roman first name.*

aureus, -a, -um, *adj.* [aurum], of gold, golden.

aurīga, -ae, *m.,* driver (*of a chariot*), charioteer.

aurum, -ī, *n.,* gold.

Aurunculeius, -ī, *m.,* Lucius Aurunculeius (â-run-kū-lē'yus) Cotta, *one of Caesar's lieutenants.*

aut, *conj.,* or; **aut . . . aut,** either . . . or.

autem, *conj.* (*never stands first in its clause*), but, on the other hand, however; furthermore, moreover.

auxilium, -ī, *n.* [augeō], help, aid, assistance, support; resource, resort; *pl.,* auxiliary troops, auxiliaries, reinforcements.

ā-vehō, -vehere, -vexī, -vectum, carry off, take away.

ā-vertō, -vertere, -vertī, -versum, turn away, turn aside, avert, divert.

avis, avis, -ium, *f.,* bird.

ā-volō, -āre, -āvī, -ātūrus, fly away; flee away, flee.

avus, -ī, *m.,* grandfather.

Axona, -ae, *m.,* the Aisne (ān), *a river of Belgic Gaul. See map, page 137.*

B

baculum, -ī, *n.,* staff, cane.

balteus, -ī, *m.,* girdle, belt; swordbelt.

barbarus, -a, -um, *adj.,* foreign, barbarous, barbarian, uncivilized, rude; *m. pl. as noun,* **barbarī, -ōrum,** barbarians.

Belgae, -ārum, *m. pl.,* the Belgae (bel'jē), the Belgians, *one of the three divisions of the Gallic peoples. See map, page 137.*

bellō, -āre, -āvī, -ātum [bellum], carry on war, wage war.

Bellovacī, -ōrum, *m. pl.,* the Bellovaci (be-lov'ā-sī), *a tribe of Belgic Gaul. See map, page 137.*

bellum, -ī, *n.,* war; **bellum īnferre,** wage war (on).

bene, *adv.* [bonus], well, rightly, successfully; quite; *compar.,* **melius,** better; *superl.,* **optimē,** best.

beneficium, -ī, *n.* [bene+faciō], kindness, favor, benefit, kind deed, service; privilege, distinction, honor.

benignē, *adv.* [benignus], kindly, courteously.

benignus, -a, -um, *adj.,* kind, courteous, agreeable.

bibō, -ere, bibī, —, drink.

Bibracte, -is, *n.,* Bibracte (bī-brak'tē), *the chief town of the Haedui. See map, page 137.*

bīduum, -ī, *n.* [bi-+diēs], a period of two days, two days.

bīnī, -ae, -a, *num. adj.,* by twos, two each, two at a time.

bis, *adv.,* twice, doubly, in two ways.

Boiī (Bōī), -ōrum, *m. pl.,* the Boii (bō'i-ī), *a tribe of Celtic Gaul. See map, page 137.*

bonus, -a, -um, *adj.,* good, worthy; kind, kindly, well-disposed; *n. as noun,* **bonum, -ī,** good, blessing, boon, advantage; **bona, -ōrum,** *n. pl.,* goods, property; *compar.,* **melior, melius,** better; *superl.,* **optimus, -a, -um,** best, excellent.

bōs, bovis (*see Gr. S., 8*), *m. and f.,* bull, ox, cow; *pl.,* cattle, oxen.

bracchium, -ī, *n.,* the forearm, arm.

brevis, -e, *adj.,* short (*of space or time*), brief, short-lived, small; **brevī** or **brevī tempore,** in a short time, quickly, soon.

Britannia, -ae, *f.,* Britain, Great Britain. *See map, page 237.*

Brūtus, -ī, *m.,* **L. Jūnius Brūtus,** Lucius Junius Brutus (jū'ni-us brö'tus), *one of the first two consuls.*

C

C., *abbr. for* **Gāius.**

Cācus, -ī, *m.,* Cacus (kā'kus), *a giant.*

cadō, -ere, cecidī, cāsūrus, fall, happen; fall (dead), be slain, perish.

caecus, -a, -um, *adj.,* blind; hidden, concealed; dark, obscure.

caedēs, caedis, -ium, *f.* [**caedō**], murder, slaughter, massacre, bloodshed.

caedō, -ere, cecīdī, caesum, cut, hew, cut down, cut to pieces, kill, slay; rout, strike.

caelestis, -e, *adj.* [**caelum**], heavenly, celestial; *m. pl. as noun,* **caelestēs, -ium,** gods, divinities.

caelum, -ī, *n.,* sky, heaven, air; climate.

caerimōnia, -ae, *f.,* religious ceremony, ceremony, rite.

Caesar, -aris, *m.,* Caesar; (*1*) **C. Jūlius Caesar,** Gaius Julius Caesar, *the conqueror of Gaul, consul in 59* B.C., *later dictator;* (*2*) **L. Caesar,** Lucius Caesar, *a distant relative of* (*1*), *who served as his lieutenant in Gaul.*

calamitās, -ātis, *f.,* disaster, calamity, loss, misfortune.

calceus, -ī, *m.,* shoe.

callidus, -a, -um, *adj.* [**calleō,** be callous, be experienced], experienced, skilful; shrewd.

Camillus, -ī, *m.,* M. Furius Camillus (ka-mil'us), *a famous Roman general of the fourth century* B.C.

campus, -ī, *m.,* plain, field; *especially* the **Campus Mārtius,** the field of Mars, *originally an exercise and parade-ground in Rome, dedicated to Mars.*

canis, -is, *m. and f.,* dog, hound.

capiō, -ere, cēpī, captum, take, take possession of, capture, seize; reach; receive, get; choose, select; adopt, conceive; assume; contain, hold; **initium capere ab,** begin at.

Capitōlīnus, -a, -um, *adj.* [**Capitōlium**], of the Capitol, Capitoline; *m. as noun,* **Capitōlīnus, -ī,** the Capitoline Hill. *See map, page 39.*

Capitōlium, -ī, *n.,* the Capitol, *the Temple of Jupiter in Rome;* the Capitoline Hill, *on which the Capitol stood.*

captīvus, -ī, *m.* [**capiō**], prisoner, captive.

Capua, -ae, *f.,* Capua (kap'ū-ä), *a city of Italy. See map, page 277.*

caput, capitis, *n.,* head; top; source *or* mouth of a river; a person, citizen, individual; a citizen's status, citizenship; chief city, capital.

Capys, Capyos, *m.,* Capys (kā'pis), *a Trojan.*

carcer, -eris, *m.,* prison, dungeon; stall at the starting-point on a race-track, barrier.

Carnutēs, -um, *m. pl.,* the Carnutes (kär'nö-tēz), *a tribe of Celtic Gaul. See map, page 137.*

carō, carnis, *f.,* flesh, meat.

carpentum, -ī, *n.,* a carriage (*with two wheels*).

carrus, -ī, *m.,* cart.

Carthāginiēnsis, -e, *adj.* [Carthāgō], of Carthage, Carthaginian; *m. pl. as noun,* **Carthāginiēnsēs, -ium,** the Carthaginians.

Carthāgō, -inis, *f.*, Carthage, *a city of northern Africa. See map, page 277.*

cārus, -a, -um, *adj.*, dear, beloved, precious; expensive.

casa, -ae, *f.*, hut, cottage.

Cassandra, -ae, *f.*, Cassandra (ka-san'drạ), *a daughter of Priam, who foretold future events correctly, but was never believed.*

Cassius, -ī, *m.*, **L. Cassius,** Lucius Cassius Longinus ((kash'ius lon-jī'nus), *consul in 107* B.C.

castellum, -ī, *n.* [*diminutive of* **castrum,** fort], fort, fortress, stronghold, redoubt.

castra, -ōrum, *n. pl.* [**castrum,** fort], camp, military encampment; **castra movēre,** break camp; **castra pōnere,** pitch camp.

cāsus, -ūs, *m.* [cadō], a falling, fall; accident, chance, occurrence; emergency; extremity; case (*in grammar*), condition; misfortune, disaster, calamity, fate; **cāsū,** *abl.*, by accident, by chance, accidentally.

catēna, -ae, *f.*, chain, shackle, fetter.

causa, -ae, *f.*, cause, reason, motive, excuse; a cause, interest; position, condition; a case (*at law*), cause, trial, lawsuit; **causā,** *with preceding gen.*, for the sake of, for the purpose of, on account of, by reason of; **causam dīcere,** plead a case.

caveō, -ēre, cāvī, cautum, beware of, beware, guard against, be on one's guard, take care.

cēdō, -ere, cessī, cessum, go away, give way, retreat, withdraw; yield, yield to, yield to in rank.

celer, celeris, celere, *adj.*, swift, speedy, sudden.

celeritās, -ātis, *f.* [celer], speed, swiftness, quickness.

celeriter, *adv.* [celer], swiftly, quickly.

cēlō, -āre, -āvī, -ātum, conceal, hide, keep secret.

cēna, -ae, *f.*, dinner.

cēnō, -āre, -āvī, -ātum [cēna], dine, dine upon.

cēnseō, -ēre, -uī, -um, assess; estimate, think, believe; propose, vote.

cēnsus, -ūs, *m.* [cēnseō], census, *enumeration of people according to wealth for purposes of taxation and military service;* census rating, wealth.

Centaurus, -ī, *m.*, centaur, *a mythical creature with a horse's body and a man's head.*

centum, *indecl. num. adj.*, a hundred.

centuriō, -ōnis, *m.* [centuria, a hundred men], centurion, *commander of a century.*

Cerberus, -ī, *m.*, Cerberus (sèr'be-rus), *the fabled watch-dog of the lower world.*

cernō, -ere, crēvī, crētum, separate, distinguish; discern, see.

certāmen, -inis, *n.* [certō, fight], struggle, battle; contest, trial, rivalry, emulation.

certē, *adv.* [certus], surely, certainly, at least, at all events.

certus, -a, -um, *adj.*, definite, settled, certain, fixed; assured, established; trustworthy, unerring, sure; (**aliquem) certiōrem facere,** to inform (someone).

cervus, -ī, *m.*, stag, deer.

(cēterus), -a, -um, *adj.* (*masculine nom. sing. not in use, chiefly plural forms employed*), the other, the rest of, the remaining; *m. pl. as noun,* **cēterī, -ōrum,** the rest, the others, the remainder, all the rest.

Charōn, -ontis, *m.*, Charon (kā'ron), *the ferryman over the River Styx.*

cibārius, -a, -um, *adj.* [cibus], pertaining to food *or* rations; *n. pl. as noun,* **cibāria, -ōrum,** provisions, rations, food.

cibus, -ī, *m.*, food.

Cicerō, -ōnis, *m.,* Cicero: (*1*) Marcus Tullius Cicero, *the famous orator;* (*2*) Quintus Tullius Cicero, *one of Caesar's lieutenants in Gaul, brother of the famous orator.*

Cimber, -brī, *m.,* a Cimbrian; **Cimbrī, -ōrum,** *pl.,* the Cimbri (sim'brī), *a people of northern Germany.*

Cincinnātus, -ī, *m.,* L. **Quīnctius Cincinnātus,** L. Quinctius Cincinnatus (kwingk'shius sin-si-nā'tus), *a famous Roman of the fifth century* B.C.

cingō, -ere, cīnxī, cīnctum, surround, encircle; gird on, gird.

Circē, -ēs, *f.,* Circe (sėr'sē), *an enchantress.*

circiter, *adv., and prep. with acc.:* as *adv.,* about, nearly, approximately; *as prep.,* about, near.

circuitus, -ūs, *m.* [**circumeō,** go around], a going around, a circuit, compass; **in circuitū,** all around, on all sides.

circum, *prep. with acc.* [**circus**], around, about.

circum-dō, -dare, -dedī, -datum, place *or* put around; trace around; surround, encircle.

circum-sistō, -sistere, -stetī, —, stand around, surround, hem in.

circum-veniō, -venīre, -vēnī, -ventum, come around, surround, outflank, encircle; get the better of, deceive.

circus, -ī, *m.,* a circle; a circus; *especially,* **Circus Maximus,** the Circus Maximus, *a famous place for chariot-racing in Rome. See map, page 39.*

citerior, -ius, *compar. adj.* [**cis,** on this side of], on this side; nearer, hither; **Gallia Citerior,** Nearer (Cisalpine) Gaul. *See map, page 137.*

citrō, *adv.* [**cis,** on this side of], to this side; **ultrō citrōque,** hither and thither, backward and forward.

cīvis, cīvis, -ium, *m.,* citizen, fellow-citizen.

cīvitās, -ātis, *f.* [**cīvis**], citizenship; the state, a state, nation; city.

clam, *adv.,* secretly, privately.

clāmō, -āre, -āvī, -ātum, cry out, shout, call out.

clāmor, -ōris, *m.* [**clāmō**], a loud cry, outcry, shout, shouting, clamor, noise, din; shout of approval, applause; **clāmōrem tollere,** set up a shout *or* cry.

clārus, -a, -um, *adj.,* bright, clear; loud; famous, renowned, distinguished.

classis, classis, -ium, *f.,* division, class; fleet.

claudō, claudere, clausī, clausum, shut, close, fasten; shut in, inclose; **agmen claudere,** to bring up the rear.

clēmentia, -ae, *f.* [**clēmēns,** gentle], gentleness, mercy, clemency.

cliēns, -entis, *m.,* a dependent, vassal, client, follower.

clientēla, -ae, *f.,* patronage; *pl.,* groups of allies, dependents.

clipeus, -ī, *m.,* shield.

coepī, coepisse, coeptum, *in perfect stem tenses only* (*see* **incipiō**), have begun, began, commenced.

cōgitō, -āre, -āvī, -ātum [**com-+ agitō**], consider carefully, think over; plan, intend, design.

cognōmen, -inis, *n.* [**com-+(g)nōmen**], cognomen, surname, last name.

cognōscō, -nōscere, -nōvī, -nitum [**com-+(g)nōscō,** learn], become acquainted with, learn about, investigate, learn, find, ascertain; *in perfect tenses,* know, be aware; be acquainted with; recognize.

cōgō, -ere, coēgī, coāctum [**com-+ agō**], bring together, collect; drive, compel, force.

cohors, cohortis, -ium, *f.,* cohort, *the tenth part of a Roman legion.*

co-hortor, -ārī, -ātus sum, encourage, urge on, exhort.

Colchī, -ōrum, *m. pl.,* the people of Colchis (kol'kis), the Colchians (kol'ki-ạns).

Colchis, -idis, *f.*, Colchis (kol′kis), *a country to the east of the Black Sea. See map, page 277.*

Collātīnus, -ī, *m.*, L. Tarquinius Collātīnus, Tarquinius Collatinus (kolạ-tĭ′nus), *one of the first two consuls of Rome.*

colligō, -ligere, -lēgī, -lēctum [com-+ legō], gather together, collect; rally; sē colligere, recover oneself, rally, recover.

collis, collis, -ium, *m.*, hill, height.

collocō, -āre, -āvī, -ātum [com-+locō, place], station, arrange; establish; place, dispose; give in marriage.

colloquium, -ī, *n.* [colloquor], conference, conversation, interview.

colloquor, -loquī, -locūtus sum [com-+ loquor], talk with, converse, confer.

collum, -ī, *n.*, the neck.

colō, -ere, coluī, cultum, cultivate, till; live *or* dwell in; inhabit; cherish, esteem; honor, worship; observe, practice.

columna, -ae, *f.*, column, pillar.

comes, -itis, *m. and f.*, companion, comrade, associate, attendant.

commeātus, -ūs, *m.* [commeō, go and come], communication, trip; furlough; supply-train, convoy; provisions, supplies.

com-memorō, -āre, -āvī, -ātum, mention, speak of, relate, state.

commendō, -āre, -āvī, -ātum [com-+ mandō], intrust, commend; recommend; surrender.

com-mittō, -mittere, -mīsī, -missum, send together, bring together; build, construct; cause, bring about; be guilty of, commit; intrust, commit; proelium committere, begin battle, engage in battle.

Commius, -ī, *m.*, Commius (kom′i-us), *a chief of the Atrebates, whom Caesar made king.*

commodē, *adv.* [commodus], conveniently, advantageously, easily, well; satis commodē, to much advantage, very easily.

commodus, -a, -um, *adj.*, convenient, suitable; *n. as noun*, commodum, -ī, convenience.

com-moror, -ārī, -ātus sum, stop, remain, sojourn.

com-moveō, -movēre, -mōvī, -mōtum, move *or* affect deeply, excite, arouse, disturb, alarm.

commūnicō, -āre, -āvī, -ātum [commūnis], make common; communicate, impart; share, divide.

commūnis, -e, *adj.*, common, in common, general, public.

commūtātiō, -ōnis, *f.* [commūtō], change; turn; interchange.

com-mūtō, -āre, -āvī, -ātum, change, alter; exchange.

com-parō, -āre, -āvī, -ātum, prepare, prepare for; get together, secure, obtain, buy.

comparō, -āre, -āvī, -ātum [compār, like], compare, match.

com-pellō, -pellere, -pulī, -pulsum, drive together, collect; drive, force.

comperiō, -perīre, -perī, -pertum, find out, find, discover, learn.

com-pleō, -plēre, -plēvī, -plētum [com-+pleō, fill], fill, fill up; fill.with men; complete.

com-plūrēs, -plūra *or* -plūria, *adj.*, several, a number of, many.

com-portō, -āre, -āvī, -ātum, bring together, collect, convey.

com-prehendō, -prehendere, -prehendī, -prehēnsum, seize, catch, grasp; arrest, take prisoner.

comprimō, -primere, -pressī, -pressum [com-+premō], press together, squeeze; hold back, restrain, repress.

cōnātus, -ūs, *m.* [cōnor], attempt, undertaking, effort, enterprise.

con-cēdō, -cēdere, -cessī, -cessum, go away, give way, retire, yield; yield precedence; grant, permit, assign.

concīdō, -cīdere, -cīdī, -cīsum [com-+ caedō], cut down, cut to pieces, kill, destroy; cut off; intersect, interrupt.

conciliō, -āre, -āvī, -ātum [concilium], bring together, reconcile; win, win over, win the favor of; bring about, establish.

concilium, -ī, n., assembly, meeting, council.

con-citō, -āre, -āvī, -ātum [conciō, call, arouse], call, summon; arouse, excite, instigate.

con-clāmō, -āre, -āvī, -ātum, cry out together, cry out loudly, shout, exclaim.

concordia, -ae, f. [concors, harmonious], harmony, agreement.

con-currō, -currere, -currī or -cucurrī, -cursum, assemble hurriedly, run together, come running, rush, hasten; encounter, charge, dash.

condiciō, -ōnis, f. [condīcō, agree], agreement; terms, conditions; state, condition, situation.

con-dō, -dere, -didī, -ditum, put together; store up; hide, conceal; found, establish, construct.

con-dūcō, -dūcere, -dūxī, -ductum, bring together, collect; induce, lead; hire.

cōn-ferō, -ferre, contulī, collātum, bring together, gather, collect; match, pit against; compare, contrast; attribute, assign; apply, devote; sē cōnferre, betake oneself, proceed, withdraw, go.

cōnfertus, -a, -um, adj. [pf. part. of cōnferciō, press together], crowded, dense, in close array.

cōnfestim, adv., at once, immediately, promptly.

cōnficiō, -ficere, -fēcī, -fectum [com-+faciō], make, compose; finish, complete, accomplish; weaken, overcome, exhaust; of troops, muster, raise; of food, masticate.

cōn-fīdō, -fīdere, -fīsus sum, be confident, believe, have confidence (in), trust, rely.

cōn-firmō, -āre, -āvī, -ātum, strengthen, confirm, corroborate; establish; develop; encourage, reassure, console; assert, declare.

cōn-flagrō, -āre, -āvī, -ātum, be on fire, be consumed, burn.

cōn-flīgō, -flīgere, -flīxī, -flīctum, dash together, collide; contend, be in conflict, fight.

congredior, -gredī, -gressus sum [com-+gradior, step], come together, meet; engage in battle with, encounter, contend.

congressus, -ūs, m. [congredior], meeting, conference, interview; encounter, conflict, charge.

conjiciō, -jicere, -jēcī, -jectum [com-+jaciō], throw together, put together; throw, hurl; force, drive.

con-jungō, -jungere, -jūnxī, -jūnctum, fasten together, join, unite.

conjūnx, conjugis, m. and f. [conjungō], a married person, husband, wife, spouse.

conjūrātiō, -ōnis, f. [conjūrō], conspiracy, plot; league, confederacy.

con-jūrō, -āre, -āvī, -ātum, take oath, league together, form a conspiracy, conspire, plot.

cōnor, -ārī, -ātus sum, try, attempt, undertake, plan.

conquīrō, -quīrere, -quīsīvī, -quīsītum [com-+quaerō], hunt for, search out, collect, get together.

cōn-sanguineus, -a, -um, adj., related by blood; m. pl. as noun, cōnsanguineī, -ōrum, kinsmen, blood-relations, relatives.

cōnscendō, -scendere, -scendī, -scēnsum [com-+scandō, climb], climb, mount; go aboard, embark on.

cōn-scrībō, -scrībere, -scrīpsī, -scrīptum, write; enroll, levy, enlist; patrēs cōnscrīptī, senators.

cōnsēnsus, -ūs, m. [cōnsentiō, agree], agreement, harmony, united action, consent.

cōn-sentiō, -sentīre, -sēnsī, -sēnsum, agree, combine, conspire.

cōn-sequor, -sequī, -secūtus sum, follow up or after, follow, pursue; overtake; accomplish, gain; ensue.

cōn-servō, -āre, -āvī, -ātum, retain, maintain, preserve; protect, save, spare; observe, regard, respect.

Cōnsidius, -ī, *m.*, **P. Cōnsidius,** Publius Considius (kǫn-sid'i-us), *an officer in Caesar's army.*

cōn-sīdō, -sīdere, -sēdī, -sessum, sit down; halt, take a position; encamp, settle.

cōnsilium, -ī, *n.*, counsel, advice; judgment, wisdom; measure, plan, purpose; advisory board, council; cōnsilium inīre, form a plan.

cōn-sistō, -sistere, -stitī, —, take one's stand, halt, make a stand; get a footing, maintain one's place; consist, be composed, depend.

cōnspectus, -ūs, *m.* [cōnspiciō], sight, view, presence.

cōnspiciō, -spicere, -spexī, -spectum [com-+speciō, look], catch sight of, look at, behold, perceive, observe.

cōnspicor, -ārī, -ātus sum, catch sight of, observe, see, behold.

cōnstīpō, -āre, -āvī, -ātum, crowd together.

cōnstituō, -stituere, -stituī, -stitū-tum [com-+statuō], place, station; set up, erect, establish, found; arrange; fix, institute, appoint; decide, determine.

cōn-stō, -stāre, -stitī, -stātūrus, stand together, stand with; stand firm, be unmoved; consist, be composed; rely, depend; agree; *impers.*, cōnstat, it is known, it is certain, it is agreed.

cōn-suēscō, -suēscere, -suēvī, -suē-tum, become accustomed; *perfect,* be accustomed, be in the habit of.

cōnsuētūdō, -inis, *f.* [cōnsuēscō], custom, habit, way, policy; manner of living; close intercourse, intimacy, friendship.

cōnsul, -ulis, *m.*, consul, *one of the two chief magistrates at Rome.*

cōnsulāris, -e, *adj.* [cōnsul], of a consul, consular.

cōnsulō, -sulere, -suluī, -sultum, deliberate, consult, ask the advice of;

consult the interests of (*with dative*), look out for; devise measures.

cōnsultum, -ī, *n.* [cōnsulō], decree, resolution, order.

cōn-sūmō, -sūmere, -sūmpsī, -sūmp-tum, devour, consume, destroy; spend, use up.

con-temnō, -temnere, -tempsī, -temp-tum, scorn, despise, disparage.

con-tendō, -tendere, -tendī, -tentum, attempt, strive for; contend, fight, struggle, vie; hasten, hurry, make haste.

contentus, -a, -um, *adj.* [*pf. part. of* contineō], satisfied, contented, content.

continenter, *adv.* [continēns], continuously, continually.

contineō, -tinēre, -tinuī, -tentum [com-+teneō], hold together; shut in, bound, surround; contain, hold; restrain, repress, control.

contingō, -tingere, -tigī, -tāctum [com-+tangō], touch, extend to, reach, adjoin; attain to, attain, arrive at; *impers.*, contingit, it befalls, happens to, falls to one's lot.

continuus, -a, -um, *adj.* [contineō], uninterrupted, successive, continuous, unbroken.

contrā, *adv., and prep. with acc.: as adv.*, on the contrary, on the other hand; opposite, on the opposite side; *as prep.*, against, over against, opposite, facing; contrary to.

con-trahō, -trahere, -trāxī, -tractum, gather, draw together; make smaller, contract.

contrōversia, -ae, *f.* [contrōversus, disputed], dispute, quarrel, controversy.

contumēlia, -ae, *f.*, insult, abuse, outrage, injury; buffeting, violence.

cōnūbium, -ī, *n.* [com-+nūbō, marry], marriage.

con-vallis, -vallis, -ium, *f.*, valley.

con-veniō, -venīre, -vēnī, -ventum, assemble, come together; meet, meet with; come to; *impers.*, convenit, an agreement is made, it is agreed.

con-vertō, -vertere, -vertī, -versum, turn about, turn; change, convert; attract the attention of; direct; turn one's attention; *pass. as reflexive*, turn oneself, turn.

con-vocō, -āre, -āvī, -ātum, call together, call, summon.

co-orior, -orīrī, -ortus sum, come forth, arise, spring up; break out.

cōpia, -ae, *f.*, abundance, supply, plenty; amount, number; chance, opportunity; *pl.*, supplies, provisions; forces, troops; **pedestrēs cōpiae**, infantry forces, infantry.

Cornēlius, -ī, *m.*, Cornelius.

cornū, -ūs, *n.*, a horn (*of an animal, also a musical instrument*); wing (*of an army*), flank.

corpus, corporis, *n.*, body, frame; dead body, corpse.

corripiō, -ripere, -ripuī, -reptum [com- +rapiō], seize, take hold of, snatch up; assault, attack; *of ground*, cover quickly, hurry over.

cotīdiānus, -a, -um, *adj.* [cotīdiē], daily; ordinary, usual.

cotīdiē, *adv.* [quot, as many as+diēs], every day, daily.

Cotta, -ae, *m.*, **L. Aurunculeius Cotta**, L. Aurunculeius (â-rung-kū-lē'yus) Cotta, *one of Caesar's lieutenants.*

Crassus, -ī, *m.*, Crassus: (*1*) Marcus Licinius (li-sin'i-us) Crassus, *a member of the First Triumvirate;* (*2*) Publius Licinius Crassus, *son of (1), one of Caesar's lieutenants.*

crēber, -bra, -brum, *adj.*, thick, repeated, numerous, frequent.

crēdō, -ere, crēdidī, crēditum, intrust, commit, consign; trust, place confidence in; believe, think, suppose.

creō, -āre, -āvī, -ātum, create, make; elect, choose, appoint.

Crēscēns, -entis, *m.*, Crescens (kres'-enz), *a charioteer.*

crēscō, -ere, crēvī, crētum, increase, grow greater, grow; prosper.

Creūsa, -ae, *f.*, Creüsa (krē-ū'sä), *wife of Aeneas.*

cruciātus, -ūs, *m.* [cruciō, to torture], torture, torment; cruelty.

crūdēlis, -e, *adj.*, cruel, unmerciful, barbarous.

crūdēlitās, -ātis, *f.* [crūdēlis], cruelty, severity, barbarity.

cultūra, -ae, *f.* [colō], cultivation.

cultus, -ūs, *m.* [colō], cultivation, culture; worship, devotion; manner of life, civilization, refinement.

cum, *prep. with abl.* (*sometimes attached to the end of a word*), with, along with, in company with, together with, at the same time with.

cum, *conj.*: *of time*, when, while, after, whenever; *of cause*, since, because; *concessive or adversative*, though, although; **cum . . . tum**, both . . . and, not only . . . but also; **cum prīmum**, as soon as.

cumulus, -ī, *m.*, heap, pile.

cupiditās, -ātis, *f.* [cupidus], eager desire, eagerness, desire.

cupidus, -a, -um, *adj.* [cupiō], desirous, eager, fond, greedy.

cupiō, -ere, cupīvī, cupītum, wish eagerly, desire, be eager, wish; be favorable, wish well (to).

cūr, *adv.*: *interrog.*, why? for what reason? *rel.*, for which reason, on which account, why.

cūra, -ae, *f.*, care, attention, diligence; object of care, concern, task; anxiety.

Curēs, -ium, *m. and f. pl.*, Cures (kū'rēz), *the chief town of the Sabines* (a people near Rome). *See map, page 305.*

cūria, -ae, *f.*, curia (*a division of the Roman people*), ward; senate-house.

Cūriātius, -ī, *m.*, Curiatius (kū-ri-ā'-shi-us), *an Alban name, name of triplet brothers who fought the Roman Horatii.*

cūrō, -āre, -āvī, -ātum [cūra], care for, take care of, attend to; provide for, arrange, cause (to be done).

currō, -ere, cucurrī, cursum, run; hasten, hurry.

currus, -ūs, *m.,* car, wagon, chariot.

cursus, -ūs, *m.* [**currō**], a running, race; pace, speed; course, way; career; journey, voyage.

custōdiō, -īre, -īvī, -ītum [**custōs**], watch, guard, defend, protect.

custōs, -ōdis, *m. and f.,* guard, guardian, keeper.

D

Danaī, *gen.* **-ōrum** *or* **-um,** *m. pl.,* the Greeks.

dē, *prep. with abl.: of place,* from, down from, away from; *of time,* from, just after, about; *of respect,* concerning, of, in regard to, in respect to, about; *of cause,* on account of, over, for; *in other relations,* from, of, on, in accordance with.

dea, -ae, *f.,* a goddess.

dēbeō, -ēre, -uī, -itum [**dē+habeō**], owe; be bound to, be under obligation to; ought, must.

dē-cēdō, -cēdere, -cessī, -cessum, withdraw, go away, retire, depart; die.

decem, *indecl. num. adj.,* ten.

dē-cernō, -cernere, -crēvī, -crētum, decide, decree, resolve, vote; decide, settle.

dē-certō, -āre, -āvī, -ātum, fight out to the end, fight a decisive battle; fight, contend.

decimus, -a, -um, *num. adj.* [**decem**], tenth.

dēcipiō, -cipere, -cēpī, -ceptum [**dē+capiō**], take in, deceive.

dēclīvis, -e, *adj.* [**dē+clīvus,** slope], sloping downward, descending, sloping; *n. as noun,* **dēclīve, -is,** a slope, declivity.

dē-currō, -currere, -cucurrī *or* **-currī, -cursum,** run down; hurry along, hasten, run; drill, maneuver.

dēditiō, -ōnis, *f.* [**dēdō**], surrender, capitulation; **in dēditiōnem venīre,** to surrender.

dēdō, -dere, -didī, -ditum [**dē+dō**], give up, surrender; devote, dedicate; **dēditus, -a, -um,** *adj.,* surrendered; given up, devoted.

dē-dūcō, -dūcere, -dūxī, -ductum, lead away *or* down, withdraw, remove; lead, bring, take, escort; draw down; *of ships,* launch; *of sails,* spread, unfurl.

dēfendō, -ere, dēfendī, dēfēnsum, keep *or* ward off, repel; defend, protect.

dēfēnsor, -ōris, *m.* [**dēfendō**], defender.

dē-ferō, -ferre, -tulī, -lātum, bring down *or* away, carry down *or* along; bring, convey, carry; confer, bestow, grant; report, announce.

dēfessus, -a, -um, *adj.* [*pf. part. of* **dēfetīscor,** grow weary], tired out, exhausted, weary.

dēficiō, -ficere, -fēcī, -fectum [**dē+faciō**], fail, run out, be insufficient; be wanting *or* missing; be exhausted; abandon, desert; revolt.

Dēianīra, -ae, *f.,* Deianira (dē-yạ-nĭ′-rạ), *the wife of Hercules.*

deinceps, *adv.,* in succession, in turn.

deinde, *adv.,* thence, from there; next, then; in the second place; afterwards.

dējiciō, -jicere, -jēcī, -jectum [**dē+jaciō**], throw *or* hurl down; slay, kill; strike *or* cut off; drive away, dislodge, expel; drive down, bring down; destroy, demolish; disappoint.

dēleō, -ēre, dēlēvī, dēlētum, blot out, efface; destroy, overthrow, annihilate.

dē-ligō, -āre, -āvī, -ātum, bind down, tie, tie up, moor.

dēligō, -ligere, -lēgī, -lēctum [**dē+legō**], choose, select.

Delphī, -ōrum, *m. pl.,* Delphi (del′fī), *a city in Greece famous for the oracle of Apollo. See map, page 61.*

dēmissus, -a, -um, *adj.* [*pf. part. of* **dēmittō,** send *or* let down], downcast, despondent.

dē-mōnstrō, -āre, -āvī, -ātum, point out, show; state, explain.

dēmum, *adv.,* at last, at length; **tum dēmum,** then at last, not until then, then only.

dēnique, *adv.,* at last, at length, finally; in short.

dēns, dentis, *m.,* tooth.

dēnsus, -a, -um, *adj.,* close, thick, dense, crowded, in close array.

dē-nūntiō, -āre, -āvī, -ātum, announce, proclaim; command, order; warn, threaten.

dē-pōnō, -pōnere, -posuī, -positum, lay down, lay aside; deposit; give up, resign; place, station.

dē-populor, -ārī, -ātus sum, lay waste, plunder, ravage.

dēscendō, -scendere, -scendī, -scēnsum [**dē+scandō,** climb], climb down, descend, come down, dismount; have recourse, resort.

dē-serō, -serere, -seruī, -sertum [serō, join], abandon, desert, forsake.

dēsertus, -a, -um, *adj.* [*pf. part. of* **dēserō**], abandoned, deserted.

dē-sīderō, -āre, -āvī, -ātum, long for, desire, demand, require; miss, need.

dēsiliō, -silīre, -siluī, -sultum [**dē+saliō,** leap], jump down, leap down; alight, dismount.

dē-sistō, -sistere, -stitī, -stitum, stop, cease, leave off; desist from, abandon.

dē-spērō, -āre, -āvī, -ātum, despair of, despair, give up hope.

dēspiciō, -spicere, -spexī, -spectum [**dē+speciō,** look], look down upon, scorn, disdain, despise.

dē-spondeō, -spondēre, -spondī, -spōnsum, pledge, promise; promise in marriage, betroth.

dē-sum, -esse, -fuī, -futūrus, be wanting, be lacking, fail.

dē-trahō, -trahere, -trāxī, -tractum, draw off, strip off, take from; remove, withdraw.

dētrīmentum, -ī, *n.* [**dēterō,** wear away], loss, injury, damage; detriment; defeat.

deus, -ī (*nom. pl.,* **dī,** *dat. and abl. pl.,* **dīs**), *m.,* a god, deity.

dēversōrium, -ī, *n.* [**dēversor,** turn aside, lodge], inn, lodging-place.

dē-vorō, -āre, -āvī, -ātum, swallow, devour.

dexter, -tra, -trum, *adj.,* right, right-hand, on the right, on the right side.

dextra, -ae, *f.* [**dexter**], the right hand; **ā dextrā,** on the right.

dī, *see* **deus.**

Diāna, -ae, *f.,* Diana (dī-an′ạ), *the goddess of hunting.*

dicō, -āre, -āvī, -ātum, proclaim.

dīcō, -ere, dīxī, dictum, say, tell, state, assert; speak, utter; mention, relate; plead (*with* **causam**); pronounce, administer, dispense (*with* **jūs**); name, call; set, appoint.

dictātor, -ōris, *m.* [**dictō,** dictate], dictator.

dictiō, -ōnis, *f.* [**dīcō**], a speaking, a pleading.

diēs, diēī, *m. and f.,* a day; time, period of time, interval; appointed time; **ad diem,** at the appointed time, punctually; **multō diē,** late in the day; **postrīdiē ejus diēī,** the next *or* following day.

differō, -ferre, distulī, dīlātum [**dis-+ferō**], carry apart, scatter; postpone, delay, put off; differ, be different.

difficilis, -e, *adj.* [**dis-+facilis**], difficult, hard, troublesome.

difficultās, -ātis, *f.* [**difficilis**], difficulty, trouble.

digitus, -ī, *m.,* a finger; a toe; an inch, *the sixteenth part of a Roman foot.*

dignitās, -ātis, *f.* [**dignus**], worth, merit; dignity, rank, honor, prestige, reputation.

dignus, -a, -um, *adj.,* worthy, deserving, fit.

dīligēns, *gen.* **dīligentis,** *adj.,* industrious, faithful, diligent.

dīligenter, *adv.* [**dīligēns**], carefully, diligently.

dīligentia, -ae, *f.* [**dīligēns**], diligence, care, faithfulness.

dī-micō, -āre, -āvī, -ātum [dis-+micō, flash], fight, contend, struggle.

dī-mittō, -mittere, -mīsī, -missum, send out; send away, let go, dismiss; give up; lose.

dīrigō, -rigere, -rēxī, -rēctum, direct, guide.

dīripiō, -ripere, -ripuī, -reptum [dis-+rapiō], tear in pieces; plunder, ravage.

dīrus, -a, -um, *adj.,* dread, dreadful, terrible.

dīs, *dat. and abl. pl. of* **deus.**

dis-cēdō, -cēdere, -cessī, -cessum, go away, withdraw, depart, leave.

discessus, -ūs, *m.* [**discēdō**], a going away, withdrawal, departure; defection.

disciplīna, -ae, *f.* [**discō**], instruction, training, teaching, discipline; a system of instruction, system.

discō, -ere, didicī, —, learn, be taught, learn to know.

discrīmen, -inis, *n.* [**discernō,** separate], a separation, difference; decisive moment; crisis, danger.

dis-pār, *gen.* **disparis,** *adj.,* unequal, unlike, ill-matched.

dispergō, -spergere, -spersī, -spersum [dis-+spargō, scatter], scatter, spread, disperse.

dissēnsiō, -ōnis, *f.* [**dissentiō,** dissent], disagreement, dissension.

distineō, -tinēre, -tinuī, -tentum [dis-+teneō], hold *or* keep apart, divide, separate, isolate.

dis-tribuō, -tribuere, -tribuī, -tribūtum, assign, divide, distribute.

dītissimus, -a, -um [*superl. of* **dīs,** rich], *adj.,* richest, wealthiest.

diū, *adv.,* long, a long time, for a long time; *compar.,* **diūtius,** longer, too long; *superl.,* **diūtissimē,** for the longest time.

diūtinus, -a, -um, *adj.,* long continued, lasting.

dī-versus, -a, -um, *adj.,* opposite, opposing; different; separate, acting separately.

dīves, *gen.* **dīvitis,** *adj.,* rich, opulent, wealthy.

Dīviciācus, -ī, *m.,* Diviciacus (di-vish-i-ā′kus); (*1*) *a chief of the Haeduans;* (*2*) *a chief of the Suessiones.*

dīvidō, -ere, dīvīsī, dīvīsum, part, divide, separate; distribute, share, allot.

dīvīnus, -a, -um, *adj.* [**dīvus,** divine], of the gods, divine, sacred.

dīvitiae, -ārum, *f. pl.* [**dīves**], riches, wealth.

dō, dare, dedī, datum, give, concede, grant, furnish; pay, suffer; **in fugam dare,** put to flight; **in mātrimōnium dare,** give in marriage, arrange a marriage for; **negōtium dare,** employ; **operam dare,** take pains, exert oneself, see to it that; give aid; **sē ventō dare,** run before the wind; **vēla dare,** set sail.

doceō, -ēre, -uī, doctum, teach, inform, instruct; show, explain, prove.

doleō, -ēre, -uī, -itūrus, grieve, suffer, be in pain; be grieved, be sorry, lament, be indignant.

dolor, -ōris, *m.* [**doleō**], sorrow, suffering, pain; distress, grief, indignation, vexation, chagrin, annoyance; **magnō dolōre afficere,** annoy greatly.

dolus, -ī, *m.,* trickery, deceit, treachery, trick.

domesticus, -a, -um, *adj.* [**domus**] of *or* belonging to the home, home (*as adjective*); one's own, private, personal; internal, civil, domestic.

dominus, -ī, *m.,* master, owner, ruler, lord.

domus, -ūs (-ī) (*see Gr. S., 8*), *f.,* house, home; household, family; *loc.,* **domī,** at home.

dōnum, -ī, *n.,* gift, present.

dormiō, -īre, -īvī, -ītum, sleep.

dōs, dōtis, *f.,* a marriage gift, dowry.

dracō, -ōnis, *m.*, serpent, dragon.

druidēs, -um, *m. pl.*, the Druids, *an ancient order of priests in Gaul and Britain*.

dubitō, -āre, -āvī, -ātum [dubius], be uncertain, doubt, hesitate, delay.

dubius, -a, -um, *adj.*, doubtful, uncertain, indecisive; *n. as noun*, **dubium, -ī**, doubt, uncertainty.

ducentī, -ae, -a, *num. adj.* [duo+ centum], two hundred.

dūcō, -ere, dūxī, ductum, lead, conduct; bring; lead (*home as wife*), marry; take on, assume; trace (*a wall or ditch*), make, construct; think, consider, regard; draw out, prolong, postpone, put off; **in mātrimōnium dūcere**, marry.

dūdum, *adv.*, a while ago, before; **jam dūdum**, a long time ago, long ago, this long time.

dum, *conj.*, while, as long as; till, until; provided.

Dumnorīx, -īgis, *m.*, Dumnorix (dum'nō-riks), *a prominent Haeduan, brother of Diviciacus.*

duo, duae, duo, *num. adj.*, two.

duodecim, *indecl. num. adj.* [duo+ decem], twelve.

duo-dē-vīgintī, *indecl. num. adj.*, eighteen.

duplex, *gen.* **duplicis**, *adj.*, double, twofold.

dūrus, -a, -um, *adj.*, hard, harsh, unfeeling, severe; uncultivated, rude; difficult, dangerous.

dux, ducis, *m.* [dūcō], leader, guide; general, commander.

Dymas, -antis, *m.*, Dymas (dī'măs), *the father of Hecuba.*

E

ē, *see* **ex**.

ecce, *interj.*, see! behold! look!

ē-dīcō, -dīcere, -dīxī, -dictum, declare, proclaim, decree, appoint.

ēditus, -a, -um, *adj.* [*pf. part. of* ēdō], raised high, elevated, lofty.

ē-dō, -dere, -didī, -ditum, put forth, give out, exhibit, display, disclose, announce, utter, bring forth; give birth to; inflict.

edō, -ere, ēdī, ēsum, eat.

ē-ducō, -āre, -āvī, -ātum, bring up, rear, train.

ē-dūcō, -dūcere, -dūxī, -ductum, lead out, march out; draw (*a sword*).

efferō, -ferre, extulī, ēlātum [ex+ ferō], bring *or* carry out, remove; carry out to burial, bury; make known; elate, excite; raise up, elevate; extol, praise.

efficiō, -ficere, -fēcī, -fectum [ex+ faciō], make, produce, accomplish, perform, finish, complete; bring about, cause, effect.

effugiō, -fugere, -fūgī, -fugitūrus [ex+ fugiō], flee from, flee, escape; escape from, avoid.

ego, *gen.* **meī** (*nom. pl.* **nōs**), *pers. pron.*, I.

ēgredior, -gredī, -gressus sum [ē+ gradior, step], go out, come out; march out, leave, depart; disembark, land.

ēgregius, -a, -um, *adj.* [ē+grex, flock], extraordinary, remarkable, unusual; distinguished, illustrious.

ē-mittō, -mittere, -mīsī, -missum, send forth *or* away, release, drop; hurl, discharge; open an outlet to; utter, say.

emō, emere, ēmī, ēmptum, buy, purchase; *sometimes in compounds*, take.

enim, *conj.*, for; really, in fact, indeed.

ēnsis, -is, *m.*, sword.

ē-nūntiō, -āre, -āvī, -ātum, assert; proclaim, reveal, disclose; report.

eō, īre, iī (īvī), **itum**, go, advance, march.

eō, *adv.* [is], on that account, therefore, for the reason; to that place, there, thither; to such an extent *or* degree.

eōdem, *adv.* [īdem], to the same place; to the same end, to the same result *or* purpose.

Epēus, -ī, *m.,* Epeus (ē-pē′us), *a Greek who constructed the wooden horse.*

epistula, -ae, *f.,* letter, epistle.

Eporēdorīx, -īgis, *m.,* Eporedorix (ep-ō-red′ō-riks), *a Haeduan leader.*

eques, equitis, *m.* [equus], horseman, cavalryman; knight; *pl.,* horsemen, cavalry; the knights, *one of the three orders of Roman society.*

equester, -tris, -tre, *adj.* [eques], of a horseman, of the cavalry, equestrian, cavalry (*as adj.*).

equitātus, -ūs, *m.* [equitō, ride], cavalry.

equus, equī, *m.,* a horse.

ērigō, -rigere, -rēxī, -rēctum [ē+regō], lift, lift up, raise; arouse, encourage, excite, bestir.

ēripiō, -ripere, -ripuī, -reptum [ē+rapiō], snatch away, snatch out, pull out; take away, remove; deprive; save, rescue, free.

errō, -āre, -āvī, -ātum, wander; go astray, be mistaken, err.

ērudiō, -īre, -īvī, -ītum [ē+rudis, rough], train, teach, instruct, educate.

ēruptiō, -ōnis, *f.* [ērumpō, break forth], a breaking out, sortie, sally.

essedum, -ī, *n.,* a war-chariot (*of the Britons*).

et, *conj., and adv.,* and; also, even, too; **et . . . et,** both . . . and, not only . . . but also.

etiam, *adv.* [et+jam], yet, even yet, still; also, too, besides, furthermore, likewise, even; **etiam atque etiam,** again and again, repeatedly; **nōn modo . . . sed etiam,** not only . . . but also; **nōn sōlum . . . sed etiam,** not only . . . but also; **quīn etiam,** moreover, nay even, nay more, more than that.

Etrūscus, -a, -um, *adj.,* Etruscan; *m. pl. as noun,* **Etrūscī, -ōrum,** the Etruscans.

et-sī, *conj.,* even if, and if, although; and yet.

Eurōpa, -ae, *f.,* Europe.

Eurystheus, -ī, *m.,* Eurystheus (ū-ris′thūs), *king of Tiryns* (*see map, page 68*).

ē-vādō, -vādere, -vāsī, -vāsum [vādō, walk, go], go away, come out; escape.

ē-veniō, -venīre, -vēnī, -ventum, come out; turn out, result, happen.

ēventus, -ūs, *m.* [ēveniō], outcome, result; event, occurrence; fate, disaster.

ex (*before vowels and some consonants*), **ē** (*only before consonants*), *prep. with abl.:* of space, out of, from; on the side of, on; of time, from, since, after; of source, out of, from; of cause, because of, in consequence of, in accordance with; in partitive expressions, of, from, from among; in other relations, from, in keeping with, according to, to judge by, by, of.

ex-animō, -āre, -āvī, -ātum, deprive of breath, exhaust, weaken; kill; **exanimātus, -a, -um,** *pf. part.,* breathless, exhausted.

ex-cēdō, -cēdere, -cessī, -cessum, go out, withdraw, retire, depart.

excipiō, -cipere, -cēpī, -ceptum [ex+capiō], take out, except; take up, catch, capture; intercept; withstand, resist; meet, greet, receive, entertain.

excitō, -āre, -āvī, -ātum [exciō, call out], call out; arouse, incite, excite; bring about, cause; erect (*towers*), raise.

ex-clāmō, -āre, -āvī, -ātum, call out, cry out, exclaim.

exemplar, exemplāris, -ium, *n.,* example, copy.

exemplum, -ī, *n.,* specimen, example; model; precedent.

ex-eō, -īre, -iī, -itum, go out, come forth, march out; go away, withdraw, retire, leave.

exerceō, -ēre, -uī, -itum [ex+arceō, inclose], engage busily, employ; train, drill, exercise; administer, preside over; execute.

exercitātiō, -ōnis, *f.* [exercitō, train], exercise, practice, training.

exercitus, -ūs, *m.* [exerceō], army.

exiguus, -a, -um, *adj.* [exigō, drive out], limited, small, slight, short, poor.

exilium (exsilium), -ī, *n.* [exul], exile, banishment.

exīstimō, -āre, -āvī, -ātum [ex+ aestimō, estimate], estimate, value; consider, judge, suppose, believe, think.

exitus, -ūs, *m.* [exeō], a going out; exit; conclusion, end, result.

expectō (exspectō), -āre, -āvī, -ātum [ex+spectō], look forward to, await, wait for; expect, antici- pate, hope for.

expediō, -īre, -īvī, -ītum, extricate, free; expedītus, -a, -um [*pf. part. as adj.*], unimpeded, free, unencumbered, light-armed, in light array; un- obstructed, open, easy.

ex-pellō, -pellere, -pulī, -pulsum, drive from *or* out, expel, remove, banish.

experior, -perīrī, -pertus sum, make trial of, try; experience; prove, test.

ex-piō, -āre, -āvī, -ātum [piō, appease], expiate, make up for.

explōrātor, -ōris, *m.* [explōrō], scout, spy.

explōrō, -āre, -āvī, -ātum, investigate, examine, reconnoiter, explore; ex- plōrātus, -a, -um, *pf. part.*, assured, certain.

ex-pōnō, -pōnere, -posuī, -positum, put *or* set forth; expose, abandon; set ashore, land, disembark; display, draw up; explain, relate.

ex-pugnō, -āre, -āvī, -ātum, take by assault, take by storm, capture, conquer.

extrā, *adv.*, *and prep. with acc.* [ex- terus, outward], outside, beyond, outside of.

extrēmus, -a, -um, *adj.* [*superl. of* exterus, outward], outermost, ex- treme, farthest, most distant, last; the end *or* last part of, extremity of; ad extrēmum, at last.

extruō (exstruō), -truere, -trūxī, -trūctum [ex+struō, heap up], pile up; rear, erect, construct.

exul (exsul), -ulis, *m.*, an exile.

F

faber, -brī, *m.*, workman, mechanic, smith, carpenter; engineer.

Fābricius, -ī, *m.*, C. Fābricius, C. Fabricius (fa̱-brish'ius), *a prom- inent Roman of the third century* B.C.

fābula, -ae, *f.*, story, tale; fable, fiction.

facile, *adv.* [facilis], easily, without difficulty, readily.

facilis, -e, *adj.*, easy, without diffi- culty; gracious, agreeable, cour- teous.

facinus, facinoris, *n.*, act, deed, mis- deed, crime, outrage.

faciō, -ere, fēcī, factum, make, do, form, construct, create, perform, commit; cause, bring about, accom- plish; act; assume, suppose; furnish; (aliquem) certiōrem facere, inform (someone); iter facere, march, make a journey; lūdōs facere, hold games; potestātem facere, grant opportu- nity *or* permission.

factiō, -ōnis, *f.* [faciō], faction, party.

factum, -ī, *n.* [*pf. part. of* faciō], deed, act, event; exploit.

facultās, -ātis, *f.* [facilis], ability, power of doing; means, opportunity; supply, abundance; *pl.*, resources.

fallō, -ere, fefellī, falsum, deceive, cheat; fail, disappoint; elude, escape; violate, break.

falsus, -a, -um, *adj.* [*pf. part. of* fallō], false, misleading, pretended, unfounded.

fāma, -ae, *f.*, common talk, report, rumor, tradition; reputation, fame.

famēs, -is, *f.*, hunger, starvation.

familia, -ae, *f.* [famulus, servant], slaves in a household; household; family, race.

familiāris, -e, *adj.* [familia], of a household, private, domestic; intimate; *m. as noun,* **familiāris, -is,** an intimate friend *or* acquaintance; **rēs familiāris,** private property, estate.

fās, *n., indecl.* [for, speak], divine sanction *or* law (*as opposed to* jūs, *human law*); the right, the proper *or* lawful thing; **fās est,** it is right, permissible, lawful, proper, the will of heaven.

fātum, -ī, *n.* [*pf. part. of* for, speak], an utterance; oracle, prophecy; fate, doom, destiny.

fēlīciter, *adv.* [fēlīx], happily, successfully, luckily, auspiciously.

fēlīx, *gen.* **fēlīcis,** *adj.,* fruitful; successful, happy, fortunate.

fēmina, -ae, *f.,* a female; a woman.

ferāx, *gen.* **-ācis,** *adj.* [ferō], productive, fertile.

ferē, *adv.,* usually, generally; nearly, almost, about.

ferō, ferre, tulī, lātum, bear, carry, bring; endure, submit to, suffer; withstand; report, say; *of laws,* propose, offer, carry, enact; **fertur,** it is said; **ferunt,** they say; **aegrē (molestē) ferre,** be indignant, resent; **signa ferre,** advance the standards, advance.

ferōx, *gen.* **ferōcis,** *adj.* [ferus], fierce, savage; spirited; aggressive; insolent.

ferrum, -ī, *n.,* iron; a weapon of iron *or* steel, spearhead; spear, sword.

ferus, -a, -um, *adj.,* wild; cruel, fierce, savage, uncivilized.

fidēlis, -e, *adj.* [fidēs], faithful, loyal, trustworthy, reliable.

Fidēnātēs, -ium, *m. pl.,* the Fidenates (fid-ē̦-nā′tēz), *the people of* Fidenae (fĭ-dē′nē), *a town near Rome.*

fidēs, -eī, *f.,* faith, belief, confidence; credit, reliance; loyalty, faithfulness, fidelity, honor; promise, pledge; protection, dependence, alliance, trust; **in fidem recipere,** take under one's protection.

fīdō, -ere, fīsus sum, *semi-deponent,* trust, rely upon, have confidence in; believe, be sure.

fīdūcia, -ae, *f.,* confidence, assurance.

fīgō, -ere, fīxī, fīxum, attach, fasten.

fīlia, -ae, *f.,* daughter.

fīlius, -ī, *m.,* son.

fingō, -ere, fīnxī, fīctum, mold, form, make up; devise, invent; imagine, fancy; control.

fīniō, -īre, -īvī, -ītum [fīnis], bound, define, limit, determine; end, finish.

fīnis, fīnis, -ium, *m. and f.,* limit, boundary; end, close; *pl.,* borders, boundaries, territory, land, country.

fīnitimus, -a, -um, *adj.* [fīnis], bordering, adjacent, neighboring; *m. pl. as noun,* **fīnitimī, -ōrum,** neighbors.

fīō, fierī, factus sum [*pass. of* faciō], be made, be done, become, come about, happen, result.

firmus, -a, -um, *adj.,* strong, vigorous, steadfast, firm, powerful.

flamma, -ae, *f.,* blaze, fire, flame.

flectō, -ere, flexī, flexum, bend, turn, turn around, incline, curve; change, alter; guide, direct.

fleō, -ēre, flēvī, flētum, weep, cry, weep for, lament.

flōs, flōris, *m.,* a blossom, flower.

flūctus, -ūs, *m.* [fluō], wave, billow.

flūmen, flūminis, *n.* [fluō], river, stream.

fluō, -ere, flūxī, flūxum, flow, run, stream, drip.

foedus, foederis, *n.,* agreement, stipulation; treaty, league, alliance.

fōns, fontis, -ium, *m.,* spring, fountain, water; origin, source.

fore (=futūrus esse), *fut. inf. of* sum.

fōrma, -ae, *f.,* form, shape, figure; appearance; beauty.

fors, fortis, *f.,* chance, accident.

fortasse, *adv.,* perhaps.

forte, *adv.* [*abl. of* fors, chance], by chance, by accident, as it happened; perhaps.

fortis, -e, *adj.*, strong, powerful; brave, courageous, bold, fearless.

fortiter, *adv.* [fortis], bravely, gallantly, boldly.

fortūna, -ae, *f.* [fors], fortune, fate, luck, good fortune; condition, state, position, chance.

forum, -ī, *n.*, an open space; marketplace; forum; *especially*, **Forum Rōmānum,** the Roman Forum. *See map, page 39.*

fossa, -ae, *f.* [fossus, dug up], ditch, trench.

frangō, -ere, frēgī, frāctum, break, wreck, shatter; weaken, wear out; overcome, dishearten.

frāter, frātris, *m.*, brother.

fraus, fraudis, *f.*, deceit, deception, fraud, trickery.

fretum, -ī, *n.*, a strait, channel; the sea.

frōns, frontis, *f.*, brow, forehead, front; face, countenance.

frūctus, -ūs, *m.*, crop; profit, income; fruit.

frūmentārius, -a, -um, *adj.* [frūmentum], of *or* pertaining to grain, of provisions; abounding in grain, belonging to grain, fruitful; **rēs frūmentāria,** grain supply, provisions.

frūmentum, -ī, *n.* [fruor, enjoy], grain; *pl.*, growing crops, standing grain.

frūstrā, *adv.*, vainly, in vain, to no purpose, without effect.

Fufetius, -ī, *m.*, **Mettius Fufetius,** Mettius Fufetius (met'i-us fū-fē'shius), *an Alban dictator.*

fuga, -ae, *f.*, a fleeing, flight; **in fugam dare,** put to flight.

fugiō, -ere, fūgī, fugitūrus, flee, run away, take to flight; run away from, avoid.

fūmus, -ī, *m.*, smoke.

funditor, -ōris, *m.* [funda, a sling], a slinger.

fundō, -ere, fūdī, fūsum, pour, pour out; scatter, rout, defeat; shed.

fundus, -ī, *m.*, bottom, lowest part; farm, estate.

furor, -ōris, *m.* [furō, to rage], rage, madness, fury, passion.

G

Gabiī, -ōrum, *m. pl.*, Gabii (gā'bi-ī), *a town of ancient Italy. See map, page 305.*

Gabīnus, -a, -ym, *adj.*, of Gabii (gā'bi-ī); *m. pl. as noun,* **Gabīnī, -ōrum,** the people of Gabii (*see map, p. 305*).

Galba, -ae, *m.*, Galba (gal'bä); (*1*) *a king of the Suessiones;* (*2*) Servius Sulpicius (sẻr'vi-us sul-pish'i-us) Galba, *one of Caesar's lieutenants in Gaul.*

galea, -ae, *f.*, a helmet (*of leather or metal*).

Gallia, -ae, *f.*, Gaul, *the country;* **Gallia Citerior,** Nearer (Cisalpine) Gaul. *See map, page 137.*

Gallicus, -a, -um, *adj.* [Gallia], of the Gauls, Gallic.

Gallus, -a, -um, *adj.*, pertaining to Gaul, Gallic; *m. as noun,* **Gallus, -ī,** a Gaul; *pl.*, the Gauls.

Garunna, -ae, *m.*, *a river of Gaul, now called the Garonne* (gä-rôn). *See map, page 137.*

gaudeō, -ēre, gāvīsus sum, *semideponent*, rejoice, be glad, take pleasure, delight.

gaudium, -ī, *n.* [gaudeō], joy, delight, pleasure.

geminus, -a, -um, *adj.* [gignō], twinborn; double, twofold; *m. pl. as noun,* **geminī, -ōrum,** twins.

Genava, -ae, *f.*, *a Gallic city on Lake Geneva, modern Geneva* (jenē'vä). *See map, page 137.*

gēns, gentis, -ium, *f.*, tribe, people, nation; clan, house.

genus, generis, *n.* [*compare* **gēns**], birth, descent, race, family; sort, class, kind, character, nature.

Germānia, -ae, *f.*, Germany.

Germānus, -a, -um, *adj.*, German; *m. as noun,* **Germānus, -ī,** a German; *pl.*, the Germans.

gerō, -ere, gessī, gestum, bear, wear, carry, wield; wage, carry on, conduct; manage, administer; do, perform; *pass., often,* go on, take place, be done; **sē gerere,** conduct oneself, behave.

Gēryōn, -onis, *m.,* Geryon (jer'i-ọn), *a fabulous monster.*

gigās, -antis, *m.,* a giant.

gignō, -ere, genuī, genitum, beget, bear, give birth to, produce.

gladiātor, -ōris, *m.,* gladiator, fighter.

gladius, -ī, *m.,* sword.

Glaucē, -ēs, *f.,* Glauce (glâ'sē), *daughter of Creon, king of Corinth.*

glōria, -ae, *f.,* glory, fame, renown, reputation.

Graecia, -ae, *f.,* Greece. *See map, page 61.*

Graecus, -a, -um, *adj.,* Greek, Grecian; *m. as noun,* **Graecus, -ī,** a Greek; *pl.,* the Greeks.

grātia, -ae, *f.* [**grātus**], favor, regard, esteem, friendship; influence, prestige; gratitude, thanks, requital; **grātiās agere,** express thanks, thank; **grātiam referre,** make requital, requite, repay; **grātiā,** *with dependent gen.,* for the sake of.

grātīs, *adv.,* for nothing, without pay.

grātulātiō, -ōnis, *f.* [**grātulor,** rejoice], congratulation; rejoicing, joy.

grātus, -a, -um, *adj.,* pleasing, acceptable; agreeable; pleased, grateful.

gravis, -e, *adj.,* heavy, weighty, heavily laden; burdensome, hard to bear, offensive, oppressive, difficult, severe, serious, grave, important, influential; dignified; *of age,* advanced.

graviter, *adv.* [**gravis**], heavily; severely, seriously; hard, with great force; with dignity.

H

habeō, -ēre, -uī, -itum, have, hold, possess, own, keep, contain; consider, regard, think; treat, use; *of a speech,* deliver, make; **sē habēre,** be situated, be.

habitō, -āre, -āvī, -ātum [**habeō**], live, dwell, reside.

Haeduus, -a, -um, *adj.,* Haeduan; *m. as noun,* **Haeduus, -ī,** a Haeduan; *pl.,* the Haedui (hed'ū-ī), the Haeduans, *a tribe of Celtic Gaul. See map, p. 137.*

Hannō, -ōnis, *m.,* Hanno, *a prominent Carthaginian.*

Harpyiae, -ārum, *f. pl.,* the Harpies, *fabulous creatures half bird and half woman.*

hasta, -ae, *f.,* spear, lance, javelin.

haud, *adv.,* not at all, by no means, not.

Hecuba, -ae, *f.,* Hecuba (hek'ū-bạ), *the wife of Priam.*

Helvētius, -a, -um, *adj.,* Helvetian (hel-vē'shiạn), of the Helvetians; *m. pl. as noun,* **Helvētiī, -ōrum,** the Helvetii, the Helvetians, *a tribe of Celtic Gaul. See map, p. 137.*

herba, -ae, *f.,* herbage, grass, herb, plant.

Herculāneum, -ī, *n.,* Herculaneum (hẹr-kū-lā'nẹ-um), *a city of Italy destroyed at the same time as Pompeii. See map, page 20.*

Herculēs, -is, *m.,* Hercules (hẹr'kū-lēz), *a famous Greek hero.*

Herdonius, -ī, *m.,* **Turnus Herdonius,** Turnus Herdonius (hẹr-dō'ni-us), *a prominent man of Aricia.*

herī, *adv.,* yesterday.

Hesperides, -um, *f. pl.,* the Hesperides (hes-per'i-dēz), *the daughters of Atlas, keepers of the golden apples.*

hīberna, -ōrum, *n. pl.,* winter-quarters.

hic, haec, hoc, *demonstr. pron. and adj., referring to what is near in space, time, or thought; as adj.,* this, *(pl.* these), the present; the following; the last named, the latter; the first named, the former; *as pron.,* he, she, it; *pl.,* they.

hīc, *adv.,* here, in this place; on this occasion; at this point; there, in that place.

hiemō, -āre, -āvī, -ātum [hiems], spend the winter, winter.

hiems, hiemis, *f.*, winter; storm, stormy weather.

Hippolytē, -ēs, *f.*, Hippolyte (hipol'i-tē), *queen of the Amazons.*

Hispānia, -ae, *f.*, Spain.

historia, -ae, *f.*, history.

hodiē, *adv.* [hic+diēs], today; now.

homō, hominis, *m.*, a human being, man, person.

honestus, -a, -um, *adj.* [honōs], honored, respected, illustrious; honorable, upright.

honor *or* honōs, -ōris, *m.*, honor, esteem, reputation, distinction; reward; office, public office, official honor.

honōs, see honor.

hōra, -ae, *f.*, an hour, hour, time.

Horātius, -ī, *m.*, Horatius (hō-rā'-shius); (*1*) *the name of three brothers who fought the Alban Curiatii*, (*2*) Pūblius Horātius, Publius Horatius, *the father of the three Horatii.*

horribilis, -e, *adj.* [horreō, shudder], dreadful, horrible, terrible.

hortor, -ārī, -ātus sum, encourage, cheer, exhort, urge, advise.

hortus, -ī, *m.*, garden.

hospes, -itis, *m.*, host; guest, visitor, stranger; friend, guest-friend.

hospitium, -ī, *n.* [hospes], entertainment, hospitality; guest-friendship.

Hostīlius, -ī, *m.*, (*1*) Hostius Hostīlius, Hostius Hostilius (hos'ti-us hostil'i-us), *a Roman commander in the time of Romulus;* (*2*) Tullus Hostīlius, Tullus Hostilius, *the third king of Rome.*

hostis, hostis, -ium, *m.*, enemy, public enemy, foe; *pl.*, the enemy.

Hostius, *see* Hostīlius.

hūc, *adv.* [hic], to this place, hither, here; besides, in addition.

hūmānitās, -ātis, *f.* [hūmānus], human nature *or* feeling; kindliness; culture, civilization, refinement.

hūmānus, -a, -um, *adj.* [homō], of man, human; kind; civilized, cultivated, refined.

humilis, -e, *adj.* [humus, ground], low, insignificant; humble, unknown, obscure.

Hydra, -ae, *f.*, the Hydra (hī'drą), *a water-serpent slain by Hercules.*

Hypanis, -is, *m.*, Hypanis (hip'an-is), *a Trojan.*

I

ibi, *adv.*, there, in that place; then, thereupon.

Iccius, -ī, *m.*, Iccius (ik'shius), *a leader of the Remi.*

ictus, -ūs, *m.*, thrust, blow; wound.

īdem, eadem, idem, *demonstr. pron. and adj.*, the same, the same one; also, too, besides, likewise.

idōneus, -a, -um, *adj.*, suitable, adapted, fit; capable, deserving.

igitur, *adv.*, therefore, then, consequently, accordingly.

ignāvus, -a, -um, *adj.* [in-+gnāvus, busy], inactive, idle; cowardly.

ignis, ignis, -ium, *m.*, fire; signal-fire.

ignōrō, -āre, -āvī, -ātum, not know, be unaware of, be unacquainted with, disregard, ignore.

ignōscō, -nōscere, -nōvī, -nōtum, overlook, pardon, forgive.

ignōtus, -a, -um, *adj.* [in-+(g)nōtus], unknown, unfamiliar, strange.

ille, illa, illud, *demonstr. pron. and adj.*, that (*pl.* those), yonder, that one; the well-known, the famous; he, she, it; *pl.*, they; *in contrast with another pronoun*, the other, the former; *more rarely*, the latter.

imitor, -ārī, -ātus sum, copy, imitate; resemble.

immolō, -āre, -āvī, -ātum [in+mola, meal], sacrifice, offer as a sacrifice.

immortālis, -e, *adj.* [in-+mortālis, mortal], immortal, undying, eternal.

impedīmentum, -ī, *n.* [impediō], impediment, hindrance; *pl.*, baggage, heavy baggage *of an army*, baggage-train.

impediō, -īre, -īvī, -ītum [in+pēs], entangle, hinder, impede, obstruct; delay; prevent.

impedītus, -a, -um, *adj.* [*pf. part. of* impediō], entangled; encumbered, impeded, hindered; difficult, obstructed, impassable.

impellō, -pellere, -pulī, -pulsum [in+pellō], drive *or* urge on, incite, induce.

imperātor, -ōris, *m.* [imperō], general, commander-in-chief, emperor.

imperātum, -ī, *n.* [*pf. part. of* imperō], order, command; **imperāta facere,** obey commands.

imperītus, -a, -um, *adj.* [in-+perītus], inexperienced, unskilled; ignorant, unacquainted.

imperium, -ī, *n.* [imperō], command, order; power, control, authority; supreme power *or* command; sovereignty, rule, government, empire.

imperō, -āre, -āvī, -ātum [in+parō], order, command, direct; demand; levy; control, rule, govern; impose.

impetrō, -āre, -āvī, -ātum [in+patrō, perform], obtain (*by request*), obtain one's request, secure, effect.

impetus, -ūs, *m.* [in+petō], attack, charge; force, impulse, violence.

impleō, -plēre, -plēvī, -plētum [in+ -pleō, fill], fill up, fill.

implōrō, -āre, -āvī, -ātum [in+plōrō, wail], beseech, entreat, implore, call for.

impōnō, -pōnere, -posuī, -positum [in+pōnō], place *or* set upon, put on, impose; mount; put on board, embark.

imprīmīs (in prīmīs), *adv.* [in+*abl. pl. of* prīmus], especially, chiefly.

īmus, -a, -um, *adj.* [*superl. of* īnferus], lowest, at the foot *or* bottom of; deepest, inmost, the depths of; humblest, lowest; *n. as noun,* **īmum, -ī,** the bottom, lowest part, depth.

in, *prep. with acc. and abl.: with acc.,* into, toward, against, upon; for; till; over; *with abl.,* in, in the midst of, on, upon, among, at, over; in the case of.

incendō, -cendere, -cendī, -cēnsum, set fire to, burn; inflame, incense, enrage.

incidō, -cidere, -cidī, — [in+cadō], fall into, fall upon, fall; happen, occur; *of war,* break out, begin.

incipiō, -cipere, -cēpī, -ceptum [in+ capiō], begin.

in-citō, -āre, -āvī, -ātum [citō, rouse], urge on, arouse, incite, instigate; hurry.

inclūdō, -clūdere, -clūsī, -clūsum [in+ claudō], shut in, inclose, confine, imprison.

incola, -ae, *m. and f.* [incolō], inhabitant, resident.

in-colō, -colere, -coluī, —, dwell in, inhabit; live.

incolumis, -e, *adj.,* unharmed, safe.

incommodum, -ī, *n.* [incommodus, inconvenient], inconvenience, loss, trouble, injury, disaster, misfortune.

in-crēdibilis, -e, *adj.,* incredible, extraordinary.

incūsō, -āre, -āvī, -ātum [in+causa], accuse, complain of; censure, upbraid.

inde, *adv.: of place,* from that place, thence; *of time,* after that, next, then; *of cause,* in consequence, therefore; *of source,* from it, of it.

in-dīcō, -dīcere, -dīxī, -dictum, proclaim, declare, appoint, set.

indignātiō, -ōnis, *f.* [indignor, resent], indignation, resentment.

indignitās, -ātis, *f.* [indignus, unworthy], unworthy treatment, indignity, outrage.

in-dūcō, -dūcere, -dūxī, -ductum, bring *or* lead in; draw on *or* over, cover, spread over; induce, move, impel; lead on, influence.

induō, -duere, -duī, -dūtum, put on (*clothing, etc.*), dress in, clothe, cover.

in-eō, -īre, -iī, -itum, go into, enter; enter into *or* upon, undertake, begin; **cōnsilium inīre,** form a plan; **initā aestāte,** at the beginning of summer.

inermis, -e, *adj.* **[in-+arma],** unarmed, defenseless.

īn-fandus, -a, -um, *adj.,* unspeakable, shocking, terrible.

īnfāns, -fantis, -ium, *m.,* baby, infant, child.

īn-fēlīx, *gen.* **-fēlīcis,** *adj.,* unhappy, luckless, ill-fated, unfortunate.

īnferior, *compar. of* **īnferus.**

īn-ferō, -ferre, intulī, illātum, bring *or* carry in; import; inflict, inflict upon, bring upon; bring forward, allege; cause, produce; **bellum īnferre,** wage war on; **sē īnferre,** advance, proceed, rush in; **signa īnferre,** advance (*to the attack*), charge.

īnferus, -a, -um, *adj.,* down, low, below; *m. pl. as noun,* **īnferī, -ōrum,** those of the lower world, the dead, the shades; *compar.,* **īnferior, -ius,** lower, lower down; inferior, weaker; *superl.,* **īnfimus, -a, -um** *or* **īmus, -a, -um,** lowest, at the foot *or* bottom of; deepest, inmost, the depths of; humblest, lowest; *n. as noun,* **īmum, -ī,** the bottom, lowest part, depth.

īnficiō, -ficere, -fēcī, -fectum [in+faciō], stain, dye, color; infect, poison.

īnfimus, *superl. of* **īnferus.**

īnfrā, *adv., and prep. with acc.,* below, under, underneath, beneath.

īnfundō, -fundere, -fūdī, -fūsum, pour into, pour upon; infuse.

ingenium, -ī, *n.,* inborn quality *or* nature, character, disposition; talent, ability, genius.

ingēns, *gen.* **ingentis,** *adj.,* enormous; vast, huge, very large, great.

ingredior, -gredī, -gressus sum [in+gradior, step], go into, enter, go forward, advance; engage in, undertake.

inimīcus, -a, -um, *adj.* **[in-+amīcus],** unfriendly, hostile; *m. as noun,* **inimīcus, -ī,** an enemy (*personal, or not in war*), foe, opponent, rival.

inīquus, -a, -um, *adj.* **[in-+aequus],** uneven, unequal; unfair, unjust; unfavorable, disadvantageous; unfriendly, unkind, hostile; discontented.

initium, -ī, *n.* **[ineō],** a going in; beginning; edge, boundary; **initium capere ab,** begin at.

injūria, -ae, *f.* **[in-+jūs],** injustice, wrong, injury, abuse; *abl. used adverbially,* unjustly, undeservedly.

(in-jussus, -ūs), *m.* **[in-+jubeō],** *only abl.* **injussū,** without command, without order.

inopia, -ae, *f.* **[inops,** without means], lack, want, scarcity; need, poverty.

inquam, inquis, inquit, —, —, inquiunt, *defective verb* (*always after one or more words of a quotation*), say.

īn-sequor, -sequī, -secūtus sum, follow up, follow after *or* close, follow, pursue.

īnsidiae, -ārum, *f. pl.,* treachery, ambush, trick, stratagem, plot.

īnsigne, īnsignis, -ium, *n.* **[īnsignis],** a mark, badge, sign, signal; decoration, honor; *pl.,* decorations, ornaments, insignia.

īnsignis, -e, *adj.* **[in+signum],** marked, distinguished, extraordinary, conspicuous; noted.

īnstituō, -stituere, -stituī, -stitūtum [in-+statuō], set in place; draw up; arrange, erect, construct, build; establish, found; prepare, prepare for, begin, undertake; determine upon, adopt, appoint; train, instruct.

īnstitūtum, -ī, *n.* **[*pf. part.* of īnstituō],** principle, custom, usage, institution.

īn-stō, -stāre, -stitī, -stātūrus, stand upon; be near, approach, be at hand; threaten; urge, insist; press on, follow after, pursue.

īn-struō, -struere, -strūxī, -strūctum, build up, construct; provide, equip, prepare; draw up, array, arrange, marshal.

īnsula, -ae, *f.,* island.

integer, -gra, -grum, *adj.* [*compare* **in-+tangō**], untouched, whole; unhurt; unimpaired, fresh, vigorous; honest, upright.

intellegō, -legere, -lēxī, -lēctum [**inter +legō**], understand, perceive, learn, know.

in-tendō, -tendere, -tendī, -tentum, stretch to; extend, direct, bend, aim, apply.

intentus, -a, -um, *adj.* [*pf. part. of* **intendō**], intent, attentive.

inter, *prep. with acc.: of space,* between, among, within; *of time,* during, in the course of; *in reciprocal relations,* with, from, by, to; **inter sē,** with *or* to each other; from one another; among themselves; *in other relations,* between, among, through.

inter-cēdō, -cēdere, -cessī, -cessum, go *or* come between, be between, intervene; veto; *of time,* intervene, pass.

intercipiō, -cipere, -cēpī, -ceptum [**inter +capiō**], intercept, catch up; cut off; take away.

interclūdō, -clūdere, -clūsī, -clūsum [**inter+claudō**], shut *or* cut off, intercept, block.

inter-dum, *adv.,* sometimes, from time to time, occasionally.

inter-eā, *adv.,* meanwhile, in the meantime.

inter-eō, -īre, -iī, -itum, be lost, perish, be killed.

interficiō, -ficere, -fēcī, -fectum [**inter +faciō**], kill, slay, destroy.

interim, *adv.,* in the meantime, meanwhile.

interior, -ius, *compar. adj.,* inner, interior.

inter-mittō, -mittere, -mīsī, -missum, leave off, interrupt, cease, suspend; let pass *or* go by, lose; *pass.* (*of time*), elapse, intervene.

interrēgnum, -ī, *n.,* interregnum, *an interval between two reigns.*

inter-rogō, -āre, -āvī, -ātum, ask, inquire of, question.

inter-sum, -esse, -fuī, -futūrus, be *or* lie between, intervene; be present at, attend, take part in; *impers.,* **interest,** it is to the interest *or* advantage, it concerns.

inter-vāllum, -ī, *n.,* intervening space, distance, interval (*of time or of space*).

intrā, *prep. with acc.,* within, inside of; into, inside.

intrō, -āre, -āvī, -ātum, go into, enter, penetrate.

intrō-dūcō, -dūcere, -dūxī, -ductum, lead into, introduce.

intro-eō, -īre, -iī, -itum, enter.

in-ūsitātus, -a, -um, *adj.,* unusual, strange, unfamiliar, extraordinary.

in-vādō, -vādere, -vāsī, -vāsum, enter; *with* **in** *and the accusative,* invade, rush in upon.

in-veniō, -venīre, -vēnī, -ventum, come upon, find, discover.

invītō, -āre, -āvī, -ātum, invite, summon, request, urge.

invītus, -a, -um, *adj.,* against one's will, unwilling.

ipse, ipsa, ipsum, *intensive pron.,* self, himself, herself, itself; *pl.,* themselves; he, she, it; *emphatic,* very, the very.

īra, -ae, *f.,* ire, anger, rage.

īrātus, -a, -um, *adj.* [*pf. part. of* **īrāscor,** become angry], angry, angered, in anger, enraged.

irrumpō, -rumpere, -rūpī, -ruptum [**in+rumpō**], break in *or* into, force one's way into, burst into.

is, ea, id, *demonstr. pron. and adj.: as adj.,* that one, this (*pl.* these), this one; such, of such a sort *or* kind; *as personal pron.,* he, she, it; *pl.,* they; **ejus modī,** of that *or* such a sort.

iste, ista, istud, *demonstr. pron. and adj., referring to that which is close to or belonging to the person addressed: as adj.*, that of yours, that (*pl.* those), that one; *as pron.*, he, she, it; *pl.*, they.

ita, *adv.*, so, thus, in this way, as follows; to such an extent, in such a way; accordingly, thus; on this condition; ut . . . ita, just as . . . so, while . . . yet.

Ītalia, -ae, *f.*, Italy.

ita-que, *conj.*, and so, accordingly, therefore, and thus.

item, *adv.*, also, likewise, too.

iter, itineris, *n.*, a way, road; passage, journey, march; right of way; line of march; **magnum iter**, a rapid *or* forced march.

iterum, *adv.*, again, a second time, once more.

Ithaca, -ae, *f.*, Ithaca, *kingdom of Ulysses, an island off the west coast of Greece. See map, page 61.*

Iūlus, -ī, *m.*, Iulus (ī-ū'lus), *also known as Ascanius, son of Aeneas.*

J

jaceō, -ēre, -uī, —, lie, be prostrate *or* fallen, lie dead.

jaciō, -ere, jēcī, jactum, throw, hurl, fling; throw about, scatter, sow; throw up, build, construct, lay (*a foundation*); drop (*an anchor*).

jactūra, -ae, *f.* [jaciō], loss, expenditure.

jam, *adv.*, already, now, by this time; soon, directly; furthermore, besides; **nōn jam**, no longer; **jam dūdum**, a long time ago, long ago, this long time; **jam prīdem**, long ago, this long time.

Jāniculum, -ī, *n.*, the Janiculum (ja-nik'ū-lum), *a hill in Rome, west of the Tiber. See map, page 39.*

jānua, -ae, *f.*, door.

Jāsōn, -onis, *m.*, Jason, *the leader of the Argonauts.*

jubeō, -ēre, jussī, jussum, order, command.

jūdicium, -ī, *n.* [jūdicō], trial, a legal trial; a court; judgment, decision; opinion.

jūdicō, -āre, -āvī, -ātum [jūdex, judge], decide, judge, think, consider.

jūgerum, -ī (*gen. pl.*, jūgerum), *n.*, a juger (*about two-thirds of an acre*).

jugum, -ī, *n.*, yoke; ridge, summit, height, crest.

Jūlius Caesar, *m.*, Gaius Julius Caesar, *the conqueror of Gaul, consul in 59* B.C., *later dictator.*

jungō, -ere, jūnxī, jūnctum, join, fasten, attach, unite, associate; harness, yoke.

jūnior, -ius, *adj.* [*compar. of* juvenis], younger.

Jūnius Brūtus, *m.*, Lucius Junius Brutus, *one of the first two consuls at Rome.*

Jūnō, -ōnis, *f.*, Juno, *sister and wife of Jupiter and the queen of the gods.*

Juppiter, Jovis, *m.*, Jupiter, *the king of the gods.*

Jūra, -ae, *m.*, the Jura (jö'rạ), *a chain of mountains between the Rhine and the Rhone. See map, page 137.*

jūrō, -āre, -āvī, -ātum [jūs], take oath, make an oath, swear.

jūs, jūris, *n.*, right, justice, law; legal right, authority; obligation, duty; prestige; *abl.*, jūre, by right, rightfully, justly.

jūs jūrandum, jūris jūrandī, *n.*, an oath.

jūstitia, -ae, *f.* [jūstus], justice, uprightness, righteousness.

jūstus, -a, -um, *adj.* [jūs], in accordance with law; just, fair, right, proper; well-grounded; regular, allotted; upright.

juvenis, -is, *adj.*, young, youthful; *m. and f. as noun,* juvenis, -is, a young person, a young man or woman (*esp. one less than forty years of age*), a youth; *compar.*, jūnior, -ius, younger.

juvō, -āre, jūvī, jūtum, aid, help, assist, serve.

L

L., *abbr. for* **Lūcius.**

Labiēnus, -ī, *m.,* **T. Labiēnus,** Titus Labienus (lā-bi-ē'nus), *Caesar's most trusted lieutenant in the Gallic War.*

labor, -ōris, *m.,* labor, toil, exertion, trouble; hardship, pain, distress, difficulty.

labōrō, -āre, -āvī, -ātum [labor], strive, labor, toil, take pains; suffer, be hard pressed, be in difficulties, be in danger; be afflicted, suffer; labor for.

lacessō, -ere, -īvī, -ītum, harass, provoke, challenge, attack.

lacrima, -ae, *f.,* a tear.

lacrimō, -āre, -āvī, -ātum, weep.

lacus, -ūs, *m.,* lake, pond.

laetus, -a, -um, *adj.,* joyful, glad, happy; with joy, with alacrity.

Lāocoōn, -ontis, *m.,* Laocoön (lā-ok'-ō-on), *a Trojan priest.*

Lāomedōn, -ontis, *m.,* Laomedon (lā-om'e-don), *a king of Troy (see map, p. 61).*

lapis, lapidis, *m.,* a stone.

lātē, *adv.* **[lātus],** widely, extensively, far and wide.

lateō, -ēre, -uī, —, lie hidden, be concealed, lurk, escape notice; hide, seek shelter.

Latīnus, -a, -um, *adj.,* of Latium, Latin; *m. pl. as noun,* **Latīnī, -ōrum,** the Latins, *a nation of central Italy. See map, page 305.*

Latīnus, -ī, *m.,* Latinus (lā-tī'nus), *a legendary king of the Laurentines.*

lātitūdō, -inis, *f.* **[lātus],** width, breadth, extent.

Latobrīgī, -ōrum, *m. pl.,* the Latobrigi (lat-ō-brī'jī), *a German tribe. See map, page 137.*

latrō, -ōnis, *m.,* robber, brigand.

lātus, -a, -um, *adj.,* broad, wide, extensive.

latus, lateris, *n.,* side; flank, wing (*of an army*).

laudō, -āre, -āvī, -ātum [laus], praise, extol, commend, approve.

laus, laudis, *f.,* praise, fame, glory, renown; superior quality, merit, excellence.

Lāvīnia, -ae, *f.,* Lavinia (lā-vin'i-ą), *daughter of King Latinus.*

Lāvīnium, -iī *or* **-ī,** *n.,* Lavinium (lā-vin'i-um), *a city of ancient Italy. See map, page 305.*

lectīca, -ae, *f.* **[lectus,** couch], a litter, *a curtained and covered couch, usually carried by slaves.*

lēgātiō, -ōnis, *f.* **[lēgō,** appoint as deputy], embassy, legation; mission.

lēgātus, -ī, *m.* [*pf. part. of* **lēgō,** appoint as deputy], representative; lieutenant, legate; ambassador, envoy, deputy.

legiō, -ōnis, *f.* **[legō],** a legion.

legō, -ere, lēgī, lēctum, gather, collect; choose, select, appoint; read.

Lemannus, -ī, *m.,* Lake Geneva. *See map, page 137.*

lēnis, -e, *adj.,* smooth, gentle; mild, kind, indulgent.

leō, -ōnis, *m.,* a lion.

levis, -e, *adj.,* light, slight, trifling, small; easy to bear, easy.

lēx, lēgis, *f.,* law, statute, enactment; terms, condition.

libenter, *adv.* **[libēns,** willing], willingly, with pleasure, gladly.

liber, librī, *m.,* a book.

līber, lībera, līberum, *adj.,* free, independent; undisturbed; permitted.

Līber, -ī, *m.,* Liber (lī'bėr), *a charioteer.*

līberī, -ōrum, *m. pl.* **[līber],** the free members of the household; children.

līberō, -āre, -āvī, -ātum [līber], set free, free, liberate, release.

lībertās, -ātis, *f.* **[līber],** liberty, freedom, independence; permission.

Libya, -ae, *f.,* Libya (lib'i-ą), *a country of northern Africa. See map, page 61. (Sometimes means Africa.)*

licet, licēre, licuit *or* **licitum est,** *impers.*, it is allowed *or* permitted, one may; **licet,** *conj.*, although, granted that.

Lichās, -ae, *m.*, Lichas (lī'kạs), *a companion of Hercules.*

ligneus, -a, -um, *adj.* [lignum], of wood, wooden.

lignum, -ī, *n.*, wood, a piece of wood; *pl.*, firewood.

Lingonēs, -um, *m. pl.*, the Lingones (ling'gō-nēz), *a people of Celtic Gaul. See map, page 137.*

lingua, -ae, *f.*, tongue; language, speech.

linter, -tris, *f.*, boat, skiff.

Linus, -ī, *m.*, Linus (lī'nus), *a centaur who instructed Hercules in music.*

littera, -ae, *f.*, a letter (*of the alphabet*); *pl.*, a letter, an epistle, letters; literature, literary accomplishments, scholarship.

lītus, lītoris, *n.*, shore, seashore, beach.

locus, -ī, *m.* (*pl. usually n.*, **loca, -ōrum**), a place, spot, point, locality; ground, earth; space, position, station, situation; room, chance, occasion, opportunity; degree, rank; *abl.*, *with dependent gen.*, in the place of, as.

longē, *adv.* [longus]: *of space,* far away, far off, at *or* to a distance; distant, away; *of degree,* by far, far, much; *of time,* for a long time, long.

longus, -a, -um, *adj.*, long, extensive; long-continued; distant; **nāvis longa,** war-vessel.

loquor, loquī, locūtus sum, say, speak, talk, converse.

lōrīca, -ae, *f.*, coat of mail; breastwork, parapet.

lotus, -ī, *m.*, the lotus.

Lūcius, -ī, *m.*, Lucius (lū'shius), *a Roman first name.*

Lucumō, -ōnis, *m.*, Lucumo (lö'-kū-mō), *an Etruscan name; the original name of* **Tarquinius Prīscus.**

lūdō, -ere, lūsī, lūsum, play, engage in sport.

lūdus, -ī, *m.*, game, play, sport, public game *or* exhibition; **lūdōs facere,** hold games.

lūmen, -inis, *n.* [lūx], light, a light, lamp, torch.

lūna, -ae, *f.*, the moon.

lūx, lūcis, *f.*, light, daylight; **ortā lūce** *or* **prīmā lūce,** at daybreak.

M

M., *abbr. for* **Mārcus.**

magicus, -a, -um, *adj.*, magical, magic.

magis, *adv.* [*compar. of* **magnopere**], more, more greatly, in a greater degree, rather.

magister, -trī, *m.*, chief, master; teacher.

magistrātus, -ūs, *m.* [magister], a public office, magistracy; magistrate, official.

magnificus, -a, -um, *adj.* [magnus+ faciō], splendid, fine, magnificent.

magnitūdō, -inis, *f.* [magnus], greatness, size, extent, magnitude.

magnopere *or* **magnō opere,** *adv.*, greatly, very much, exceedingly; earnestly; *compar.*, **magis,** more, more greatly, in a greater degree, rather; *superl.*, **maximē,** in the highest degree, most of all, exceedingly, chiefly, especially.

magnus, -a, -um, *adj.*, great, large, of great extent, much, considerable; loud; **magnum iter,** a rapid *or* forced march; *m. as noun,* **Magnus, -ī,** the Great, *a name of Pompey; compar.*, **major, majus,** greater, larger; *superl.*, **maximus, -a, -um,** greatest, largest.

major, majus, *adj.* [*compar. of* **magnus**], greater, larger; **major nātū,** older, elder.

majōrēs, -um, *m. pl.*, ancestors, forefathers.

male, *adv.* [malus], badly, ill, wrongly, wickedly; *compar.,* **pejus,** worse; *superl.,* **pessimē,** worst, most unkindly.

maleficium, -ī, *n.* [maleficus, doing wrong], an evil deed; harm, mischief, injury.

mālō, mālle, māluī, — [magis+volō], prefer, choose rather.

malum, -ī, *n.* [malus], evil, calamity, misfortune, harm; punishment.

malus, -a, -um, *adj.,* bad, evil, wicked, criminal; *compar.,* **pejor, pejus,** worse; *superl.,* **pessimus, -a, -um,** worst, most wicked.

mandātum, -ī, *n.* [*pf. part. of* mandō], command, order, instruction, commission.

mandō, -āre, -āvī, -ātum [manus+dō], hand over, give over, give; intrust, commit, consign; order, commission, command.

maneō, -ēre, mānsī, mānsum, remain, stay, stop.

Mānlius, -ī, *m.* (*1*) M. **Mānlius,** Marcus Manlius Capitolinus (kap-i-tō-lī'nus), *who saved the Roman Capitol in the Gallic War, a consul in 392* B.C.; (*2*) L. **Mānlius Vulsō,** Lucius Manlius Vulso (vul'sō), *a consul in 256* B.C.

manus, -ūs, *f.,* the hand; force; a force, band of armed men, troop.

Mārcella, -ae, *f.,* Marcella.

Mārcius, -ī, *m.,* Ancus **Mārcius,** Ancus Marcius (ang'kus mär'shius), *the fourth king of Rome.*

Mārcus, -ī, *m.,* Marcus, *a Roman first name.*

mare, maris, -ium, *n.,* the sea.

maritimus, -a, -um, *adj.* [mare], of the sea, maritime, on the sea, along the coast.

marītus, -ī, *m.* [mās, masculine], husband.

Mārs, Mārtis, *m.,* Mars, *the Roman god of war; figuratively,* war, battle.

Mārtius, -a, -um, *adj.* [Mārs], of Mars; of the month of March; **Campus Mārtius,** the field of Mars, *originally an exercise and parade-ground in Rome, dedicated to Mars. See map, page 39.*

māter, -tris, *f.,* mother; **mātrēs familiae,** matrons.

māteria, *acc.,* **-am,** *or* **māteriēs,** *acc.,* **-em,** *f.* [māter], stuff, material, timber.

mātrimōnium, -ī, *n.* [māter], marriage, wedlock; **in mātrimōnium dare,** give in marriage, arrange a marriage for; **in mātrimōnium dūcere,** marry.

Matrona, -ae, *f.,* the Marne (mårn), *a river of Gaul. See map, page 137.*

mātūrō, -āre, -āvī, -ātum [mātūrus], set about early, hasten, hurry.

mātūrus, -a, -um, *adj.,* ripe, full grown, matured, of proper age, mature; early, speedy.

maximē, *adv.* [*superl. of* magnopere], in the highest degree, most of all, exceedingly, chiefly, especially.

maximus, -a, -um, *adj.* [*superl. of* magnus], greatest, largest; *especially,* **Circus Maximus,** the Circus Maximus, *a famous place for chariot-racing in Rome. See map, page 39.*

Mēdēa, -ae, *f.,* Medea (mē-dē'ä), *wife of Jason.*

medicus, -a, -um, *adj.* [medeor, heal], of healing, medical; *m. as noun,* **medicus, -ī,** physician, surgeon.

mediocris, -e, *adj.* [medius], medium, ordinary, moderate, mediocre.

medius, -a, -um, *adj.,* middle, the middle of, the midst of; in the middle *or* midst; intervening; *n. as noun,* **medium, -ī,** the middle, the intervening space, the midst.

melior, melius, *adj.* [*compar. of* bonus], better.

melius, *adv.* [*compar. of* bene], better.

membrum, -ī, *n.,* limb, member, part.

memoria, -ae, *f.* [**memor,** mindful], memory, recollection, remembrance; memory, time.

Menapiī, -ōrum, *m. pl.,* the Menapii (mẹ-nā'pi-ī), *a tribe of Belgic Gaul. See map, page 137.*

Menelāus, -ī, *m.,* Menelaus (men-e-lā'us), *a king of Sparta.*

Menēnius Agrippa, *m.,* Menenius Agrippa (mẹ-nē'ni-us a-grip'ä), *a prominent Roman of the early Republic.*

mēns, mentis, *f.,* the mind, understanding, judgment, reason; spirit; purpose, intention.

mēnsa, -ae, *f.,* table; meal, course; dish.

mēnsis, mēnsis, -ium *or* **-um,** *m.,* month.

mercātor, -ōris, *m.* [**mercor,** to trade], trader, merchant.

Mercurius, -ī, *m.,* Mercury, *the messenger of the gods and god of traders.*

mereō, -ēre, -uī, -itum, *and* **mereor, -ērī, -itus sum,** deserve, earn, acquire.

mergō, -ere, mersī, mersum, plunge, sink, dip, overwhelm.

merīdiēs, -ēī, *m.* [**medius+diēs**], midday, noon; the south.

meritum, -ī, *n.* [*pf. part. of* **mereō**], merit, desert, service; favor, benefit.

meritus, -a, -um, *adj.* [*pf. part. of* **mereō**], meriting, deserving; merited, deserved, just.

Messāla, -ae, *m.,* **M. Messāla,** Marcus Valerius Messala (vạ-lē'ri-us me-sā'lä), *a consul in 61* B.C.

mēta, -ae, *f.,* turning-post, goal.

mētior, -īrī, mēnsus sum, measure; deal *or* measure out, distribute.

Mettius, -ī, *m.,* Mettius Fufetius, Mettius Fufetius (met'i-us fụ-fē'-shius), *an Alban dictator.*

metuō, -ere, -uī, — [**metus**], fear, dread, be afraid of, be in fear.

metus, -ūs, *m.,* fear, terror, anxiety.

meus, -a, -um, *poss. adj.* [**mē**], my, mine, my own, of mine.

mī, *masculine singular vocative of* **meus.**

migrō, -āre, -āvī, -ātum, remove, move, migrate.

mīles, mīlitis, *m.,* soldier, soldiery.

mīlitāris, -e, *adj.* [**mīles**], of a soldier, of war, military; **rēs mīlitāris,** warfare, the art of war, military science.

mīlle, *num. adj.* (*pl.* **mīlia, -ium,** *neuter noun*), a thousand; **mīlle passūs,** a thousand paces, a mile.

Minerva, -ae, *f.,* Minerva, *the Roman goddess of wisdom and of the arts and sciences.*

minimē, *adv.* [*superl. of* **parum**], least, very little; by no means, not at all, no.

minimus, -a, -um, *adj.* [*superl. of* **parvus**], smallest, least, very small.

minor, minus, *adj.* [*compar. of* **parvus**], smaller, less, inferior, of less importance.

minuō, -ere, -uī, -ūtum, lessen, diminish, weaken, impair; *of the tide,* ebb.

minus, *adv.* [*compar. of* **parum**], less; **nihilō minus,** none the less; nevertheless; **quō minus** *or* **quōminus,** so that not, from; **sī minus,** if not.

mīrābilis, -e, *adj.* [**mīror**], wonderful, strange, marvelous.

mīror, -ārī, -ātus sum [**mīrus**], wonder at, admire, be astonished, wonder.

mīrus, -a, -um, *adj.,* wonderful, astonishing, surprising, strange.

miser, -era, -erum, *adj.,* wretched, unhappy, miserable, pitiful.

mittō, -ere, mīsī, missum, send, dispatch; dismiss, release; cast, hurl; omit, pass over.

modo, *adv.* [**modus**], only, merely; just now; **nōn modo . . . sed etiam,** not only . . . but also.

modus, -ī, *m.,* measure, size; limit, amount; way, manner, method, kind, sort, character; **ejus modī,** of that *or* such a sort; **quem ad modum,** in what way, how; as.

moenia, -ium, *n. pl.,* city walls, walls.

molō, -ere, -uī, -itum [mola, grind-stone], grind; *pf. part.*, **molitus, -a, -um**, ground; **molita cibāria**, meal, flour.

moneō, -ēre, -uī, -itum, remind, advise, warn.

mōns, montis, -ium, *m.*, a mountain, a range of mountains.

mōnstrō, -āre, -āvī, -ātum [mōnstrum], show, exhibit; point out.

mōnstrum, -ī, *n.* [moneō], a warning, omen, portent, miracle; monster.

mora, -ae, *f.*, delay, stopping; hindrance.

Morinī, -ōrum, *m. pl.*, the Morini (mor'i-nī), *a tribe of Belgic Gaul. See map, page 137.*

morior, morī, mortuus sum, die.

moror, -ārī, -ātus sum [mora], delay, linger, wait, tarry; stop, retard, hinder.

mors, mortis, *f.*, death.

mortuus, -a, -um, *adj.* [*pf. part. of* morior], dead; *m. as noun*, **mortuus, -ī**, a dead person; *pl.*, the dead, the slain.

mōs, mōris, *m.*, custom, habit, practice, manner, usage; *pl.*, character, disposition.

mōtus, -ūs, *m.* [moveō], movement, motion; disturbance, tumult; impulse, motive.

moveō, -ēre, mōvī, mōtum, move, stir; remove, expel; excite, affect, arouse, influence; **castra movēre**, break camp.

mox, *adv.*, soon, presently, before long, then, afterwards.

mulier, -eris, *f.*, woman, female.

multitūdō, -inis, *f.* [multus], multitude, large number, crowd, throng; the crowd, the common people, population.

multō, *adv.* [multus], by much, much, by far, far.

multum, *adv.* [multus], much, greatly, especially, very; often, frequently; *compar.*, **plūs**, more; *superl.*, **plūrimum**, most, very, for the most part, generally.

multus, -a, -um, *adj.*, many, many a; much, abundant, a great quantity of; extensive, great; *m. pl. as noun*, **multī, -ōrum**, many, many persons; **multum, -ī,** *n.*, much.

mūniō, -īre, -īvī, -ītum [moenia], wall in, fortify, guard, defend, protect; build (*a road*), construct, pave.

mūnītiō, -ōnis, *f.* [mūniō], fortification, intrenchment, works, defenses, rampart; the work of fortifying.

mūnus, mūneris, *n.*, service, office; duty, task, function; gift, present.

mūrus, -ī, *m.*, wall, city wall.

mūtō, -āre, -āvī, -ātum, change, transform; replace, exchange.

N

nam, *conj.*, for, inasmuch as.

nam-que, *conj.*, for, for in fact; inasmuch as.

nancīscor, nancīscī, nactus sum, happen upon, meet with, find; get, obtain.

Nantuātēs, -um, *m. pl.*, the Nantuates (nan-tū-ā'tēz), *a Gallic tribe in the Alps. See map, page 137.*

nārrō, -āre, -āvī, -ātum, report, relate, tell, say, describe.

nāscor, nāscī, nātus sum, be born *or* produced; rise, arise, spring up, grow; be found; **nātus, -a, -um,** *pf. part.*, often with a numeral, at the age of, aged, old.

nātiō, -ōnis, *f.* [nāscor], nation, tribe, people, race.

nātūra, -ae, *f.* [nāscor], nature, character, quality.

(nātus, -ūs), *m.* [nāscor], only in abl. sing., **nātū**, birth, age; **major nātū**, older, elder.

nātus, -ī, *m.* [*pf. part. of* nāscor], a son, child.

nauta, -ae, *m.* [*for* nāvita], sailor.

nāvicula, -ae, *f.* [nāvis], a small boat, skiff.

nāvigō, -āre, -āvī, -ātum [nāvis+agō],
set sail, sail.

nāvis, nāvis, -ium, *f.*, ship, vessel,
boat; **nāvem appellere,** bring to
land, bring up, come to land, put
ashore; **nāvis longa,** war-vessel; **nāvis onerāria,** freight-ship, transport-
ship, transport; **nāvem** *or* **nāvēs
solvere,** set sail, weigh anchor.

-ne, *enclitic adv., and conj.: as adv., a
sign of direct questions that may be
answered by "yes" or "no"; as
conj., introducing indirect questions,
whether.*

nē, *adv., and conj.: as adv.,* not; **nē
. . . quidem,** not . . . even, not . . .
either; *as conj.,* that . . . not, in
order that . . . not, in order not to,
for fear that; *after verbs of fearing,*
that, lest; **nē quis,** in order that
no one.

Neāpolis, -is, *f.,* Naples. *See map,
page 20.*

nec, *see* neque.

necessārius, -a, -um, *adj.* [necesse],
necessary, inevitable; urgent, press-
ing, critical; *m. pl. as noun,* **necessā-
riī, -ōrum,** close friends, kinsmen.

necesse, *indecl. adj.,* necessary.

necō, -āre, -āvī, -ātum [nex], kill,
put to death, slay.

neglegō, -legere, -lēxī, -lēctum [nec+
legō], disregard, neglect, despise,
slight.

negō, -āre, -āvī, -ātum, say no, say
that not; deny, refuse.

negōtium, -ī, *n.* [ōtium], business,
undertaking; task, duty, affair; difficulty, trouble; **negōtium dare,** employ.

nēmō, *dat.* nēminī, *acc.* nēminem, *no
gen. or abl., m. and f.* [ne+homō],
no one, nobody.

nepōs, -ōtis, *m.,* grandson.

ne-que *or* nec, *conj.,* and not, nor;
neque . . . neque *or* **nec . . . nec,**
neither . . . nor.

Nerviī, -ōrum, *m. pl.,* the Nervii
(nĕr'vi-ī), *a tribe of Belgic Gaul.
See map, page 137.*

ne-sciō, -scīre, -scīvī, —, not know, be
ignorant, be at a loss; **nesciō quis,
nesciō quid,** someone or other, something or other, somebody, something.

Nessus, -ī, *m.,* Nessus, *the name of a
certain centaur.*

neuter, -tra, -trum, *adj.* [ne+uter],
neither; *m. pl. as noun,* **neutrī,
-ōrum,** neither side *or* party.

nē-ve *or* neu, *conj.,* and not, nor, and
not to, and that not.

nex, necis, *f.,* death, murder, slaughter.

nī, *see* nisi.

nihil, *n., indecl.* [nihilum], nothing;
as adv., not at all; **nōn nihil,** something; *as adv.,* somewhat, to some
extent.

nihilum, -ī, *n.* [ne+hilum, a particle],
nothing at all, not a bit, nothing;
*especially, in the abl. with a compar.,
e.g.,* **nihilō minus,** none the less,
nevertheless.

nisi *or* nī, *conj.* [ne+sī], if not, unless;
after a neg. or interrog., except.

nōbilis, -e, *adj.* [nōscō], well-known,
famous; of noble birth, noble; excellent; *m. pl. as noun,* **nōbilēs,
-ium,** the nobles, the nobility.

nōbilitās, -ātis, *f.* [nōbilis], fame, renown, superiority; high *or* noble
birth, high rank, nobility; *as a collective noun,* the nobility, the nobles.

noceō, -ēre, -uī, -itum, harm, damage,
injure, hurt; **nocēns, -entis,** *pres.
part.,* guilty.

noctū, *adv.* [nox], by night, at night.

nocturnus, -a, -um, *adj.* [nox], of *or*
by night, nightly, nocturnal.

nōlō, nōlle, nōluī, — [ne+volō], not
wish, be unwilling; *imperative,* **nōlī,**
pl., **nōlīte,** do not.

nōmen, -inis, *n.,* a name; reputation,
fame; account, sake; pretext, excuse.

nōn, *adv.,* not; **nōn jam,** no longer; **nōn nihil,** something; **nōn numquam,** sometimes, a few times.

nōn-dum, *adv.,* not yet.

nōn-ne, *used to introduce a question and to imply the answer "yes."*

nōn-nūllus, **-a,** **-um,** *adj.,* some, several.

nōnus, **-a,** **-um,** *num. adj.* [novem], ninth.

nōs, *pers. pron.* [*pl. of* ego], we.

nōscō, **-ere,** **nōvī,** **nōtum,** become acquainted with, learn, recognize; *pf.,* know.

noster, -tra, -trum, *adj.* [nōs], our, ours, our own; *m. pl. as noun,* **nostrī, -ōrum,** our men, troops, soldiers.

nōtus, **-a,** **-um,** *adj.* [*pf. part. of* nōscō, learn, know], known, familiar, well-known.

novem, *indecl. num. adj.,* nine.

novus, **-a,** **-um,** *adj.,* new, young, recent, last, latest; novel, strange, unusual; **rēs novae,** a change of government, revolution; *superl.,* **novissimus,** **-a,** **-um,** last, the end of, rear; **novissimum agmen,** the rear, rear line *or* column; *m. pl. as noun,* **novissimī, -ōrum,** those at the rear, the rear ranks *or* line.

nox, noctis, -ium, *f.,* night.

nūbēs, nūbis, -ium, *f.,* cloud, mist.

nūdō, -āre, -āvī, -ātum [nūdus], strip, uncover, make *or* lay bare; expose, bring to light; strip of, deprive of, empty.

nūdus, **-a,** **-um,** *adj.,* naked, lightly clad; bare, exposed, unprotected.

nūllus, **-a,** **-um,** *adj.,* no, not any, none; *m. pl. as noun,* **nūllī, -ōrum,** none.

num, *interrog. adv.: with a direct question to which a negative answer is expected,* is not so, is |it? *Often best rendered by the inflection of the voice; with indirect questions,* whether.

Numa, **-ae,** *m.,* **Numa Pompilius,** Numa Pompilius (nū'mǎ pom-pil'-ius), *the second king of Rome.*

numerus, **-ī,** *m.,* a number; amount, quantity; account, estimation; *abl. with dependent gen.,* in the number of, as.

Numitor, **-ōris,** *m.,* Numitor (nū'-mi-tôr), *a king of Alba.*

numquam, *adv.* [ne+umquam], never, not at all; **nōn numquam,** sometimes, a few times.

nunc, *adv.,* now, at present; at this time; as things now are, in present circumstances.

nūntiō, -āre, -āvī, -ātum [nūntius], announce, give news, report, narrate, relate; give orders, direct.

nūntius, **-ī,** *m.,* messenger, courier; news, message; order, command.

nūper, *adv.,* lately, recently, not long since.

nusquam, *adv.* [ne+usquam, anywhere], nowhere, in no place.

nympha, **-ae,** *f.,* nymph; *pl.,* the nymphs, *female deities that inhabited the seas, fountains, woods, and mountains.*

O

Ō, *interj.,* O! oh!

ob, *prep. with acc.,* toward, against; on account of, by reason of, because of; **ob eam rem,** for this reason, therefore; **quam ob rem,** on account of which, wherefore, therefore; why; why?

objiciō, -jicere, -jēcī, -jectum [ob+jaciō], throw before, throw to, throw against, offer, expose; interpose, oppose.

obscūrus, **-a,** **-um,** *adj.,* dark, dim, obscure.

obses, obsidis, *m. and f.,* hostage, pledge, security.

obsideō, -sidēre, -sēdī, -sessum [ob+sedeō], hem in, beset, obstruct, blockade, besiege.

obsidiō, -ōnis, *f.* [ob+sedeō], siege, blockade.

obtineō, -tinēre, -tinuī, -tentum [ob+teneō], hold, occupy, possess, have; be in charge of, govern, administer; hold fast, gain, obtain, acquire.

occāsiō, -ōnis, *f.* [ob+cadō], occasion, opportunity, fitting moment.

occāsus, -ūs, *m.* [occidō], a falling, setting; downfall, ruin; **sōlis occāsus,** sunset, the west.

occidō, -cidere, -cidī, -cāsum [ob+cadō], fall down, fall, die, perish, be killed; set (*applied to the sun*).

occīdō, -cīdere, -cīdī, -cīsum [ob+caedō], cut down, kill, slay.

occultō, -āre, -āvī, -ātum [occulō, hide], hide, conceal.

occultus, -a, -um, *adj.* [*pf. part. of* occulō, hide], hidden, concealed, secret; *n. as noun,* **in occultō,** in secret, in concealment.

occupō, -āre, -āvī, -ātum, take possession of, occupy, seize; cover, fill; employ, engage, keep busy; **occupātus, -a, -um,** *adj.* [*pf. part. of* occupō], occupied, employed, engaged, busy.

occurrō, -currere, -currī, -cursum [ob+currō], run against, run to meet, meet, encounter, oppose; meet with, fall in with.

Ōceanus, -ī, *m.,* the (Atlantic) Ocean.

octāvus, -a, -um, *num. adj.* [octō], eighth.

octō, *indecl. num. adj.,* eight.

oculus, -ī, *m.,* eye.

ōdī, ōdisse, ōsūrus, *defective verb,* hate, detest, loathe.

offerō, -ferre, obtulī, oblātum [ob+ferō], bring before, offer, present, bring against, expose; **sē offerre,** expose oneself.

officium, -ī, *n.* [faciō], service, favor, kindness; duty, official duty, obligation, sense of obligation, allegiance, obedience.

ōlim, *adv.,* once, formerly, of old, once upon a time.

omittō, -mittere, -mīsī, -missum [ob+mittō], let go, give up, neglect, let slip; cease, stop; cease to speak of, say nothing of, omit.

omnīnō, *adv.* [omnis], altogether, wholly, entirely, in all, only; *with negatives,* at all.

omnis, -e, *adj.,* all, every; *n. pl. as noun,* everything.

onerārius, -a, -um, *adj.* [onus], fitted *or* suitable for burdens; **nāvis onerāria,** freight-ship, transport-ship, transport.

onus, -eris, *n.,* load, pack, burden, weight; cargo; care, responsibility.

opera, -ae, *f.* [opus], work, pains; effort, labor, toil; attention; aid, help; **operam dare,** take pains, exert oneself, see to it that; give aid.

opīniō, -ōnis, *f.* [opīnor, suppose], opinion, view, belief, expectation; reputation, impression.

oportet, oportēre, oportuit, *impers.,* it is necessary *or* obligatory, it is proper, it behooves; (one) must, (one) ought.

oppidānus, -a, -um, *adj.* [oppidum], of *or* pertaining to a town; *m. pl. as noun,* **oppidānī, -ōrum,** townspeople, inhabitants of a town.

oppidum, -ī, *n.,* town, stronghold, city.

opportūnē, *adv.* [opportūnus], opportunely.

opportūnus, -a, -um, *adj.* [ob+portus], fit, suitable, opportune, seasonable, at the right time, convenient, advantageous, favorable.

opprimō, -primere, -pressī, -pressum [ob+premō], press *or* weigh down, burden, crush, overpower, overwhelm, destroy; suppress, put down; surprise.

oppugnātiō, -ōnis, *f.* [oppugnō], a taking by storm, attack, assault, siege.

oppugnō, -āre, -āvī, -ātum [ob+pugnō], attack, assault, try to storm, besiege.

(ops), opis, *f.* [*no nom. or dat. sing.*], aid, help; power; *pl.*, power, influence, resources, wealth, riches.

optimē, *adv.* [*superl. of* **bene**], best.

optimus, -a, -um, *adj.* [*superl. of* **bonus**], best, excellent.

opus, operis, *n.*, work, labor, toil; task; deed, achievement; structure, siege-work, fortification; want, need, necessity; **opus est,** there is need of, it is necessary; **magnō opere,** greatly, very much, exceedingly; earnestly; **quantō opere,** how much? how greatly?

ōra, -ae, *f.*, margin, border, edge; **ōra maritima,** coast, seacoast, shore, seashore.

ōrāculum, -ī, *n.* [**ōrō**], an oracle, prophecy.

ōrātiō, -ōnis, *f.* [**ōrō**], oration, speech, discourse, harangue.

orbis, orbis, -ium, *m.*, circle, ring; **orbis terrārum,** the earth, the world.

Orcus, -ī, *m.*, Orcus, *the lower world, or the god of the lower world.*

ōrdō, ōrdinis, *m.*, row, rank, line; order, arrangement; an order, class, rank.

Orgetorīx, -īgis, *m.*, Orgetorix (ôr-jet'-ō-riks), *a Helvetian chieftain.*

orior, -īrī, ortus sum, arise, rise, spring; come forth, appear, begin, break out; be born, be descended, spring from; **oriēns,** *pres. part.*, rising; **ortā lūce,** at daybreak.

ōrnātus, -a, -um, *adj.* [*pf. part. of* **ōrnō,** equip], furnished, equipped, fitted out; illustrious, distinguished.

ōrō, -āre, -āvī, -ātum [**ōs**], speak; entreat, pray, plead, beg.

ōs, ōris, *n.*, mouth; opening; the face, countenance, look, expression.

ōsculor, -ārī, -ātus sum [**ōsculum,** a kiss], kiss.

ostendō, -tendere, -tendī, -tentum [**obs**+**tendō**], display, hold out, show, point out; disclose, make known; state, declare, affirm.

ōstium, -ī, *n.* [**ōs**], door; mouth, entrance.

ōtium, -ī, *n.*, leisure, idleness, ease; peace, quiet.

P

P., *abbr. for* **Pūblius.**

pābulor, -ārī, -ātus sum [**pābulum**], forage, collect forage.

pābulum, -ī, *n.* [**pāscō,** feed], food; fodder, pasture, grass, forage.

pācō, -āre, -āvī, -ātum [**pāx**], make peaceful, render peaceful, pacify, subdue.

paene, *adv.*, nearly, almost.

pāgus, -ī, *m.*, district, division, canton; clan.

palam, *adv.*, openly, in public.

Palātīnus, -a, -um, *adj.*, of *or* belonging to the Palatine; **mōns Palātīnus,** the Palatine Hill, *one of the seven hills of Rome. See map, page 39.*

Palātium, -ī, *n.*, the Palatine Hill, *one of the seven hills of Rome. See map, page 39.*

pālus, -ī, *m.*, stake.

palūs, -ūdis, *f.*, swamp, marsh.

pandō, -ere, pandī, passum, spread, stretch out, extend; *of hair,* dishevel; **passīs manibus,** with outstretched hands.

Panthūs, -ī, *m.*, Panthus, *a nephew of Hecuba.*

pār, paris, *adj.*, equal, like, similar; well-matched; fitting, suitable; *m. as noun,* **pār, paris,** a match, an equal.

parātus, -a, -um, *adj.* [*pf. part. of* **parō**], prepared, equipped, ready.

parcō, -ere, pepercī, parsūrus, spare, preserve, show mercy to.

parēns, parentis, *m. and f.* [**pariō**], parent, father, mother.

pāreō, -ēre, -uī, —, obey, be subject to, yield, submit.

pariō, -ere, peperī, partum, obtain, bear.

parō, -āre, -āvī, -ātum, prepare, make ready, prepare for, equip; get, obtain, acquire.

pars, partis, -ium, *f.,* part, share, division; rôle, side, direction, quarter; party, faction; **ūnā ex parte,** on one side.

partim, *adv.* [**pars**], partly, in part; **partim ... partim,** partly ... partly, some ... others.

partior, -īrī, -ītus sum [**pars**], share, divide, distribute.

parum, *adv.* [**parvum**], too little, not enough, insufficiently; *compar.,* **minus,** less; *superl.,* **minimē,** least, very little; by no means, not at all, no.

parvus, -a, -um, *adj.,* small, little, slight, insignificant; humble; *compar.,* **minor, minus,** smaller, less, inferior, of less importance; *superl.,* **minimus, -a, -um,** smallest, least, very small.

passus, -ūs, *m.,* step, pace, stride; **mīlle passūs,** a thousand paces, a mile.

pāstor, -ōris, *m.* [**pāscō,** feed], shepherd, herdsman.

patefaciō, -facere, -fēcī, -factum [**pateō**+**faciō**], lay open, open, throw open; bring to light, expose, reveal.

pateō, -ēre, -uī, —, lie *or* be open, stretch out, extend; be open *or* exposed; be evident *or* plain.

pater, patris, *m.,* father; *pl. often,* forefathers, ancestors; senators; **patrēs cōnscrīptī,** senators.

patior, patī, passus sum, suffer, endure, bear, submit to; allow, permit.

patria, -ae, *f.* [*fem. of adj.* **patrius,** of a father, *with* **terra** *understood*], fatherland, country, one's country, native country *or* land.

paucitās, -ātis, *f.* [**paucus**], fewness, scarcity, small *or* scanty number.

paucus, -a, -um, *adj.,* few; *usually pl.,* few, a few, a small number of; *m. pl. as noun,* **paucī, -ōrum,** a few, only a few, few people; *n. pl. as noun,* **pauca, -ōrum,** a few things, a few words.

paulātim, *adv.* [**paulum,** little], little by little, gradually.

paulisper, *adv.* [**paulum,** little+**per**], for a short time, for a little while.

paulō, *adv.* [*abl. of* **paulum,** a little], (by) a little, a little, somewhat.

paulum, *adv.* [*acc. of* **paulum,** a little], a little, slightly, somewhat.

pavor, -ōris, *m.* [**paveō,** be afraid], trembling, terror, alarm, anxiety.

pāx, pācis, *f.,* peace.

pectus, pectoris, *n.,* the breast; heart, mind, feelings.

pecūnia, -ae, *f.* [**pecū,** cattle], wealth, money, a sum of money.

pecus, pecoris, *n.,* cattle, flock, herd.

pecus, pecudis, *f.,* a beast, animal; a sheep; a head of cattle; *pl.,* cattle.

pedes, peditis, *m.* [**pēs**], foot-soldier, infantryman; *collect. or pl.,* infantry.

pedester, -tris, -tre, *adj.* [**pēs**], on foot, pedestrian, of a foot-soldier; on *or* by land; **pedestrēs cōpiae,** infantry forces, infantry.

peditātus, -ūs, *m.* [**pedes**], infantry, foot-soldiery, foot-soldiers.

pejor, pejus, *adj.* [*compar. of* **malus**], worse.

pejus, *adv.* [*compar. of* **male**], worse.

Peliās, -ae, *m.,* Pelias (pē'li-ạs), *uncle of Jason.*

pellis, pellis, -ium, *f.,* skin, hide, pelt.

pellō, -ere, pepulī, pulsum, beat, strike; drive out *or* away, expel, banish; rout, repulse, defeat.

pendō, -ere, pependī, pēnsum, weigh, weigh out; pay, pay out; suspend; *with* **poenam,** pay, undergo, suffer.

per, *prep. with acc.:* of *space,* through, among, amid, throughout; along, at; over, across; *of time,* throughout, during; *of cause,* by reason of, on account of; *of agency,* by means of, through the agency of, through, by; **per sē,** of oneself; *in oaths,* by; *in other relations,* through, of, by, at.

percipiō, -cipere, -cēpī, -ceptum [per+ **capiō**], seize, get, receive; perceive, notice; learn, hear; feel.

percutiō, -cutere, -cussī, -cussum [per +**quatiō,** shake], thrust *or* pierce through, transfix; strike.

per-dūcō, -dūcere, -dūxī, -ductum, lead *or* bring through, bring, conduct, lead; prolong; extend, construct; win, induce.

peregrīnus, -a, -um, *adj.* [**peregrē,** abroad], from abroad, strange, foreign; *m. as noun*, **peregrīnus, -ī,** a foreigner, stranger.

per-eō, -īre, -iī, -itūrus, go through; pass away, be lost, disappear; perish, be destroyed, die.

per-facilis, -e, *adj.*, very easy.

per-ferō, -ferre, -tulī, -lātum, bear through; bring, carry, convey; bear, endure, suffer, submit to, tolerate; bring news, report, relate; carry *or* enact (*a law*).

perficiō, -ficere, -fēcī, -fectum [per+ **faciō**], accomplish, carry out, complete, finish; cause, bring about.

perfidia, -ae, *f.* [**perfidus**], faithlessness, treachery, perfidy.

perfidus, -a, -um, *adj.*, treacherous, faithless.

perfuga, -ae, *m.* [**perfugiō**], deserter.

per-fugiō, -fugere, -fūgī, —, flee for refuge, flee to, desert.

perīculōsus, -a, -um, *adj.* [**perīculum**], dangerous, perilous.

perīculum, -ī, *n.*, trial, test, attempt; danger, peril, risk.

perītus, -a, -um, *adj.*, experienced, skilled, familiar with, accustomed to, acquainted.

per-maneō, -manēre, -mānsī, -mānsum, continue, stay through, remain, abide, last, be permanent.

per-mittō, -mittere, -mīsī, -missum, let go; give over, commit, intrust; surrender; permit, allow.

per-moveō, -movēre, -mōvī, -mōtum, move strongly *or* deeply, disturb, alarm; influence, induce.

perpetuus, -a, -um, *adj.*, continuous, unbroken, constant, perpetual, lasting; the whole of; **in perpetuum,** for all time, forever.

per-scrībō, -scrībere, -scrīpsī, -scrīptum, write in full, write out, describe fully; record, register.

per-sequor, -sequī, -secūtus sum, follow up, follow through *or* after; follow; pursue.

Perseus, -ī, *m.*, Perseus (pèr′sūs), *a Greek hero, son of Danaë.*

perspiciō, -spicere, -spexī, -spectum [per+**speciō,** look], see *or* look through, perceive clearly; examine, inspect, become acquainted with, understand; see, observe, ascertain.

per-suādeō, -suādēre, -suāsī, -suāsum, persuade, convince, induce.

per-terreō, -terrēre, -terruī, -territum, frighten *or* terrify thoroughly, terrify.

pertineō, -tinēre, -tinuī, -tentum [per+ **teneō**], stretch, extend, reach; lead to; tend, lead; relate, pertain, concern, belong to.

perturbātus, -a, -um, *adj.* [*pf. part. of* **perturbō**], disturbed, alarmed, dismayed.

per-turbō, -āre, -āvī, -ātum, disturb greatly, throw into confusion *or* disorder, disturb; dismay.

per-veniō, -venīre, -vēnī, -ventum, come through *or* to, come up, arrive, reach, come.

pēs, pedis, *m.*, the foot; *as a measure,* a foot; **pedem referre,** retreat, withdraw, retire.

pessimus, -a, -um, *adj.* [*superl. of* **malus**], worst, most wicked.

petō, -ere, petīvī, petītum, pursue, strive after, aim at, seek; thrust at, assail; repair to, make for, go to; demand, require, ask for, ask; beseech, beg, entreat; canvass (*for office*).

phalānx, -angis, *f.*, phalanx, *a military formation in close order.*

Phīneus, -ī, *m.,* Phineus (fin'ē-us), *a king of Salmydessus. See map, page 68.*

pīlum, -ī, *n.,* pike, spear, heavy javelin, javelin.

Pīsō, -ōnis, *m.,* Piso: (*1*) **M. Pīsō,** Marcus Pupius Piso (pū'pi-us pī'sō), *a consul in 61* B.C.; (*2*) **L. Pīsō,** Lucius Calpurnius (kal-pèr'ni-us) Piso, *a consul in 58* B.C.; (*3*) **L. Pīsō,** Lucius Calpurnius Piso, *a Roman commander, grandfather of* (*2*).

placeō, -ēre, -uī, -itum, please, be pleasing, suit; *impers.,* **placet,** it is resolved *or* decided, it is thought best.

plācō, -āre, -āvī, -ātum, soothe, appease, placate, pacify.

plānitiēs, -ēī, *f.* [**plānus,** level], level ground, a plain.

plēbs, plēbis, *or* **plēbēs, -eī** *or* **-ī,** *f.,* the common people, populace, plebs, plebeians.

plērumque, *adv.* [**plērusque**], for the most *or* greater part, very often, commonly, generally.

plērusque, plēraque, plērumque, *adj.* [**plērus,** very many], most; *pl.,* very many, the greater part of, most of, most, the most, majority.

plūrēs, plūra, *pl. adj.* [*compar. pl. of* **multus**], a number of, several.

plūrimum, *adv.* [*superl. of* **multum**], most, very, for the most part, generally; **plūrimum posse,** be most powerful.

plūrimus, -a, -um, *adj.* [*superl. of* **multus**], most, very many, very large, abundant, of great volume; *n.,* **plūrimum, -ī,** very much.

plūs, plūris, *n.* [*compar. of* **multus**], more; *pl. as adj.,* **plūrēs, plūra,** a number of, several; *m. pl. as noun,* **plūrēs, -ium,** more, the majority.

plūs, *adv.* [*compar. of* **multum**], more.

pōculum, -ī, *n.,* cup.

poena, -ae, *f.,* punishment, penalty; **poenam pendere,** pay the penalty, undergo *or* suffer punishment.

Poenus, -a, -um, *adj.,* Punic, Carthaginian; *m. as noun,* **Poenus, -ī,** a Phoenician, a Carthaginian; *pl.,* the Phoenicians, the Carthaginians.

poēta, -ae, *m.,* poet.

Polītēs, -ae, *m.,* Polites (pō-lī'tēz), *son of Hecuba and Priam.*

polliceor, -ērī, -itus sum, promise, offer.

Polyphēmus, -ī, *m.,* Polyphemus (pol-i-fē'mus): (*1*) *one of the Argonauts;* (*2*) *a Cyclops.*

Pompeiī, -ōrum, *m.,* Pompeii (pompā'yē), *a city of ancient Italy. See map, page 20.*

Pompilius, -ī, *m.,* **Numa Pompilius,** Numa Pompilius (nū'mā pom-pil'ius), *the second king of Rome.*

pōmum, -ī, *n.,* fruit, apple.

pondus, ponderis, *n.* [*compare* **pendō**], a weight (*of a scale*); weight, mass, load; heaviness.

pōnō, -ere, posuī, positum, put, place, set up, lay, fix, station, arrange, post; deposit, store away, lay away; lay aside, set aside; *pass.,* be situated; **arma pōnere,** lay *or* throw down one's arms, surrender; **castra pōnere,** pitch camp, encamp.

pōns, pontis, -ium, *m.,* bridge.

populor, -ārī, -ātus sum, devastate, lay waste, plunder, ravage.

populus, -ī, *m.,* a people, nation; the people, the citizens, the populace.

porcus, -ī, *m.,* swine, hog.

porta, -ae, *f.,* gate, city gate; door, entrance.

portō, -āre, -āvī, -ātum, convey, carry, bring, bear, transport.

portus, -ūs, *m.,* harbor, port.

poscō, -ere, poposcī, —, demand, call for, claim, require, beg, desire, ask.

possessiō, -ōnis, *f.* [**possīdō,** occupy], a possessing, occupation; possession, property.

possideō, -sidēre, -sēdī, -sessum [**por** =**prō**+**sedeō**], have possession of, possess, have, hold, occupy; acquire.

possum, posse, potuī, — [**potis,** able+
sum], be able, can; have power,
strength, influence; **plūrimum posse,**
be most powerful.

post, *adv., and prep. with acc.:* as
adv., behind, in the rear; after,
afterwards, later; *as prep.,* behind,
back of; after, since.

post-eā, *adv.,* afterwards, after that,
later, subsequently, hereafter, thereafter.

posteā-quam, *see* **postquam.**

posterus, -a, -um, *adj.* [**post**], following, ensuing, later, next; *m. pl. as
noun,* **posterī, -ōrum,** coming gen-
erations.

post-quam *or* **posteā-quam,** *conj.,*
after, as soon as, when.

postrēmō, *adv.* [**postrēmus,** last], at
last, last of all, at length, finally.

postrīdiē, *adv.* [*locative* **posterī+diē**],
next day, the day after, the fol-
lowing day; **postrīdiē ejus diēī,** the
next *or* following day.

postulō, -āre, -āvī, -ātum, demand, require, ask for, request.

potēns, *gen.* **-entis,** *adj.* [*pres. part. of*
possum], powerful, strong, influen-
tial, able.

potentia, -ae, *f.* [**potēns**], power, political influence *or* power, influence,
authority.

potestās, -ātis, *f.* [**potis,** able], power,
authority; privilege, opportunity,
possibility; permission; **potestātem
facere,** grant opportunity *or* permission.

potior, -īrī, -ītus sum [**potis,** able],
become master of, gain possession
of, get power over, get control of,
capture; acquire, obtain; possess,
hold.

potius, *compar. adv.* [**potis,** able],
rather, preferably.

prae, *prep. with abl.,* before, in front
of, ahead of; in comparison with.

prae-acūtus, -a, -um, *adj.,* sharp in
front *or* at the end, sharpened,
pointed.

praebeō, -ēre, -uī, -itum [**prae+
habeō**], hold forth, offer; display,
show; afford, furnish.

prae-cēdō, -cēdere, -cessī, -cessum,
go before, precede; surpass, excel.

praecipiō, -cipere, -cēpī, -ceptum
[**prae+capiō**], enjoin upon, instruct,
direct, give directions, order, advise.

praeda, -ae, *f.,* booty, plunder, prey,
spoil.

prae-dicō, -āre, -āvī, -ātum [**dicō,** pro-
claim], proclaim, declare, assert,
relate; boast.

praedō, -ōnis, *m.* [**praeda**], robber,
plunderer, pirate.

praefectus, -ī, *m.* [*pf. part. of* **praeficiō**],
commander, officer, prefect, captain.

praeficiō, -ficere, -fēcī, -fectum [**prae+
faciō**], place over *or* in charge of,
place in command of, put at the
head of.

prae-mittō, -mittere, -mīsī, -missum,
send forward, send ahead.

praemium, -ī, *n.,* reward, prize, recom-
pense.

praesēns, *gen.* **-entis,** *adj.* [*pres. part.
of* **praesum**], at hand, present, in
person; of the present (time), immediate, for the moment.

praesertim, *adv.,* especially, particu-
larly.

praesidium, -ī, *n.* [**praeses,** a protec-
tor], defense, assistance, protection;
garrison, guard; detachment; fortification, stronghold.

praestāns, *gen.* **-stantis,** *adj.* [*pres. part.
of* **praestō**], surpassing, superior,
distinguished, remarkable, excellent.

prae-stō, -stāre, -stitī, -stitum, stand
before; be superior, surpass, excel;
exhibit, show; supply, furnish; perform; **praestat,** *impers.,* it is better *or*
preferable.

prae-sum, -esse, -fuī, -futūrus, be
ahead; be in command *or* in charge
of, command, preside over, rule over.

praeter, *prep. with acc.* [**prae**], past,
by, beyond, before, along; besides,
except; in addition to; contrary to.

praeter-eā, *adv.*, in addition, besides, besides this, moreover, further, furthermore.

praetor, -ōris, *m.* [*for* **praeitor**, *from* **praeeō,** go in front], (leader); praetor, *a Roman magistrate charged with judicial duties.*

prehendō, -hendere, -hendī, -hēnsum, grasp, seize.

premō, -ere, pressī, pressum, press, press hard; burden, weigh down.

prex, precis, *f.*, prayer, entreaty, request.

Priamus, -ī, *m.*, Priam (prī'am), *king of Troy.*

prīdem, *adv.*, long ago, long since; **jam prīdem,** long ago, this long time.

prīdiē, *adv.* [*compare* **prior** *and* **diēs**], (on) the day before, the preceding day.

prīmō, *adv.* [**prīmus**], at first, in the first place, first.

prīmum, *adv.* [**prīmus**], first, first of all, in the first place; **cum prīmum** *or* **ubi prīmum,** as soon as; **quam prīmum,** as soon as possible.

prīmus, -a, -um, *adj.* [*superl. of* **prior**], first, foremost, earliest; first part of; first, principal, chief; distinguished, eminent; *m. pl. as noun,* **prīmī, -ōrum,** the leading *or* foremost men; **in prīmīs (imprīmīs),** especially, chiefly, in particular.

prīnceps, *gen.* **prīncipis,** *adj.* [**prīmus** +**capiō**], first, foremost, chief; *m. as noun,* **prīnceps, prīncipis,** leader, chief, leading man *or* citizen.

prīncipātus, -ūs, *m.* [**prīnceps**], first place, leadership, supremacy.

prior, prius, *adj.* [*compar.*], former, prior, preceding, previous, first; superior.

prīscus, -a, -um, *adj.*, of early *or* former times, former, ancient, oldtime; *m. as noun,* **Prīscus, -ī,** the Elder, *applied to Tarquin, the fifth king of Rome, as a last name.*

prīstinus, -a, -um, *adj.* [*compare* **prior**], former, of old, old-time, original; preceding, previous.

prius, *adv.* [**prior**], before, previously, earlier, sooner, first; **prius ... quam,** before, sooner than.

prius-quam, *conj.*, before, until.

prīvātus, -a, -um, *adj.* [*pf. part. of* **prīvō,** deprive], private, individual, personal, apart; *m. as noun,* **prīvātus, -ī,** a private citizen.

prō, *prep. with abl.*, before, in front of; in behalf of, for the sake of, in favor of, in defense of, for; in place of, in return for, in exchange for; instead of; in the character *or* guise of, as; in accordance with, in proportion to, in view of, considering.

probō, -āre, -āvī, -ātum [**probus,** good], test, try; prove, show; approve, approve of.

prō-cēdō, -cēdere, -cessī, -cessum, go forward, go on, advance, proceed.

procul, *adv.*, at a distance, in the distance, afar; distant, far distant.

prō-dō, -dere, -didī, -ditum, bring forth, display; reveal; hand down, record, relate; give over, betray, surrender.

prō-dūcō, -dūcere, -dūxī, -ductum, lead *or* bring forth, lead forward, bring out; draw up (*troops*); protract, prolong.

proelium, -ī, *n.*, battle, engagement; **proelium committere,** begin battle, engage in battle.

profectiō, -ōnis, *f.* [**proficīscor**], a setting out, departure.

prō-ferō, -ferre, -tulī, -lātum, bring forth *or* forward, exhibit, produce; mention, make known; extend, defer.

prōficiō, -ficere, -fēcī, -fectum [**prō**+**faciō**], carry out, accomplish, effect; make progress, be of assistance, avail; gain.

proficīscor, proficīscī, profectus sum [**prōficiō**], set out *or* forth, start, go, march, proceed; spring, arise.

pro-fugiō, -fugere, -fūgī, -fugitūrus, flee from *or* before, flee, escape.

profugus, -a, -um, *adj.* [profugiō], fleeing, fugitive; *m. as noun,* **profugus, -ī,** fugitive, refugee, exile.

prōgredior, -gredī, -gressus sum [prō+ **gradior,** step], go on *or* forward, step forward, proceed, advance.

prohibeō, -hibēre, -hibuī, -hibitum [prō+habeō], hold back; restrain, keep, keep out *or* away from; prevent, hinder from.

pro-inde, *adv.*, therefore, accordingly, hence.

prōjiciō, -jicere, -jēcī, -jectum [prō+ **jaciō**], hurl forward *or* down; throw, throw away, abandon; drive away, cast out, banish.

prō-mittō, -mittere, -mīsī, -missum, promise, assure, give hope of.

prō-nūntiō, -āre, -āvī, -ātum, announce, declare, proclaim, report.

prope, *adv.*, *and prep. with acc.: as prep.*, near, near-by, near to; *as adv.*, nearly, almost, about; *compar.*, **propius,** nearer; *superl.*, **proximē,** nearest, very near; last, most recently.

prō-pellō, -pellere, -pulī, -pulsum, drive forward *or* forth; dislodge, drive off, repel, put to flight, rout.

properō, -āre, -āvī, -ātum [properus, speedy], hasten, hurry, be in haste; do hastily.

propinquus, -a, -um, *adj.* [prope], near, near-by, neighboring; *m. and f. as noun,* **propinquus, -ī,** *and* **propinqua, -ae,** a relative, kinsman, kinswoman.

propius, *adv.* [*compar. of* **prope**], nearer.

prō-pōnō, -pōnere, -posuī, -positum, put *or* set forth, point out; exhibit, display, explain, report; offer, propose.

proprius, -a, -um, *adj.*, one's own, private, appropriate, characteristic.

propter, *prep. with acc.*, near, close to; because of, on account of.

propter-eā, *adv.*, for this *or* that reason, on account of this, on that account, therefore; **proptereā quod,** for the reason that, because.

prō-sequor, -sequī, -secūtus sum, follow after, pursue; escort, attend; address; honor, adorn.

Prōserpina, -ae, *f.*, Proserpina (prō- sėr′pi-nä), *or* Proserpine (pros′ėr- pin), *the queen of the lower world, wife of Pluto.*

prō-sternō, -sternere, -strāvī, -strā- tum, throw down, overthrow, lay prostrate.

prō-sum, prōdesse, prōfuī, prōfutūrus, be of service, be of benefit, help, profit.

prōtinus, *adv.*, next, then; at once, immediately.

prō-videō, -vidēre, -vīdī, -vīsum, foresee; make provision for, care for, provide.

prōvincia, -ae, *f.*, province.

proximē, *adv.* [*superl. of* **prope**], nearest, very near; last, most recently.

proximus, -a, -um, *adj.* [*superl. of* **propior,** nearer], nearest, next, very near; the next preceding *or* following; the most closely connected *or* related.

prūdēns, *gen.* **prūdentis,** *adj.* [**prōvidēns**], prudent, wise, discreet.

prūdentia, -ae, *f.* [**prūdēns**], foresight, prudence, discretion, wisdom.

pūblicē, *adv.* [**pūblicus**], in the name of the people *or* state, officially; for the state, at public expense.

pūblicus, -a, -um, *adj.* [**populus**], belonging to the people *or* state, common, general, public, official; **rēs pūblica, reī pūblicae,** *f.*, the state, commonwealth, government, constitution, public interests, general welfare.

Pūblius, -ī, *m.*, Publius (pub′li-us), *a Roman first name.*

puella, -ae, *f.* [*diminutive of* **puer**], girl, maiden.

puer, puerī, *m.*, boy, lad, child; *pl.*, boys, children.

pugna, -ae, *f.*, battle, fight.

pugnō, -āre, -āvī, -ātum [pugna], fight, engage in battle, contend.

pulcher, -chra, -chrum, *adj.,* beautiful, handsome; noble, honorable.

Pullō, -ōnis, *m.,* **T. Pullō,** *Titus Pullo, a centurion in Caesar's army.*

pulsō, -āre, -āvī, -ātum, beat, knock at.

pulvis, -eris, *m. and f.,* dust, cloud of dust.

pūrgō, -āre, -āvī, -ātum [pūrus, clean +agō], cleanse, clean, clear; excuse, exonerate.

putō, -āre, -āvī, -ātum, (clean, clear up, trim); consider, judge, think, believe, suppose.

Pyrrhus, -ī, *m.,* Pyrrhus (pir'us), *a king of Epirus* (*see map, p. 61*), *son of Achilles.*

Pȳthia, -ae, *f.,* Pythia (pith'ĭ-ạ̈), *the priestess who gave oracles in the temple of Apollo at Delphi* (*see map, p. 61*).

Q

Q., *abbr. for* **Quīntus.**

quā, *adv.* [quī], where, by which *or* what way *or* road.

quadrāgintā, *indecl. num. adj.,* forty.

quadringentī, -ae, -a, *num. adj.* [quattuor+centum], four hundred.

quaerō, -ere, quaesīvī, quaesītum, seek, search *or* hunt for; seek to obtain, strive for; ask, inquire.

quaestor, -ōris, *m.* [quaerō], quaestor, *a Roman magistrate connected with state finances.*

quam, *adv.,* to what degree, how, how greatly; how? *after comparatives,* than; *with superlatives,* as . . . as possible; **ante quam,** *conj.,* before; **prius . . . quam,** before, sooner than; **quam prīmum,** as soon as possible; **tam . . . quam,** so much . . . as.

quam-quam, *conj.,* although, though; *in a corrective sense,* and yet, yet, nevertheless.

quantum, *adv.* [quantus]: *rel.,* as much as, as far as, to such an extent as; *interrog.,* how much? how far? to what an extent? **tantum . . . quantum,** as much . . . as.

quantus, -a, -um, *adj.: interrog.,* how large? how great? how much? **quantō opere,** how much? how greatly? *rel.,* as great (*especially after* **tantus**); **tantus . . . quantus,** as (so) great . . . as, as large . . . as, as much . . . as; *n. as noun,* **quantum, -ī,** as much as, all that.

quā-rē, *adv.: rel.,* for which reason, wherefore, on account of which, why, therefore; *interrog.,* why? for what reason? on what account?

quārtus, -a, -um, *num. adj.* [quattuor], fourth.

qua-sī, *adv.,* as if, as though, as it were, almost.

quattuor, *indecl. num. adj.,* four.

-que, *enclitic conj.,* and.

queror, querī, questus sum, complain; complain of, find fault with.

quī, quae *or* **qua, quod,** *indef. adj.,* some, any.

quī, quae, quod, *rel. pron.,* who, which, what, that; *rel. adj.,* which.

quī *or* **quis, quae, quod,** *interrog. adj.,* what? which?

quia, *conj.,* because.

quicquam, *see* **quisquam.**

quīcumque, quaecumque, quodcumque, *indef. pron.,* whoever, whatever, whichever, everyone who, everything that.

quīdam, quaedam, quoddam *or* **quiddam,** *adj.,* a certain, some; a kind of; *pron.,* a certain one, a certain person, somebody, someone, something; *pl.,* certain ones, some.

quidem, *adv.: postpositive,* indeed, in truth, certainly, at least, even; *with concessive force,* it is true, to be sure; **nē . . . quidem,** not even, not . . . either.

quiēs, -ētis, *f.,* quiet, repose, rest; peace.

quiētus, -a, -um, *adj.* [*pf. part. of* **quiēscō,** keep quiet], quiet, peaceful, free from toil, at rest, idle.

quīn, *conj. and adv.* [**quī,** how+**ne**], so that not, but that; *as conj., after words of doubt,* that, that not; *after words of hindering,* from; *as adv.,* nay, nay even, indeed, moreover, furthermore; **quīn etiam,** nay even, moreover, nay in fact, nay more, more than that.

Quīnctius, -ī, *m.,* **L. Quīnctius Cincinnātus,** L. Quinctius Cincinnatus (kwingk'shius sin-si-nā'tus), *a famous Roman of the fifth century* B.C.

quīndecim, *indecl. num. adj.* [**quīnque**+**decem**], fifteen.

quīngentī, -ae, -a, *num. adj.* [**quīnque**+**centum**], five hundred.

quīnque, *indecl. num. adj.,* five.

quīntus, -a, -um, *num. adj.* [**quīnque**], fifth.

Quīntus, -ī, *m.,* Quintus, *a Roman first name.*

quis, quid, *indef. pron.,* anybody, anyone, anything; **nē quis,** so *or* in order that no one; **sī quis,** if any, if anyone, whoever.

quis *or* **quī, quae, quod,** *interrog. adj.,* what? which? what kind *or* sort of? **quem ad modum,** in what way, how; as.

quis, quid, *interrog. pron.,* who? which? what? **nesciō quis, nesciō quid,** someone or other, something or other, somebody, something.

quis-quam, quicquam *or* **quidquam,** *indef. pron.,* anyone, anything, anyone *or* anything at all; *as adj.,* any.

quisque, quaque, quodque, *indef. adj.,* each, each one.

quis-que, quid-que, *indef. pron.,* each one, every one, each person, each, every.

quō, *interrog. adv.* [**quī**], whither? where? to what place? in what direction? *rel.,* to which place *or* point, whither; because.

quō, *conj.,* in order that, that; **quō minus** *or* **quōminus,** so that not, from, lest.

quo-ad, *adv.,* as long as, so long as, till, until.

quod, *conj.* [**quī**], because; as to the fact that, whereas; the fact that, that; **proptereā quod,** for the reason that, because; **quod sī,** but if, now if, and if.

quōminus, *see* **quō** (*conj.*).

quondam, *adv.,* formerly, once.

quoniam, *conj.* [**quom**(=**cum**)+**jam**], since, because, as, seeing that, inasmuch as.

quoque, *conj.,* also, too.

quotannīs, *adv.* [**quot,** how many + *abl. pl. of* **annus**], every year, yearly.

quotiēns, *adv.* [**quot**]: *rel.,* as often as; *interrog.,* how often? how many times?

R

rapiō, -ere, rapuī, raptum, seize, carry off, steal; plunder, lay waste.

ratiō, -ōnis, *f.* [**ratus,** thought out], account, reckoning; regard, consideration; method, way, manner, plan, course; art, theory, system, science; reason, motive, ground; affair, transaction.

recēns, *gen.* **-entis,** *adj.,* new, fresh, recent, late.

recessus, -ūs, *m.,* retreat, chance of retreat.

reciperō, *see* **recuperō.**

recipiō, -cipere, -cēpī, -ceptum [**re-**+**capiō**], take, get *or* bring back, regain, recover; take to oneself, welcome, admit, receive; take upon oneself, undertake, stand good for, assume; **in fidem recipere,** take under one's protection; **sē recipere,** recover oneself, recover; betake oneself, withdraw, retire, retreat.

recuperō *or* **reciperō, -āre, -āvī, -ātum,** win *or* get back, recover, regain.

recūsō, -āre, -āvī, -ātum [**re-**+**causa**], refuse, decline.

red-dō, -dere, -didī, -ditum, give back, return, restore; give up, hand over; answer back; pay back; render, make, cause to be.

red-eō, -īre, -iī, -itum, go back, return, come back; **ad sē redīre,** recover consciousness.

redigō, -igere, -ēgī, -āctum [red-+ agō], drive back; bring under, reduce, subdue; render, make; collect, raise (*money*).

redimō, -imere, -ēmī, -ēmptum [red-+ emō], buy back, redeem, ransom; buy up, contract for.

reditus, -ūs, *m.* [**redeō**], a going back, return.

re-dūcō, -dūcere, -dūxī, -ductum, lead back, conduct *or* bring back; restore.

re-ferō, -ferre, rettulī, relātum, carry *or* bring back; give *or* pay back, repay; reply, answer; relate, tell, announce, report; refer, lay before; refer to, measure by; report, register, record; **grātiam referre,** make requital, requite, repay; **pedem referre,** withdraw, retire, retreat; **sē referre,** betake oneself, go back, return.

reficiō, -ficere, -fēcī, -fectum [re-+ faciō], make over, remake, renew, refresh, recruit; repair, refit, rebuild; reëlect.

re-fugiō, -fugere, -fūgī, -fugitūrus, flee back; flee away, escape, flee for refuge.

rēgia, -ae, *f.* [**rēgius**], royal palace, palace.

rēgīna, -ae, *f.* [**rēx**], queen.

regiō, -ōnis, *f.* [**regō**], line, direction; region, district, territory.

rēgius, -a, -um, *adj.* [**rēx**], of a king, kingly, royal, regal.

rēgnō, -āre, -āvī, -ātum [rēgnum], be king, reign, rule.

rēgnum, -ī, *n.* [**rēx**], royal authority *or* power, kingship; sovereignty, supremacy, dominion, rule; kingdom, throne.

regō, -ere, rēxī, rēctum, guide, direct, control; govern, rule.

Rēgulus, -ī, *m.,* **M. Atīlius Rēgulus,** Marcus Atilius Regulus (a-til′i-us reg′ū-lus), *a consul in 256* B.C.

rejiciō, -jicere, -jēcī, -jectum [re-+ jaciō], throw *or* hurl back, drive *or* force back, beat off, repulse, repel; reject, refuse.

religiō, -ōnis, *f.,* reverence, piety; religion; scruple; religious observance.

re-linquō, -linquere, -līquī, -lictum, leave behind, leave, desert, abandon.

reliquus, -a, -um, *adj.* [**relinquō**], left, left behind, remaining, rest *or* remainder of; remaining, future; *n. as noun,* **reliquum, -ī,** a remainder, something left.

re-mittō, -mittere, -mīsī, -missum, send back, throw *or* hurl back; let go, relax; remit, abate, discontinue.

re-moveō, -movēre, -mōvī, -mōtum, move back *or* away, push away; take away, remove, withdraw, drive off *or* away.

Remus, -ī, *m.,* Remus, *brother of Romulus.*

Rēmus, -a, -um, *adj.,* of the Remi (rē′mī); *m. as noun,* **Rēmus, -ī,** one of the Remi; *pl.,* the Remi, *a tribe of Belgic Gaul* (*see map, p. 137*).

rēmus, -ī, *m.,* an oar.

re-novō, -āre, -āvī, -ātum, renew, refresh, restore.

re-nūntiō, -āre, -āvī, -ātum, bring back word, report, announce; proclaim, declare the election of.

re-pellō, -ere, reppulī, repulsum, drive back *or* away, repulse, repel, avert; refuse, reject.

repente, *adv.* [**repēns,** sudden], suddenly, unexpectedly.

repentīnus, -a, -um, *adj.* [**repēns,** sudden], sudden, unexpected, hasty.

reperiō, -īre, repperī, repertum, find, discover, meet with; find out, learn.

re-portō, -āre, -āvī, -ātum, carry back; carry off, win.

rēs, reī, *f.*, thing (*the exact meaning to be determined by the context*); matter, fact, affair, event; act, exploit; circumstance, case, condition; truth, actuality; interest, property, possession; **ob eam rem,** for this reason, therefore; **quā ex rē,** and so; **quam ob rem,** on account of which, wherefore, therefore; why; why? **rē vērā,** in reality, in fact, in truth; **rēs familiāris,** private property, estate; **rēs frūmentāria,** grain supply, provisions; **rēs mīlitāris,** warfare, the art of war, military science; **rēs novae,** a change of government, revolution; **rēs pūblica,** the state, commonwealth, government, constitution, public interests, general welfare.

re-servō, -āre, -āvī, -ātum, keep back, save up, reserve.

re-sistō, -sistere, -stitī, —, stand still, stop, halt, make *or* take a stand; resist, withstand, oppose, offer resistance.

respiciō, -spicere, -spexī, -spectum [re-+speciō, look], look back, look back at, look at, regard, have regard for, consider.

re-spondeō, -spondēre, -spondī, -spōnsum, answer, reply, respond.

respōnsum, -ī, *n.* [respondeō], a reply, answer, response.

rēs pūblica, *see* rēs.

restituō, -stituere, -stituī, -stitūtum [re-+statuō, station], put *or* place back, restore, replace, reinstate, renew, revive, form again.

retineō, -tinēre, -tinuī, -tentum [re-+teneō], hold *or* keep back, retain, detain; restrain, curb; keep up, maintain.

re-vertō, -vertere, -vertī, — (*active regularly in pf. tenses only*), turn back, go back, return.

re-vertor, -vertī, -versus sum, turn back, go back, return.

rēx, rēgis, *m.* [regō], king.

Rhēnus, -ī, *m.*, the Rhine. *See map, page 137.*

Rhodanus, -ī, *m.*, the Rhone. *See map, page 137.*

rīpa, -ae, *f.*, bank (*of a stream*), shore.

rogō, -āre, -āvī, -ātum, ask, question; ask for, request, beg.

rogus, -ī, *m.*, funeral pyre.

Rōma, -ae, *f.*, Rome.

Rōmānus, -a, -um, *adj.*, Roman; *m. as noun,* **Rōmānus, -ī,** a Roman; *pl.,* the Romans.

Rōmulus, -ī, *m.*, Romulus (rom'ū-lus), *the founder of Rome.*

rosa, -ae, *f.*, a rose.

rōstrum, -ī, *n.* [rōdō, gnaw], beak, snout, bill; beak (*of a ship*); *pl.,* **rōstra, -ōrum,** the Rostra, *a platform for speakers in the Forum, adorned with beaks of captured ships.*

ruīna, -ae, *f.* [ruō], downfall, overthrow, ruin, destruction, calamity; *pl.,* ruins.

rūmor, -ōris, *m.*, hearsay, rumor, report, gossip.

rumpō, -ere, rūpī, ruptum, break.

ruō, -ere, ruī, ruitūrus, rush; fall, fall in ruins.

rūpēs, -is, *f.* [rumpō], rock, cliff.

rūrsus *or* rūrsum, *adv.* [*contraction for* reversus *or* reversum, *pf. part. of* revertor], again, back again, once more; in turn, further.

Rutulī, -ōrum, *m. pl.*, the Rutuli (rut'ū-lī) *or* Rutulians, *a nation of central Italy.* *See map, page 305.*

S

Sabīnus, -a, -um, *adj.*, Sabine; *m. pl. as noun,* **Sabīnī, -ōrum,** the Sabines, *a people of central Italy.* *See map, p. 305.*

Sabīnus, -ī, *m.*, **Quīntus Titūrius Sabīnus,** Quintus Titurius Sabinus (kwin'tus tĭ-tū'ri-us sā-bī'nus), *one of Caesar's lieutenants.*

saccus, -ī, *m.*, sack, bag.

sacer, -cra, -crum, *adj.*, dedicated, sacred, consecrated, holy; *n. usually pl. as noun*, sacrum, -ī, sacred rite, religious custom *or* observance; sacer mōns, the Sacred Mount, *a hill near Rome.*

sacerdōs, -ōtis, *m. and f.* [sacer], priest, priestess.

sacrificium, -ī, *n.* [sacrificus, sacrificial], a sacrifice.

sacrum, *see* sacer.

saepe, *adv.*, often, frequently, repeatedly.

saevus, -a, -um, *adj.*, savage, fierce, cruel, harsh.

sagitta, -ae, *f.*, arrow.

sagittārius, -ī, *m.* [sagitta], a bowman, archer.

sāl, salis, *m.*, salt.

salūs, -ūtis, *f.*, health; welfare, safety; salutation, greeting.

salveō, -ēre, —, —, be well *or* in good health; salvē, *imperative (in greetings)*, hail to you, greetings, how are you?

salvus, -a, -um, *adj.*, safe.

sānctus, -a, -um, *adj.* [*pf. part. of* sanciō, make sacred], sacred, holy, inviolable.

sanguis, sanguinis, *m.*, blood, bloodshed; stock, descent, race.

sapientia, -ae, *f.*, wisdom.

satis, *indecl. adj., and adv.*: *as adj.*, enough, sufficient; *as noun*, enough, a sufficiency, a plenty; *as adv.*, enough, sufficiently, quite, somewhat; satis commodē, to much advantage, very easily.

satis-faciō, -facere, -fēcī, -factum, do enough, give satisfaction, make reparation, apologize.

saxum, -ī, *n.*, a rock, stone.

scaena, -ae, *f.*, scene.

scapha, -ae, *f.*, a small boat, skiff.

scelerātus, -a, -um, *adj.* [*pf. part. of* scelerō, make wicked, pollute], wicked, criminal, infamous.

scelus, sceleris, *n.*, evil *or* wicked deed, crime, sin, wickedness.

scientia, -ae, *f.* [sciēns, knowing], knowledge, skill, science.

sciō, -īre, -īvī, -ītum, know, be aware, understand, know how.

scrībō, -ere, scrīpsī, scrīptum, write, write out, compose.

scūtum, -ī, *n.*, shield.

sē-cēdō, -cēdere, -cessī, -cessum, go apart *or* away, retire, withdraw, depart.

secundus, -a, -um, *adj.* [sequor], following, second; favorable, successful.

sed, *conj.*, but, on the contrary.

sēdecim, *indecl. num. adj.* [sex+decem], sixteen.

sedeō, -ēre, sēdī, sessum, sit, be seated, sit down; settle, sink; rest, be settled.

sēdēs, -is, *f.* [sedeō], seat, chair; settlement; residence, home; ground, place, spot.

semper, *adv.*, always, ever, perpetually.

senātor, -ōris, *m.* [senex], senator, one of a council of elders.

senātus, -ūs, *m.* [senex], senate, council *or* body of elders.

senex, *gen.* senis, *adj.*, old, aged; *m. as noun*, senex, senis, old man, elder.

sententia, -ae, *f.* [sentiō], thought, feeling, opinion, judgment; meaning, intention, effect.

sentiō, -īre, sēnsī, sēnsum, perceive, feel, realize, know; observe; think, judge, suppose.

septem, *indecl. num. adj.*, seven.

septentriōnēs, -um, *m. pl.* [septem+triōnēs, plowing oxen], the stars of the Big Dipper, the north.

septimus, -a, -um, *num. adj.* [septem], seventh.

sepultūra, -ae, *f.* [sepeliō, bury], burial, interment.

Sēquana, -ae, *f.*, *now* the Seine, *a river in France. See map, page 137.*

Sēquanus, -a, -um, *adj.*, of the Sequani (sek'wạ-nĭ), Sequanian; *m. as noun,* Sēquanus, -ī, a Sequanian; *pl.*, the Sequani, the Sequanians, *a tribe of Celtic Gaul (see map, p. 137).*

sequēns, *gen.* -entis, *adj.* [*pres. part. of* sequor], following, next, succeeding.

sequor, sequī, secūtus sum, follow, follow after, pursue; ensue, result, agree with.

Ser., *abbr. for* Servius.

sermō, -ōnis, *m.* [serō, bind], talk, conversation, discourse.

serpēns, -entis, *f.* [*pres. part. of* serpō, crawl], serpent, snake.

servitūs, -ūtis, *f.* [servus], slavery, servitude.

Servius Tullius, *m.*, Servius Tullius (sėr'vi-us tul'i-us), *the sixth king of Rome.*

servō, -āre, -āvī, -ātum, observe, watch, guard, keep, preserve, save; be on guard.

servus, -ī, *m.*, slave, servant.

sex, *indecl. num. adj.*, six.

sextus, -a, -um, *num. adj.* [sex], sixth.

Sextus, -ī, *m.*, Sextus, *a Roman first name.*

sī, *conj.*, if, in case, in the event that; to see if; quod sī, but if, now if; sī minus, if not; sī quis, if any, if anyone, whoever.

Sibylla, -ae, *f.*, Sibyl, *a female soothsayer.*

sīc, *adv.*, thus, so, in this way *or* manner; so, to such an extent *or* degree; yet, still; ut . . . sīc, as . . . so, while . . . yet, though . . . still.

Sicilia, -ae, *f.*, Sicily. *See map, page 277.*

sīc-ut *or* sīc-utī, *adv.*, just as, as; as it were.

significō, -āre, -āvī, -ātum [signum+faciō], announce, point out; indicate, show, mean.

signum, -ī, *n.*, token, emblem, mark, sign; signal; **signa ferre,** advance the standards, advance; **signa inferre,** advance *to the attack*, charge; *military* standard, banner; statue, image.

silentium, -ī, *n.* [sileō, be still], silence, quiet, peace.

silva, -ae, *f.*, forest, wood, woods.

similis, -e, *adj.*, like, similar, resembling; **vērī simile,** likely, probable.

simul, *adv.*, at the same time, together; simul atque, as soon as.

simulō, -āre, -āvī, -ātum [similis], make like; pretend, feign.

sīn, *conj.* [sī+ne], but if, if however.

sine, *prep. with abl.*, without.

singulāris, -e, *adj.* [singulī], single, alone; singular, unusual, extraordinary; one by one.

singulī, -ae, -a, *pl. num. adj.*, one at a time; one on a side, one each, each, every.

sinister, -tra, -trum, *adj.*, left, léft-hand, on the left.

sinistra, -ae, *f.* [sinister], the left hand; ā sinistrā, on the left-hand side.

Sinōn, -ōnis, *m.*, Sinon (sī'nọn), *a Greek who allowed himself to be captured by the Trojans in order that he might make possible the capture of Troy.*

situs, -ūs, *m.*, site, situation, position.

sī-ve *or* seu, *conj.*, or if; sīve . . . sīve, if . . . or if, whether . . . or.

societās, -ātis, *f.* [socius], alliance, association, partnership.

socius, -ī, *m.*, associate, partner, ally, comrade, accomplice, companion.

sōl, sōlis, *m.*, the sun, (*as a proper name, capitalized*) the Sun-god; sōlis occāsus, sunset, the west.

soleō, -ēre, solitus sum, *semi-deponent*, be accustomed; be in the habit of.

solitus, -a, -um, *adj.* [*pf. part. of* **soleō**], accustomed, customary, usual.

sollicitō, -āre, -āvī, -ātum [**sollicitus,** agitated], agitate, incite, stir up, excite; tempt, test.

sōlum, *adv.* [**sōlus**], only, merely, alone; **nōn sōlum . . . sed etiam,** not only . . . but also.

sōlus, -a, -um, *adj.,* alone, only, the only, sole, single.

solvō, -ere, solvī, solūtum [**se-+luō,** to loose], loosen, untie, unbind, release, set free; exempt, absolve; relax; *of ships, with or without* **nāvem** *or* **nāvēs,** set sail, weigh anchor.

somnus, -ī, *m.,* sleep, slumber.

sonus, -ī, *m.,* sound, noise.

soror, -ōris, *f.,* sister.

sors, sortis, -ium, *f.,* a lot, casting of lots; prophecy, oracular response; lot, fortune, fate.

spargō, -ere, sparsī, sparsum, scatter, sprinkle, strew.

spatium, -ī, *n.,* space, extent, room; interval, distance, lap; space of time, time.

speciēs, -ēī, *f.* [**speciō,** look], sight, spectacle; appearance, aspect.

spectāculum, -ī, *n.* [**spectō**], a spectacle, show, exhibition.

spectātor, -ōris, *m.* [**spectō**], spectator, onlooker.

spectō, -āre, -āvī, -ātum [**speciō,** look], watch, look at, view, see; consider, regard; observe; face, lie, be situated; look to, tend.

spēlunca, -ae, *f.,* cave, cavern.

spernō, -ere, sprēvī, sprētum, despise, scorn, spurn.

spērō, -āre, -āvī, -ātum [**spēs**], hope, hope for, expect.

spēs, speī, *f.,* hope, expectation, anticipation.

spīna, -ae, *f.,* barrier; spina, *low wall dividing the circus lengthwise.*

spoliō, -āre, -āvī, -ātum [**spolium,** booty], strip, despoil, plunder.

(spōns, spontis), *f.,* *only abl.,* **sponte, with suā, meā, tuā,** of one's own (my own, your own) accord, voluntarily; without help, unaided, alone.

spōnsus, -ī, *m.* [*pf. part. of* **spondeō,** promise], betrothed, lover.

stabulum, -ī, *n.* [**stō**], stable, stall.

statim, *adv.* [**stō**], at once, immediately, forthwith.

statiō, -ōnis, *f.* [**stō**], military post, station; picket, guard; outpost; **in statiōne esse,** to be on guard.

statuō, -ere, statuī, statūtum [**status,** a standing], set up, make stand; stop, halt; set in place, station, place; determine, decide.

statūra, -ae, *f.* [**status,** a standing], stature, height, size.

stīpendium, -ī, *n.,* tax, tribute; a soldier's pay; campaign, service.

stō, stāre, stetī, stātūrus, stand; stop, halt; stand still; endure, stand by, abide by.

strepitus, -ūs, *m.* [**strepō,** make a din], din, clatter, noise, uproar, confusion.

studeō, -ēre, -uī, —, desire, be eager *or* anxious; be devoted (to), apply oneself, devote oneself, give attention (to), study; favor, wish well to, be friendly to.

studium, -ī, *n.* [**studeō**], zeal, eagerness, enthusiasm; good-will, loyalty, devotion; pursuit, occupation, study, branch of study.

stultitia, -ae, *f.* [**stultus,** foolish], folly, foolishness; imbecility.

Stymphālus, -ī, *m.,* Stymphalus (stimfā'lus), *a town of Greece. See map, page 68.*

suādeō, -ēre, suāsī, suāsum, urge, exhort, advise, recommend.

sub, *prep. with acc. and abl.: with acc., of place,* under, beneath, into; up to, close to, toward; *of time,* just before, toward, on the eve of, during; **sub vesperum,** toward evening; *with abl., of place,* under, beneath, at the foot of; *of time,* in, at, within; *of relation,* under the control *or* dominion of.

sub-dūcō, -dūcere, -dūxī, -ductum, lead *or* draw up, beach (*ships*); withdraw, lead away *or* under.

sub-eō, -īre, -iī, -itum, come up (*from below*), come up (to), approach, advance; enter, advance into; go under, take up; undergo, endure, submit to.

subitō, *adv.* [**subitus,** sudden], suddenly, unexpectedly.

subjiciō, -jicere, -jēcī, -jectum [**sub**+ **jaciō**], hurl beneath; place below *or* under; hurl from beneath; subject, expose.

sub-levō, -āre, -āvī, -ātum, lift *or* hold up, support; relieve, assist.

sub-mittō, -mittere, -mīsī, -missum, lower, let down, drop; stoop; send up *or* under, send as aid *or* reinforcement; yield.

sub-sequor, -sequī, -secūtus sum, follow up *or* after, follow, follow closely.

subsidium, -ī, *n.* [**sub**+**sedeō**], aid (*held in reserve*), assistance, help, support, relief; *pl.*, reserves, reinforcements, aid.

succēdō, -cēdere, -cessī, -cessum [**sub** +**cēdō**], go under; come up to, approach, advance, draw near; succeed, take the place of, come next.

Suēbus, -a, -um, *adj.*, of the Suebi (swē′bĭ); *m. pl. as noun,* **Suēbī, -ōrum,** the Suebi, *a people of Germany. See map, p. 137.*

Suessiōnēs, -um, *m. pl.*, the Suessiones (swes-i-ō′nēz), *a tribe of Belgic Gaul.*

suī, sibi, sē, sē, *third pers., sing. and pl., reflexive pron.,* of himself, herself, itself, themselves; *in acc. as subject of inf.,* him, her, it, them, *or* he, she, it, they; *reciprocal,* each other, one another.

sum, esse, fuī, futūrus, be, exist.

summa, -ae, *f.* [**summus**], top, summit; highest sum, total, sum total, sum; chief place *or* control, supreme command, supremacy; **summa imperiī,** supreme command.

summoveō (submoveō), -movēre, -mōvī, -mōtum [**sub**+**moveō**], move from under, send away; dislodge, drive away, remove, ward off.

summus, -a, -um, *adj.* [*superl. of* **superus**], highest, uppermost, highest part of, top of; chief; *n. as noun,* **summum, -ī,** the top, summit.

sūmō, -ere, sūmpsī, sūmptum [**sub**+ **emō**], take, take to oneself, take up; take on, assume, adopt; claim; consume, spend.

superbus, -a, -um, *adj.*, haughty, proud, arrogant; *m. as noun,* **Superbus, -ī,** the Proud, *applied to the second King Tarquin as a last name.*

superior, -ius, *adj.* [*compar. of* **superus**], higher; superior, better, stronger; *of time,* earlier, former, previous.

superō, -āre, -āvī, -ātum [**superus**], rise above *or* higher than; surpass, outdo; subdue, conquer, defeat, overcome; be victorious, be superior; survive.

super-sum, -esse, -fuī, -futūrus, be left *or* over, survive, remain over.

superus, -a, -um, *adj.* [**super,** above], high, high up, upper; *m. pl. as noun,* **superī, -ōrum,** the gods above, gods; **Mare Superum,** the upper sea, i.e., the Adriatic.

supplicium, -ī, *n.* [**supplex,** suppliant], punishment; execution.

supportō, -āre, -āvī, -ātum [**sub**+ **portō**], bring *or* carry up, carry *or* convey to.

suprā, *adv., and prep. with acc.* [**superus**]: *as adv.,* above, before, earlier, formerly; *as prep.,* of place, above, on, over, beyond; *of time,* before, earlier than.

suscipiō, -cipere, -cēpī, -ceptum [**subs** +**capiō**], take up, take upon oneself, undertake.

suspīciō, -ōnis, *f.* [**sub**+**speciō,** look], suspicion, distrust.

suspicor, -ārī, -ātus sum [*compare* **suspiciō**], suspect, surmise, conjecture.

sustineō, -tinēre, -tinuī, -tentum [**subs+teneō**], uphold, support, sustain, bear up under; withstand, resist, endure, bear; check, stop, restrain; hold out, endure; **sē sustinēre,** hold oneself up, stand up, hold up.

suus, -a, -um, *poss. adj., reflexive, third person* [*compare* **suī**], his own, her own, its own, their own; his, her, hers, its, theirs; one's own, one's; *m. pl. as noun,* **suī, -ōrum,** one's (his, their) own men, troops, friends, people, party; *n. pl. as noun,* **sua, -ōrum,** one's (his, her, their) own possessions, his (her, their) possessions *or* property.

Symplēgadēs, -um, *f.,* the Symplegades (sim-pleg'ạ-dēz), *the Clashing Rocks, situated, according to legend, at the entrance to the Black Sea.*

Syrācūsae, -ārum, *f. pl.,* Syracuse, *a city in Sicily. See map, page 61.*

Syrācūsānus, -a, -um, *adj.,* Syracusan; *m. as noun,* **Syrācūsānus, -ī,** a Syracusan; *pl.,* the Syracusans.

T

T., *abbr. for* **Titus.**

tabernāculum, -ī, *n.* [**taberna,** hut], a tent.

taceō, -ēre, -uī, -itum, be silent, keep silent about, pass over unnoticed.

tālis, -e, *adj.,* such, of such a kind *or* sort.

tam, *adv.,* thus, so, so much, to such an extent.

tamen, *adv.,* nevertheless, still, yet, however.

tam-quam, *adv.,* as if, just as if; on the ground that.

Tanaquil, -īlis, *f.,* Tanaquil (tan'ạ-kwil), *wife of Tarquinius Priscus.*

tandem, *adv.,* at last, at length, finally.

tangō, -ere, tetigī, tāctum, touch; border on; come to, reach; affect, influence, move.

tantulus, -a, -um, *adj.* [**tantus**], so small, so little, so unimportant.

tantum, *adv.* [**tantus**], so much, so greatly, to such an extent, so far; this much, only, alone, merely; **tantum . . . quantum,** as much . . . as.

tantus, -a, -um, *adj.,* so great, so large, of such a size, of such an extent; **tantus . . . quantus,** as (so) great . . . as, as large . . . as, as much . . . as; *n. as noun,* **tantum,** so much.

tardō, -āre, -āvī, -ātum [**tardus**], make slow, retard, hinder, check.

tardus, -a, -um, *adj.,* tardy, slow, sluggish, spiritless.

Tarquinius, -ī, *m.,* Tarquinius (tär-kwin'i-us), Tarquin, *name of a Roman royal family, supposed to be of Etruscan origin:* (*1*) **L. Tarquinius Prīscus,** L. Tarquinius Priscus (pris'kus), *fifth king of Rome;* (*2*) **Lūcius Tarquinius,** Lucius Tarquinius, *son of Priscus and afterwards king himself with the added name* **Superbus;** (*3*) **Arrūns Tarquinius,** Arruns (ar'unz) Tarquinius, *a son of Priscus;* (*4*) **Arrūns Tarquinius,** Arruns Tarquinius, *a grandson of Tarquinius Priscus and nephew of* (*3*); (*5*) **Sextus Tarquinius,** Sextus Tarquinius, *a son of Superbus;* (*6*) **L. Tarquinius Collātīnus,** L. Tarquinius Collatinus (kọl-ạ-tī'nus), *one of the first two consuls at Rome.*

taurus, -ī, *m.,* bull.

tēctum, -ī, *n.* [*pf. part. of* **tegō**], roof; shelter, dwelling, house.

tegō, -ere, tēxī, tēctum, cover, shelter, protect; conceal, hide.

tēlum, -ī, *n.,* missile, weapon, javelin, dart.

temerārius, -a, -um, *adj.* [**temere**], imprudent, rash, indiscreet.

temere, *adv.,* rashly, indiscreetly, recklessly.

tempestās, -ātis, *f.* [**tempus**], time, season, period; good *or* bad weather; storm, tempest.

templum, -ī, *n.,* temple, shrine.

temptō, -āre, -āvī, -ātum [**tendō**], test, try, make trial of; venture, attempt; assail, attack; tamper with, tempt.

tempus, temporis, *n.,* time; a time, period, season; (the) time, chance, opportunity, occasion; circumstances, times, condition; crisis; **brevī tempore,** in a short time, quickly, soon; **ex tempore,** without preparation, offhand.

tendō, -ere, tetendī, tentum, stretch, aim, direct; make one's way, go.

teneō, -ēre, -uī, —, hold, possess; occupy, dwell in; control, restrain.

tergum, -ī, *n.,* the back; rear; **tergum vertere,** flee, take to flight.

terra, -ae, *f.,* the earth, the land; land, soil; territory, region; **orbis terrārum,** the earth, the world.

terreō, -ēre, -uī, -itum, frighten, terrify, alarm.

terribilis, -e, *adj.* [**terreō**], frightful, terrible, dreadful.

terror, -ōris, *m.* [**terreō**], terror, fright, panic, fear, alarm, dread.

tertius, -a, -um, *num. adj.* [**ter,** three times], third, the third.

testis, -is, -ium, *m. and f.,* a witness.

testūdō, -inis, *f.* [**testa,** shell, hard covering], a tortoise; *as a military term, a shed for the protection of besiegers, or a close formation of troops with overlapping shields.*

Teutonī, -ōrum, *or* **Teutonēs, -um,** *m. pl.,* the Teutons, *a German people.*

Thēbae, -ārum, *f. pl.,* Thebes, *a city of ancient Greece. See map, page 68.*

Thessalia, -ae, *f.,* Thessaly (thes'a-li), *a country forming a part of Greece. See map, page 116.*

Thymoetēs, -ae, *m.,* Thymoetes (thim-ō-ē'tēz), *a Trojan.*

Ti., *abbr. for* **Tiberius.**

Tiberis, -is, *m.,* the Tiber, *the river on which Rome is situated. See map, page 305.*

Tiberius, -ī, *m.,* Tiberius, *a Roman first name; especially, the second Roman emperor.*

timeō, -ēre, -uī, —, fear, dread, be afraid of; be afraid, be alarmed.

timidus, -a, -um, *adj.* [**timeō**], afraid, fearful, timid, cowardly.

timor, -ōris, *m.* [**timeō**], fear, dread, alarm, timidity.

Titūrius, -ī, *m.,* **Q. Titūrius Sabīnus,** Quintus Titurius Sabinus (tī-tū'ri-us sạ-bī'nus), *one of Caesar's lieutenants.*

toga, -ae, *f.* [**tegō**], toga, *an outer garment worn by Roman men in civil life.*

tollō, -ere, sustulī, sublātum, lift, raise, take up; take on board; exalt, glorify, extol; take away, remove, carry off; do away with, make way with, abolish; **ancoram tollere,** weigh anchor, set sail; **clāmōrem tollere,** set up a shout *or* cry.

tormentum, -ī, *n.* [**torqueō,** twist], torment, torture; *also, a military engine or machine for hurling missiles; hence, pl.,* artillery.

tot, *indecl. num. adj.,* so many.

totidem, *indecl. num. adj.* [**tot**+**idem**], the same number of, just as many.

tōtus, -a, -um, *adj.,* whole, the whole (of), all, entire, total, wholly.

trabs, trabis, *f.,* a beam, timber, log.

trādō, -dere, -didī, -ditum [**trāns**+**dō**], give *or* hand over, deliver up, surrender; hand down, transmit, report, tell; teach.

trādūcō, -dūcere, -dūxī, -ductum [**trāns**+**dūcō**], lead across *or* over, bring across, transfer, conduct.

trāgula, -ae, *f.,* javelin, dart, *a light javelin thrown by a strap, used by the Gauls.*

trahō, -ere, trāxī, tractum, draw, drag, draw along *or* away.

trājiciō, -jicere, -jēcī, -jectum [trāns+ jaciō], hurl across *or* through; transfix, pierce; transport, take across; go over, cross, pass over.

trāns, *prep. with acc.*, across, beyond, on the other side of, to the other side of.

trāns-eō, -īre, -iī, -itum, cross, go over, go across *or* through, pass through; pass by, outstrip; *of time*, pass by, pass.

trāns-fīgō, -fīgere, -fīxī, -fīxum, transfix, pierce.

trāns-portō, -āre, -āvī, -ātum, carry *or* take across, transport, convey, remove.

trecentī, -ae, -a, *num. adj.* [trēs+centum], three hundred.

trēs, tria, *gen.* trium, *num. adj.*, three.

Trēverī, -ōrum, *m. pl.*, the Treveri (trev'e̥-rī), *a people of Belgic Gaul. See map, p. 137.*

tribūnus, -ī, *m.* [tribus, tribe], a tribune, *title of a Roman official.*

tribuō, -ere, tribuī, tribūtum [tribus, tribe], allot, assign, grant, bestow; pay, render; ascribe, attribute.

trīduum, -ī, *n.*, a period of three days, three days.

trīgintā, *indecl. num. adj.*, thirty.

triplex, *gen.* -icis, *adj.* [ter, three times +plicō, fold], threefold, triple, in three divisions *or* lines.

Trōja, -ae, *f.*, Troy, *a city in Asia Minor. See map, page 277.*

Trōjānus, -a, -um, *adj.*, of Troy, Trojan; *m. pl. as noun*, Trōjānī, -ōrum, the Trojans.

tū, *gen.* tuī (*nom. pl.*, vōs), *pers. pron.*, you.

tuba, -ae, *f.*, a trumpet.

tueor, -ērī, tūtus sum, look *or* gaze at; watch, guard, protect.

Tulingī, -ōrum, *m. pl.*, the Tulingi (tū-lin'jī), *a German tribe. See map, page 137.*

Tullia, -ae, *f.*, Tullia (tul'i-ą), *the name of a woman or girl; especially, the two daughters of King Servius Tullius.*

Tullius, -ī, *m.*, Servius Tullius, Servius Tullius (sȇr'vi-us tul'i-us), *the sixth king of Rome.*

Tullus Hostīlius, *m.*, Tullus Hostilius (tul'us hos-til'i-us), *the third king of Rome.*

tum, *adv.*, then, at that time; thereupon, next; cum . . . tum, both . . . and, not only . . . but also; tum dēmum, then at last, not until then, then only.

tumultus, -ūs, *m.* [tumeō, swell], uproar, confusion, disorder; an uprising, insurrection, rebellion.

tumulus, -ī, *m.* [tumeō, swell], mound, hillock, small hill.

turbō, -āre, -āvī, -ātum [turba, confusion], disturb, confuse, agitate; throw into confusion.

Turnus, -ī, *m.*, Turnus (tȇr'nus): (*1*) king of the Rutuli (rut'ū-lī); (*2*) Turnus Herdonius, Turnus Herdonius (hȇr-dō'ni-us), *a chief of Aricia.*

turpis, -e, *adj.*, ugly, unsightly; shameful, disgraceful, dishonorable, discreditable, base.

turris, turris, -ium, *f.*, a tower.

tūtus, -a, -um, *adj.* [*pf. part. of* tueor], protected, safe, secure, in safety; *n. as noun*, tūtum, -ī, safety, place of safety.

tuus, -a, -um, *poss. adj.* [tū], your, yours (*referring to one person*).

U

ubi, *adv.: rel.*, where, in which place; when, whenever; ubi prīmum, as soon as; *interrog.*, where?

Ubiī, -ōrum, *m. pl.*, the Ubii (ū'bi-ī), *a German tribe. See map, page 137.*

ulcīscor, ulcīscī, ultus sum, take vengeance on, avenge, punish.

Ulīxēs, -is, *m.*, Ulysses (ū-lis'ēz), *a famous Greek leader.*

ūllus, -a, -um, *adj.*, any; *m. as noun*, ūllus, ūllīus, anyone, anybody.

ulterior, -ius, *compar. adj.*, farther, beyond, more distant, ulterior.

ultimus, -a, -um, *adj.* [*superl. of* **ulterior**], farthest, most remote *or* distant; last, extreme; last part of, end of.

ultrā, *adv., and prep. with acc.: as adv.,* on the other *or* far side, beyond, farther, in addition; *as prep.,* on the other side of, beyond, past.

ultrō, *adv.,* beyond; of one's own accord, voluntarily; without reason *or* cause, without provocation; **ultrō citrōque,** hither and thither, backward and forward.

umerus, -ī, *m.,* shoulder.

umquam, *adv.,* at any time, ever.

ūnā, *adv.* [**ūnus**], at the same time, along with, together.

unde, *adv.: rel.,* from which place, whence; from which cause, from which; *interrog.,* whence? from what place *or* direction? from what cause?

ūndecimus, -a, -um, *num. adj.* [**ūndecim,** eleven], eleventh.

undique, *adv.* [**unde**+**que**], from all sides *or* directions, on all sides, all around, everywhere.

unguentum, -ī, *n.* [**unguō,** anoint], ointment, unguent.

ūniversus, -a, -um, *adj.* [**ūnus**+**versus,** toward], all together, all, whole, entire, universal.

ūnus, -a, -um, *num. adj.,* one, single; only, alone; the same, common; **ad ūnum,** to a man.

urbs, urbis, -ium, *f.,* city; *especially,* the City, i.e., Rome.

ūrō, -ere, ussī, ustum, burn, burn up, consume.

usque, *adv.,* all the way, even to, even, as far as; all the time; **usque ad,** up to, till.

ūsus, -ūs, *m.* [**ūtor**], use, enjoyment; service, use, advantage, profit; practice, experience, knowledge, skill; **ūsuī** *or* **ex ūsū,** of advantage, of service, of use; **ūsus est,** there is need *or* occasion, it is necessary.

ut *or* **utī,** *adv. and conj.: as adv.,* as, when, since, as soon as; as, just as; since, inasmuch as, seeing that; though, although, even if, as if; how (*introducing indirect questions*); **ut . . . ita,** just as . . . so, while . . . yet; **ut . . . sīc,** as . . . so, while . . . yet, though . . . still; *as conj.: with clauses of purpose,* that, in order that, so that, in order to; *with clauses of result,* that, so that.

uter, -tra, -trum, *pron.: interrog.,* which (of the two)? which? *indef.,* whichever of the two, whichever.

uter-que, utraque, utrumque, *adj.,* each (of two), both; *pl., of two parties,* each side, both sides *or* parties, both.

ūtilis, -e, *adj.* [**ūtor**], useful, advantageous, serviceable, expedient.

ūtor, ūtī, ūsus sum, use, make use of, employ, enjoy; take advantage of, adopt, accept, avail oneself of; exercise, practice, observe; be on close terms with, associate with.

uxor, -ōris, *f.,* wife.

V

vacuus, -a, -um, *adj.* [**vacō,** be empty], empty, vacant, unoccupied, devoid.

vadum, -ī, *n.,* shallow place, shallow, shoal; ford.

vae, *interj.,* ah! alas!; *with dat.,* woe! woe to!

vagor, -ārī, -ātus sum [**vagus,** roving], range, roam, wander.

valeō, -ēre, -uī, -itūrus, be strong *or* powerful; have strength *or* power, have influence; be valid; avail, succeed; *imperative,* **valē,** *pl.,* **valēte,** good-by.

validus, -a, -um, *adj.* [**valeō**], well, strong, vigorous.

vallēs, vallis, -ium, *f.,* valley.

vāllum, -ī, *n.* [**vāllus,** stake], intrenchment, rampart, earthwork.

varius, -a, -um, *adj.,* differing, different, various; changing.

vās, vāsis (*pl.,* **vāsa, -ōrum**), *n.,* dish, vessel, utensil.

vāstō, -āre, -āvī, -ātum [vāstus, waste], lay waste, devastate, ravage.

vehemēns, *gen.* -entis, *adj.*, violent, vehement, impetuous, furious, strong, vigorous.

vehementer, *adv.* [vehemēns], violently, fiercely; vigorously, severely, strongly, very much, greatly.

vehō, -ere, vexī, vectum, carry, convey, bring, bear, transport; *pass.*, be carried, ride, sail.

Veiēns, *gen.* -entis, *adj.*, of Veii (vē′yī); *m. pl. as noun,* Veientēs, -ium, the Veientes (vē̞-yen′tēz), the people of Veii (*see map, p. 305*).

Veiī, -ōrum, *m. pl.*, Veii (vē′yī), *a city of the Etruscans, about twelve miles from Rome. See map, page 305.*

vel, *conj.*, or; vel . . . vel, either . . . or.

vellus, velleris, *n.*, fleece, pelt.

vēlum, -ī, *n.*, a covering, veil; awning, curtain; a sail; vēla dare *or* facere, set sail.

vēnātiō, -ōnis, *f.* [vēnor, hunt], hunting, hunting expedition.

vēndō, -dere, -didī, -ditum [vēnum, sale+dō], offer for sale, sell.

Venellī, -ōrum, *m. pl.*, the Venelli (vē̞-nel′ī), *a tribe of Celtic Gaul. See map, page 137.*

venēnum, -ī, *n.*, drug, poison, venom.

Venetī, -ōrum, *m. pl.*, the Veneti (ven′ē̞-tī), *a tribe of Celtic Gaul. See map, page 137.*

veniō, -īre, vēnī, ventum, come, go; in dēditiōnem venīre, to surrender.

venter, -tris, *m.*, the belly, stomach.

ventus, -ī, *m.*, the wind.

Veragrī, -ōrum, *m. pl.*, the Veragri (ver′ā̞-grī), *a Gallic tribe in the Alps. See map, page 137.*

verbum, -ī, *n.*, a word, saying, expression; *pl.*, words, discourse, conversation; verba facere, speak.

Vercingetorīx, -īgis, *m.*, Vercingetorix (vėr-sin-jet′ō̞-riks), *a leader of the Arverni, commander-in-chief of the Gallic forces in the uprising against the Romans in 52* B.C.

vereor, -ērī, -itus sum, reverence, respect; fear, dread.

vērō, *adv.* [vērus], in truth, in fact, indeed; however, but, but in fact.

versō, -āre, -āvī, -ātum [vertō], turn often, turn.

versor, -ārī, -ātus sum, be engaged *or* involved, be situated, be busy, be employed *or* occupied; live, dwell.

vertō, -ere, vertī, versum, turn, turn around; change, transform; tergum vertere, flee, take to flight; *pass. as reflexive,* turn (oneself), turn one's attention.

vērus, -a, -um, *adj.*, true, real, actual; right, fair, just, proper; rē vērā, in reality, in fact, in truth; *n. as noun,* vērum, -ī, the truth.

vesper, -erī (-eris), *m.*, the evening star, evening; sub vesperum, toward evening.

vester, -tra, -trum, *poss. adj.* [vōs], your, yours (*referring to more than one person*).

vēstīgium, -ī, *n.* [vēstīgō, trace out], footprint, footstep, track, trace.

vestis, -is, -ium, *f.*, covering, cover; clothing; *pl.*, clothes, garments.

vetus, *gen.* veteris, *adj.*, old, ancient, long standing, former, of former times.

vetustus, -a, -um, *adj.*, old, ancient, long established.

via, -ae, *f.*, way, road, street; journey, march; Via Appia, -ae, *f.*, the Appian Way.

viātor, -ōris, *m.* [via], a traveler.

vīcīnus, -a, -um, *adj.* [vīcus], neighboring, near.

victima, -ae, *f.*, a victim, an animal for sacrifice.

victor, -ōris, *m.* [vincō], victor, conqueror; *as adj.*, victorious.

victōria, -ae, *f.* [victor], victory.

victus, -a, -um, *adj.* [*pf. part. of* vincō], defeated, vanquished; *m. pl. as noun,* victī, -ōrum, the vanquished.

vīcus, -ī, *m.*, street, quarter; village.

videō, -ēre, vīdī, vīsum, see, perceive, understand; see to, take care; *pass.*, be seen, be noticed; (*very frequently*) seem, appear; (*sometimes*) seem good or right.

vigil, vigilis, *m.*, sentinel.

vigilia, -ae, *f.* [**vigil**, awake], being awake, wakefulness, watching; guard, night watch; a watch (*as a division of time*), a fourth part of the night.

vīgintī, *indecl. num. adj.*, twenty.

vīlicus, -ī, *m.* [**vīlla**], steward, farm-manager.

vīlla, -ae, *f.*, country house, farm-house, villa; country estate, farm.

vinciō, -īre, vīnxī, vīnctum, bind, fasten, fetter; check, restrain.

vincō, -ere, vīcī, victum, conquer, overcome, defeat, subdue; be victorious, win; *m. pl. as noun*, **victī, -ōrum,** the vanquished, the conquered.

vinculum, -ī, *n.* [**vinciō**], a fastening; bond, fetter, chain.

vīnea, -ae, *f.* [**vīnum**], vineyard, vine-arbor; a shed (*used in sieges*).

vīnum, -ī, *n.*, wine.

violō, -āre, -āvī, -ātum [**vīs**], violate, harm, injure, dishonor, outrage.

vir, virī, *m.*, a man, a male person; husband.

virgō, -inis, *f.*, maiden, virgin, young girl.

Viridovīx, -īcis, *m.*, Viridovix (vi-rid'-ō-viks), *a chief of the Venelli* (*see map, p. 137*).

virtūs, -ūtis, *f.* [**vir**], manliness, courage, valor, bravery; virtue, worth, value, excellence.

vīs (*see Gr. S., 8*), *f.*, force, violence, strength, power; essence; *pl.*, strength; **vim facere,** use violence or force.

vīta, -ae, *f.*, life; way of life, manner of living.

vītō, -āre, -āvī, -ātum, avoid, shun, escape.

vīvō, -ere, vīxī, vīctum, live; subsist, feed; dwell, reside.

vīvus, -a, -um, *adj.* [**vīvō**], alive, living.

vix, *adv.*, hardly, barely, scarcely, with difficulty.

vocō, -āre, -āvī, -ātum [**vōx**], call, summon, call together, convoke; call by name, call, name.

volō, -āre, -āvī, -ātūrus, fly.

volō, velle, voluī, —, will, wish, be willing, intend.

Volscī, -ōrum, *m. pl.*, the Volsci (vol'sī), the Volscians, *a people of Latium. See map, page 305.*

volucer, -cris, -cre, *adj.* [**volō,** fly], flying, winged; *f. as noun*, **volucris, -is,** a bird.

voluntās, -ātis, *f.* [**volō,** wish], will, wish, desire; consent, approval, sanction; good-will, favor; willingness.

voluptās, -ātis, *f.* [**volō,** wish], pleasure, enjoyment, delight.

Volusēnus, -ī, *m.*, **C. Volusēnus,** Gaius Volusenus Quadratus (gā'yus vol-ū-sē'nus kwạ-drā'tus), *a military tribune in Caesar's army.*

Vorēnus, -ī, *m.*, **L. Vorēnus,** Lucius Vorenus (vō-rē'nus), *a centurion in Caesar's army.*

vōs, *pers. pron.* [*pl. of* **tū**], you.

voveō, -ēre, vōvī, vōtum, vow, devote, promise solemnly; wish for, wish, desire.

vōx, vōcis, *f.*, voice, sound; word, saying, utterance, cry, shout.

Vulcānus, -ī, *m.*, Vulcan, *the god of fire.*

vulgus, -ī, *n.*, the common people, common crowd, the multitude, the public.

vulnerō, -āre, -āvī, -ātum [**vulnus**], wound, injure.

vulnus, vulneris, *n.*, a wound, injury; **vulnera facere,** inflict wounds.

Vulsō, -ōnis, *m.*, **L. Manlius Vulsō,** L. Manlius Vulso (mān'li-us vul'-sō), *consul in 392* B.C.

vultus, -ūs, *m.*, expression, countenance, look, features, face.

A

(able), be able, possum, posse, potuī, —.

accomplish, cōnficiō, -ficere, -fēcī, -fec-tum; efficiō, -ficere, -fēcī, -fectum; prōficiō, -ficere, -fēcī, -fectum.

(account), on account of, propter, *prep. with acc.*

advance, prōcēdō, -cēdere, -cessī, -cessum.

(afraid), be afraid, timeō, -ēre, -uī, —; vereor, -ērī, -itus sum.

Africa, Āfrica, -ae, *f.*

after, post, *prep. with acc.*

again, iterum, *adv.*

aid, auxilium, -ī, *n.*

Aisne, Axona, -ae, *m.*

all, omnis, omne.

ally, socius, -ī, *m.*

Alps, Alpēs, -ium, *f. pl.*

also, etiam, *adv.*

although, cum, *conj.*

always, semper, *adv.*

Amazons, Amāzones, -um, *f. pl.*

ancestors, majōrēs, -um, *m. pl.*

and, et, -que, atque, *conjs.*

announce, nūntiō, -āre, -āvī, -ātum.

another, alius, alia, aliud.

approach, appropinquō, -āre, -āvī, -ātum (*takes dat., or* ad *with acc.*).

Aquileia, Aquileia, -ae, *f.*

archer, sagittārius, -ī, *m.*

Argonauts, Argonautae, -ōrum, *m. pl.*

Ariovistus, Ariovistus, -ī, *m.*

arise, orior, -īrī, ortus sum.

arms, arma, -ōrum, *n. pl.*

army, exercitus, -ūs, *m.*

arrest, comprehendō, -prehendere, -prehendī, -prehēnsum.

arrival, adventus, -ūs, *m.*

arrive, perveniō, -venīre, -vēnī, -ven-tum; arrive at, perveniō in, *w. acc.*

arrow, sagitta, -ae, *f.*

ascend, ascendō, -scendere, -scendī, -scēnsum.

Asia, Asia, -ae, *f.*

ask, quaerō, -ere, quaesīvī, quaesītum.

ask for, rogō, -āre, -āvī, -ātum.

assemble, conveniō, -venīre, -vēnī, -ventum.

Athens, Athēnae, -ārum, *f. pl.*

Atlas, Atlās, -antis, *m.*

at last, postrēmō, *adv.*

at once, statim, *adv.*

attack (*noun*), impetus, -ūs, *m.*

attack (*verb*), oppugnō, -āre, -āvī, -ātum.

at this time, nunc, *adv.*

authority, auctōritās, -ātis, *f.*

avoid, vītō, -āre, -āvī, -ātum.

(away), be away, absum, -esse, āfuī, āfutūrus.

B

baggage, impedīmenta, -ōrum, *n. pl.*

barbarian, barbarus, -ī, *m.*

battle, proelium, -ī, *n.*

be, sum, esse, fuī, futūrus.

beam (*noun*), trabs, trabis, -ium, *f.*

bear, ferō, ferre, tulī, lātum.

beautiful, pulcher, -chra, -chrum.

because, quod, cum, *conjs.*

before (*conj.*), priusquam.

Belgians, Belgae, -ārum, *m. pl.*

believe, crēdō, -dere, -didī, -ditum.

bird, avis, avis, avium, *f.*

boldness, audācia, -ae, *f.*

book, liber, librī, *m.*

boy, puer, puerī, *m.*

brave, fortis, forte.

bravely, fortiter, *adv.*

bridge, pōns, pontis, -ium, *m.*

bring, ferō, ferre, tulī, lātum; addūcō, -ducere, -dūxī, -ductum.

Britain, Britannia, -ae, *f.*

brother, frāter, frātris, *m.*

building, aedificium, -ī, *n.*

burn, incendō, -ere, -cendī, -cēnsum.

but, sed, *conj.*

buy, emō, -ere, ēmī, ēmptum.

by, ā, ab, *prep. with abl.*

C

Caesar, Caesar, Caesaris, *m.*

call, vocō, -āre, -āvī, -ātum; appellō, -āre, -āvī, -ātum.

camp, castra, -ōrum, *n. pl.*

camp-follower, cālō, -ōnis, *m.*

can, be able, possum, posse, potuī, —.

captive, captīvus, -ī, *m.*

capture, capiō, -ere, cēpī, captum.

careful, dīligēns, *gen.* -entis.

carry, ferō, ferre, tulī, lātum.

Carthage, Carthāgō, -inis, *f.*

catch sight of, cōnspicor, -ārī, -ātus sum.

cavalry, equitātus, -ūs, *m.*

centurion, centuriō, -ōnis, *m.*

change, mūtō, -āre, -āvī, -ātum.

children, līberī, -ōrum, *m. pl.*

choose, dēligō, -ligere, -lēgī, -lēctum.

citizen, cīvis, cīvis, -ium, *m.*

city, urbs, urbis, -ium, *f.*

close, claudō, -ere, clausī, clausum.

cohort, cohors, cohortis, -ium, *f.*

collect, condūcō, -dūcere, -dūxī, -ductum; cōgō, -ere, coēgī, coāctum.

come, veniō, -īre, vēnī, ventum.

command, imperō, -āre, -āvī, -ātum (*takes dat.*); be in command of, praesum, -esse, -fuī, -futūrus (*takes dat.*).

common people, plēbs, plēbis, *f.*; vulgus, -ī, *n.*

companion, comes, comitis, *m.*

congratulations, grātulātiō, -ōnis, *f.*

conquer, vincō, -ere, vīcī, victum.

consul, cōnsul, cōnsulis, *m.*

convenience, commodum, -ī, *n.*

convenient, commodus, -a, -um.

copper, aes, aeris, *n.*

country, terra, -ae, *f.*

country, native country, patria, -ae, *f.*

courage, virtūs, virtūtis, *f.*

cowardly, ignāvus, -a, -um.

crime, scelus, sceleris, *n.*

cross, trānseō, -īre, -iī, -itum.

crowd (*verb*), cōnstīpō, -āre, -āvī, -ātum.

cruel, crūdēlis, -e.

cruelty, crūdēlitās, -ātis, *f.*

custom, mōs, mōris, *m.*

D

danger, perīculum, -ī, *n.*

dangerous, perīculōsus, -a, -um.

dare, audeō, -ēre, ausus sum.

dark, obscūrus, -a, -um.

daughter, fīlia, -ae, *f.*

day, diēs, diēī, *m. and f.*; every day, cotīdiē, *adv.;* the day before, prīdiē, *adv.*

dear, cārus, -a, -um.

decide, dēcernō, -ere, -crēvī, -crētum.

deep, altus, -a, -um.

deer, cervus, -ī, *m.*

defeat, superō, -āre, -āvī, -ātum; vincō, -ere, vīcī, victum.

defend, dēfendō, -ere, -fendī, -fēnsum.

delay (*noun*), mora, -ae, *f.*

delay (*verb*), moror, -ārī, -ātus sum; tardō, -āre, -āvī, -ātum.

delayed, tardātus, -a, -um.

demand, postulō, -āre, -āvī, -ātum.

depart, discēdō, -ere, -cessī, -cessum.

desire, cupiō, -ere, -īvī, -ītum; studeō, -ēre, -uī, — (*takes dat.*).

desirous, cupidus, -a, -um.

despise, dēspiciō, -spicere, -spexī, -spectum.

destroy, dēleō, -ēre, -ēvī, -ētum.

(devoted), be devoted to, studeō, -ēre, -uī, — (*takes dat.*).

differ, differō, -ferre, distulī, dīlātum.

difficult, difficilis, -e.

difficulty, difficultās, -ātis, *f.*

direction, pars, partis, -ium, *f.*

dog, canis, canis, *m.*

downward-sloping, dēclīvis, -e.

dragon, dracō, -ōnis, *m.*

drive back, repellō, -ere, reppulī, repulsum.

drive from, expellō, -pellere, -pulī, -pulsum.

Dumnorix, Dumnorix, -īgis, *m.*

dust, pulvis, -eris, *m. and f.*

E

(each other), to *or* with each other, inter sē.

easily, facile, *adv.*

easy, facilis, -e.

eighth, octāvus, -a, -um.

either . . . or, vel . . . vel.

elect, creō, -āre, -āvī, -ātum.

embassy, lēgātiō, -ōnis, *f.*

encourage, cōnfirmō, -āre, -āvī, -ātum.

enemy, hostis, hostis, -ium, *m.; inimī-cus, -ī, m.*

entreat, obsecrō, -āre, -āvī, -ātum.

entrust, commendō, -āre, -āvī, -ātum.

envoy, lēgātus, -ī, *m.*

escape, effugiō, -fugere, -fūgī, -fugitūrus.

Etruscans, Etrūscī, -ōrum, *m. pl.*

Europe, Eurōpa, -ae, *f.*

every day, cotīdiē, *adv.*

everything, omnia, -ium, *n. pl.*

explain, expōnō, -pōnere, -posuī, -positum.

extend, pateō, -ēre, -uī, —.

F

faithful, fidēlis, -e.

famous, clārus, -a, -um.

far, longē, *adv.*

farmer, agricola, -ae, *m.*

father, pater, patris, *m.*

favor, faveō, -ēre, fāvī, fautum (*takes dat.*).

fear (*noun*), timor, timōris, *m.*

fear (*verb*), timeō, -ēre, -uī, —; vereor, -ērī, veritus sum.

few, paucī, -ae, -a.

field, ager, agrī, *m.*

fight, pugnō, -āre, -āvī, -ātum.

finally, postrēmō, tandem, *advs.*

find, inveniō, -venīre, -vēnī, -ventum; reperiō, -īre, repperī, repertum.

fire, ignis, ignis, -ium, *m.*

flee, fugiō, -ere, fūgī, fugitūrus.

fleece, vellus, velleris, *n.*

flight, fuga, -ae, *f.*

follow, sequor, sequī, secūtus sum; persequor, -sequī, -secūtus sum.

folly, stultitia, -ae, *f.*

food, cibus, -ī, *m.*

for, ad, *prep. with acc.;* dē, *prep. with abl.*

for a long time, diū, *adv.*

forage, pābulor, -ārī, -ātus sum.

forces (*of soldiers*), cōpiae, -ārum, *f. pl.*

forest, silva, -ae, *f.*

fortification, mūnītiō, -ōnis, *f.*

fortify, mūniō, -īre, -īvī, -ītum.

found, condō, -dere, -didī, -ditum.

four, quattuor, *indecl. num.*

friend, amīcus, -ī, *m.*

friendly, amīcus, -a, -um.

friendship, amīcitia, -ae, *f.*

frighten, terreō, -ēre, -uī, -itum.

frightened, territus, -a, -um.

from, ā, ab; ē, ex; dē, *preps. with abl.*

from all sides, undique, *adv.*

G

gain possession of, potior, -īrī, potītus sum (*takes abl.*).

gate, porta, -ae, *f.*

Gaul (*the country*), Gallia, -ae, *f.*

Gauls, Gallī, -ōrum, *m. pl.*

general, imperātor, -ōris, *m.*

generous, amplus, -a, -um.

Geneva, Genava, -ae, *f.*

Germans, Germānī, -ōrum, *m. pl.*

giant, gigās, -antis, *m.*

girl, puella, -ae, *f.*

give, dō, dare, dedī, datum; **give back,** reddō, -dere, -didī, -ditum.

go, eō, īre, iī, itum; **go out,** exeō, -īre, -iī, -itum; **go away,** abeō -īre, -iī, -itum.

golden, aureus, -a, -um.

good, bonus, -a, -um.

grain, frūmentum, -ī, *n.*

great, magnus, -a, -um.

greatly, magnopere, *adv.*

Greeks, Graecī, -ōrum, *m. pl.*

guard, custōdiō, -īre, -īvī, -ītum.

H

happen, accidō, -cidere, -cidī, —.

happy, contentus, -a, -um.

harbor, portus, -ūs, *m.*

hasten, properō, -āre, -āvī, -ātum; contendō, -tendere, -tendī, -tentum.

have, habeō, -ēre, -uī, -itum.

he, is, *gen.* ejus.

hear, audiō, -īre, -īvī, -ītum.

heavy, gravis, -e.

height, altitūdō, -dinis, *f.*

helmet, galea, -ae, *f.*

help (*noun*), auxilium, -ī, *n.*

help (*verb*), juvō, -āre, jūvī, jūtum.

Helvetians, Helvētiī, -ōrum, *m. pl.*

Hercules, Herculēs, -is, *m.*

here, hīc, *adv.*

high, altus, -a, -um.

hill, collis, collis, -ium, *m.*

(of) himself, herself, themselves, *reflexive,* suī, *gen.* (*dat.* sibi; *acc. and abl.* sē *or* sēsē).

hindrance, impedīmentum, -ī, *n.*

his, *when reflexive,* suus, -a, -um; *when not reflexive,* ejus (*gen. sing. of* is).

home, domus, -ūs, *f.*

honor, honor, honōris, *m.*

honorable, honestus, -a, -um.

hope, spēs, speī, *f.*

Horatius, Horātius, -ī, *m.*

horse, equus, -ī, *m.*

horseman, eques, equitis, *m.*

hostage, obses, obsidis, *m. and f.*

house, tēctum, -ī, *n.*

I

ill, aeger, -gra, -grum.

(importance), it is of importance, interest.

in, in, *prep. with abl.*; in, *prep. with acc.*

incredible, incrēdibilis, -e.

infantry, peditēs, -um, *m. pl.*

influence, auctōritās, -ātis, *f.*

inhabitant, incola, -ae, *m. and f.*

injure, noceō, -ēre, -uī, -itum (*takes dat.*).

insult, contumēlia, -ae, *f.*

interpreter, interpres, interpretis, *m.*

into, in, *prep. with acc.*

invite, invītō, -āre, -āvī, -ātum.

iron, ferrum, -ī, *n.*

island, īnsula, -ae, *f.*

it, is, ea, id.

Italy, Ītalia, -ae, *f.*

J

Jason, Jāsōn, -onis, *m.*

javelin, pīlum, -ī, *n.*

jump down, dēsilio, -silīre, -siluī, -sultum.

K

kill, interficiō, -ficere, -fēcī, -fectum; necō, -āre, -āvī, -ātum.

kind, genus, generis, *n.*; modus, -ī, *m.*

king, rēx, rēgis, *m.*

kingdom, rēgnum, -ī, *n.*

kinsman, necessārius, -ī, *m.*

know, sciō, scīre, scīvī, scītum; **not know,** ignōrō, -āre, -āvī, -ātum.

knowledge, scientia, -ae, *f.*

L

Labienus, Labiēnus, -ī, *m.*

lake, lacus, -ūs, *m.*

land, terra, -ae, *f.*; ager, agrī, *m.*

language, lingua, -ae, *f.*

large, magnus, -a, -um.

lay waste, vāstō, -āre, -āvī, -ātum.

lead, dūcō, -ere, dūxī, ductum.

lead across, trādūcō, -dūcere, -dūxī, -ductum.

leader, dux, ducis, *m.*
learn, discō, -ere, didicī, —.
leave, relinquō, -ere, -līquī, -lictum.
legion, legiō, -ōnis, *f.*
letter, epistula, -ae, *f.*
liberty, lībertās, -ātis, *f.*
lieutenant, lēgātus, -ī, *m.*
live, habitō, -āre, -āvī, -ātum.
long (*adj.*), longus, -a, -um; **a long time, for a long time,** diū, *adv.*
longer, diūtius, *adv.*
lose, āmittō, -mittere, -mīsī, -missum.
loss, dētrīmentum, -ī, *n.*
loyal, fidēlis, -e.

M

magistrate, magistrātus, -ūs, *m.*
make, faciō, -ere, fēcī, factum.
make reparations, satisfaciō, -facere, -fēcī, -factum (*takes dat.*).
make war on, bellum īnferre (*takes dat.*).
man, vir, virī, *m.*; homō, hominis, *m.*
many, multī, -ae, -a (*pl. of* multus).
Marcus, Mārcus, -ī, *m.*
Marseilles, Massilia, -ae, *f.*
measure out, mētior, -īrī, mēnsus sum.
Medea, Mēdēa, -ae, *f.*
messenger, nūntius, -ī, *m.*
mile, mīlle passūs, *pl.*, mīlia passuum.
money, pecūnia, -ae, *f.*
month, mēnsis, mēnsis, -ium *or* -um, *m.*
mother, māter, mātris, *f.*
mountain, mōns, montis, -ium, *m.*
move, moveō, -ēre, mōvī, mōtum.
my, meus, -a, -um.

N

name, nōmen, nōminis, *n.*
nation, gēns, gentis, -ium, *f.*; nātiō, -ōnis, *f.*
native country *or* land, patria, -ae, *f.*
nature, nātūra, -ae, *f.*
never, numquam, *adv.*
new, novus, -a, -um.
night, nox, noctis, -ium, *f.*
ninth, nōnus, -a, -um.

no (*adj.*), nūllus, -a, -um, *gen.* nūllīus.
noise, strepitus, -ūs, *m.*
no one, nēmō.
not, nōn, *adv.*; **that . . . not,** nē.
nothing, nihil, *indecl., n.*
notice, animum advertere.
now, nunc, *adv.*
number, numerus, -ī, *m.*
nymph, nympha, -ae, *f.*

O

obey, pāreō, -ēre, -uī, — (*takes dat.*).
often, saepe, *adv.*
old, vetus, *gen.* veteris.
old man, senex, senis, *m.*
on, in, *prep. with abl.*
on account of, propter, *prep. with acc.*
one, ūnus, -a, -um, *gen.* ūnīus.
one . . . another, alius . . . alius.
only (*adj.*), sōlus, -a, -um.
only (*adv.*), omnīnō.
open, aperiō, -īre, aperuī, apertum; patefaciō, -facere, -fēcī, -factum.
or, an, aut, vel, *conjs.*
order, jubeō, -ēre, jussī, jussum.
Orgetorix, Orgetorīx, -īgis, *m.*
other, another, alius, -a, -ud; **others,** aliī, -ōrum, *m.*; **the other, the rest (of),** reliquus, -a, -um.
our, noster, -tra, -trum; **our men,** nostrī, -ōrum, *m. pl.*
outside, outside of, extrā, *prep. with acc.*
overthrow (*noun*), ruīna, -ae, *f.*

P

part, pars, partis, -ium, *f.*
peace, pāx, pācis, *f.*
Perseus, Perseus, -ī, *m.*
persuade, persuādeō, -suādēre, -suāsī, -suāsum (*takes dat.*).
Phoenicians, Poenī, -ōrum, *m. pl.*
picture, pictūra, -ae, *f.*
place (*noun*), locus, -ī, *m.* (*pl.* loca, -ōrum, *n.*).
place (*verb*), pōnō, -ere, posuī, positum.

(place), to the same place, eōdem, *adv.*

place in command of, praeficiō, -ficere, -fēcī, -fectum (*takes dat.*).

plan (*noun*), cōnsilium, -ī, *n.*

plan (*verb*), cōgitō, -āre, -āvī, -ātum.

please, placeō, -ēre, -uī, placitum (*takes dat.*).

pleasing, grātus, -a, -um.

(pleasure), be a pleasure to, placeō, -ēre, -uī, placitum (*takes dat.*).

plunder, praedor, -ārī, -ātus sum.

poet, poēta, -ae, *m.*

(possession), gain possession of, potior, -īrī, potītus sum (*takes abl.*).

(possessions), their possessions, sua, -ōrum, *n. pl., reflexive.*

praetor, praetor, -ōris, *m.*

praise, laudō, -āre, -āvī, -ātum.

prepare, parō, -āre, -āvī, -ātum.

prepared, parātus, -a, -um.

promise, polliceor, -ērī, pollicitus sum.

protection, praesidium, -ī, *n.*

province, prōvincia, -ae, *f.*

prudent, prūdēns, *gen.* -entis.

punishment, poena, -ae, *f.*

(purpose), for the purpose of, causā, *preceded by genitive.*

Q

queen, rēgīna, -ae, *f.*

quickly, celeriter, *adv.*

R

rampart, vāllum, -ī, *n.*

read, legō, -ere, lēgī, lēctum.

reason, causa, -ae, *f.*

receive, accipiō, -ere, -cēpī, -ceptum.

recent, recēns, *gen.* -entis.

refinement, hūmānitās, -ātis, *f.*

regain, recuperō, -āre, -āvī, -ātum.

region, regiō, -ōnis, *f.*

Regulus, Rēgulus, -ī, *m.*

reinforcements, subsidium, -ī, *n.*

remain, maneō, -ēre, mānsī, mānsum.

(reparations), make reparations, satis-faciō, -ere, -fēcī, -factum (*takes dat.*).

report, renūntiō, -āre, -āvī, -ātum.

resist, resistō, -sistere, -stitī, — (*takes dat.*).

rest, the rest of, reliquus, -a, -um.

restore, reddō, -dere, -didī, -ditum.

(result), it results, fit, fierī, factum est.

return, redeō, -īre, -iī, -itum; revertor, -vertī, -versus sum.

reward, praemium, -ī, *n.*

Rhine, Rhēnus, -ī, *m.*

Rhone, Rhodanus, -ī, *m.*

river, flūmen, flūminis, *n.*

road, iter, itineris, *n.*

robber, latrō, -ōnis, *m.*

Romans, Rōmānī, -ōrum, *m. pl.*

Rome, Rōma, -ae, *f.*

Romulus, Rōmulus, -ī, *m.*

rout, dispergō, -ere, -spersī, -spersum.

run, currō, -ere, cucurrī, cursum.

S

safe, tūtus, -a, -um.

Saguntum, Saguntum, -ī, *n., a city of Spain.*

sailor, nauta, -ae, *m.*

same, īdem, eadem, idem.

save, servō, -āre, -āvī, -ātum.

say, dīcō, -ere, dīxī, dictum.

scorn, spernō, -ere, sprēvī, sprētum.

scout, explōrātor, -ōris, *m.*

sea, mare, maris, *n.*

see, videō, -ēre, vīdī, vīsum; cōnspiciō, -spicere, -spexī, -spectum.

seek, petō, -ere, petīvī, petītum.

seem, videor, -ērī, vīsus sum.

seize, occupō, -āre, -āvī, -ātum; capiō, -ere, cēpī, captum.

self, himself, herself, itself, *pl.,* themselves, *when reflexive,* suī, *gen.* (*dat.* sibi, *acc. and abl.* sē *or* sēsē); *when not reflexive,* ipse, ipsa, ipsum.

send, mittō, -ere, mīsī, missum.

separate, dīvidō, -ere, dīvīsī, dīvīsum.

set out, proficīscor, proficīscī, pro-fectus sum.

Sextus, Sextus, -ī, *m.*

share, partior, -īrī, -ītus sum.

shed, fundō, -ere, fūdī, fūsum.

shepherd, pāstor, -ōris, *m.*

shield, scūtum, -ī, *n.*

ship, nāvis, nāvis, -ium, *f.*

shout, shouting, clāmor, -ōris, *m.*

show, mōnstrō, -āre, -āvī, -ātum.

Sicily, Sicilia, -ae, *f.*

(sides), from all sides, undique, *adv.*

sight, cōnspectus, -ūs, *m.*

(sight), catch sight of, cōnspicor, -ārī, -ātus sum.

signal, signum, -ī, *n.*

since, cum, *conj.*

sister, soror, sorōris, *f.*

six, sex, *indecl. num.*

slave, servus, -ī, *m.*

slinger, funditor, -ōris, *m.*

small, parvus, -a, -um.

so, tam, ita, *advs.*

so great, tantus, -a, -um.

so large, tantus, -a, -um.

soldier, mīles, mīlitis, *m.*

so many, tot.

some, quīdam, quaedam, quoddam *or* quiddam; nōnnūllī, -ōrum, *m. pl.*

some . . . others, aliī . . . aliī, *pl.*

sometimes, interdum, *adv.*

son, fīlius, -ī, *m.*

soon, mox, *adv.*

sound, sonus, -ī, *m.*

Spain, Hispānia, -ae, *f.*

spear, hasta, -ae, *f.*

speed, celeritās, -ātis, *f.*

stand, stō, stāre, stetī, stātūrus.

stature, statūra, -ae, *f.*

still, tamen, *adv.*

storm, tempestās, -ātis, *f.*

story, fābula, -ae, *f.*

street, via, -ae, *f.*

strong, firmus, -a, -um.

sufficiently, satis, *adv.*

summer, aestās, -ātis, *f.*

supply, cōpia, -ae, *f.*

surpass, praecēdō, -cēdere, -cessī, -cessum (*takes dat.*).

surrender, trādō, -dere, -didī, -ditum; dēdō, -dere, -didī, -ditum.

surround, circumdō, -dare, -dedī, -datum; circumveniō, -venīre, -vēnī, -ventum.

swamp, palūs, -ūdis, *f.*

swift, celer, -eris, -ere.

sword, gladius, -ī, *m.*

T

take, capiō, -ere, cēpī, captum.

task, negōtium, -ī, *n.*

tear, lacrima, -ae, *f.*

temple, templum, -i, *n.*

tent, tabernāculum, -ī, *n.*

tenth, decimus, -a, -um.

territory, fīnes, -ium, *m. pl.*

that (*conj.*), ut; nē (*after verbs of fear*).

that (*dem.*), ille, illa, illud; is, ea, id; iste, ista, istud.

that (*rel.*), quī, quae, quod.

that . . . not, nē.

their, *when reflexive,* suus, sua, suum; *when not reflexive,* eōrum, eārum (*gen. pl. of* is).

then, tum, *adv.*

Thessaly, Thessalia, -ae, *f.*

thing, rēs, reī, *f.*

think, arbitror, -ārī, -ātus sum; putō, -āre, -āvī, -ātum.

third, tertius, -a, -um.

this, hic, haec, hoc; is, ea, id.

thousand, mīlle, *pl.* mīlia, -ium.

three, trēs, tria.

through, per, *prep. with acc.*

throw, jaciō, -ere, jēcī, jactum.

(time), a long time, for a long time, diū, *adv.*

tired, tired out, dēfessus, -a, -um.

to, ad, in, *preps. with acc.*

today, hodiē, *adv.*

top of, highest part of, summus, -a, -um.

touch, tangō, -ere, tetigī, tāctum.

town, oppidum, -ī, *n.*

townspeople, oppidānī, -ōrum, *m. pl.*

treacherous, perfidus, -a, -um.

treachery, perfidia, -ae, *f.*

tribune, tribūnus, -ī, *m.*

Trojans, Trōjānī, -ōrum, *m. pl.*

Troy, Trōja, -ae, *f.*

trumpet, tuba, -ae, *f.*

trust (*noun*), fidēs, fideī, *f.*

trust (*verb*), cōnfīdō, -fīdere, -fīsus sum (*takes dat.*).

try, cōnor, -ārī, -ātus sum.

twice, bis, *adv.*

two, duo, duae, duo.

U

Ulysses, Ulīxēs, -is, *m.*

understand, intellegō, -legere, -lēxī, -lēctum; comprehendō, -hendere, -hendī, -hēnsum.

undertake, suscipiō, -ere, -cēpī, -ceptum.

until, dum, *conj.*

unwilling, invītus, -a, -um; **be unwilling,** nōlō, nōlle, nōluī, —.

urge, hortor, -ārī, -ātus sum.

use, ūtor, ūtī, ūsus sum (*takes abl.*).

V

Vercingetorix, Vercingetorīx, -īgis, *m.*

victory, victōria, -ae, *f.*

village, vīcus, -ī, *m.*

violent, vehemēns, *gen.* -entis.

voice, vōx, vōcis, *f.*

W

wage, gerō, -ere, gessī, gestum.

wait, wait for, expectō, -āre, -āvī, -ātum.

walk, ambulō, -āre, -āvī, -ātum.

wall, mūrus, -ī, *m.*

wander, vagor, -ārī, -ātus sum.

war, bellum, -ī, *n.*; **make war on,** bellum īnferre (*takes dat.*).

warn, moneō, -ēre, -uī, -itum.

watch (*noun*), vigilia, -ae, *f.*

watch (*verb*), spectō, -āre, -āvī, -ātum.

way, via, -ae, *f.*

we, nōs.

wealth, dīvitiae, -ārum, *f. pl.*

weapon, tēlum, -ī, *n.*

what (*interrog. adj.*), quis *or* quī, quae, quod.

when, cum, ubi, *conjs.*

where, ubi, quō, *advs.*

which (*rel. adj.*), quis *or* quī, quae, quod.

which, what (*interrog. adj.*), quī *or* quis, quae, quod.

who, which, what, that (*rel. pron.*), quī, quae, quod.

who, which, what (*interrog. pron.*), quis, quid.

whole, tōtus, -a, -um, *gen.* tōtīus.

whose (*rel. pron.*), cujus.

why, cūr, *adv.*

wide, lātus, -a, -um.

winter, hiems, hiemis, *f.*

wisdom, sapientia, -ae, *f.*

wise, sapiēns, *gen.* sapientis.

wish, cupiō, -ere, cupīvī, cupītum; volō, velle, voluī, —; **not wish, be unwilling,** nōlō, nōlle, nōluī, —.

with, cum, *prep. with abl.*

withdraw, excēdō, -cēdere, -cessī, -cessum; discēdō, -cēdere, -cessī, -cessum.

without, sine, *prep. with abl.*

withstand, sustineō, -tinēre, -tinuī, -tentum.

woman, fēmina, -ae, *f.*; mulier, mulieris, *f.*

wonder, wonder at, mīror, -ārī, -ātus sum.

word, verbum, -ī, *n.*

work, labōrō, -āre, -āvī, -ātum.

worthy, dignus, -a, -um (*takes abl.*).

wound (*verb*), vulnerō, -āre, -āvī, -ātum.

write, scrībō, -ere, scrīpsī, scrīptum.

writer, auctor, -ōris, *f.*

Y

year, annus, -ī, *m.*

yesterday, herī, *adv.*

you, tū, tuī; *pl.* vōs, vestrum *or* vestrī.

young man, juvenis, juvenis, *m.*

your, *of one person,* tuus, -a, -um; *of more than one person,* vester, -tra, -trum.

INDEX OF GRAMMAR

(Numbers refer to pages.)

ABLATIVE CASE
  absolute, 109, 392 (Section 85)
    translation of, 109, 392 (Section 85*a*)
  of accompaniment, 391 (Section 80), 392
    (Section 80*a*, *b*)
  of agent, 389 (Section 66*a*), 391 (Section
    76)
  of cause, 393 (Section 88)
  of comparison, 391 (Section 77)
  with *cōnfīdō*, 181 (n. 4)
  of degree of difference, 392 (Section 84)
  with *dē* or *ex* instead of genitive, 54
    (n. 7), 85 (n. 4), 388 (Section 53*a*)
  with deponents, 149, 393 (Section 89)
  of description, 87, 393 (Section 87)
  of manner, 73, 392 (Section 81)
  of means, 392 (Section 82)
  of place, 391 (Section 78)
  of place from which, 77, 391 (Section 75)
  with prepositions, 407 (Sections 152-153)
  of respect, 73, 393 (Section 86)
  of route, 392 (Section 83)
  of separation, 391 (Section 74)
  of specification, *see* respect
  of time, 391 (Section 79)
ac (*atque*), with words of likeness and unlikeness, 156 (n. 4), 193 (n. 12)

ACCUSATIVE CASE
  of direct object, 390 (Section 67)
  of duration of time, 390 (Section 68)
  of extent in space, 89, 390 (Section 69)
  of place to which, 71, 94 (n. 11), 390
    (Section 70)
  with prepositions, 390 (Section 71), 407
    (Sections 153-154)
  with *propius*, 177 (n. 8), 238 (n. 4)
  with *proximus*, 182 (n. 1)
  as subject of infinitive, 390 (Section 72),
    401 (Section 125)
  two accusatives with verbs of naming,
    etc., 390 (Section 73)
  with compounds of *trāns*, 390 (Section
    73*a*)

ADJECTIVES
  adherent, 394 (Section 92)
  with adverbial force, 394 (Section 96)
  agreement, 387 (Section 47)
  comparative
    declension of, 363 (Section 18)
    translation of, 394 (Section 97)
  comparison of
    regular, 363 (Section 16)
    irregular, 363 (Section 17)
  with dative, 389 (Section 60)

  declension of
    first, 43, 361 (Section 9)
    second, 43, 361 (Section 9)
    third, 43, 362 (Sections 10-13)
    comparatives, 363 (Section 18)
  demonstrative, 366 (Section 26)
  denoting a part, 394 (Section 95)
  with genitive in -*īus*, 363 (Section 15)
  identifying, 366 (Section 27)
  indefinite, 368 (Section 32)
  intensive, 367 (Section 28)
  interrogative, 367 (Section 31)
  numeral, 364-365 (Section 21)
  possessive, 366 (Section 25)
  predicate, 394 (Section 93)
  substantive use of, 394 (Section 94)
  superlative, 394 (Section 97)

ADVERBS
  comparative and superlative, translation
    of, 394 (Section 97)
  comparison of, 364 (Sections 19-20)

AGREEMENT
  of adjectives, 387 (Section 47)
  of appositives, 387 (Section 49)
  of gerundives, 113
  of participles, 55, 57, 387 (Section 47)
  of relative pronouns, 285 (n. 6), 387 (Sec-
    tion 48)
  of verbs, 319 (n. 12), 387 (Section 50)
aiō, conjugation of, 386 (Section 46)
aliquis, declension of, 368 (Section 32)
antequam, with anticipatory subjunctive,
  398 (Section 110*a*)

APPOSITIVES, 387 (Section 49)
atque (*ac*), with words of likeness and
  unlikeness, 156 (n. 4), 193 (n. 12)
bōs, declension of, 361 (Section 8)
causā
  with dependent genitive, 299 (n. 11)
  with gerund, 58, 404 (Section 137*a*)

CAUSAL CLAUSES
  cum, 89, 398 (Section 113)
  quod, quia, quoniam, 400 (Section 120)
coepī, 386 (Section 46)
  passive, with passive infinitive, 193 (n. 14)

COMMANDS
  imperative, 400 (Section 121)
    in indirect discourse, 403 (Section 131, 2)
  negative
    with *nē*, 400 (Section 122*a*)
    with *nōlī*, 400 (Section 122)

COMPARATIVE ADJECTIVES
declension of, 363 (Section 18)
translation of, 394 (Section 97)

COMPARISON
of adjectives, 363 (Sections 16-17)
of adverbs, 364 (Sections 19-20)

COMPOUND VERBS
with dative, 105, 389 (Section 65)
prefixes, 59, 105

CONCESSIVE CLAUSES, 85, 398 (Section 114), 399 (Section 114*b*)

CONDITIONS
contrary to fact, 402 (Section 130)
future less vivid, 402 (Section 129)
future more vivid, 402 (Section 128)
translation of, 402 (Section 128*a*)
non-committal, 401 (Section 127)

cōnfīdō
with ablative, 181 (n. 4)
with dative, 181 (n. 4), 285 (n. 8)

-cum, enclitic, 71 (n. 7), 407 (Section 152)

cum CLAUSES
anticipatory, 398 (Section 110*a*)
causal, 89, 398 (Section 113)
concessive, 85, 398 (Section 114)
descriptive, 95, 203 (n. 3), 399 (Section 115)

cum prīmum, with perfect, 190 (n. 6)

DATIVE CASE
with adjectives, 389 (Section 60)
of agent, 111, 389 (Section 66)
with compounds, 105, 389 (Section 65)
with *cōnfīdō*, 181 (n. 4), 285 (n. 8)
of indirect object, 388 (Section 59)
of possession, 147, 389 (Section 62)
of purpose, 119, 389 (Section 63)
of reference, 119, 389 (Section 64)
with special verbs, 69, 389 (Section 61)

dē with ablative, used instead of genitive, 54 (n. 7), 85 (n. 4), 388 (Section 53*a*)

DEFECTIVE VERBS, 386 (Section 46)

DEMONSTRATIVES, 366 (Section 26)

DEPONENT VERBS
conjugation
first, 51, 378-380 (Section 38)
second, 51, 378-380 (Section 38)
third, 53, 378-380 (Section 38)
fourth, 53, 378-380 (Section 38)
ablative with, 149, 393 (Section 89)
genitive with, 141 (n. 4), 393 (Section 89*a*)
gerund of, 56 (n. 7)
infinitives of, 79
participles of, 55, 57, 403 (Sections 132*a* and 136*a*)
perfect participle as passive, 146 (n. 2)
semi-deponent, 380 (Section 38)

DESCRIPTION, relative clause of, 398 (Section 112)

DESCRIPTIVE CLAUSES OF SITUATION, 95, 203 (n. 3), 399 (Section 115)

DISTRIBUTIVE NUMERALS, 364 (Section 21)
instead of cardinals, 284 (n. 2), 303 (n. 6)

domus
declension of, 361 (Section 8)
in place-from-which construction, 77, 391 (Section 75)
in place-to-which construction, 71, 94 (n. 11), 390 (Section 70)
in place-where construction (locative), 81, 393 (Section 91)

dum
with anticipatory subjunctive, 115, 398 (Section 110*a*)
in clauses of proviso, 398 (Section 111)
with present indicative, 16 (n. 2), 49 (n. 2), 405 (Section 144)

dummodo, 398 (Section 111)

duo, declension of, 365 (Section 22)

ENCLITICS
-cum, 71 (n. 7), 407 (Section 152)
-ne, 123 (n. 4)

eō, conjugation of, 130, 384 (Section 43)
infinitives of, 131

ex with ablative, used instead of genitive, 54 (n. 7), 85 (n. 4), 388 (Section 53*a*)

FEAR, clauses of, 125, 397 (Section 109)
translation of, 397 (Section 109*c*)

ferō, conjugation of, 49, 382-383 (Section 42)
compounds of, 49

fīō, conjugation of, 130, 139, 384-385 (Section 44)
infinitives of, 131

fore, used instead of *futūrus esse*, 116 (n. 1)

GENITIVE CASE
with deponents, 141 (n. 4), 393 (Section 89*a*)
of description, 87, 388 (Section 54), 393 (Section 87*a*)
with *interest*, 192 (n. 14)
of material or composition, 388 (Section 57)
of measure, 388 (Section 54*a*)
objective, 388 (Section 55)
partitive, 387 (Section 53)
of possession, 387 (Section 52)
with *potior*, 141 (n. 4), 393 (Section 89*a*)
with *refert*, 192 (n. 14)
subjective, 388 (Section 56)
with verbs, 388 (Section 58)
of the whole, 387 (Section 53)
after *mīlia*, 74 (n. 6)
replaced by ablative with *dē* or *ex*, 54 (n. 7), 85 (n. 4), 388 (Section 53*a*)

GERUNDIVES, 113, 404 (Section 138)
agreement, 113
case uses
genitive, 113, 404 (Section 138*a*)
with *meī, tuī*, etc., 176 (n. 2)
accusative, 113, 404 (Section 138*a*)
ablative, 113, 404 (Section 138*a*)
distinction between gerund and gerundive, 113, 404 (Section 139)
GERUNDS, 57, 113, 131, 404 (Section 137)
case uses
genitive, 57, 58, 404 (Section 137*a*)
dative, 58, 404 (Section 137*b*)
accusative, 58, 404 (Section 137*c*)
ablative, 58, 93 (n. 8), 312 (n. 4), 404
(Section 137*d*)
of deponent verbs, 56 (n. 7)
distinction between gerund and gerundive, 113, 404 (Section 139)
hic, declension of, 366 (Section 26)
īdem, declension of, 366 (Section 27)
IDENTIFYING PRONOUN OR ADJECTIVE, 366
(Section 27)
ille, declension of, 366 (Section 26)
for special emphasis, 56 (n. 3)
IMPERATIVE MOOD, 400 (Section 121)
IMPERSONAL VERBS
with genitive, 192 (n. 14)
with infinitive as subject, 401 (Section
124)
passive of intransitive used impersonally, 107 (n. 5), 119 (n. 2)
INDEFINITES, 368 (Section 32)
INDICATIVE
in causal clauses, 400 (Section 120)
after certain conjunctions, 395 (Section
99)
in clauses with *cum* meaning "when,"
399 (Section 115*a, b, c*)
in *dum* clauses, 405 (Section 144)
in future more vivid conditional sentences, 402 (Section 128)
in main clauses, 395 (Section 98)
in non-committal conditional sentences,
401 (Section 127)
in noun clauses with *quod*, 395 (Section
101)
in relative clauses, 395 (Section 100),
398 (Section 112*b*)
with words meaning "until" or "before,"
398 (Section 110*b*)
INDIRECT DISCOURSE, 401 (Section 125, 1),
402 (Section 131)
commands in, 403 (Section 131, 2)
informal (implied), 111 (n. 11), 324
(n. 2, 4), 400 (Section 119)
subordinate clauses in, 403 (Section 131, 3)
tense of infinitives in, 83

INDIRECT QUESTIONS, 103, 400 (Section
117)
double questions, 179 (n. 3)
INFINITIVE
present, 77, 79, 131
perfect, 77, 79, 131
future, 77, 79, 131
complementary, 401 (Section 123)
of deponents, 79
historical, 214 (n. 14), 401 (Section 126)
as nominative of gerund, 404 (Section
137)
sometimes omits *esse*, 121 (n. 10)
as subject, 401 (Section 124)
with subject accusative, 390 (Section 72),
401 (Section 125), 402 (Section 131, 1)
tense of, in indirect discourse, 83
used instead of gerund as accusative,
404 (Section 137)
with verbs of promising, 321 (n. 9)
INFORMAL INDIRECT DISCOURSE, 111
(n. 11), 324 (n. 2, 4), 400 (Section 119)
inquam, conjugation of, 386 (Section 46)
INTENSIVE, 367 (Section 28)
INTERROGATIVE PRONOUN AND ADJECTIVE,
367 (Sections 30-31)
ipse, declension of, 367 (Section 28)
IRREGULAR VERBS, see *eō, ferō*, etc.
is, declension of, 366 (Section 26)
equivalent to definite article, 220 (n. 12)
jubeō, with infinitive clause, 397 (Section
107*c*), 401 (Section 125, 2)
LOCATIVE CASE, 81, 393 (Section 91)
mālō, conjugation of, 385-386 (Section 45)
meminī, 386 (Section 46)
mīlia, declension of, 365 (Section 22)
modo, in clauses of proviso, 398 (Section
111)
MOOD, see INDICATIVE, etc.
-ne, 123 (n. 4)
nē
in a negative command, 400 (Section
122*a*)
with noun clauses of desire, 107, 397
(Section 107)
with noun clauses of fear, 125, 397 (Section 109)
with optative, 396 (Section 103, 3*a*)
with purpose clauses, 105, 396 (Section
104)
after verbs of hindering, 191 (n. 9), 399
(Section 116, 2)
with volitive, 395 (Section 102*a*)
NEGATIVE COMMANDS
with *nē*, 400 (Section 122*a*)
with *nōlī* and infinitive, 400 (Section 122)

nēve, between subjunctives denoting an idea of wish or desire, 316 (n. 4)

nōlī, 400 (Section 122)

nōlō, 49, 385, 386 (Section 45)

NOMINATIVE CASE
as subject, 387 (Section 51), 401 (Section 126*a*)
as predicate, 387 (Section 51*a*)

nōn
in noun clauses of fact, 397 (Section 108)
in optative clauses, 396 (Section 103, 3*a*)
in result clauses, 396 (Section 106)

NOUN CLAUSES
of desire, 107, 397 (Section 107)
translated with infinitive, 397 (Section 107*a*)
after verb of commanding, persuading, or warning, 114 (n. 3), 139 (n. 5), 397 (Section 107*c*)
of fact, 139, 397 (Section 108)
of fear, 397 (Section 109)
dependent on *perīculum est*, 397 (Section 109*b*)
with *quod*, 395 (Section 101)

NOUNS
first declension, 42, 359 (Section 1)
second declension, 42, 359 (Section 2)
third declension, 42, 359-360 (Sections 3-5)
fourth declension, 42, 361 (Section 6)
fifth declension, 42, 361 (Section 7)
irregular, 361 (Section 8)

num, 123 (n. 6)

NUMERALS
cardinal, 364-365 (Section 21)
distributive, 364-365 (Section 21)
ordinal, 364-365 (Section 21)

ōdī, 66 (n. 2), 386 (Section 46)

PARTICIPLES, 403 (Section 132)
present, 55, 57, 111, 131, 403 (Section 133)
declension of, 55, 362 (Section 14)
perfect, 57, 111, 131, 403 (Section 134)
declension of, 403 (Section 134)
future active, 57, 111, 131, 403 (Section 135)
declension of, 57, 403 (Section 135)
with *sum*, 57, 403 (Section 135)
future passive, 111, 131, 403 (Section 136)
declension of, 111, 403 (Section 136)
as gerundive, 113, 404 (Section 138)
translation of, 111
with *sum*, 111, 403 (Section 136)
agreement, 55, 57, 387 (Section 47)
of deponents, 55, 57, 403 (Sections 132*a* and 136*a*)

PASSIVE VOICE
used impersonally, 107 (n. 5), 237 (n. 12)
used in reflexive sense, 81 (n. 6)

patior
with infinitive and subject accusative, 177 (n. 2), 401 (Section 125, 2)
with noun clause as object, 177 (n. 2)

PERSONAL PRONOUNS, 365 (Section 23)

PLACE CONSTRUCTIONS
locative, 81, 393 (Section 91)
place from which, 77, 391 (Section 75)
place to which, 71, 390 (Section 70)
place where, 391 (Section 78)

plūs, declension of, 363 (Section 18)

POSSESSIVES, 366 (Section 25)

possum, conjugation of, 130, 381-382 (Section 40)
present subjunctive, 121, 130
imperfect subjunctive, 87, 130
perfect subjunctive, 130
past perfect subjunctive, 130
infinitives of, 131

postquam
with indicative, 395 (Section 99)
with perfect translated as past perfect, 107 (n. 3)

potior
governing ablative, 149, 393 (Section 89)
governing genitive, 141 (n. 4), 393 (Section 89*a*)

PREFIXES, 59, 218
whose compounds take dative, 105, 389 (Section 61)

PREPOSITIONS
cases with, 407 (Sections 152-154)
with gerunds, 58, 404 (Section 137*d*)
as prefixes, 105, 218

priusquam, with subjunctive, 398 (Section 110*a*)

PRONOUNS
demonstrative, 366 (Section 26)
identifying, 366 (Section 27)
indefinite, 368 (Section 32)
intensive, 367 (Section 28)
interrogative, 367 (Section 30)
personal, 365 (Section 23)
possessive, 366 (Section 25)
reflexive, 365 (Section 24)
relative, 367 (Section 29), 387 (Section 48)

propius, with accusative, 177 (n. 8), 238 (n. 4)

prōsum, conjugation of, 382 (Section 41)

proximus, with accusative, 182 (n. 1)

PURPOSE
  clauses of, 105, 396 (Section 104)
    translations of, 396 (Section 104*b*)
    with *quō*, 144 (n. 5), 396 (Section 105)
    with relative, 105, 396 (Section 104*a*)
  gerundive with *ad*, 113, 140 (n. 3)
  supine, 145 (n. 15)

quam
  with comparatives, 391 (Section 77*a*)
  force of, with superlative, 143 (n. 5)

quamquam, 395 (Section 99)

quī, declension of, 367 (Section 29)

quīdam
  declension of, 368 (Section 32)
  with ablative, instead of genitive of
    the whole, 54 (n. 7), 85 (n. 4), 388
    (Section 53*a*)

quīn
  with subjunctive, after verb of doubting,
    141 (n. 1), 399 (Section 116, 1)
  with subjunctive, after verb of hinder-
    ing, 191 (n. 9), 399 (Section 116, 2)

quis, declension of, 367 (Section 30)

quisquam, declension of, 368 (Section 32)

quisque, declension of, 368 (Section 32)

quō, in clauses of purpose, 144 (n. 5), 396
    (Section 105)

quod
  causal, with indicative and subjunctive,
    400 (Section 120)
  with indicative, 395 (Section 101)
  introducing substantive clause, 196 (n.
    12), 395 (Section 101*a*)

quōminus, after verbs of hindering, 191
    (n. 9), 399 (Section 116, 2)

REFLEXIVE PRONOUN, 365 (Section 24)

RELATIVE CLAUSES
  of description, 398 (Section 112)
  with indicative, 395 (Section 100)
  preceding antecedent, 104 (n. 14)
  of purpose, 105, 396 (Section 104*a*)

RELATIVES, 367 (Section 29)
  agreement, 285 (n. 6), 387 (Section 48)
  in causal clauses, 398 (Section 113*a*)
  in concessive clauses, 399 (Section 114*b*)
  in purpose clauses, 105, 396 (Section
    104*a*)
  translated by personal pronouns, 107
    (n. 12)

RESULT CLAUSES, 93, 396 (Section 106)

SEMI-DEPONENTS, 380 (Section 38)

SEQUENCE OF TENSES, 123, 406 (Section
    150), 407 (Section 151)

SUBJUNCTIVE, 85
  present
    active, 121, 128
    passive, 121, 129

imperfect
  active, 85, 128
  passive, 87, 129
perfect
  active, 123, 128
  passive, 123, 129
past perfect
  active, 95, 128, 406 (Section 148)
  passive, 129
anticipatory, 115, 398 (Section 110)
by attraction, 169 (n. 2), 400 (Section 118)
in conditions
  contrary to fact, 402 (Section 130)
  future less vivid, 402 (Section 129)

cum
  causal clauses, 89, 398 (Section 113)
  concessive clauses, 85, 398 (Section
    114)
  descriptive clauses of situation, 95,
    399 (Section 115)
of desire or will, 395-396 (Sections 102-
    103)
in indirect discourse
  commands, 403 (Section 131, 2)
  subordinate clauses, 403 (Section
    131, 3)
in indirect questions, 103, 400 (Section
    117)
in informal (implied) indirect discourse,
    111 (n. 11), 324 (n. 2, 4), 400 (Section
    119)
with *necesse est*, 401 (Section 124*a*)
in negative commands, 400 (Section
    122*a*)
in noun clauses of desire, 107, 397 (Sec-
    tion 107)
in noun clauses of fact, 139, 397 (Section
    108)
in noun clauses of fear, 125, 397 (Section
    109)
optative, 395-396 (Section 103, 1, 2, 3)
after *perīculum est*, 397 (Section 109*b, c*)
in clauses of proviso, 398 (Section 111)
in clauses of purpose, 105, 396 (Section
    104)
  with relative pronouns, 105, 396 (Sec-
    tion 104*a*)
  with *quō*, 144 (n. 5), 396 (Section 105)
  possible translations of, 396 (Section
    104*b*)
in clauses with *quīn*
  after verbs of doubting, 141 (n. 1), 399
    (Section 116, 1)
  after verbs of hindering, 191 (n. 9), 399
    (Section 116, 2)
in *quod* causal clauses, 400 (Section 120)
in relative clauses of description, 398
    (Section 112)
in clauses of result, 93, 396 (Section 106)
volitive, 395 (Section 102)

SUFFIXES, 245

sum, conjugation of, 130, 380-381 (Section 39)
  present subjunctive, 121, 130
  imperfect subjunctive, 87, 130
  perfect subjunctive, 123, 130
  past perfect subjunctive, 130
  with future active participle, 57
  with future passive participle, 111
  infinitives of, 131

SUPERLATIVE, translation of, 394 (Section 97)

SUPINE, 79, 405 (Section 140)
  accusative, 145 (n. 15), 405 (Section 140)
  ablative, 405 (Section 141)

SYNOPSIS OF VERBS, 378 (Section 37)

tamen, in main clause to which concessive clause is attached, 85, 296 (n. 9), 399 (Section 114*a*)

TENSES, 405 (Section 142)
  present, 136 (n. 2), 405 (Section 143)
    with *cum primum*, 190 (n. 6)
    with *dum*, 405 (Section 144)
    with future force, 405 (Section 143*b*)
    historical, 405 (Section 143*a*)
  imperfect, 405 (Section 145)
    in repeated or habitual action, 67 (n. 2), 189 (n. 2), 405 (Section 145*a*)
    translation of, 405 (Section 145*b*)
    subjunctive uses, 405 (Section 145*c*)
  future, 406 (Section 146)
    in future more vivid conditional sentences, 402 (Section 128)
    indicative as substitute for imperative, 94 (n. 4)
    translation of, with certain conjunctions, 406 (Section 146*a*)
  perfect, 406 (Section 147, 1, 2)
    in future less vivid conditional sentences, 402 (Section 129*a*), 406 (Section 147, 2*a*)
    with *postquam* translated as past perfect, 107 (n. 3)
  past perfect, 406 (Section 148)
  future perfect, 406 (Section 149)
  sequence of, 123, 406 (Section 150)
    exceptions, 406 (Section 151)

trēs, declension of, 365 (Section 22)

ubi, indicative with, 395 (Section 99)

ut
  with indicative, 114 (n. 6)
  with subjunctive
    in noun clauses of desire, 107, 397 (Section 107)
    in noun clauses of fact, 139, 397 (Section 108)
    in clauses of fear, 125, 397 (Section 109)
    in clauses of purpose, 105, 396 (Section 104)
    in clauses of result, 93, 396 (Section 106)

utinam, 395 (Section 103)

ūtor, with ablative, 149, 393 (Section 89)

utrum, introducing double question, 179 (n. 3)

VERBS
  first conjugation, 44-45, 128-129, 369-372 (Sections 33-34)
  second conjugation, 44-45, 128-129, 372-378 (Sections 35-36)
  third conjugation, 44-45, 128-129, 372-378 (Sections 35-36)
  fourth conjugation, 44-45, 128-129, 372-378 (Sections 35-36)
  agreement, 319 (n. 12), 387 (Section 50)
  defective, 386 (Section 46)
  deponent, 51, 53, 378-380 (Section 38)
  irregular, 380-386 (Sections 39-45)
  semi-deponent, 380 (Section 38)
  synopsis, 378 (Section 37)

vetō, with infinitive clause, 397 (Section 107*c*), 401 (Section 125, 2)

vīs, declension of, 361 (Section 8)

VOCATIVE, 393 (Section 90)
  position of, 393 (Section 90*a*)

volō, conjugation of, 49, 130, 385-386 (Section 45)
  infinitives of, 131

WISHES, mood and tenses, 395-396 (Section 103. 1, 2, 3)

WORD ORDER
  emphatic word between *nē . . . quidem*, 191 (n. 4)
  ille following noun for special emphasis, 56 (n. 3)
  position of monosyllabic preposition, 71 (n. 2), 407 (Section 155)
  relative clause preceding antecedent, 104 (n. 14)